ARGUMENT WITHOUT END

Argument Without End

IN SEARCH OF ANSWERS
TO THE VIETNAM TRAGEDY

Robert S. McNamara,
James G. Blight, and Robert K. Brigham

WITH THOMAS J. BIERSTEKER
AND COL. HERBERT Y. SCHANDLER (U.S. ARMY, RET.)

PublicAffairs   NEW YORK

Library of Congress Cataloging-in-Publication Data
McNamara, Robert S., 1916–
Argument without end : in search of answers to theVietnam tragedy / Robert S. McNamara, James G.
Blight, and Robert K. Brigham.—1st ed.
p.   cm.
Includes index.
ISBN 1–891620–87–8
1. Vietnamese Conflict, 1961–1975—United States. 2. Vietnam—History—1945–1975. 3. United States—
History—1945–   . 4. United States—Foreign relations—Vietnam. 5. Vietnam—Foreign relations—
United States. I. Blight, James G. II. Brigham, Robert K. (Robert Kendall), 1960–   . III. Title.
DS558.N439   1999
959.704'3373—dc21
                                                                                        99–11830
                                                                                           CIP

10   9   8   7   6   5   4   3   2   1

To jML and LLL, the "back-channel,"

who made everything possible

History is an argument without end

—————

Pieter Geyl, Debates with Historians, 1955

Contents

6

Negotiating Initiatives, 1965–1967:
Why Did They Fail?

7

U.S. Military Victory in Vietnam:
A Dangerous Illusion?

8

Learning from Tragedy:
Lessons of Vietnam for the Twenty-First Century

PREFACE

The publication of *In Retrospect* in 1995 stimulated enormous interest with comments ranging from harsh and widespread criticism to warm praise. I was often asked whether I was surprised by the controversy created by the book. My answer was no. It was clear that our nation had not yet either fully understood or fully come to terms with Vietnam. Many readers—I would say most—recognized that the lessons of Vietnam, if properly drawn, would be applicable to the world of today—to Bosnia and Kosovo, for example—and will continue to be applicable to the world of tomorrow. But it was clear I was presenting only a part of the story. Many U.S. officials, both civilian and military, who participated in decisions relating to the conflict had yet to be heard from. And there had been few extensive contacts with their counterparts in Vietnam, China, and Russia. I anticipated that, as more documents were released, more memoirs written, and more scholarly research conducted, my conclusions, in particular the lessons to apply to the future, would change. To hasten that process I asked Leslie Gelb, president of the Council on Foreign Relations in New York, to probe the willingness of Vietnamese scholars and former policymakers to meet with their American counterparts to review the decisionmaking of both sides. In particular, I hoped to examine a hypothesis that had gradually taken shape in my mind: Both Washington and Hanoi had missed opportunities to achieve our geopolitical objectives without the terrible loss of life suffered by each of our countries. There were, I hypothesized, opportunities either to have avoided the war before it started or to have terminated it long before it had run its course. Were there such opportunities? If so, why were they missed? What lessons can we draw to avoid such tragedies in the twenty-first century?

"History," said the Dutch historian Pieter Geyl, is "an argument without end." This book is another chapter in that argument about the lessons of the Vietnam War.

ROBERT S. MCNAMARA

Washington, DC
April, 1999

Biographical Sketches of Participants in the U.S.-Vietnamese Dialogue

Six sets of meetings were held in Hanoi, Vietnam, between November 1995 and February 1998, involving U.S. and Vietnamese scholars and former civilian and military officials. In preparing for the meetings, we created briefing notebooks to summarize the available documentation and scholarship regarding each topic on our common agenda. In addition, Vietnamese and American participants met in July 1998, along with an international cast of scholars, at a conference at the Rockefeller Foundation's Bellagio, Italy, conference center. In Bellagio, an earlier draft of the manuscript of this book was reviewed. In the lists that follow, the Vietnamese participants have not been separated into scholars and former officials (as have the U.S. participants), because all of the Vietnamese participants, including those who are now Vietnam's top scholars of the war, participated in the events under reexamination and thus bring to the discussions firsthand knowledge of Hanoi's decisionmaking, in addition to their scholarly expertise.

The Vietnamese language is an anomaly in that it is a tonal Asian language deriving in part from Chinese roots, but (due to an edict of the French colonial authorities during the early twentieth century) it uses a Roman alphabet rather than traditional Chinese characters. The Roman alphabet is, in addition, augmented with an array of diacritical marks. This has traditionally caused confusion to Westerners who attempt to pronounce Vietnamese names based only on their spelling. Therefore, the names of the Vietnamese participants in the dialogues, listed below, are followed by phonetic spellings set in *italics* that approximate the English spelling of the way the names *sound* in Vietnamese.

The phonetic spelling of each Vietnamese participant is provided for this reason: We believe that the information in the U.S.-Vietnamese dialogues found in this book will make it difficult, if not impossible, hereafter to understand the history of many aspects of the Vietnam War from an exclusively American perspective. Thus, as authors, we want to avoid making a mistake similar to that made by many U.S. officials during the war who did not take sufficient interest in the Vietnamese communists—their views, their history, or even the names and backgrounds of their principal adversaries—and thus did not understand them, leading to many missed opportunities to avoid the war or terminate it earlier than proved possible at the time. We believe that knowing, however imperfectly, how to say (thus perhaps to remember) the names of our Vietnamese colleagues is the beginning of a new kind of understanding of the war in the West.

U.S. Participants

FORMER OFFICIALS

ROBERT S. MCNAMARA. Secretary of Defense to Presidents John F. Kennedy and Lyndon B. Johnson, 1961–1968. McNamara came to the U.S. Department of Defense in 1961 from his post as President of the Ford Motor Company in Detroit. He played critical roles in all the crises of the Kennedy period, including those centered on Laos (March 1961), Berlin (August–October 1961), and the Cuban missile crisis (October 1962). He was deeply involved in Vietnam planning from the beginning of the Kennedy administration. He is the author of *In Retrospect: The Tragedy and Lessons of Vietnam* (1995), in which he describes the evolution of his views. By late 1965 he had become an advocate of a negotiated settlement; by the summer and fall of 1967, he took the unusual step of directing, from the Pentagon, a significant peace initiative involving Henry Kissinger, then a Harvard University professor, using a channel to Hanoi via Paris. On his exploratory trip to Hanoi in November 1995, during which the Vietnamese formally agreed to the collaborative project on the war, McNamara became the highest ranking former U.S. official from the war ever to visit Hanoi. He is 82 years old and lives in Washington, D.C.

FRANCIS M. BATOR. Deputy Special Assistant to the President for National Security Affairs, 1965–1967. During his service in the Johnson White House, he assumed principal responsibility for European affairs and U.S. trade policy. After leaving government, he returned to the John F. Kennedy School of Government at Harvard University, where he is now Professor Emeritus. He is writing a book on President Johnson's decisionmaking style and strategy. He is 76 years old and lives in Cambridge, Massachusetts.

CHESTER L. COOPER. A representative of the Office of Strategic Services in China during World War II, he became a Central Intelligence Agency analyst for Southeast Asia, 1953–1963. During that period he was a participant in the Geneva conferences on Vietnam in 1954 and on Laos in 1961. After his return from Geneva, Cooper joined the staff of the National Security Council, 1963–1966, where he was a deputy to National Security Adviser McGeorge Bundy with responsibility for Vietnam affairs, including coordination of the various peace initiatives then under way between Washington and Hanoi. He was a Special Assistant to U.S. Special Envoy for Vietnam W. Averell Harriman, 1966–1968. He is the author of *The Lost Crusade: America in Vietnam* (1970), a scholarly memoir of the war. He is now Deputy Director of the Pacific Northwest National Laboratories in Washington, D.C. He is 81 years old and lives in Chevy Chase, Maryland.

NICHOLAS DEB. KATZENBACH. Deputy Attorney General under Robert F. Kennedy, 1961–1963, he became Acting Attorney General, 1964–1965, following Kennedy's departure from the Johnson administration. Katzenbach became centrally involved in Vietnam policymaking as Deputy Secretary of State, 1966–1969. During 1966–1967 he was, along with Robert McNamara, a principal advocate of a negotiated settlement of the war. Now retired, he is 78 years old and lives in Princeton, New Jersey.

GEN. WILLIAM Y. SMITH. A graduate of West Point and a former U.S. Air Force fighter pilot, he was shot down over North Korea during the Korean war but escaped before he could be captured. While serving in the Pentagon, he became a Special Assistant to Gen. Maxwell D. Taylor, Chairman of the Joint Chiefs of Staff (JCS), a key figure in U.S. policy toward Vietnam during this period. General Smith worked with Taylor from 1961, when President Kennedy named him Chairman of the JCS, until Taylor's departure to Saigon as Ambassador in mid-1964. General Smith was a participant in the Cuban missile crisis project, on which the Vietnam War project is modeled, and he is coauthor (with Gen. Anatoly Gribkov) of *Operation Anadyr* (1994), on the military aspects of the missile crisis. He retired from the Air Force with the rank of general (four star) and is also the retired president of the Institute for Defense Analyses. He is 75 years old and lives in Falls Church, Virginia.

GEN. DALE VESSER. A graduate of West Point and a former Rhodes Scholar, he served two tours of duty in Vietnam, one as a commander of infantry, the other as a U.S. adviser to the South Vietnamese Army. He also served on the staff of the National Security Council and on the staff of the Office of the Secretary of Defense, where he participated in the writing of the study known as the *Pentagon Papers*. General Vesser retired from the Army with the rank of lieutenant general (three star). He recently chaired an interservice panel investigating health issues deriving from the Gulf War. He is 64 years old and lives in McLean, Virginia.

SCHOLARS

THOMAS J. BIERSTEKER. Director, Thomas J. Watson Jr. Institute for International Studies, and Henry Luce Professor of Transnational Organizations, Brown University. Educated at the University of Chicago and Yale University, he is the former Director of the School of International Relations at the University of Southern California. His principal scholarly interests are in international relations theory, including concepts of sovereignty and hegemony, and the role of historical counterfactuals; and in the impact of globalization on markets, security, and other issues. Together with Hayward Alker over the past twenty years, he has published a series of seminal pieces on world order including the classic "The Dialectics of World Order" (1984).

JAMES G. BLIGHT. Professor of International Relations (Research), Thomas J. Watson Jr. Institute for International Studies, Brown University. A cognitive psychologist by training, James Blight, along with Joseph S. Nye, was the founder and director of the missile crisis project at Harvard's Kennedy School of Government (1986–1989) and at Brown's Watson Institute (1990–1993). He is the author or coauthor of six books on the Cuban missile crisis. His most recent books are *Politics of Illusion: The Bay of Pigs Invasion Reexamined* (1998, with Peter Kornbluh) and *Intelligence and the Cuban Missile Crisis* (1998, with David A. Welch). He is the director of the Vietnam War project at the Watson Institute.

ROBERT K. BRIGHAM. Associate Professor of History and Director, Program in International Relations, Vassar College. Uniquely trained in the history of U.S. decisionmaking during the Vietnam War while at the University of Kentucky, and in decisionmaking in Hanoi and among the National Liberation Front (NLF) while at Cornell, he has published widely on the war in both English- and Vietnamese-language journals. His most recent book is *Guerilla Diplomacy: The NLF's Foreign Relations and the Vietnam War* (1998). He is currently writing a book on the South Vietnamese Army.

GEORGE C. HERRING. Alumni Professor of History, University of Kentucky. He is a past president of the Society for Historians of American Foreign Relations and is, in addition, the most widely read and cited American historian of the Vietnam War, having written scores of articles and nearly a dozen books on the war over the past quarter century. *America's Longest War: The United*

States and Vietnam, 1950–1975 (3d ed., 1996) is the most influential text in the field for college students. He is the editor of *The Secret Diplomacy of the Vietnam War: The Negotiating Volumes of the Pentagon Papers* (1983), which, until the dialogues presented in Chapter 6 of this book became available, represented virtually all that was known about the secret peace initiatives between 1965 and 1967. Among his recent books is *LBJ and Vietnam: A Different Kind of War* (1994).

JAMES G. HERSHBERG. Associate Professor of History, George Washington University. He was the Founding Director of the Cold War International History Project, the Woodrow Wilson Center, Washington, D.C., and the editor of its *Bulletin*, 1991–1997. In addition to having published widely on the Cuban missile crisis and other episodes in the history of the Cold War, he is the author of the prize-winning *James B. Conant: Harvard to Hiroshima and the Making of the Nuclear Age* (1993).

CHARLES E. NEU. Professor and Chairman, Department of History, Brown University. He is a member of the Executive Board of the Watson Institute at Brown University. Trained in diplomatic history at Harvard University, he has written widely in essays and reviews on many aspects of the Cold War, including the Vietnam War. He is currently editing for publication the spring 1998 lectures on the Vietnam War given at Johns Hopkins University, and he is at work on a textbook of the war. He is a regular reviewer for *Reviews in American History* on issues related to the Vietnam War.

JOHN PRADOS. Independent scholar, Takoma Park, Maryland. He was a founder of the National Security Archive in Washington, D.C., and is one of the most prolific American writers on the war, focusing mainly on military issues. Among his works dealing with Vietnam are *Presidents' Secret Wars: CIA and Pentagon Covert Operations from World War II Through Transcam* (1986), *Valley of Decision: The Siege of Khe Sanh* (1991, with Ray W. Stubbe), *The Hidden History of the Vietnam War* (1995), and, most recently, *The Blood Road: The Ho Chi Minh Trail and the Vietnam War* (1999).

COL. HERBERT Y. SCHANDLER (U.S. Army, Ret.). Professor in the Department of Grand Strategy, Industrial College of the Armed Forces, National Defense University, Washington, D.C. A graduate of West Point, he served two tours of duty in Vietnam between 1966 and 1970, following which he earned a Ph.D. from the Government Department, Harvard University (1974). He has published widely in military journals on the Vietnam War, and his book, *The*

Unmaking of a President: Lyndon Johnson and Vietnam (1977), is widely regarded as the classic study of the impact of the war on the Johnson presidency in the pivotal year of 1968.

DAVID A. WELCH. Associate Professor of Political Science, University of Toronto, and Director of the Graduate Program in International Relations, University of Toronto. He is the coauthor of several books on the Cuban missile crisis, including, most recently, *Intelligence and the Cuban Missile Crisis* (1998, with James G. Blight). He has also published widely on the political psychology of crisis decisionmaking and on the impact of moral considerations on decisions, including his prize-winning *Justice and the Genesis of War* (1993).

Vietnamese Participants

NGUYEN CO THACH (*Nwinn Co Tock*). Retired Foreign Minister of Vietnam, 1980–1989. Nguyen Co Thach joined the anti-French resistance at age fourteen. During the French war, 1945–1949, he was principal private secretary to Gen. Vo Nguyen Giap, commander of the Vietminh Army, later serving as a provincial chairman in the Third Zone (the Red River Delta area). In 1954 he was named Director General of the Ministry of Foreign Affairs (the executive officer). In October 1954 he became Director of the Bureau of Foreign Affairs of the Military and Political Commission, which took over the administration of Hanoi from the French. He returned to the Foreign Ministry in 1956, serving in New Delhi as Consul General. In 1960 he was named Deputy Foreign Minister (for Laos, Cambodia, and the United States), and he participated in the 1961–1962 Geneva conference on Laos. From 1962 to 1968, Nguyen Co Thach had principal oversight in the Foreign Ministry for policy toward the United States and he was the senior Foreign Ministry official involved in Hanoi's participation in the many peace initiatives at that time. From 1968 to 1973, he was the principal deputy in Paris to Xuan Thuy and Le Duc Tho during the peace talks. Nguyen Co Thach was head of the Vietnamese delegation to the June 1997 conference. He died in April 1998. He was 78 years old.

BUI THANH SON (*Bwee Tonn Sone*). Deputy Director for Research, Institute for International Relations (IIR), Ministry of Foreign Affairs, Hanoi. Bui Thanh Son participated in all six sets of discussions in Hanoi and was the Vietnamese chair at the February 1998 meetings. He is a graduate of the IIR and also has an M.A. in political science from Columbia University (1993). He is 35 years old.

GEN. DANG VU HIEP (*Dahng Voo Heep*). Deputy Director General, General Political Department, Vietnamese Army. He is a historian of the war, having written several studies of various battles and campaigns occurring toward the end of the war. In early 1965, he was a People's Army of Vietnam (PAVN, or North Vietnamese Army) adviser to the People's Liberation Army Forces (PLAF) in the Central Highlands and, in this capacity, was closely involved with two events of pivotal significance in the escalation of the war: the February 7, 1965, attack at Pleiku, and a similar attack at Qui Nhon on February 10. Contrary to U.S. assessments at the time, General Hiep revealed at the June 1997 conference that both attacks were planned and carried out by the local commander, without consultation with Hanoi. He is 66 years old.

DAO HUY NGOC (*Dow Wee Nawk*). Recently retired as Director General, Institute for International Relations (IIR), Ministry of Foreign Affairs, Hanoi, Dao Huy Ngoc has been the principal coordinator of the collaborative project on the war on the Vietnamese side. He served as Principal Chair for the June 1997 conference for the Vietnamese team. Immediately before becoming Director General of the IIR, he served as Ambassador to Japan. He is 65 years old.

DINH NHO LIEM (*Deen No Leem*). Upon his retirement, Dinh Nho Liem was Ambassador to the Soviet Union and a Deputy Foreign Minister. In the late 1940s, he was the supervisor of Thanh Hoa Province. In 1954 he went to Poland and in 1959 to India, serving in New Delhi as Consul General. After serving in Cairo during the early 1960s, he returned to Hanoi to serve as head of the "Solutions" Division of the U.S. affairs department in the Foreign Ministry (after 1968). He participated in the Paris Peace Conference at various periods. At the June 1997 conference in Hanoi, Dinh Nho Liem gave the formal Vietnamese presentation on the issue of a neutral solution for the Saigon government, arguing that such a solution was indeed possible, but only after the removal of Ngo Dinh Diem and Ngo Dinh Nhu in November 1963. He is 77 years old.

GEN. DOAN CHUONG (*Zwann Chong*). Director, Institute of Strategic Studies, Ministry of Defense, Hanoi. Gen. Doan Chuong is a specialist in military strategy and tactics and has written widely on military issues in both the French and U.S. wars, in both of which he participated as a member of the People's Army of Vietnam. At the June 1997 conference in Hanoi, he made the principal Vietnamese presentation on several issues concerning Hanoi's military preparedness: the possibility that the United States would have radically escalated the war by: cutting off the Ho Chi Minh Trail; a radical escalation of the bombing of the North; and a U.S. invasion north of the 17th parallel. He is 64 years old.

LUU DOAN HUYNH (*Loo Zwann Hwinn*). Senior Researcher, Institute for International Relations, Ministry of Foreign Affairs, Hanoi. Luu Doan Huynh is Vietnam's outstanding historian of the war currently publishing in English. He is the coeditor (with Jayne S. Werner) of *The Vietnam War: Vietnamese and American Perspectives* (1993). He joined the Vietnam People's Army in 1945 as a teenager. After joining Hanoi's Foreign Ministry, Luu Doan Huynh served throughout South Asia and Southeast Asia (in Delhi, Bangkok, and Canberra). Due in part to his fluency in English, he served in 1966 as an intelligence analyst in the Department of U.S. Affairs; later, he was part of a five-person team that prepared the basic documents for entering negotiations with the United States. Luu Doan Huynh participated in all six of the meetings between Vietnamese and U.S. participants (1995–1998). He is 71 years old.

LUU VAN LOI (*Loo Von Loy*). A retired journalist and Foreign Service officer, Luu Van Loi is Vietnam's foremost historian of Vietnam's negotiations with the United States. He has written (with Nguyen Anh Vu) on the abortive secret diplomacy between the Hanoi government and Washington prior to the Paris Peace Conference, and is coauthor (with Nguyen Anh Vu) of *The Le Duc Tho–Kissinger Negotiations in Paris*, published in English in 1995. He was an army officer during the anti-French resistance. In 1954 he joined the mission of the Vietnam People's Army to the International Control Commission, where he became a deputy to Hanoi's principal delegate, Ha Van Lau. In 1961 he was named Deputy Director of South Vietnam Affairs in the Ministry of Foreign Affairs; in that capacity, he participated in the Geneva Conference on Laos from 1961–1962. Between February and April 1965, Luu Van Loi helped draft the Four Points, which remained Hanoi's basic negotiating stance from that point forward. Following the announcement of the Four Points on April 8, 1965, he monitored all of the secret peace probes between Hanoi and Washington from the Foreign Ministry in Hanoi. From 1968 to 1973, he was in Paris and participated in all phases of the peace talks. He was subsequently appointed the head of the Borders Commission and entrusted with the task of negotiating with Vietnam's neighbors in Indochina. He is 85 years old.

NGUYEN DINH PHUONG (*Nwinn Deen Fong*). Upon his retirement, he was Director of European Affairs in the Foreign Ministry. Nguyen Dinh Phuong was also a teacher during the anti-French resistance war. During the mid-1950s, he was a delegate to the International Control Commission. Later he became an interpreter and assistant to the Foreign Ministry's head of U.S. affairs, Ha Van Lau. In this capacity, he worked on several of the peace initiatives involving secret Washington-Hanoi talks. He served in Paris for the entire duration of the Peace Conference, acting as principal English-Vietnamese interpreter for Le Duc Tho and Xuan Thuy. Later, he became Ambassador to Sweden; he was director of the European Division of the Foreign Ministry when he retired. Nguyen Dinh Phuong participated in both the June 1997 and the February 1998 conferences in Hanoi. He is 77 years old.

GEN. NGUYEN DINH UOC (*Nwinn Deen Ook*). Director, Institute of Military History, Ministry of Defense, Hanoi. Throughout the French and American wars, Nguyen Dinh Uoc was a military journalist and writer on a wide variety of military affairs, retiring with the rank of major general. He is Vietnam's outstanding authority on the vexing issue of casualties—how to define "casualty," how to distinguish between combatant and noncombatant casualties, and other such issues arising from the nature of the war in Vietnam. He was a cochair of the June 1997 conference. He is 73 years old.

NGUYEN KHAC HUYNH (*Nwinn Kok Hwinn*). Senior Researcher, Institute for International Relations, Ministry of Foreign Affairs, Hanoi. He joined the anti-French resistance while in high school and, after 1954, joined the Foreign Ministry as an analyst. Beginning in 1967, Nguyen Khac Huynh was a principal coordinator of information relating to U.S. affairs, including the many peace initiatives occurring via third-country intermediaries. In 1968 he moved to Paris to participate in the peace talks, working closely with Nguyen Van Hieu, the National Liberation Front representative to the Paris talks. Upon his retirement, he was Ambassador to Mozambique. Since his retirement from the Foreign Service, Nguyen Khac Huynh has become one of Vietnam's most active historians of the French and U.S. wars. He is 75 years old.

MADAME NGUYEN THI BINH (*Nwinn Tee Binn*). Madame Nguyen Thi Binh is Vice President of Vietnam's Council of State. A southerner by birth, she became a resistance fighter at an early age and was one of the founding members of the National Liberation Front (NLF) in December 1960. During the American War, she became a leading member of the NLF and held various posts in the Provisional Revolutionary Government (PRG). She went to Paris during the latter phases of the peace talks and signed the Paris Peace Accords on behalf of the NLF as its Foreign Minister. Madame Nguyen Thi Binh participated in discussions with the U.S. team in November 1995, during which the collaborative project on the war was launched. She is 78 years old.

COL. QUACH HAI LUONG (*Kwok Hy L'wong*). Senior Researcher, Institute of Strategic Studies (ISS), Ministry of Defense, Hanoi. During the American

War, he was an artillery officer, trained to operate Soviet surface-to-air missiles protecting the city of Hanoi. Since joining the ISS, Col. Quach Hai Luong has become one of Vietnam's leading specialists on U.S. strategy during the war. He participated in both the June 1997 and February 1998 meetings, including (in February 1998) a series of dialogues on the military strategy of Hanoi and Washington with Col. Herbert Y. Schandler. He is 63 years old.

TRAN NGOC KHA (*Tron Nawk Kah*). A journalist specializing in foreign affairs. During the mid-1960s, Tran Ngoc Kha was a deputy and English-language interpreter for Mai Van Bo, head of the Democratic Republic of Vietnam (DRV) Commercial Delegation in Paris (and the DRV's top official in France). He worked with Mai Van Bo on the several peace initiatives between 1965 and 1967 that used Paris as a venue, including the "XYZ" channel, about which Tran Ngoc Kha made the formal Vietnamese presentation at the June 1997 conference. He is 60 years old.

TRAN QUANG CO (*Tron Kwong Cuh*). Retired (in 1996) as the First Deputy Foreign Minister of Vietnam. Before joining the Ministry of Foreign Affairs in 1959, Tran Quang Co was an officer in the People's Army of Vietnam. In 1954 he became a member of the teaching staff of the Foreign Affairs College of the Foreign Ministry. In 1964 he became First Secretary of the embassy in Jakarta, returning to Hanoi in 1966 to work in the "Solutions" Division of the U.S. affairs department in the Foreign Ministry. During 1966–1968, he was centrally involved in drafting the DRV's negotiating stance in what would become in April 1968 the Paris Peace Talks. Later, he participated with Nguyen Co Thach and Richard Holbrooke of the U.S. State Department in (unsuccessful) negotiations with the United States (1977–1979) to normalize relations between the United States and Vietnam. In 1986 he was made a member of the Central Committee, and was named First Deputy Foreign Minister in 1991. At the June 1997 conference, Tran Quang Co gave the formal presentations from the Vietnamese side on the peace initiatives and the lessons of the war. He is 78 years old.

GEN. VO NGUYEN GIAP (*Vuh Nwinn Zee-ap*). Retired four-star General of the Army and former Defense Minister, Gen. Vo Nguyen Giap is the most eminent living Vietnamese official from the American War. He was born into a revolutionary family. His father was executed by the French, and a sister died of privation in a French prison. In addition, his first wife was executed by the French. Originally trained in French schools as a history teacher, General Giap joined the anti-French resistance and quickly rose to become a principal associate of Ho Chi Minh. He was commander of the Vietminh forces throughout the anti-French resistance war and directed the forces at the pivotal siege and battle of Dien Bien Phu in May 1954. General Giap became, during the late 1950s and early 1960s, a leading writer on military strategy, becoming known as the leading exponent of "People's War" in Vietnam, which drew on, but was in many ways different from, the Chinese variant of resistance war. By the mid-1960s, as Defense Minister, he had delegated many strictly military responsibilities to Gen. Van Tien Dung and others, but in July 1967, with the death of Gen. Nguyen Chi Thanh, he took principal responsibility for the planning and execution of the Tet offensive of early 1968. He participated in two meetings with the U.S. team (November 1995 and June 1997) at the Ministry of Defense in Hanoi. He is 86 years old.

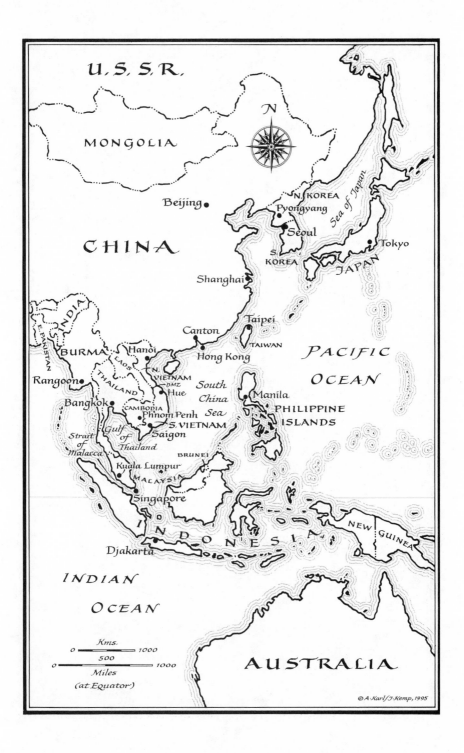

ARGUMENT WITHOUT END

At the end of World War I, President Wilson believed, as did many other Americans, that we had won a war to end all wars. How wrong they were. The twentieth century has become the bloodiest in all of human history. Must we repeat that carnage in the twenty-first century? This book will draw lessons from the Vietnam War to reduce that risk.

1

The Theme and Structure of the Book

Most men look at things as they are and wonder why. I dream of things that never were and ask why not?

George Bernard Shaw[1]

From *In Retrospect to Argument Without End*

The Vietnam War, with which I was personally involved for more than seven years as U.S. secretary of defense (1961–1968), was among the bloodiest in all of human history. It is estimated that something on the order of 3.8 million Vietnamese (North and South, military and civilian) were killed. The United States lost 58,000. Had the United States lost in proportion to its population the same percentage as Vietnam, 27 million Americans would have died. Many times these numbers were wounded. During the course of the war, in addition, North and South Vietnam were nearly destroyed as functioning societies, and America was torn asunder by issues related to the war. Ironically, each principal combatant achieved its objectives: The Hanoi government reunified Vietnam under its leadership; and to the United States, the "dominoes" did not fall, as communism and Soviet and Chinese hegemony did not spread across Southeast Asia.

The thesis of this book is that the war was a tragedy for both sides. Both Washington and Hanoi could have accomplished their purposes without the appalling loss of life. There were missed opportunities, either for avoiding the war before it started or for terminating it before it had run its course. I speculated along these lines in my memoir of the war, *In Retrospect: The Tragedy and Lessons of Vietnam.*[2] But lacking access to former officials and documents from the Hanoi government, I could not pursue the matter further at that time.

Since then, however, this thesis has been buttressed by an analysis of formerly unavailable, newly translated Vietnamese and Chinese documents, as well as the six sets of discussions in Hanoi over more than two years between Vietnamese and U.S. scholars and former officials. For the first time, I believe, an understanding has begun to emerge regarding which of the decisions on each side were made on the basis of an accurate understanding of the motives and capabilities of the adversaries, and which were made on the basis of misperceptions, miscalculations, and misjudgments. On the basis of what our analysis adds to the historical record, we propose lessons that should be drawn for advancing peace among nations in the twenty-first century.

The Twenty-First Century: A Bloody Repetition of the Twentieth?

My earliest memory as a child is of a city exploding with joy. The city: San Francisco. The date: November 11, 1918—Armistice Day. I was two years old. The city was celebrating not only the end of World War I but also the belief, held so strongly by President Wilson—and many other Americans— that the United States and its allies had won a war to end all wars.

They were wrong, of course. The twentieth century was on its way to becoming the bloodiest, by far, in all of human history. During the century soon to end, 160 million people will have been killed in conflicts—within nations and between nations—across the globe. If we wish to avoid a repetition in the next century of the tragedy of the twentieth, the time to start is now.

As a first step, we should begin by establishing a realistic appraisal of the problem. It is readily apparent, very complex, and very dangerous. A recent report, titled "Carnegie Commission on the Prevention of Deadly Conflict," chaired by David A. Hamburg and Cyrus R. Vance, stated it very clearly:

> Peace—will require greater understanding and respect for differences within and across national boundaries. We humans do not have the luxury any longer of indulging our prejudices and ethnocentrism. They are anachronisms of our ancient past. The worldwide historical record is full of hateful and destructive behavior based on religious, racial, political, ideological, and other distinctions—holy wars of one sort or another. Will such behavior in the next century be expressed with weapons of mass destruction? If we cannot learn to accommodate each other respectfully in the twenty-first century, we could destroy each other at such a rate that humanity will have little to cherish.[3]

The Carnegie Commission is saying, in effect, that the end of the Cold War in 1989 did not, and will not, in and of itself result in an end to conflict. We see the truth of this statement on all sides—in the Iraqi invasion of Kuwait, the civil war in the former Yugoslavia, the turmoil in northern Iraq, the tension between India and Pakistan, the unstable relations between North and South Korea, and the conflicts across the face of sub-Saharan Africa in Angola, Somalia, Sudan, Rwanda, Burundi, Zaire, Sierra Leone, and Liberia. These all make clear that the world of the future will not be without conflict. Racial, religious, and ethnic tensions will remain. Nationalism will be a powerful force across the globe. Political revolutions will erupt as societies advance. Historic disputes over political boundaries will endure. And economic disparities among and within nations will increase as technology and education spread unevenly around the world. The underlying causes of Third World conflict that existed long before the Cold War began remain now that it has ended. They will be compounded by potential strife among states of the former Soviet Union and by continuing tensions in the Middle East. During the past fifty years, these very tensions have contributed to 125 wars causing 40 million deaths. So, in these respects, the world of the future will not be different from the world of the past: Conflicts within nations and conflicts among nations will not disappear.

In such a world many political theorists, in particular those classified as "realists," predict a return to traditional power politics. They argue that the disappearance of ideological competition between East and West will trigger a reversion to traditional relationships based on territorial and economic imperatives. They say that the United States, Russia, Western Europe, China, Japan, and perhaps India will seek to assert themselves in their own regions while also competing for dominance in other areas of the world where conditions are fluid. This view has been expressed, for example, by Harvard University professor Michael Sandel, who has written: "The end of the Cold War does not mean an end of global competition between the superpowers. Once the ideological dimension fades, what you are left with is not peace and harmony, but old-fashioned global politics based on dominant powers competing for influence and pursuing their internal interests."[4] In contrast to Sandel, Carl Kaysen, former director of the Institute for Advanced Study at Princeton, states: "The international system that relies on the national use of military force as the ultimate guarantor of security, and the threat of its use as the basis of order, is not the only possible one. To seek a different system . . . is no longer the pursuit of an illusion, but a necessary effort toward a necessary goal."[5]

Sandel's conception of relations among nations in the post–Cold War world may be historically well-founded. But I would argue that it is inconsistent with our increasingly interdependent world. No nation, not even the United States, can stand alone in a world in which nations are inextricably entwined with one another economically, environmentally, and with regard to security. I believe, therefore, that the United Nations charter offers a far more appropriate framework for international relations in the future than does the doctrine of power politics.

I would also argue that Sandel's emphasis on balance-of-power politics in the twenty-first century assumes we will be willing to continue to accept a foreign policy that lacks a strong moral foundation. I am aware that the majority of political scientists, particularly those of the realist school, believe morality—as contrasted with a careful calculation of national interests based on balance-of-power considerations—is a dangerous guide for establishing foreign policy. They would say that a foreign policy driven by moral considerations promotes zealousness and a crusading spirit, with potentially dangerous results. But the United States has defined itself in highly idealistic and moral terms throughout its history. A leading contemporary figure in the discussion of the role of morality in foreign policy is Joseph Nye, who served in both the Carter and first Clinton administrations. Currently the dean of Harvard's Kennedy School of Government, he writes: "Americans are a moralistic people, and their concern carries over into foreign policy. . . . Given the nature of the American political culture, there will always be a demand for moral expression in foreign policy. To ignore it in one period is likely to lay the grounds for exaggerating it in the next."[6]

But simply including morality as a variable is not a solution. Many of the most controversial foreign policy debates in the United States have found both sides basing their arguments on moral considerations. U.S. policy toward Cuba today is justified on moral grounds by supporters saying it is immoral to support dictators who abuse human rights. And it is attacked, on moral grounds, by critics saying it leads to suffering by the mass of the Cuban people. Similarly, a U.S. policy toward China that placed primary emphasis on support of individual civil rights might well weaken the Chinese government's ability to increase the population's access to advances in nutrition, education, and health.

Moreover, moral considerations do not offer a clear guide to action in many other foreign policy disputes, for example, the conflicts today in the Middle East and Bosnia. Peoples of different religions and cultures, confronting common problems, often arrive at different moral judgments relating to conflicts between individual and group rights, between group rights and national rights, and between the rights of individual nations. And even where the moral objective may be clear—as in Rwanda or Burundi, where there was near universal agreement that the killing should stop—we may lack the capability to achieve it. We are learning that external military force has limited power to restore a failed state.

But surely, in the most basic sense, one can apply a moral judgment to the level of killing that has occurred in the twentieth century. *There is no jus-tification for it today, and there can be no justification for its continuation into the twenty-first century!*

So, can we not agree that there is one area of foreign policy in which moral principles should prevail yet have not? And that is in relation to the settlement of disputes within nations and among nations without resort to violence. To move in this direction, should not the nations of the world—the United States in particular—establish as their overarching foreign policy goal the reduction of fatalities from conflict within and among nations?

Learning from History: Missed Opportunities and Lessons

As I have said, wars between great and lesser powers, and conflicts within nations, are certain to occur, but can we not reduce their frequency and severity by learning from history—by identifying missed opportunities, drawing lessons, and applying the lessons to the future? Although I believe the answer is that we can, such a proposition remains highly controversial among historians.

Many would argue that nonrecurring, broad historical forces determine the course of relations among nations, including wars. They would say that the U.S. intervention in Southeast Asia during the 1960s—the Vietnam War—was the result of such pressures. In effect, they say history is predetermined, that missed opportunities do not really occur and therefore history has few if any lessons to teach succeeding generations: Historical events are determined by forces larger than individual people making individual choices.

I believe such a view is contradicted by common sense and by everyday experience. We all make choices. We observe the results. If we are consci-entious, we examine our experience for clues as to opportunities we may have missed, and we look for ways to make fewer mistakes in the future. Do we not believe that our lives are the sum of the choices we make? And is this not our principal means of assuming our share of responsibility for our own conduct—and for the welfare of those who come after us? I believe it is.

Many scholars share my view. For example, the distinguished Stanford diplomatic historian Gordon A. Craig notes the prevalence of this tendency in his fellow historians, then tells us what is wrong with their approach:

> In our historical explanations we are biased in favor of great impersonal forces and long-term trends and dominant political and cultural developments, and are

uneasy with the contingent, the unexpected, and the accidental. . . . The trouble with this kind of explanation is that it tends to be deterministic and to give the impression that what happened had to happen and that there were no alternatives.[7]

Craig, a specialist on modern Germany, is thus keenly aware of the many unlikely circumstances, especially the many rooted in misunderstanding and misjudgment that in combination made possible Hitler's rise to power.

British historian H. R. Trevor-Roper is even more forceful on this point. He criticizes his fellow historians for "keeping the corpse [of history] unburied and refrigerated, on a cold mortuary slab, for anatomical demonstration."[8] Instead of becoming caretakers of a living history, a history in which events are seen as the "result of particular . . . decisions or events that in themselves were not necessary," many historians become, in effect, the undertakers of that history.[9]

Historians who think in this way are concerned about what they call "counterfactual" history. They fear that instead of writing the history of what actually happened, historians, memoirists, and others may simply engage in speculation about "what if" or "what might have been" without paying due attention to the historical record of what actually occurred.

This relates directly to our attempt in this book to identify missed opportunities and draw lessons from them. The historians fear, in other words, that efforts like ours will become mired in what they believe the record shows are impossible or low-probability outcomes—like avoiding a U.S. war in Vietnam or ending it much earlier than was the case.[10] They would say, for example, that any outcome that did not occur should not be taken seriously, because the "outcome" seems possible only in retrospect.

I want to be absolutely clear that *my primary concern is with raising the probabilities of preventing conflict in the future.* The missed opportunities we examine are, we argue, due primarily to mutual misperception, misunderstanding, and misjudgment by leaders in Washington and Hanoi. We therefore ask: *If each side had known the truth about the other's reality, might the outcome have been less tragic?* This permits us to focus on the lack of knowledge, on what prevented each side from acquiring such knowledge, and thus to draw lessons about how to prevent ignorance from producing such tragedies in the future.[11]

I believe, therefore—and my coauthors of this book agree with me—that history is not immune from human initiative. I agree with Columbia University political scientist Robert Legvold, who argues as follows:

> History is neither determined, nor a set of dramatic turning points, but rather should be understood as the accumulation of marginal human choices

made by real leaders, in real time, operating under real-world constraints. Or to put it another way, in every situation there are not only broad historical forces at work, there are also highly specific aspects which one could imagine having been very different at the time. Moreover, if in the light of the historical record the difference had occurred, a different outcome might have been made more probable.[12]

Does it matter whether one believes that human decisions make a difference? I believe it does, for two reasons: first, because such a view encourages us to search for *missed opportunities* that (had they been grasped) would have led to a better result; and second, because the analysis of missed opportunities often points to lessons aimed at preventing missed opportunities in the future.

Of course, outside pressures exist that limit actions. And I know from personal experience in the Kennedy and Johnson administrations that these pressures can be excruciating. Time is short. Information is sparse or inconsistent. And the stakes are high, as is often the case in matters of foreign policy, because the nation's vital interests seem threatened. These pressures are often difficult to overcome.

On Vietnam, this has led some historians to leap to a conclusion I find unacceptable: Individual initiative and choice were of little consequence in determining the course of the war. For example, the distinguished Harvard historian Ernest May has written that "given the assumptions generally shared by Americans in the 1960s, it seems probable that any collection of men or women would have decided as did members of the Kennedy and Johnson administrations."[13] In other words, leaders from these two administrations, myself included, are said to have been pushed along, like leaves before the wind, by forces no one could have resisted. More recently, when commenting on *In Retrospect*, professor May, though he praised the book, characterized it as "a little like a memoir by a Crusader who cannot remember why he particularly cared about the fate of Jerusalem."[14] He felt I had been too critical of myself and my colleagues, too intent on identifying missed opportunities to have avoided the war or ended it earlier, with less tragic results. I was, therefore, in his view, insufficiently appreciative of the forces that led us to our failed policies.

But—and this is a fundamental point—leaders are supposed to lead, to resist pressures or "forces" of this sort, to understand more fully than others the range of options and implications of choosing such options. This is what Pres. Franklin Roosevelt did when he convinced the American people that the United States should help its allies fight the Nazis. I believe this is what

President Kennedy did during the Cuban missile crisis when he resisted
heavy pressure—public and private—to attack the Soviet missile sites in
Cuba. And I believe this is what President Johnson and his associates,
including myself, should have done to resist the pressure—from the public,
the media, academicians, and the Congress—toward a military solution to
the problem of Vietnam.[15]

The Method: Critical Oral History

But on what basis, and through the application of what principles, can we
learn from history to avoid the mistakes of the past? The method of retrospective review of conflict by opponents—what the scholars call "critical
oral history"—was created specifically to address these questions. It was
developed first at Harvard's Kennedy School of Government, in the context
of a project on the Cuban missile crisis. That project moved to Brown University's Watson Institute for International Studies in 1990. The Watson
Institute has subsequently been responsible for organizing other projects on
the recent history of U.S. foreign policy. These have included reexamina-
tions of the Bay of Pigs and the collapse of U.S.-Soviet détente during the
1970s. Since late 1995 it has acted as principal organizer of "Missed Opportunities," the joint U.S.-Vietnamese project on the Vietnam War, the data
from which provide the basis of this book.

The approach requires the simultaneous interaction of *documents* bearing
on the paper trail of decisions for issues and events under reexamination;
memories of those who participated in the decisions; and *scholars*, whose
business it is to know the relevant aspects of the written record.

As formerly secret documents become available, we begin to understand
more clearly than before the way events unfolded. Yet documents have a
weakness of their own: They do not supply their own context. To a large
extent, then, the memories of the participants help to supply missing context
to the documents, and in turn the documents supply many of the facts that
human memories distort or forget. In concert, several people's memories
may test and correct each individual's memory, so that errors in recollection
or egregious distortions can be reduced—all the more so if the parties to a
discussion are known to have divergent views of the event. (This is especially true, as one would expect, in the case of former adversaries, whose
views of an event usually are not just discrepant but often contradictory.)
Unlike conventional oral history, in which people merely tell their stories,
critical oral history subjects these stories to multidimensional analysis and

criticism. Thus, a particular story—not only a policymaker's recollection of his experience but also, perhaps, a scholar's favorite theory—must answer to three judges: the documentary record, the expertise of specialists in the field, and the recollections of those who lived through the event in positions of official responsibility.[16]

The Cuban Missile Crisis Project and the Vietnam War Project

The Cuban missile crisis of October 1962 was the first event analyzed by the method of critical oral history. Five major conferences were held between 1987 and 1992. I participated in all five, including the final meeting, in Havana, Cuba, chaired by Cuban Pres. Fidel Castro. That project proved that the crisis was more dangerous than is generally recognized even today—and that its lessons have yet to be learned.

The crisis began when the Soviets moved nuclear missiles and bombers to Cuba—secretly and with clear intent to deceive—in the summer and early fall of 1962. The missiles were to be targeted against cities along America's East Coast, putting 90 million Americans at risk. Photographs taken by a U-2 reconnaissance aircraft on Sunday, October 14, 1962, brought the deployments to President Kennedy's attention. He and his security advisers—military and civilian—believed that the Soviets' action posed a threat to the West. Kennedy therefore authorized a naval quarantine of Cuba to be effective Wednesday, October 24. Preparations also began for air strikes and an amphibious invasion. The contingency plans called for a "first-day" air attack of 1,080 sorties— a huge attack. An invasion force totaling 180,000 troops was assembled in southeastern U.S. ports. The crisis came to a head on Saturday, October 27, and Sunday, October 28. Had Soviet leader Khrushchev not publicly announced on that Sunday that he was removing the missiles, I believe that on Monday a majority of Kennedy's military and civilian advisers would have recommended launching the attacks.

By the conclusion of the third Cuban missile crisis conference, in Moscow in 1989, it had become clear that the decisions of each of the three nations before, during, and after the crisis had been distorted by misinformation, miscalculation, and misjudgment. At the time, some of us—particularly President Kennedy and I—believed that the United States faced great danger.[17] The Moscow meeting confirmed that judgment. But during the Havana conference we learned that we had seriously underestimated those dangers. While in Havana, we were told by the former Warsaw Pact chief of staff, Gen. Anatoly

Gribkov, that in 1962 the Soviet forces in Cuba possessed not only nuclear warheads for their intermediate-range missiles targeted on U.S. cities but also nuclear bombs and tactical warheads.[18] The tactical warheads were to be used against U.S. invasion forces. At the time, as I mentioned, the Central Intelligence Agency (CIA) was reporting no warheads on the island.

In November 1992—thirty years after the event—we learned more. An article appeared in the Russian press stating that at the height of the missile crisis Soviet forces on Cuba possessed a total of 162 nuclear warheads, including at least ninety tactical warheads. Moreover, it was reported that on October 26, 1962—a moment of great tension—warheads were moved from their storage sites to positions closer to their delivery vehicles in anticipation of a U.S. invasion.[19] The next day, Soviet Defense Minister Rodión Malinovsky received a cable from Gen. Issa Pliyev, the Soviet commander in Cuba, informing him of this action. Malinovsky sent it to Khrushchev. Khrushchev returned it to Malinovsky with "Approved" scrawled across the document. Clearly, there was a high risk that in the face of a U.S. attack—which, as I have said, many in the U.S. government, military and civilian alike, were prepared to recommend to President Kennedy—the Soviet forces in Cuba would have decided to use their nuclear weapons rather than lose them.[20]

We need not speculate about what would have happened in that event. We can predict the results with certainty.

Although a U.S. invasion force would not have been equipped with tactical nuclear warheads—President Kennedy and I had specifically prohibited that—no one should believe that had American troops been attacked with nuclear weapons the U.S. would have refrained from a nuclear response. And where would it have ended? In utter disaster.[21]

What lesson should we draw from these stunning data—data suggesting that our brush with nuclear catastrophe in October 1962 was extraordinarily close? The lesson was clear to me from that moment in Havana when we first began to learn, from General Gribkov, about Soviet preparations for nuclear war in the event of a U.S. invasion. Near the conclusion of that session, I asked Fidel Castro two questions:

(a) Were you aware of it—the Soviet deployment of tactical nuclear warheads, and plans for their use; and

(b) What was your interpretation or expectation of the possible effect on Cuba? How did you think the U.S. would respond, and what might the implications have been for your nation and the world?[22]

Castro's answer sent a chill down my spine. He replied:

Now, we started from the assumption that if there was an invasion of Cuba, nuclear war would erupt. We were certain of that . . . we would be forced to pay the price, that we would disappear. . . . [23] Would I have been ready to use nuclear weapons? Yes, I would have agreed to the use of nuclear weapons. . . . I would have agreed, in the event of the invasion you are talking about, with the use of tactical nuclear weapons. . . . If Mr. McNamara or Mr. Kennedy had been in our place, and had their country been invaded, or their country was going to be occupied . . . I believe they would have used tactical nuclear weapons.[24]

I hope that President Kennedy and I would not have behaved as Castro suggested we would have. His decision would have destroyed his country. Had we responded in a similar way, the damage to our own would have been disastrous.

But human beings are fallible. We know we all make mistakes. In our daily lives, mistakes are costly, but we try to learn from them. In conventional war mistakes cost lives, sometimes thousands of lives. But if mistakes were to affect decisions related to the use of nuclear forces, there would be no learning period. They would result in the destruction of nations. The indefinite combination of human fallibility and nuclear weapons carries a very high risk of a potential nuclear catastrophe.[25]

This lesson—and I regard it as the most important substantive lesson by far deriving from the Cuban missile crisis project—has also been endorsed by many distinguished civilian and military leaders around the world.[26]

The Cuban missile crisis project also taught me what I will call a "methodological" lesson: Through extensive dialogue with one's former enemies it is possible to learn a good deal about decisionmaking on "the other side" in pivotal events involving U.S. foreign policy. We had gambled that going to Moscow in 1989, and to Havana in 1992, would yield knowledge about the missile crisis to an extent that would silence the many critics who warned that we would be dealing with communists, who were still our adversaries, if not our enemies; that our counterparts would not be forthcoming and that we would, in effect, be "duped." But the gamble paid off. We learned things in Moscow and Havana that were astonishing (and which subsequent investigations have substantially verified) and that point to important lessons.[27]

Therefore, while I was writing *In Retrospect*, but before it was published, I began to wonder whether a process could be initiated with the Vietnamese from which might come some answers to questions I could pose only rhetorically in my memoir. Some of these questions were debated by me, and by the two presidents I served, throughout my involvement with the Vietnam War, questions such as: Would China intervene militarily, as it had in Korea, if the United States should attempt to invade North Vietnam and occupy the country;[28] were any of our attempts to establish a cease-fire and move to negotiations between 1965 and 1968 taken seriously in Hanoi; if so, why did they fail?[29] About all such questions, I wrote, "We may never know."[30]

I began an attempt to initiate an inquiry to sound out Vietnamese interest in a project modeled on the missile crisis project by contacting Leslie Gelb in February 1995. Mr. Gelb is president of the Council on Foreign Relations in New York and had worked with me as general editor of the Pentagon Papers project nearly thirty years before. Mr. Gelb expressed interest, and made inquiries with Mr. Le Van Bang, who was then the Vietnamese representative to the United Nations (and who would later become, in July 1995, Vietnam's first postwar ambassador to the United States).

Le Van Bang thought the idea had merit, but he also said that the suggestion of a seminar setting in which former enemies exchanged views on issues of common interest would probably strike the traditionally secretive and hierarchical Vietnamese leadership as strange. He said, for example, it was hard for him to imagine the Vietnamese leadership handing over sensitive documents relating to the war, such as one finds in the *Pentagon Papers*. Nevertheless, he told Mr. Gelb that the idea would be taken seriously, in part because of my personal involvement, but also because the Vietnamese government, then on the verge of achieving full diplomatic relations with the United States, was conscious of the need to demonstrate to the U.S. public that it was willing to sit down with Americans and discuss our once bitterly fought war with calmness and credibility.

With that, Mr. Gelb agreed that the Council on Foreign Relations would sponsor an exploratory trip to Hanoi, with the caveat that I personally lead the group going to Hanoi.

I then contacted professor James Blight of Brown University's Watson Institute, who along with Joseph Nye had organized the missile crisis project. I asked him whether he would also act as principal organizer of a Vietnam War project. He said he would. One of professor Blight's first calls was to professor Robert Brigham, Vassar College historian of decisionmaking on the war in both Washington and Hanoi (and fluent in Vietnamese). Professor Brigham agreed to join the team, as did several others, and the project was launched.

Our group met throughout the summer and fall of 1995 in preparation for a November trip that had been approved by the Vietnamese government. I arrived in Hanoi on November 7 and met with Vietnamese officials and scholars the following day, November 8. On Saturday, November 9, I appeared at a press conference held at the Vietnamese Ministry of Foreign Affairs, announcing our agreement to work toward a conference on the war. I left Hanoi that evening, following a visit to the U.S. chief of mission in Hanoi, Desaix Anderson, who also endorsed the project.[31]

Unknown to me, *In Retrospect* had been translated into Vietnamese, published in Vietnam months earlier in a pirated edition, and become a bestseller. The net effect of this was that all of the people with whom we discussed the project had read the book and spoke in an informed way about its contents.[32] There was, in fact, resistance in some quarters in Hanoi to focusing on *joint* responsibility for missed opportunities. But it was clear that some Vietnamese officials and scholars also strongly supported the idea.[33] So my colleagues and I returned to the United States cautiously optimistic that the success of the missile crisis project might be repeated.

The trip to Hanoi proved to be at least as controversial as my previous participation in the Havana conference. The considerable publicity generated by the trip backfired, leading to substantial criticism from the American press of the project and my participation in it. Regretfully, the Council on Foreign Relations withdrew from the project.

Fortunately, the Watson Institute believed the project had the potential to yield lessons from the past that could be applied in the future. Its director, professor Thomas Biersteker, gave his support to the project and has become a contributor to this book. From time to time, political pressure from the left and right was applied to professor Biersteker and to Brown University to drop the project. But they never wavered in their support; without it, the project would have been terminated.

Following an enormous amount of preparation, lasting two years and involving a half-dozen trips to Hanoi by professors Blight, Brigham, Biersteker, and their colleagues, a conference was convened in Hanoi, June 20–23, 1997. Its title reflected my original intended focus: "Missed Opportunities: Revisiting the Decisions of the Vietnam War." I led the U.S. delegation, which also included two former senior U.S. generals, one of whom had spent 500 days in the Vietnamese jungles, other former civilian officials involved with the war, and a team of outstanding U.S. scholars on the war. The Vietnamese delegation was led by Nguyen Co Thach, deputy foreign minister throughout the Vietnam War (later foreign minister, 1980–1989), and included an impressive array of former military and civilian leaders and scholars of the war.[34]

Two things were clear from the outset—and throughout the Hanoi conference. First, the Vietnamese government had established limits to the candor of its participants. For example, though the Vietnamese entered enthusiastically into discussions of what they considered to be missed opportunities by the United States, nothing but stony silence followed our repeated attempts to draw them out and to admit that misperceptions, misunderstandings, and misjudgments had been mutual. This was not merely frustrating. The Vietnamese government's desire to control the conference nearly caused the conference to be canceled, just as it began, when the Vietnamese reneged—or tried to renege—on their prior agreement to let the Cable News Network (CNN) film the meetings in preparation for a documentary. A compromise was eventually reached, whereby CNN filmed one entire day of proceedings and received exclusive interviews with Nguyen Co Thach and the second ranking Vietnamese participant, Tran Quang Co, following the conference.

Second, it was also clear from the outset that some of the Vietnamese participants were trying to circumvent the gag rule that had been imposed by their government. One could see this in discussions that took place during breaks, over lunches (which were taken together with the Vietnamese), and eventually in the sessions themselves. For example, Nguyen Co Thach, who seemed to be acting as the "policeman" in charge of limiting candor, increasingly was challenged by Vietnamese scholars who began their interventions by saying that they had been reviewing documents relevant to the issues in question and that they had a different perspective from Mr. Thach. These were then followed up by ever more explicit and revealing comments outside the conference room, some even beginning with open admissions of Hanoi's joint responsibility for missed opportunities. Finally, in one private conversation with me, Thach volunteered that he had come to accept that position. These admissions were given further credence by reference to details that had never before been revealed about Hanoi's decisionmaking.

Those Vietnamese participants who seemed most informed and open asked the U.S. organizers from Brown University to meet after the conclusion of the conference to plan a small follow-up meeting in Hanoi at which these issues could be discussed further. But there was a catch: I personally must be excluded from the participants in the proposed follow-up meeting. Jim Blight went to Hanoi just before Christmas 1997 to ask the Vietnamese organizers why they felt it was desirable that I stay away.

They answered as follows: Mr. Thach was very ill and would not be able to attend the follow-up meeting (he died in April 1998). To avoid "imbalance" in the delegations, it would be wise for McNamara to be absent.

Just as I had gambled in going to Havana in January 1992, this time I gambled that in staying away from the meeting our team would have a better chance of breaking new ground in understanding the missed opportunities—and lessons—associated with the war. And so, during February 23–26, 1998, our group and a Vietnamese team met in Hanoi to go over the ground covered in the June 1997 meeting and to extend the discussion beyond that point. I believe—and my coauthors believe—that this gamble has paid off handsomely.

Missed Opportunities in Vietnam

Were there not missed opportunities, for each side, to have achieved its geopolitical objectives without the terrible loss of life suffered in the war—missed opportunities either for avoiding the war before it started or for terminating it before it had run its course? In Hanoi, I suggested there were at least six, and I asked whether these truly were missed opportunities. If so, why weren't they grasped? I put the six in the form of questions for discussion, by both sides:

1. A Neutral Vietnam.
   If, in 1961–1964, the United States had supported the concept of neutralization then under discussion between France and North Vietnam, would the result have been a viable, "neutral" Vietnam allied to neither East nor West?

2. The Survival of the Diem Regime in South Vietnam.
   If the United States had given its full support in 1963 to Ngo Dinh Diem's regime, and if Diem had survived and remained leader of South Vietnam, would he have asked for, or permitted the introduction of, large numbers of U.S. combat troops?

3. The Possibility of a U.S. Military "Victory."
   Was it ever feasible? Could it have been achieved without genocide or involving China, Russia, and the United States in a massive war?

4. A U.S. Withdrawal.
   In September 1967 the director of the CIA, Richard Helms, presented to President Johnson a secret memorandum stating that the United States could probably have withdrawn from Vietnam at that time without a significant adverse effect on its geopolitical status and security around the world. Was this judgment correct? Might a U.S. withdrawal have resulted in a unified Vietnam but not in a communist takeover of the rest of the region?

5. The Failed Negotiations.
   During the years I was secretary of defense, there were at least seven major attempts by the U.S. government, several formulated by me, to

initiate negotiations with the Hanoi government. Why did all of these efforts at negotiations fail?

The discussions in Hanoi in June 1997 and February 1998 focused on this agenda. Likewise, the organization of this book derives from it.

There were two significant exceptions—additions, really—placed onto the agenda by the Vietnamese. Beginning with my first visit to Hanoi in November 1995, all our Vietnamese interlocutors, without exception, told us that two missed opportunities were absent from the U.S. agenda. Vice President Madame Nguyen Thi Binh concluded our discussion on November 8, 1995, by asking me: "Why, in 1945, did the United States spurn Chairman Ho Chi Minh's attempts to reach out to President Truman?[35] And why, in 1954, did the United States become our enemy, taking the place of the French imperialists?"[36]

The period before 1961—before President Kennedy came to office—also came up several times in my conversation with Gen. Vo Nguyen Giap during the same November 1995 visit to Hanoi. What began as a discussion about the escalation of the war during the 1960s was shifted by Giap back to the earlier period, especially 1954, the year President Eisenhower first articulated what became known as the "domino theory"—that is, if South Vietnam fell to communism, all of Indochina would fall, "like a row of dominoes."[37] Giap commented: "Dominoes, dominoes, dominoes—this theory was an illusion. Whatever happened in Vietnam had nothing to do with what happened in Laos, to say nothing of Indonesia. . . . I am amazed that even the brightest people—people like yourself—could have believed it." I assured him that we did believe it but that I took his point and now believed that the pre-1961 period needed to be on the agenda for our conference.

I felt that this emphasis by the Vietnamese, contrasted with my own initial preference to begin our analysis of events with the period following President Kennedy's inauguration, showed how differently some Americans and Vietnamese still viewed the events in question, with different starting points, and certainly with different views as to which missed opportunities were the most important.

Tran Quang Co, a former first deputy foreign minister, formulated a sixth category of possible missed opportunities as follows:

6. Misunderstandings, 1945–1960.
The first occurred in 1945–1946. If the Truman administration had adhered to the concept of self-determination; and had responded to the letter that Ho Chi Minh sent to President Truman in September 1945; and

had prevented the French occupation of Vietnam; then an opportunity would have presented itself to achieve Vietnamese independence and unification, without the French and American wars.

The second missed opportunity took place in 1954, with the Geneva Accords. The Geneva Conference was intended to be an historic meeting that would put an end to war in Indochina and restore long-lasting peace to Vietnam. The Geneva Accords endorsed free elections, which, if they had occurred in 1956, would have provided a basis for the peaceful reunification of Vietnam. However, in 1954 the U.S. administration, fearing that free elections involving communists were unlikely, supported the installation of Ngo Dinh Diem as president of a new entity called "South Vietnam."

The basic question put to participants in the Hanoi meetings—and to readers of this book—is this: In the light of what now can be learned from the historical record, what U.S. and Vietnamese decisions might have been different and what difference would they have made in the course of the war—*if each side had judged the other side's intentions and capabilities more accurately?*

Would not a discussion of these missed opportunities, of the U.S. and Vietnamese mindsets that lead to them, and of the lessons to be drawn from such an analysis help avoid similar conflicts in the twenty-first century? That was my hope as I boarded the plane for Hanoi, and that remains my hope now.

AUTHOR'S NOTE

My coauthors and I will proceed as follows. Each chapter opens and closes with brief "Introduction" and "Conclusions" sections written by me. Apart from these beginning and ending sections, the text of Chapters 2–6 was written by professors Blight and Brigham, based in part on transcripts of our meetings in Hanoi. Chapter 7, apart from my Introduction, was written by Col. Schandler; the Introduction and Conclusions sections of Chapter 8 were written by me, and the remaining text was cowritten by professor Biersteker and me. All of the principal authors—professors Blight, Brigham, and I—share in the conclusions to each chapter and the book as a whole, as summarized in Chapter 8. Following each chapter introduction, a second section, titled "Monologues in Real Time," will summarize the evolving views that Washington and Hanoi held toward each other during this period. They were, indeed, monologues in the sense that virtually no meaningful communication occurred between the two sides during the entire period. Each side, therefore, drew conclusions about the other based on very limited and biased information, and neither had any sensitivity whatever to what actually drove decisions on the other side. In each chapter, the Monologues section is organized into two subsections, titled "The View from Washington" and "The View from Hanoi"; these are based on our understandings of the available sources, and they have been informed as well by discussions of the sources with our Vietnamese collaborators. The Monologues sections are followed by sections titled "A Dialogue in Retrospect," which contain highlights of the two principal conferences, which were held in Hanoi during June 1997 and February 1998. The transcripts are derived from audio recordings of the conferences. The transcriptions and translations—both phrasing and substance—have been checked and cleared by all participants on both sides.

The discussions were frank and tough throughout, as befits the first-ever discussion by former enemies of this tragic war. Had this dialogue occurred in real time, rather than in retrospect, I believe the tragedy could have been prevented. The Vietnamese contributions to the dialogues contain much that is being put on the record in the West by the Vietnamese for the first time. Selections from these "Additions to History" are summarized in Appendix A.

April 7, 1954. "You have what you would call the 'falling domino' principle. You have a row of dominoes set up, you knock over the first one and what will happen to the last one is the certainty that it will go over very quickly. . . . So the possible consequences of the loss [of Vietnam] are just incalculable to the free world."

October 4, 1957. Following the launch of the Soviet "Sputnik" satellite, Soviet leader Nikita Khrushchev stated to U.S. leaders: "We will bury you."

January 20, 1961. "Let every nation know—we shall pay any price, bear any burden, meet any hardship, support any friend, oppose any foe to assure the survival and the success of liberty."

2

Enemies: Washington's and Hanoi's Mindsets by January 1961

Each day the crises multiply. Each day their solution grows more difficult. Each day we draw nearer the hour of maximum danger, as weapons spread and hostile forces grow stronger. . . . In Asia, the relentless pressures of the Chinese Communists menace the security of the entire area—from the borders of India and South Viet Nam to the jungles of Laos, struggling to protect its newly won independence. . . . Life in 1961 will not be easy.

John F. Kennedy, January 30, 1961[1]

The present South Vietnamese regime is a camouflaged colonial regime dominated by the Yankees, and the South Vietnamese government is a servile government, implementing faithfully all the policies of the American imperialists. Therefore this regime must be overthrown and a government of national and democratic union put in its place . . . and thus bring about . . . the peaceful unification of the country.

Founding Program of the South Vietnamese National Liberation Front, January 29, 1961[2]

Introduction

Press coverage of my initial visit to Hanoi in November 1995 emphasized that former enemies would be meeting. This journalistic "hook" found its embodiment in what, for the reporters, was the high point of the visit—a November 9, 1995, meeting between former North Vietnamese Defense Minister Gen. Vo Nguyen Giap and me. "A remarkable meeting of two old adversaries" and "old foes meet" were typical headlines.[3] General Giap, who was 84 at the time, and I, aged 79, joked about the double meaning in such headlines. We decided we liked the phrase "former enemies" better than "old foes."

In fact, we were the bitterest of enemies during what we call the "Vietnam War," what the Vietnamese call the "American War." As I recalled vividly, we considered each other to be irreconcilable opponents from the moment the Kennedy administration took office on January 20, 1961.

It was here, I believed—with Washington's and Hanoi's mindsets toward each other—that any U.S.-Vietnamese dialogue on the war must begin. We must first ask ourselves: What were our most basic assumptions toward each other by January 1961, when the Kennedy administration came to office? Each side should have an opportunity to present systematically its views of the other side. And each side should be permitted ample opportunity to respond to these presentations, during the course of which, I hoped, each side would be able to see more clearly what it got wrong and what it got right in assessing the nature and extent of the threat the other represented.

What was our mindset in January 1961? We saw South Vietnam as a fledgling country, one we had pledged to assist and sustain in the 1954 SEATO Treaty signed by Britain, France, and the United States. In other words, we believed Hanoi, via its ally the National Liberation Front (NLF), was seeking to make South Vietnam the next "domino" to "fall" in Southeast Asia. We believed that if the South Vietnamese domino fell, then all of Southeast Asia—Thailand, Indonesia, Malaya, the Philippines, even Japan—could be at risk. Therefore, the vital interests of the West would be in jeopardy.

My colleagues and I in the Kennedy and Johnson administrations had failed to ask the necessary hard questions about our U.S. mindset. There were four:

- Was it true that the fall of South Vietnam would trigger the fall of all Southeast Asia?

- Would that constitute a grave threat to the West's security?

- What kind of war—conventional or guerrilla—might develop?

- Could we win it with U.S. troops fighting alongside the South Vietnamese?[4]

When I went to Hanoi in November 1995, the biggest question in my mind was this: Will the Vietnamese really want to play this game by our rules? Would they agree to take a critical look at their own mindset, which labeled the Kennedy and Johnson administrations as "neocolonialists" and "neoimperialists" whose primary motive was to destroy the Hanoi government? I knew—without question—that if this was their mindset they were *dead wrong!* But would these committed communists in Hanoi really agree to reexamine not only Washington's mindsets, in search of mistakes, but also their own?

My discussion with General Giap revealed immediately that such a result would not easily or immediately be accomplished. Giap and I began by discussing the Tonkin Gulf incident of August 1964. I wanted to know whether, in addition to the August 2, 1964, attack by North Vietnamese forces against the U.S. ship *Maddox*, there was also an attack on August 4. I told him I thought such an attack was "probable but not certain."[5] He informed me that there had been no attack on August 4; and that the August 2 attack had been ordered not from Hanoi, which is what we in Washington assumed at the time, but by a local commander.

This was an important confirmation by Giap. Because we mistakenly believed that both attacks had occurred and had been initiated by orders from Hanoi, we believed that the leadership of North Vietnam had, for whatever reason, decided to escalate the conflict by targeting U.S. personnel and assets in the area. Had we known—had I personally been able to prove—that only one attack had taken place and that it had been ordered by a local commander (who believed North Vietnam's territorial waters had been violated both by the *Maddox* and *Turner Joy* as well as by covert operations carried out by the South Vietnamese with U.S. assistance) it is likely that President Johnson would not have ordered the first U.S. retaliatory air strike on the North—sixty-four sorties in all against what were believed to be the home bases of the attacking patrol boats and their supporting oil complex.[6]

Giap and I then turned to the subject of our joint project. Here is part of the record of our conversation:

Robert McNamara: General, I want us to examine our mindsets, and to look at specific instances where we—Hanoi and Washington—may each have been mistaken, have misunderstood each other, such as in the Tonkin Gulf episode we've been discussing.

Gen. Vo Nguyen Giap: I don't believe we misunderstood you. You were the enemy; you wished to defeat us—to destroy us. So we were forced to fight you—to fight a "people's war" to reclaim our country from your neoimperialist ally in Saigon—we used the word "puppet," of course, back then—and to reunify our country.

Robert McNamara: General, I am interested—and my U.S. colleagues are interested—in putting a claim such as you have just made to the test at our conference. Were we—was I, was Kennedy, was Johnson—a "neoimperialist" in the sense you are using the word? I would say *absolutely not!* Now, if we can agree on an agenda focused on episodes like Tonkin Gulf, where we may have misunderstood each other, then—

Gen. Vo Nguyen Giap: Excuse me, but we *correctly* understood you—what you were doing in the Tonkin Gulf. You were carrying out sabotage activities to create a pretext that would allow you to take over the war from the Saigon government, which was incompetent.

Robert McNamara: That is totally wrong, General. I assure you: There was no such intent. None. But this is why we need to reexamine each other's misunderstandings—for two reasons. First, we need to identify missed opportunities; and second, we need to draw lessons which will allow us to avoid such tragedies in the future.

Gen. Vo Nguyen Giap: Lessons are important. I agree. However, you are wrong to call the war a "tragedy"—to say that it came from missed opportunities. Maybe it was a tragedy for you, because yours was a war of aggression, in the neocolonialist "style," or fashion, of the day for the Americans. You wanted to replace the French; you failed; men died; so, yes, it was tragic, because they died for a bad cause.

But for us, the war against you was a noble sacrifice. We did not want to fight the U.S. We did not. But you gave us no choice. Our people sacrificed tremendously for our cause of freedom and independence. There were no missed opportunities for us. We did what we had to do to drive you and your "puppets"—I apologize, Mr. McNamara, for again using the term "puppet"—to drive you and your puppets out. So I agree that *you* missed opportunities and that *you* need to draw lessons. But us? I think we would do nothing different, under the circumstances.

Robert McNamara: Well, General, I hope you'll agree to put issues like that—our mindsets, yours and ours—on the agenda.

Gen. Vo Nguyen Giap: Yes, of course. We have nothing to fear.[7]

So this was how it began—my effort and the efforts of our U.S. group—to begin a discussion, leading to at least one major conference, which would *begin* at the *beginning*, with a discussion of Washington's and Hanoi's mindsets in January 1961. Our Vietnamese colleagues agreed to do so, in more or less the same spirit as that in which General Giap agreed to the idea. That is, they would be pleased to listen to the U.S. participants, such as myself, reflect on how and why we may have missed, in real time, the overriding significance of Vietnamese nationalism. They would be delighted, in fact, to participate in such a conversation.

But what they did not anticipate, I believe, was the extent to which our side would press them hard and repeatedly to reflect critically on their own mind-set, on their own conviction at the time, that U.S. motives were fundamentally indistinguishable from those of the hated French colonialists. They would make two discoveries in the dialogues that ensued: first, that their view of the U.S. mindset and motives was *wrong*; and second, that their misunderstanding of the U.S. mindset and motives may have led the Hanoi government to take actions that, in retrospect, were *mistakes*, which led to missed opportunities, and which contributed to the tragedy of the war we fought.

Many—not all, but many—of our Vietnamese colleagues would therefore ultimately disagree profoundly with Giap's self-satisfied assessment. This would occur over time, as they became more familiar with our point of view, and as mutual trust and respect began to counteract the corrosive effects of our relations during the period under reexamination—when we were the bitterest of enemies.

Monologues in Real Time: Enemies, January 1961

The View from Washington

Some recent analyses of John F. Kennedy's Vietnam policy would seem to support Hanoi's mindset in January 1961: that Washington was seeking aggressively to throw its weight around in Southeast Asia. Such assessments often begin by citing Kennedy's inaugural address of January 20, 1961, in which he said that America would "pay any price, bear any burden . . . to assure the success of liberty."[8] It is true that few Americans old enough to remember Kennedy's delivery of that speech can fail to recall the youthful, articulate president calling on his fellow citizens to fulfill what he said was the historic U.S. mission: to lead the effort to popularize and spread Western liberal values throughout the world.

Did this imply that Kennedy and his foreign policy team saw themselves in January 1961 as preparing to go on the *offensive*, in Vietnam and elsewhere, as (what General Giap called) "neoimperialists"? This myth—which has several variations—has persisted throughout the nearly four decades since Kennedy's inaugural and must be accounted for. Historians who subscribe to it cite Kennedy's address as evidence of what they take to be his aggressive, dangerous, anticommunist brinkmanship.

From the left side of the political spectrum, the recent book *Pay Any Price* tells us that Kennedy's approach to foreign policy in general, and to Vietnam in particular, led to dangerous "crisis management" improvisation in Southeast Asia.[9] In a similar vein, other historians have written of what they judge to be Kennedy's foolhardy "quest for victory" at any cost, in Vietnam and elsewhere.[10] To these historians, the Kennedy foreign policy team is portrayed as a group of hardened, aggressive cold warriors. They were dangerous "imperialists," in more or less the same way that Vo Nguyen Giap understands the term.

From the right side of the political spectrum, Henry Kissinger, noting the "soaring language" of Kennedy's inaugural, has recently passed the following judgment on the foreign policy confusion he believes is embedded in Kennedy's inaugural message: "The sweeping global commitment was not related to any specific national-security interest and exempted no country or region of the world. Kennedy's eloquent peroration was the reverse of Palmerston's dictum, that Great Britain had no friends, only interests. America, in the pursuit of liberty, had no interests, only friends."[11] The "domino theory" to which the Kennedy foreign policy team subscribed, according to Kissinger, "was not so much wrong as it was undifferentiated. The real issues posed by Vietnam were not whether communism should be resisted in Asia, but whether the 17th parallel was the right place to draw the line. . . . That issue," he argues, "was never carefully examined in terms of geopolitics."[12] (In retrospect, Kissinger says he would have preferred Laos as the place to draw the line in Southeast Asia.)

To Kissinger, as to some other theorists and practitioners of realpolitik— members of the "realist" school of international politics—Kennedy and his team were inexperienced and overconfident in foreign affairs, too much infused with American optimism to understand the balance and use of power in the real world into which they were thrust on January 20, 1961. They therefore risked giving the impression of being "imperialists," according to Kissinger, without having the know-how to follow through successfully.

These assessments, however popular they may be among some historians, have nothing in common with what may be called the "psychological reality" in which Kennedy and his foreign policy team operated from January 20, 1961, onward. The record is clear and unambiguous. They did not gather in those first days to draw up plans for plucking lost dominoes off the shelf of the communists. There was no overconfidence about any supposed ease of the tasks ahead. Moreover, there also seems to have been an acute awareness in Kennedy himself that the United States was everywhere on the defensive— was in danger of losing the battle against communism. This was, after all, part of his presidential campaign message in 1960, and the American people, by and large, believed him. The motives driving U.S. foreign policy in the Kennedy administration appear to have been almost entirely *defensive*.

Historian George Herring describes the mood in Washington then as a "siege mentality," which captures something of the somber sentiment in which the Kennedy team approached its foreign policy tasks.[13] As Deputy National Security Adviser Walt W. Rostow recalls:

> The general image of Kennedy's first days as president is sometimes projected as one of light-hearted improvisation until the sobering experience of the Bay of Pigs [April 18–20, 1961]. For those engaged intimately with him in foreign affairs, it was a sober—even somber—time from the beginning, although confronted with the certain visceral good cheer. He once greeted McGeorge Bundy and me as we came into his office: "What's gone against us today?"[14]

What was the intended message, then, behind the "soaring language" of the inaugural, the stated willingness to "pay any price, bear any burden"? It seems it was meant, at least in part, as a message to Moscow and Beijing, urging *them* not to be overconfident, urging *them* not to take foolish risks, in case they thought the new administration in Washington too new and ineffectual to resist. This is the same message Kennedy would try to impart to Nikita Khrushchev, a known risktaker of historic proportions, at their June 1961 summit in Vienna, though Kennedy felt afterward that he had not gotten through to the Soviet leader.

It is impossible to understand the foreign policy mindset in Washington during January 1961 without appreciating the extent of the nuclear threat that colored every significant point of contention between East and West. Now that the Cold War is over, and the threat of a U.S.-Russian nuclear confrontation has subsided, it takes a considerable imagination to reenter this most pervasive and gnawing aspect of the American mindset of January 1961. The nuclear balance between the United States and the Soviet Union was far from clear. Khrushchev was already infamous for making nuclear threats over such seemingly disparate issues as the status of West Berlin, the Cuban Revolution, and U.S. spy planes. John Kennedy and his advisers did not merely imagine this threat; they heard and read it as the rhetoric emerged from Khrushchev's Kremlin.

In January 1961 John Kennedy and his team first began to understand what it meant to bear responsibility for preventing a nuclear holocaust. But how did one do this? There was no defense against ballistic missiles, so one was forced to rely on deterrence—on making credible threats to the Soviet adversary to retaliate in kind if ever it should launch its nuclear weapons against the United States or its allies. But what was a "credible" threat? Who knew? Rostow acutely describes Kennedy's dilemma: "Kennedy was not a morbid man. But those close to him knew he was haunted by the fear that he might be the man whose decisions led to nuclear war. It was a good deal to ask of a human being—to protect the possibility of civilization by putting it at risk. . . . The burden was most harsh and explicit in Kennedy's time."[15]

Who knew which erupting crisis, in which part of the world, might, because of misunderstanding between Washington and Moscow and its presumed ally in Beijing, escalate unmanageably into nuclear holocaust? Concern in Washington about Third World instability was reinforced by a speech Khrushchev delivered on January 6, 1961, just before Kennedy assumed office. Khrushchev seemed to offer carte blanche support to insurgents everywhere, saying:

> Liberation wars will continue to exist for as long as imperialism exists, as long as colonialism exists. These are revolutionary wars. Such wars are not only admissible but inevitable, since the colonialists do not grant independence voluntarily. . . .
>
> What is the attitude of Marxists toward such uprisings? A most positive one.[16]

According to a Kennedy White House aide, Arthur Schlesinger, the president-elect was deeply affected by this speech. He studied it carefully, and according to Schlesinger, some of the more hawkish-sounding passages in the inaugural, and in the State of the Union address delivered the following week, derive from Kennedy's reading and rereading of Khrushchev's January 6 speech.[17] In Vietnam, the type of war Khrushchev alluded to was already in progress. Assistant Secretary of State William P. Bundy recalled the feeling all through the administration: "What was going on in Vietnam seemed the clearest possible case of what Khrushchev in January had called a 'war of national liberation.'"[18]

Vietnam was a special problem for Washington, for it was the only state in Southeast Asia that was essentially the *creation* of the United States. In a June 1956 speech, Kennedy himself had made this point. "If we are not the parents of little Vietnam," he said, "then surely we are the godparents . . . this is our offspring."[19] As a U.S. senator, Kennedy had in 1954 supported the selection of Ngo Dinh Diem as head of the new South Vietnamese government and opposed the plan for all-Vietnam elections in July 1956, as mandated by the Geneva Accords two years earlier.[20] South Vietnam, as he saw it, was a testing ground for U.S. values and for the capacity of those values to survive and flourish in the face of what he, and most U.S. officials of his generation, saw as new and ever more insidious forms of communist aggression in the newly emerging states of former colonies of the European powers.

But it would be the landlocked and theretofore virtually unknown kingdom of Laos, Vietnam's western neighbor, that would provide the first concrete test in Southeast Asia of the principles Kennedy had enunciated in his inaugural. On January 19, his last full day in office, Dwight Eisenhower had told Kennedy that Laos was the place to hold the line against the spread of communism in Southeast Asia. He reported that both Moscow and Hanoi were assisting the communist Pathet Lao forces, following a right-wing coup on December 8, which Washington supported.[21] Three weeks before his meeting with Kennedy, Eisenhower had told the National Security Council: "We cannot let Laos fall to the Communists, even if we have to fight, with our allies or without them."[22] To Kennedy, Dean Rusk, and McNamara, Eisenhower stressed on January 19 that Laos was the "key to the whole area" and that if the communists take over in Laos "it would be just a matter of time until South Vietnam, Cambodia, Thailand and Burma would collapse."[23] In other words, all the dominoes would fall.

What was so worrisome about Laos? Certainly the United States had little intrinsic interest in or knowledge of Laos as such. The fear rested in the communist *connections* that Washington believed existed, a metaphorical "extension cord" reaching all the way from Moscow (believed to be the true source of power) to communist Pathet Lao forces in Laos by way of Beijing and Hanoi. These were the ostensible mechanics of the domino theory, and the danger was obvious: An otherwise local conflict, in an out-of-the-way place, on the other side of the world, becomes linked in the minds of Washington policymakers to the policies of their nuclear-armed enemy in Moscow. Suddenly, in this far-off kingdom, fundamental U.S. interests appear not only to be involved but also threatened. Only much later, after the Cold War had ended, would it become clear that during this period *both* Moscow and Washington operated on the basis of a fear of aggression by the other. But in early 1961, few in Washington dissented from the view that Moscow, Beijing, and Hanoi were on the offensive in Southeast Asia, that they were winning, and the United States had better do something about it quickly.

Events later during spring 1961 would point to a possible "neutralist solution" for Laos, which Washington regarded more or less as Mao Zedong had proclaimed it: "The objective of a neutralist government," Mao said, "is to destroy the neutralist government."[24] For the moment, Laos had not yet "fallen" to the communists, though who knew how long the neutralist solution would hold up? And if Laos provided ostensible proof that the communists were intent on knocking over the dominoes in Southeast Asia, South Vietnam would provide Washington with a place and a cause to make its stand.

Still, the complicated task would be far from easy. Kennedy and his foreign policy team took a complex view of the situation in South Vietnam and other former colonial areas in turmoil, one that was not merely, or even mainly, focused on military solutions. In their view, a great revolution was occurring—the births of dozens of new nations, whose constituents would have to choose between totalitarian communism and U.S.-style democracy. Given accurate information and a free choice, they believed, rational people would never choose communism over "freedom"—to use Kennedy's favorite idiom. The problem was that the communists knew this too and sought at every opportunity to seize power by force of arms and to exercise control over people in the developing world, in part by brainwashing them with Marxist-Leninist dogma.

On his trip to Saigon in May 1961, Vice Pres. Lyndon Johnson described Diem as the "Winston Churchill of Southeast Asia." For many Americans, this was their first exposure to Diem, even to Vietnam.[25] Whether or not Kennedy believed Diem to be a Churchill, he did nothing to discredit Johnson's dubious description. Also, on May 11 Kennedy approved what was called the "Presidential Program for Vietnam," which included not only military assistance but also "supporting actions of a . . . political, economic, psychological and covert character" for the "defense of South Vietnam."[26] Thus did the Kennedy administration begin to act on its belief that in addition to helping the South Vietnamese Army defend its borders it would "arm" the South Vietnamese people, in classrooms, in the countryside, in churches and temples, with *ideas* that might compete successfully with communist propaganda.

It was in this context that the enemy—the National Liberation Front (NLF) and the Hanoi government—began to come into sharper focus. In his inaugural, Kennedy had not mentioned Vietnam, though his pledge that "one form of colonial control shall not have passed away only to be replaced by a far more iron tyranny"[27] certainly applied to South Vietnam. On April 20, as the last members of the Cuban invasion brigade were still being rounded up at the Bay of Pigs, Kennedy had spoken publicly about the Cuban fiasco. But he added: "We dare not fail to grasp the new concepts, the new tools, the new sense of urgency we will need to combat it—whether in Cuba or South Vietnam. . . . Now it should be clear," he concluded, "that our security may be lost piece by piece, country by country, without the firing of a single missile, or the crossing of a single border."[28] Kennedy was clearly refining Eisenhower's domino theory. These new dominoes would fall,

Kennedy believed, not through occupation by Soviet troops, as in Eastern Europe, but via communist insurgencies, led by committed communists who learned their trade in, and took orders from, Moscow and/or Beijing.

On May 25, 1961, Kennedy gave an extraordinary address to a joint session of Congress. His assistant and speechwriter, Theodore Sorensen, called the speech a "unique second State of the Union address." It was motivated almost entirely by the administration's feeling that it needed additional resources to deal with a rapidly growing list of major international crises.[29] (Sorensen lists fifteen such crises during the first eight months of 1961.) In this context, before Congress and on national radio and television, Kennedy *began* with Vietnam, taking dead aim at the extension cord that connected the potential domino (South Vietnam) to the NLF, Hanoi, Beijing, and Moscow:

> For the adversaries of freedom did not create the [anticolonial] revolution; nor did they create the conditions which compel it. But they are seeking to ride the crest of its wave—to capture it for themselves.
>
> Yet their aggression is more often concealed than open. They have fired no missiles; and their troops are seldom seen. They send arms, agitators, aid, technicians and propaganda to every troubled area. But where fighting is required, it is usually done by others—by guerrillas striking at night, by assassins striking alone—assassins who have taken the lives of four thousand civil officers in the last twelve months in Vietnam alone—by subversives and saboteurs and insurrectionists, who in some cases control whole areas inside of independent nations.[30]

If in retrospect the inaugural address seems somewhat bellicose, these passages strike closer to the heart of what Kennedy and his foreign policy team believed they faced. The language was not as soaring, yet the mindset was clearer: We are in danger of losing the race for the "hearts and minds" to our communist enemies; the Vietnamese communists are among the most brutal, devious, and effective of our enemies; and if we were to lose to the communists in Vietnam, the security of the West will be at risk.

THE VIEW FROM HANOI

While leaders in Washington by January 1961 feared a falling domino in South Vietnam, leaders in Hanoi had fears of their own about the course of events in the South. They never seemed to waver in their commitment to reunifying Vietnam under Hanoi's communist leadership, even after it was clear that the United States would back Ngo Dinh Diem's government to an extent they had not anticipated. Nevertheless, for many in Hanoi, events in the South in 1959 and early 1960 seemed to be moving too quickly, too chaotically. Their fear was that an uprising or revolt against Diem might occur prematurely, before Diem's political apparatus and military capability were sufficiently weakened. One result of a premature political revolt in the South would be the alienation of moderates and members of the professional class, which the resistance needed to complement its largely (though far from exclusively) communist adherents. Were this to occur, their joint cause—Hanoi's and the southerners'—might be set back many years. A second possibility was a direct American intervention. U.S. forces might provide backup support for Diem's forces—the South Vietnamese Army. And then—this was the doomsday scenario in Hanoi—U.S. forces, having secured the South for their "neoimperialist puppet," might attempt to crush the Hanoi government and occupy the country north of the 17th parallel. Thus, for the communists, timing and careful *political* calculations were the keys to success. Le Duan, a southerner who became Party secretary in 1960, put it this way: "How far we win, how far they lose, must be calculated and measured precisely."[31]

Although Ho Chi Minh and Vo Nguyen Giap were better known in the West, Le Duan was the Hanoi leader most responsible for coordinating events in the North and South in such a way as to maintain this delicate balance. On the one hand, as a southerner who traveled throughout the South clandestinely during the late 1950s, he saw firsthand the brutal effects of Diem's campaign to eradicate the southern resistance. It was important that the southerners understand that they had not been forgotten by Hanoi and that they receive tangible support for resisting Diem. On the other hand, sensing the strong commitment Washington had made to Diem, Le Duan had to worry about inadvertently inviting American intervention. Le Duan and John Kennedy had this in common: Each leader groped for ways to support his ally in South Vietnam without encouraging the enemy superpower to intervene, thus causing the conflict to spiral out of control.

On January 31, 1961, the North Vietnamese Politburo, at the urging of Le Duan, produced a new guiding document on revolutionary war strategy in the South. For the first time, the Politburo endorsed armed struggle in the South as an essential element of overthrowing Diem and reunifying Vietnam. U.S. historian and former Foreign Service official William Duiker describes the mindset at that moment in Hanoi and among its southern allies:

By the beginning of 1961, the southern insurgents, stimulated from the North, were on the march. Several provinces, including a number in the

Mekong delta and along the central coast, had come under the partial control of the revolutionary forces. In Hanoi, the initial confusion over policy had been at least temporarily resolved and the foundations of a coherent revolutionary strategy were beginning to emerge. In the world at large, the insurgents now appeared to possess the vocal support of the socialist countries and the sympathy of many others. A new stage of the Vietnamese revolution was about to begin.[32]

In the Maoist lexicon favored by war planners in Hanoi, the "special war" with the United States, and its South Vietnamese ally, was now under way. This critical decision was taken almost simultaneously with the Kennedy administration's arrival in Washington.

The Vietnamese concept of "people's war" had evolved over a millennium of invasion and occupation by great powers. In a sense, the goal of such revolutionary warfare is to gradually weaken and "outlast" the forces of the great power—whether Mongol, Chinese, Japanese, or French. But rather than being a strategy for guerrilla warfare, the kind given notoriety during the 1960s by Argentinian revolutionary Che Guevara—an ostensible strategy for all oppressed peoples, at any time, in any place or situation—the Vietnamese doctrine focused only on the Vietnamese task: the expulsion of larger powers that occupied it.

The object of Vietnamese strategy was thus to retake control of Vietnamese people and territory rather than to conquer others. In addition, the emphasis was on political consolidation, on building a core of revolutionaries who were committed to a long-term struggle and had the capacity to lead, by example, to a similar commitment from others. According to the most famous exponent of Vietnamese people's war, Vo Nguyen Giap, "The military line of our party derives from and always follows its political line."[33] Giap's writing on people's war is opaque at best, but it is clear that primacy of what he calls the "political line" requires a rigidly hierarchical decision process led by those who take a longer, broader view of the situation than is possible from the battlefield.

Truong Chinh, who was Party secretary in Hanoi until 1956 and later head of the National Assembly, put the issue in terms that would apply directly to the situation in the South by the beginning of the 1960s:

> There are those who have a tendency only to rely on military action. . . . They tend to believe that everything can be settled by armed force; they do not apply political mobilization, are unwilling to give explanations and to convince people; . . . fighting spiritedly, they neglect political work; they do

not . . . act in such a way that the army and the people can wholeheartedly help one another.[34]

In other words, the goal is to create a revolutionary movement *first*, before engaging the enemy in the field. Only in this way, it is argued, can one expect partisans to make the kinds of sacrifices, and demonstrate the degree of militant spirit, needed to defeat a larger, militarily more powerful enemy. This is the critical difference between guerrilla warfare and revolutionary warfare, as adapted by the Vietnamese communists in their wars against the French and the Americans.[35]

To a certain extent, Kennedy and his associates understood the point, which was that they must find a way to win the hearts and minds of the South Vietnamese people in order to create the conditions under which they would choose Western values and thus fight and win what was essentially their own war against communist insurgents. The difference, of course—and it was decisive—was that people like Vo Nguyen Giap, Truong Chinh, Le Duan, and their compatriots knew intimately the hearts and minds of the people they sought to organize. In addition, they were in no particular hurry taking the long view as long as they could retain the allegiance and cooperation of the southern resistance, then being hit hard by Diem's "To Cong" forces, which were ruthlessly destroying their human infrastructure.

But if the pace of the southern war was constrained by revolutionary doctrine and Hanoi's wariness about Washington's response, it was nevertheless propelled inexorably forward by the spiral of violence in the South. At the Fifteenth Plenum in January 1959, under pressure from Le Duan, the Party leadership in Hanoi had approved Resolution 15, which first elevated armed struggle to equal status with political struggle in the South. Bui Tin, who would later become editor of the Party's daily newspaper, *Nhan Dan* (The People), was among those involved in the early infiltration efforts. He recalls:

> During 1959 and early 1960, we did not send whole units to the South, but instead secretly selected individuals from among those southerners who had re-grouped to the North in 1954. . . . Those chosen to go South had to be brave, physically fit and preferably unmarried. At the time, they also had to volunteer to go. . . . I had to explain to them about the directives of the 15th Plenum and the political situation in the South which, according to Le Duan, was rapidly changing as a result of this infiltration programme.[36]

In this way, Hanoi attempted gradually to increase pressure on the Diem government, in ways that were consistent with the doctrine of people's war.

But in early 1960, a series of uprisings took place that were not sanctioned and ordered by Hanoi. A major insurrection occurred in Ben Tre, in the central Mekong Delta, during January 17–20.[37] Another attack on Diem's forces occurred at Tay Ninh, also in the central delta.[38] Official histories refer to these and similar events in late 1959 and early 1960 as the period of "partial and spontaneous uprisings." They emphasize that the purpose was to seize control of the government at the local level, replace Diem's people with resistance forces, and then move on to the next hamlet or village.

The reactions to these developments in Hanoi and Saigon were diametrically opposed. Diem and his circle saw signs of ominous escalation by the North and attributed everything to northern "mercenaries." The U.S. military mission was worried, too. At Tay Ninh, insurgents killed twenty-three South Vietnamese soldiers and captured a substantial amount of weapons and ammunition. The head of the U.S. Military Advisory Group, Lt. Gen. Samuel Williams, called it a "severe blow to the Vietnamese Army and an indication of the VC [Vietcong—the resistance] ability to stage large-size and well-planned attacks."[39] In addition, the U.S. embassy in Saigon would report more than 700 assassinations of government officials during the last half of 1960. Resistance fighters in the South referred to this as the "extermination of traitors" campaign, and it was ferocious, as the casualties indicate.[40] However, at Ben Tre, and probably elsewhere, local activists had acted in defiance of the guidelines of Resolution 15. Sometime in March 1960, a group in the South had issued a declaration calling on the masses to rise up at once and overthrow the Diem government. On March 28, 1960, the Regional Committee for the South—which coordinated resistance activities—issued a warning to its compatriots. It cautioned them that such actions as had been taken were premature.[41]

What did all this furious activity signify? Did it reveal evidence of Sino-Soviet manipulation of the Vietnamese communists by the Kremlin? Was it confirmation that the communist extension cord was channeling power from Moscow to such places as Ben Tre and Tay Ninh? Was the Vietnamese communist mindset that of a domino?

It was not. In retrospect, we can see that Hanoi often had great difficulty getting its ostensible southern Vietnamese domino to topple the enemy at the appropriate time. Instead, the NLF's founders seem to have been, for the most part, idealistic and aggrieved members of various groups who had run afoul of Diem and his circle. Years later, former NLF founder and leader Truong Nhu Tang recalled the peculiar circumstances of that moment:

> Replacing the French despots with a Vietnamese one [Diem] was not a
> significant advance. . . . Among my circle of friends, there was anger and pro-

found disappointment at this turn of events. We were living, we felt, in historic times. A shameful, century-long era had just been violently closed out, and a new nation was taking shape before our eyes. Many of us agreed that we could not acquiesce in the shape it was taking. If we were not allowed a say about it from within the government, we would have to speak from without. . . .

Among us we also had people with close ties to the sects, the legal political parties, the Buddhists. In each group we made overtures, and everywhere we discovered sympathy and backing.[42]

Organizers such as Truong Nhu Tang—educated, patriotic, embarrassed by Diem—were *nationalists*. Some were communists; many were not. Many had not been politically active before. But Diem's tactics had forced them to take a stand.

The classic formulation of this phenomenon is due to Isaiah Berlin:

Nationalism . . . is a pathological form of self-protective resistance. . . . It animates revolts . . . for it expresses the inflamed desire of the insufficiently regarded to count for something among the cultures of the world. The brutal and destructive side of modern nationalism needs no stressing in a world torn by its excesses. Yet it must be recognized for what it is—a world-wide response to a profound and natural need on the part of newly liberated slaves—"the decolonized"—a phenomenon unpredicted in the Europe-centered society of the nineteenth century.[43]

Writing in 1960 for a Soviet publication on the occasion of the anniversary of Lenin's ninetieth birthday, Ho Chi Minh said that "at first patriotism, not yet communism, led me to have confidence in Lenin." Why? Because, as he recalled his youth in 1920s Paris, where he first encountered Lenin's ideas, Lenin was the only author Ho read who began with this question: "If you do not condemn colonialism, if you do not side with the colonial people, what kind of revolution are you waging?"[44] More than any other single person, Ho Chi Minh would ensure that Vietnam would "count for something among the cultures of the world" in the twentieth century.

In North and South, the leaders were Vietnamese nationalists who had found in Leninism a way to focus, articulate, and implement their shame and anger. The fates of the Hanoi government and the southern resistance were officially joined on December 20, 1960, at a secret location in the Mekong Delta, where the NLF was founded. The NLF was dominated by communists but also contained many other anti-Diem elements as well. Its formation did not, however, signal that Hanoi had given the go-ahead for an all-out offensive. Quite the reverse, in fact. It meant Hanoi's alternative governing structure was taking shape and that the time had come to unite "partial and spontaneous uprisings" with a systematic strategy to take over the South, beginning with the rural areas, and, only when these were secured, to move to the cities.

Le Duan explained what had to be done in a February 1961 letter to Nguyen Van Linh, chairman of the Regional Committee for the South. The war must be carried forward, he said, *"in the Vietnamese way, that is, by partial insurrections, the formation of revolutionary bases, launching guerrilla warfare and then culminating in a general insurrection,* mainly through the use of political forces combined with armed forces to seize power for the people."[45] Hanoi would seek to micromanage (a term sometimes used to characterize Washington's conduct of the Vietnam War) all aspects of the war in the South, but "in the Vietnamese way." Southern resistance fighters would thus have considerable leeway as to targets and timing, simply because their communications infrastructure was primitive. That being said, the line, as it were, would be laid down by Hanoi, who would thereafter demand that the line was followed.

It was in this paradoxical context of carefully constrained but exceedingly lethal violence in South Vietnam that Radio Hanoi announced, via an English broadcast monitored in Saigon and Phnom Penh on January 29, 1961, that the NLF had been created. The NLF was formed, the broadcast said, "by various forces opposing the fascist Ngo Dinh Diem regime." It also called on "the entire people" to rise up and evict the "American imperialists" who were "subjugating the southern part of our country through a disguised [or camouflaged] colonial regime."[46] In eight of the ten points in its founding program, NLF urged the Vietnamese people to overthrow Diem and the "camouflaged imperialist" or "colonialist" regime of the United States.[47] Here is article 1:

> The present South Vietnamese regime is a camouflaged colonial regime dominated by the Yankees, and the South Vietnamese government is a servile government, implementing faithfully all the policies of the American imperialists. Therefore this regime must be overthrown and a government of national and democratic union put in its place . . . and thus bring about . . . the peaceful unification of the country.[48]

In fact, there is an implicit assumption permeating the NLF platform that it will have to reckon with the United States at some point. But, in January 1961, few could guess how costly the reckoning would ultimately become.

By January 1961, then, the United States had become every bit as much the enemy as Diem, yet few Vietnamese outside Saigon had ever seen an American. Why was the United States in this position? Truong Nhu Tang gives part of the answer: Hanoi and NLF leaders believed, perhaps understandably, not only that the Americans had *replaced* the French but also that they were *just like the French*, interested only in subjugating and exploiting the Vietnamese people. In any case, Washington backed Diem, and the big friend of their number-one enemy was also their number-one enemy. This was their mindset as they marched off to war in January 1961.

A Dialogue in Retrospect: Former Enemies, June 1997

PROLOGUE: DOMINOES, NO! IMPERIALISTS, YES!

According to an agreement worked out in Hanoi three weeks before the June 1997 conference, the first session would be taken up with presentations on the mindsets of the U.S. and Vietnamese sides.

The initial presentation was by Robert McNamara. It had been circulated in advance and was already familiar to the participants at the table (though not to the many observers). His oral presentation was somewhat shorter than the written document. Both the paper and oral presentation were straightforward attempts to open an inquiry into the basic assumptions—the mindsets—of former enemies in one of the bloodiest wars of the century. McNamara admitted that he and his colleagues may well have misjudged Hanoi's motives and intentions due to the obsessive focus in Washington on the fear of falling dominoes. He concluded by inquiring as to whether Hanoi's estimate of Washington's intentions might have been similarly mistaken and thus connected to possible missed opportunities.

Former Foreign Minister Nguyen Co Thach gave the first Vietnamese presentation. He gave no ground whatsoever. The war was caused, he said, by the U.S. desire to become "master of the world." Because the United States backed the brutal and incompetent Diem, he added, it was forced to fight a war against the NLF and Hanoi. Thach agreed with McNamara that the U.S. mindset focused on dominoes as such was wrong. But Hanoi, he concluded, had the correct mindset—that the Americans were the "new imperialists." Nguyen Co Thach delivered this broadside with considerable emotion, and the audience in the large conference hall was utterly silent when he concluded. One wondered: Is it not possible, some four decades after events have transpired, to break into a genuine dialogue about mindsets—about the basic assumptions each side held about the other? The answer: yes—but not quite yet.

The second Vietnamese presentation was by former First Deputy Foreign Minister Tran Quang Co. He began by making a point that was to have considerable impact on the U.S. participants, one that would be made by all the Vietnamese participants: In order to understand the war, one must go back to 1945, not just to January 1961, when Kennedy came to office. He then listed the principal mistakes, as he saw them, in the U.S. mindset toward Vietnam leading to the war. The mood lightened somewhat during a humorous exchange in which Tran Quang Co and McNamara recalled the latter's first visit to Hanoi in November 1995, when he was presented with several pirated editions of the translated *In Retrospect*—but no royalties. Then Tran Quang Co berated several U.S. administrations for betraying traditional American values in the way they approached Vietnam. Finally, Tran Quang Co asked: Did Hanoi make any mistakes during the period in question? He answered himself in the affirmative; Hanoi did make one mistake. Ho Chi Minh and his colleagues had believed—wrongly—that the United States alone among the big powers was anticolonialist.

Following are lengthy excerpts from what participants referred to as the "predialogue" that started off our talks. Robert McNamara begins:

Robert McNamara: My thesis is that we must not permit the twenty-first century to repeat the slaughter of the twentieth; underlying any attempt to reduce the risk of future conflict, will be a better understanding of how past conflicts originated, and what steps might have been taken to avoid them or shorten them.

A retrospective study of the Cuban missile crisis made very clear that the decisions of the Soviet Union, the U.S. and Cuba, before and during the crisis, had been distorted by misinformation, miscalculation, and misjudgment.[49]

Did similar forces shape the decisions of the United States, North Vietnam, and South Vietnam—and hence the course of the Vietnam War—during the 1960s? I now believe so. If that had been understood at the time, would the outcome have been different? Surely the answer must be yes. So I conclude that by studying the misjudgments that affected the course of the war in Vietnam, we can draw lessons which will help prevent similar tragedies in the future. At my request the Council on Foreign Relations, and later, as we've heard, Brown University, in particular the Watson Institute at

Brown University, undertook to ascertain the interest of the Vietnamese government in such a project. And I was delighted when your government responded favorably and agreed to this conference. . . .

Now a major factor, of course, shaping the course of the war was the "mindset" that underlay the decisions of each of the participants. This is the subject of our first session this morning.

Before discussing the U.S. mindset, I want to state, and I want to state it quite frankly, that if I had been a Vietnamese communist in January 1961, when the Kennedy administration came to office, I might well have believed, as I judge they did, that the United States's goal in Southeast Asia was to destroy the Hanoi government and its ally the NLF—that the U.S. was an implacable enemy whose goal, in some fashion, was victory over their country.

Now why might I have believed that? Because the U.S. had:

- Rejected or ignored friendly overtures to President Truman from Ho Chi Minh in the summer and fall of 1945, following the defeat of the Japanese.

- Supported post–World War II French claims to its former colonies in Southeast Asia and had, in addition, throughout the early 1950s financed much of the French war against the Vietminh insurgents, led by Ho Chi Minh.

- Refused to sign the Geneva Accords of 1954, which thus thwarted the planned Vietnamese elections for 1956 that were mandated by the Geneva Agreement.[50]

However, if I had been a Vietnamese communist and had held those views, I would have been totally mistaken. We in the Kennedy administration had no such view; we had no such aims with respect to Vietnam. On the contrary, we believed our interests were being attacked all over the world by a highly organized, unified communist movement, led by Moscow and Beijing, of which we believed, and I now think incorrectly, that the government of Ho Chi Minh was a pawn.

So put very simply, our mindset was indeed one of the fear of "falling dominoes."

Throughout the Kennedy and Johnson administrations, we operated on the premise that the loss of South Vietnam to North Vietnam would result in all of Southeast Asia being overrun by communism and that this would threaten the security of both the United States and the entire noncommunist world. Our thinking about Southeast Asia in 1961 differed little from that of many of the Americans of my generation who, after fighting during World War II to help turn back German and Japanese aggression, had witnessed the Soviet takeover of Eastern Europe following the war and the attempted move into Western Europe. We accepted the idea that had been advanced first by George Kennan in that famous 1947 "X" article anonymously published in *Foreign Affairs*: the view that the West, led by the United States, must guard against communist expansion through a policy of containment.[51] That was the foundation of our decisions about national security and the application of Western military force for the next quarter-century.

Like most Americans, we saw communism as monolithic. We believed that the Soviets and the Chinese were cooperating and trying to extend their hegemony. In hindsight, of course, it's clear that they had no such unified strategy after the late 1950s. We—or at least I, and I think I was far from alone—didn't recognize that. But their split grew slowly and it became apparent only very gradually. At the time, communism still seemed on the march. Don't forget that Mao Zedong had aligned China to fight with Korea against the West in 1953. In 1961 Nikita Khrushchev had predicted communist victory through "wars of national liberation" in the Third World. Earlier he had told the West: "We will bury you."[52] And that threat had gained credibility when in 1957 the USSR launched Sputnik, demonstrating its lead in space technology. The next year Khrushchev started turning up the heat on West Berlin. Castro followed by transforming Cuba into a potential base for subversion in the Western Hemisphere. And Ho Chi Minh, with the help of the Chinese, had driven the French forces out of Indochina.

So it seemed obvious to us that the communist movement in Vietnam was closely related to the guerrilla insurgencies being carried on in the 1950s in Burma, Malaya, and the Philippines. We viewed those conflicts not as nationalistic movements—as I think they were, with hindsight—we viewed them as signs of a unified communist drive for hegemony in Asia. That way of thinking led Dean Acheson, President Truman's secretary of state and one of our ablest and wisest statesmen, to call Ho Chi Minh "the mortal enemy of independence in Indochina."[53] This shows the mindset that was common amongst us at the time.

We also knew that the Eisenhower administration had accepted the Truman administration's view that Indochina's fall to communism would threaten U.S. security. Therefore the Eisenhower administration had sounded the warning of the Chinese threat clearly and often. In 1954, it was President Eisenhower who coined that term "falling dominoes"; he said that if Indochina fell, the rest of Southeast Asia would indeed fall like a "row of dominoes."[54] And he had added that "the possible consequences of that loss are just incalculable to the free world." And it was on January 19, 1961, Eisenhower's last full day in office, at a meeting with President Kennedy, a meeting which I attended, that he warned us that "if Laos [and by implication

Vietnam] is lost to the Free World, in the long run we will lose all of Southeast Asia."[55]

Eisenhower wasn't alone in those thoughts. During his years in the Senate, John F. Kennedy had echoed Eisenhower's assessment of Southeast Asia. He had said—and I quote Kennedy's words in a speech he made in 1956: "Vietnam represents the cornerstone of the Free World in southeast Asia. It's our offspring. We can't abandon it, we can't ignore its needs."[56] So we felt beset. We felt at risk. And that fear underlay the Kennedy administration's involvement in Vietnam.

You will remember in his inaugural address President Kennedy had called on America and the West to bear the burden of a long struggle—a long struggle against communist hegemony extending across the world. Kennedy said, and I quote: "Let every nation know, whether it wishes us well or ill, that we shall pay any price, bear any burden, meet any hardship, support any friend, oppose any foe to assure the survival and success of liberty."[57] But in applying that resolve in Southeast Asia, I now believe we badly misread both China and Vietnam. We misjudged China's objectives, we mistook its bellicose rhetoric to imply a drive for regional hegemony. And I believe we also greatly underestimated the nationalistic element and aspect of Ho Chi Minh's movement. We saw him first as a communist and only secondarily as a Vietnamese nationalist.

Now when I say "we misjudged" I'm not talking only of the two presidents and their senior advisors, but of many of the experts in and outside government, and across the nation. For example, the National Intelligence Estimates (NIEs), which were produced throughout the period 1961–68, and which provided the foundation of much of the thinking of the president and his senior advisors, supported these conclusions. A National Intelligence Estimate dated June 9, 1964, stated—and I want to quote it at some length:

> The loss of South Vietnam and Laos to the communists would be profoundly damaging to the U.S. position in the Far East, most especially because the U.S. has committed itself persistently, emphatically, and publicly to preventing a communist takeover of the two countries. Failure here would be damaging to U.S. prestige, and would seriously debase the credibility of U.S. will and capability to contain the spread of communism elsewhere in the area. Our enemies would be encouraged and there would be an increased tendency among other states to move toward a greater degree of accommodation with the communists. The chief effect would be upon communist China, both in boosting its already remarkable self-confidence and in raising its prestige as a leader of world communism. Peiping has already begun to

advertise South Vietnam as proof of its thesis that the underdeveloped world is ripe for revolution, that the U.S. is a paper tiger, and that local insurgency can be carried through to victory without undue risk of precipitating an international war. To some degree, this will tend to encourage and strengthen the more active revolutionary movements in various parts of the underdeveloped world.[58]

That was a fair statement of the views of the major policymakers of the U.S. government at that time. We did indeed believe the threat of communist aggression to be real. But—and I want to stress this—although we may have exaggerated the threat, we had some cause to be concerned. We not only saw the increasing belligerence of both China and the Soviet Union in the 1950s, but during the 1960s, during my seven years as secretary of defense, we came close to armed conflict with the Soviets on at least three occasions. And if you doubt that, I urge you to read a new book published just this week. The book is *One Hell of a Gamble*, by Aleksandr Fursenko and Timothy Naftali.[59] It shows how close you came, and we came—the whole world came—to nuclear war during the Cuban missile crisis. And that was but one of three occasions on which we came—we, the U.S. and the Soviets—came close to armed conflict: over Berlin in August of sixty-one, over Soviet missiles in Cuba in October of sixty-two, and over the Middle East war in June of sixty-seven.

As for North Vietnam, it appeared to us to be closely associated with the Chinese and the Soviets in their effort to extend communist control across the world. Let me just mention two or three points that led us to that view— an erroneous view I am convinced today—but I want you to understand why we held it then:

- We saw the affinity for the communist movement and its leaders demonstrated by Ho Chi Minh and his colleagues in Moscow and, after 1949, in Beijing.

- We took note of Truong Chinh's 1949 statement that "the U.S. would be defeated in Indochina as it had been in China," which indicated, to U.S. leaders, the intention to force communist governments on all the countries of Indochina.

- We were familiar with the content, and saw the results of, the Politburo's Resolution 15 of May 1959. You'll remember that this was the resolution which stated that armed struggle was to be the policy of the anti-Diem resistance in the South.[60]

- From the late 1950s, we saw the evidence of Hanoi's support for the

Pathet Lao insurgency in neighboring Laos, supported in 1961 by Soviet aircraft and weapons.

These actions confirmed our fears that communist countries, large and small, were bent on extending their hegemony over neighboring states.

But perhaps you may ask: Why did we fail to consider China and Vietnam in the same light as we did Yugoslavia? This is an absolutely *fundamental* question! There were several reasons. Tito appeared to us to be unique. He and Stalin had publicly quarreled. In contrast, China's and North Vietnam's rhetoric made us think they sought to work together to achieve regional hegemony. And Cuba, by embracing the Soviet Union, seemed illustrative of how ostensibly independent Third World nations could quickly place themselves within the communist orbit. And as Castro said to me when we met with him in Havana: "We then [1962] were seeking to subvert the established governments of the Western Hemisphere." So we equated Ho Chi Minh not with Marshal Tito, as I think we should have, but with Fidel Castro.[61]

The view I have set out here was a view shared by the majority of the American people, the media, and the foreign policy experts. It is widely believed today that in the early and mid-1960s, there was strong opposition in our press, our public, and academic circles as well as the Congress to U.S. involvement in Vietnam. That view is not correct. In 1995, Richard Harwood, a *Washington Post* reporter, wrote an article that dealt with this issue. I quote from it, as follows: "The *New York Times* hailed the Tonkin Gulf Resolution in 1964 as proof of our united determination to support the cause of freedom in Southeast Asia—against" what he called "the mad adventure by the North Vietnamese communists." And he went on to say that—this is Harwood now reporting in 1995—that David "Halberstam," who later wrote one of the major critiques of U.S. involvement in Vietnam, "published a few months later," in 1964–65, "a book in which he opposed any American abandonment of South Vietnam because, he said, 'Vietnam is a legitimate part of America's global commitment . . . it's perhaps one of only five or six nations in the world that are . . . vital to U.S. interests.'"[62]

Later in the same article, Harwood wrote that the thesis that I've just elaborated had been studied in 1970 by Susan Welch, a political scientist at the University of Illinois. She stated, based on her analysis, that the American public "viewed the war as a struggle between communism and the Free World, vital to the preservation of all of Southeast Asia and perhaps all of Asia."[63] She said that the major newspapers, academic circles, and the Congress had not deviated from that view until the latter part of the 1960s.

So this was our mindset. I think that it was an erroneous mindset, but I wanted all of us to start this meeting by understanding what it was and why it evolved.

This retrospective review of the U.S. mindset raises, I think, two fundamental questions:

1. If we had believed then what I believe today—that is to say, that this U.S. mindset was incorrect in essential respects—could we have obtained public support for a policy of noninvolvement or withdrawal from Vietnam?

2. Is the view which I now hold correct—that our security would not have been threatened had we not intervened in Vietnam?

The first question is not on the agenda this morning, so I simply want to say a word in passing because many of my associates have said, "Well, McNamara, you might be right, our view was wrong, but if the leaders of the country had held that divergent view, they could not have persuaded the American people to go along with it." I don't believe that. If Kennedy and Johnson and their associates had believed that a North Vietnamese victory did not threaten the security of the West, it would have been our responsibility to persuade the public of the merit of our views. And I think we could have done so. One does not, or should not, contrary to what you sometimes read, govern a country or govern the U.S., on the basis of polls. We didn't, and I think we would have prevailed if we had held the view that I now believe was the correct view. I believe strongly that we could have persuaded the American public to follow that view.

But the other question—"would our security have been threatened had we not intervened?"—was very much an issue in the 1960s, it remains so today. Walt W. Rostow, who was a senior official under President Kennedy and later became President Johnson's National Security Adviser, wrote in 1995: "Mr. McNamara's view that our security would not have been threatened had we not intervened, or had withdrawn earlier than we did, depends heavily on his view of the importance of Asia to the United States and the extent to which withdrawal from Vietnam would affect the balance of power in Asia."[64] He basically says today that we were justified in doing what we were doing, and I am wrong to think otherwise because I don't understand Asia and I don't understand where we'd be in Asia had we not intervened. He continues to believe that we would be much weaker today had we not intervened. And he implies that the rapid economic and social advance throughout Southeast Asia that has been realized in the 1970s and 1980s could not have been achieved without the U.S. action. And by the way, Rostow is not the only one who believes that. Singapore's Lee Quan Yew, a very wise statesman, believes the same thing.

I think they are both wrong. Would the balance of power in Asia today be different than it is had we not intervened? How would China and the Soviet Union have behaved in that event? Would they have sought to extend their hegemony south and east? Would North Vietnam have permitted a unified Vietnam to be used for that purpose? Even without Chinese and Soviet attempts to extend communist control, might not surrounding countries such as Malaysia, Thailand, Indonesia—might they not have sought geopolitical accommodation with the communist regimes in the region, much as Castro intended that the nations of Latin America would disassociate themselves from the U.S. when he sought to subvert their governments?

In sum, then, these were our "mindsets," which were the basis throughout the 1960s for U.S. military intervention in Southeast Asia, as well as for North Vietnam's refusal to negotiate—were these two mindsets correct? I think not. Is it not more probable that:

• By January 1961, each side was mistaken in its assessments of the motives and intentions of the other?

• These mistaken views convinced both sides that each other's principal goal was to attack the vital interests of the other?

• If each side had known the true motives, intentions, and fears of the other, each would have understood that defensive motives predominated in the thinking of each?

• Opportunities to avoid or terminate the conflict were missed by both sides out of ignorance, bias, prejudice, and other limitations on human assessment and action?

Finally, cannot lessons be drawn from a review of the missed opportunities which can apply today and tomorrow to the goal of preventing, or at least reducing the risk, of deadly conflict in the twenty-first century?

Nguyen Co Thach: I want to thank Mr. McNamara for his remarks and for giving us such a clear picture of the U.S. mindset toward Vietnam—toward the government in Hanoi I mean, after the country was split into two parts at Geneva in 1954. And it is true that Ho Chi Minh and his followers were very attracted to the United States. Mr. McNamara is quite correct in this, as evidenced by Ho Chi Minh's appeal to the U.S. Declaration of Independence after the August Revolution of 1945.

In my way of thinking, the principal problem in the evolution of these mindsets was that—especially in the 1950s and 1960s—the U.S. seemed to want to become the world's policeman. Mr. McNamara correctly quotes President Kennedy's inaugural address as evidence of a certain anticommunist mind-set—a fear that communism would overrun the U.S., or something of the sort. Actually, it seemed to us that in Kennedy's inaugural, he was asserting that the U.S. wished to become something like the "master of the world." In this way, the U.S. would replace the British and the French, who had previously based their policies on such a wish. In our part of the world, this "fear of falling dominoes" was joined to the "threat of the yellow skin"—so those were two reasons, or excuses, really, why the U.S. felt justified in taking over as the new imperialists.

Now, where did the war come from—from what did the American War emerge? The answer is not difficult to find. In Geneva in 1954, other countries—large and powerful countries, not only the U.S.—decided that Vietnam should be divided into two countries. The U.S. installed Ngo Dinh Diem in Saigon and decided to keep him in power at all costs, because of the fear of the communists in the North, ignoring the fact that many, many people in the southern part of Vietnam did not want Diem, would not have voted for Diem, in fact feared Diem. When Diem, backed by the U.S., became increasingly brutal, the people in the South organized themselves, at last, to fight Diem, because they were given no alternative by the U.S.-backed dictator. And so, beginning with the struggle against Diem, the conflict grew, as the U.S. gradually took over Diem's functions, including the military ones, eventually, and the southern resistance—the NLF—turned to its northern allies for assistance in their struggle. That is more or less how the war came about, I think. There is no big mystery about it.

Therefore, I would say, with all due respect to Mr. McNamara, that the U.S. mindset, as he says, was incorrect, but also that the Vietnamese mindset—our assessment of the U.S.—was essentially correct. Essentially correct. That is all.

Tran Quang Co: I agree that the conference should be aimed at drawing the lessons so we can avoid tragic wars, like the Vietnam War, in the twenty-first century. I agree with Mr. McNamara that miscalculation and misjudgment are two of the factors that led to the conflict between the U.S. and Vietnam. So I agree with that part of Mr. McNamara's presentation in which he says that the war could have been avoided, or terminated earlier, if the U.S. had correctly assessed the goals of North Vietnam. I agree with this.

Mr. McNamara, however, wishes to focus only on the period after the Kennedy administration came to office. But I think in order to understand the problems that led to the war in the 1960s, we must go back farther in history than January 1961. The process of U.S. involvement in Vietnam began—seriously began—with the Truman administration and continued more or less uninterrupted through five presidents. The Kennedy administration merely followed the path of its predecessors with readjustments made in accordance with the international context and the realities of the war at that time. In 1945, Vietnam turned to the U.S. with the hope of obtaining some sympathy and support from the West but the Truman administration, which completely misunderstood Vietnam, turned its back on Vietnam.

This misunderstanding, which continued from the Truman administration until at least the end of the Vietnam War in 1975, fell into the following four categories:

1. On the unity of Vietnam and the will of the Vietnamese people to reunify their country. The Vietnamese people completely rejected the idea of "two Vietnams."

2. On the character of the revolutionary movement of Vietnam (which was basically a national liberation movement).

3. On the primary goals of the struggle of Vietnam (national independence and unity, not the overthrow of other governments in the region).

4. On the relations between Vietnam and the USSR, and Vietnam and China (which were based on mutual interests, not the dependence of Vietnam).

These were the four principal errors in the U.S. mindset toward Vietnam. According to my understanding, all U.S. administrations, from Truman's to Nixon's, committed these mistakes.

All the leaders in these administrations made these mistakes, but—and this is very significant for us—only Mr. McNamara has been brave enough to admit making them. For this, he has earned the respect of the Vietnamese people. As he learned when he was last in the country, *In Retrospect*, his memoir of the war, is very popular in this country. However, he also learned that he was not getting any royalties from book sales in this country. All he got was a few free copies of his book in the Vietnamese language. [Laughter.]

Robert McNamara: You're right about that. I'm still waiting for the royalties, too. [Laughter.]

Tran Quang Co: Yes, but I'm afraid it may take Vietnamese publishers a long time to learn about the concept of royalties. [Laughter.]

Mr. McNamara admits mistakes, which we admire, but he unfortunately attributes most mistakes to misjudgments and miscalculations. But we must also ask: *What about values and intentions?* As I understand it, the right to self-determination—the independence of a nation—belongs to the general values of the world community. What about U.S. support of the French colonialists after World War II, in defiance of its own democratic traditions? What about the direct U.S. military intervention in Vietnam—I mean sending U.S. soldiers to find and kill Southern Vietnamese? And what about the U.S. policy seeking to divide Vietnam for good and to "bomb North Vietnam back to the Stone Age"? We must ask: Are *these* policies consistent with these moral values? Mr. McNamara says that the Kennedy administration did not seek to destroy the NLF. But we must respect history; we must face the historical facts. Isn't this *exactly* what the U.S. tried to do—to destroy the NLF by bombing or any other means at its disposal? Isn't this why the U.S. soldiers were in Vietnam in the first place?

The question arises as to whether Vietnam—the government in Hanoi—also made such mistakes about the U.S. Was the Vietnamese mindset wrong in some way about the Americans? Yes, in one way, the Vietnamese mindset was wrong. What was our mistake? Prior to September 1945, the Vietnamese people perceived the U.S. to be a world leader in the fight against fascism. At that time, the Vietnamese people considered the U.S. to be the only powerful Western country that opposed colonialism. Because of this, Vietnam had hoped that the U.S. would sympathize with the Vietnamese people's legitimate struggle for independence, freedom, and happiness. Unfortunately, reality proved that it was not so.

Here is another point that must be considered. Objectively speaking, Vietnam could not choose whether or not to fight a war. I mean, Vietnam had no choice, to fight or not to fight, unless it was willing to give up its desires for national independence and accepted, instead, the status of an enslaved country. From the Vietnamese perspective, the outbreak of war was not due to any Vietnamese misunderstanding of France or the United States. Instead, we believe war was brought to Vietnam by outside countries, in spite of the fact that Vietnam wanted to obtain national independence through peaceful means. I stress "through peaceful means." Vietnam did not want war.

Therefore, Mr. McNamara's argument that the outbreak of war was a direct result of "misjudgments, miscalculations, and misinformation" about the other side is only applicable to the U.S. side. Vietnam had no choice but to fight. The war came about, as we understand it, due to a serious conflict of basic interests. That was at the heart of the problem.

I think Mr. McNamara's idea of "missed opportunities" is an interesting one that needs some consideration. While the outbreak of war is a result of a conflict of interests between countries, in general terms the war could have been terminated in two ways:

1. The first possibility would have been the military victory of one side over the other, the result being that one side would successfully achieve its desired goals, but at the expense of the other.

2. A second possibility would have required that both sides acknowledge a need to negotiate and to change their objectives sufficiently to reach a mutually acceptable compromise.

These seem to me to be the two broad possibilities for avoiding the missed opportunities about which Mr. McNamara speaks.

I believe we have all agreed with each other that the purpose of this conference is to draw lessons that will prevent the twenty-first century from repeating the bloody wars of the twentieth century. I think, therefore, that we should only discuss the missed opportunities that are stipulated in the second possibility. I am afraid that if we seek to draw lessons from the missed opportunities consistent with the first possibility—i.e., a U.S. military victory—then the twenty-first century is bound to be characterized by more violence where powerful countries try to destroy weaker, smaller countries.

❖

What some began calling the "predialogue" had begun. It would take some time before the Vietnamese would begin to respond to McNamara's admonition that they look more closely at their own mindset, at the core of which was the conviction that Washington's aims in Vietnam were neoimperialist aims, that North Vietnam and the NLF were its victims and, since their view of the U.S. was correct, they had made no mistakes and therefore missed no opportunities. Their views, like those of the Americans, would become far more complex than this as the discussion progressed.

The Dialogue Begins

It is hardly surprising that those who fought a brutal war against each other—whose everyday reality during the war seemed to confirm their assumptions regarding the enemy—that these former officials would only with difficulty, and over time, begin to probe the veracity of their decades-old mindsets.

This especially applies to the Vietnamese. To them, the U.S. was what may be called a "first order" aggressor or enemy. Americans came to their country and killed their people. As they saw it, this was without provocation on their part. As Tran Quang Co said, the Vietnamese did not ask for the war; it was brought to them by the American imperialists. Evidence of U.S. "imperialism," according to this view, is still everywhere to be seen in the unrepaired damage in Vietnamese cities and the countryside.

To the Americans, the Hanoi government was a "second order" aggressor or enemy that had invaded a U.S. ally. It did no direct damage to the United States as such. The damage the war did to the United States was real and is certainly still present, but it is less tangible than that to which the Vietnamese bear witness. Still, even to the participating former U.S. officials, there was a difficulty in facing, for the first time in most cases, in Hanoi, senior representatives of that ostensible "domino" that they had tried unsuccessfully to subdue.

The surprise was that real dialogue began soon after the break following the formal presentations. After some back-and-forth about the fallacy of falling dominoes, and several more attempts by some Vietnamese participants to establish the U.S. imperialist-colonialist "credentials," suddenly the ice was broken.

Chester Cooper, frustrated by the repetition of "imperialist" epithets, turns to the Vietnamese side—to anyone who cared to respond—and asks whether it is possible that they misread the United States. Luu Doan Huynh responds by saying that Hanoi did not want to fight a war with the United States—that they hoped to set up a coalition government in Saigon acceptable to all parties. He does not say Hanoi failed to do so, but that is what he meant, as he later clarified. Robert Brigham then asks the Vietnamese side whether they did not miss an opportunity to explain this to the United States. Nguyen Khac Huynh responds that they tried but that they lacked the sophistication and experience to know how to inform the United States without appearing to be weak.

From that moment, the discussion of missed opportunities, and of mistaken mindsets, became more reciprocal, a joint exploration by colleagues, rather than a latter-day confrontation of wary former enemies.

❖

Luu Doan Huynh: . . . Between the early 1950s and the beginning of the Kennedy administration, the U.S. mindset toward Vietnam was influenced by some sort of irrational apprehension or nightmare. You know, there is something that they call the "blindness of history" that can be applied here. Everything, it seems, was perceived through the lens of Cold War politics. It was because of this that you gentlemen could not understand the rise of nationalist movements throughout the Third World, movements that became powerful in the 1950s and 1960s. These nationalist movements would eventually change the face of international relations. . . .

All those events spoken about by Mr. McNamara . . . meant to you gentlemen that Soviet influence was increasing everywhere. In particular, Mr. McNamara mentioned Resolution 15, according to which the leadership in Hanoi committed itself to the armed struggle in the South. But, really, Resolution 15 had nothing whatsoever to do with the Soviets. In Vietnam, Resolution 15 indicated the desire for self-determination. No more, no less. Our strategy with respect to the struggle in South Vietnam would be independent from the Soviets and Chinese, though we would endeavor to remain friendly to both. I believe that Americans, if they would simply have "read the fine print," they would be able to distinguish nationalist movements from Cold War politics.

Nicholas Katzenbach: I have found this discussion so far very interesting regarding mindsets and their misconceptions. This is interesting, I think, because of what's been said about unintended consequences of actions—actions taken for one reason which have a different impact—different consequences—than were originally intended. For example, I think that it should have been clear to everyone that the United States was opposed to colonialism after World War II, even if some of the policies of the United States tended to support the colonial powers in some parts of the world, such as here, in Vietnam. Obviously, you who live in this part of the world were totally focused on what happened here. What you seem to be telling us is that you therefore drew the conclusion that the United States was procolonial. This seemed valid to you, even though almost everything that we did and said opposed colonialism in most parts of the world.

So I think one of the reasons for the misconceptions in these various mindsets comes from the fact that you were all very much focused—each country is focused—on its own problems. This means that they did not necessarily see that the problem on which they are focused arises from some unintended consequences of an action taken for reasons that have nothing to do with them. The U.S. support of France after the war is a good example. Now, in that connection, I think that if you believe another country has a misconception about what it is that you are trying to do, then you should try to cure that misconception—to correct that mistake in the mindset. It would seem to be in your interest—in everybody's interest—to do so.

Dinh Nho Liem: . . . Mr. Katzenbach has asserted that the U.S. opposed colonialism. That may be the way it looked in Washington. But we believed—it was obvious—that the U.S. was opposed to Vietnam's national independence. We saw U.S. policy as it related to our history—Vietnamese history, which has been devoted to the struggle for the maintenance of Vietnamese independence against any opposition. This was not just an issue of misperception or misinformation. No. The main point is that the objectives of both sides were different. Vietnam went to war to defend its national independence. The U.S. opposition was based on the belief that if Vietnam gained its independence this would lead to the spread of communism throughout Southeast Asia. That U.S. perception was wrong. . . .

Gen. Nguyen Dinh Uoc: . . . I wonder if it is really true that, as Mr. Katzenbach said, the U.S. was opposed to colonialism. In 1963 and 1964, there were fourteen coups attempted against the Saigon regime. Why did the U.S. continue to come to the rescue of the Saigon government? Isn't it obvious? Because they wanted a puppet government in Saigon that could be manipulated. That is what we saw in the relationship between the U.S. and the Diem government.

Forgive me for saying so, but what was the rationale behind the creation of strategic hamlets? The basis of this program was that the U.S. displaced peasants and put them into fortified camps that were nothing more than jails by another name. If that was not colonialism, then what is? That is very clear. The hamlets were like jails surrounded by barbed wire where one must get permission to move about. So how could the peasants stand it? An individual's right, a citizen's right to freedom, where has that gone? It is obvious that this was the imposition of colonialism.

Chester Cooper: During the last hour or two, I have heard several of my American colleagues point out that—or suggest—that some parts of our U.S. mindset about the world in general and about Vietnam in particular were *wrong!* And I've heard many of my friends on the other side of the table comment that many of the U.S. mindsets about Vietnam were wrong. But I would like to ask you whether any of your mindsets, any of your perceptions of the U.S. may have been wrong. [Laughter.]

Dao Huy Ngoc: Well, on this point, Mr. Tran Quang Co has already stated that before 1945 the Vietnamese wrongly believed the U.S. to be an anti-colonial power.

Luu Doan Huynh: I will speak about our mindset in 1960, at about the time the Kennedy administration came into office. We tried to be realistic. We tried to take a realistic view of the U.S. So our mindset was as follows: to conduct political and armed struggle in the South with the hope of gradually bringing about the collapse of the Saigon army. A corollary of this was to get the U.S. and Saigon government to agree to the creation of a coalition government committed to a policy of peace and neutrality. And that government would request that the U.S. terminate its intervention and assume normal relations.

If history had unfolded in that manner, the revolution in Vietnam would have avoided a big war with the U.S., which is exactly what we wanted.

Robert Brigham: . . . This points to a possible missed opportunity, possibly even a mistaken policy, on the part of the Hanoi government. That missed opportunity, or mistake, was in doing little or nothing to explain to the American policymakers the sorts of considerations just mentioned by Mr. Luu Doan Huynh, such as the desire for a neutral solution in the South, and certainly the desire to avoid a war with the Americans.

What *did* the Americans hear, or read, about your motives? Well, they heard about you from the Chinese. The rhetoric coming out of Beijing immediately after the formation of the Front, just before the Front's Second Party Conference in February 1962, was quite clear: Beijing saw the creation of the NLF as the first of many united fronts to be created in Southeast Asia. Did the Washington policymakers believe this? You bet they did. Why not? It was consistent with their view of the history of the Cold War since the end of World War II, and it confirmed some of their worst fears about the Chinese communists in particular—that they were especially interested in a multi-front confrontation with the West. I have studied your available literature carefully, and I know of nothing you produced that would tend to dissuade the American policymakers from this doomsday view of the meaning of the creation of the NLF in 1960. Nothing. I'm not saying they were right and you were wrong. I'm saying that you did little or nothing to convince them *then*, in real time, that they were mistaken.

Nguyen Khac Huynh: First, I want to say something about this issue of whether or not the U.S. was a "colonialist" power—of whether the U.S. was a colonialist power in Vietnam. Mr. McNamara has said the U.S. did not have colonialist aims. Let me put the matter in the following way: The U.S. did not precisely follow the example of the English or French. When the English or French conquered an area, they established a colonial governor. The governor was all-powerful. If there was already a king or an emperor in place, then they usually retained him as a puppet, as long as he was compliant.

The U.S. had a slightly different approach. It set up a puppet regime through the use of economic and military assistance that was under U.S.

control. In this regime, the U.S. ambassador played the role of a French or British governor-general. The U.S. ambassador took the orders he received from Washington and passed them on to the puppet government in Saigon. In case the government did not satisfy the U.S., the U.S. would not hesitate to replace it. . . .

Here is the second point. . . . In the resistance war against the French, we lived in the jungles for nearly ten years and eventually defeated them without having much information about their policies and strategies. We nevertheless knew more about the French than the U.S., since we had to be with them for nearly a hundred years. But our knowledge about the U.S., which became our enemy, was far from sufficient. That is true. It was natural that we did not know much about U.S. internal affairs, the role your domestic politics played in the war, especially in the early days of the war. And our knowledge about the U.S. relationship with the rest of the world, which Mr. McNamara has referred to as the "geopolitical factor," was quite limited. We therefore formulated our strategies and policies principally on the basis of our assessment of the actual situation on the battlefield.

In these circumstances, what more could we do to make the U.S. understand us? Truly, we did not know how to do it. . . .

MISTAKEN MINDSETS: "IT TAKES TWO TO TANGO"

At the end of the first day—which had been taken up entirely with the discussion of mindsets—it was clear that there was still much work ahead. It had been especially difficult to get the Vietnamese participants to entertain the possibility that their mindset with regard to the United States—especially to the Kennedy administration—had been incorrect. A comment from Dao Huy Ngoc toward the end of the first day's discussion revealed an important reason for this. He said that perhaps both the U.S. and Soviet Union believed the domino theory. This "bloc" mentality, he concludes, may account for why and how small countries like Vietnam got caught in the middle and had to choose. Yet he still does not appear to fully credit the remarks of the U.S. participants who have described their mindset as motivated by defensive considerations—that this is the essence of the domino theory—of falling dominoes. One senses how difficult it must be for a citizen of a small country like Vietnam to appreciate that for leaders of a gigantic superpower like the United States, it was fear of losing, not imperialist avarice, that accounts for its involvement in Vietnam.

This prompted Robert McNamara to revisit his opening remarks, stressing that the domino theory subscribed to by U.S. officials in those days was profoundly defensive and, however misguided its application may have been in Vietnam, was nevertheless rooted in the same kind of idealism that appealed to Ho Chi Minh. That being the case, he says, labeling the U.S. "imperialists" betrays a fundamental misunderstanding of the U.S. mindset, which stressed defending basic ideals, which Washington believed were threatened in South Vietnam.

Does this matter? It matters a great deal, says McNamara. Those ideals are fundamental, he says, and "I don't think you appealed to them." The implication, one that was taken up in subsequent sessions, is that if the Vietnamese had found a way credibly to appeal to ideals both sides apparently shared, the tragedy might have been avoided or minimized. The reverse, of course, is also true—that Washington also failed to communicate its mindset to Hanoi. But this does not, McNamara argues, eliminate Hanoi's portion of the responsibility for the tragedy.

As the delegations were leaving the conference after the grueling and emotionally draining first day of discussions, Nguyen Co Thach, head of the Vietnamese team, turned to the U.S. participants and said: "So, you think it takes two to tango, eh? Maybe. We will talk more about this."

❖

Dao Huy Ngoc: . . . I wonder if the greatest mistake of the U.S. was in devising a scheme for dominating the world. It seems that after World War II the U.S. and the USSR both decided that they wanted to dominate the world. Now, it is clear that if the communists had not won in China in 1949, and if the USSR had not taken its action in 1950, then I believe that U.S. relations with Southeast Asia could have been different. But because the big powers were trying to establish blocs, U.S. actions toward Vietnam did not really relate specifically to Vietnam, but to the mindset of establishing blocs. Maybe each side—U.S. and USSR—had its own domino theory. Maybe for the U.S., Vietnam was regarded as a kind of domino.

Robert McNamara: I would like one last word in relation to mindsets and misunderstandings, particularly in relation to Ambassador Ngoc's point. We certainly misunderstood Vietnam. But I believe in the discussions this morning and this afternoon, there has been strong evidence that you did then—and I suspect even today—that you misunderstood our evaluation of the situation in Vietnam. I think I can speak for Presidents Kennedy and Johnson, with whom I was very close. I can certainly speak for myself. And I know I can speak for Averell Harriman on this particular point, because he and I discussed it many times. We were *not* opposed to an independent, unified Vietnam. We were *not!*

I want to make that very, very clear. I don't think you understood it then, and I'm not sure you understand it today. And if you didn't understand it then, and you don't understand it today, I am willing to accept that this is due to a deficiency on our part—a failure on our part to convince you.

So let me try again and I want to be blunt. What we feared was a Vietnam that was a pawn in the hands of the Soviets and/or the Chinese, exactly the same way that Castro told me in 1992 that Cuba would have been a pawn in the hands of the Soviet Union for penetration of the Western Hemisphere and a weakening of U.S. security in our hemisphere. Now I suspect that our fears may have been unwarranted with regard to North Vietnam—to a communist Vietnam. But I also want to say to you that I think you were wrong in not presenting to us more clearly and strongly then the kind of remarks we heard today: that you were not intending—you did not act and you were not intending to act—as an instrument of, or as an extension of, Chinese and Soviet power.

So I come away from today—and we are at the end of the session today—with a feeling I brought with me to Vietnam—that I brought into the session this morning. I believe we misunderstood each other. I think it is a tragedy. We were not opposed to your independence. Ho Chi Minh was correct when he quoted our Declaration of Independence in his early statements, in 1945, when he formed this country. We believed those sentiments then [in 1776], and we believe them today. I know we don't always act in accordance with those beliefs, but those are our fundamental beliefs. I don't think you appealed to them. I don't think you understood them. And I am damn certain we didn't understand that that was your belief. So I think it's a tragedy that we allowed that misunderstanding to exist and I hope we won't allow it to continue in the future.

Conclusions

Near the end of his famous novel of the French war in Indochina, *The Quiet American*, Graham Greene has the cynical English narrator say this about the naive American of the title: "He was impregnably armoured by his good intentions and his ignorance."[65] The same could be said of leaders in both Washington and Hanoi by January 1961. Each did far too little to penetrate the armor of the mistaken mindsets of its enemy—to refute them in ways that would have permitted both to understand that neither Washington nor Hanoi was threatened by each other's *real* objectives. If each had found a way to get through the other's armor of fear, the tragedy could have been avoided.

The opening discussion of mindsets established a precedent in the conference for bluntness, tempered with the willingness to listen on both sides. I was fascinated by the Vietnamese presentation of their view of alleged U.S. "imperialism" or "colonialism"—by how elaborate the theory was, and how many diverse instances seemed to them to prove by January 1961 that the United States was the reincarnation of the French. It really struck home when Nguyen Khac Huynh said that it was more or less obvious in Hanoi that Ngo Dinh Diem was the equivalent of the French colonial governor, put in place by the United States to do its bidding. This is not just incorrect. To those of us on the U.S. team who had dealt with Diem, such a view is *incomprehensible*.

In my introduction to this chapter, I listed the four basic questions that we in Washington should have asked, but did *not* ask, regarding our own "falling dominoes" mindset. Now, with the benefit of the June 1997 discussion of mindsets, of countless other discussions between representatives of our two sides, and on the basis of related research we have carried out, I would like to propose some tentative answers to those initially unasked questions. Beginning with the United States and its mindset, here are the questions and the answers I would give today:

1. Enemy's Objective. Was it true that the fall of South Vietnam would trigger the fall of all Southeast Asia? Answer: Probably not. Hanoi's overriding objective was to unify the country.

2. Assessment of the Enemy Objective. Would that constitute a grave threat to the West's security? Answer: No. At worst Southeast Asia would have been mostly neutral, which was acceptable.

3. Nature of the War. What kind of war—conventional or guerrilla—might develop? Answer: Neither. We encountered something called "people's war," which we did not anticipate or understand.

4. Estimated Cost of Victory. Could we win it with U.S. troops fighting alongside the South Vietnamese? Answer: No. We could not win it at acceptable cost.

5. Mistakes/Missed Opportunities. Should we not have known the answers to all these questions before deciding whether to commit troops? Answer: Yes. Without question.

What about Hanoi? Similar questions should have been asked by them in 1961. Here are a set of such questions and what I believe would have been the correct answers, based on what we now know:

1. Enemy's Objective. Was it true that the U.S. goal was to establish some sort of colonial empire in Indochina and subjugate the Vietnamese people? Answer: No. The U.S. goal was to prevent the collapse of an ally.

2. Assessment of the Enemy Objective. Was the U.S. presence in South Vietnam necessarily a threat to the security of Hanoi and its southern sympathizers? Answer: No. The Hanoi government was not seen by the U.S. as a threat in itself, only as part of the "row" of communist dominoes.

3. Nature of the War. What kind of war might develop? Answer: Hanoi was tragically wrong about the kind of war they believed they would have to wage with the United States, which included a land war in the South and a massive bombing campaign in the North.

4. Estimated Cost of Victory. Was the outcome worth the sacrifice? Not if it could have been achieved at a lesser cost.

5. Mistakes/Missed Opportunities. Should Hanoi have known the answers to all these questions before deciding whether to challenge the U.S. militarily? Answer: I would say yes, without question. The high probability is that North Vietnam could have achieved its political objectives without the human, social, and material costs of a fifteen-year war.

In summary, by 1961 the mindsets of both sides were gross distortions of reality.

The remainder of this book will analyze these mistaken mindsets, leading to the identification of missed opportunities and the drawing of lessons. Though it sounds simple, it is worth pointing out that missed opportunities are not just negotiations that fail to come to fruition; there are also those situations that participants did not even realize were potential opportunities. As we began to speak with our Vietnamese counterparts, one such missed opportunity—something we have not previously thought of as a chance to avert the war—came up again and again, forcing us to reconsider both the origin of the war and the Vietnamese themselves. That opportunity was missed at Geneva in July 1954, and we shall turn to it next.

September 2, 1945. Ho Chi Minh began his inaugural address to the citizens of newly independent Vietnam by quoting Thomas Jefferson's Declaration of Independence, then said: "The entire Vietnamese people are determined to sacrifice all their lives and property in order to safeguard their independence and liberty."

Geneva, July 1954. The United States alone among the great powers refused to sign the Geneva Accords under which China, Russia, Western European nations, and Ho Chi Minh agreed on a temporary partition of Vietnam, with elections to be held in 1956. U.S. Secretary of State John Foster Dulles refused even to shake hands in Geneva with communist representatives of Vietnam and China.

3

The Evolution of Washington's and Hanoi's Mindsets, 1945–1960

We must be clear-sighted in beginnings, for, as in their budding we discern not the danger,

so in their full growth we perceive not the remedy.

Michel de Montaigne, Essays, 1580

Introduction

In Chapter 2, we explored the mindsets of the leaders of Washington, Hanoi, and the National Liberation Front (NLF) as they related to Southeast Asia at the start of the Kennedy administration. But what we failed to understand when the administration assumed office on January 20, 1961, is that "the Vietnam problem" already had a history of its own that antedated John F. Kennedy's presidency by many years. Not one of the top officials in government was intimately familiar with that history, and our government lacked high-level experts who were known to and in constant communication with senior officials. When the Berlin crisis occurred in 1961, and during the Cuban missile crisis of 1962, President Kennedy was able to turn to senior people like Llewellyn Thompson, Charles "Chip" Bohlen, and George Kennan, who knew the Soviets intimately. There were no senior officials in the Pentagon or State Department—with continuing access to the president, the secretaries of state and defense, and the national security adviser—with comparable knowledge of Southeast Asia.[1]

As our discussions with Vietnamese officials and scholars evolved, I became keenly aware of how ignorant we had been. This first became apparent during our initial visit to Hanoi, in November 1995. At that time I conceived the period to be covered by the project would be the same as *In Retrospect*— that is, it should begin in January 1961, when the Kennedy administration came to office. That was what interested me. My tenure as secretary of defense was a period of escalation of the war. It was this period that I wanted to try to understand, and I went to Vietnam to propose that they join our group in the effort.

On November 8, 1995, I gave a preliminary presentation of our ideas at Hanoi's Institute for International Relations. In attendance was a group of about fifty Vietnamese, including current and former cabinet ministers, high-ranking military officers, and their top scholars of the war. Following my presentation, the floor was given to Nguyen Co Thach, former longtime foreign minister of postwar Vietnam and a key official during the war. He said that he supported the project, except for one flaw, which if not corrected would prevent it from being successful. "The flaw," said Thach, in a refrain we were to hear throughout all our subsequent discussions in Hanoi, "is that the most important missed opportunities happened before January 1961."

In particular, he mentioned two episodes that Vice Pres. Madame Nguyen Thi Binh would also bring up later in our visit: (1) Ho Chi Minh's unanswered appeals for support to Pres. Harry Truman in 1945 and 1946; and especially (2) the failure to implement the Geneva Accords of 1954—specifically, the failure to hold all-Vietnam elections in July 1956, which, he believed, would have permitted the reunification of Vietnam at that point. Thach's remarks were followed by those of Tran Quang Co, then the first deputy foreign minister, who supported Thach and who himself emphasized the singular significance of Geneva. "Without understanding Geneva, and the way we felt about it," Co said, "you will never understand our side of the Vietnam war."

Another member of our U.S. group intervened to say that, with all due respect, the former officials we were proposing to bring to a conference in Vietnam had no relevant experience during the earlier Truman and Eisenhower periods. In any case, he said, most of the relevant participants are dead. At this point Thach, who had been speaking in Vietnamese, intervened in English. Turning to Vietnamese scholar Luu Doan Huynh, seated next to him, Thach said: "Excuse me Huynh, are you dead? You're not dead, are you?" When Huynh reassured Thach on this point, Thach turned to me and said: "You see, he is not dead. And I am not dead either.[2] Many of us on this side of the table are not dead. We would be happy to discuss the significance of the Geneva Conference with anyone you send to Hanoi who is not dead."

Of course, once his remarks were translated, the entire room fell into a fit of laughter, which helped to stimulate discussion following my presentation. But it also made a point that has remained vividly in my mind ever since: The Vietnamese see our conflict within a much longer span of time than we tend to in the United States. Our cabinet-level officials enter and leave government every four or eight years at most. The majority don't last that long. But many of the Vietnamese who would ultimately participate in our project had spent the better part of their long lives engaged in the singular task of fighting for Vietnamese unification and independence: against the French colonialists during the 1930s, the Japanese during in the early 1940s, the French again during the 1950s, and later the Americans during the 1960s and 1970s. They thus had long memories and saw connections we needed to know more about if we were to understand their mindset during the 1960s, when the war escalated to an American war.

I recalled the point made by Nguyen Co Thach and Tran Quang Co somewhat later, after we had agreed to include "Geneva, 1954" in our joint agenda. Instinctively, I opened *In Retrospect* to the index and looked up "Geneva," just to see what I had said about it in my memoir. But I discovered that "Geneva" is not an entry in the index. It now seems ironic to me that I had begun the second chapter of that book, "The Early Years," with an epigraph from Montaigne: "We must be clear-sighted in beginnings, for, as in their budding we discern not the danger, so in their full growth we perceive not the remedy."[3] We begin this chapter with the same epigraph, to emphasize the necessity of understanding how conflict begins as viewed by both sides. Why both sides? Because I had been equally struck on that first visit to Hanoi by the relative lack of knowledge—and even lack of interest—of the Vietnamese leaders in U.S. thinking during the 1950s and 1960s.

I have already described Washington's and Hanoi's 1961 mindsets in Chapter 2, as presented at our June 1997 conference in Hanoi. This chapter seeks to identify the historical origins of those mindsets, as follows:

- *Becoming Enemies:* What drove Washington and Hanoi during the 1945–1960 period to conclude that they were enemies?

- *Disaster at Geneva:* What happened at Geneva in 1954 that contributed to the suspicion and enmity with which Washington and Hanoi regarded each other?

- *Post-Geneva Perceptions:* What events immediately preceding the arrival in Washington of the Kennedy administration produced the situation as we found it in January 1961—with Washington and Hanoi already locked into a spiral of escalation toward war?

These are fundamental questions. They have never before been addressed by Americans and Vietnamese *together* in a context as informed and frank as that in which our seven sets of discussions—six in Hanoi, one in Bellagio, Italy—have taken place over the past three years. In this chapter, my coauthors and I provide what we believe is the first authoritative, *two-sided* account of missed opportunities by both Washington and Hanoi, 1945–1960, that put both on a collision course toward war.

Monologues in Real Time: Collision Course

THE VIEW FROM WASHINGTON

World War II ended in August 1945 when Japan surrendered unconditionally following the atomic bombings of Hiroshima and Nagasaki. Almost
immediately, the number-one task in U.S. foreign policy became the
rebuilding of Western Europe, including Germany, under what became the
Marshall Plan. An important part of this effort involved finding ways to bol-
ster the French in Europe and elsewhere, in return for French participation
on the side of the West in the emerging confrontation with the Soviet Union,
which was proving impossible to dislodge from the Central European countries it occupied after Germany surrendered on May 8, 1945. France, which
had capitulated in 1940 and was occupied throughout the war by Germany,
was in political turmoil. To policymakers in Washington, including President Truman and the man who would become his secretary of state in 1949,
Dean Acheson, even liberated France might be at some risk of a communist
takeover, by electoral or other means. Fear of this scenario led the United
States to initiate a series of proposals that would, on April 4, 1949, lead to
the formation of the North Atlantic Treaty Organization (NATO), with the
United States and France among the signatories.

An important French quid pro quo for agreeing to participate in NATO
and related collective security arrangements in Europe was U.S. assistance
to France in reclaiming colonies in Indochina, including Vietnam. Incre-
mentally, the United States acquiesced, despite its anticolonial past and
inclinations. Dean Acheson later recalled:

> The U.S. came to the aid of the French in Indochina not because we
> approved of what they were doing, but because we needed their support for
> our policies in regard to NATO and Germany. The French blackmailed us. At
> every meeting when we asked them for greater effort in Europe they brought
> up Indochina. . . . They asked for our aid for Indochina but refused to tell me
> what they hoped to accomplish or how. Perhaps they didn't know.[4]

In this way, with almost no thought given to the fate of Vietnam itself, Truman, Acheson, and their colleagues in Washington struck a Faustian bargain,
by which the United States would eventually become the guarantor and
underwriter of the unsuccessful French effort to reclaim its prewar colonies
in Indochina. This was how U.S. involvement with Vietnam began: absent-

mindedly, almost as a kind of "throwaway" in a grand bargain for the heart of Europe, to appease its defeated, temperamental, and proud French ally.

As seen in Washington, the stakes in Vietnam had risen dramatically by 1949. That year, the Soviets successfully tested their first atomic bomb, and the communists under Mao Zedong had simultaneously triumphed in China, raising the specter of a Soviet-Chinese effort to subvert U.S. interests in Asia, as well as Europe. The situation was deemed so dire that Acheson felt compelled to personally resolve a debate then in progress within the U.S. government about the true nature of Ho Chi Minh and his followers. In a May 1949 cable, he declared: "Question whether Ho as much nationalist or commie is irrelevant. All Stalinists in colonial areas are nationalists."[5] Vietnam was about to become a pawn on the great global chessboard of the nascent East-West Cold War.

In mid-January 1950, "Red" China, as it quickly became known, recognized the Vietminh resistance in Vietnam, led by Ho Chi Minh. Ho's government became known as the Democratic Republic of Vietnam (DRV), even though the French still controlled the major Vietnamese cities of Hanoi, Saigon, and Haiphong. A few days after their formal recognition by Beijing, Ho Chi Minh and his colleagues reciprocated, recognizing the communist government in China. This led Acheson to proclaim in response that recognition of the DRV by the Soviet bloc (including Red China) "should remove any illusion as to the nationalist character of Ho Chi Minh's aims and reveals Ho in his true colors as the mortal enemy of native independence in Vietnam."[6] In a countermove on February 7, the United States recognized the government in Saigon of the dissolute and ineffectual former emperor, Bao Dai, brought back by the French from Hong Kong in an attempt to provide a degree of legitimacy for their presence in Vietnam. So rather than recognizing French suzerainty over Vietnam, the United States chose to recognize the French puppet government.

By mid-1950, the momentum had increased even further toward more active and extensive U.S. involvement in Vietnam. In April, a National Security Council report, NSC–68, declared a national emergency in the face of the communist threat. "The issues that face us," it said, "are momentous, involving the fulfillment or destruction not only of this Republic but of civilization itself."[7] In May and June 1950, the United States agreed to underwrite the French effort to subdue Ho Chi Minh and his followers. At a ministerial meeting in Paris on May 8, Acheson agreed to begin massive economic and military aid to the French. And on June 27, hard on the heels of the outbreak of the Korean War, President Truman signed into law the aid package to the French for their war in Indochina, which was coupled with authorization for U.S. military engagement on the Korean Peninsula.

As Dwight Eisenhower, Truman's successor, would soon discover, underwriting the French effort in Indochina was a "dead-end alley."[8] The French capitulation to Vietminh forces at the pivotal battle of Dien Bien Phu in May 1954 left Eisenhower administration officials unsure as to how they should proceed. Just before the French surrendered, but after it was clear they would be defeated, Secretary of State John Foster Dulles gave the U.S. interpretation of the significance of the French capitulation: "The propagandists of Red China and Russia," he said, "make it apparent that [their] purpose is to dominate all of Southeast Asia."[9] On this point Dulles, as fervent an anticommunist as ever existed, had not the slightest doubt. The problem was, as he saw it, in "letting the communist aggressor know in advance where his aggression could lead him."[10] In the American foreign policy vernacular popularized by Dulles, these were the salient questions: how to "contain" communism (in this case, in Southeast Asia); and how, once contained, might it be "rolled back"?

The "containment" problem in Southeast Asia would be dealt with first in Geneva, at an international conference cochaired by the British and the Soviets. At first, the United States, Dulles in particular, wanted no part of an international conference cochaired by the Soviets that included communist Chinese participation on an equal footing with the other big powers. When it was clear, however, that the conference would unavoidably be the venue for deciding the Indochina question in the wake of the French defeat, the United States agreed to participate, as an "observer."

Whereas jockeying among the big powers consumed Dulles, the more mundane task of researching the Vietminh fell to Chester Cooper, a young CIA specialist on Southeast Asia. His first task, he later recalled, was to answer this question authoritatively: "Was there really a Ho Chi Minh—or more precisely, was the original Ho Chi Minh still alive?"[11] Such was the level of Washington's knowledge of, and interest in, the Vietminh.

Dulles himself stayed only briefly in Geneva, conducting himself, as one of his biographers put it, like a "puritan in a house of ill repute," around the likes of the old Bolshevik, Vyacheslav Molotov, and "Long March" veteran Zhou Enlai, to say nothing of the representatives of the Vietminh guerrillas, who were still at war with the U.S. French ally in Indochina.[12] Dulles was heard to remark that the only way he would ever meet Zhou, who led the Chinese delegation, was if their cars collided.[13] As if to prove his point, Dulles actually refused to shake hands with Zhou, in one of the more notable diplomatic nonevents of the conference. Chester Cooper later recalled that "like Shakespeare's whining schoolboy, the American delegation 'crept like a snail unwillingly' to Geneva."[14]

The Geneva Conference was driven by a deadline: If an agreement satisfactory to the principal participants was not reached by July 20, the new and fragile French government of Pierre Mendes-France would resign. This, it was generally believed, would completely destabilize the situation not only in France but also in Indochina, where the military and political situation was obviously far from resolved. Such a predicament might therefore lead to a military intervention by one or more of the big powers, possibly producing in Indochina a Geneva "solution" potentially more disastrous than the original problem the conference was convened to resolve. And though this deadline produced a sense of urgency, it did not lead to any increased inclination by the United States to deal directly with the principal parties to disputes that concerned not only Vietnam but also Laos and Cambodia.

From Washington's point of view, then, the result of the Geneva Conference was precisely the sort of disaster that had been feared. Among the provisions worked out at the last minute under the pressure of the July 20 deadline, the two most disturbing to the U.S. delegation were these: First, Vietnam would be partitioned at the 17th parallel, north of which the Vietminh would establish a "regroupment area" centered in Hanoi, and south of which France and the United States would organize a "regroupment area" centered in Saigon; and second, all-Vietnam elections would be held two years hence, on July 20, 1956, and based on the results, Vietnam would be reunified and a government established based on the results of the elections. In Washington, this could mean only one thing: A significant part of Vietnam was now "lost" to communism. On July 23, Dulles spoke about "the loss in Northern Vietnam."[15] Walter Bedell Smith, head of the U.S. delegation, refused to sign the Geneva Accords, agreeing only to "take note" of these odious provisions. Smith felt compelled in the aftermath to deny publicly that Geneva was another Munich. But the analogy to the British attempt to appease the Nazis seemed all too apt in Washington.[16]

Washington responded in two ways to this "loss" of part of a Free World "asset" in Indochina. First, the United States would establish the Southeast Asia Treaty Organization, on the model of NATO, for collective security from communist subversion in the area. But the more important and fateful move was to bring back to Vietnam Ngo Dinh Diem, a Roman Catholic Vietnamese expatriate who had been residing in the United States, to establish a government in Saigon that would provide a "democratic" alternative to the communist DRV. Arriving in early July 1954, Diem, financially underwritten by the United States, moved quickly to consolidate his control of the chaotic situation in South Vietnam—this new entity formally created in Geneva.

With money pouring in from Washington, with the South Vietnamese security forces being advised by the U.S. Military Assistance and Advisory Group in Saigon, and with a tough determination to prevail, Diem at first seemed to be the great foreign policy success Washington had been looking for ever since the Soviet bloc had begun taking assets after World War II. He was hailed as an "Asian liberator" who had succeeded in stopping the spread of communism in Indochina.

However, Diem would prove to be something of a Frankenstein's monster for Washington. The brutality of his regime increased, led by Diem's brother, Ngo Dinh Nhu, who directed internal security in South Vietnam. Predictably, such brutality backfired, and by the late 1950s a communist-led guerrilla movement, with close ties to the Hanoi government, was already in control of parts of the South Vietnamese countryside. Moreover, Diem proved to be remarkably impervious to advice and counsel, even if it came from Washington. A mandarin, he believed he ruled with "the mandate of heaven," an attitude that infuriated his American underwriters and estranged his fellow Vietnamese. And so a vicious cycle was created. Diem used ever more brutal and arbitrary means to eliminate suspected communists, which in turn led to increased guerrilla activity. In response to the increased guerrilla threat, more American advisers were sent to Saigon, only to be rebuffed or ignored by an increasingly isolated, brutal, and unresponsive Diem. Nevertheless, throughout the 1950s, Washington ignored Diem's arbitrariness and brutality, for the most part, because it was believed that he, and he alone, could transform South Vietnam into a bulwark against the spread of communism from the North.

On October 26, 1960, President Eisenhower sent congratulations to Diem on the occasion of the fifth anniversary of the establishment of South Vietnam. But on November 11, just days after John Kennedy was elected U.S. president, a coup attempt against Diem by a group of his elite paratroopers nearly succeeded. And, as mentioned earlier, in December the NLF was established. Diem was already on the ropes, although years would pass before Washington perceived this to be the case.

THE VIEW FROM HANOI

In March 1945, the Japanese unilaterally ended French rule in Indochina and established a fictitious "independent" Vietnam under the emperor, Bao Dai. Meanwhile, the Vietminh, led by Ho Chi Minh, continued to gain strength, especially in the North and its major city, Hanoi. Following Japan's unconditional surrender on August 15, 1945, the Vietminh moved quickly in the chaos that followed to take the reins of government. During August 18–28, Vietminh-led insurrections occurred throughout Vietnam. Bao Dai abdicated on August 30. With the speed and efficiency of a blitzkrieg, the Vietminh movement had accomplished what would come to be known as the August Revolution. In less than a month, they had triumphed over the French colonialists, the Japanese invaders, and the imperial pretender.

On Sunday, September 2, after consulting with an American official in Hanoi about the wording of some phrases he wished to use from Jefferson's Declaration of Independence, Ho Chi Minh addressed a euphoric crowd of Vietnamese in Hanoi. He began and ended his remarks as follows:

> "All men are created equal. They are endowed by their Creator with certain inalienable rights; among these are Life, Liberty, and the pursuit of Happiness."
>
> This immortal statement was made in the Declaration of Independence of the United States of America in 1776. In a broader sense, this means: All the peoples on the earth are equal from birth, all the peoples have a right to live, to be happy and free. . . .
>
> We, members of the Provisional Government of the Democratic Republic of Vietnam, solemnly declare to the world that Vietnam has the right to be a free and independent country—and in fact is so already. The entire Vietnamese people are determined to mobilize all their physical and mental strength, to sacrifice their lives and property in order to safeguard their independence and liberty.[17]

This was neither the first nor last time that Ho Chi Minh would reach out to Washington for support in the Vietminh's anticolonial struggle against the French. Ho was encouraged by what he saw as a common cause with the United States—both historically, as former colonies, and during World War II, in their joint fight against the Japanese. But Ho was unmindful of the postwar priorities in Washington, and for this reason his efforts to obtain U.S. support would come to nothing. Ho wrote at least eight poignant cables and letters to President Truman between October 1945 and February 1946, making the case for Vietnamese independence. But to no avail. None of the letters received a reply.[18] At this stage, and for some years to come, Washington regarded France as the principal actor in the unfolding drama in Indochina. The indigenous Vietminh movement was perceived, if at all, as a "native" bit player.

By early 1950, the war against the French had settled into a grinding stalemate, with the Vietminh controlling much of the countryside, the

French forces still holding the three major cities of Saigon, Hanoi, and Haiphong. Although the absence of U.S. support for the August Revolution was disappointing, and even though it was known that the United States was providing some support for the French effort in Indochina, Ho Chi Minh and his followers at this point still seem to have regarded the French, and only the French, as their enemy. It seems that after sending the original flurry of letters and cables to Truman, Ho and his colleagues more or less forgot about the United States. In fact, by early 1950, the Vietminh had made important gains, and it was unclear how much longer the French could hold out. Victory seemed close, even without U.S. support.

The mutual diplomatic recognition in January 1950 (that is, between the government led by Ho Chi Minh and the triumphant forces of Mao Zedong in Beijing) was an interesting and encouraging development. But a millennium of animosity and suspicion between China and Vietnam was scarcely to be overcome by an exchange of letters and diplomats. When criticized for negotiating a five-year term for continued French military presence in Vietnam in March 1946, Ho defended his position by implying that the alternative was to accept Chinese Kuomintang occupation forces of Chiang Kai-chek. He explained: "You fools. . . . The last time the Chinese came they stayed one thousand years. . . . As for me, I prefer to smell French shit for five years, rather than Chinese shit for the rest of my life."[19]

Whatever illusions Ho Chi Minh may have had regarding assistance, or at least benign neglect, from Washington were exploded on May 8, 1950, when U.S. Secretary of State Dean Acheson announced that the United States would hereafter contribute to financing the French in Indochina. In reaction, Ho seems to have jumped to a doomsday conclusion: that the real reason for U.S. assistance to the French was Washington's desire to recolonize Indochina, in some fashion, for themselves. According to Ho:

> The U.S. imperialists have of late openly interfered in Indochina's affairs. It is with their money and weapons and their instructions that the French colonialists have been waging war in Vietnam, Cambodia and Laos.
>
> However, the U.S. imperialists are intensifying their plot to discard the French colonialists so as to gain complete control over Indochina. . . . Therefore to gain independence, we, the Indochinese people, must defeat the French colonialists, our number-one enemy. At the same time, we will struggle against the U.S. interventionists.[20]

From this point forward—roughly from mid-1950—the Vietminh seem to have regarded Washington as a kind of deus ex machina of the French war effort. There would be no more citations of Jefferson and no more plaintive telegrams to the U.S. president. First, they must deal with the French.

But as Ho Chi Minh would soon discover, the interests of his Vietminh resistance were no safer with his fraternal Soviet and Chinese "allies" than they were with the French "number-one enemy" or the U.S. "interventionists." For in March 1954, when Vietminh forces under Gen. Vo Nguyen Giap were still dug in at the siege of Dien Bien Phu, discussions had already begun—discussions about which the Vietminh leadership knew little or nothing—among the French, British, Soviets, and Chinese regarding the terms under which the war in Indochina might be settled. They had agreed that the venue would be Geneva and had tacitly agreed that the best outcome—best for the big powers, that is— would involve a partition of Vietnam. China, in any case, would not object to such a partition, as long as its traditional zone of security in North Vietnam was established as fraternally communist. The Vietminh leaders, including Ho Chi Minh, having fought in the jungles of Vietnam for nearly a decade, knew nothing about these discussions. At Geneva, they would get a rude awakening as to how the game of diplomacy is played by the big powers.

Just as the French were surrendering at Dien Bien Phu (May 7, 1954), the Vietminh sent a delegation to Geneva headed by the acting minister of foreign affairs, Pham Van Dong. He was sent, as it were, to claim the spoils of military victory: a unified Vietnam, from which French troops would be withdrawn according to a fixed schedule. Then, and only then, according to the Vietminh proposal, would a cease-fire go into effect. In other words, the Vietminh would stop fighting if, and only if, the French had already left, and the Vietminh was in charge of administration and elections.[21] Pham Van Dong made these proposals at the second plenary session in Geneva on May 10.

Such proposals were anathema to the Western delegations. The French were being asked to quietly fall on their sword, and their allies were being asked to assist the French in doing so. Of course, to the hardened guerrilla fighters representing the Vietminh in Geneva, the logic of their proposal must have been self-evident. They had won the war and now came to Geneva to take back their country. In theory, if they failed to get their way in Geneva, they could open a final offensive and physically drive the French out. However, the question such a possibility would pose was this: What will Washington do in response?

That question—would the Americans intervene?—may have provided the Soviets and the Chinese with all the leverage they needed with their nascent Vietnamese ally, as they repeatedly pressed Pham Van Dong and his team to agree to compromise after compromise. The French delegate to Geneva, Jean Chauvel, had the impression, he said, "that the Vietminh were really on the end of a string being manipulated from Moscow and Beijing. When they moved forward too quickly Zhou Enlai and Vyacheslav Molotov were always at hand to pull them back to a more accommodating position."[22] Zhou and Ho Chi Minh met July 3–5 in Liou-Chow, on the Vietnam-China border, to discuss the Geneva talks, reportedly so Zhou could press Ho personally on the necessity for the Vietminh to accept a temporary partition of Vietnam and thereby avoid a U.S. military intervention.[23]

Finally, they agreed. It must have been a doubly bitter pill to swallow for Ho and his compatriots, since the settlement was virtually identical to the one they had struck with the French in March 1946, with the temporary partition then being at the 16th parallel. Never again, one imagines, would the Vietnamese communists trust their big friends to look out for their interests. In fact, at the Paris Peace Conference, which settled the U.S. war in 1973, there were neither Soviets nor Chinese.[24] They were not invited.

Ho Chi Minh claimed a partial victory on July 15 at a meeting of the Party's Central Committee. He said he understood that the burden of the Geneva settlement would fall hardest on his southern compatriots. He called on them, nevertheless, to "place national interests above local interests and permanent interests above temporary interests" over the following two years, until the elections leading to reunification would be held.[25]

In spite of exuding what must have been forced optimism to buoy his southern comrades, Ho could not avoid expressing his deep concern that the United States was "becoming our main and direct enemy."[26] His fear was prescient. As noted, there would be no elections. The Diem regime would turn out to be more efficient than expected at crippling the resistance movement in the South. As it happened, the situation in the South would become so desperate that Hanoi would be forced to abandon its line of pure political struggle and agree to direct support of an armed revolt south of the 17th parallel.

This shift happened in stages. First, with the passing of the deadline for the elections called for by the Geneva Accords, Le Duan, the Party's chief in the Nam Bo district in southern Vietnam (and destined to be named Party secretary in Hanoi in 1960), in 1956 had published an influential pamphlet called "The Path of Revolution in the South." Although not specifically endorsing armed struggle as the only path in the South, he implied strongly that the conditions there might soon warrant it. "The line of revolutionary movement must," he said, "be in line with the inclinations and aspirations of the people." And what are these, for the southern comrades? "With the cruel repression and exploitation of U.S.-Diem [as the regime was called by many of its foes within Vietnam], the people's revolutionary movement will definitely rise up. The people of the South have known the blood and fire of nine years of resistance war, but the cruelty of the U.S.-Diem cannot extinguish the spirit of struggle in the people."[27] That is to say, the southerners aren't going to take it much longer. Later, returning to Hanoi from a clandestine tour of the South in 1958, Le Duan reported to the Hanoi leadership that many Party organizations had been nearly destroyed by Diem's security forces.

In January 1959, the Party held its Fifteenth Plenum in Hanoi and passed what came to be known as Resolution 15. Declaring "the basic path of development of the revolution in the South is to use violence," Resolution 15 essentially permitted southerners to protect themselves and to fight back when necessary.[28] In May 1959, Group 559 was formed, responsible for establishing the Truong Son Route, or Ho Chi Minh Trail, by which the North would resupply the resistance in the South.[29] The momentum pulling Hanoi into the middle of an increasingly violent situation in the South culminated on December 20, 1960, with the formation of the NLF at a meeting in a secure area of Nam Bo (in the South). The formation and platform of the NLF was announced in an English-language broadcast over Radio Hanoi on January 29, 1961.[30]

Hanoi officials had also apparently learned the lesson of Geneva. Hanoi's official history of the period indicates that in May 1960 the Chinese had exerted pressure on Hanoi to dampen enthusiasm in the South for armed revolt. The entry concludes defiantly: "Masters of their own destiny, the people of Vietnam strongly advanced the revolutionary war in the South."[31] China, however, was only a big bully of an ally. The United States was now the big enemy, as indicated in Article 1 of the NLF Platform: "Overthrow the camouflaged colonial regime of the American imperialists and the dictatorial power of Ngo Dinh Diem, servant of the Americans, and institute a government of national democratic union."[32]

It is worth noting what had caused a direct military confrontation between Washington and Hanoi to draw ever closer. The definitions of *Washington* and *Hanoi* had over the years become enlarged, in both cases, to include the intentions and capabilities of their respective allies in South Vietnam. Neither Washington nor Hanoi understood all the ramifications of this development at the time. But the brutality and arbitrariness of Diem's regime had, by the time of Kennedy's election, begun to pull the United States more directly into the civil conflict in the South. Likewise, it is unclear if, when, and under what conditions, Hanoi would have agreed to Resolution 15 and the formation of the NLF, if it hadn't had its hand forced—as it clearly was—by desperate southern colleagues. Hanoi saw the writing on the wall, took the necessary steps, and thus established control over the resistance war in the South.

It has long been obvious that during the course of the war that followed Washington underestimated the resilience of its adversary *in Hanoi*. But what was the state of mind among those in the South who were most eager to move to armed struggle? Did they understand, as Ho Chi Minh surely understood, that an all-out armed struggle *in the South* carried a high risk of a devastating U.S. response, not only in the South but also the North?

The answer seems to be that the southerners *did* understand the likely consequences, but they were willing to pay the ultimate price, if it came to that. This is particularly evident in what we know of Nguyen Chi Thanh, a southerner who rose to become the most powerful figure in the NLF. At the time of his death in summer 1967, Nguyen Chi Thanh was secretary of the Central Office South Vietnam (COSVN), the mobile nerve center established for the leadership of the southern resistance, and commander of the People's Liberation Army Forces (PLAF). One can glean some of the key assumptions, and some of the back-against-the-wall abandon of the southern cause, in the following selections from a piece he wrote in July 1963, two years before the introduction of U.S. combat troops.

> In 1954, the U.S. imperialists, taking advantage of the French colonialists' defeat at Dien Bien Phu, drove the French out of southern Vietnam and set up a puppet regime headed by Ngo Dinh Diem. In essence, this meant that U.S. neocolonialism replaced French colonialism and become dominant in south Vietnam.
>
> It appears that southern Vietnam is the focus of many contradictions. The United States should have used algebra in gauging the situation there; instead it used simple arithmetic. Consequently it has run into a blind alley.
>
> We do not have any illusions about the United States. We do not underestimate our opponent—the strong and cunning U.S. imperialism. But we are not afraid of the United States. . . . If, on the contrary, one is afraid of the United States, and thinks that to offend it would court failure, and that firm opposition to U.S. imperialism would touch off a nuclear war, then the only course left would be to compromise with and surrender to U.S. imperialism.[33]

The NLF was founded, in other words, because the southern allies of Hanoi were desperate, were angry, and, as they saw it, had nothing to lose and everything to gain by taking on Diem *and the United States* in a winner-take-all war. Nguyen Chi Thanh, in the above passage, seems in fact to say that for southerners the options boiled down to these: risk total annihilation—even nuclear war—or unconditionally surrender to the United States.

In deciding to support, supply, and direct this war, "Hanoi" thus became *radicalized* beyond anything that was appreciated in Washington for many years. In this way of thinking, the United States was a colonial power, like France, that must be driven into the sea; it was ignorant as well as powerful, and thus it was vulnerable in the long run. This was a state of mind bound by a kind of solemn oath to fight to the death. If nuclear war resulted and Vietnam was destroyed in the process, then, at least to someone with this viewpoint, it couldn't be helped. At least they would go down honorably, fighting for what they believed was a just cause.

One wonders whether, if leaders in Washington had understood *this* "Hanoi," the Hanoi whose decisions must ultimately respond to the desperation and commitment of their southern compatriots—they would have altered their calculations after January 29, 1961, when the existence of the NLF was announced by Hanoi. And one wonders whether leaders in Hanoi might have calculated somewhat differently had they known how high a price all the Vietnamese—North and South—would ultimately have to pay for their embrace not only of the southern cause—of liberation and unification—but also of southerners, over whom the shadow of Geneva hung like a death sentence and who *next time* would resist any deal that would not guarantee them the same rights and privileges as those obtained by their northern compatriots.

A Dialogue in Retrospect: Collision Course

GENEVA: THE BIGGEST MISSED OPPORTUNITY?

By June 1997, at our first Hanoi conference on the war, our Vietnamese colleagues remained unconvinced that we on the U.S. side fully grasped their view that important missed opportunities to avoid a U.S. war in Vietnam occurred before the Kennedy administration came to office. They were, we now believe, correct in this assessment.

Nevertheless, the joint planning meetings before that conference often involved a kind of tug-of-war between the two sides over whether missed opportunities might, in theory, have existed during the 1960s, as well as the 1950s. The Vietnamese, although not denying the possibility, ultimately took a middle position: The most important missed opportunity was said to have occurred in Geneva in 1954 and in the failure to implement the elections mandated by the Geneva Accords in 1956. The chief spokesman for this view at the June 1997 conference was Nguyen Khac Huynh, a fiery former ambassador who has embarked on a second career as a historian.

Nguyen Khac Huynh: First, about the Geneva Accords. I would have to say that we on the Vietnamese side regard the failure to implement the Geneva Agreement as the *biggest*—as the greatest and most important— missed opportunity to avoid the war. In retrospect, we can see that the Geneva Accords had wide support. The agreement responded to the hopes of the Vietnamese people and also corresponded, we believe, with the general international trend at that time. All participating countries approved of the agreement. Even the United States did not formally object, although the U.S. did not sign the document.

The implementation of the elections of 1956, as stipulated in the Geneva Accords, would, we believe, have been the best solution of all. Why do we say this? Because: First, the conflict would have been resolved in a free and open manner by all the people of Vietnam; and second, the elections would have been consistent with international law. If this had happened, then the so-called "Vietnam problem" for the U.S. would never have arisen again. Never again. Vietnam would have been unified and free, and thus no conflict among the different sides would have taken place. Mr. McNamara speaks in his book of the "tragedy" of the Vietnam war. The failure to implement the Geneva Accords is, we believe, the origin and main cause of the tragedy. . . .

Our American colleagues wish to begin the serious search for missed opportunities in 1961—in January 1961—when Kennedy came to office, when Mr. McNamara came to office. But we do not begin with 1961. That was not the beginning of the problem, not the beginning where the biggest opportunities were lost. Historians must begin at the beginning, and the beginning—or at least where we believe it is fruitful to begin—is with the failure to implement the Geneva Accords. To do otherwise, we believe, would be doing an injustice to history.[34]

Despite the overwhelming significance attached by the Vietnamese to the missed opportunity at Geneva, the Geneva Conference as such was not discussed at the June 1997 conference, though it was alluded to quite often. There were various reasons for this, including an overly ambitious agenda and a marked asymmetry with regard to knowledge about the technical details of the Geneva process. By mutual agreement, therefore, we decided to emphasize the Geneva Conference in the follow-up conference in Hanoi in February 1998.

BECOMING ENEMIES, 1945–1960

The U.S.-Vietnamese dialogue on Geneva began in earnest at the February 1998 conference in Hanoi.[35] The entire first day—more than seven hours—was devoted to it. The excerpts that follow in this section derive from that dialogue.

From almost the first moments, the dialogue on Geneva focused on a central question: How did these two countries, with little common history and less common knowledge of each other, become during the post–World War II period the bitterest of enemies, who would fight one of the bloodiest wars of the twentieth century? Clearly Ho Chi Minh could not imagine this in September 1945, when he cited the Declaration of Independence as the model for Vietnamese independence. Just as clearly, Franklin Roosevelt and Harry Truman, overwhelmed with the post–World War II tasks of rebuilding Europe and Japan, could never have imagined it. Yet it happened. Why? By what process did these "total strangers," as one participant put it, become "mortal enemies"?

Nguyen Khac Huynh, with his historian's passion for accurate chronology, begins by explaining the evolution of thinking in Hanoi about Hanoi's relation to the United States. He cites three turning points, which we referred to earlier: (1) the failure of the Truman administration to respond to Ho Chi Minh's 1945–1946 appeals for support against the French; (2) the U.S. "intervention" in mid-1950, when the United States began to underwrite the French war effort in Indochina; and (3) the Geneva Conference, at which he admits that Washington and Hanoi were largely ignorant of each other, except for Hanoi's assessment—which he contends was accurate—that the United States had become its number-one enemy.

The following dialogue illuminates what might be called the narcissism of great powers and small adversaries. U.S. participants, led by Chester Cooper, say in various ways that Washington did not view Hanoi as an enemy. In fact, the U.S. participants say, the United States had hardly any view at all of Hanoi, which at the time mattered little to them. What mattered was that Washington needed to support its European ally, France. And it also mattered that Hanoi appeared to be taking orders from Moscow and Beijing and was therefore avowedly seeking to undermine U.S. interests in the region. This is why, as Cooper says, all the Hanoi representatives had to do was come forward at some point—the earlier the better, but surely by the time of the Geneva Conference—and explain to the United States that they were nationalists who sought an independent line from the communist powers, as Tito had done in Yugoslavia.[36]

The Vietnamese respond somewhat testily, making the point that of course the United States was its enemy, because it supported the French, with whom Hanoi was at war. Nguyen Khac Huynh is joined by Luu Doan Huynh, an energetic and polymathic scholar known to the U.S. side by his nickname, "Pepperpot," and Luu Van Loi, a journalist-diplomat whose experience with Vietminh-DRV foreign policy antedates the August Revolution of 1945. As participants in a movement in one of the poorest regions in the world, they say in various ways that they did not, and in fact could not, imagine that U.S. support for France derived from Washington's interest in anything beyond their own borders—beyond the putative U.S. wish to destroy them. Luu Doan Huynh is eloquent on the naïveté of the Vietminh during the 1940s, attempting to explain their views to the United States via a low-level contact in Bangkok; and about how their hands were tied in Geneva, where their Soviet and Chinese friends did their talking for them, something they now regret, because they see that they should have been talking to the United States— communicating with the United States.[37]

And so the tragic tale unfolded: With Washington listening mainly to Hanoi's rhetoric and monitoring its connections with the Sino-Soviet bloc; and with Hanoi seeing evidence of a more tangible kind all around them that the United States was the enemy because "blood," as Luu Doan Huynh points out, "speaks with a terrible voice."

❖

Nguyen Khac Huynh: I want to go back to this question: When did the United States first make the mistake of getting involved in Indochina? It seems to me this is important to discuss, because our views of it—the U.S. view and the Vietnamese view—are so different. It is important, I think, to give you an accurate picture of the way we saw the U.S., and its role, at that time, immediately after World War II.

In 1945, Truman met de Gaulle and made a commitment to support France in Indochina. This should be seen as the beginning of the involvement. But as I see it, this was just a *political* mistake. The Truman administration had not yet committed itself to specific actions in support of the French colonial policy. U.S. intervention became clearer with the actions, as follows:

1. The U.S., as Mr. Robert Brigham said, began to assist the French with money and arms, beginning in mid-1950. Why is this significant? Because the U.S. basically rescued the French at that time. Without the U.S. aid, we believe we would have defeated the French in 1950, or 1951

at the latest. If we had—if the U.S. had not rescued the French in 1950, just imagine: It is possible that there would have been no partition, no U.S.-backed Diem regime, and no U.S.-Vietnam war.

2. The second concrete action of significance taken by the U.S. was its recognition of Bao Dai and his puppet regime established by the French on February 7, 1950. I believe that U.S. scholars and policymakers alike understand—and that they understood then—that this was a puppet regime. Yet the U.S. recognized this regime and pressured its allies to follow suit.

According to our understanding, it was at this critical point—in 1950—that we say the United States first "intervened" in Vietnam. After this first "intervention," the Vietnamese people perceived both the French and the Americans as the enemy. Mr. Chester Cooper has suggested that the United States and Vietnam did not understand each other at Geneva in 1954. Of course, there were many things about one another that we—you and we—did not understand. But we did understand one fundamental fact: that the United States was the enemy—the enemy of the Vietnamese people. True, we hardly knew one another, so to speak. But we knew you had already intervened against us, and that you were the enemy—the new enemy. After 1950, we had a slogan: We must defeat the French "aggressors" and the U.S. "interventionists."

Chester Cooper: I fail to see how the events at Geneva in 1954 convinced you that the U.S. was your enemy. I'd go further than that: I think—and I was not the only one at Geneva who thought this—that you should have regarded the Soviets and the Chinese as your enemies. . . .

So my question is: What did the Soviets and the Chinese say to you to get you to accept the 17th parallel when, the way it looked to us, you could have gotten a much better deal?

Luu Van Loi: Here is what happened. Pham Van Dong, who had originally demanded the 13th parallel, said the 16th would be acceptable. But at a meeting held in the afternoon of July 20 between the foreign ministers of the four big powers and Pham Van Dong, Vietnam had to accept, under pressure, the 17th parallel and nationwide elections two years hence. Also, on the same day, Zhou Enlai gave up his demand for the neutralization of all of Indochina. But we were not satisfied with the 17th parallel. Not at all. We were convinced that the balance of forces between ourselves and France was at that time greatly in our favor. Had it been left to us, we would never have accepted the 17th, under those circumstances.

Chester Cooper: This is absolutely fascinating. But it only reinforces my point, which is that we weren't your enemy at Geneva. If you had enemies, they were the Russians and the Chinese. They were the ones who applied the pressure on the issue of the parallel.

Nguyen Khac Huynh: I am surprised at Mr. Chester Cooper's remark that by the time of the Geneva Conference the United States was not Vietnam's enemy but rather China and USSR. Who helped us beat the French and who helped the French? I insist that the distinction between friend and foe lies on the battlefield and not merely in our minds. If Mr. Chester Cooper is right, then I am afraid his logic is too high for us to understand. But according to our ordinary logic, those who help us are our friends and those who fight us are our enemies.

Chester Cooper: I apologize for being facetious. But I was being only partly facetious. Of course, for the reasons you mention, we were enemies— certainly we weren't friends. I was just trying to point out that in connection with the 17th parallel issue we would have given you the 16th not as a gift but because we would have been willing to concede the 16th parallel.[38] So in that respect, when you think about Geneva—well, we didn't take the 16th parallel away from you. The Chinese and the Russians did. . . .

You mistakenly concluded in 1954 that we were already your sworn enemy; and that we were the big winner in Geneva, mainly because the results would allow us—would allow the U.S.—to bring you to heel, to defeat you. But that was *wrong!* It was *wrong!* But because you assumed you were right, you acted in ways that convinced us that you were the enemy, and that it was necessary to defeat you in some decisive sense.

I am not blaming you and I am not blaming us. But you have to understand this: Your reading of our reading of the Geneva Conference was dead wrong. That is a fact. . . .

In the fifties or the sixties, why didn't you come to us and say: "Look, don't believe the Chinese and Soviet propaganda. It doesn't apply to us. We assure you that we are anxious to pursue an independent policy. We think that we should have some discussions about who is the true enemy of whom. Let's talk about this and get things cleared up." Our problem was that we believed the Soviets and the Chinese. We shouldn't have. But you could have helped us and, in the process, helped yourselves. Why didn't you come forward and assert your independence from the Moscow and Beijing line?

Luu Doan Huynh: In 1947, Ho Chi Minh sent Vice Minister Pham Ngoc Thach to Bangkok to explain to your embassy about the Vietnamese policy. Later on, in 1948, Mr. Thach invited a U.S. representative to visit our base area to see our resistance—to see for himself—what we were fighting for and so on. But the invitation was refused.

There is something else. In 1949, we were preparing the trip of Pres. Ho Chi Minh to China to seek help. At that time, a U.S. journalist asked: "Can Vietnam be neutral like Switzerland?" That was in September 1949. The man who asked was Sol Sander. Ho Chi Minh's answer was, "Why not?" It seems to me that in comments like these it is obvious that Ho Chi Minh, speaking for the whole leadership, earnestly hoped that the U.S. would remain neutral. That was what they hoped. It is also obvious in the lack of strong criticism of the U.S. at that time by the resistance leaders and the radio broadcast station of the resistance. It seems to me you in the U.S. might have noticed this too.

I want to speak frankly: to say that, before Geneva, and just after Geneva, the American government knew nothing about Vietnam, that they cared little or not at all about Vietnam—this is wrong. I say this because already in 1946, 1947, and 1948 many of your Foreign Office [State Department] officials spoke about Ho Chi Minh. What did they say? They said, "Yes, he is a communist, but he is a nationalist first." A nationalist first and a communist second. That is what they said. That is a correct view, a wise view. During these years—the late 1940s—you were neutral about the war in Vietnam. I am speaking about 1945, 1946, 1947, 1948. You were more or less neutral. Maybe not 100 percent. Maybe 80 percent neutral. Okay. To us, 80 percent neutral was acceptable.

But then, you know, in 1950, you discarded all these correct and sensible views of U.S. officials and you said that the struggle of the DRV is a part of the Chinese expansionist game in Asia. There you were wrong. If I may say so, you were not only wrong, but you had, so to speak, lost your minds. Vietnam a part of the Chinese expansionist game in Asia? For anyone who knows the history of Indochina, this is incomprehensible. This is why I say: *This* is the initial "original sin"—if I may use the Catholic term—the "original sin" of the United States. In 1950, not before, not after, is when you began your downfall.

Col. Herbert Schandler: You have stated a Vietnamese view of this very eloquently. As I was listening to you speak, Mr. Huynh, I could sense how confusing it must have been, in 1950, for you to try to figure out why this country that you knew almost nothing about, the United States, had for some reason decided to become your enemy.

But—and this seems to be something that was very hard for you in Vietnam to grasp, for obvious reasons—the United States was taking a *world* view of all these issues. The Iron Curtain was falling all across Europe. This was shocking. We had fought a bloody war in Europe, and had won, only to have half of Europe reconquered by a totalitarian system. Communism, we felt, had to be stopped. The Iron Curtain then fell in Asia in 1954 with the armistice in Korea and with the Geneva Accords. Like Chet Cooper, I remember the 1950s and Chet is right: Sometimes it looked to us like we were on the losing side of history.

David Welch: Did the Vietnamese delegation in Geneva realize that by letting the Soviets and the Chinese take the lead that it would be more difficult later to convince the United States that North Vietnam was not a communist "puppet"?

Luu Doan Huynh: What will happen to our relations with the U.S.? This was—I would say—a very important question in our minds. What will happen when the world's biggest power becomes our enemy? But we could not discuss this in Geneva. In hindsight, I think, we should have tried to find a way to meet you—the Americans—explain to you our national objectives and find out about your attitude. Of course, in the situation that obtained then, this was no simple matter, but it was perhaps necessary to do so.

But in those days, we were all confined—all of us, you too—by policies coming from the need not to offend our friends—you, the French, and British and we, the Chinese, and Soviets.

David Welch: . . . In Geneva, the Vietnamese delegation was not concerned about future relations with the U.S.? Or you *were* concerned, but the situation in Geneva did not permit you to discuss your relations with the U.S. productively?

Luu Doan Huynh: The latter; yes, the latter. We were *very* concerned about you—that you will be our main enemy in the future, after Geneva. Immediately after Geneva, in March 1955, the Central Committee of the Vietnamese Workers' Party declared that from then on the United States is our leading and most dangerous enemy. They know that. They are absolutely convinced about this. We were in great difficulty. But we were severely restricted in what we could say at Geneva.

Nguyen Khac Huynh: . . . It was obvious to us—to anybody—that among the five powers, we had two allies: the Soviet Union and China. They had helped us defeat the French at Dien Bien Phu. The French were our defeated enemy of long standing. The U.S. was the enemy on the horizon. The British we knew little about, except we thought they and the U.S. generally agreed on almost everything.

Chester Cooper: I hope I have disabused you of at least that mistaken belief. [Laughter.]

Nguyen Khac Huynh: Not entirely, not entirely. I am not talking about hatred between Dulles and Eden. I am talking about policies.

What about Vietnam? We had spent ten years in the jungle—in the jungle—fighting the French. We were not well versed in international affairs. We did not yet have any experience with diplomacy or multilateral discussions, such as those that took place in Geneva. Please try to understand our situation in 1954. Literally, we were stepping out of the jungle and going to Geneva, at the invitation of our friends, our allies, the Chinese and Soviets. This is not like today in Hanoi, here at the Institute of International Relations, where we train our young diplomats. We knew nothing about diplomacy, about how to conduct ourselves, what to ask for, what to demand, how to "maneuver" in that kind of environment.

David Welch: May I ask a clarification? Did you say that Molotov or Zhou Enlai told Pham Van Dong that if Vietnam did not agree to the temporary division of Vietnam at the 17th parallel then the United States would intervene militarily? Was that the Soviet and Chinese assessment?

Luu Doan Huynh: You see, all the deliberations between the socialist countries in Geneva were dominated by an important issue—I would say one urgent necessity. This is: We must reach an agreement in Geneva in order to prevent the United States from carrying out a military intervention in Indochina. This was one of the main issues in all our conversations in Geneva "behind closed doors." . . .

The Soviets and Chinese tried to convince us of the imminence of U.S. military intervention. And so we were watching developments in France. We were concerned about what would happen if the government collapsed. If I may say so, this concern was not helped by the U.S. refusal to participate fully in the Geneva process. We asked ourselves: Why? One reason we could think of was that they wanted to be free of Geneva's restrictions on foreign involvement, so they could intervene militarily if they wanted to. That was what we thought.

Nguyen Khac Huynh: I would like to provide you with the accurate documentation on this issue. I would like to read from the historical record.
. . . When did we start to regard the United States as our enemy? Here is your
answer: "At the Eighth Plenum of the Party in August 1955 it was concluded
that the governing force in the South at that time were American and pro-American forces." In other words, France was not worth consideration at the time.
I have the official document right here. [Points to materials on table.]

Chester Cooper: . . . This leads me to propose a theory, and the theory has
two parts.

1. You were a victim of what we used to call "communist propaganda." *You*
   were the victims, not us. . . . You are telling us—and I appreciate your honesty and respect for history when you tell us this—you are saying that you
   had concluded, firmly concluded, that we were your enemy and we were
   preparing to attack you in Vietnam. Ladies and Gentlemen: While I
   respect your honesty in saying these things, that belief was absolutely without foundation. *It was absolutely false—totally wrong!* Here is my second
   proposition—the second part of my theory, which applies to our side:

2. We were victims of our own propaganda too. . . . Based on what I have
   learned in the course of our discussions—last June and now, in February—
   I now believe we exaggerated, or even completely misjudged, the extent to
   which Vietnam would be a stepping-stone—or a pawn—for the Chinese in
   Southeast Asia. I think we were wrong to believe that. Dead wrong.

Col. Herbert Schandler: I want to remind everyone that in 1954, when
the French asked for American military assistance in Vietnam, the United
States specifically refused their request. The Eisenhower administration
went even further than this and told the French government that the U.S.
was not going to intervene in any way during, or after, the battle of Dien Bien
Phu. So the U.S. government took a hard look at military intervention in
Vietnam. That is true. But they decided against it. That's the important
point. The U.S. decided in the spring of 1954, just before the Geneva Conference that we have been talking about, against any form of direct military
intervention in Vietnam.[39]

Chester Cooper: So the question is: What was it that made you think in
this period that the United States was your enemy? Was it propaganda from
the Soviets and Chinese? Was it Dulles? Was it something else . . . ?

Luu Van Loi: Now, as to our beliefs, our conclusions: I take Col. Schandler's point, and similar points about specific U.S. actions at the time we are discussing, the early and mid-1950s. The French asked for a U.S. military intervention at Dien Bien Phu, the U.S. refused, and that was that. Yes, of course. But I suggest that we not be quite so literal in our analysis of U.S. policy at the time. One can always find examples after the fact to support one's views. You see, our understanding was based not on your having taken specific actions—or not taking actions, in the case raised by Col. Schandler. (In fact, I doubt we knew about the U.S. refusal to help the French until years later, though I could be wrong.) No. Our calculations and judgments were based on this fact, which we saw every day in our country: *The U.S. was intervening in Vietnam, replacing the French imperialists, providing critical support for Ngo Dinh Diem, and had thus become, by these means, the enemy of the Vietnamese people!*

Therefore, Mr. Cooper, I am afraid I fail to see how, or in what way, we were wrong in our assessment of the U.S. That is my answer. Does this answer satisfy you?

Chester Cooper: Not quite. I think you are reading too much backwards into the history we are discussing. Yes, of course, eventually we became enemies, as we well know. But I am telling you authoritatively, as a member of the U.S. government at the time we are talking about, and as one who dealt every day with these issues, that you were wrong in your assessment *then*, in the mid-1950s. Wrong, wrong, wrong! We had made no such decision to intervene. But—and this is the critical point, I think—because you *assumed* that we were hostile, and were seeking to destroy you, then you did things, and you made statements, that appeared to us to confirm the views of people like John Foster Dulles that *you* were our mortal enemy.

That is what I am saying. I can see better now, thanks to your explanation, how you reached your conclusions in 1954–55. But I am telling you: You were wrong.

Are you satisfied with *my* answer? [Laughter.]

Luu Van Loi: I still think you are right about the Americans and wrong about the Vietnamese. [Laughter.]

Luu Doan Huynh: May I say something about this? I will concede one point to you: that in 1954 we made a mistake. In 1954, we were not knowledgeable enough, not wise enough, to understand that you were not then capable, and not then willing, to undertake an all-out military intervention in Vietnam. We did not understand this. Why did we make this mistake? Because we did not correctly read the international situation. That was one reason. Also—we cannot deny this—we were misled by our friends. Okay? . . .

But at the end of 1954 and early '55, things changed. The French are leaving. Now it is *you*, the Americans, who are in South Vietnam supporting Diem, who has refused to hold elections, who is persecuting our people. So you then become the bulwark of Diem, who is the enemy—who opposes—our goal of reunification. It seems to me that in every struggle you know who is your friend, who is your enemy, and who is so and so. So on that I don't think we were wrong.

Nguyen Khac Huynh: Excuse me, but our evidence is the millions of U.S. dollars that the United States gave to France. At the end of 1953 and the beginning of 1954, U.S. assistance to France accounted for 80 percent of the entire French military effort in Indochina—*80 percent!* And, as I said earlier, the United States recognized the puppet regime of Bao Dai set up by the French. I know we have run over the time limit for this session, but if there was more time, I could continue to provide you with this kind of evidence. But as for the United States not regarding Vietnam as an enemy—where is the evidence?

Robert Brigham: To U. S. policymakers providing 80 percent of France's financial commitment in Indochina, was, in relative terms, a very small price to pay for France's support in Europe. For instance, in 1947, President Truman asked Congress for aid to Greece, Turkey, and Iran for fighting communist insurgencies. In dollar terms, this was more costly than what we were spending on the French in Indochina. As Herb Schandler said earlier, the U.S. turned down France's request—and it was an urgent request, made at the highest levels—for a U.S. military intervention at Dien Bien Phu. They turned it down for military reasons and for fiscal reasons. The 83rd and 84th [Congresses] wouldn't appropriate any funds for more direct intervention in 1954.

The historical record in the U.S. strongly suggests that policymakers wanted to give France, through 1954, just enough support to keep their allegiance in Europe, and not a dollar more than that. They certainly did not see their mission—or any part of their mission—as tipping the balance in Indochina in favor of the French. That's why we—why people like Chet Cooper—would never have perceived themselves as a "first-class enemy" of the resistance forces fighting the French. Maybe a "second-class enemy," but only in the rather vague sense that those guys the French are fighting are supposed to be communists, and we are against communists.

Luu Doan Huynh: But really, your bullets are the killers of our people. We see that this is America's gift to Vietnam—allowing the French to kill our people. This is the most convincing evidence we have of America's loyalties in this affair. So how can we conclude that you are not our enemy? That is impossible. How can we believe that?

I can tell you a story. We had a lot of soft-liners toward America in the jungle areas of Viet Bao, the central seat of the government—a lot of intellectuals who were very sympathetic to Americans. In 1951, one of these intellectuals went on an inspection trip with the inspector general of the government. During the visit, B-26 bombers began shooting with their machine guns at our people. (They can machine-gun you from a great distance, before you can hear the noise of the engine.) The inspector general was killed in the attack. This person—the intellectual—returned to Viet Bao and told the other intellectuals: "You see, we cannot be soft on Americans anymore."

So you see, we understand all your arguments about U.S. interests with the French and so on. We believe Mr. Chester Cooper when he says that he did not consider Vietnam an enemy. But please try to understand me when I say: *Blood speaks with a terrible voice!*

Geneva's Shadow Over Hanoi

It was obvious to all participants in Geneva in 1954, including U.S. observers, that the DRV delegation headed by Pham Van Dong was disappointed by the results: a partition of Vietnam at the 17th parallel and the promise of all-Vietnam elections and reunification two years later. In the course of our February 1998 dialogue, however, it became clear that the Geneva experience was extraordinarily traumatic—the clinical sense of that term seems appropriate here—for the Hanoi leadership and for all Vietnamese communists. One is tempted to say that from July 20, 1954, forward, or not later than July 1956 (the date when the elections were to have taken place), every major decision and action relative to the U.S. had to pass this requirement: It must not lead to another Geneva.

Because of the retrospective horror with which it regarded the outcome at Geneva, Hanoi's diplomatic and military flexibility would be severely constricted in their appraisal and interactions with the United States. At Geneva, they listened to their big friends, the Soviets and Chinese. In the future, they would not. At Geneva, they compromised in order to secure a promise, which was broken. In the future, their willingness to compromise would seem virtually nonexistent to Washington. At Geneva, they tried to play the game of diplomacy with the big powers and lost. In the future, "diplomacy" with the United States would be conducted only between Washington and Hanoi—or not at all. And most importantly, one suspects, at Geneva they felt they had, in effect, betrayed their compatriots south of the 17th parallel, who had already suffered most in the war with the French. After the formation of the NLF on December 20, 1960, Hanoi would neither seek nor accept any settlement in which the North and South received unequal portions. This anti-Geneva stance was institutionalized in 1960 when Le Duan, a tough southern revolutionary, was made Party secretary and assumed overall command of the war effort throughout Vietnam.

In response to a query from Thomas Biersteker, Luu Doan Huynh and Nguyen Khac Huynh describe the aftermath and implications of the shadow of Geneva:

◈

Thomas Biersteker: . . . I think all of us on the U.S. side would like to know more about the connections—the connections *you* made between Geneva and the 1965–1968 period. Did you, for example, learn one or more lessons from Geneva that you sought to apply in the period we are now discussing?

Luu Doan Huynh: I would like to say this. The Geneva Agreements contained certain fundamental clauses about independence, unity, and other things which helped us legitimize the political battle for the liberation of [South] Vietnam. But all in all, the 1954 Geneva Agreement was a disaster for us. It represented for the Vietnamese people a diplomatic scheme which resulted in a long-term division of the country and in much suffering to our people. The big powers, including the U.S., were the architects of the Geneva Agreement of 1954. Vietnam was their victim.

Therefore, we did not want a Geneva-type conference for the solution of the Vietnam-U.S. war. We wanted direct, bilateral Vietnam-U.S. talks so we could speak for ourselves and act in our own interests. But, you know, we could not say this openly because that would jeopardize the support given to North Vietnam by the USSR and China who, unfortunately, had a stake in a new Geneva-type conference. . . .

But I can tell you that even after the conclusion of the Paris Agreement, many Vietnamese—particularly those from and in South Vietnam—still raised questions. They wanted to know whether the post-Paris situation would be similar to the post-Geneva disaster. It was not until 1975—until the victory in the South—that their fears began to subside. Do you see my point? They were afraid of being abandoned again. And why not? Who can blame them?

Nguyen Khac Huynh: . . . The Geneva Agreement had a big impact on the conduct of our struggle over the next twenty-one years. There were three reasons:

1. . . . Psychologically, I would say, this was very important to us—to work with all our resources to achieve the final objective of the Geneva Accords, which was the unification of Vietnam.

2. . . . We observed (and preserved) the legal validity of the Geneva Agreement for twenty-one years. It was on this basis that we tried to get the United States involved—using the Geneva Agreement as a kind of diplomatic "leverage." . . .

3. . . . At Geneva we were squeezed between the big powers. But by the time of the negotiations with the United States we had escaped from that "box."

I would say that those are the three most important points—or lessons— that we took away from Geneva.

WINNERS AND LOSERS AT GENEVA

Ironically, both Washington and Hanoi believed they had "lost" at Geneva. John Foster Dulles lamented the loss of Vietnam north of the 17th parallel. Ho Chi Minh worried about having "lost" the Vietminh compatriots south of the 17th parallel. However, propagandists on both sides felt compelled, as is usually the case, to declare victory. And also as usual, leaders on both sides fell for each other's propaganda. Each worried that its enemy was growing overconfident. This led to worst-case thinking in both Washington and Hanoi.

As can be seen in the following discussion, it is far from easy, even now, for Americans and Vietnamese to believe that each side actually believed then, in 1954, that the other was the big winner at Geneva.

Chester Cooper: . . . In fact, the U.S. government didn't even want to send a delegation of observers to Geneva. They didn't want anything to do with it. The only reason we went was because of Korea—because Geneva was also the venue, as I am sure all of you recall, for formalizing the cease-fire in Korea. We were there almost entirely to look after our interests on the Korean question. . . . We didn't want to be there. We got nothing out of it, one way or the other. . . .

Luu Doan Huynh: But I don't understand. You say that the U.S. did not like Geneva. But we know that as a result of the Geneva Agreement the U.S. was the biggest winner. After all, you—the United States—replaced the French. You took over everything in Indochina. So how do we reconcile these two things: that you gained the most, but somehow you did not like the outcome. I don't understand this.

Chester Cooper: We gained the most? What did we gain? Can you tell me what benefit we got from the Geneva Conference?

Luu Doan Huynh: Well, the U.S. gained a lot. Then what did Vietnam get?

Chester Cooper: That is a different question, which I will let you and your colleagues answer. But the only benefit I got based on the Geneva Conference of 1954 is to be able to come to Hanoi last June and now in February to explain to you that the U.S. got no benefit whatever from the Geneva Agreement. [Laughter.]

Luu Doan Huynh: I understand that there was a certain loss of face for America in Asia because you backed colonial France, then France lost the battle of Dien Bien Phu and then everything else.
   Okay. But look at what you gained at Geneva:

1. Half of Vietnam, most of Laos, and all of Cambodia still remained under Western influence—by this time, that meant mainly *U.S.* influence.

2. France was out of Indochina—this was important—and the field was open for the United States to control everything.

3. The process of consultation and talks and the results of Geneva were seen by some in the United States as a demonstration of the effectiveness of the well-known "brinkmanship" policy championed by Dulles. Dulles seems to have viewed it that way, as evidenced in his statement to *Life* magazine in 1956 that "Dien Bien Phu was a blessing in disguise."[40]

For these reasons, it seems not only that *we* thought the U.S. was the big winner in Geneva. It seems that the U.S.—that Dulles—thought so too.

Col. Herbert Schandler: . . . What did we gain in Geneva? We "gained" —if that is the right word—the responsibility for propping up a weak, inept government in South Vietnam. Its one saving grace to us was that we saw it as a bulwark against communist domination of all of Southeast Asia.

Who Sabotaged the Geneva Agreement?

Beginning in the period following the Geneva Conference, Washington and Hanoi began accusing each other of "aggression" south of the 17th parallel. Washington's view—and there was little or no dissent from this view at the time—was that the insurgency in the South was conceived and directed by Hanoi and ultimately underwritten by Hanoi's allies in Moscow and Beijing. Thus, the members of the resistance to Ngo Dinh Diem's regime were considered to be "mercenaries," even though they were Vietnamese. Hanoi's view—equally unanimous, one guesses—was that the repressive measures of Diem were conceived, directed, and financed by Washington as part of a plan whose ultimate aim was to crush the DRV itself.

From the outset of the post-Geneva maneuvering, therefore, each side accused the other of beginning its "aggression" first, requiring a "defensive" reaction. Chester Cooper supervised the CIA's analysis of Hanoi's support for the southern resistance. Nguyen Khac Huynh recently reviewed relevant Vietnamese documents. And Robert Brigham is familiar with the documentation from both sides. As the following exchange indicates, the jury is still out on who first sabotaged the spirit and letter of Geneva.

❖

Chester Cooper: I want to comment on problems with implementing the Accords. No one was "pure" about implementing the Accords. You had political cadres from the North heading to the South right after the agreement was signed. Doesn't this indicate that you already believed that the elections would never take place? Bob Brigham cited Pham Van Dong to this effect. But isn't this another kind of evidence that you understood in 1954—that you didn't wait until 1956—to conclude that you were going to have to fight to reunify the country?

Luu Doan Huynh: Excuse me. Are you saying these cadres were going South immediately after Geneva, in the summer of 1954?

Nguyen Dinh Phuong: From North to South?

Chester Cooper: Yes to both of you. I am talking about the Hanoi government sending its cadres to the South—North to South—immediately after the Geneva Conference concluded.

Nguyen Khac Huynh: I will respond to Mr. Chester Cooper's accusation about the movement of troops. With regard to sending troops, I can tell you, as an objective historian, we did not send any troops South. . . .

Chester Cooper: Cadres, not troops.

Nguyen Khac Huynh: No cadres. I remember the situation and I have recently reviewed our documents on this period. Here is the chronology:

1954–56:   No troops, no cadres were sent to the South. In fact, we did everything in our power to comply with the Geneva Accords and to make sure our compliance was noticed.

1958:   We began to organize self-defense units at the grassroots level. . . . Acts of terrorism were being carried out on a large scale, and our people needed some means of at least protecting themselves.

1960:   The military forces in the South had by this time been trained by U.S. advisers and had become much more adept at repression. And so in 1960 we began to send some military specialists.

1963:   At the end of the year in 1963, we began to send combat troops to the South, in an effort to achieve a quick victory, after Diem's assassination, before the Americans would be able to take over the war against our people.

That is the chronology. It is in our documents.

Robert Brigham: From our limited access to Vietnamese documents from that period, it seems that the government in the North actively sought not to deploy any forces in the South. This seems to have been confirmed at a Politburo meeting in April 1956.

Luu Doan Huynh: Yes, you see, in 1956 the Politburo still wanted to pursue the political path to reunification. Of course, some others, especially in the South, had some different ideas, that's true.

Moving to Armed Struggle in the South

By the late 1950s, a renewal of armed conflict was deemed inevitable by members of the southern resistance. They had, on orders from Hanoi, refrained from taking up arms in the two years between the Geneva Conference and the passing of the date for the mandated elections. Washington attributed the increasing violence after mid-1956 to the usual sources: Hanoi, on orders from Moscow and Beijing. Hanoi, likewise, was reconfirmed in its conviction that the Americans were behind the Diem regime's mounting brutality. Neither Washington nor Hanoi was able to appreciate the extent to which local factors were driving the escalation of violence, namely Diem's insensitivity as a leader, and various disenfranchised groups in the South who were reassembling themselves into a coalition to resist.

Recalling her girlhood in the South during this period, Le Ly Hayslip remembered, "We learned that, like the French, men of another race called Americans wanted to enslave us. 'Their allies are the traitorous Republicans of Ngo Dinh Diem!' the Viet Cong shouted."[41] In the following exchange, Nguyen Khac Huynh and Luu Doan Huynh explain to a perplexed Chester Cooper why it seemed logical to conclude that when Diem's forces moved against its enemies in the South the strings of these Vietnamese "puppets" had been pulled by their big enemy in Washington.

❖

Nguyen Khac Huynh: . . . By 1956, we realized that peaceful reunification was not possible. Therefore, our leaders in both regions had to reassess the situation—led by Le Duan in the South and Ho Chi Minh in the North. The combined efforts of Le Duan and Ho Chi Minh resulted in the passage of Resolution 15 in January of 1959. As you know, this signaled that we had given up a strategy of purely political struggle, which could not succeed, due to Ngo Dinh Diem's brutal tactics against our people. Resolution 15 had overwhelming support in the North and the South. Our greatest difficulty was gaining support from the Soviet Union and China for our new policy of struggle for reunification. As you know, almost at the same time Resolution 15 was passed, the Soviets and Chinese began to have problems between themselves. It took all of Ho Chi Minh's great skills to obtain support from both Moscow and Beijing for Resolution 15.

To conclude: We were forced to take up arms in the South because the United States and Diem's regime forced us to. We wanted a peaceful solution, but it was not possible to have reunification without arms. . . .

Chester Cooper: . . . I think it's fair to say we wished him [Diem] well. He inherited a very difficult situation in the South, and we were amazed at the extent to which he was able to solidify his control. We gave him no direct military help that I can recall. We did provide some economic assistance because the South was in difficult shape. And if I recall correctly, between 1954–1956 there was no U.S. military presence in Vietnam. . . . [42]

During the period you are asking about [1954–1956], I don't recall that we even followed Diem's activities, such as they were, regarding the communists of South Vietnam.

Luu Doan Huynh: Okay, this is interesting. So you were pretty sure that Diem wouldn't be able to last. That was your perception right at first. But from our point of view, this is what happened. Already in 1955 Diem began executing people, lots of people, all sorts of people. . . . Diem's security forces were trained in the U.S. And there were many other things that indicated to us that Diem was the U.S.'s puppet—was taking orders from the U.S. Now Mr. Chester Cooper says that the orders to kill our people in 1955 did not come from Washington. Okay. But how could we know this? He was your guy, and he was killing our people. You see, blood again—blood speaks loudly when you are the one who is bleeding.

Conclusions

Throughout the period 1945–1960, I was an executive in the Ford Motor Company in Detroit, Michigan. I knew almost nothing about Vietnam. I did know, or thought I knew, that Ho Chi Minh was an enemy of the West, though I could have said little as to why this was the case, other than to identify Ho's North Vietnamese government as a communist "domino" that had already "fallen" to the Sino-Soviet bloc. My senior associates in the government, including, for example, President Kennedy, Vice-Pres. Lyndon B. Johnson, Secretary of State Dean Rusk, National Security Adviser McGeorge Bundy, and Chairman of the Joint Chiefs Gen. Lyman Lemnitzer, though somewhat more knowledgeable than I, were equally convinced that Russia and China sought to use Vietnam as a stepping-stone to communist control of Southeast Asia.

As for the Hanoi government, throughout more than half the same period, Ho and his colleagues were fighting a guerrilla war against the French in the jungles of Vietnam. During the latter part of the period—after the Geneva Conference in 1954—they supported another guerrilla war in South Vietnam. On the basis of the discussions excerpted above (see the third section, "A Dialogue in Retrospect: Collision Course") it seems that leaders in Hanoi believed during this period that the United States had become their number-one enemy, because Americans were thought to be "imperialists" bent on crushing the Hanoi government and occupying Vietnam.

But what was the reality? *Hanoi was no domino! Washington was no imperialist!* These fundamental misunderstandings would ultimately lead to a tragic war. In 1961 the North Vietnamese leadership and the Kennedy administration saw each other through this thick fog of simplistic Cold War rhetoric that had been accumulating over fifteen years. At the time, the United States had gone much farther down the path to military conflict than the new administration realized. This in no way excuses me and my colleagues in the Kennedy administration, or the leaders in Hanoi, from having to share the responsibility for failing to halt the momentum toward war after January 20, 1961. We—all of us—therefore became to one degree or another culpable for the oncoming tragedy.

I find the revelations in this chapter both fascinating and appalling. Our Vietnamese colleagues went on record for the first time in revealing many of the difficulties, uncertainties, and missteps along the way, especially in their relations with the Soviets and Chinese. This degree of candor is fascinating and important and possible only now, with the Cold War behind us. But the history discussed above, from both the Washington and Hanoi points of view, is so fraught with missed opportunities—with decisions made on the basis of insufficient reflection and utterly mistaken beliefs—as to be almost unbelievable. Some historians may say that it couldn't be helped, that the pressure of Cold War politics drove leaders to do what they did. But as I see it, leaders did not reexamine their fundamental beliefs. Such a reexamination would have made clear that the beliefs were in error and would have been the first step toward changing them. Leaders of both countries succumbed to the pressures that existed, in Washington and in Hanoi. And this is what makes the revelations so appalling. Why were these opportunities missed?

- *Becoming Enemies, 1945–1950.* There is no question that the United States missed opportunity after opportunity to probe Ho Chi Minh and the Vietminh in order to discover their nationalist roots. In addition, U.S. leaders erred in not doing their homework on Vietnam's historical relationship with China. They had been adversaries for a thousand years before either one became communist. Dean Acheson's excuse was that the French "blackmailed" the United States into supporting them in Indochina strikes me as unconvincing, in retrospect. Leaders in Washington should have stuck with their basic moral values rather than allow themselves to be blackmailed. Acheson's and Truman's decision in mid-1950 to underwrite the French war effort in Indochina was a mistake, a very, very costly mistake.

But Ho Chi Minh and his colleagues also missed opportunities during this period. Much was said by our Vietnamese colleagues in each of the conferences about the difficulties involved in emerging from jungle warfare into the world of international geopolitics. Fair enough. But I do not understand why Ho did not pursue the issue with the Truman administration. Since when does "no answer" mean "you are my enemy"? In this case, as we have seen, it only meant "I am too busy" or "I am not interested." If the Vietminh represented primarily a nationalist movement, then Ho and his associates should have found a way to get through with that message. My impression is that they allowed themselves to be blackmailed into doing otherwise, first by the Soviets, then by the Chinese, much to their eventual regret.

- *Disaster at Geneva, 1954–1956.* The Geneva Conference and aftermath are filled with missed opportunities by both sides. The U.S. refusal to fully participate in the conference, and its refusal to endorse the compromise outcome, were inexcusable. This behavior presages the U.S. effort during the 1960s to escalate the war in Vietnam even though most of our key allies opposed it. It also points to a lesson that will be taken up in Chapter 8: the need for collective action, not unilateral punitive measures by the United States—whether military or political or economic—against an ostensible enemy.

   Our Vietnamese colleagues said a good deal about the difficulties they encountered with regard to "maneuvering" at Geneva. It must have been a shock to emerge from a bloody war—a war thought all but won—only to be "invited" by your big "friends" to participate in a conference at which your country will be split in half and, as a result of which, you will be forced in effect to betray your compatriots in the South. But as Luu Doan Huynh argued at the February 1998 conference, this was all the more reason for the DRV delegation in Geneva to seek out the Americans, to talk to them, to explain their situation. As Chester Cooper said at the June conference, he never could figure out who the DRV delegates were "reporting" to in Geneva—the Chinese or the Soviets. Based on all this, it seems to me that Hanoi's representatives weren't so much "reporting" as they were being "blackmailed" by "friends." This, in turn, leads me to wonder why, having been treated this way by China and the Soviet Union, they didn't try to make the Americans understand this, rather than come away telling themselves that the United States was Hanoi's "number-one enemy." Why didn't Hanoi take the initiative? I just don't understand it.

- *Post-Geneva Perceptions, as of January 1961.* Were opportunities missed at the outset of the Kennedy administration to head off the momentum toward war? Without question—and they were missed by both Washington and Hanoi. Let me focus on one piece of evidence—an amazing coincidence of which I was unaware until my involvement in our collaborative project with the Vietnamese. On January 28, 1961, one week after taking office, President Kennedy approved the main provisions of a counterinsurgency plan for South Vietnam that had been developed in the waning months of the Eisenhower administration.[43] On January 28 in Hanoi, Radio Hanoi announced the formation of the NLF, along with its founding ten-point program. Within twenty-four hours, Washington and Hanoi had taken actions each felt was in its interest; but they were based on misperceptions of the other side and would prove to contribute importantly to the magnitude of the tragedy to follow.

Why was this a missed opportunity? Because neither Washington nor Hanoi chose to use the relative flexibility provided by the change in American administrations to renew attempts to investigate the *real*, as opposed to the *imagined*, motives and intentions of each other—that is, to establish a direct and credible channel of contact. Instead of talking to each other, Washington and Hanoi each endorsed its own particular version of covert war against the other's allies in South Vietnam. Each was based on a fundamental misreading of the other. Neither country troubled to recheck the accuracy of its assumptions by discussing it with the other.

The counterinsurgency program was based on Washington's assumption that the southern resistance movement could be eliminated merely by upgrading the South Vietnamese Army and having U.S. advisers give South Vietnamese administrators technical advice about how to run a government. The problem was defined as a lack of technical competence in the South Vietnamese officials. This assessment was based on fantasy, rather than reality, as regards both the strength of the resistance and the capabilities of the Diem government. By November 1961, Gen. Maxwell Taylor would recognize this. Upon his return from a fact-finding trip to Vietnam, he advised President Kennedy that U.S. troops might eventually be needed to deal with the resistance.[44]

But Hanoi likewise erred tremendously in not taking advantage of the situation: a young, open-minded, intellectually curious president had just come to office in Washington with a good deal of interest in and sensitivity to foreign policy. But instead of attempting to contact the president, Hanoi embraced Article 1 of the NLF Platform, which called on its partisans to "overthrow the camouflaged colonial regime of the American imperialists."[45] This reflects a fundamental misunderstanding of U.S. motives and intentions in January 1961. John Kennedy was no "imperialist," and his administration had not the slightest interest in establishing a neocolonial regime in Saigon. Hanoi failed to make clear to the Kennedy administration that its characterization of the NLF was wrong.

At the conclusion of the June 1997 conference in Hanoi, the Vietnamese scholar Luu Doan Huynh reflected on such jointly missed opportunities as those listed above:

> . . . As I have listened to the discussion in this conference, I ask myself: How could two countries have so many wrong ideas about each other? I am not just talking about mindsets. They were bad enough. But all the way through—all the way through this bloody affair, we had many wrong ideas about each other. I ask myself: How is this possible?[46]

I concur with Luu Doan Huynh's assessment. Obviously the "wrong ideas" he refers to have many historical and cultural causes. The tragedy is that leaders in both Washington and Hanoi missed so many opportunities for correcting mistakes before they led to war.

4

A Neutral Solution: Was It Possible?

Footfalls echo in the memory

Down the passage which we did not take

Towards the door we never opened

Into the rose-garden.

T. S. Eliot, "Burnt Norton"[1]

Introduction

In 1963, U.S. Pres. John F. Kennedy asked Canadian Prime Minister Lester Pearson, whom Kennedy personally disliked, for advice on Vietnam. "Get out," was Pearson's succinct reply. With equal succinctness, Kennedy responded: "That's a stupid answer. Everybody knows that. The question is: How do we get out."[2] By 1963 the president had already begun to ruminate about the answer to that question of *how* the U.S. could get out. Much U.S. prestige and many resources had already been sunk into our efforts to give the people of South Vietnam the option of a noncommunist government. Getting out would not be easy. Robert Kennedy later recalled, in 1967, the outline of JFK's answer to his own hard question. Bobby said the solution, according to his brother, must involve "some form of coalition government with people who would ask us to leave."[3] Implicit in Bobby's statement, of course, was the assumption that such a coalition government in Saigon would be supported by Hanoi and would be sufficiently durable to survive.

We believed at the time that failing to keep such a commitment as we had made in South Vietnam would erode the confidence of our other allies and lead to potentially disastrous effects on the security of the West worldwide. But if we pulled out of Vietnam, what chance would we have that whatever coalition government was in place, a neutral government in East-West terms, would remain neutral long enough—would be able to resist communist domination by Hanoi long enough—to flourish on its own and thus also protect us from charges of abandoning an ally?

August 29, 1963. French President Charles de Gaulle stated publicly that France stood ready to assist any serious effort to achieve a neutral solution for "all of Vietnam," pledging French efforts toward "independence" as well as "peace and unity" in Indochina.

The answer of most senior U.S. officials? *Zero.* We had no confidence in such an outcome because we believed at the time that Hanoi, like communist governments everywhere, backed up by Moscow and Beijing, would seek to subvert any such arrangement at the first available opportunity, by whatever means were necessary. We believed that Hanoi had done just that in Laos and that Hanoi's and the National Liberation Front's (NLF) public endorsements of a neutral solution in Saigon were pure propaganda. So we never took their pronouncements seriously. Therefore, throughout the Kennedy administration and well into the Johnson administration, my colleagues and I—and, as the polls showed, the vast majority of the American public—believed that there was no neutral solution to the governance of South Vietnam because Hanoi and the NLF would not permit it. We believed we had no choice, therefore, but to continue to pursue the original goal of the Eisenhower administration: preserving an anticommunist bulwark in Saigon.

Moreover, we did not take neutrality seriously when it was proposed to us by others, including American officials (such as Sen. Mike Mansfield and U.S. Ambassador to India John Kenneth Galbraith); leaders of important U.S. allies (for example, French Pres. Charles de Gaulle); or even UN Secretary General U Thant. We took none of their proposals seriously because none appeared to be based on realistic appraisals of probable North Vietnamese behavior. Their authors were a small minority. The conventional wisdom among top U.S. civilian and military officials was that if the U.S. supported a neutral government in South Vietnam, then Laos would almost certainly come under Hanoi's domination; Cambodia might exhibit a facade of neutrality but would in fact accept communist Chinese domination; and Thailand would become very shaky, as would Malaysia, already beset by Indonesia. Even Burma would see the developments as a clear sign that the whole area now had to accommodate completely to communism (with serious consequences for India as well). Neither the U.S. State Department nor the CIA's National Board of Estimates criticized the conventional wisdom, and the National Security Council never even scheduled the subject for debate.

In May 1967, in a memo to President Johnson, I suggested a combined political-military strategy that raised the possibility of compromise with a more flexible bargaining position while actively seeking a political settlement. But Walt Rostow, the national security adviser, strongly disagreed and reported to the president that my memorandum "aroused strong feelings" within the government.[4] The memo unleashed a storm of controversy, the result being that the possibility of a neutral government in Vietnam was not properly debated in the upper levels of our government. In September 1967, Averell Harriman, then a senior official in the State Department, and I agreed that the United States "must make up our minds that the only way to settle the conflict is by moving to a coalition [i.e., a neutral] government."[5] But again, the issue was not debated in the National Security Council.

My point in referring to the repudiation of various neutral solutions is not that my colleagues and I were wrong, though I believe we *were* wrong, as the revelations in this chapter demonstrate without question. My point is that we didn't properly analyze the *idea* of a neutral solution. It wasn't taken seriously. It was simply rejected. And that, I believe, was a basic mistake—a failure of imagination, a failure to explore the possibilities, to test the limits of the option in each concrete situation where it arose, from whatever source.

But were Mansfield and Galbraith (and, later, Harriman and I) right? Was de Gaulle right? Was a neutral solution to the problem of the government in Saigon a *real* possibility, on terms that we in Washington could have lived with? In other words: *Would Hanoi and the NLF have agreed to, and worked to sustain, a neutral Saigon government made up of a coalition from across the political spectrum in South Vietnam?* During the period 1961–1967, the majority view, received wisdom that was widely accepted, was absolutely not. By 1995, when *In Retrospect* was published, all I could say was that I had no idea whether a neutral solution would have been practical, because I lacked access to Hanoi and NLF officials and documents.

This is why in November 1995 I suggested, during my first visit to Hanoi, that "A Neutral Solution?"—with the question mark—be placed on the agenda of our collaborative project on possible missed opportunities. Specifically, I asked that our group consider the following questions:

- What was the thinking in Hanoi and in the NLF regarding a neutral solution in Saigon? Was it merely useful as propaganda, or was it serious?

- If it was serious, why might Hanoi and the NLF have favored it as something other than just a quick transition to communist domination?

- In light of what can be learned about the evolution of views in both Washington and Hanoi, what appear to be the major missed opportunities for achieving a neutral solution?

Questions such as these should have been posed by Washington and Hanoi to each other during the 1960s. As it was, it took another three decades before we discovered the surprising answers.

Monologues in Real Time: A Neutral Solution?

THE VIEW FROM WASHINGTON

The reaction of Secretary of State John Foster Dulles to the Geneva Agreement was scarcely concealed panic. To Dulles, Asia was slipping away to the communists, who seemed to be on the march across the region. The West had now "lost" Vietnam north of the 17th parallel, via the Geneva Agreement, just as the U.S. had "lost" the mainland of China when Mao's forces triumphed in 1949. The doctrine of containment seemed to be failing miserably in the region. At best, the Geneva Conference provided a means for "saving" the southern portion of Vietnam, though for how long was anyone's guess.

Thus, on September 7, 1954, less than two months after the Geneva Accords were signed, Dulles successfully convened a conference in Manila where delegates signed an agreement creating the Southeast Asia Treaty Organization (SEATO). Modeled on NATO, its objective was to bind the Asian countries still in the "free world," to use the Washington lexicon of 1954, into an explicitly anticommunist alliance. The members were, in addition to the United States, Great Britain, France, Australia, New Zealand, Thailand, Pakistan, and the Philippines. France blocked an effort by Dulles to include the newly independent members of its former colonial empire—Laos, Cambodia, and Vietnam—as full members. The French pointed out that under the Geneva Accords participation in military alliances was expressly forbidden. As a compromise, a separate protocol was signed, according to which the member nations extended their protection to Laos and "the free territory under the jurisdiction of the State of Vietnam"—that is, what would in 1955 be rechristened as the Republic of South Vietnam, or South Vietnam. (Cambodia refused such protection.)[6]

In follow-up testimony before the Senate, Dulles explained the purpose of SEATO:

> If there is a revolutionary movement in Vietnam or in Thailand, we would consult together [with other members of SEATO] as to what to do about it, because if that were a subversive movement that was in fact propagated by communism, it would be a very grave threat to us. But we have no undertaking to put it down; all we have is an undertaking to consult together as to what to do about it.[7]

The U.S. Senate ratified the SEATO treaty in February 1955. On October 26, with U.S. backing, Ngo Dinh Diem proclaimed the Republic of South

Vietnam, a new entity evidently in contradiction to Article 6 of the Geneva Accords, which had declared that "the military demarcation line [the 17th parallel] is provisional and should not in any way be interpreted as constituting a political or territorial boundary."[8] The action was justified on the grounds that *prior* communist aggression from North Vietnam proved that *they* had already violated the Geneva Accords, necessitating the action taken by the United States.

Vietnam south of the 17th parallel was not the only area being contested. In Laos, a theretofore obscure, landlocked mountain kingdom, the Eisenhower administration became concerned over the success of a group known as the Pathet Lao, which had close ties to Hanoi. Its leader, Prince Souphanouvong, had close personal ties to Ho Chi Minh. His half-brother, Souvanna Phouma, was head of the Laotian government in the capital, Vientiane. In October 1957 the two half-brothers negotiated the so-called Vientiane Agreements, which established Laos as a neutral country, run by a coalition government that had Pathet Lao representation in both the civilian and military leadership.

To Dulles, who "thought coalitions with communists were halfway houses to perdition," this seemed the precursor of another "loss" to communism because, as he saw it, communists were never satisfied until they had eliminated all members of a coalition who were not communist.[9] For this reason, as George Ball has written, through Dulles's "astigmatic" vision, "Laos loomed large as a 'bulwark against communism' and a 'bastion of freedom.'"[10] Using the SEATO treaty as justification, the United States invested nearly $300 million in Laos by the end of 1960, with 85 percent going to the right-wing forces (chiefly the army), headed by Gen. Phoumi Nosavan, whom Dulles's brother, CIA Director Allen Dulles, had discovered in France.

In this way, a local dispute in an out-of-the-way place escalated in a remarkably short period of time into a potential superpower confrontation, as the Soviets backed and supplied the Pathet Lao and the U.S. supported Phoumi Nosavan and the Royal Laotian Army. On January 1 and 7, 1961, Pathet Lao forces, now joined by forces loyal to a former paratrooper named Kong Le, scored decisive victories over Phoumi's forces. In Washington, Laos seemed, despite the massive infusion of American resources, to be on the brink of a communist takeover.[11] Were a takeover to occur, it was feared that U.S. prestige and influence in Southeast Asia would sink even lower and thus provide additional proof, to the few in Washington who might have required any, that a neutral solution, though less bloody than a communist coup, leads to the same disastrous result—a communist takeover. This was the context in which Eisenhower's Laos problem was handed off to Kennedy.

As noted in Chapter 2, on January 19, 1961, Kennedy was briefed by Eisenhower on the eve of the new president's inauguration. Kennedy asked about prospects for a Laotian coalition that included Pathet Lao representation. Christian Herter, Dulles's successor as secretary of state, told Kennedy that "any proposal which would include communists in the government would end up with the communists in control."[12] In response to a direct question from Kennedy, Eisenhower told him that "it would be far better to intervene through SEATO" than to seek a coalition with communists. Eisenhower went even further, to emphasize the gravity of the situation. He said he would prefer *unilateral* U.S. intervention to any kind of neutralist arrangement because "the loss of Laos would be the loss of the 'cork in the bottle' and the beginning of the loss of most of the Far East."[13]

During the first two months of his administration, Kennedy would spend more time on Laos than any other single issue.[14] The situation looked bleak. The Soviets were airlifting an estimated forty-five tons of arms out of Hanoi each day to Pathet Lao forces, who daily expanded the territory they had conquered and now occupied. After weeks of study and discussion, Kennedy and his advisers saw the following options:

1. Do nothing. Let the Pathet Lao take over.

2. Do everything needed to crush the Pathet Lao.

3. Accept a division of Laos, on the model of Korea.

4. Negotiate to restore a neutral coalition government.[15]

Rejecting Eisenhower's dire warnings, Kennedy decided that a neutral solution was his best option, if it could be obtained. On March 23, he spoke publicly about his determination to seek a neutral solution, still mispronouncing the name of the unfamiliar and exotic hot spot as "LAY-oss" rather than "Louse"—which rhymes with "house"—a sign of the utter bizarreness of the unfolding events.[16] In addition, he ordered U.S. Marines in Japan and Okinawa to prepare to move to the Thai border with Laos. The Seventh Fleet was alerted. Against this background of a stated preference for negotiations, augmented by apparent preparations for a U.S. military intervention, a cease-fire was reached. On May 16, 1961, the Geneva Conference was reconvened to consider the future of Laos, the ostensible goal being to reestablish a neutral coalition government in Vientiane. Two weeks later, in an otherwise stormy and difficult meeting with Soviet Premier Nikita Khrushchev in Vienna on June

3–4, 1961, Kennedy and the Soviet leader agreed to scale back what both agreed were overcommitments in Laos. Kennedy and his advisers could only hope that the cork had been stuffed back in the bottle, at least provisionally, as they turned their attention to what they saw as the far more important, and qualitatively different, problem: South Vietnam.

Throughout 1961, the situation in South Vietnam seemed to deteriorate. In spite of a growing sense of urgency, however, Kennedy and his senior officials could give the problem but intermittent attention. The year was filled with crises, including the debacle of the Bay of Pigs invasion in April; the brutal summit with Khrushchev in Vienna in early June, at which Khrushchev threatened war in lieu of a settlement on Berlin; the Berlin crisis itself; the erection of the Berlin Wall, beginning on August 13; the U.S.-Soviet tank confrontation in Berlin in late October. As the situation in Vietnam worsened, Americans, worried about matters closer to home, purchased bomb shelters in record numbers. The poet Robert Lowell wrote in "Fall 1961" of "the chafe and jar of nuclear war" in which "we have talked our extinction to death."[17] By and large, Vietnam would have to wait for a break in what seemed in Washington, and throughout the United States, like a frightening increase in the danger of a nuclear attack from the Soviet Union.

Finally, in October, Kennedy ordered Gen. Maxwell Taylor, chairman of the Joint Chiefs of Staff, and Walt Rostow, deputy to National Security Adviser McGeorge Bundy, to lead a fact-finding trip to South Vietnam and make recommendations for how to proceed. They spent a week there, October 18–25, flying afterward to the Philippines to draft what became known as the Taylor Report. It was submitted to Kennedy on November 11.[18] The president met with the Taylor group, together with other senior officials, the same day. He met again with Robert McNamara and Dean Rusk on November 14. The report emphasized the gravity of the situation and the need for a wide range of reforms by the Saigon government, along with increased U.S. military assistance.

By November 15, Kennedy made his most important decisions so far with regard to Vietnam. He agreed to most components of the concrete military assistance package recommended in the report. However, Kennedy, a president who famously disliked premature foreclosure of options, made no irrevocable U.S. commitments to any specific policy. He decided *not* to sanction the use of U.S. combat forces in Vietnam; *not* to seek a negotiated settlement at that time; and *not* to provide the kind of all-out, do-or-die commitment to preserving the Diem regime sought by some of his military advisers. Kennedy's decisions were formalized on November 22 in National Security Action Memorandum 111 (NSAM 111).[19]

Several commentators, including Kennedy's White House aide, Arthur

Schlesinger, have commented on the composition of the Taylor group, particularly its lack of a senior State Department official. According to Schlesinger, the choice of Taylor and Rostow to lead the group "expressed a conscious decision by the Secretary of State to turn the Vietnam problem over to the Secretary of Defense."[20] Schlesinger believes that this may have been appropriate in November 1961, when the military situation seemed so desperate as to warrant an all-out effort to reverse the situation on the battlefield. But Schlesinger adds: "The effect, however, was to color future thinking about Vietnam in both Saigon and Washington with the unavowed assumption that Vietnam was primarily a military rather than a political problem."[21] Decoded, the phrase *political problem* implied a neutral solution of some sort in Saigon, perhaps on the model of what was then being negotiated regarding Laos.

Was there, in November 1961, a neutral solution available to Kennedy? There was, at least in principle, and it was proposed informally to the president as an alternative to the Taylor recommendations. The most important backers were Averell Harriman and Chester Bowles, both from the State Department. The secretary of state, Dean Rusk, did not present a recommendation to the president. Bowles had for several months been promoting the enlargement of a neutral and independent Laos so as to include the rest of Southeast Asia (minus North Vietnam): Burma, Thailand, South Vietnam, Cambodia, and Malaya. Bowles argued that if the communists tried to take advantage of any or all of these proposed neutral governments, Washington would find it easier to marshal international support in opposition than would otherwise be the case.[22]

Harriman wrote a personal memorandum to Kennedy on November 11, the same day the Taylor group submitted its report. Harriman argued for a negotiated solution via a "strengthened and modernized" version of the Geneva Accords of 1954, which might mean reunification and elections, as originally mandated in Geneva.[23] In a handwritten cover note marked "Personal," Harriman told Kennedy, "I have given a copy of this draft memorandum to Dean Rusk. He asked me to tell you his comment. 'It is a matter of timing' bearing in mind 'other communications' on the same subject."[24] Kennedy read it, and on November 14 he asked for responses from others. In a memo dictated for McGeorge Bundy, he said, "I would like to have you consider the proposals made by Governor Harriman."[25]

Did Kennedy seriously consider this neutral solution as an alternative to the Taylor group's recommendations? Probably not, though it is impossible to say one way or the other with confidence. What we do know is that at this critical moment Kennedy focused instead on the more immediate need, as he saw it, to improve the Diem government's relative military position in its struggle with the Hanoi-backed NLF. In his memorandum of November 14 to Rusk and McNamara, Kennedy lifted key passages without alteration from Walt Rostow's nearly apocalyptic response to Harriman's proposal:

> If we postpone action in Vietnam to engage in talks with the communists, we can surely count on a crisis of nerve in Viet-Nam and throughout Southeast Asia. The image of U.S. unwillingness to confront Communism—induced by the Laos performance—will be regarded as definitely confirmed. There will be panic and disarray. . . . If we negotiate now—while infiltration continues—we shall in fact be judged weaker than in Laos; for in that case we at least first insisted on a cease-fire.[26]

Of the Bowles-Harriman neutral solution, Schlesinger remarks: "It was an imaginative proposal, but it seemed either too early or too late."[27] Ironically, as we shall see below, it may actually have come at exactly the *right* time. Historian George Kahin writes: "There is no way of knowing whether Harriman was aware how strikingly close in several respects his prescription was to that being advanced by the NLF."[28] However that may be, Kennedy's November 15 decisions meant that for the time being he would agree to no neutral solution in Saigon.

With regard to Laos, however, a neutral solution was the *objective*. In Laos, as elsewhere, many U.S. officials viewed a neutralist coalition as undesirable because of what was referred to as communists' "nibbling" tactics—piecemeal acquisition of territory—under the guise of a cease-fire or even with a neutral government in place. In Laos, a cease-fire had been declared on May 3, 1961, and was, theoretically, in effect from that point forward. In reality, all sides jockeyed for position, as the negotiations went on in Geneva. During May 2–6, 1962, Pathet Lao forces overwhelmed U.S.-backed units of Phoumi Nosavan at Nam Tha in northwest Laos.[29]

Several days later, on May 9, a Special National Intelligence Estimate was issued, in line with what was considered to be the seriousness of the new situation. It offered a doomsday prediction following the sought-after neutral solution in Laos:

> The attack and the manner in which it was conducted provide further proof of the decreasing military role and strength of the "neutralist" forces in Laos and the increasing tendency for the communist troops to assume exclusive jurisdiction. The attack underscores the weakness of [neutralist Prince Souvanna Phouma's] influence. It also reinforces the view previously expressed that Souvanna would be increasingly unlikely to be able to prevent communist control of a coalition government.[30]

In response, the Kennedy administration moved U.S. Marines and other combat personnel in Thailand up to the Laos border and sent naval and air force detachments into the area. State Department intelligence chief Roger Hilsman reported: "Over the next three days the intelligence reports showed no further troop movement."[31] According to White House special assistant Theodore Sorensen, the administration believed that "the Pathet Lao stopped, convinced that the United States meant business."[32] The episode, in any event, did nothing to build U.S. confidence in neutral solutions, either for Laos or for South Vietnam.[33]

If it accomplished nothing else, the episode at Nam Tha may have forced U.S. officials to encourage their demonstrably inept ally, Phoumi Nosavan, to get serious about a political solution in Laos. On July 23, 1962, the Declaration of Neutrality was signed, giving roles in the new government to the Hanoi-backed Pathet Lao, headed by Prince Souphanouvong, to Phoumi Nosavan's royalists, and a neutralist group led by Souvanna Phouma, who would lead the government. Chester Cooper, a U.S. participant in the Geneva negotiations, later recalled: "The agreement stimulated some hope but few illusions."[34] Cooper says the U.S. participants doubted that Hanoi would really comply with the provision in the agreement prohibiting foreign troops in Laos. (Several thousand North Vietnamese troops were present inside Laos at the time of the signing.) The hope, according to Cooper, derived from the possibility that Averell Harriman, who headed the U.S. delegation, may have convinced the head of the Soviet delegation, Deputy Foreign Minister Georgi M. Pushkin, to use Moscow's influence to prevent Hanoi from trying to bring down Souvanna's neutral government. But nothing was put on paper in Geneva. Pushkin died shortly after the signing, and Moscow would not admit afterward to having made any such commitment.[35]

Much later, however, it was learned that Kennedy had personally authorized Harriman to meet with Ung Van Khiem, Hanoi's foreign minister, who was in Geneva to sign the accords on behalf of the Hanoi government. The meeting took place on July 23, the day of the signing, in the hotel suite of the Burmese delegation to the conference. Ung Van Khiem and one aide met with Harriman and his deputy, William Sullivan. The meeting went nowhere and broke down in a cascade of charges and countercharges. "We got absolutely nowhere," Sullivan recalled in 1980. "We hit a stone wall."[36]

Harriman, according to Sullivan, had the following scenario in mind:

Once you get the Laotian settlement . . . you might be able to expand it into a larger area of understanding, and particularly if you got the Soviets to recognize that it united their interests as well as ours to try to neutralize the whole Indochina area, that otherwise it might fall prey to the Chinese, and that we might be able to build therefore on the Laos settlement. . . . [Kennedy] was constantly looking for opportunities to see if we could expand from the Laos agreement.[37]

The failure of this initiative seemed to confirm the views of the many senior officials in the administration who at that point were already deeply skeptical about a neutral solution for South Vietnam.[38]

Moreover, Washington became convinced immediately after the signing at Geneva that Hanoi was already violating the accords. U.S. intelligence, for example, counted approximately 6,000 North Vietnamese troops in Laos by July 1962. They counted several hundred leaving, but no more.[39] With the support of Hanoi's forces, the Pathet Lao managed to maintain control of the two northern provinces it had "liberated" before the signing of the Geneva Accords. According to Chester Cooper: "What emerged was a de facto partition of the country, with [only] two-thirds of the population living under government control."[40]

Did the U.S. perception of massive violations of the neutral "solution" in Laos really affect Washington's views about the possibility of a neutral solution in South Vietnam? Or were Hanoi's violations merely a convenient excuse to dismiss an option few liked anyway? Dean Rusk, a straightforward man seldom given to exaggeration or hyperbole, was unequivocal. He recalled: "With any semblance of North Vietnamese adherence to the accords, we could have entertained the idea of a neutralized South Vietnam. In view of Hanoi's wholesale violation of the accords, we didn't believe Hanoi would accept a neutral South Vietnam."[41] After Geneva, for Rusk—and for many others as well—a "neutral *solution* in Saigon" became a contradiction in terms. The feeling was this: If Hanoi cannot be trusted to keep its commitments in Laos, why should they be trusted in South Vietnam? Even the few senior officials in the Kennedy administration who favored a neutral solution found it difficult, if not impossible, to answer this question satisfactorily. Most officials in Washington had altogether lost interest in the idea.

Beginning in May 1963, however, the idea was revitalized, though Washington was not directly involved. On May 8, Ngo Dinh Nhu ordered his security police to break up a rally of Buddhists in Hue, in northern South Vietnam. Their alleged offense was flying Buddhist flags on this, the Buddha's birthday. An ugly incident ensued, resulting in the deaths of one woman and eight children. The Buddhists, led by a monk named Thich Tri Quang, mobilized with remarkable speed and efficiency and organized protests and demonstrations throughout South Vietnam. These, in turn, were broken up, often brutally, by Nhu's police. Then, on June 11, a Buddhist monk named Quang Duc, aged sixty-six, immolated himself in the middle of a busy Saigon street. Photographs and stories about the event dominated the news worldwide for days. Other immolations followed. Ngo Dinh Nhu's wife, Tran Le Xuan (known as Madame Nhu), a militant Roman Catholic, declared the self-immolations to be a Buddhist "barbecue." She told an interviewer, "Let them burn, and we shall clap our hands."[42] These statements were also widely reported.

Washington was furious with Nhu and with the Diem government in general. They had staked their money, advice, and prestige on Diem and Nhu, and Washington had been embarrassed by the Saigon government's increasingly brutal and all too visible actions. The demonstrations escalated in number throughout the summer. Diem and Nhu became, from Washington's point of view, surly and uncooperative. Soon, what had begun as a dispute between the Catholic Diem government and the Buddhist majority in South Vietnam escalated to a confrontation between the Saigon government and Washington. Nhu became increasingly visible in this dispute, and the already reclusive Diem retreated even further from view. Nhu printed bizarre stories in a newspaper he controlled, *Times of Vietnam*, for example, that Washington had paid millions to the NLF in a plot to organize a coup; and rumors were repeated that various members of the U.S. mission in Saigon were on an "assassination list" that Nhu himself had prepared.[43]

Publicly, the U.S. response to these events was critical but muted. But privately, those most directly responsible for Vietnam policy were furious. Doubts began to surface over the summer about how viable the Diem regime actually was. Roger Hilsman, the State Department's action officer on Vietnam, confided the following on September 3 in a memorandum of conversation: "All this I have been saying for months. . . . Nhu beat up the Buddhist Pagodas. . . . The purpose was to lead the U.S. around by the nose to demonstrate to all Vietnam that we were controllable. . . . It is true that we don't have the leverage that some think we do in calling the tune in a country we are helping, but we are not and cannot be their complete puppets."[44] An irreversible process of estrangement had begun between the Diem government and the Kennedy administration.

In this hot-house atmosphere of threats and counterthreats between Saigon and Washington, a mediated conversation was initiated between Saigon and Hanoi regarding the possibility of a neutral solution—some kind of rapprochement between North and South. The idea may have originated with Buu Hoi, a scientist who lived in Paris and had access to French Pres. Charles de Gaulle. De Gaulle, at Buu Hoi's urging, sent instructions to Roger Lalouette, the French ambassador in Saigon, to find a way to facilitate a conversation between Hanoi and Saigon. Lalouette chose as the intermediary Mieczyslaw Maneli, the Polish representative on the International Control Commission, which was established in 1954 to oversee compliance with the Geneva Accords. Because of his position, Maneli enjoyed unrestricted transit between North and South Vietnam. And because Maneli was from a communist country, Lalouette believed his access in Hanoi would be enhanced.

Maneli, who defected to the West in 1968, recalled his discussions in the North and South in a memoir, published in English in 1971.[45] Additional details were later divulged by Ellen Hammer in her 1987 book *A Death in November*, based on extensive interviews with many of the participants.[46] Here, in brief, seems to have been the situation that drove mortal enemies toward a neutral solution in Saigon: Diem was on the ropes by late summer 1963. Most believed he would be removed, either by his generals or outright by the United States. His immediate problem, from his point of view, was *the Americans*. Ho Chi Minh and his colleagues were also in trouble. North Vietnam was suffering through its worst drought in memory. (Maneli reported, for example, that Hanoi suggested beginning the rapprochement with a barter of northern coal for southern rice.)[47] Its leaders were beginning to understand that South Vietnam could only be reconquered by force but that this would involve a possibly catastrophic war with the United States. Finally, old animosities were resurfacing between the Chinese and northern Vietnamese. In particular, Mao was relentless in pushing Hanoi toward military confrontation with the United States, and it was understood in Hanoi that the Chinese would not mind if the Hanoi government was weakened as a result, so long as it survived as a communist buffer next door to China.

On August 29, amid these exchanges, President de Gaulle stated publicly that France stood ready to assist any serious efforts to achieve a neutral solution for Vietnam.[48] Following de Gaulle's announcement, rumors began to fly in Saigon that a French-brokered deal was imminent. A common thread in all the scenarios was aptly described by Francis Winters: "Independence [in North and South] would be an all-Vietnamese dream, not a Cold War mirage."[49]

Three principal questions arise in retrospect regarding these accounts. First, was something like this Saigon-Hanoi rapprochement actually discussed, via Maneli? Evidence from Western sources suggests its authenticity. Second, what kind of neutral solution might have been achieved? Is it possible that Hanoi would have tolerated leaving Diem in charge in Saigon? Several years after the publication of his memoir, Maneli recalled the pivotal moment of discussions about arrangements in Saigon. He said: "I asked if such a government could be headed by Mr. Diem. In the summer of 1963, the answer was finally yes."[50] Third, assuming good faith on the part of Hanoi and Saigon, by what means would the Americans and Chinese have become convinced that it was in their respective interests to remove themselves from the scene? Any answer is of course speculative, especially on the Hanoi-Beijing side. Arthur Schlesinger's reflection on Washington's reaction, however, is hopeful but possibly realistic: "A Diem-Ho deal could have been the means of an American exit from Vietnam in 1963, though the life expectancy of a Diem government in Saigon would have been minimal thereafter. An opportunity of some sort was perhaps missed in the autumn of 1963."[51]

Diem and Nhu were abruptly assassinated following a U.S.-backed coup on November 1. A group of generals, led by Duong Van Minh, nicknamed "Big Minh," with the advice and support of the U.S. embassy, overthrew the Ngo brothers and took control of the government. The change in leadership, however, did nothing to quell speculation about the possibility of a neutral solution in Saigon. On the contrary, the new junta, including General Minh, seemed inclined from the moment they took power to be probing for a possible neutral arrangement. Their natural proclivities in this direction were given encouragement from a variety of sources. On November 8, the NLF put out a conciliatory manifesto calling for the formation of a coalition government "composed of representatives of all forces, parties, tendencies and strata of the South Vietnamese people."[52] Prince Norodom Sihanouk of Cambodia reiterated his call for an international conference that would consider a neutral "federation" of Southeast Asian nations, including South Vietnam, a notion the NLF endorsed on December 13. Also in December, French President de Gaulle issued another of his periodic offers to facilitate any neutralist arrangement in Saigon.

Disquieted by this swirl of rumors, proclamations, and proposals, President Johnson sent the following warning to the Minh junta, disguised as a New Year's greeting. He told Minh: "We shall maintain in Vietnam American personnel and material as needed to assist you in achieving victory. . . . Neutralization of South Vietnam is unacceptable [and] would only be another name for a communist take-over."[53] In fact, Johnson administration officials were mortified by the possibility that Diem's successors might be looking for a neutral solution. McGeorge Bundy and Walt Rostow both delivered scathing attacks in early January on a proposal from Mike Mansfield that suggested, in essence, taking seriously the idea of a neutral solution in Saigon.[54] Cable traffic between the Saigon embassy and Washington was also filled with fulminations against the neutralist tendencies of the junta.[55]

The Minh junta was itself thrown out in a coup on January 30, 1964, led by Gen. Nguyen Khanh. The Nguyen Khanh group was supported by many in the U.S. embassy in Saigon who had expressed frustration with General Minh and his colleagues for failing to prosecute the war against the NLF with sufficient enthusiasm and skill. But in light of what we now know about the *political* objectives of the junta, it is possible that their behavior was at least partially purposeful, their fatal miscalculation being an overestimate of Washington's interest in, or at least toleration of, a neutral solution in Saigon and an accommodation with the NLF.

What did they believe and what was their objective? General Minh insisted that he and his colleagues were *noncommunist* rather than *anticommunist*. "You must understand the distinction," he said, "because it is an important one."[56] Their strategy, in short, seems to have been an incremental accommodation with the NLF. Minh's brother was a member of the NLF, but the junta also had many other lines of communication to the NLF, especially the noncommunist membership. In 1970 the Minh junta's prime minister, Nguyen Ngoc Tho, recalled their outlook in late 1963:

> The strategy of the new government was first to consolidate itself with . . . minorit[ies] and then to bring the NLF out of opposition and into support of what would be termed a government of reconciliation. At this time [1963–1964], the NLF was overwhelmingly noncommunist. . . . The effort envisaged was to try to bring over the most detachable elements within the NLF. . . .
>
> The second step envisaged was for the launching of a government of reconciliation, which would be one wherein all elements of the NLF would be welcome to participate in an electoral process. The NLF was then sufficiently free of Hanoi's control to have made this process quite possible. We would have striven for a neutral government—not a government without an army, but one without foreign troops or bases and one whose neutrality in international affairs would incline towards the West.[57]

Thus it would not have been in the interest of the junta to carry out the policy required by Washington, which was often referred to as "breaking the back of the Vietcong" (using the epithet for the NLF). In any case, they were removed at the end of January and replaced by those the Saigon embassy and Washington believed were more determined to carry out *American* policy in South Vietnam.

The late January coup signaled the end of any serious intent in Saigon, let alone capability, for pursuing a neutral solution. Throughout 1964, coup followed coup. Each successor government in Saigon was deemed more or less acceptable in Washington based solely on the U.S. estimate of its compatibility with U.S. strategy for prosecuting the war. Unlike Diem and Nhu, and unlike Duong Van Minh and his junta, the successors had no neutralist tendency. Its absence, instead, became one of the prerequisites for the job.

George Ball was sent by President Johnson to consult with President de Gaulle in June 1964 and to ask for his support, in case the United States saw fit to escalate the war. Ball later recalled what de Gaulle told him: "We would never succeed by force, only by negotiation. . . . Vietnam, he said—and I shall never forget the phrase—is 'rotten country.' France [de Gaulle added] had learned that to its sorrow."[58] Having given up on a neutral solution, the U.S. would now learn this lesson.

THE VIEW FROM HANOI

Compared with other communist leaders of the twentieth century, Ho Chi Minh must rank as one of those least constricted by rigid communist ideology. His genius lay in his pragmatism—in the way he was able to combine Vietnamese history, anticolonial rhetoric, quasi-Leninist organizational tactics, the patience of Job, and a common demeanor and manner that belied great sophistication and cleverness. His goal, and the goal of his organization, the Vietminh, was a unified, independent Vietnam. That was the goal in 1930 at the founding and remained the goal during the American War in 1969, when he died. He was a communist, of course. But like Cuba's Fidel Castro, Ho seems in retrospect to have married his movement to communism as a means, not an end, all the Marxist-Leninist rhetoric notwithstanding. Among the many names he called himself, the one that may be closest to the heart of his life's project is Nguyen Ai Quoc—"Nguyen the Patriot."

Ho's pragmatism was evident in the way he and his colleagues approached the issue of "neutralism." After the August Revolution in 1945 and for several years thereafter, including the early years of the resistance war against the French, the Vietminh had a more or less neutral foreign policy, to the extent they had any at all. In 1947, for example, Ho was effusive in his praise of Switzerland, the most famously neutral of European countries.[59] But he also liked to quote Jefferson and Lenin. One sees in this attitude the natural neutralism of a cosmopolitan, uncommonly literate Third World revolutionary. Ho and most of his colleagues, in fact, may be said to have been "psychologically neutral" even toward France, their colonial oppressor and enemy at the time. They would fight the French forever, if necessary, of course. But many were also Francophiles, in their way—fluent in French, educated either in France or in French schools in Vietnam, and well read in French history and literature. Gen. Vo Nguyen Giap, for example, began his professional life as a history teacher, and he was equally conversant with French and Vietnamese history. He still enjoys being interviewed in French.

This casual phase of Vietnamese "neutralism" ended abruptly in 1949, with the triumph of Mao's communist forces in China. Vietnam had been only mildly interesting to Stalin and his Soviet colleagues following World War II. The Soviet Union had its own problems, and Stalin was focused on consolidating his acquisitions in Eastern Europe and in challenging U.S. supremacy in the global ideological battle between East and West. But China had been a Vietnamese nemesis for a millennium or more, and the new communist government in Beijing began almost immediately in 1949 to make demands on Ho and his movement. As a result, the Vietnamese resistance publicly recognized the primacy of the Communist Party as the source of all ideological wisdom. This occurred at the Second National Congress in early 1951. Yet in a move that exemplified his pragmatic nationalism, Ho Chi Minh stipulated that the Party be named Lao Dong. This is almost always translated as "Workers' Party." But an equally accurate translation, one possibly more in keeping with Ho Chi Minh's pragmatic intentions, is "Labor Party." And naming the state the Democratic Republic of Vietnam reflected in part the fact that the Vietnamese Revolution drew on resources more extensive than merely communist ideology.[60]

During the early 1950s, Ho Chi Minh seems to have self-consciously evolved a second kind of East bloc neutrality—a balance in Vietnam's relations with Moscow and Beijing and a high degree of independence, before and after the split between the two communist giants became evident at the end of the decade. Hanoi's situation was much more complex than most officials in Washington understood. The Soviets were the acknowledged leaders of the world communist movement. They were a superpower, with nuclear weapons and other sophisticated armaments. But they were also far away, geographically speaking. In addition, Vietnam shared little or no history or culture with the Russians, who were utterly alien to the Vietnamese in these respects (as they would be to the Cubans, later on). But when Mao's communists came to power in China, Ho's pragmatism was severely tested. Few statesmen in recent history could have faced a more difficult challenge than he faced with regard to China: dealing with a gigantic, historic enemy and colonial oppressor (as the Vietnamese view China) that becomes, almost overnight, one's "fraternal" ally and principal supplier of goods and services necessary to complete one's own revolution.

Soviet motives in aiding the Vietminh, and later the government in Hanoi, were clearly ideological. What else would they be? But Chinese motives in assisting Ho's movement and, later, his government, were mixed up with the antagonistic history the two nations shared. Chinese aid always had strings attached. The trick for the Vietnamese lay in discovering *which* strings—why, exactly, the Chinese were offering to be helpful. Published statements from leaders in Hanoi do not, of course, condemn the Chinese. But one suspects that from 1949 onward Vietnamese leaders became extraordinarily vigilant regarding Chinese motives, which had historically led them to seek to occupy northern Vietnam and treat it as a kind of buffer state. Vietnamese communists suspected that Chinese aid, in whatever form, would be calculated in Beijing to keep the Hanoi government strong enough to survive and remain a buffer between China and U.S.-dominated South Vietnam yet not strong enough to secure true independence from Beijing. Transcripts of discussions from the 1960s between leaders of Beijing and Hanoi are striking, in fact, in the degree to which Mao Zedong, Zhou Enlai, and others speak condescendingly to their Vietnamese counterparts, almost in the tone of parent to child. But perhaps more striking is Vietnamese compliance in the presence of Mao and Zhou.[61]

This natural tendency of Ho Chi Minh and his colleagues toward neutral solutions to specifically Vietnamese problems received a boost due to the neutral policies of Laos, Indonesia, and Burma and with the founding of the Non-Aligned Movement (NAM) in Belgrade in 1961.[62] Official Washington regarded the NAM with skepticism. "Neutrality" was seen as a camouflage for incipient communism—what was often called "creeping socialism" in those days. When avowedly communist countries (especially North Vietnam after 1954 and Cuba after 1961) claimed to embrace the NAM's principle of "peaceful coexistence" as its own, Washington regarded them as charlatans. But at that time, Washington had little or no appreciation of the delicate balancing act leaders such as Ho Chi Minh had to perform in order to carve out a margin of independence from Moscow and Beijing.

By the mid-1950s, however, it was clear in Hanoi that finding a different kind of neutral solution would soon become Hanoi's most important foreign policy goal. Sometime after the Geneva Accords were signed in July 1954— probably not long after they were signed—leaders in Hanoi realized that Washington regarded the 17th parallel as marking a permanent rather than a temporary division of Vietnam. At that moment, for every North Vietnamese leader, reaching a neutral solution in Saigon became a goal that was seldom far from their minds over the next twenty years. Why? Because the United States was not only a big power; it had the means, and possibly the will, to destroy North Vietnam utterly and completely. This was understood. So the United States could not be defeated in the South, in the customary meaning of the word *defeated*.

Second, Ho Chi Minh and other leaders in Hanoi believed it might not be possible to convince the Soviet Union or China to back them to the extent necessary to actually convince the Americans to leave. They understood that neither communist power sought a direct confrontation with the United States, which might very well result from a Washington-Hanoi confrontation and could conceivably involve the use of nuclear weapons.[63]

Third, some leaders in Hanoi, though perhaps not all, understood that the partition of Vietnam had introduced an ugly fact of life into their own calculations: From 1954 onward, the situation of the southern communists would be *fundamentally* different than for those north of the 17th parallel. In the North, the government would build socialism. In the South, socialists would be hunted, harassed, tortured, and killed in significant numbers, all with U.S. backing. If and when the partition was erased, therefore, the South would, to an extent, be alien territory to northerners. In this situation, the *southern* communist comrades could rightly claim to be the best judges of their own destiny. Thus, a neutral solution in Saigon, as part of an overall strategy for expelling the United States and the government it supported in Saigon, became a paramount and ineradicable element of Hanoi's policy. The number-one goal of Hanoi, in a sense, was to arrive at a neutral solution *in order to avoid a catastrophic escalation of the conflict with the United States.*[64]

This realization was evident even at the pivotal Fifteenth Party Plenum in 1959, at which Le Duan first presented what would become the blueprint for the war in the South. Resolution 15 officially recognized political and armed struggle as a legitimate strategy for liberating the South. But even Resolution 15 shows awareness of the need for somehow arriving at a political solution in Saigon without unduly antagonizing the Americans. In this regard, a sobering admonition can be discovered submerged in the standard socialist rhetoric of the time:

> To defend world peace is the common aspiration of all countries and is in keeping with the requirements of the development of revolution in the world as seen by our camp. In order to coordinate the struggle of Vietnam with the revolutionary movement of the world's people, our Party advocates the solution of Vietnam's reunification by the path of peace. . . . The 15th Plenum predicts that the revolution in the South has the possibility to develop peacefully by gradually transforming the situation—the political situation—in a favorable way to revolution. Although such a possibility is very small, we do not discard it. Instead, we must grab it.[65]

Such statements were regarded in Washington—to the extent anyone was aware of them—in one of two ways: as pure propaganda; or as attempts by

Hanoi to straddle the increasingly wide ideological gulf between Moscow and Beijing. They doubtless served these purposes. But there is no reason to suspect that the Vietnamese communists were immune from the iron law of governing: All politics is local. And the local situation on the horizon alluded to by the author of the above passage in Resolution 15 is bound to be difficult. Hence the exhortation to find a political solution in the South before so much damage has been done that there is nothing meaningful left to "solve."

A neutral solution in Saigon—including both a neutralist foreign policy and a coalition government—was from the start part of the public platforms of the NLF and the Hanoi government. Article 1 of the NLF Founding Program called for "a government of national and democratic union . . . composed of representatives of all social classes, of all nationalities, of the various political parties, of all religions." Article 8 called for "a foreign policy of peace and neutrality . . . in accordance with the principles of peaceful coexistence adopted at the Bandung Conference."[66]

So once again we see the convergence of Hanoi's objectives around a neutral solution in Saigon. At a minimum, such a program as that put forward by the NLF was designed to widen their base of support in countries not formally committed to one bloc or the other. As a Party official in Hanoi argued: "We can gain a tremendous diplomatic advantage and put the United States at a huge disadvantage by promoting the neutralization of South Vietnam."[67] Such advantages would accrue within South Vietnam, where communists were, and would for some time remain, a minority among NLF membership. Such an approach would also help to ease the burden on governments being leveraged by Washington to fall in line behind U.S. policy in Vietnam. And the stated policy was compatible with that of many countries with which the United States itself had normal and peaceful relations, from avowedly neutral but Soviet-inclined India to avowedly communist but famously independent Yugoslavia.

An NLF neutral solution in Saigon was also realistic in light of the differences in the experience, after 1954, of northerners and southerners. According to two Vietnamese historians of the NLF: "The neutrality of the South means for Vietnam a divergence of political character each side of the 17th parallel, while our country has always constituted a single entity. . . . Yet neutralism is the solution acceptable to all patriots, and would constitute an important step forward compared with the present disguised colonial regime."[68] The neutral solution would thus be a transitional phase, presumably, to reunification of some kind between North and South. But who knew precisely what form, how many stages, or how long the transition would take?

By late 1961, the Kennedy administration had stepped up military aid to South Vietnam and had launched a new phase in the propaganda campaign with the release of a White Paper, "A Threat to Peace: North Vietnam's Effort to Conquer South Vietnam."[69] In response, Hanoi called the NLF's first Party Congress in February 1962 to approve an emergency program with the promotion of a neutralist foreign policy as its centerpiece. The NLF was directed by the Party to establish the Foreign Relations Commission, headed by Nguyen Van Hieu, a southerner and longtime Party member, who would lead the diplomatic-propaganda effort. The commission served as the NLF's Foreign Ministry until 1969, when the Provisional Revolutionary Government was established.

The number-one priority of the new commission was to promote the establishment of a coalition government in Saigon with a neutral foreign policy.[70] This campaign would, to the extent it succeeded, tend to contradict the claim in the Kennedy administration's White Paper that the NLF was only a "tool" of Hanoi that was engaged in an attempt to "conquer" South Vietnam. Hieu's commission would promote the NLF as a separate entity not controlled by Hanoi, one that would ask the Americans to leave after achieving power in Saigon. Nguyen Van Hieu explained: "All of our dreams, goals and aspirations are meaningless unless we can remove the foreigners from our land. We must adopt any means necessary to accomplish this task, including the promotion of a coalition government in South Vietnam."[71] Was this propaganda? Of course. Was it *only* propaganda? No. The nature of the southern situation and experience, together with the heterogeneous membership of the NLF, pointed to some sort of neutral solution in Saigon.

By the beginning of 1962, it appears that the idea of a neutral solution in Saigon, one that would achieve all reasonable goals of Hanoi, *including* avoiding a big war with the United States, was moved by the leadership from a mere hope to a concrete plan of considerable ingenuity. Prospects for a neutral solution seemed to be improving. Le Duan was the driving force behind the plan. As a southerner in the Hanoi leadership, and the leader most directly responsible for the conduct of the war in the South, he seems to have become persuaded, based largely on his reading of the ongoing Laos conference in Geneva, that Washington was amenable to a neutral solution—not only in Laos, but in South Vietnam. Le Duan's strategy was to be one of *entrapment.*

The year 1962—especially from February through August—might in fact be thought of as the year of the "neutrality offensive" by Hanoi. Nguyen Van Hieu's Foreign Relations Commission provided the propaganda element of the strategy. But that was only the beginning of what seems to have been a comprehensive and carefully calibrated effort to lead Washington slowly but surely into a cul-de-sac, at the end of which would be a neutral solution in Saigon acceptable to all the relevant parties; this would permit the United States to withdraw from Vietnam without engaging in a major war with the NLF and the Hanoi government.

Sometime in February 1962, while the NLF was holding its First Congress, the Politburo in Hanoi sent secret instructions to its Central Office South Vietnam, directing it to contact any South Vietnamese who might be acceptable to Washington in a coalition government but who were known to be privately sympathetic to the NLF and the Hanoi government. The idea behind this "under-the-blanket" strategy was to build a list of senior figures whose names would be entered onto the list of candidates during the ensuing bargaining over the precise constituency of the new governing coalition. Similar instructions were sent to Paris, where a significant Vietnamese émigré community was located. In this way, the Hanoi leadership hoped to pack the eventual coalition with people who could be counted on to be sympathetic to Hanoi's inclinations with regard to the Saigon government.[72]

The critical prerequisite to making Hanoi's strategy effective was the successful conclusion of the ongoing Geneva Conference on Laos. By May 1962, the delegates had been meeting for a year without tangible results. Le Duan, in particular, believed that a Laos settlement could be used as a "model" for an analogous settlement in South Vietnam. In Hanoi's view, the problem was the reluctance of the rightist, U.S.-backed forces under Phoumi Nosavan to come to the table in Geneva prepared to discuss a neutral solution.

According to sources in Hanoi, an attempt was therefore made to force Washington's ally to the table by means of an attack on Phoumi Nosavan's forces, which took place during May 2–5, 1962, at Nam Tha in northwest Laos. The idea was to provide proof that the rightists' position in the field was deteriorating, thereby giving them an incentive—and giving the United States the incentive—to come quickly to an agreement.

Special care was taken by Hanoi to keep the communist Pathet Lao forces on a short leash. (The Vietminh and Pathet Lao had become close allies in 1946; Vietnamese and Laotian communists remained close in 1962.) The Pathet Lao seized outposts at Muong Sing and Muong Long, then held their positions. They made no attempt to enter Luang Prabang, the royal capital at that time. The troops were also forbidden even to appear on the banks of the Mekong River, due to known U.S. sensitivities. Hanoi was pleased when Washington's response seemed more or less what they had hoped for. Although it did send U.S. Marines to the Thai border in a show of force, the United States nonetheless pressured Phoumi Nosavan to come to an agreement on a neutralist government in Vientiane, which was signed in July by all parties. So far, so good, as Hanoi saw it.[73]

Hanoi's strategy and tactics were explained in detail to the NLF via letter from Le Duan to southern leader Nguyen Van Linh in July. Le Duan knew the question would arise as to why Hanoi's forces and Pathet Lao forces didn't take advantage of the situation in May and make an effort to take over the entire country by force. He explained:

> If military activities were escalated to a much higher level, the situation might have become complicated, and might even work against our goal of victory. . . . Then the war would not involve only the Phoumi Nosavan forces, but also American forces. . . . If we go beyond that level, the correlation of forces on the battlefield would be difficult, and this would not be beneficial to the Lao revolution at this stage.[74]

In other words, the goal was not just to improve the temporary position on the battlefield in Laos but also to avoid provoking the United States into active participation. In fact, the whole objective was to get the Americans to leave voluntarily, that is, *not* to stay and fight.

In the same letter, Le Duan explained the application to South Vietnam itself. "In South Vietnam," he wrote, "we must restrain the increasing U.S. intervention, and prevent the U.S. from turning the special war [NLF versus Diem's forces] into a local war [involving U.S. combat forces], which would expand the war into the whole country. We must know how to defeat the enemy within South Vietnam." He theorized that if the Americans cannot achieve a decisive victory, then "the U.S. must either replace Diem or negotiate with us and accept a coalition government."[75] Le Duan goes on to state that an acceptable coalition could contain elements loyal to the NLF, the United States, France, and perhaps others.

The Geneva Declaration of Neutrality on Laos was signed on July 23. The following day, *Nhan Dan*, the Hanoi Party daily, carried an editorial presumably written under the supervision of Le Duan. Once again it is possible to see, among the required socialist rhetorical flourishes, that Hanoi's objectives in Laos have implications closer to home:

> The success of the Geneva Conference on Laos shows . . . that the peace forces can struggle efficiently against the launching of local wars by imperialists.
>
> The peaceful solution of the Lao problem . . . also proves that *many other problems* can be solved by peaceful negotiations provided the peace loving forces are united. . . .

The Vietnamese people fully support the struggle of the Lao national coalition in the new stage designed to strengthen peace in Laos.[76]

In this way, and in less than twenty-four hours following the signing of the Geneva pact, Le Duan had gone public with his Laotian "model" of a neutral solution in Saigon.

The capstone of the neutrality offensive occurred on August 10, when the NLF issued a new, fourteen-point statement outlining its position. One cannot avoid the impression that the document is really the NLF's negotiating stance—the opening gambit intended to draw the United States into an immediate discussion, based on the Laos solution, of the future of South Vietnam. Here are some of its more relevant demands:

- Withdrawal of all foreign troops.

- South Vietnam can have its own army, but its task is just to defend its borders.

- South Vietnam will be independent both domestically and in its foreign policy.

- Foreign residents will be permitted to remain in South Vietnam and to do business, providing they respect its laws.

- South Vietnam will stand ready to join Cambodia and Laos in establishing a zone of peace and neutrality in Southeast Asia.

- South Vietnam's neutrality must be guaranteed by Southeast Asian countries, and by representatives of the two blocs, in a formal treaty.[77]

This statement was hardly noticed in Washington and has received little retrospective attention in the West. Was it serious? Sources in Hanoi confirm that it was regarded as utterly serious at the time in both Hanoi and by the NLF. Its authors hoped that it would begin a concrete discussion with Washington that would, in turn, result in an agreement that allowed the United States to leave honorably, with a neutral solution in place in Saigon. For how long? Who knew? Retrospective estimates by sources in Hanoi who were involved at the time range from years to decades.

In his memoir *Following Ho Chi Minh*, Bui Tin, the former editor of *Nhan Dan*, writes unflatteringly of Le Duan that "he was very self-confident and thought a lot of himself."[78] Bui Tin knew Le Duan well and worked with him for more than a decade. He tends to the view that Le Duan may have overcompensated for his relative lack of education and experience by a combination of bullying tactics and constant emphasis on his status as the sole southerner in the top leadership (at least for many years). This status, in turn, may have led him to suppose that his wisdom regarding the war in the South was, if not infallible, at least more reliable than the views of the others in the leadership, not excluding Ho Chi Minh.

Compensatory overconfidence on the part of Le Duan may help to explain a series of monumental errors of judgment associated with Hanoi's efforts in 1962 to bring the United States to the negotiating table. In a way, they are the mirror image of the errors made in Washington later on, after the introduction of U.S. combat troops and the bombing of the North in 1965. Washington's policymakers sought to carefully calibrate the level of violence that was inflicted, so as to bring Hanoi to the negotiating table. It failed, just as Hanoi failed to bring Washington to the table through its own strategy of carefully calibrated violence in Laos. In retrospect, Le Duan and his colleagues seem in 1962 to have been intoxicated with the possibilities of the Laos model. The problem, of course, is that they neglected to take into account the *U.S. perception* of what was happening in Laos. The strategy was exceedingly clever—but utterly uninformed.

First, Hanoi made a fundamental *misinterpretation*. Leaders in Hanoi, led by Le Duan, failed to understand Washington's motives for entering into the Laos negotiations. The Kennedy administration was involved primarily in order to extricate itself from a mess it had inherited from the previous administration. Laos was a sideshow, an exotic "operetta," as George Ball called it—a huge waste of time and resources.[79] Hanoi deluded itself into believing that Laos mattered to the Americans. But it didn't. The whole point of U.S. participation in Geneva was to relegate Laos to the status of an issue that did *not* matter. In short, to Washington, Laos was not a model for anything.[80]

Second, Hanoi made at least three fundamental *miscalculations*. Hanoi regarded their action at Nam Tha in early May 1962 as limited, and they seem to have convinced themselves that Washington would also see it that way. Instead, predictably to anyone who knew anything about the prevailing views in Washington, it was seen as a simple, gross violation of the cease-fire of a year earlier—no more, no less. In addition, by not withdrawing the bulk of their troops from Laos, in violation of the terms of the agreement of July 23, 1962, Hanoi effectively killed any possibility that senior officials in Washington might take a chance on a neutral solution in South Vietnam. Possibly motivated by the understandable need to protect its own border—a problem Washington obviously did not have and for which it had little empathy—Hanoi drastically underestimated the extent to which Washington would regard the Laos model as a *failed* model. Finally, it is difficult to understand the reasoning by which Hanoi would have convinced itself that their expanded efforts to supply the NLF via the Ho Chi Minh Trail through Laos, in violation of the Geneva Agreement, would pass either unnoticed or unremarked in Washington. That particular violation mattered greatly in Washington and was another reason that the U.S. government regarded the Laotian experiment as a failure, not to be repeated in South Vietnam.

Third, it is possible that the initiative, despite having been based on mis-interpretations and miscalculations, might still have borne fruit but for an additional *oversight*. That oversight concerns the meeting on July 23, 1962, following the signing of the Declaration of Laotian Neutrality in Geneva. The U.S. report of the meeting, by Harriman deputy William Sullivan, is given in the previous section. Until now, however, it has never been clear why Hanoi's foreign minister, Ung Van Khiem, did not take advantage of his meeting with Harriman, Washington's strongest and most influential supporter of a neutral solution in Saigon, to begin a dialogue on the issue. Instead, Khiem began with anti-U.S. accusations; Harriman reciprocated in kind, then reported to President Kennedy that Hanoi was apparently uninterested in a negotiated settlement. This is also the view of historian William Duiker, who speculates that the "balance of forces" in the South was not yet such that Hanoi felt confident enough to enter negotiations with the United States.[81]

But having seen the elaborateness of Le Duan's plan to snare the Americans immediately following the Geneva Conference, this explanation—that Hanoi was uninterested—doesn't ring true. What happened? Why didn't Ung Van Khiem explain Hanoi's position on Nam Tha or any of the other issues that Hanoi and Washington found contentious?

According to Vietnamese sources the foreign minister was unaware of his government's ultimate objectives in Geneva. *He literally did not know his government was pursuing a neutral solution on the Laos model!* How is this possible? Sources in Hanoi have explained it thus: First, Ung Van Khiem, even though a member of the Central Committee, was not privy to decisions taken by the ruling Politburo *unless the Politburo issued an order deriving from its deliberations that required specific action by the foreign minister.* Otherwise, he was left completely in the dark. Second, Le Duan seems to have written his critical letter to Nguyen Van Linh, and the editorial in *Nhan Dan*, *after* Ung Van Khiem departed for Geneva in mid-July. (He flew to Geneva with Chen Yi, China's foreign minister.) In fact, the Foreign Ministry knew at the time that there was a neutralization project *only* from Article 8 of the NLF Founding Program—nothing more. The ministry had no knowledge whatever of the ongoing *Letters to the South*, sent by Le Duan to the

Central Office South Vietnam, for distribution as needed within the NLF. In other words, in the absence of instructions to the contrary, he assumed his job following the signing of the pact in Geneva was to harangue Averell Harriman. And so he did.

When in 1963 Ung Van Khiem was replaced by Xuan Thuy, the Foreign Ministry had slightly better access to Hanoi's policymaking. But only after Xuan Thuy became ill and was replaced in 1964 by Nguyen Duy Trinh, a Politburo member, was the Foreign Ministry for the first time "in the loop" of foreign policy decisionmaking. Even then, Nguyen Duy Trinh, who also had other duties in the government, did not have his office at the Foreign Ministry, and communication was poor between him and his staff. Only later would Foreign Ministry personnel be encouraged to study a problem on their own initiative. But in July 1962, Ung Van Khiem was not supposed to know what Le Duan was up to—and he didn't. In contrast, Averell Harriman, his interlocutor, had open and frequent access to President Kennedy. Harriman naturally assumed that Hanoi's foreign minister, who technically outranked him by several notches, would have at least a working knowledge of Hanoi's policy toward the United States. So when Harriman was subjected to his harangue, he drew the only rational conclusion possible, given his understanding of who he was dealing with: Hanoi was not interested in a neutral solution for Saigon. And that is exactly what he told Kennedy.

Looking back, the Harriman-Khiem fiasco has great poignancy, when one considers that it was the last meaningful face-to-face opportunity *until 1968* for ranking (if not fully informed) North Vietnamese and U.S. diplomats to explore the possibilities and limits of a negotiated settlement—a neutral solution, a coalition government—for South Vietnam. Six years would elapse and hundreds of thousands of people would die before the same Averell Harriman sat down in Paris with Hanoi's representatives during the late spring of 1968.

Another conundrum arises: Given the stakes for Hanoi, and given the elaborate planning to maneuver the Americans into accepting a neutral solution, why did Hanoi not attempt to follow up the Harriman-Khiem travesty—to explain their position and set things right? There appear to have been four principal reasons. In their presumed order of significance for Hanoi's leaders, they are:

1. *Fear of appearing weak.* This comes up repeatedly in discussions with those familiar with the process in Hanoi during those days. Le Duan, in particular, was fearful on this score. He believed that any approach by Hanoi to Washington might be misread as preemptive capitulation, which

would encourage U.S. hawks to try to escalate the war in pursuit of a military victory. This fear became especially strong later, between 1965 and 1967, during the flurry of attempts by Washington to use intermediaries to probe Hanoi's interest in a negotiated settlement.

2. *Fear of offending the Chinese.* By 1962, Beijing was on public record condemning Soviet "revisionism" and accommodation to the West. Le Duan was the Politburo member in Hanoi closest to the Chinese, and Le Duan ran the war. We now know that the Chinese applied relentless pressure on Hanoi throughout the 1960s to avoid any and all possibilities for negotiation with the United States.

3. *Fear of giving false hope.* At the 1954 Geneva Conference, Hanoi had reluctantly capitulated to Chinese pressure to partition Vietnam—temporarily, as it was falsely hoped—at the 17th parallel. Southerners remembered this and would thereafter remain skeptical about all arrangements engineered in Hanoi. Thus, if Hanoi were to order the NLF into negotiations with the United States, and the talks were to fail or the NLF membership were to withdraw on its own, getting the NLF back in the fold and reunifying the country would be infinitely more difficult than it would have been if they hadn't tried to negotiate prematurely.

4. *Blind faith in the Laos model.* It is unclear to what extent Le Duan's faith in his scheme to apply the Laos model to South Vietnam was shared by others in the leadership. But the conspicuous absence of any meaningful probes regarding a neutral solution by Hanoi from mid-1962 to mid-1963 would seem to indicate that Hanoi was waiting—waiting for the U.S. to reach a level of frustration less than would cause Washington to escalate the war but more than enough to instill interest in a neutral solution for Saigon.[82]

Any one of these factors could have prevented Hanoi from being more aggressive in seeking to implement their carefully conceived follow-up of the Laos agreement. Taken together, they seem to have induced diplomatic paralysis.

It seems that even a year later Hanoi was *still* waiting for Washington to take the lead. In May 1963, Ho Chi Minh gave a speech to the National Assembly during which he appealed personally to President Kennedy to try to understand that the situation in South Vietnam was analogous to the American struggle for independence from England. It seems that Ho may have been casting around in an attempt to develop some sort of private channel between himself and Kennedy. In any case, it is highly unlikely that news of this speech—with its vaguely pedagogical exhortation, possibly masking an invitation—would ever have reached the White House under any circumstances. But Ho also had the misfortune to deliver his speech on May 8, 1963, at almost the very hour that Ngo Dinh Nhu's police had their first fatal altercation with Buddhist protesters in Hue. Ho's speech would have been lost in the all-out effort that followed to limit the damage from that episode. In any case, it is unknown when the Hanoi leadership finally decided that the Laos model had failed—or whether they ever came to such a final judgment.

It is equally difficult to untangle the web of intrigue regarding a neutral solution—an all-Vietnam solution—spun by Ngo Dinh Nhu during the desperate summer and early autumn of 1963. Sources in Hanoi report that none of his personal representatives, nor Nhu himself, were ever received in or by Hanoi. The feeling in Hanoi seems to have been that Nhu was merely trying to apply pressure on the United States for reasons of his own. Mieczyslaw Maneli *was* received in Hanoi—several times—as he attempted to carry out his mission of shuttle diplomacy between Saigon and Hanoi. Ho Chi Minh is even said to have told Ramchundur Goburdhun, the Indian chairman of the International Control Commission in Vietnam, in 1963 that he—Ho—considered Diem to be "a patriot, in his way."[83] But this seems to have been motivated by a desire to detach Diem and Nhu from the Americans, making the Ngos more vulnerable to the NLF.

The various offers to facilitate from President de Gaulle, between August 1963 and the spring of 1964, seem to have reached Hanoi only via the newspaper. Sources in Hanoi have said that de Gaulle's messengers, beginning with Roger Lalouette, the French ambassador in Saigon, seem only to have been in touch with Saigon, not with Hanoi. This seems also to have been true for the period immediately following the November 1 coup and assassination of Diem and Nhu and their replacement by the junta led by Gen. Duong Van Minh. A week after the coup, the NLF issued—reissued, actually—a conciliatory statement calling for a cease-fire and free general elections, followed by the formation of a coalition government.[84] This time, the NLF went out of its way to emphasize that reunification with the North would be neither quick nor automatic. It would be realized, they said, "step-by-step on a voluntary basis, with consideration [given] to the characteristics of each zone, with equality, and without annexation of one zone by another."[85] To prove they meant business, the NLF reduced its level of military activity in December and early January, a fact noticed by the CIA.[86]

But the evidence suggests that by December 1963 the Hanoi leadership, led by Le Duan, had acknowledged the failure of the plan to draw Washington into negotiations over a neutral solution in Saigon. Momentous decisions based on this premise were taken at the Ninth Plenum of the Party in Hanoi in December. They concluded that the United States, for whatever reasons, had committed itself to enlarging the war on the ground in the South and possibly in the North as well. In January, Le Duan, Le Duc Tho, and poet To Huu traveled to Moscow to try to appease Khrushchev and other Soviet leaders, who they knew would disagree with Hanoi's decision to, in effect, escalate the war preemptively in the hope of winning before the Americans could respond effectively.

Predictably, the Soviets disagreed, in part no doubt because in their paranoia they thought the Chinese were behind the move. They were not. The Vietnamese communists were playing in the same game they had been in since the early 1950s, attempting to balance costs and benefits with their fraternal but warring big brothers, China and the USSR. During the summer of 1964, nearly a year before the arrival of the first American combat troops, Deng Xiaoping offered a massive aid program to Hanoi on the condition that they refuse all future aid from the Soviets. Hanoi declined.[87] And so it went: Having failed to arrive at a neutral solution to their conflict with Washington, Hanoi strove all the harder, as the stakes and level of violence increased, to find a neutral solution to their problems with their fraternal allies.

A Dialogue in Real Time: A Neutral Solution?

THE LAOS MODEL, 1962

The concept of neutrality was a somewhat arcane topic, much-loved by East-West negotiators during the Cold War. Issues arose repeatedly as to whether a country claiming neutral status was really pro-Western, procommunist, independent, or really neutral. Moreover, since the neutral solution in Saigon never materialized, the issue presented participants in the June 1997 Hanoi conference with perhaps the purest example of a *counterfactual*—an analysis of a presumably possible but nonoccurring event of considerable significance. Despite its abstractness and apparently speculative nature, however, discussion of neutrality in Hanoi was unexpectedly volatile, with much finger-pointing.

Luu Doan Huynh: North Vietnam at the end of the 1950s had a view that it believed was realistic: neutrality for South Vietnam, reaching minimum objectives without a big war with the U.S. And the years 1961–1962 augured well for us: The U.S. also agreed on the neutralization of Laos. We had high hopes that this could be extended to South Vietnam. The U.S. did not understand that we were trying to create the conditions for a neutral government in Saigon or the reasons why we thought this would be acceptable to the U.S. And contrary to our wishes, a big war broke out between North Vietnam and the U.S. Why was that?

I think that the views of the U.S.—of Washington—are probably the most significant in this matter. But is there any other contributing factor, any shortcoming, however slight, on the part of North Vietnam? In hindsight, I regret that because of inadequate expertise Vietnam's diplomatic service could not contribute effectively to the neutralization of South Vietnam. In truth, there had been no direct contact between North Vietnam and the U.S. from 1954–1964. I am sure this lack of contact led to mutual misunderstanding of many kinds. No one—not your side and not our side—took necessary steps to establish contact—[speaking in English] "to establish channels of communication." [Resumes in Vietnamese.] I will give several examples so that we can examine whether, or the extent to which, both sides misunderstood each other. . . .

After the conclusion of the Geneva Conference on Laos (July 20, 1962), the U.S. and North Vietnam basically ceased to have any more contact with one another. The U.S. did not feel the need to contact us again, and North Vietnam also did not seek any private meetings with the U.S. Mr. Le Duan's *Letters to the South* give me the impression that he wanted negotiations with the U.S. at some critical stage but that the initiative must come from the U.S. side. He emphasized that North Vietnam should take the initiative to respond to U.S. overtures by preparing in advance a number of South Vietnamese, pro-NLF personalities whose political predilections had not been detected by the enemy. Such people would then be encouraged to join the multicomponent neutral government. Such a government, according to Mr. Le Duan, might come about either through negotiations with South Vietnamese circles and the U.S. or through a victorious uprising. The idea was for the South Vietnamese to set up a government which the U.S. could accept and with whom they would agree to negotiate. In this way, Mr. Le Duan gave more emphasis to the "internal" side of the neutrality formula and less emphasis to seeking talks with the U.S.

I now feel that if, in the early 1960s, the U.S. had initiated talks with us, had taken the initiative, we would have accepted such a proposal. It seems that, in retrospect, we should have taken the initiative, because of the importance of gaining mutual understanding and thus avoiding a widening of the conflict.

One year after Geneva, in the middle of 1963, Kennedy appears to have believed that the kind of neutrality established in Laos could not succeed in Vietnam, because, in his view, North Vietnam was a great danger to Laotian neutrality. . . .

But, you see, in the meantime, we still believed that Laotian neutrality was possible and that neutrality in the South was possible.

Chester Cooper: Mr. Nguyen Co Thach and I were both at the Laos Conference in Geneva. I was very close to Gov. Averell Harriman then, and later became his deputy for Vietnam negotiations. And I have to tell you that Governor Harriman had a great stake in the neutrality issue—the true neutrality of Laos. It was he who insisted to the State Department and to President Kennedy that we negotiate a solution with Souvanna Phouma. When Harriman realized that this was not to be—that Laos was not going to be a neutral country in the sense that we at least interpreted the word "neutral"—he began to think that perhaps he had failed in this negotiation. I want you to understand this. Harriman cared about this issue, and he understood the importance of it for the Vietnam case.

Nguyen Co Thach: On the subject of Laos: Between North Vietnam and the United States there was far from a complete correspondence. You see, at the time, the United States wanted a pro-Western neutrality in Laos, while North Vietnam of course did not want a pro-Western neutrality for Laos. Of course, North Vietnam wanted a neutrality for Laos that was pro-Vietnamese or procommunist. [Laughter.] Now, the issue of Laos was very complex and difficult. Very difficult.

I agree that in Geneva there may have been an opportunity to come to a mutual agreement. I mean on the topic of neutrality in Laos. From what has been said here today, it may well be that if such an agreement could have been reached with Mr. Harriman the "atmosphere" for discussions of similar subjects between North Vietnam and the U.S. might have changed for the better. But this did not happen. So it was definitely a missed opportunity. But it has to be said that these issues—the neutrality of Laos and the possible neutrality of the Saigon government—these were very different. Even if we had agreed to some formula for Laos, this does not guarantee that we could agree to a similar formula for South Vietnam.

Gen. Dale Vesser: Sir, you distinguished between a Western neutrality and a Vietnamese, or a communist neutrality. I would like to know what the practical difference was between these two forms of neutrality from the perspective of your country.

Nguyen Co Thach: The Vietnamese wanted a neutrality . . . at this time, we and the United States could not agree on one definition of neutrality—that both sides could accept. This was the difficulty. To have a realistic chance at a solution—well, of course both sides must find a way to agree to it. The conference in Geneva on Laos in 1961–1962 was a chance for both to have possibly come to an agreement. . . .

Gen. Dale Vesser: . . . If I could follow up, sir: There has been some discussion earlier about a possible Laos solution being a model for the kind of neutrality that would have been acceptable to Vietnam in a neutralization of the South. What would you see as the compromise that was possible given the discussion we've had thus far for such a neutrality? What would have been the formula?

Nguyen Co Thach: I have given you my answer. We wanted a pro-Vietnamese neutrality. You wanted a pro-U.S. neutrality. It would have been difficult to combine these, but perhaps not impossible. How? Why speculate? It did not occur.

Chester Cooper: I worked very hard with Governor Harriman in 1961 and 1962 on the Laos Agreement. I think I mentioned earlier that Governor Harriman had a lot of difficulty convincing Washington that we ought to deal with Souvanna Phouma. In order for Harriman to sell his case to Washington, he made a deal with a man named G. M. Pushkin, head of the Russian delegation in Geneva. There was something called the Harriman-Pushkin Agreement. It was a "gentleman's agreement." I don't even know if there was anything in writing. But they agreed that each of them would try very hard to make sure that the Laos Agreement—the letter and the spirit of the Laos Agreement—would be observed.

As I have looked back on these events, it is clear that we should have dealt with you, not with Pushkin. Pushkin died shortly after the conference was over. We were never even sure whether Pushkin ever informed his government of his deal with Harriman. But second—and this is the important point—your delegation and our delegation should've gotten together to work out some arrangement. There and then we should have worked out a deal to ensure that the Laos Agreement was observed, but we didn't. I think that was a tremendous missed opportunity. I know there were reasons why we didn't do it—why it would have been difficult. But you had Averell Harriman totally committed to making it work, and Harriman had clout in Washington with President Kennedy and his senior advisers. I think Bob McNamara and Nick Katzenbach would agree with this.

While working at CIA, I *knew* that you did not return all your troops in Laos to North Vietnam. That's a matter of record. You know that and I know that. I am more convinced than ever that if the Laos Agreement had produced what we could have accepted as a neutral Laos, then we would've been much more inclined to look seriously at the possibility of a neutral Vietnam.

Now you might ask: How might such a discussion have taken place—I mean, what would have been the terms of such a discussion of "neutrality"? Well, this is one of the problems. Neutrality is a very hard concept to pin down—to discuss productively—in diplomatic circles. To be honest about it, when we talked about neutrality, we thought of Switzerland and Sweden. That was our definition of neutrality. When the nonaligned nations referred to themselves as "neutral," we reluctantly accepted that designation, even though in our view they weren't really neutral. . . .

So in light of these considerations, all this history, let me ask: Do you [gesturing toward Vietnamese participants] believe that we could have made the Laos Agreement robust enough to make a neutral solution in Saigon a real possibility?

Luu Doan Huynh: Now with regards to the issue of the neutrality of Laos: Yesterday I already made a long comment on it, but I'd like to remind you of what I said. There is this issue: If you look at the period from 1962–1975, three forces were fighting over Laos; Laos was never divided and was not occupied by any outside force.

The Pathet Lao and North Vietnam never tried to bring about a complete change of the status quo in Laos between 1962 and 1975. But if the Pathet Lao were attacked, then of course they had to protect themselves and retaliate. Each party must respect the area under the control of the other.

Now, in my opinion, we should discuss the potential for a neutral South Vietnam. As for Laos, we have already discussed that yesterday, okay? We discussed Laos yesterday, and I think that we have explained everything to you. We have tried our best.

Chester Cooper: I know this was discussed yesterday, but I am not sure you understand how much the failure of the Laos Agreement meant to the Kennedy administration. I mean, the fact that you didn't keep your side of the agreement. I don't think the Pathet Lao was disarmed. The Pathet Lao forces should have been disarmed after that accord, but they weren't disarmed.

Luu Doan Huynh: How can they be disarmed?

Chester Cooper: They were all turned into civilians? I don't think so.

Luu Doan Huynh: But there is some confusion here—something which you don't understand about the situation. The Pathet Lao were to be reintegrated into the Laotian Royal Army only under the 1954 Geneva Accords, not under the 1962 agreement. There was no provision about reintegration or disarming in the 1962 agreement. No, no!! Look at the agreements in Laos in '62—there is no such provision. You have confused it with the 1954 Geneva Agreements on Laos. In '62, only the departure of foreign troops was required, but not the disarming of the Pathet Lao. I think you confuse the 1962 and the 1954 Geneva Agreements.

Chester Cooper: Excuse me, but are you telling me that all the DRV [North Vietnamese] troops—that all your forces—left Laos in 1962?

Luu Doan Huynh: Yeah ... well, okay, you can criticize us on that. Alright. [Laughter. Applause.] But disarming the Pathet Lao in 1962? No. There was no such provision, okay?

WHAT KIND OF NEUTRAL SOLUTION?

For a variety of reasons, the Vietnamese participants were reluctant at first to discuss aspects of their policymaking process even when—as is the case with the neutral solution—it did not lead to the outcome of interest. Vietnamese reticence, whatever the motives may have been, inevitably struck many U.S. participants as a lack of candor, possibly indicating that they were under instructions not to yield any information to the Americans about their own planning process. The session on neutrality was a breakthrough, in this respect: Most Vietnamese participants—with the significant exception of their leader, Nguyen Co Thach—began to discuss their planning process. Moreover, they did so in a way that had the effect of encouraging the Americans to ask even more probing questions. In response, the Vietnamese began to disagree with one another publicly, for the first time.

◆

Robert Brigham: It was one thing to preach "neutralism" abstractly, and another thing to get down to specifics. . . . We really have no clear idea of what the NLF meant by *neutrality*, in the sense of what sort of neutralist government in Saigon would have satisfied them. I wonder if any of our Vietnamese colleagues can clarify this.

Nguyen Co Thach: When discussing the issue of neutrality, I don't recall any concrete opinions, or plans, being put forward about what a neutral South Vietnam would be like. I am talking about the big nations. This is an issue that should've been discussed. Plans should have been proposed, but they were not, as I remember.

Luu Doan Huynh: . . . I think there exists a pretty firm concept of the neutralization of South Vietnam—of what it would look like. I mean—it is not very detailed, but it is a kind of skeleton, a blueprint of how it should work.

It is like this. It would involve a coalition government which is broadly based. It would be comprised of—in addition to NLF and other non-NLF patriots—pro-French and some pro-U.S. elements—that is, some members of the Saigon government. Such a broad-based composition would have been important. Why? To make the new government accessible to the U.S. so that it could facilitate the work of negotiating a U.S. troop withdrawal. The coalition government would be set up in one of two ways: either by negotiations held between the NLF, various South Vietnamese figures, and the U.S.; or by the South Vietnamese people after a successful uprising. All that was put on paper. Okay?

Robert Brigham: Well, after de Gaulle and Prince Sihanouk met in October 1962, de Gaulle in an interview in *The New York Times* proposed a neutral solution for South Vietnam. . . . Secretary Rusk said, "But the kind of coalition government that the NLF proposes today would be one in which they would dominate and they would simply ask the Americans to leave— well, that's no coalition government. That's not neutrality."

Nguyen Khac Huynh: I would like to speak about this issue. I can affirm that in our documents from this period there exists no concrete plan for the neutralization of the South. None exists—in the documents. Later, from the image of a neutral Laos in 1962, some in Hanoi had ideas about how to achieve a neutral South Vietnam. However, to my knowledge, no one was given the task of formulating a kind of detailed blueprint for a neutral South Vietnam.

However, due to the neutralization of Laos in 1962, and taking that as a kind of model, the following seemed to some in Hanoi to be the main provisions for a neutral solution:

1. First, no foreign troops and no foreign intervention.

2. Second, the coalition government must have representation from all the major political forces.

3. Third, the coalition government must be recognized by the world—first and foremost by the major powers, in order to provide it with stability.

These are the broad requirements. But the documents do not present a more detailed plan. Why is this? I believe this was because of the difficulties over Laos. Perhaps Hanoi and the NLF believed that the U.S. was not interested in this issue and therefore they did not pursue it in further detail. So the documents verify what Mr. Nguyen Co Thach said: The discussions of neutrality were never very detailed or specific. . . .

I would also like to respond to Mr. Chester Cooper's question: "What is a neutral solution?" I would answer you this way: A neutral solution, by definition, regardless of where it is being applied, must be a solution according to which neither side can defeat the other, but rather the sides must agree with each other—must *bargain* with each other, must reach some sort of compromise. Once one side has defeated the other, then that is not a neutral solution. This is not a situation of "neutrality." Let us remember what we were talking about back in those days. Neutrality was of interest to many—was regarded as desirable—because being "neutral" lowered the odds that there would be some kind of outside intervention against you, from one of the big powers or somebody else. That is the point of a neutral solution: to establish some kind of equilibrium that will prevent such things. But for this to work, power must truly be shared and must be accepted by the outside parties. That is what I wanted to say.

Gen. Nguyen Dinh Uoc: I want to speak about why, perhaps, as Mr. Nguyen Co Thach and others have said, no thought—or not much thought—was given to the concrete details of a neutral solution in the South.

At the Geneva Conference on Laos in 1962, we heard, for the first time, that the U.S. might be willing to accept a coalition government with communist participation. This was extremely interesting to us. This was something new that North Vietnam had to consider. Of course, we are not talking about a neutrality like Switzerland, as mentioned by Mr. Cooper. That is different. But a kind of neutrality was suggested which included or recognized the participation of the three factions. I am not sure, but this was maybe the first time we had ever heard of this, or believed that the U.S. might actually accept communist participation in such a formula. It was only after this, I think, that the North Vietnamese leadership believed it had to do some analysis of the situation in South Vietnam.

Washington's Fear: A Sham Neutrality (Part 1)

Encouraged by their Vietnamese counterparts in the meeting in Hanoi in June 1997, the U.S. side soon began to ask more pointed questions about neutrality and the prospects for a coalition government in Saigon. This was important because the deepest reservations in Washington about a neutral solution were not related to the structure of any agreement, or how many groups would be included, although these factors would of course have been taken into account. Washington's abiding reservation was that *whatever* arrangement was worked out, Hanoi would violate it and quickly move in and take over. In other words, the feeling in Washington was that any neutrality agreed to by Hanoi would be a sham, a fake, a ruse, its only purpose being to get the Americans to leave.

Francis Bator goes straight to the heart of the matter by posing the question directly. He says Washington feared a quick takeover by Hanoi, and he asks the Vietnamese participants whether this was a legitimate fear or not. Luu Doan Huynh immediately replies that it was *not* a legitimate fear. In a marvelous metaphor he compares any neutral government in Saigon to "many bedfellows and different dreams." He then assigns blame to both Washington and Hanoi for preventing the bedfellows from eventually getting together.

Nicholas Katzenbach then pursues a line of thought begun by Bator, in asking specifically: How would a really neutral government in Saigon have fit with Hanoi's "dream" of reunification of Vietnam under Hanoi's leadership? Nguyen Co Thach, visibly irritated by the question, lashes out by saying that Katzenbach's question was a good one during the early 1960s, but not now. He says the Americans should have asked these questions back then. But instead, he says, they refused to negotiate with Hanoi. Gen. W. Y. Smith tries twice to convince Nguyen Co Thach that questions like

Katzenbach's lay at the heart of the rationale of the conference, which is to identify missed opportunities and draw lessons from them. Nguyen Co Thach will have none of it and expresses his regret, once again, that Washington lacked the will to ask these kind of questions during the 1960s, when it really mattered.

Nguyen Co Thach's refusal to be drawn into the discussion initiated by Francis Bator offended some on the U.S. side. Yet his defiant demurral turned out to be an important contribution to the education of the U.S. participants. For they had not known, or perhaps had insufficiently appreciated, that Foreign Ministry negotiators like Nguyen Co Thach had virtually no authorization to initiate *any* kind of discussion with the Americans, and their superiors in Hanoi did not give them the kind of detailed information that would have been necessary for success, even if they had attempted to initiate discussions. Therefore, the only way a person like Nguyen Co Thach, who participated actively in the 1962 Geneva Conference, could have contributed to avoiding Hanoi's catastrophic war with the United States was on the condition that the United States must initiate the discussion. One can only try to imagine how frequently over the years, and how poignantly, Nguyen Co Thach must have privately condemned his U.S. colleagues for not coming forward and thus helping him help his countrymen avoid a war with the United States. In June 1997, his was an anger fueled by deep regret.

❖

Francis Bator: There was an American view—held by most of us, I think, at the time—about the inevitable consequences of a coalition government in Saigon. Very simply, the view was that a coalition government would perform one, and only one, function, which would be to ask the Americans to leave. . . . Then, if the Americans left, the next step in the process would be the unification of all Vietnam, alright, but with the Hanoi government in firm control of all essential matters. And the result of *that* would be that the South would simply be absorbed into what was not a neutral country—by no stretch of the imagination, a neutral country. This was the fear, I think—and I am putting this in somewhat caricatured terms—the fear was that the Saigon government and all of South Vietnam would be quickly swallowed up by the communist bloc. And so my question is: Was it unreasonable, on the part of Americans, to foresee that sequence?

Luu Doan Huynh: I want to say something about this. I think that by saying a coalition government, in the South, would require a withdrawal of Americans—if you are saying this, then I don't think that you are being precise. Why do I say this? Because a coalition government would request the withdrawal of U.S. troops—*U.S. troops*—not all Americans. All the Americans do not have to leave. The neutral solution would only have required the withdrawal of troops. Only the troops. We are not talking about a withdrawal of all influence in terms of politics and culture and economics. This would not happen.

So please, let us think more precisely about how this would work. As I see it, once a neutral government has been formed—a peaceful and neutral South, a coalition government—what we would have is like a big bed with many sleeping together but with individual dreams that differ from each other, but they can still sleep together. [Laughter.] "Many bedfellows and different dreams." [Laughter continues.] This is how I understand it. . . .

Really, I think it was mostly your fault. You did not perceive things objectively. It was your mindset. We had this in mind, but we did not come up with a diplomatic démarche in those days to push this through. And then, when your troops arrived and your bombers started flying, it was too late.

So there are these two reasons for the failure of neutrality in South Vietnam: The primary reason is because of you gentlemen, over there [gestures at U.S. participants]. And second, we did not have the political means to push it through.

Nicholas Katzenbach: I want you to understand that I am the most objective person that I know, Mister—[Laughter.]

Luu Doan Huynh: [Interrupting.] Everyone claims that. You are not alone.

Nicholas Katzenbach: Let's just say I am as objective as you are. [Laughter.]

Luu Doan Huynh: Okay, Okay. You and I are objective. But not these other guys. [Makes wide gesture at all other participants. Laughter.]

Nicholas Katzenbach: Agreed. . . . Okay. Now the solution—we have referred to a neutral "solution" in South Vietnam. If it were to occur, it might possibly be much like the one you [Luu Doan Huynh] talked about—with representation from the National Liberation Front, and with representation from other groups.

Now, I'm sure you still have the objective of reunification. The question I have is: What does the government in Hanoi do next? What would "neutrality" in South Vietnam mean? Would it mean, "Alright that's fine, we will not send any weapons, we will do nothing of that kind, we will do nothing to attempt to influence that government in South Vietnam." Let's say that would have been your intent. What kinds of guarantees would you have been prepared to offer the U.S.? Or is this just a sham arrangement to get those—16,000 or so—U.S. advisers out of the country so you can move in and take over? Is that what it's about?

Nguyen Co Thach: With regard to the period between '63 and '64, I'm glad that Mr. Katzenbach has raised this for discussion. You know, back then, the U.S. did not want to discuss this idea, this scenario. So how can we say anything? How can we respond? If the U.S. had been as insightful back then as Mr. Katzenbach is today, then they would have raised this issue for discussion back then. That would be great. But I would say to you: Because there was no discussion then, there's nothing, really, to talk about now. Forget it. It's just idle speculation.

Nicholas Katzenbach: Are you suggesting that I talk too much, or that I'm idle, or both? [Laughter.]

Nguyen Co Thach: No, no, neither. [Laughter.] I don't think that you are wrong. In fact, you are right—absolutely right. If the U.S. had raised the same points then that you raised today, I—all of us—would have welcomed more discussions.

Nguyen Khac Huynh: Yes, it could have been discussed further.

Nguyen Co Thach: But back then it was not discussed. The U.S. actually rejected negotiations about neutrality in the South. So, back then the U.S. was wrong and today Mr. Katzenbach is right. [Laughter.] Mr. Katzenbach, you are right, but the United States was wrong. [Laughter.]

Gen. W. Y. Smith: . . . I don't think it is adequate for you just to say: "Well, it didn't happen and therefore, who knows, and it's not important." Our whole point in coming over here for this conference is to look into things that *didn't* happen, and *therefore* they *are* important—or might be important—because they may point to lessons for the future.

You have said you would have accepted a coalition government in South Vietnam of some sort. But you have not answered Nick's [Katzenbach] questions, which were: How long did you expect the coalition government to last?

How much freedom did you expect to permit in such a Saigon government? Did you intend to harass the government—to make things difficult for it? Were you going to help it? If so, *how* would you help it—help it to do what? I think these are important questions.

Nguyen Co Thach: But General Smith, I already answered Mr. Katzenbach. I have already responded to you gentlemen. Let me try again. If back then Mr. Katzenbach—if the Americans—had asked those kinds of questions, then that would have been great, it might have led to something fruitful. But the Americans did not do this. They rejected our suggestions. They chose not to negotiate. It was obvious then, to us—to me—that you did not care to learn what we thought, what we were trying to do, what we might agree to. If you do not negotiate and discuss—discuss, as we are discussing today—then how could you know what we think?

But now it is too late. Why bother? The time has passed. Even if in the end we all agree on something, what difference will it make? It will make no difference.

I have finished.

Gen. W. Y. Smith: Pardon me, Mr. Thach, but I'd like to respond to that. I think our conclusions may matter a lot, if you believe—as I do, as we on the U.S. side do—that we need to understand history if we are going to avoid some of the things we've gotten into in the past. I'm not asking you and your colleagues for a confession or anything. I am just asking you to help us figure out the answer to Mr. McNamara's question: You know, whether we missed some opportunities—together—to avoid the war. That's all I'm trying to say.

Nguyen Co Thach: I have already responded. You should have asked these questions thirty-five years ago. Then, maybe the war could have been avoided. Now, it is too late.

A MAJOR MISSED OPPORTUNITY

During the period under discussion—roughly 1961 to 1963—Robert McNamara was not as involved in attempts to explore a possible negotiated solution in Vietnam, as he was later on, from 1965 to 1968. Like some of the other U.S. participants, therefore, he was surprised to hear that each side, Washington and Hanoi, seemed to have dropped the ball at a point in the confrontation *before* it became a U.S.-Vietnam war.

◆

Robert McNamara: When we asked that the subject of neutrality—neutrality for the South—be placed on our conference agenda, we did so with a preconceived idea based on limited knowledge of that time. The preconceived idea was that General de Gaulle was serious about finding a neutral solution for the Saigon government. Now de Gaulle was concerned about the security of the West. To some degree, France had the same obligations that we did, because France was a signatory of the SEATO treaty, whose purpose was, more or less, to avoid domination of South Vietnam by communist China and communist Russia. I personally did not know much about de Gaulle's initiative and the whole business of the "neutral solution" generally. So I personally wanted it on our agenda because I didn't believe you, and I didn't believe we, had properly considered it.

All I've heard this afternoon simply confirms that conclusion. I have heard nothing—*nothing!*—indicating that this idea was seriously considered, debated, articulated, or proposed by either side—by your side or by our side. Now, I appreciate that some of the issues are complex, involve conflicting chronologies of who said what to whom and when. Fine. But I have heard Minister Nguyen Co Thach say repeatedly that the idea was just not given much thought in Hanoi. And Mr. Cooper has given reasons, as an American intimately involved in these matters, why we did not give this serious consideration.

So I suggest to you that this was a *major* missed opportunity. Together— and I stress *together*—we failed to grasp what appears to be, looking back, an opportunity to avoid much of the tragic bloodshed that followed. . . .

We have heard people on both sides discuss why it would have been difficult to get such a solution for South Vietnam; why the complexities would have overwhelmed the efforts anyway, had they been made; why the bad experience of Laos early in the period may have played a role in discouraging people from taking the idea seriously and from pursuing it. I accept all that. I have no problem with that. But from what we have heard here today— what I have heard here today: *We did not, and you did not, explore the "neutralist solution" fully.* Now you may say that there are good reasons—good historical reasons—why neither side chose to pursue it. Fine. But my god, in looking back on what followed—on the tragedy in which both of our countries became engaged—doesn't it make sense to examine why that opportunity was missed and what might be done in the future to avoid missing similar opportunities?

Washington's Fear: A Sham Neutrality (Part 2)

The February 1998 conference in Hanoi was private and small. The goal of the U.S. participants was to ask some questions arising from the June 1997 discussions in Hanoi that were either too detailed or too politically sensitive to deal with in June, when many observers and some U.S. press representatives were present. Not to miss an opportunity, the U.S. side subjected the Vietnamese participants to what one called "genial interrogation," reflected by freewheeling give-and-take, outlined below in a question-and-answer format, with speakers' dialogue following.

❧

How Long Would It Last?

Question: What was the projected duration of a transitional coalition government in Saigon?

Answer: Answers varied, but perhaps ten to twenty years.

Luu Doan Huynh: . . . Mr. Le Duan wrote to NLF officials in the South in July 1962, in which he said the following:

1. In South Vietnam we must restrain the increasing U.S. intervention in order to prevent the U.S. from turning the special war into a local war. (Mr. Le Duan is expressing his fear of an "Americanized war.")

2. The U.S. will be ever more bogged down in a long, drawn-out special war in South Vietnam, without a way out, and under these conditions, we might compel the enemy to negotiate with us on a coalition government.

Robert Brigham: . . . There was great skepticism, especially in the U.S., about the tenability of any neutralist solution. Le Duan may have believed that neutrality had a chance in South Vietnam. But U.S. Secretary of State Dean Rusk did not. Rusk, for example, said in the fall of 1962 that "this kind of neutralism is no neutralism at all. It is tantamount to surrender." That was his view.

So my question is: Was Dean Rusk's reading correct? Was neutralism supposed to be just a short, temporary phase leading to unification under the socialist banner? . . . Is it true that this coalition government—let's say it was composed of former Saigon regime officials, former NLF officials, and some "third force"—would, as its first order of business, demand that the Americans leave the country?

Nguyen Khac Huynh: . . . Was neutrality permanent or temporary? I will tell you frankly how we thought about it: We considered the neutrality of South Vietnam to be just a transitional phase toward the reunification of Vietnam. But this by no means implied anything like what Mr. Brigham suggests—that the *first* thing the government would do is ask the Americans to leave. This is a misconception of our views. We saw reunification as a *gradual* process. We also believed that during the transitional period we would have a unified government but two regimes—the socialists in the North and the neutralists in the South. It would be like China and Hong Kong today— one country with two systems—not forever, but for a limited period.

You will ask: How long was this period to be? Of course the leaders of Vietnam had no way of knowing how long that period would last. I will give you my view, and I can say that this view is not only my view but represents, more or less, our conversations on this issue at the time. How long would the neutralist transition last? *From ten to twenty years.* Something like that.

How Would Reunification Work?

Question: Assuming a neutral coalition had governed in Saigon, the capital of an independent South Vietnam, how would it be reunified with the North, and how complete would be the reunification?

Answer: No one knew the answer, because it was impossible to predict the conditions in the South. Once the country became independent and free from U.S. troops, there was in fact no guarantee that Saigon and Hanoi would ever be completely reunified.

Luu Doan Huynh: You know, this question of the *process* of setting up a neutralist coalition government was given a great deal of thought at the time. At our June 1997 conference, Mr. Nguyen Co Thach said that little or nothing was written down by the Hanoi leadership on this problem in the 1962–1964 period. Still, much thought went into it, because it was the preferred solution—or part of the preferred solution.

It was seen—the process of neutralization of South Vietnam—as having these three stages:

1. The first stage: The neutralization of South Vietnam, involving the formation of a coalition government committed to independence based on neutrality.

2. The second stage: U.S. military "withdrawal with honor," as we called it
   at the June conference.

3. The third stage: Normal and friendly relations with the U.S. . . .

The DRV obviously hoped that the situation in South Vietnam would
evolve and gradually shift in favor of the NLF and CPV [the Communist
Party of Vietnam]. Eventually, we looked forward to reunification, thanks to
the patriotism of the people and the political activities of the NLF. . . .

But how would this turn out in the long run? Nobody knew for sure.
Reunification? Continued partition with more or less friendly and stable
relations between the two parts? An uneasy peace in South Vietnam? That is
a matter that would depend essentially on the internal situation—economic
and political—in North and South Vietnam. And everything would depend
on the activities of the parties directly involved to prevent the recurrence of
war. This would be necessary for many reasons, but mainly because the success of any such arrangement would be accompanied by some clause about
policing the agreement with international supervision. You—the Americans—would never be so unwise as to drop this requirement, I am sure.

Okay, so what does all this add up to? Three things: We did not want a big
war with the United States; we believed the neutralist solution was the way
to do this; and a neutral government in the South might last for a long time,
but in any case, it would evolve peacefully. You know—as you now can see,
when the genie is out of the bottle, it may have a life of its own, which you
cannot control, or cannot control to the extent you thought you could.

So do you see the point? Don't for one minute take for granted that any
plan from our side would succeed 100 percent in the political field.

How Much Control by Hanoi?

Question: Is it possible that the experience of the southerners would have
led them, within the framework of an independent Saigon government,
actively to oppose reunification with the North?

Answer: There were two answers: Probably not, for as history records, it did not happen, because the Vietnamese people have always thought of themselves as one nation. The second answer: Yes, it could have happened, and might have happened, but for the U.S. war, which created conditions for reunification totally different than would have existed without it.

Robert Brigham: . . . This is a very sensitive question and I hesitate to ask it, but it is important for our understanding of events in Vietnam during this period. As you know, the United States viewed the NLF and Hanoi as a monolith taking instructions from outside the borders of Vietnam. As a student of Vietnam and the war I've always been interested in the regionalism within the Party. And listening to what we've been discussing about neutralism this afternoon, it seems to me that what you're suggesting is that a coalition government—made up of NLF forces, a third force, and former Saigon officials—would have a certain southern view that wouldn't necessarily correspond to the northern view of how events should evolve. The southerners' experience was, after all, very different from that of northerners after 1954. Did this play a part in your thinking about how a "neutralist solution" might evolve into a unified Vietnam?

Nguyen Dinh Phuong: I understand what you are saying: that perhaps a neutralist government in Saigon might have different ideas about the conditions for unification, whenever that would have come about. In answer, I would say, yes, it could have turned out that way, but in fact it did not. As you know, the South has different economic and cultural traditions from the North. And I would say, yes, there were people who wanted to separate South Vietnam from Hanoi.

But you must not forget that the struggle for national independence was conducted under the leadership of one party. The policies and the guidelines for national unity set by the Party met the wishes and desires of the people in the South as well as the North. A slogan became popular at that time: "Vietnam is only one nation. The Vietnamese people are one. The river may be without water. The mountains may have eroded. But Vietnam will always be one country."

Luu Doan Huynh: Ah, but there are always these centrifugal and centripetal forces operating in the political environment. Politicians always think they can control these forces. But often, they overestimate their control. The American mistake—one American mistake—was to believe that just because we say we want to do this and that, that we know how to do it— that we know how to control everything and make it come out just the way we

want. You took for granted that because somebody said we had these intentions, or wishes, that we had a good plan to implement them. You should not
have taken that for granted. Do you understand what I am saying?

Robert Brigham: Yes, I think so. Thank you.

Luu Doan Huynh:
No, don't thank me. You are very courageous for asking such a question.

Conclusions

In my introduction to this chapter, I posed three questions that, collectively, seemed to me ought to guide our research into whether missed opportunities occurred with regard to a neutral solution in Saigon during the early
1960s. When I posed them, I had no idea whether we would ever be in a
position to answer them with confidence because I did not know whether our
Vietnamese counterparts would be able and willing to join our effort.

I now believe we can answer those questions, and when the answers are
combined with what we know about U.S. decisionmaking on this issue, they
point to missed opportunities that are numerous; that were potentially
avoidable; and are, therefore, in retrospect, collectively a tragic reminder of
the disastrous effects of human misperception, misunderstanding, and misjudgment.

Let me repeat my original questions and give my personal responses,
based on research conducted by my coauthors and me, during three years:

Question: What was the thinking in Hanoi and in the NLF regarding a neutral solution in Saigon? Was it merely useful as propaganda, or was it serious?

Answer: The answer is more sophisticated than the question: Hanoi's and
the NLF's embrace of neutrality and a coalition government in Saigon was
both propaganda *and* a serious attempt to head off the war. The revelations
about the NLF's neutralist "campaign" were not known to me before but did
not surprise me. Yet some of the details of the behind-the-scenes thinking
about Le Duan's project to apply the Laos model to South Vietnamese were
stunning. Why? Because *we never knew!* I certainly knew nothing about this.
Moreover, I discussed these matters with Averell Harriman on dozens of
occasions, and I am convinced that Averell never knew either. He and I
were the strongest advocates of a neutral solution, and had we even an

inkling of what we now know, we would have pursued it vigorously with both President Kennedy and President Johnson.

Also, I am aghast at the shallowness of our own thinking on the issue of a neutral solution. Why didn't we ask Hanoi for a full explanation of the process they foresaw? If we had asked, and if they had convinced us, for example, that they foresaw reunification taking years, even decades, my god we would have, or should have, jumped at it. But we didn't know. We didn't ask. It is true that Hanoi was, as some of their representatives now acknowledge, much too reticent in providing us with this kind of information. But I am struck by how much we could have learned if we simply had kept asking until we got a plausible answer.

Question: If we had been serious about a neutral solution, why might Hanoi and the NLF have favored neutrality as something other than just a quick transition to communist domination?

Answer: This was a major stumbling block at the time. We could think of a hundred reasons—most having to do with "falling dominoes"—why Hanoi would *not* favor a neutral solution—a truly neutral solution, one that was not a sham arrangement. But according to the revelations from our Vietnamese colleagues, neutrality provided a good option for both Hanoi and for the NLF. It would have permitted Hanoi to more easily avoid potentially damaging breaches with either the Soviets or the Chinese. Also, the southern experience was vastly different from that of the North after 1954, which is something we in Washington should have focused on but didn't, believing that communist ideology would override any regional differences that might have arisen. Particularly fascinating was the implication—maybe more than an implication—at the February 1998 conference that it was entirely possible that South Vietnam might *never* be reunified with the North and that this was understood by at least some in Hanoi.

One of the most poignant sets of revelations, for me, concerns the connections Hanoi and the NLF made between a neutral solution in Saigon and the avoidance of a war with the United States. This puts a human face, so to speak, on an issue I confess I have never understood: why the Vietnamese— Hanoi and the NLF, North and South—were seemingly unconcerned, even thoughtless, about what in the world they were getting themselves into when they chose to fight a war with the most powerful nation on earth in which, according to their figures, 3.8 *million* Vietnamese were killed. One can say they were brave and patriotic, and these judgments are, I believe, necessary and correct. But still, as we saw it in Washington at the time, the Vietnamese communists seemed all too much like the Japanese kamikaze pilots whom those of us in the Pacific theater dealt with during World War II. But this, on the basis of what we learned about their efforts to pull the United States into a neutral solution *in order to head off the war*, turns out to be a false analogy. They did not want a war. Neither did we. But neither side knew enough about the other to avoid it.

Question: In light of what can be learned about the evolution of views in both Washington and Hanoi, what appear to be the major missed opportunities for achieving a neutral solution?

Answer: One could plausibly argue that the entire 1961–1964 period was a huge missed opportunity and let it go at that. Thinking about it now, the fundamental problem was obviously each side's inability and unwillingness to communicate its beliefs to the other in convincing ways, and this did not change throughout the period. But three moments stand out in my mind.

First, the rationale behind the North Vietnamese–Pathet Lao action at Nam Tha in early May 1962 makes sense, in retrospect, but was utterly incomprehensible in Washington at the time. If anyone close to Kennedy had speculated in his presence that the attack was really a tactic to raise the odds of a negotiated neutral solution in Saigon, the individual would have been laughed out of the room. Apparently, the Hanoi leadership, in ordering the action, thought its motives would be transparent to us, because they did not, so far as I know, attempt to communicate it to us. They should have.

Second, the Vietnamese revelations regarding the disastrous meeting on July 23, 1962, in Geneva are among the most interesting and disturbing to have emerged from our joint project. We did not know about any of this— that the foreign minister knew nothing and didn't matter in Hanoi's policy process; that Hanoi did not communicate its intentions to the foreign minister while he was in Geneva meeting with Averell Harriman and other Americans; or that the foreign minister would assume that his duty would be, hard on the heels of signing an important agreement with the United States, to gratuitously insult the top-ranking U.S. representative at the Geneva Conference.

I never spoke to Averell about that meeting, to my recollection. I still have difficulty squaring what appears to have been Le Duan's intense interest in a neutral solution, on the one hand, and the abject ignorance of his chosen representative in Geneva on the other. When a U-2 pilot accidentally overflew the Soviet Union during the Cuban missile crisis, President Kennedy remarked that "there's always some sonofabitch who doesn't get the word."[88] Almost unbelievably, to me, it appears that Hanoi's foreign minister wasn't supposed to get the word, and this doomed a discussion that might have initiated serious, direct discussions about a neutral solution.

Third, and finally, I believe we should have explored the idea of a neutral solution with the French. It is true that de Gaulle was difficult to deal with. But in matters of war and peace, these things just have to be put aside. There may have been some way, with French intervention, to work out something between Diem and Nhu, on the one hand, and Hanoi on the other. But French participation would have been especially useful, based on our current analysis, with the junta of Gen. Duong Van Minh. It appears as if he and his colleagues had a plan for a neutral solution that might have led somewhere. But we'll never know because we never explored it with them.

Why were these opportunities missed? Because, even though Kennedy wanted a neutral solution, he didn't believe Hanoi could be trusted; because Hanoi wanted it but felt it couldn't initiate the discussion with the United States for fear of appearing weak or of laying themselves open to charges of "revisionism" from the Chinese; because Diem and Nhu wanted it, but we wouldn't hear of it, and, in addition, they were instinctively opposed to sharing power with anyone outside their family; and because the NLF wanted it, but they did not have the autonomy required to come forward on their own, except under Hanoi's aegis.

I was struck in June 1997 by Luu Doan Huyhn's metaphor for the way the neutral solution was envisaged by Hanoi: *many bedfellows, different dreams.* As I understand him, this is exactly the way we envisaged it as well. The poet W. B. Yeats wrote: "In dreams begins responsibility."[89] Neither Hanoi nor Washington acted responsibly with regard to their common dream of a neutral solution in Saigon. Opportunities were missed by both. The result was disastrous.

5

Escalation: 1961–1965

We are not trying to wipe out North Vietnam. We are not trying to change their government. We are not trying to establish permanent bases in South Vietnam. . . . We are there because we are trying to make the Communists of North Vietnam stop shooting at their neighbors . . . to demonstrate that guerrilla warfare, inspired by one nation against another nation, can never succeed. . . . We must keep on until the Communists in North Vietnam realize the price of aggression is too high—and either agree to a peaceful settlement or to stop their fighting.

Pres. Lyndon B. Johnson, July 1966[1]

If by "final victory" you mean the departure of the Americans, then we will fight to final victory. Everything depends on the Americans. If they want to make war for twenty years then we shall make war for twenty years. If they want to make peace, we shall make peace and invite them to tea afterwards.

Pres. Ho Chi Minh, December 1966[2]

Introduction

As I look back on my service in government, I am haunted by two recollections. I find it almost incredible that we escaped the Cuban missile crisis without a major war with the Soviet Union.* I was not confident when I went to bed on the evening of Saturday, October 27, 1962, that, as I put it at the time, I would live to see another Saturday. But I find it equally incredible that we did not find a way to halt and reverse escalation toward a major war in Vietnam. The missile crisis haunts me—and it should concern everyone—because of what *might* have happened (and we have not yet acted to ensure that it might not happen again).

*It was, I believe, the "best managed" crisis of the last half of the century, but we were very lucky as well.

December 1964. President Johnson said: "We are in bad shape in Vietnam—we can't afford to, and we will not, pull out." Later he said: "I knew I was bound to be crucified either way I moved."

May 1965. A factor limiting President Johnson's actions in Southeast Asia was his determination to avoid a war with China. Unbeknownst to the United States, Ho Chi Minh had traveled to China to request and receive from Mao Zedong a pledge to intervene on North Vietnam's behalf, if the United States invaded the North, or if U.S. planes bombed targets in China.

November 9, 1995. General Vo Nguyen Giap told Robert McNamara in Hanoi that what the U.S. believed had been a second attack on a U.S. naval vessel in the Gulf of Tonkin on August 4, 1964, had not occurred. The erroneous U.S. belief triggered the start of U.S. bombing of North Vietnam and a congressional resolution authorizing U.S. military action in Southeast Asia.

But the tragic war in Vietnam also haunts me—as I believe it should concern everyone—because it *did* happen. In this chapter, my coauthors and I address a major part of the problem—the process of escalation—and we do so having had unprecedented access to former officials and documentation from *both* sides.

I recounted in my memoir, *In Retrospect*, how Pres. John F. Kennedy asked all his senior national security officials to read Barbara Tuchman's *The Guns of August*, soon after it was published in early 1962.[3] Tuchman's book is a powerful indictment of the European leaders who allowed the crisis of July 1914, initiated by the assassination of Austrian Archduke Franz Ferdinand in Sarajevo, to escalate into World War I.[4] Kennedy had already, in his first year as president, been through the Bay of Pigs fiasco, the Berlin Wall crisis, and, as described in Chapter 4, a crisis over Laos. He chose *not* to escalate any of these confrontations. The president told us after we had read Tuchman's book: "I don't ever want to be in that position. We are not going to bungle into a war."[5]

He followed his own advice later in 1962, during the Cuban missile crisis. On that Saturday, October 27, probably the single, most dangerous moment of the crisis, the president and his brother, Attorney General Robert Kennedy, discussed the events of the day. Alluding to Tuchman's book, the president told Bobby: "I am not going to follow a course which will allow anyone to write a comparable book about this time, *The Missiles of October*."[6] That crisis did not lead to war—a war with tremendous risk of further escalation to nuclear conflict—in large part because of the prudent decisions made under great pressure by John Kennedy.[7]

In one sense, the Vietnam War and the missile crisis were similar: Each side, by its actions, created a result neither side had foreseen or desired. In October 1962, this process resulted in a close call to nuclear catastrophe, a near miss, perhaps a last-minute escape. Yet with regard to Vietnam, the result was a crisis not resolved at the last minute but rather a tragic war for both sides. Why?

It has become fashionable among U.S. journalists and scholars to put the blame on Pres. Lyndon Johnson. Some have claimed that he was too ignorant about the world to understand the issues. Others have said he didn't care about anything except his domestic program. Still others have expressed the view that President Johnson was obsessed with not losing a war associated with John Kennedy, in whose shadow he had the misfortune to govern but whose savvy in foreign affairs he is supposed to have lacked. And so on.[8]

Those who would lay all the blame on Johnson are wrong on at least three scores. First, what we now call the "Vietnam War" was escalating—slowly but unmistakably—long before Lyndon Johnson became president. Second, they are wrong about Johnson's interest in foreign affairs. He devoted a major part of his time and effort to international issues, including Vietnam. Third, it takes two to escalate in the way that the Vietnam War escalated in the 1960s, and therefore any explanation of the escalation must take into account decisions made in Hanoi in addition to those made in Washington.

The Johnson administration inherited an intractable problem. Few were as determined as Johnson to solve it without military escalation. But, until very recently, little was known in the West regarding Hanoi's decisionmaking, which until now has rendered any attempt at a two-sided analysis of the escalation risky at best and purely speculative at worst.

1. On the History of the Escalation.

I have said that I knew little about the history of U.S.-Vietnam relations before becoming secretary of defense in January 1961. Few of us did. In fact, I was unfamiliar with many of the events and issues discussed in Chapters 3 and 4. Virtually all the senior officials were in the same boat. There was then—and I fear there is now—little, if any, institutional memory. As evidenced in the recently released transcripts of audiotapes secretly made by Johnson in the White House, my historical innocence was apparently no secret. On May 27, 1964, the president called Sen. Richard Russell, Democrat of Georgia and chairman of the Senate Armed Services Committee, to ask for his advice on Vietnam. Russell, who spoke in the same slangy, southern vernacular for which Johnson was famous, was also, like Johnson, one of the cleverest politicians of his time. Here is part of Russell's response to Johnson:

> The thing [Vietnam] is going to be a headache to anybody that tries to fool with it. Now you got all the brains in the country, Mr. President. You better get ahold of them. I don't know what to do about this. . . . We're there. You've got over there McNamara . . . And he's a can-do fellow. But I'm not too sure he understands the history and background of those people out there as fully as he should. But even from his picture, the damn thing ain't getting any better and it's getting worse.[9]

Russell was absolutely right about my (I should say *our*) lack of historical knowledge of Vietnam. And years later, it is obvious how the historical naïveté of myself, my colleagues, including Senator Russell, and the American public got us into trouble.

2. On Johnson's Grasp of the Issues Connected with Vietnam.

Although Lyndon Johnson's diction may not have been perfect, a shrewder political mind is hard for me to imagine. To put the blame for the escalation of the war on Johnson is to betray ignorance of the difficulty of the problem he, as president, actually faced back then. "Advice" such as Russell provided was common: Vietnam was "going to be a headache to anybody that tries to fool with it." That's not advice, it's sympathy from one who has no advice. And Lyndon Johnson was the man who, as president, would have to "fool with it"—to stop the escalation toward a U.S.-Vietnam war without betraying America's allies around the world.

One can get a clear picture of President Johnson's grasp of the central dilemma of Vietnam in the tapes and transcripts. The tapes are very high-quality recordings. As I listened to them while I was preparing *In Retrospect*, the voice of the president came through so vividly that I felt I could almost see him sitting across from me, asking all his senior advisers, in his Texas drawl, what in the *hell* he was supposed to *do* about "VEET-Naam," as he called it. Here is the president and National Security Adviser MacGeorge Bundy, also on May 27, 1964:

LBJ: I'll tell you the more that I stayed awake last night thinking of this thing, the more I think of it, I don't know what in the hell—it looks to me like we're getting into another Korea. It just worries the hell out of me. I don't see what we can ever hope to get out of there with, once we're committed. I believe that the Chinese communists are coming into it. I don't think we can fight them ten thousand miles from home. . . . I don't think it's worth fighting for and I don't think we can get out. It's just the biggest damned mess I ever saw.

Bundy: It is. It's an awful mess.

LBJ: And we just got to think about—I was looking at this sergeant of mine this morning. Got six little kids . . . and he bringing me my things and bringing me my night reading . . . and I just thought about ordering his kids in there and what in the hell am I ordering him out there for? What the hell is Vietnam worth to me? What is Laos worth to me? What is it worth to this country? No, we've got a treaty but, hell, everybody else's got a treaty out there and they're not doing anything about it. Of course, if you start running from the Communists, they may just chase you right into your own kitchen.

Bundy: Yeah, that's the trouble. And that is what the rest of that half of the world is going to think if this thing comes apart on us. That's the dilemma.[10]

This conversation brings home like nothing else the difficulty of Johnson's position. He does *not* want to escalate U.S. involvement in Vietnam. He does *not* want to tempt China into a major confrontation. He does *not*—and this came through literally hundreds of times in my interactions with him in those years—he does *not* want to send U.S. soldiers to Vietnam to fight for a cause he himself cannot fully articulate or justify to his own satisfaction.

And yet what would happen if the United States pulled out? Like the rest of us, he worried about a communist takeover in the region and possible escalation to a major East-West confrontation as a result. As Mac Bundy said later in the same conversation: "I think you're constantly searching, if I understand you correctly, for some means of stiffening this thing that does not have this escalating aspect to it."[11] That's *exactly* what he was searching for, but neither Mac, nor I, nor Senator Russell—nor anybody else—could tell him how to solve the problem! We didn't want to escalate. We didn't think we could pull out. Later in the conversation, Mac lays it out for the president—not advice, but an objective that seemed, in and of itself, inherently contradictory: "The main objective is to kill as few people as possible while creating an environment in which the incentive to react is as low as possible. But I can't say to you this is a small matter."[12] Indeed, the "main objective" proved to be unattainable.

3. On Hanoi's Decisionmaking.

We knew almost nothing about it at the time. Moreover, until my November 1995 trip to Hanoi, it had been impossible for U.S. and Vietnamese scholars and former officials to *compare* their understandings of the process of escalation. In other words, at which points did each side come to believe the other was escalating the conflict? One of our first tasks became the joint identification of "crossroads"—of points in time when each side believed a major step was taken in the escalation of the war by the other side. Our objective was to arrive at a short list that might be discussed in detail at the June 1997 and February 1998 Hanoi conferences.

In each case of escalation, each side believes the *other* takes a hostile action, or is preparing to take hostile action, and this necessitates a *response* of some sort. Of course, the other side believes the situation is reversed, which is what gives unchecked escalation its spiral-like quality, as it seems to spin out of control. The Vietnam War proved to be no different. The Vietnamese and American members of our joint project quickly concluded that it would be productive to reexamine the crossroads that had been traversed, as the confrontation escalated to a U.S.-Vietnam war. Four of these will be discussed in this chapter.

A problem arose, however, regarding what to label each crossroad. Each side had become accustomed to referring to the crossroads in question *by what the other side was presumed to have done, or was believed to be preparing to do, which warranted a response.* The key point, of course, is that in each case, it was the other side that was presumed to have escalated. One's own action was just a response. After discussing the matter at length with our Vietnamese colleagues, it became clear that the crossroads were the "same" events to both sides only in the sense that both agreed on the timing. The four crossroads that follow are phrased so as to conform with both Washington's and Hanoi's views of each set of events:

- *January 1961:* Washington *responds* to the rapidly expanding *civil war* in the South with increased military support and counterinsurgency advisers; Hanoi *responds* to increasing brutality of the U.S.-backed government of Ngo Dinh Diem by announcing the founding in South Vietnam of the NLF to oppose the U.S.-backed Saigon government's *special war* in the South.

- *November–December 1963:* Washington *responds* to the chaos following the assassinations of Diem and Nhu in November by assuming greater responsibility for the de facto *proxy war* in the South; Hanoi, at the Ninth Party Plenum in December, *responds* to the increasing chaos in South Vietnam by greatly increasing its support for the NLF in an attempt to pre-empt a *protracted special war* with the new U.S.-backed Saigon government.

- *July 30–August 5, 1964:* Washington *responds* to an attack on a U.S. ship in the Tonkin Gulf on August 2—and what it believed to be additional attacks on August 4—with a reprisal bombing of North Vietnamese port and oil facilities on August 5; North Vietnam *responds* to covert *provocations* by the United States and South Vietnam on July 30 and 31—commando raids and electronic spying—with an attack on the U.S. destroyer *Maddox* in the Tonkin Gulf on August 2.

- *February 1965:* Washington *responds* to attacks on American advisers at Pleiku on February 7, and Qui Nhon on February 10, with reprisal bombing and sustained bombing of the North and, on February 26, by ordering two battalions of U.S. Marines to Danang; Hanoi *responds* to U.S. initiation of a *war of destruction*—sustained bombing of North Vietnam on February 8 and 11—with an all-out effort to defeat Saigon's forces before Washington can intervene.

Within this framework, we present our principal findings:

1. Washington's and Hanoi's assessments of each other at the time.

2. Significant errors in the assessments by each side of the other's intentions.

3. The contributions these errors—misperceptions, misjudgments, and misunderstandings—made to the process of escalation.

In light of these findings, I will identify in my conclusions to this chapter what appear to have been the major missed opportunities to stop and reverse the spiral of escalation toward a U.S.-Vietnam war.

Monologues in Real Time: Escalation

THE VIEW FROM WASHINGTON

The Strategy of Conflict. Washington's approach to the problem of escalation in Vietnam must be understood in relation to the primary U.S. national security issue of the era: preventing a catastrophic war that might well escalate into nuclear war with the Soviet Union. When they assumed office on January 20, 1961, John F. Kennedy and his senior national security advisers became the first U.S. leaders to face what became the defining three-part conundrum of the nuclear age. First, in a Cold War atmosphere of deep mistrust between Washington and Moscow, a crisis might erupt anywhere, anytime that fundamental U.S. and Soviet interests seemed to conflict. Second, due to miscalculations or misjudgments, any conflict might escalate out of control and into a direct East-West, or U.S.-Soviet, military confrontation, which would greatly raise the odds of nuclear war. Third, in the event of nuclear war, the U.S. plan—the Single Integrated Operational Plan (SIOP)—called for unleashing a massive nuclear strike against the entire Sino-Soviet bloc.

This was the horrifying reality that confronted President Kennedy and his associates in briefings during their first several weeks in office. The possibility of a crisis escalating to catastrophic nuclear war was therefore a major concern of the new Kennedy administration. Nuclear danger was palpable to Kennedy and his people, and they immediately set out to reduce the risk of such escalation. For example, in long private conversations with President Kennedy—repeated later with President Johnson—Robert McNamara had recommended, without qualification, that the president never initiate under any circumstances the use of nuclear weapons. McNamara believed they accepted his recommendation. But neither they nor he could discuss their positions publicly because they were totally contrary to established NATO policy.[13] Inevitably, any crisis or conflict, including the ongoing struggle in Vietnam, was evaluated by the political leadership of the United States in terms of its potential to escalate to nuclear doomsday.

The Kennedy administration's attempt to solve this problem, formulated by McNamara, was known variously as "flexible response," "limited options," and by other labels. At the heart of this new doctrine was the belief that decisionmakers should have the option of responding in crises at a low level of violence or in other ways that might not quickly escalate to nuclear holocaust. If necessary, the decisionmaker—the president himself, if nuclear weapons themselves came to be involved—could move up the "rungs" of a "ladder" of escalation, until such time as the adversary chose to cease and desist its activities—Soviet- or Chinese-backed aggression— rather than face the consequences at the next highest level of escalation. This view had many sources, including the seminal writing of Gen. Maxwell Taylor, who had resigned from the U.S. Army during the Eisenhower administration, in part over the lack of credible military options with which to oppose communist aggression. Taylor would later become Kennedy's chairman of the Joint Chiefs of Staff and ambassador in Saigon.[14] Flexible response was formally proposed by McNamara, in classified form, as the official policy of the Kennedy administration at a NATO meeting in Athens on May 5, 1962.[15]

Considerable influence was also exerted during the Kennedy years by so-called defense intellectuals. For example, Harvard professor Thomas Schelling, in papers on nuclear strategy collected in his 1960 book *The Strategy of Conflict*, stated with characteristic pithiness:[16]

> "Strategy of conflict" sounds cold-blooded, [but] the theory is not concerned with the efficient *application* of violence or anything of the sort; it is not essentially a theory of aggression or of resistance or of war. *Threats* of

war, yes, or threats of anything else; but it is the employment of threats, or of threats and promises, or more generally of the conditioning of one's own behavior on the behavior of others, that the theory is about.[17]

This view penetrated the civilian leadership under Kennedy, and later Johnson, to a remarkable degree. In this view, a conflict is as much *psychological* as physical, with the upper hand gained by the side with the most credible threats conditioned on *future* actions. Thus, acts of war are chosen in part for their *signaling* value as well as their capacity to disable an opponent. It is *cautious* when confronting a nuclear opponent because of the ever-present fear of escalation to nuclear war. It is concerned with *limited objectives*, not with the destruction of the opponent. And, at times, it is *reactive*: It is the *other* side that must decide whether to escalate and face the consequences.[18] The objective is to bend an opponent's will via the threat to continue on up the ladder of escalation.

Inherent in the formulation and application of this doctrine was major participation of civilians. Kennedy had arrived at the presidency somewhat skeptical of military advice. His skepticism was reinforced after going ahead with the Bay of Pigs invasion, largely on the basis of rosy, unrealistic scenarios from his CIA and military advisers, and after his experience with the Joint Chiefs regarding military operations in Laos. It was this background that caused him—and McNamara—to maintain such tight control over military operations during the missile crisis in 1962. Civilian control to this extent was not appreciated by some military leaders. A notable exception was General Taylor. Gen. William Westmoreland, U.S. field commander in Vietnam between 1964 and 1968, writing in 1976 of his years in Saigon, said: "Many of the errors could be traced to strong control of the conduct of the war from Washington."[19] Later, in 1991, at a conference on Vietnam at the LBJ Library, referring to the constraints that kept the Vietnam War "limited," he said, "At the time I felt that my hands were tied" but that "we have to give President Johnson credit for *not* allowing the war to expand geographically."[20]

Lyndon Johnson proved to be just as determined as Kennedy to retain control of the war, and for exactly the same reason: fear of uncontrolled escalation to disaster with either the Soviet Union, China, or both.

January 1961: Response to Civil War in South Vietnam. For a time during the 1950s, the survival of Ngo Dinh Diem and his U.S.-backed government was considered in Washington to be something of a miracle, proof for the then fashionable idea of "nation-building" as a means for containing com-

munism in the developing world. Indeed, with the critical assistance of his
U.S.-trained security police, directed by his brother, Ngo Dinh Nhu, Diem's
South Vietnamese government appeared by 1957 to have begun to eliminate
the troublesome communist-led insurgency. In May of that year, Diem made
a triumphal visit to the United States, which included discussions with President Eisenhower and his inner circle, with members of the Rockefeller
family and other influential backers of the South Vietnamese "experiment."
In general, the Eisenhower administration was pleased with the return on its
investment: In exchange for mere money and a few Americans in Saigon to
offer advice of various sorts, communism was being contained at the 17th
parallel in Indochina. In 1963, speaking of Diem's work during the 1950s,
Sen. Mike Mansfield, a former professor of East Asian history, said: "His
[Diem's] personal courage, integrity, determination, and authentic nationalism were essential forces in forestalling a total collapse in South Vietnam
and in bringing a measure of order and hope out of the chaos, intrigue and
widespread corruption."[21]

As it happened, May 1957 would be Diem's finest hour. His regime began
its slow, inexorable collapse during the following year. A National Intelligence
Estimate (NIE) of May 26, 1959, revealed many of the sources of discontent.
"The government," the NIE reported, "is in fact essentially authoritarian," and
"members of the executive branch are little more than the personal agents of
Diem," whereas the legislature has no real power at all. Finally, it reported:
"No organized opposition, loyal or otherwise, is tolerated, and critics of the
regime are often repressed."[22] Diem's and Nhu's repressive "solutions" only
added to their problems. In 1959 they instituted a "fortified" resettlement program in which peasants were removed to "safe" areas. The peasants hated the
program, which forcibly moved them from what they considered to be the
sacred ground of their ancestors. This was followed by something called the
"Agroville" program, which was also quickly abandoned. (This propensity to
put walls around peasants would emerge yet again, in late 1961, in the
strategic hamlet program, which also failed.)[23]

Resistance to Diem began to mobilize, tentatively at first, but unmistakably. In July 1958, French scholar and journalist Bernard Fall published the
results of his field research in South Vietnam, in which he mapped the pattern of assassinations and other politically motivated terrorism in the South.
On the basis of the dramatic increases he identified, he announced "the
onset of a new war" in the South.[24] Between May 1957 and May 1958, Fall
found evidence for at least 700 assassinations of Diem's low-level
appointees in the villages of South Vietnam. (By May 1959, the figure would
rise to 1,200; by May 1960 to 2,500; and by May 1961 to 4,000.)[25]

Finally, Fall cleverly and painstakingly correlated rebel activities with complaints lodged with the International Control Commission, which had ostensible oversight of adherence to the Geneva Accords of 1954. Based on his findings, Fall wrote: "The conclusion is inescapable, that there must be some coordination between the rebels and the North Vietnamese government."[26] In a retrospective study, U.S. Information Agency analyst Douglas Pike drew the same conclusion but noted: "Insurgency efforts in the 1958–1960 period involved violence such as assassinations but few armed attacks."[27] The rebels were still feeling their way forward and were not yet, by later standards, well organized.

Even so, they were beginning to evince a characteristic they called *dau tranh*, which is usually translated as "struggle," as in "political struggle" or "armed struggle." But, as one of the rebels explained, "struggle" does not do justice to what the South Vietnamese government and its U.S. backers would have to contend with from this point forward. *Dau tranh*, he said, "is all important to a revolutionist. It marks his thinking, his attitudes, his behavior. His life, his revolutionary work, his whole world is *dau tranh*. The essence of his existence is *dau tranh*."[28] To American sensibilities, this appeared to be an extreme and lethal form of fanaticism, and the capacity of the rebels to sustain it throughout the war would be a continuing source of fear and wonderment to U.S. personnel on the ground in South Vietnam.

In an attempt to demean the rebel movement, the Diem government began calling it the "Vietcong," or Vietnamese communists, even though it was clear that many of its members were not communists. Douglas Pike has described the nature of the transition to civil war with the founding of the NLF, as it was understood in Washington:

> There is a vast difference between a collection of clandestine opposition political groups and the organizational weapon that emerged, a difference of kind, not just degree. The National Liberation Front was not simply another indigenous covert group, or even a coalition of such groups. It was an organizational steamroller, nationally conceived and nationally organized, endowed with ample cadres and funds, crashing out of the jungle to flatten the GVN [South Vietnamese government]. . . . The creation of the NLF was an accomplishment of such skill, precision and refinement that when one thinks of who the master planner must have been, only one name comes to mind: Vietnam's organizational genius, Ho Chi Minh.[29]

This phenomenon—the NLF—with its origins in an inchoate southern resistance, would now be organized, directed, controlled, and supplied by

Hanoi. It would present Diem's U.S. backers with a new and (what turned out to be) insoluble problem: how to assist a fundamentally incompetent, unpopular authoritarian ruler in his efforts to put down a civil war masterminded by Hanoi. Washington's initial response, the planning for which was begun in 1960 under Eisenhower, was two-pronged: It would provide training in *counterinsurgency* for Diem's forces; and it would attempt to place conditions on future aid to Diem that would force him to make his government more responsive to the people of South Vietnam, who would then (in theory) become less susceptible to blandishments and coercion by the NLF. On January 28, 1961, just one week after assuming the presidency, Kennedy approved the main provisions of the counterinsurgency plan. Negotiations with Diem to implement it began on February 13. The administration was optimistic that further escalation of U.S. involvement would be unnecessary.[30]

The plan approved by Kennedy, however, contained what would turn out to be a fateful caveat: "That the Government of South Viet-Nam has the basic potential to cope with the Viet Cong guerrilla threat *if necessary corrective measures are taken and adequate forces are provided.*"[31] Corrective measures were not taken. And one of the most destructive military campaigns in history proved inadequate to defeat the combined forces of the NLF and Hanoi's army.

November–December 1963: Response to Proxy War in the South. During the summer of 1963, the Diem government came unglued, but initially it had little to do with the NLF's civil war. On May 8, Ngo Dinh Nhu sent his security police into Hue to order Buddhists to take down their flags, which had been hung in honor of the Buddha's birthday. When the dust settled on the ensuing riot, women and children were dead, the Buddhist monks began to organize, and the pace of Diem's and Nhu's march to oblivion quickened. All summer long, the world's newspapers and televisions were filled with horrifying images of Buddhist monks incinerating themselves in protest over the government's harsh treatment of the Buddhists. In this last act of an oft–played out scenario, U.S. officials tried to pressure Diem and Nhu to make various kinds of reforms, the Ngo brothers resisted, and the two allied governments became estranged, even hostile, toward each other by the end of the summer. On November 1 the brothers would be removed in a palace coup led by Gen. Duong Van Minh, who had gotten assurance from U.S. Ambassador Henry Cabot Lodge that Washington would not oppose a coup. Minh ordered Diem and Nhu executed the same day.

This chapter addresses not the details of the coup, or U.S. culpability in it, which is well documented.[32] Rather, the issue is this: Did the removal of the

Ngo brothers affect the escalation of the war? The answer is that it *did*. With the removal of Diem, the only bona fide South Vietnamese nationalist capable of holding South Vietnam together (other than the NLF), the U.S. was led to begin to transcend its role as the backer, tutor, and underwriter of whatever Saigon regime might be in place. The many successor regimes would prove unstable and incompetent, and their fighting units were no match in the field for the Hanoi-backed NLF forces. But Washington had sunk costs in Saigon and, in any case, felt it had somehow to prevent a communist takeover. The NLF, by now directed by the Politburo in Hanoi, would continually seek to take advantage of the void in South Vietnamese leadership. In this way, Washington would find itself increasingly in a role analogous to Hanoi's: as the "patron" of a "proxy" government—actually a whole series of more or less pliant but incompetent governments—whose politicians and fighting units were increasingly under the direction and control of U.S. advisers.

Would Diem ever have requested, or accepted, U.S. combat troops in South Vietnam? Put another way: If Diem had remained in charge, would the conflict in Vietnam have escalated to a U.S.-Vietnam war? Almost surely, the answer is no. Had Diem remained in charge, one of three scenarios would likely have been played out. First, though theoretically possible, it is quite unlikely that Diem could have rallied his forces and put down the civil war in the South, which was of course why many in Washington and the U.S. embassy in Saigon wanted him removed. A second scenario is more likely, in the event that Diem had tried, but failed, to crush the NLF's civil war: Sometime in 1964, the NLF forces would have removed him, and a neutral coalition government would have been established in Saigon with close ties to Hanoi. Either way, the escalation to an American war would not have occurred.

But there is also a third scenario that is intriguing: that Diem would have sought, or been amenable to, rapprochement with Hanoi. Diem had theretofore exhibited none of the skills and attitudes required for building such a coalition. Yet there is evidence that he might have tried it. Certainly, many of the Americans in the Saigon embassy were worried that he might.

On August 7, 1963, amid the Buddhist crisis and under intense pressure from Washington to negotiate with the Buddhists, Diem exploded in an interview with American journalist Marguerite Higgins:

> What am I to think of the American government. . . . ? Am I merely a puppet on Washington's string? . . . If you order Vietnam around like a puppet on a string, how will you be different . . . from the French? I hope . . . that your government will take a realistic look at these young generals plotting to take my place. . . . I am afraid there are no George Washington's in our military.

. . . Gradually, when the war ends, we can move to greater democracy on a national level. . . . But it is impossible—a delusion—to think that a solution for Asia consists in blindly copying Western methods. . . . The key to good relations between the United States and Vietnam . . . is respect for the substance of sovereignty. . . . The Americans are breaking Vietnamese psychology and they don't even know what they are doing.[33]

This is not the mentality of a leader who is inclined to fight a proxy war, accepting troops and marching orders, along with material resources.

The Americans weren't the only people who believed Diem would neither request nor accept U.S. combat troops with the loss of his power and South Vietnamese sovereignty that was implied by such a move. Hanoi's leaders also believed this, basing their conclusion in part on the reports of a well-placed spy in Saigon. Vu Ngoc Nha (code name "Hai Nha"—or "Nha no. 2"), a Catholic who served Diem as "presidential adviser," resided at Gia Long Palace (and in fact also served Diem's successors until he was disgraced in 1968). At about the same time as Diem's interview with Higgins, Diem also consulted Nha about the issue of U.S. troops. Bui Tin, former editor of the Hanoi party daily *Nhan Dan* and a former North Vietnamese colonel, later interviewed Vu Ngoc Nha and has described the report by Nha of his conversation with Diem:

> When the U.S. administration pressed Diem to allow American ground troops to be based in the South, he turned to his adviser one evening and said, "Nha, this question is very important. If we let the troops come here, they are foreigners and in no time they will be shooting and bombing. They will be taking military action on our soil and staying here. So if there are ever talks about reunification, what could we say to Ho Chi Minh?"[34]

Bui Tin adds his own postscript to this account. "I believe," he says, "the Americans considered this necessary in order to move from special warfare to all-out war and the intervention of U.S. ground forces in Vietnam, *which the Ngo brothers would have opposed.*"[35] In this sense, the removal of Diem and Nhu was a tragedy for both Washington *and* Hanoi, if one believes that some accommodation between the Saigon and Hanoi governments was in the offing, or at least possible. The available evidence suggests that both may have been true.

With the removal of Diem, an autocratic, even brutal but patriotic Vietnamese nationalist, the momentum toward two-sided proxy war in the South increased rapidly. On November 26, just four days after President Kennedy's assassination, President Johnson approved National Security Action Memorandum 273. It provided for continuity with the Kennedy administration's policies. Washington's objective, it asserted, was "to assist the people and Government of South Vietnam to win their contest against the externally directed and supported communist conspiracy."[36] President Johnson also approved planning for a covert action program that later became known as Operational Plan (OPLAN) 34-A, which would play an important role in the July–August 1964 events in the Tonkin Gulf. Secretary of Defense McNamara was sent to Saigon in December to assess the situation. His December 21, 1963, report to the president ended this way: "*Conclusion.* My appraisal may be overly pessimistic. . . . But we should watch the situation very carefully, running scared, hoping for the best, but preparing for more forceful moves if the situation does not show early signs of improvement."[37]

In light of what followed, the appraisal was in fact overly *optimistic*. The junta that removed Diem and Nhu would be removed in another coup the following month, ushering in a period of chronic instability in Saigon that would remain for the remainder of the war. Estimated infiltration from the North, which had leveled off somewhat in 1963, would nearly double in 1964 from 7,906 to 12,424.[38] These were still "regroupees"—southerners who had settled north of the 17th parallel following the Geneva Accords of 1954. They knew the territory. They had been trained, outfitted, and indoctrinated in the North. And they came south on Hanoi's behalf. A civil war was fast becoming a proxy war. "More forceful moves" by the United States would in fact be called for, and soon.

August 2–4 1964: Response to Provocation in the Tonkin Gulf. At 3:40 A.M. (EDT) on Sunday, August 2, 1964, the U.S. destroyer *Maddox* was attacked by North Vietnamese patrol boats in the Gulf of Tonkin off the North Vietnamese coast. *Maddox*, joined by aircraft from the U.S. aircraft carrier *Ticonderoga*, damaged two of the attacking boats and disabled another. President Johnson, when informed of the incident, chose not to retaliate, though he issued a protest and warning to the Hanoi government. Maxwell Taylor, now U.S. ambassador in Saigon, saw a chance to raise morale in the always shaky South Vietnamese government by retaliating against the North. Failure to respond, he cabled to Secretary of State Dean Rusk on August 3, would signal to Hanoi "that the U.S. flinches from direct confrontation with the North Vietnamese."[39] Johnson, however, chose not to retaliate as Taylor recommended.

Two days later, on the morning of Tuesday, August 4, Secretary of Defense McNamara called the president to tell him that *Maddox* was again reporting the presence of hostile boats and that, based on information derived from North Vietnamese radio communications, an attack might be imminent. This was the beginning of a day-long series of transpacific telephone conversations involving a host of people, from McNamara to Commander John J. Herrick, the commander of the task group to which *Maddox* belonged. The question—and it assumed immense importance by late in the day—was whether an attack had actually occurred on *Maddox* and another U.S. ship, *Turner Joy*.

The details of the complex tale need not concern us here, where our objective is to trace the two-sided escalation of the war. However, sources in Hanoi, including Hanoi Defense Minister Gen. Vo Nguyen Giap, have recently revealed that Washington erred on two counts. The revelations were made in a conversation with Robert McNamara in Hanoi on November 9, 1995. First, according to Giap, the August 2 attack was ordered by a local commander, not by Hanoi, as was assumed in Washington at the time. It was carried out, he said, in retaliation for U.S.-backed South Vietnamese commando raids on two North Vietnamese islands nearby on July 30 and 31, according to OPLAN 34-A; and in retaliation for so-called DeSoto patrols, designed to spy electronically on North Vietnamese communications facilities. In addition, the second "attack" on August 4, which U.S. officials believed was highly probable but were never able to confirm positively, never occurred.[40] It appears that on August 4 the appearance of an attack may have derived from poor visibility, anxious U.S. sonar operators, and mistaken analyses of intercept data from North Vietnamese communications. (The significance of these two apparent U.S. misperceptions are taken up in the third section below and in the fourth section, in which the connections between these events and missed opportunities are addressed.)

However, having reached a determination that the attack was "probable but not certain," President Johnson decided that since the attack probably *had* occurred, this time it would *not* go unanswered.[41] Just before midnight (EDT) on August 4, President Johnson announced on radio and television that a retaliatory strike was then under way on North Vietnamese port and oil facilities that were associated with the activities of the torpedo boats that had attacked the U.S. ships. On Friday, August 7, Congress approved the Southeast Asia Resolution, better known as the Tonkin Gulf Resolution. The House vote was 416–0; the Senate vote was 88–2 (with ten affirmative absentees). This became a de facto go-ahead from Congress for the Johnson administration's deepening involvement in the war in Vietnam.

Verbatim notes of the discussion at the president's meeting with the National Security Council on August 4 reveal a good deal about the way the episode galvanized Johnson to retaliate. After a briefing by Robert

McNamara on the operational details of the presumed attack, Dean Rusk opens discussion on the question of what Washington's response should be and why. The answer is that it should be one that sends a particular *signal*:

Secretary Rusk: An immediate and direct reaction by us is necessary. The unprovoked attack on the high seas is an act of war for all practical purposes. We have been trying to get a signal to Hanoi and Peking. Our response to this attack may be that signal. We are informing NATO, SEATO and the UN. As an indication of Hanoi's intentions the second attack was a more serious decision for the North Vietnamese than the decision to make the first attack.

President Johnson, however, cautiously inquires of CIA Director John McCone about the likelihood that the North Vietnamese purposely provoked the Americans, because they want to escalate the war *now*.

The President: Do they want a war by attacking our ships in the middle of the Gulf of Tonkin?

McCone then gives Johnson his best guess as to what the event was actually about, from the other side's point of view. Although he does not specify where he believes the order came from—a local commander or from Hanoi—he gives the North Vietnamese rationale concisely:

CIA Director McCone: No. The North Vietnamese are reacting defensively to our attacks on their off-shore islands. They are responding out of pride and on the basis of defense considerations. The attack is a signal to us that the North Vietnamese have the will and determination to continue the war. They are raising the ante.

This appears to be all that Johnson needs to hear.

The President: Are we going to react to their shooting at our ships over 40 miles from their shores? If yes, we should do more than merely return the fire of the attacking ships. If this is so, then the question involves no more than the number of North Vietnamese targets to be attacked.

Bromley Smith, the notetaker, closes the account by noting: "A draft statement by the President was revised. It is to be made public by the President as soon as the U.S. attack planes are over target."[42] So a "signal" will be sent. It will acknowledge that Hanoi has raised the ante. It will be a major step in what the *Pentagon Papers* analysis of the Tonkin Gulf episode calls "an essentially psychological campaign to convince Hanoi that the United States meant business."[43]

President Johnson was elected on his own in November 1964, defeating Barry Goldwater by the largest margin in U.S. history. Days before, on November 1, NLF forces had carried out an attack on the U.S. air base at Bien Hoa, killing five Americans, wounding seventy-six, and causing considerable damage to U.S. aircraft.[44] The Joint Chiefs recommended a severely punitive response, far beyond what could reasonably be called a "reprisal," the culmination of which was to be a B-52 strike against Phuc Yen, the principal airfield near Hanoi. President Johnson decided not to retaliate. But the attack on Bien Hoa was the most visible evidence yet that Americans were being targeted and that Johnson's military advisers wanted to send a signal of their own to Hanoi that this was not acceptable.

Just after the election, an interagency task force was assembled, chaired by William P. Bundy, the assistant secretary of state for Far Eastern affairs. Ambassador Maxwell Taylor returned at that time and gave an important briefing to the group on November 27. Taylor's tone was strident: "But with all, we are tired of standing by and seeing the unabashed efforts of the DRV [Democratic Republic of Vietnam—North Vietnam] to absorb South Vietnam into the communist orbit against its will. We know that Hanoi is responsible and that we are going to punish it until it desists from this behavior."[45] Taylor concludes his briefing for the Bundy group: "We must leave negotiating initiatives to Hanoi. . . . Whatever the course of events, we should adhere to these principles: a. Do not enter into negotiations until the DRV is hurting. . . . b. Never let the DRV gain a victory in South Vietnam without having paid a disproportionate price."[46]

It thus fell to William Bundy's interagency group to hammer out a policy based on this general get-tough approach to the situation in Vietnam. They recommended a two-phase program. Phase 1 would consist of "an intensification of earlier 'signals' to Hanoi that it should cease supporting the insurgency in the South or face progressively higher costs and penalties."[47] It would last about thirty days. Phase 2, however, would be "a continuous program of progressively more serious air strikes, possibly running from two to six months."[48] Between the lines of the statement of the overall objectives of the two-phase bombing program one finds many of the principles espoused by U.S. civilian strategists such as Thomas Schelling:

> The U.S. must be willing to pause to explore negotiated solutions, should North Vietnam show any signs of yielding, while maintaining a credible

threat of still further pressures. In the view of the working group, the prospect of greater pressures to come was at least as important as any damage actually inflicted, since the real target was the *will* of the North Vietnamese government to continue the aggression in the South rather than its *capability* to do so. But even if it retained the capability, North Vietnam might elect to discontinue the aggression if its anticipated future costs and risks were greater than it had bargained for.[49]

The formulation is elegant, clear, coherent, and—as events later proved—wrong in every important respect. There would be no sign of yielding from Hanoi. Its will was never broken, or even bent. At the end of the struggle, it had both the capability and the will to proceed with its plan. All this, despite having absorbed the heaviest bombing in history from the most powerful nation on earth.

A story circulated at Harvard during the 1960s that a missed opportunity had occurred when Harvard failed to offer a scholarship to Ho Chi Minh, in order that he might have the opportunity to study with professor Schelling. If he had, according to the Cambridge pundits, he would have known that Washington was trying to send him a *signal* via the bombing. As it was, Ho and his colleagues, in their ignorance, thought the United States was trying to destroy their country.

February 1965: Pleiku and Qui Nhon—the American War Begins. The Tonkin Gulf incident had provoked an immediate reprisal against North Vietnamese targets and the planning for Phase 1 and Phase 2. Yet by the end of December 1964, it had done nothing to improve the course of the war in the South. While the planning went on, the situation in South Vietnam went from bad to worse. The Saigon government came apart yet again on December 21, with Gen. Nguyen Khanh, who seemed to be the real powerbroker, siding with the so-called Young Turks in the South Vietnamese Army in their fight with the political leadership. On December 23, Dean Rusk threatened to withdraw all aid to the Saigon government. The immediate reply from Nguyen Khanh was that the South Vietnamese government could survive without U.S. funds. On December 24, Christmas Eve, the NLF attacked the Brinks Hotel in Saigon, killing two Americans and wounding fifty-two. And forty miles southeast of Saigon, at Binh Gia, the South Vietnamese forces engaged NLF forces beginning on December 28 in a major battle that lasted well into early January. When it was over, the NLF had soundly beaten the South Vietnamese forces, even though they were backed by U.S. helicopters, advisers, and weapons. Finally, once again the Buddhists seemed to some U.S. officials to be nearing some sort of deal with the

South Vietnamese government, such as it was, and the NLF, to create a coalition government that once established would ask the Americans to leave. All of these factors together summed to what became known in Washington by the euphemism "the situation" in South Vietnam.[50]

President Johnson had made a tough decision after the bombing of the Brinks Hotel *not* to engage in Phase 1 reprisal bombing against targets in North Vietnam. He believed that a prerequisite to reprisal bombing of the North was a government in Saigon that seemed at least minimally stable and in charge. He worried that the United States would appear as if it were "trying to shoot its way out of an internal Saigonese crisis."[51] However, by the end of December, officials in Washington, and in the U.S. embassy in Saigon, began to believe that they needed to reverse the sequence of events if they were to have any chance of regaining the initiative, that is, the United States should *first* show its support of the South Vietnamese civilians and military personnel with whom the United States was allied by launching a bombing campaign against the North, especially if (as everyone expected) Hanoi-backed and -directed targeting of Americans continued. Perhaps, *then*, the argument went, the South Vietnamese would muster the courage to take charge of their situation.[52]

The problem was described by McGeorge Bundy and Robert McNamara in a January 27, 1965, memorandum to President Johnson—a memo that became known as the "fork in the road" paper. Increased U.S. military pressure on Hanoi, they speculated, might just get the South Vietnamese to "pull up their socks":

> The underlying difficulties in Saigon arise from the spreading conviction that the future is without hope for anti-communists. . . . Our best friends have been somewhat discouraged by our own inactivity in the face of major attacks on our own installations. . . . They feel that we are unwilling to take serious risks. In one sense all of this is outrageous, in the light of all we have done and all that we are ready to do if they will only pull up their socks. But it is a fact—or at least so McNamara and I now think.[53]

Having laid out the problem, Bundy and McNamara then go to the heart of the matter—the fork in the road that confronted the president:

> *We see two alternatives.* The *first* is to use our military power in the Far East to force a change of Communist policy. The *second* is to deploy all our resources along a track of negotiation, aimed at salvaging what little can be preserved with no major addition to our military risks. We tend to favor the

first course, but we believe that both should be carefully studied and that alternative programs should be argued out before you.[54]

Finally, they say, "You should know that Dean Rusk does not agree with us." Rusk, they say, would rather try to make the current policy work. "This would be good," Bundy concludes, "if it was possible. We do not think it is."[55]

The memorandum was discussed with the president late on the morning of January 27, 1965, but there was no consideration of "deploying all our resources along a track of negotiation—with no major addition to our military risks." Instead, the president decided to send McGeorge Bundy to South Vietnam—his first visit—as President Johnson's personal representative to assess the situation and return with recommendations for the president that would assist him in deciding which fork in the road to take.

The trip was fateful indeed. At 2:00 A.M. on February 7, the last day of the Bundy team's visit to Saigon, the NLF ended the Tet holiday truce by bombing the U.S. airfield at Pleiku, in northern South Vietnam, and the U.S. helicopter base at Camp Holloway, four miles away. Of the 137 Americans wounded, nine died and seventy-six had to be evacuated. There was also heavy damage to equipment. As a result, the National Security Council was called into session in Washington. Following four lengthy telephone consultations with Bundy and others in Saigon, the president ordered reprisal attacks on North Vietnam in an operation called "FLAMING DART I."[56]

Chester Cooper was a member of the Bundy delegation in Saigon on that fateful trip. Later he recalled: "On our return trip to Washington we heard the White House statement over the plane's radio":[57]

> Today's joint response was carefully limited to military areas which are supplying men and arms for attacks in South Viet-Nam. As in the case of the North Vietnamese attacks in the Gulf of Tonkin last August, the response is appropriate and fitting.
>
> As the U.S. government has frequently stated, we seek no wider war. Whether or not this course can be maintained lies with the North Vietnamese aggressors.[58]

Cooper recalls that at that moment, "in early February 1965 the die was cast. The war was about to be changed in kind rather than in degree."[59]

Just after the Bundy group returned to Washington, on February 10, the NLF struck again at Qui Nhon, killing twenty-three American soldiers and wounding twenty-one others. President Johnson again ordered a reprisal bombing on a group of targets called for in a targeting package code-named

"FLAMING DART II." Three days later, the president ordered a "program of measured and limited air action," which would be called ROLLING THUNDER and remain in effect for the next three and a half years. On February 26, the president approved the dispatch of two U.S. Marine battalions to Danang as a security force to protect the U.S. air base there. Those Marines would be only the first installment of what would become approximately 2 million U.S. combat personnel who would serve, at one time or another, in South Vietnam during the next decade.

At the time, there was little doubt in Washington that Hanoi had ordered the attack at Pleiku specifically to send a signal of its own to the United States while the Bundy team was visiting Saigon. An intelligence report from the aftermath of Pleiku, for example, states: "Whether Hanoi specifically ordered the Pleiku attack or whether the NLF merely received Hanoi's blessing for the attack remains speculative. There can be little doubt, however, that Hanoi had . . . ample reason to favor the notion."[60] In addition, there was speculation in the U.S. intelligence community that the attack had been planned by Hanoi for an additional reason: to embarrass Soviet Premier Alexei Kosygin, who was in Hanoi at the time, as a way to compel the Soviets to forsake their notions of a peace initiative.[61] Either hypothesis leads to the conclusion that, in Lyndon Johnson's locution, Hanoi did indeed "seek a wider war" via attacks such as were carried out at Pleiku.

History, however, may be both more mundane and less conspiratorial than either of these explanations suggests. Revelations by Gen. Dang Vu Hiep at the June 1997 conference in Hanoi clearly indicate that the attacks on both Pleiku and Qui Nhon were planned by field commanders who had no idea that Bundy was in Saigon or that Kosygin was in Hanoi. Moreover, at the February 1998 Hanoi conference, Col. Quach Hai Luong, of Hanoi's Institute for Strategic Studies, reported that *NLF forces at Pleiku were unaware that U.S. personnel were present at the time of the attack!* In other words, the Pleiku attack was not targeted at Americans, was not ordered by Hanoi, and was not designed by Hanoi to send a signal of any kind to anybody.

The authors of the *Pentagon Papers* captured the pivotal significance of these events by beginning their analysis of the U.S. air war over North Vietnam with a section called: "Introduction—Pleiku pulls the trigger."[62] Within a week of the attack, the bombing of the North was a fact of daily life. McGeorge Bundy is supposed to have said that "Pleikus are streetcars," implying that Pleiku, though obviously not designed as a pretext to initiate the bombing, was nonetheless a convenient reason to deepen U.S. involvement, a development that many saw as inevitable.[63] Perhaps. But if Gen. Dang Vu Hiep and Col. Quach Hai Luong are correct—and we have no reason to doubt them—then the authors of the *Pentagon Papers* were surely not justified in describing the Qui Nhon bombing as "an act of defiance."[64] It was not an act of defiance or a signal to Washington. It was an act of war—no more, no less— by the same NLF group in Interzone 5 that had carried out the Pleiku attack.

It appears that U.S. decisionmakers running the air war from the White House—including President Johnson, who was centrally involved—mistakenly, perhaps without being fully conscious of it, came to believe that the NLF's war on the ground was also run *with the same degree of detailed control* from the leadership headquarters in Hanoi. It was not. Thus, strictly speaking, Pleiku and Qui Nhon did not pull the "trigger" that initiated an American war. Washington pulled the trigger itself—it took the momentous step, based on a misunderstanding of NLF command and control procedures, thinking that their counterparts in Hanoi had *already* done so.

The View from Hanoi

The Strategy of Defeating the U.S. "Aggressive Will." From the moment the United States brought Ngo Dinh Diem to Saigon as its designated architect for South Vietnamese "nation-building," the main objective of the Hanoi government was to dislodge Diem and replace him, but with one overriding caveat: Do not provoke the United States into a U.S.-Vietnam war. One of the ironies of the history of the escalation to a U.S.-Vietnam war is that the major objective of *both* Washington and Hanoi was, initially, to *avoid* escalation to this level—in which U.S. and North Vietnamese combat forces would be fighting each other directly. An additional irony is that Hanoi's strategy of achieving its twin objectives—replacing Diem with a neutral coalition government friendly to Hanoi and avoiding an American war—was in many respects the mirror image of Washington's "strategy of conflict." The goal in dealing with the awesome power of the United States would be to continually deny Washington its objectives, as it proceeded up the rungs of the ladder of escalation, until U.S. leaders at some point made a sensible, rational decision to cease and desist and, at last, to withdraw.

As with many other aspects of Vietnamese culture and history, leaders in Hanoi borrowed initially from the Chinese, then made critical adjustments that reflected important differences between China and Vietnam. At first, during the French war, the Vietminh appear to have seen their task akin to that of Mao and his forces in China. The strategic model in use had three stages: *strategic defensive*, in which a power base would be built in the countryside; *strategic parity*, a kind of equilibrium of the balance of forces; and finally *general counteroffensive*—the final march to victory.[65] In essence, the problem with this scheme for the Vietnamese, even during the French war, was that the size of the French commitment, combined with the Vietminh's relatively small forces, which were spread over a large area, meant that the last stage, the glorious victory, never materialized. Worse, on several occasions, the Vietminh acted *as if* the moment had arrived, attacked with abandon, and suffered grievously as a result.

They needed a different approach that took account of their small size and the much more powerful enemy—a model that allowed them to use perhaps the most effective weapon they had: *time*. They had waited a thousand years to dislodge the Chinese. So they would resist until the exhausted French decided to leave, which they did, beginning in 1954. Le Duan, who became the principal architect of Hanoi's war in the South after 1959, drew these lessons for the war against Diem and his U.S. backers:

> The revolution in the South will not follow the path of protracted armed struggle, surrounding the cities by the countryside and advancing to the liberation of the entire country by using military forces, as China did, but will follow a Vietnamese path. . . . There will be a guerrilla war leading to a general uprising which will primarily use political force in coordination with armed forces to grasp political power in the hands of the people.[66]

The NLF was by no means primarily a military organization but was, rather, something like a mobile, nascent government-in-waiting, from the leadership at the Central Office South Vietnam (COSVN) all the way down to the local villages. The degree of emphasis by these revolutionaries on political education and governance is perhaps unprecedented in the modern era.

As Le Duan implies, there was a reason for this: Vietnam was *not* China. It was not a huge country that had never been colonized by a European power, in the way that the French colonized Vietnam. The NLF, and their comrades in Hanoi, had to be prepared to engage in revolution over the long haul.

One of the great figures in the southern resistance was Gen. Tran Van Tra, who rose to be commander of People's Liberation Army Forces in the B2 theater (the southern part of South Vietnam, including Saigon). Tran Van Tra believed that the critical moment of the struggle in the South had been January 1961, when the Kennedy administration came to office. The understanding in the South and in Hanoi, according to Tra, was as follows:

> When the strategy of "massive retaliation," based on a monopoly of nuclear weapons, was bankrupted . . . the United States had to shift over to a

strategy of "flexible response" with its three types of war—special, limited and general—in order to take the initiative and win under any circumstances, and especially to oppose the national liberation wars. . . . That strategy was applied on the Vietnam battlefield in 1961.[67]

This was Hanoi's and the NLF's view of the Kennedy administration's strategic decisions regarding Vietnam: The United States would endeavor first to win a *special war* (victory in the South using only South Vietnamese forces and U.S. advisers and equipment); failing that, the United States would resort to a *limited war*, using its own combat forces and air power, in both North and South; finally, if this failed to subdue Hanoi and the NLF, Washington might resort to the riskiest strategy of all, *general war*, in which the war would be widened beyond the borders of Vietnam, risking intervention by China, the Soviet Union, or both.[68]

By January 1961, Tra and his colleagues had formed the view that the U.S. strategy, as they applied it in Vietnam, was an *offensive* strategy, designed to annihilate the opponent. According to Tran Van Tra, Washington, "like a greedy, addicted gambler . . . continued to lurch from one defeat to another. After they had escalated to the top-most rung, they of course had to de-escalate."[69] In other words, it was Washington that chose, at each rung on the ladder, to escalate the war, in order to satisfy its insatiable neocolonialist determination to eliminate communist governments and peoples.

Historian David Elliott has analyzed this approach so as to highlight the remarkable similarities between Washington's and Hanoi's understandings of escalation. "The fundamental objective," he writes of Hanoi's strategy, "was to understand the options open to the United States for maintaining its interests in South Vietnam and formulate ways of eliminating these options."[70] This means, according to Elliott, "the key was to defeat the '*aggressive will*' *(y chi xam luoc)* of the United States—a psychological objective more than a military one."[71] Another historian of Vietnamese decisionmaking, William Duiker, gives Hanoi's bottom line in this strategy. "The objective," he says, "would not be to inflict a total defeat on the enemy, but to create a 'no-win' situation and lead Washington to accept a political settlement and the formation of a coalition government including the NLF in Saigon."[72]

There is no doubt that Le Duan, Tran Van Tra, and their colleagues saw *flexible response* in this way by 1961 and thereafter. But this is manifestly *not* the way most U.S. leaders viewed their position or mission in Vietnam, and this misunderstanding had dire consequences for both sides. It meant that each side had articulated, ostensibly in response to the actions of the other (but fundamentally misunderstanding the approach of the other), a *strategy of attrition*, according to which each, in effect, waited for the other to run up a white flag, indicating it had had enough and was preparing to leave the field of battle. The objective of *both* Washington and Hanoi was this: to break the will of the other at the lowest possible rung on the ladder of escalation and to do so not by gaining an outright victory but by preventing the other from winning. Neither believed that the other's strategy was reactive and defensive. Thus each saw all actions taken by the other as threatening and escalatory. By the time the parties left the battlefield in Vietnam, millions would be dead, Vietnam would lay in ruins, and American society would suffer from intense internal conflict.

Finally, it must be recognized that Hanoi had to take the possible actions of China into its calculations, just as the United States did. No Vietnamese leader looked forward to a Chinese intervention in Vietnam, such as had occurred in Korea in 1950. Inevitably, in light of the long and difficult history between China and Vietnam, the Vietnamese leadership viewed such a prospect with horror—a Chinese invasion and occupation, rather than a liberation. China itself did not yearn for a confrontation with the United States but would nevertheless fight to protect its traditional buffer zone in northern Vietnam from U.S. occupation. This made Hanoi's calculations regarding the escalation of the war in the South all the more delicate. For if Washington were to escalate the war—to bomb near the Chinese border or to mount a land invasion north of the 17th parallel—Hanoi did not doubt that Beijing would intervene.

Bui Tin has recalled a conversation about this from December 1961: "Peking's main worry, as I heard Defense Minister General Luo Jui-ching explain during a visit to Vinh with his delegation, was that if we provoked the Americans into counter-attacks close to the Chinese border, they would have to intervene as had happened in Korea."[73] This was yet another reason, a very important reason, why, as Le Duan said, "How far we win, how far they lose, must be calculated and measured precisely." Unfortunately, calculations in Hanoi and in Washington would fail Le Duan's test for precision by a wide margin, principally because neither understood the motives of the other.

January 1961: Response to Special War in South Vietnam. Soon after the Geneva Conference ended in July 1954, it became clear that Ngo Dinh Diem, with advice and support from Washington, had no intention of participating in all-Vietnam elections in mid-1956, as mandated by the accords. Vietminh supporters and sympathizers south of the 17th parallel faced an agonizing choice: They could "regroup" to the North, where they would find political refuge, but that would require them to leave family, friends, and territory; or they could remain where they were and hope that the Diem regime would at some point agree to participate in the mandated elections. Some regrouped to the North. Most stayed in the South.

For those who stayed and remained committed to the cause of reunification, life became progressively more difficult. It mattered little whether one had communist sympathies or not, if one's admiration for Diem was deemed insufficient. Diem found it convenient to regard all people who disagreed with him as, more or less, "communists." He and his security chief–brother, Ngo Dinh Nhu, also found it expedient to take state-sponsored, punitive action against such people—action that became increasingly arbitrary and brutal.

It began with organized, stylized verbal abuse. In the summer of 1955, Diem launched his so-called Anti-Communist Denunciation Campaign. Citizens were classified into various groups according to their presumed degree of sympathy for the Vietminh cause. Those who were deemed in need of Diemist enlightenment—and there were many such people—were called before citizens' committees to foreswear their mistaken allegiance to communism and, often, to relate tales of communist atrocities they had seen or heard of or possibly invented for the occasion. Often, they were also required to throw various kinds of Vietminh symbols on the ground and stamp on them. In February 1956, according to the *Pentagon Papers*, "tens of thousands of Saigon citizens assembled to witness the 'conversion' of 2,000 former Vietminh cadres."[74] The author notes ominously, however, that "for many peasants the Anti-Communist Campaign was considerably more than theatrics."[75] For those unwilling to submit to such charades, life would become dangerous in the coming months and years.

As the prescribed time for the all-Vietnam elections passed in the summer of 1956, the Diem regime continued to persecute suspected Vietminh sympathizers. Hanoi's response was to commission Le Duan, who was still living in the South and was head of the Nam Bo Regional Committee (in the southernmost part of South Vietnam), to prepare a pamphlet called *The Path of Revolution in the South*. Although it acknowledged widespread persecution of cadres in the South by Diem's forces, it still did not yet condone violence as a path to revolution in the South. "Conflict," it stated, "was to be carried on by means of political activity." And although it acknowledged that many horrors had been perpetrated by U.S. "imperialists" and Diem's "feudalists," it still urged its loyalists not "to provoke war" with the enemy.[76]

In spite of Hanoi's refusal to authorize organized violence, however, apparently spontaneous uprisings were occurring frequently by mid-1957. These isolated events soon evolved into something known informally among the rebels as the "extermination of traitors" program, which involved the kidnapping and execution of local officials of the Saigon government. One objective of this campaign was to deter Diem's local officials from carrying out orders to execute, round up, incarcerate, or kill Vietminh sympathizers.[77] In the summer of 1958, under pressure from southern rebels, Hanoi gave its authorization to organize a base area in northern South Vietnam (Interzone 5) in which to train revolutionaries. A key event in the escalation to armed conflict was the already mentioned Fifteenth Plenum of the Party Central Committee in January 1959. Still, the Hanoi leadership appeared uncomfortable with its own decision to authorize violence. They waited until May 1959 to actually issue the new directive to its southern cadres.

At almost exactly the same time, Diem struck back with the most repressive—and most frightening—measures he had yet taken. On May 6, 1959, Diem signed Law 10/59, which, in an ironic bow to the former French colonial masters, inaugurated the era of death by beheading, as Diem's lieutenants traveled the countryside with mobile guillotines and platforms, looking for "communists."[78] Article 1 of Law 10/59 called for "sentence of death, and confiscation of the whole or part of his property" for anyone convicted of crimes ranging from murder to stealing farm implements and water buffalo. Article 3 proclaimed that anyone belonging to "an organization designed to help to prepare or to perpetrate" such crimes "will be subjected to the sentences provided for"—that is, they will also be beheaded. People charged with any of these myriad crimes who decided to turn over incriminating evidence to the state, however, could "enter a plea of extenuating circumstances." Article 16 announced: "The decisions of the special military court are not subject to appeal, and no appeal is allowed to the High Court." Finally, in Article 20 came the coup de grâce: "All legal provisions which are contrary to the present law [Law 10/59] are hereby repealed."[79]

The year 1959 was, according to Hanoi historian Tran Van Giau, "the darkest period" for the revolution in the South.[80] Gen. Tran Van Tra has been one of the very few high-ranking southern communists to publish his bitter feelings toward Hanoi during that dark hour.[81] Southerners, according to Tra, called the entire 1954–1959 period the time of "unilateral war, because we acted in accordance with the appeal of President Ho Chi Minh . . . to wage only political and peaceful struggles . . . not to resort to armed struggle."[82] Years later, Tra reflected on that time:

> In 1959, the most difficult period of the revolution in South Vietnam, the Ngo Dinh Diem puppet regime dragged the guillotine everywhere and carried out a bloody fascist repression. There was only one army—that of

Diem—holding sway on the battlefield, like a martial arts performer demonstrating his skills in a ring without an opponent.[83]

During this period, Tra recalls, "those who resorted to arms to defend themselves were disciplined by the Party for erratic behavior, while those who refrained from violence were captured and/or killed."[84] This continued, he said, until the spontaneous uprisings began, along with assassinations of Diem's local chiefs. This demonstrated, according to Tra, "that the situation had developed beyond the limits of self-restraint."[85] Elsewhere Tra wrote: "In my heart I still mourn the many comrades who fell in battle—with weapons in hand but not daring to fire—during that period, and mourn the many local movements that were drowned in blood."[86]

Why? Why did Hanoi adhere for so long to the line of "political struggle"? And why, from 1954–1959, did Hanoi expressly forbid southerners from taking up "armed struggle"—the use of violence? Principally because they feared *escalation*—that resort of violence would be *premature*, resulting in a protracted struggle that the United States might use to escalate to a "limited" war, that is, to a U.S.-Vietnam war. Timing and preparation were everything. To leaders in Hanoi, resort to violence should come at a time when their own strength was sufficient to finish off the South Vietnamese government of Diem quickly and completely, giving Washington insufficient time to intervene. That they held the line against armed struggle until 1959 only demonstrates how disciplined and determined they were to avoid provoking the United States prematurely or unnecessarily, thereby setting back the cause of revolution in the South by years or decades.[87]

November–December 1963: Preempting Protracted (Special) War. Hanoi closely followed the developments in South Vietnam throughout the summer of 1963. The Buddhist movement seemed to be playing into their hands, in the sense that the movement and Diem's crackdown only added to whatever measures the NLF forces might take to weaken Diem. Evidence suggests, however, that Hanoi did not anticipate the coup and assassination of Diem and Nhu in early November. Immediately following the coup, they escalated NLF activity by as much as 50 percent, and U.S. intelligence believed infiltration from the North rose accordingly. Then, as suddenly as it began, NLF-inspired incidents tapered off to a much lower level than before the coup, and Hanoi put feelers out to the junta of Gen. Duong Van Minh to determine its interest in a neutral solution. When the junta spurned the feelers, and after determining that the junta was fundamentally incompetent, leaders in Hanoi decided it was time to take stock and discuss how to proceed.[88]

But the events in Saigon provided only part of the backdrop for the drama that was unfolding in Vietnam. In addition, a struggle had been under way for some time in Hanoi for the soul of the Party. The outcome of the contest would greatly affect decisions made in Hanoi in the wake of the assassinations of Diem and Nhu. This dispute, which seems to have been extremely bitter, was rooted in the increasingly confrontational Sino-Soviet split—a development much feared by small socialist countries such as North Vietnam, which would at some point be forced to side with one big communist ally or the other.

U.S. military historian and former senior U.S. intelligence officer Gen. Philip Davidson has called the two warring factions in Hanoi the "North Vietnam Firsters" and the "South Vietnam Firsters."[89] The leaders of the first group were northerners: Truong Chinh and Vo Nguyen Giap. In their view, socialism needed a firmer base in the North *first*, before Hanoi would be in a position to ensure the success of the revolution in the South, the outcome of which seemed to them in 1963 still very much in doubt. These men were thought to have close ties to Moscow, which under Nikita Khrushchev had undertaken a policy of peaceful coexistence with the West, the United States in particular. (During the summer of 1963, for example, Washington and Moscow signed the Limited Test Ban Treaty, to great fanfare.) With regard to the pursuit of the "military struggle" in the South, the North Vietnam Firsters were the doves—cautious, wary of taking risks when so little was known about how or when the great superpower in Washington would respond.

The South Vietnam Firsters were led by a powerful triumvirate: Le Duan, the Party secretary; Gen. Nguyen Chi Thanh, commander of all communist forces in South Vietnam and, besides Giap himself, Hanoi's only *dai tuong* (General of the Army); and Le Duc Tho, the Party organizational secretary, who was influential in making high-level appointments. To these men, the liberation of South Vietnam was an emotional issue, just as it was for their fellow southerner, Gen. Tran Van Tra (who, it will be recalled, was commander of the southern B2 region of South Vietnam). Their home region had suffered through the abandonment by the northerners in Geneva in 1954 and the persecution of Diem after that. Their mission, or part of it, was to see to it that this did not happen again. They gave top priority, therefore, to completing the revolution in the South as soon as possible. Hardly by coincidence, all three had close ties to Beijing and were not above charging even revered revolutionaries like Giap with "revisionism," which in those days was a considerable epithet, connoting disinterest in promoting world revolution and far too much tolerance for the capitalist infidels in the West. As to the military struggle in the South, these men were the hawks—looking for opportunities to win a quick, decisive victory over Diem's forces before the United States could respond effectively.[90]

It was into this already emotionally charged atmosphere that the news arrived in early November 1963 that the Ngo brothers were dead and that a junta of their former officers was in charge of the Saigon government. There was obviously both risk and opportunity in the unexpected and chaotic situation in the South at that moment. It was at this critical moment in the war that the hawks stepped forward and took charge of the Ninth Party Plenum in December 1963. It was a stormy meeting, and it took more than a week to debate the ideological issues then tearing the world communist movement apart. It took several days longer to approve a draft resolution from the Politburo. Bui Tin has described what happened: "Le Duan inclined towards China and gradually carried the whole Politburo and Central Committee with him because nobody wanted to be labeled a 'revisionist' or 'anti-Party.' According to Confucian tradition, those in a weak position try to appease heaven. So Truong Chinh did not react in any way when the Politburo tended increasingly towards the Maoist view."[91] There would be no revisionism in the policy of North Vietnam toward the South now that Le Duan was running the war from Hanoi. And there would be no revisionism among the southern communists either, with Gen. Nguyen Chi Thanh commanding the armed struggle in the South.

As if to prove Bui Tin's point about Confucian tradition, Truong Chinh, the Moscow-tilting alleged revisionist, was selected to present the Plenum's hawkish, China-friendly recommendations. He summed up the policy: "It is time for the North to increase aid to the South; the North must bring into fuller play its role as a revolutionary base for the whole nation."[92] In plain terms: The People's Liberation Army Forces (PLAF) in the South, under Gen. Nguyen Chi Thanh, were about to launch an all-out offensive in an attempt to bring the southern revolution to a triumphant conclusion *before the United States was able to mobilize and intervene successfully*. For the time being, this effort would not involve any units of the North Vietnamese Army.

No doubt Le Duan, Nguyen Chi Thanh, and their supporters were excited about what they saw as a real possibility of finishing off the South Vietnamese government before the Americans could meaningfully respond. But in the resolution that derived from the Ninth Plenum, one senses that the South Vietnam Firsters—that is, the hawks—may have let their enthusiasm for a quick victory override their good sense. Le Duan, who seemed to have been intoxicated for some two years with the possibility for a neutral solution acceptable to the United States, suddenly seemed equally intoxicated with the possibility of winning *everything*—full reunification, and soon—without having to endure a transitional period for the working out of a neutral solution.

Throwing caution to the wind, the resolution is remarkably casual in its discussion of possible U.S. responses. Any sort of drastic U.S. reactions are, according to the resolution, "only remote possibilities . . . because the U.S. realizes that if she is bogged down in a large-scale and protracted war, she will be thrown into a very passive position in the world."[93] It pays only lip service to what was soon to become a cataclysmic reality for North Vietnam—so-called limited war, meaning an American war with North Vietnam: "However, we must always be vigilant," added the resolution, "and prepared to cope with the U.S. if she takes the risk of turning the war into a limited war."[94] What about a general war, possibly a nuclear war, if the conflict spreads beyond the borders of Vietnam? This is very unlikely, according to the resolution: "The possibility that a limited war in South Viet-Nam would turn into a world war is almost nonexistent because the purpose and significance of this war cannot generate conditions leading to a world war."[95]

In short, this document, nearly hallucinatory in its optimism, says: First, look for a quick victory in the South, where the situation is suddenly and unexpectedly advantageous. We will win before Washington knows what hit their allies in Saigon. *That is the principal goal: to preempt a protracted war involving the United States.* Second, it is possible that this won't happen, but we in Hanoi, being doctrinally of sound mind and schooled in the tough Chinese ways, will win any *protracted* war and we will win it within the parameters of "special" war, that is, before the Americans can escalate to a Washington-Hanoi war. Third, even if this scenario is too rosy, we must and will have the fortitude to defeat the United States in a direct military confrontation with U.S. combat forces in Vietnam, and we are prepared to have the Americans spread the war at least as far as North Vietnam. Fourth and finally, because the Vietnam War is of no great consequence outside of Southeast Asia, there is virtually no chance that any limited war the United States might wage will escalate to an unlimited, general, possibly nuclear confrontation involving Soviet or Chinese armed forces. "We were," as Bui Tin recalled that moment, "completely lightheaded in the firm belief that victory was ours."[96]

But Hanoi would *not* win a preemptive special war against the South Vietnamese government. Moreover, it would not win a protracted war against it simply because the ensuing stage of the conflict was *not* protracted—the "limited" American War began scarcely more than a year later. Hanoi would win that war, but it would take ten years, and they would pay an enormous price for fighting that mutual war of attrition. In fact, the entire preemptive strategy adopted by the southern hawks in December 1963 was based on a fundamental misunderstanding of Washington's view of escalation. Washington's approach, like Hanoi's, was reactive. In this sense, there was nothing and no one to preempt. By their actions, however, Hanoi's hawks inadvertently raised the level of hawkishness of the enemy in Washington. When Lyndon Johnson and his advisers examined the results of Hanoi's December 1963 decisions, they felt an urgent need to respond, which they did. Such were the fruits borne of Washington's ill-conceived removal of Ngo Dinh Diem in November 1963 and the equally ill-advised decisions taken at Hanoi's Ninth Plenum.

July 30–August 5, 1964: Response to U.S. Provocations. In Washington, some were offended by the effrontery of the August 2 attack by three patrol boats on the U.S. destroyer *Maddox*. Others were amazed at what seemed like the stupidity of a torpedo boat attacking a destroyer with nearby air support. Still others believed the attack opened up an opportunity to respond in a way that might boost the morale of the government in Saigon. Still others were dismayed, because they worried that any reprisal would only move Washington and Hanoi closer to a war that few wanted and might still be avoidable. All these reactions were accentuated on August 4, when another attack was believed to have occurred and which led to the U.S. reprisal bombings of August 5.

Hanoi's official chronology of military events of the war describes a mood very different from Washington's during the Tonkin Gulf affair. Between the lines of socialist bravado and the terseness of the chronology, one senses a nation under siege, whose sovereignty is being violated on a daily basis by their principal enemy, whose options for responding are limited. These are the relevant entries giving Hanoi's view of the events:

- On July 30 U.S. warships violated our coastal waters and fired on Hon Ngu Island (Nghe Tinh Province) 4 kilometers from the coast, and Hon Me Island (Thanh Hoa Province), 12 kilometers from the coast. (These were "34-A" operations.)

- On July 31 the U.S. destroyer *Maddox* entered the zone south of Con Co Island to begin its "tour" of reconnoitering and threatening along our coast.

- On July 31 and August 1 1964 U.S. airplanes based in Laos bombed the border defense post at Nam Can and Nong De Village in Nghe Tinh

Province, which were situated 7 to 20 kilometers from the Vietnamese-Laotian border. [These also were 34-A operations.]

- Faced with that situation, the local naval commanders adopted the policy of striking back at and punishing the pirates who violated our waters and our people's security.

- At noon on Sunday, August 2 1964, our navy's Squadron 3, consisting of three torpedo boats, was ordered to set out and to resolutely punish the "acts of piracy" of the U.S. imperialists, and to attack the destroyer *Maddox*, which had penetrated deeply into our coastal waters in the area between Hon Me Island and Lach Truong in Thanh Hoa Province.[97]

One gets the impression that the commander of Squadron 3 was weary of standing idly by while, as he saw it, U.S. ships and planes and South Vietnamese commandos routinely violated the sovereignty, not to say the dignity, of his country. He was fed up, and so he struck back with the only available weapons—his three torpedo boats. No one knows what assumptions, if any, he made about U.S. retaliation to his attacks.

Sources in Hanoi report that leaders in Hanoi found out about the episode in the same way that leaders in Washington did—via the telephone. The Hanoi leadership was not displeased. The leader of Squadron 3 was not punished for provoking the retaliatory U.S. air strike. On the contrary, one finds the following, curious entry in the official Hanoi history: "August 5 1964: The Vietnamese People's Navy makes the date of its first merit in defeating the U.S. navy and air force in the North as its tradition day."[98] Why? Apparently for luring the United States into making the reprisal air strike, during which the air defense forces were able to shoot down an A-4 Skyhawk piloted by Navy Lt. Everett Alvarez Jr. at Hon Gay on August 5, 1964.[99] In other words, for carrying out what was essentially a suicide mission against the *Maddox*, the torpedo boat operators—in fact the entire North Vietnamese navy—were honored.

Although the exact dates and details of the proceedings remain unclear, it appears that the Party Central Committee convened an extraordinary session during the week following the events in and around the Tonkin Gulf.[100] At the top of the agenda was a reevaluation, in light of more recent events, of a report delivered several months earlier by Gen. Nguyen Chi Thanh, the southern field commander, in which he had concluded that war with U. S. combat forces—so-called limited war—was *inevitable*.[101] As a result of that report, North Vietnamese Army units had been training for several months to head to the South, whenever the command was given. Now, the first northern-born unit, the 808th battalion, was dispatched to the South in early September; the 95th regiment headed south several weeks after that. Their objective: to provide the first phalanx of Hanoi's combat troops that would enable it to "achieve a decisive victory in the next one to two years."[102] Gen. Nguyen Chi Thanh would command the combined North Vietnamese and PLAF in the South. Gen. Tran Van Tra now became commander of PLAF forces.

The August 5 U.S. air strike on the North had thus induced the southern hawks in the leadership to begin to traverse the last crossroads on the way to a direct confrontation with the United States—a conflict that Gen. Nguyen Chi Thanh had long regarded as inevitable. In fact, the greater significance of the reprisal air strike of August 5 may have been this: The southerners were at last able to begin to bring the war home to the North, to begin to allow northerners to feel their vulnerability to U.S. military power—a feeling that had existed south of the 17th parallel for many years—and thus to build a psychological bridge from North to South that was damaged by the post-Geneva separation of the two Vietnams. Now northern soldiers were headed South to fight. Soon, perhaps, northern citizens would be at daily risk of bombing attacks. In the event of military victory over the United States—defined as closing off all U.S. options other than withdrawal—Vietnam might conceivably be unified by force of arms on terms dictated by the Hanoi leadership. A neutral solution might not be necessary.

One suspects, therefore, that although the attack on *Maddox* was not a pretext created by Hanoi to advance to the next rung on the ladder of escalation, the air strike on August 5 nevertheless served to silence skeptics, especially Gen. Vo Nguyen Giap, who doubted that PLAF forces were ready to confront U.S. forces.[103] It did so by convincing those who were not yet convinced that Washington had either already decided to plunge into a limited war—a U.S.-Vietnam war—or was on the brink of doing so. Having concluded thus, Hanoi then felt it had to "respond" to a decision it believed imminent or already taken in Washington. The Americans were proving to be more stubborn than some in Hanoi initially had predicted. So, it actively prepared for what might be, from the point of view of Hanoi, all-out war with the United States. But first Le Duan would try one more time to induce the United States to exit before a U.S.-Vietnam war began in earnest.

February 1965: Response to Limited War and the War of Destruction. The galvanizing effect of the August 5, 1964, U.S. air strike notwithstanding, Le Duan and his colleagues still paused rather than cross the road to open war with the United States. The dilemma they faced was acute. On the one hand, a limited war with the United States was not guaranteed to stay limited. If it did not—if it spread to other countries in Southeast Asia—Moscow would be furious with Hanoi for creating a situation with the potential for a U.S.-Soviet confrontation. In addition, if Washington were to carry the air war far to the North, or decided to invade North Vietnam above the 17th parallel, a Chinese intervention was very likely, and this was something everyone in Hanoi hoped to avoid. Who knew, really, what sort of war Washington had in mind?

On the other hand, the Hanoi leadership, Le Duan in particular, greatly feared what would happen if, in effect, they downgraded the war in the South, even temporarily. This specter was to haunt Hanoi's leaders until the end of the war: the fear of the catastrophic effect of giving the appearance of caving in to U.S. pressure, at any time, under any circumstances. Moreover, Hanoi's commitment to the southern cause by the end of 1964 was considerable and growing daily. So it was clear that something had to be done, something imaginative and forceful, yet something that would send a signal to Washington that a Washington-Hanoi war need not be inevitable. But what?

The clue as to how to proceed came to Le Duan via the battle of Binh Gia, forty miles southeast of Saigon, during December and January 1964–1965. Gen. Nguyen Chi Thanh and Gen. Tran Van Tra, their PLAF forces newly equipped with modern mortars, rifles, and rocket launchers, attacked units of the South Vietnamese Army at Binh Gia on December 5, 1964. The battle ebbed and flowed for several weeks, but when the dust had settled, PLAF forces had more than held their own.[104] Le Duan, perhaps prematurely, referred to the battle of Binh Gia as "a small Dien Bien Phu," recalling the climactic battle with the French in May 1954.[105]

In a letter to Gen. Nguyen Chi Thanh in early February 1965, Le Duan explained to his southern commander his last-ditch plan to head off a direct confrontation with the United States based on the success at Binh Gia. The plan had these elements:

- Quicken the pace of infiltration to the South. Binh Gia proved that PLAF were competent when adequately armed. But there were too few of them at present to overcome the South Vietnamese army.

- Defeat the South Vietnamese forces by drawing them out of the cities and destroying them.

- Prepare a countrywide uprising all over the South to occur on the heels of the annihilation of the South Vietnamese forces.

- Encourage Washington to withdraw in the face of the South Vietnamese collapse by proposing a neutral solution in Saigon that is acceptable to both sides.

- Hold the NLF forces in the countryside until a neutral solution is reached.

- Finally, after agreement is reached on a neutral solution, bring key elements of the NLF into the cities from the countryside, to ensure that the NLF's program is put into effect and that the Saigon government is progressive and friendly to Hanoi.[106] Such a neutralist coalition government was projected to last a minimum of ten to fifteen years.[107]

Le Duan admitted to Nguyen Chi Thanh that the odds of this plan succeeding were unknown. He quoted Napoleon: "Let's act, then see."[108] It is not known whether Le Duan's letter was delivered to Nguyen Chi Thanh before or after the NLF attack at Pleiku on February 7.

Gen. Dang Vu Hiep, current deputy chief of the general political department of the Vietnamese Army and a participant in the June 1997 Hanoi conference on the war, was a young officer of the People's Army of Vietnam (PAVN, or North Vietnamese Army) in Interzone 5, near Pleiku, on February 7, 1965. He revealed at the conference that contrary to U.S. assumptions at the time those who planned the attack on Pleiku were simply midlevel officers like himself, looking for advantage over the South Vietnamese troops after the end of the Tet holiday cease-fire. They did not know that McGeorge Bundy was in Saigon at the time or that Soviet Premier Alexei Kosygin was in Hanoi. Subsequently, he and others confirmed that the NLF cadres who carried out the attack did not even know for sure that any Americans were present at the site of the Pleiku attack. In any case, the so-called targeting of Americans, according to Gen. Dang Vu Hiep, had nothing to do with the planning for the attack. The objective, he said, was to destroy the South Vietnamese forces in the area or get them to defect, in order to split South Vietnam in two and thereby facilitate the collapse of the Saigon government. (See the third section, below, for the dialogue that these revelations generated.)

Allen Whiting, then the director of research and analysis for the Far East at the U.S. State Department, had forecast before Bundy departed for Saigon that the NLF would attempt to launch an assault on an American installation during the visit.[109] In fact, Whiting and his associates predicted that the attack would occur at one of three bases: Tan Son Nhut, Bien Hoa, or Pleiku.[110] Moreover, according to Whiting, the reprisal air strike following the attack on Pleiku (FLAMING DART I) was *preplanned* on the basis of his intelligence analysis and forecast.[111] Normally, according to Whiting, one would expect heavy NLF activity immediately following the Tet holiday cease-fire. This is one reason why some in the State Department urged Bundy to postpone his visit until the post-Tet situation stabilized. In any case, due to "preprogramming," within fourteen hours of the attack on Pleiku forty-nine navy jets from the U.S. aircraft carriers *Coral Sea* and *Hancock* bombed a guerrilla training base at Dong Hoi, forty miles north of the border between North and South.[112]

The NLF attack on Pleiku seemed to U.S. officials to be confirmation not only of the forecast of the attack but also of the rationale behind the prediction—that Americans would be targeted in order to drive home the point to the Bundy team that Washington should pick up and go home. But according to Gen. Dang Vu Hiep, who was there, this conclusion is absurd, given the primitive command-and-control arrangements of the NLF operating in the Central Highlands around Pleiku. According to General Hiep, units were often out of touch with their base areas for long periods. And even when they were in touch communications were minimal, for reasons of security. This is confirmed in a general way by Bui Tin, who has reported that North-South communication during this period was almost nonexistent. (Bui Tin lost touch with his sister in the South for six years and only heard at last that she was alive via a mutual contact in Paris.) He also points out that in Hanoi itself contact of any kind with the outside world during 1964–1965 was rare with but one dubious exception: "the so-called fraternal countries which sent us delegations."[113]

Thus, if Hanoi did not order the attack at Pleiku, and given the speed of the reprisal, the FLAMING DART I attack on North Vietnam *had* to seem like a pretext to North Vietnamese leaders. What else could it be? Then on February 11, ostensibly in reprisal for an attack the day before at Qui Nhon, came FLAMING DART II, a heavier bombing raid than its predecessor, lasting three hours, also preplanned. In Hanoi, this was viewed as just another pretext. On February 13, President Johnson authorized ROLLING THUNDER which, as noted, would continue for three and a half years. The North Vietnamese would call this "the war of destruction," which they would maintain was unprovoked—simply evidence of Washington's determination to destroy North Vietnam. Hard on the heels of the initiation of the bombing of the North, the first U.S. Marines arrived in Danang in March. Once again, the plans of Le Duan and his colleagues to preempt U.S. escalation were overtaken by events.

In Hanoi, the Party Central Committee held its Eleventh Plenum, March 25–27, 1965. Even at this point, however, the leadership did not choose to cross the path and openly admit a state of war existed with the United States. The resolution approved by the Plenum hedged its bets. It held that the enemy's strategy had changed to "a high-level special war with some characteristics of limited war."[114] The drafter of the resolution, presumably Le

Duan, even speculated that wily leaders in Washington were expanding the war, to include the bombing of the North and the ground war in the South, in order to enhance their bargaining position regarding a neutral solution in Saigon. It never occurred to them that the real rationale for U.S. activity might actually be the one given by President Johnson: reprisals for killing Americans. In fact, leaders in Hanoi could not imagine Washington making *reprisals* for anything. In this respect, their view of the enemy was the mirror image of the Americans' view of themselves—and equally erroneous.

A Dialogue in Real Time: Escalation

DUAL STRATEGIES OF ATTRITION

One of the most interesting aspects of the February 1998 conference in Hanoi was the peripatetic dialogue of the military historians on each team. Col. Quach Hai Luong served during the war as an antiaircraft officer in the North, rising eventually to command the batteries in the Hanoi area. He is now deputy director of the Institute for Strategic Studies in Hanoi, the research arm of the Vietnamese Army. His colleague was Col. Herbert Y. Schandler, a former U.S. Army officer who served two tours of duty in Vietnam, first as an adviser in the pacification program, later as an infantry commander. Colonel Schandler is now a professor in the Department of Grand Strategy at the National Defense University in Washington, D.C., and the author of several books on the Vietnam War.

"The colonels," as they were called at the conference, sometimes exchanged views in the conference sessions themselves. At other times, they left the sessions with an interpreter from each side and went off alone to discuss issues of mutual interest. Still other conversations occurred over lunch and dinner. (The conversations were audio-taped.)

The following excerpted dialogue begins with striking evidence of how—even today—Americans and Vietnamese lack a common set of terms to begin sorting out the war. Colonel Quach explains to Colonel Schandler that the key strategic concept on which Vietnamese and Americans disagreed was whether Vietnam was one or two countries. Behind this commonplace observation lay some interesting implications. Schandler asks Quach whether they saw the war in the South as a civil war. His reply: the Vietnamese do not have the concept of "civil war."

The most unexpected intervention comes from the two interpreters: Le Hong Truong, from Hanoi's Institute for International Relations, asks permission at one point to relate the story of a class he took while he was a student in the United States; his point is reinforced by Kathy Le, who is from the Watson Institute at Brown University. Young as they are, they already understand the reasons why the bombing of North Vietnam strengthened, rather than weakened, the will of the Hanoi government and its people.

Finally, the colonels find their way to the issue of "reprisal" bombing by the United States and finish in a moment of dual insight: Each side found itself in a war of attrition that it did not, at the time, fully comprehend.

❖

Col. Quach Hai Luong: I want to ask you: What do you think the American objectives were in Vietnam?

Col. Herbert Schandler: Our objectives in Vietnam, as stated by our various presidents, were the following. First, to establish an independent, noncommunist South Vietnam whose people had the ability to choose their own leaders and form of government. A second objective was to *convince* North Vietnam—not to defeat or crush or obliterate North Vietnam—but to *convince* North Vietnam not to impose its will on the South by means of military force. We had no burning desire even to harm North Vietnam in any way. We just wanted to demonstrate to you that you could not win militarily in the South.

Col. Quach Hai Luong: But Colonel Schandler, if I may say so, this was a critical difference between your understanding of the situation and our understanding of it. Let me put it this way: your fundamental assumption is that Vietnam was two distinct—two rightfully independent—countries. On that basis, your objectives and strategies follow. We did not make that distinction. We saw only one country. All our strategies were based on this basic premise: that Vietnam is one country, unfortunately and artificially divided in two. Our war was for the purpose of protecting our independence and maintaining our national unity.

Col. Herbert Schandler: How did the special war strategy—with U.S. advisers posted in Special Forces camps in the mountains—affect the DRV [i.e., North Vietnam] and the NLF? Did you attack that specifically?

Col. Quach Hai Luong: Oh yes. We had to. But I still have the feeling we are talking about tactics, not national strategies. From our point of view, the big picture was like this: In the South, Vietnamese were being used to resist

Vietnamese. Vietnamese were fighting Vietnamese. That was the essence, as we saw it, of your special war strategy.

The French had also used this strategy some eighty years before. At that time, the French were, like you later on, dispersed around the country in small numbers. They also used the forces of a puppet regime to oppress the people.

Col. Herbert Schandler: I see. So in your view, the American advisory effort was directed, in large part, at making "our" Vietnamese—the forces of the South Vietnamese government in Saigon—more effective at fighting other Vietnamese.

Col. Quach Hai Luong: Yes. Exactly. You used Vietnamese to fight against other Vietnamese.

Col. Herbert Schandler: So are you saying that you saw the conflict right from the beginning as a civil war? I mean, we saw it that way too, only from the other side. We were trying to assist an ally which was trying to suppress a violent rebellion. But you were assisting the other side, which was trying to overthrow the existing government, right?

Col. Quach Hai Luong: No. This is the rhetoric of other countries. We are not familiar with "civil war." In our understanding, we have never had what you call a "civil war"—I mean, with Vietnamese rebels rising up of their own accord against a Vietnamese government of the whole country. This has never happened.

Col. Herbert Schandler: Sure, but after all, it *was* a situation in which Vietnamese were fighting other Vietnamese. During the entire period before 1965, when U.S. combat troops got involved, that was the situation.

Col. Quach Hai Luong: But we do not use that concept of "civil war" to describe that situation.

Col. Herbert Schandler: What concept do you use—reunification?

Col. Quach Hai Luong: Our understanding was as follows: You—the United States—were trying to implement a special war strategy, in which the Americans did not get directly involved in the fighting. We call this a war that used Vietnamese against Vietnamese, not a "civil war."

Col. Herbert Schandler: I see. So you saw the Vietnamese we were advising purely as "puppets" of the American government. Is that right?

Col. Quach Hai Luong: In a sense, but not exactly. A better image might be this: The forces of the Saigon government at that time were more like something the U.S. pulled out of its sleeve. [Gestures, as if pulling something from far up his sleeve. Laughter.]

.   .   .

Col. Herbert Schandler: Do you think the war might have ended more favorably to the Americans if we had brought in a lot more combat troops, and maybe attempted to take the land war north of the 17th parallel?

Col. Quach Hai Luong: No. In that case, I believe you would have lost the war sooner.

Col. Herbert Schandler: You do? Why?

Col. Quach Hai Luong: Because you would have done exactly what the French had done years before. You would have spread yourselves out widely and put yourselves in an unfavorable position. You see, just as we saw Vietnam as one country, we saw the battlefield as *one and only one* battlefield. Now, the U.S. had tremendous military strength, of course. We could not deny this. If you concentrated your strength in only a few areas—like the French did, at the last, in the three major cities—then you would have an advantage in those areas.

But if the war is a *war of attrition*, which the war between our countries definitely was, and you have to maintain your forces all over the country, then we will last longer than you. We know this. We have not the slightest doubt about this. Military strategists always try to avoid being spread out in a war of attrition, which is, in a way, a Vietnamese type of war.

Col. Herbert Schandler: But suppose we had also concentrated our bombing, early in the war, on critical targets in the North—targets closely associated with your war effort. Would that have made a difference?

Col. Quach Hai Luong: But how would you know where such targets are located? How would you know where to send your pilots?

Col. Herbert Schandler: I think we had reasonably good intelligence from aerial reconnaissance and other sources on where your physical war resources were located. We held back on the bombing primarily because we wanted to try to give you an incentive to halt your assistance to the war in the South. And of course, we were also concerned about the possibility of a Chinese intervention, if the air war in the North was carried too close to the Chinese border.

Col. Quach Hai Luong: I understand that there are Americans who believe that early, massive air strikes on the North would have won the war for the U.S. Maybe this would have been a good strategy for you in World War II, against heavily industrialized countries like Germany and Japan. But when you are bombing an almost totally agricultural country like Vietnam, then your bombs just hit the ground and kill a little rice. In the 1960s, our country ran much like it had run 100 or 500 years before. Not entirely, of course. But even today, we are more than 80 percent rural.

Col. Herbert Schandler: I understand that. But as you know, our strategy for the air war was based on the belief that we could destroy the will of the people in North Vietnam to continue to support the war in the South.

Mr. Le Hong Truong: May I intervene? When I studied in the United States, I took a course in which my professor taught the Vietnam War as a case study. He said that if the U.S. had bombed more aggressively, more actively, the U.S. might have succeeded in breaking the will of the people. So I stood up and had to disagree with him. I had to explain: No, it did not work like that. The more you bombed, the more the people wanted to fight you.

Ms. Kathy Le: And at the June 1997 conference, several of the Vietnamese participants compared the U.S. bombing of North Vietnam to the German air raids on London during World War II. They pointed out that the bombing only served to strengthen the resolve of the British to fight.

Col. Quach Hai Luong: You see? These two young people have already answered your question. [Laughter.]

Col. Herbert Schandler: Yes. It bodes well for future. [Laughter.] Let me ask about the reprisals. The signal we were trying to send to Hanoi was this: If you increase your participation in the war in the South, we will bomb you. So if you want us to stop the bombing, all you have to do is decrease your support for the war in the South. We said that, in effect, *you* controlled the level of bombing by your level of support for the NLF in the South.

Col. Quach Hai Luong: Let me give you our understanding of your "reprisal" bombing you have mentioned. When you were losing in the South, you bombed the North with more intensity. We noticed this. Of course, we had to alter our tactics somewhat, moving things around and so on. But it did not affect our *strategy*. You see, we understood *your* message, turned it around, and used it against you. Every time you bomb the North, we said, we know we are succeeding in the South. More than this: Every time *you* escalate the bombing in the North, in our understanding, we in the North are forcing you to use resources that you cannot expend in the South.

Let me put it another way, using your concept of "reprisal." We said, in a way, that *you* controlled the amount of support we would give to our friends in the South. How? By the level of your bombing. By the use of your troops. If you stop bombing and withdraw your troops, we will be pleased to cease assistance to the South. But that is the only way you can get us to do it.

Col. Herbert Schandler: It really was a war of attrition all the way around, wasn't it? We both said, "We'll stop if you only quit first."

Col. Quach Hai Luong: Until you quit. Then we stopped.

Col. Herbert Schandler: Yes.

January 1961: Civil War/Special War

The agenda for the June 1997 conference was worked out jointly between the U.S. and Vietnamese teams. Even so, there was a tendency for the Americans to "lapse" and forget that the confrontation between the United States and North Vietnam did not begin with President Kennedy's inaugural on January 20, 1961. As the Vietnamese participants emphasized, there was a long history of increasing hostility, going back at least to World War II. One particularly important piece of that history for people in Hanoi was their experience with, and views of, Ngo Dinh Diem, whom the Americans installed in Saigon in mid-1954. Although Kennedy would ultimately choose not to intervene in the chain of events leading to Diem's assassination in November 1963, Kennedy's own history of relations with Diem tended to emphasize Diem's courage in heroically trying to build the nation of South Vietnam under very difficult circumstances. Several members of the U.S. delegation in June 1997 had known Diem personally and had found him difficult yet fundamentally committed to an independent South Vietnam.

Several members of the Vietnamese team thought it might be useful if the Americans were enlightened as to other views of Diem and his brother, Ngo Dinh Nhu, the head of security until he was killed along with Diem. What evolved was akin to a Quaker meeting, with various Vietnamese participants offering their views, briefly stated, of a man they regarded as a war criminal. Their task was made delicate by the fact they that were sitting directly across from several of Diem's former American colleagues. Gen. Nguyen Dinh Uoc leads off, followed by Dinh Nho Liem. The final excerpt is from Luu Doan Huynh. This was the message: Diem was evil; he betrayed the Vietnamese people; and it was profoundly liberating when, by virtue of decisions taken in Hanoi in 1959 and 1960, the southern colleagues of our panelists were given the right to defend themselves, to fight back, to begin to reunify the country.

❖

Gen. Nguyen Dinh Uoc: At the end of 1956, we could have attacked Saigon, because it refused to carry out the Geneva Accords of 1954 on Indochina. At that point, Saigon could not really defend itself. But North Vietnam wanted to avoid war. In fact, we continued to try to consult with Saigon and the U.S. in an effort to find a means for reunification. We avoided war between 1955 to 1959, but there was horrible suffering due to repression by Ngo Dinh Diem. In the Mekong River Delta, nine out of every ten resistance cadres were killed. Over 90,000 people were captured, put in jail, and interrogated.

Dinh Nho Liem: To carry out the American policy, Diem did not follow the Geneva Accords. Diem prevented, with American backing, a national referendum to unify the country. This was contrary to the wishes of the Vietnamese people who, after so many years of fighting the French, were angered that Diem would now cut their country into two parts. Also, Diem was an autocrat of the old sort. A half-dozen or so of his brothers and other family members held most of the power in Saigon and in the central and southern parts of Vietnam. He not only favored people with connections to his family, but he was also a zealous Catholic who oppressed other religions and other groups. Diem, therefore, was not well-liked even by many of those who benefited from his favors, much less the people in the countryside, whom Diem seldom saw. Diem did not have a foundation within the people. When the strategic hamlets were organized, then the people of the South began living in conditions that were "hell on earth." Let's not mince words. They were prisons, and bad prisons, at that.

After five years of struggling for peace legally, according to the Geneva

Accords, the people of South Vietnam could no longer tolerate Diem's treatment of them. As we heard from other speakers, the NLF was formed so the
people could defend themselves—in an organized way, could defend themselves. After that, the result was more or less inevitable, at least as far as
Diem was concerned. The people would never tolerate him again. If the
American government did not replace Diem, then the people would overthrow Diem. My feeling is that even if he would have been around for a few
more months—or even a year or two—he did not have the power to survive.
One way or the other, he would be gone.

Luu Doan Huynh: In the 1950s—the late 1950s—when Diem and Nhu
were going around killing all our people, the southern resistance got very
discouraged and angry because of the policy of peaceful reunification. It was
the new line, embodied in Resolution 15 of 1959, which strengthened our
unity, which was an essential prerequisite for victory. With Resolution 15,
and the organizing of the NLF, it became okay for them to fight—to fight for
their rights and independence, because this is the only way they have to get
rid of Diem. That was in 1959.

NOVEMBER–DECEMBER 1963:
THE SIGNIFICANCE OF DIEM'S ASSASSINATION

In August 1963, and later, Robert McNamara, Robert Kennedy, General
Taylor, and several others opposed those in Washington and in the Saigon
embassy who favored giving the green light to the generals around Diem who
wanted to overthrow him. McNamara's views did not prevail, however, and
Diem and his brother, Nhu, were assassinated in early November 1963.*
During his first visit to Hanoi, in November 1995, McNamara had some conversations with Vietnamese scholars and officials who informally confirmed
something he had long suspected: that overthrowing Diem had not only been
a mistake because, as it happened, his successors were an incompetent and
fractious lot; but, in addition, Diem's death undercut plans for a neutral
solution—and a relatively peaceful transition in Saigon, which Hanoi
favored. These plans were developed on the assumption that Diem's government would survive for a year or so longer than it did. Alas, the Hanoi

---

*In his book *In Retrospect*, McNamara points out that those who opposed the overthrow of Diem were as
much at fault in relation to it as were those who supported it. After the August 24 cable to Lodge from the
State Department, which initiated the coup, there was ample time for those who opposed it to stop it
before it occurred on November 2.

government, like the Diem government, misjudged the potential of the Buddhist crisis of mid-1963 to speed Diem's demise.

At the June 1997 conference, McNamara restates the question for the record he put privately to some Vietnamese in November 1995: Would Diem have requested, or would he have accepted, U.S. combat troops in South Vietnam in anything like the numbers that later arrived? If the answer is no, then a major missed opportunity may have been identified. Nguyen Co Thach responds immediately and angrily that the only regret he has about Diem is that he died "too late." He restates his response in English, so as not to be misunderstood.

It was a question that was, even after all the intervening years, more sensitive in Hanoi than the Americans realized. (But as one U.S. observer pointed out at the time: "General Sherman is still not well-loved in Georgia.")

❖

Robert McNamara: I want to go back to this issue of the assassination of Diem. There is no question in my mind but what the U.S. was implicated in the coup and the ultimate assassination of Diem. Nothing I have to say is meant to deny this. I think it is a fact that we were culpable.

But I understand—and I have been told by some of the Vietnamese present here today—and I believe that there is a record which I have never seen, a document in Hanoi which indicates that several of the leaders of North Vietnam, including Ho Chi Minh, were deeply distressed by the coup and assassination of Diem? Why? Because they believed that, for whatever else Diem was, he was also a nationalist. As a Vietnamese nationalist, therefore, he would not have wished to yield the control of his country to the U.S., which is essentially what happened when we placed 500,000 troops there. The belief, therefore—again, I have only heard this in conversation here in Hanoi, I have never seen the documents—the belief, therefore, is that he never would have requested, nor would he have accepted, large numbers of U.S. combat troops. I understand this was appreciated by many of the leaders in Hanoi and that they were very distressed by the coup and the assassination. Why? Because they foresaw what was to follow—that the Americans would, in a sense, take over, and that the war would escalate beyond anything that would have been conceivable, had the American troops not arrived in large numbers. I understand that there is documentary evidence of that, and I'd like this confirmed.

Nguyen Co Thach: We were disappointed because the assassination was so late. Too late. Okay?

Robert Brigham: We have for some time in the United States had access—limited access, but access nevertheless—to documents from the Party Plenum that took place in December 1963, one month after the assassination of Diem and Nhu. My reading of those documents suggests that there was concern because Diem's own officers brought about his demise and that the "objective conditions" had not yet been met in the South for Diem's removal from power. As Mr. McNamara has stated, there appears to have been deep concern in Hanoi. After all, if Diem's own officers had brought him down, what did that say about the course of the war in the South?

In other words—this is my interpretation, and the interpretation of several others—Diem was an enemy, but he was a useful enemy to the revolution in many ways. He not only helped to push people into the southern cadres, but you knew who you were dealing with in Diem. The uncertainty following his death—brought about not by the revolution but by his subordinates—must have produced considerable consternation in Hanoi. That's the way we've read the documents that we have from that Party Plenum in December of '63. Minister Thach, I wonder if you would speak to this.

Nguyen Co Thach: I already answered that. We were quite saddened because he died too late.

Nguyen Khac Huynh: I can say a few things about Diem and Nhu concerning the issues you have just raised. It seems to me that there are important issues on which the perceptions of U.S. researchers differ from ours.

First, the U.S. analysts, including Mr. McNamara, express regret about the death of Diem and Nhu. They are of the opinion that if they had remained alive, they would not have requested U.S. troops, in large numbers, to take part in the war. But I agree with Ambassador Dinh Nho Liem that the days of Diem and Nhu were numbered and could not be prolonged. At that time, we saw clearly that Diem and the entire Ngo family would not be able to survive much longer. Our view was that even if the Saigon government did not overthrow them with Washington's backing, the Saigon military would have done it even without a green light from Washington. On the other hand, eventually the NLF and the people's movement in the South would soon have become strong enough to topple the Diem government. Therefore, the question posed by Mr. McNamara as to whether Diem would have requested U.S. combat troops to fight the war in the South—this question is not very significant. Whether U.S. troops came or not did not depend on whether Diem and Nhu remained alive or not.

In February 1998, far from the press and the observers who filled the Hanoi conference room the previous June, a much smaller and lower-profile group of U.S. and Vietnamese participants took up the issue once more. After Robert Brigham reposes the question first asked by Robert McNamara in June, the Vietnamese respond in a qualitatively different way. Luu Doan Huynh says that this is history and, no matter what one thinks of Diem, one needs to speak one's mind about the reality of the time. Luu Doan Huynh says that his government may not fully agree with his view *but*: Diem's assassination was, in fact, a very unfortunate event and was viewed with alarm in Hanoi. Why? Because it greatly raised the odds of a direct American intervention, a subject that was taken up at the Ninth Plenum of the Party in December 1963. The decision: to try to win the war against the Saigon government before the Americans could mount a successful intervention. They failed, and both sides got the war neither side wanted.

Luu Van Loi then turns the question on its head. He says that possibly the greatest missed opportunity to head off the war occurred just *after* Diem and Nhu were removed. Hanoi, he implies, tried its best to interest the Saigon junta and, indirectly, Washington as well, in a neutral solution then and there. But the United States refused and thus missed what, in retrospect, was a major opportunity to avoid the oncoming war.

❖

Luu Doan Huynh: Now, following the Geneva Agreement in 1954 we applied the line of peaceful reunification to all our dealings with Diem. This was our main objective—to secure Diem's agreement to hold consultations—first—and thereafter his cooperation in holding the elections. To this end, we were prepared to give Diem and some of his colleagues important posts in the all-Vietnam government. Early in 1955, officials of the DRV Foreign Ministry were given oral briefings on the possibility that Diem might become vice chairman of a unified Vietnam. You know very well how he behaved, and so we had to fight with some people in the NLF who tried, as you know, to assassinate him. But their efforts were unsuccessful.

But through 1962, Diem's harsh persecution paradoxically helped us to rally broad segments of the people for the NLF. Also, we could see increasing contradictions between Diem and the U.S. In particular, we noticed Diem's refusal to toe the U.S. line in many respects, including the issue of the use of U.S. combat troops in the war in South Vietnam. Diem rejected these troops, even under heavy pressure from the U.S.

Diem was very complicated. Through his behavior from 1954 to around 1960, one could see that while relying heavily on the U.S., and opposing communism in an uncompromising way, Diem essentially represented narrow and extremist nationalism coupled with autocracy and nepotism. Diem dictated *everything*, both in the country and inside his family. As a result we found that the longer Diem stayed in power the better it was for the struggle for liberation in South Vietnam. This was not only because his autocratic and brutal behavior increased the ranks of the revolution but also because he rejected direct U.S. military intervention for a long time. This was very helpful to the NLF—very helpful—because their goal was, at the right moment, to seize a decisive victory and preempt U.S. direct military intervention. That was the goal, and Diem paradoxically helped the NLF to reach it.

(Now that this history is in the distant past, then I can tell you some things—what I know or think, which do not necessarily represent the views of some other colleagues.)

You may ask: What were we going to do with Diem if this scenario had actually happened? I think that if Diem could have helped to bring about such a happy outcome, a gradual victory of the revolution, and no big war with the U.S., he would have made an important contribution. In that case, I think he would have been offered a place in the new government. His presence would also have given a face-saving solution to the U.S. and thus have made the U.S. more amenable to a neutral solution in South Vietnam. In the long run, Diem might have continued to have a place but would not play a decisive role in the government.

But Diem's overthrow and death in the coup of November 1963 increased the danger of U.S. direct military intervention. This danger was emphasized and discussed in the Resolution of Plenum 9 of the Central Committee, in December 1963.

Luu Van Loi: By 1963, the White House could no longer ignore the crisis Diem's tactics and style had created. They decided, eventually, that they must get rid of Nhu or Diem (or both) in order to stabilize the situation in the South. There were many different formulas suggested for doing this. Finally it was suggested that they should try to separate Nhu from Diem—essentially to get rid of Nhu, who at that time ran the brutal internal security apparatus in South Vietnam. But this proved to be difficult. Nothing had been done by the time of the Buddhist crisis and repression in Hue in the summer of 1963. That was the "final straw." Diem was proving to be an embarrassment to the U.S. and he therefore had to go.

Now, what impact did the assassination of Diem and Nhu have on the course of events in the South? It led to a series of crises, as one coup followed another, throughout 1964. From the other side, the NLF called on all parties in the South to establish a coalition government—immediately! The settlement in Laos in 1962 was to have been the model.

Luu Doan Huynh: Excuse me, yes: The solution, at least the temporary solution, was to have been an entente.

Luu Van Loi: Yes, exactly. But the generals in charge in Saigon, following orders from Washington, rejected all overtures from the NLF, from de Gaulle, and even from some people within the U.S. government.[115] Thus did the U.S. miss an opportunity opened up by the death of Diem and Nhu. This is how I see it: The death of Diem and Nhu *created* an opportunity, a very realistic opportunity, for a coalition government, then and there, if only the U.S. had forced their South Vietnamese generals to come to the table. The NLF was ready and eager to do so at that point. With Diem, a coalition government seemed to many like some kind of fantasy, because of Diem's autocratic tendencies. But now, in the immediate aftermath of Diem's ouster, there was an opportunity. But you missed it.

JULY–AUGUST 1964: PROVOCATIONS IN THE TONKIN GULF

On August 4, 1964, officials in Washington spent nearly twelve continuous hours trying to determine if the so-called second attack of North Vietnamese torpedo boats had occurred in the Gulf of Tonkin. If it had, President Johnson was ready to respond with a reprisal air strike. In the conversation that follows from the June 1997 conference, Gen. Nguyen Dinh Uoc, director of Hanoi's Institute of Military History, answers that the alleged attack on August 4 did *not* occur! His source: Former Defense Minister Vo Nguyen Giap, who he says had consulted his personal diaries just to be sure and who had made the same statement to Robert McNamara during their meeting in Hanoi in November 1996. In the most obvious sense, therefore, this constitutes a missed opportunity, since the U.S. air strike was predicated on the assumption that, as Robert McNamara said in his memoir, *In Retrospect*, the second attack was "probable but not certain."[116]

Yet another question—one that went unasked in Washington in August 1964—turns out to have implications that are in some ways more interesting than the first. McNamara asks it in his memoir: Whether there were one or two attacks by North Vietnamese boats, was the U.S. reprisal strike justified? His answer: "Probably."[117] But now the conference is told by General Uoc that the attack was not ordered by the central authority in Hanoi but rather by the commander of the torpedo boat squadron in the Tonkin Gulf. Since the reprisal air strike was supposed to send a signal to Hanoi not to repeat such actions as the attack on U.S. ships, the reprisal, in retrospect, was clearly a mistake as originally conceived. In fact, Hanoi could not read the signal, because it did not order the attack. Leaders in Washington, it seems, were projecting their own, highly centralized approach to command and control onto one of the world's poorest, least-developed countries. These issues are discussed in the following excerpt.

◆

Robert McNamara: The first question I have is: Was there an attack on the *Maddox* on August 2, 1964? The answer to that is almost surely "yes." I say this because I have a fragment of a North Vietnamese shell that I took off the deck of the *Maddox*, so I think there had to be an attack. But I'd like this on the record. I see my Vietnamese colleagues nodding agreement. Okay, We'll accept that.

Now, the more important question, the one that is very interesting to me, and it relates to the discussion this morning, is: Who ordered it? Was it a local commander, or did the order come from a central authority?

Gen. Nguyen Dinh Uoc: Now, as to whether or not the North Vietnamese attacked the American ship *Maddox* on August 2: Gen. Vo Nguyen Giap said that one of the responsibilities of the Vietnamese navy in Thanh Hoa was to guard against any vessels violating the national waters of Vietnam. And if there were violations, the navy had the right to attack in order to protect those waters. That was the general policy adopted by the central authority to defend the country's sea coast, at the time. It was not a decision made centrally. That is the answer.

Robert McNamara: Thank you for a very clear answer. It points to something that certainly we did not understand or anticipate at the time. . . . There was a far greater decentralization of authority and command with respect to the North Vietnamese military than we understood at the time. I think it's an important point, because it now seems as if we may have drawn unwarranted conclusions, based on our misunderstanding of your command-and-control arrangements.

Second question: Did the presumed second attack occur on August 4— on the *Turner Joy* and the *Maddox*? General Giap said no. I wonder if you can confirm this, on the record of this conference.

Gen. Nguyen Dinh Uoc: I will give you my opinion. Several days ago, when I met with him, Gen. Vo Nguyen Giap did say very clearly that the August 4 "incident" positively did not occur. And the general also said that his private journal testifies that the August 4 "incident" did not occur. And that is the truth.

Gen. W. Y. Smith: On this question of decentralization of authority: Were these sorts of orders in effect right from the beginning, or was there some point in the '63–64 period where your orders were changed to grant greater authority to local commanders?

Nguyen Co Thach: You must keep in mind that our economy is an agricultural economy, not an industrial economy, nor did it develop like the U.S. economy. Our economy is very basic, even primitive. We now think the Vietnamese economy is rapidly industrializing. But as you see, after many years of industrialization, you gentlemen come here and notice that there remains a lot of agriculture and not much industry. [Laughter.] With an agricultural economy there is always decentralization, because communication is so difficult. But industrialization leads to urbanization and centralization. So you see: You were very centralized in your decisions and commands, and we were very decentralized in ours.

◆

At the June 1997 Hanoi conference, the Tonkin Gulf incident was discussed almost exclusively in military terms: torpedo attacks; air strikes; command and control; and so on. This was natural, since officials in Washington involved in that crisis were understandably preoccupied with whether an attack—a second attack—had actually occurred or not.

Americans had strong reactions then, and since, to the Tonkin Gulf events, and the follow-up Tonkin Gulf Resolution giving President Johnson de facto war powers. But Americans sometimes forget that in Vietnam events of this sort affect people personally, in ways with which Americans are unfamiliar. At the February 1998 conference, Luu Doan Huynh reflected on the impact of the Tonkin Gulf incident as it touched him, his family, and his fellow citizens. For it was at that time that children were evacuated from the cities, and every citizen of North Vietnam was left to ponder what was felt to be an absolute certainty: The bombing of the North—what was called in the North the "war of destruction," was about to begin. And life as they had known it in the North since 1954 was about to end.

◆

Luu Doan Huynh: We understood that the bombing was designed to curb the fighting will of North Vietnam; and also to halt supplies to the South. That is true. We did see those motives behind the decision to bomb the North.

But I would add to this that there was something else that we saw—that was indicated by the bombing. This was a signal—as we saw it—showing that you have not only extended the war to the North, but you were also going also to expand the war in the South. You were going to "Americanize" the war. Based on this assessment, we believed that very important decisions would soon be made in Washington. So we have to be careful. We have to be ready to face the possibility of an imminent escalation to a big war with the U.S. This worried us a lot.

In fact, we expected the bombing of North Vietnam to begin sometime in 1963. Yes, I said "1963." One of your high officials, according to your documents, claimed in 1963 that we were using "salami tactics" to avoid your bombing. Anyway, so the bombing began. After the bombing started in early 1965, Pres. Ho Chi Minh made a statement calling on all Vietnamese to fight for the liberation of the country. This is a very significant statement—very significant, and I am not sure the Americans understood the meaning of it at the time. It means that since you have extended the war to North Vietnam, we are now saying—officially saying—that we are entering the war in the South. . . .

I told you before that since 1963 we were anticipating the bombing. I don't mean that we thought the bombing was going to begin in 1963. Maybe yes, maybe no. What I mean is that was when we concluded that *at some point* you will begin the bombing. Why? Because at some point, you will see that you are losing ground in the South. So we decided to stand ready.

Now I am talking about August 5, 1964, and the bombing right after. After August 5, the children in Hanoi were ordered to go to the countryside for dispersal. My young son was among these children who were quickly moved to the countryside, because we knew that the bombing—the real bombing in earnest—could begin at any time. Our Foreign Ministry, and many other ministries, organized boarding houses in the countryside for the children.

So, this means that in 1963 we realized—I would say for the first time— that the bombing is coming, at some point. In August 1964, we went on alert, so to speak, and evacuated children from Hanoi, in anticipation of the bombing. And the bombing began the following February.

FEBRUARY 1965:
THE AMERICAN WAR/WAR OF DESTRUCTION BEGINS

Chester Cooper was a member of the team McGeorge Bundy brought with him to Saigon in early February 1965. He believed then, and he still believes, that if the attack on Pleiku had not occurred, a chance remained to reverse the escalatory process as late in the game as February 1965. Cooper begins the discussion of Pleiku by re-creating the mood among the members of the U.S. delegation in Saigon at the time. He then asks the Vietnamese participants what Hanoi expected the U.S. response to be. This, as Cooper said later, was "diplomatese" for "What in the hell did you expect us to do?"

Suddenly, with the response of Gen. Dang Vu Hiep, the entire conference seems to change gears. Hiep says he had been there, near Pleiku, when the attack occurred and was familiar with the details of the event. Before answering, however, he has a question of his own for the American side. He asks them whether Pleiku was just a pretext to begin the bombing, a decision that Hiep presumed had been made much earlier.

After a coffee break, Hiep is asked by session chairman George Herring to relate the details of the Pleiku attack, as he understands them. He says he and the others did not know McGeorge Bundy was in Saigon or that Alexei Kosygin was in Hanoi. It was a small operation. Americans were not targeted. Stunned by this revelation, Robert McNamara assures Hiep that Cooper is correct in saying that no decision had been made, one way or the other, to begin the bombing. In fact, he says, the principal purpose of Bundy's trip to Saigon was to help the U.S. president make that very decision. Cooper completes the circle by telling General Hiep that this may have been the greatest missed opportunity of all, because it never occurred to the Americans that an attack with the significance of the one at Pleiku could have been planned and executed by a local commander, without consultation with Hanoi.

Gen. Dale Vesser, himself a veteran of more than 500 days of combat in the Vietnamese jungles, then directs a pointed criticism at the Vietnamese: that their loose command-and-control procedures must, in light of what General Hiep has revealed, be judged partly to blame for the escalation of the war. Gen. W. Y. Smith agrees, and he challenges the Vietnamese to respond. Then follows an emotional response from Nguyen Khac Huynh, who asks General Vesser in plain terms what he would have had them do. Vesser responds by saying his point is that Hanoi *must* share the responsibility for the escalation in light of what General Hiep said about Pleiku. Nguyen Khac Huynh, in a powerful riposte to Vesser, explains that Hanoi "escalated" only in defense, only after the bombs began falling on their heads. General Hiep concludes the session by accepting General Vesser's point and by observing, philosophically: "So it goes in wars; if you escalate, then I must also escalate."

❖

Chester Cooper: In early 1965, there was great uncertainty in Washington about how to proceed. So President Johnson asked McGeorge Bundy to go to Vietnam and see for himself the progress of the war and come back with some recommendations. I went along with Mr. Bundy and several other members of the National Security Council staff on that fateful trip. . . .

Before Mr. Bundy left, he was given three possibilities to examine—given them by the president.* One was to expand the American activities—American support for the South Vietnamese government and its army. A second alternative was to proceed as we were doing, more or less without pushing ahead or pulling back. It was "more of same." The third option was to diminish the American presence and prepare to close it out. Those were the three options that Mac Bundy, my boss at the time, carried with him to Saigon in early February 1965.

. . .

I think there was a genuine chance that if Bundy came back and recommended that we decrease the level of American activity, I believe this would have been very seriously considered.

However, as you know, when we were in Saigon, there was this attack on Pleiku. A lot of Americans were killed or wounded in the attack. We flew up to Pleiku and saw the aftermath. It had quite an impact on all of us, especially on Mac Bundy. . . . What did you think we would do after that attack on Pleiku? I mean, what did you think our response would be?

Gen. Dang Vu Hiep: At this time, I was in Area 5, which was not far from Pleiku.

If I may, I would like to ask a question of the U.S. participants. The attack of U.S. troops at Pleiku by Vietnamese troops on February 7: How was it perceived—as an attack ordered by a local field commander, or in response to a command from Hanoi? I have never fully understood this—why that incident should give rise, overnight, to the bombing of the North. Why did the U.S. government regard this attack, which was more or less a normal battlefield activity, to be—well—so provocative? The logical conclusion, it seems to me, is that Pleiku was just an excuse, a pretext, for Johnson to order the bombing to begin, which is something he had probably wanted to do for some time.

George Herring: If I could ask follow-up questions regarding Pleiku, General Hiep: When was the attack on Pleiku planned? By whom? Was there an awareness that Bundy was in Saigon, or would be in Saigon? What would happen after the attack? Was there a reprimand afterward or was there a criticism for launching the attack?

*These are essentially the three choices McNamara and Bundy had outlined in their January 27, 1965, fork-in-the-road memorandum to President Johnson.

Gen. Dang Vu Hiep: The attack was actually ordered by the office of command of the forces in Pleiku itself. The South Vietnamese commanders were organizing their troops to fight against us. The plan was for a long-term offensive. The attack used only thirty people, not a full-scale attack. For a huge attack, there would need to be a lot of preparation. But not for a quick attack like that one.

Only later—now—after reading McNamara's book do I know that Bundy was in Saigon. And only after reading General Westmoreland's memoir did I learn that Alexei Kosygin was in Hanoi. You have asked whether we attacked because Kosygin was in Hanoi and Bundy was in Saigon, just to provoke the U.S. Clearly not. Those of us in the area who planned the attack had no idea they were in the country. This was war and we just attacked. The attacking unit was not criticized. It was decorated.

James Hershberg: Did your instructions at the time of Pleiku urge you to specifically hit American targets and kill American soldiers? Or were you supposed to avoid killing American soldiers and hitting American targets? Or did your instructions not distinguish between what you called "puppet" targets and American targets?

Gen. Dang Vu Hiep: No, we considered everyone—South Vietnamese troops, U.S. troops—to be the enemy. It made no difference. There was no discrimination. This was war, and our job—as soldiers in the field—was to destroy the enemy. This was our job.

Robert McNamara: It's conceivable the war would have proceeded as it did without Pleiku. But it is not correct to say that the decisions to bomb the North—via Operation "ROLLING THUNDER"—had been made before Pleiku. That is not correct. The fact is that roughly four weeks before Pleiku, McGeorge Bundy and I wrote a memorandum to the president, and we said we didn't know whether the U.S. should increase its effort or reduce its effort and that both deserved debate and discussion. The debate and discussion was never held properly. It certainly had not yet taken place, let alone concluded, when Mr. Cooper and Mr. Bundy were sent to Vietnam. One of the purposes the president had in mind in sending them was to enrich that debate and reach a conclusion. So Pleiku came at a particularly delicate moment, and it did affect the course of the war. That is a fact.

Chester Cooper: The Pleiku incident was a missed opportunity. You have to understand this. Mr. McNamara wrote up the terms of our trip. I was there when we discussed that. I was in Pleiku with Mr. Bundy, just after the attack came. I was on the plane coming home discussing it. I was in the White House when the implications of that attack occurred. You have to believe that this was a missed opportunity. It was, to use an American expression, "the straw that broke the camel's back." Once the bombers were sent north, there was no turning back.

Gen. Dale Vesser: One must also ask what North Vietnam was doing throughout this period. You were, by your own account, winning the special war, which led to the intervention by our forces to protect our bases such as the one at Pleiku, which had been under attack. But from our point of view, we were responding to the introduction of not just your individual replacements but also main-force units, first at battalion, then at regimental and finally at divisional level. Throughout this period, much fighting went on. We were very impressed by your fighting forces—especially those like myself who spent over 500 days in the jungle fighting against you through this period. So let us be clear that the United States was not the only country which was escalating its use of force through this period.

Gen. W. Y. Smith: . . . Now, as I have understood the discussion this morning, you have said that the Vietnamese philosophy has been to "fight, fight, talk, talk." If I understood you correctly, you would be fighting and talking simultaneously. General Vesser noted that at least the "fight, fight" goal was being pursued. . . . General Vesser reminded all of us that Hanoi was reinforcing in the South and, thereby, increasing the level of hostilities. He said that on the U.S. side, it looked as if we needed to respond—to respond to what you-all were doing.

I don't think I heard an adequate response to his point, which was that your actions carried consequences. You have been very critical throughout this conference of the fact that we—on the U.S. side—were "fight, fighting"—and you keep reminding us of the U.S. bombing and troop levels during this period. Now that's fine. But I haven't heard you address the fact—and it is a fact, as General Vesser said—that you were doing the same thing, which is a lot of fighting and not much talking. I would like some response to General Vesser's point.

Nguyen Khac Huynh: Before responding directly to his question, may I ask General Vesser a question: If you were in our position, and your country were being bombed in the North, and hundreds of thousands of foreign soldiers in the South were killing your people, what would you do? What would you have us do? If you were in our position what would you do? Please help me in answering this question.

Gen. Dale Vesser: Well, I would answer that question this way: Once you allowed your local commanders to make attacks on our forces as part of your special war, then you opened yourself to decisions for retaliation by our highest—by decisions of our highest leadership. One of your generals said to me yesterday that I didn't understand people's war. I think that I understand people's war. I suggest that you may not have understood the dire consequences of making those attacks. They entailed reactions on our part that made use of the forces and means that were available to the United States in carrying the fight to North Vietnam. And as you learned, these forces included bombers.

Nguyen Khac Huynh: But General Vesser, we were escalating *in defense!* In the South as well as in the North, we were undertaking national defense. We were not escalating with the intent to be hostile. Please distinguish clearly between these two situations. If you say that we escalated in order to defend the North and counter the U.S. bomber planes, then this is true. In the North, for example, we increased artillerymen. We escalated in defense. In the South, the more the U.S. intervened, the more the NLF, with the aid of reinforcements and other support from the North—i.e., the Democratic Republic of Vietnam—escalated the struggle in order to defeat the counteroffensive and General Westmoreland's "search and destroy" strategy. Therefore, yes, we "escalated" the war, in a sense. But the sense was this: There was an escalation of the determination to fight for our self-defense.

Gen. Dang Vu Hiep: General Vesser has said that there was Vietnamese escalation as well as U.S. escalation. The question arose yesterday as to when northern troops came into the picture in the South. It was only *after* the U.S. bombed the North and brought troops into the South—in other words, *after* it was clear that the U.S. was escalating—that we began to support the South with regular regiments. I said yesterday that in 1965 the NLF in the Central Highlands received three regiments from the North. Those three regiments fought against the U.S. in the November 1965 battle in the Ia Drang Valley. After that, many more regiments were sent.

But our policy was really nothing more than retaliation. So it goes in war: If you escalate, then I must also escalate, and then so, again, must you escalate, and so on. You know, at the time, there was a saying in the South: Every time you bomb the North, then the South will step up its retaliation. It was a well-known saying: "If the North calls, the South will answer." This is how it worked. This is why we "escalated" the war—in retaliation.

❖

The attack on Pleiku was revisited at the February 1998 Hanoi conference. Chester Cooper was one of McGeorge Bundy's deputies at the time and, in fact, he helped Bundy draft the so-called airborne memorandum to President Johnson, after Pleiku, on the flight from Saigon to Washington. That fateful memorandum contained the rationale for the "air war," as it was called in Washington, or the "war of destruction," as it was called in Hanoi. This is the key message from Bundy to Johnson:

> There is no way of unloading the burden on the South Vietnamese themselves, and their is no way of negotiating our way out of Vietnam which offers any serious promise at present. It is possible that at some future time a neutral non-communist force may emerge, perhaps under Buddhist leadership, but no such force currently exists, and any negotiated U.S. withdrawal today would mean surrender on the installment plan.
>
> The policy of graduated and continuing reprisal . . . is the most promising course available, in my judgment.[118]

Johnson repeats this section of the Bundy memorandum verbatim in his own memoirs, as if to plead that this was the advice he was given, so what else could he do?[119]

The Vietnamese had remained skeptical, even after the June 1997 conference, as to whether Pleiku was anything more than simply a pretext. Chester Cooper, in an intervention some of the Vietnamese participants find persuasive, then "rewrites" the memorandum he could have drafted—and would have tried to draft—for McGeorge Bundy, if only the Pleiku attack had not occurred during the February 1965 visit. Finally, following up a corridor conversation, Cooper asks whether it is true that the NLF force that attacked Pleiku *did not even know Americans were present*. True, responds Col. Quach Hai Luong. They did *not* know. Cooper concludes in a barely audible voice, full of emotion, that this is very important information. Unstated, but felt by all the scholars in the room, Vietnamese and American, is the feeling that one of the pivotal moments in the tragic war has been identified. But for Chet Cooper, the feeling of discovery is overwhelmed by the sudden illumination that he and his boss, Mac Bundy, wrote the "wrong" memo to President Johnson in February 1965—the memo that did much to launch the American War in Vietnam—due to a misunderstanding of the circumstances at Pleiku.

Chester Cooper: . . . It has been argued that if we hadn't begun the bombing at the time of Pleiku we would have bombed on another occasion—we would have used some other pretext—later, because we were ready. That may be correct. *However*, I can imagine events turning our very differently, based on a report that Mac Bundy did *not* write, due to Pleiku. I would have loved to help him write that report, let me tell you.

That report would have said the following: (a) the political situation in South Vietnam has deteriorated beyond repair; (b) the Tet cease-fire held while our group was in Vietnam; and (c) we have some reason to believe this means the North might be ready and willing to discuss an arrangement satisfactory to both sides. *Then*, I don't know what would have happened. But I guarantee you that Johnson would have had to take such a report very, very seriously. Because of Pleiku, no one could even consider writing a report like that.

I have a follow-up question for Col. Quach Hai Luong. Did you say that the attack on the Americans at Pleiku was, more or less, an *accident*? Was the target really South Vietnamese Army forces? If that is the case, we really do have an interesting—

Col. Quach Hai Luong: Yes, exactly. It was an accident. Nobody knew the Americans were there. Your people interpreted it otherwise, which was a fateful misjudgment.

Chester Cooper: This is probably the most important thing that I have heard in the two meetings so far.

Conclusions

The great British historian Sir Herbert Butterfield laid stress on what he called the "security dilemma," in which the unintended and undesired consequences of one's state's actions are mistakenly seen as hostile by another:

> You yourself may vividly feel the terrible fear that you have of the other party, but you cannot enter into the other man's counter-fear, or even understand why he should be particularly nervous. For you know that you yourself mean him no harm, and that you want nothing from him save guarantees for your own safety; and it is never possible for you to realize or remember properly that since he cannot see the inside of your mind, he can never have the same assurance of your intentions that you have. As this operates on both

sides the Chinese puzzle is complete in all its interlockings and neither party can see the nature of the predicament he is in, for each only imagines that the other party is being hostile and unreasonable.[120]

This being the case, American political scientist Robert Jervis concludes that "from this perspective, the central theme of international relations is not evil but *tragedy*."[121] Looking back at those days, in light of all this new information—much of which neither I nor any other senior U.S. official knew anything about at the time—I am stunned by the number of opportunities that were missed to head off the war before it became a confrontation between Hanoi and Washington. The decisions taken, the judgments made—are so overloaded with missed opportunities as to be unbelievable. I am not the only one who feels this way. Many of our Vietnamese colleagues agree completely with this assessment. Our goal must be to prevent such tragedies in the future.

Our two strategies relating to the *process* of escalation seemed to combine perversely to make its reversal much more difficult than it would otherwise have been. There seem to me to be six principal reasons for this perverse interaction.

1. Both Washington and Hanoi relied on strategies of *attrition*. The objective of each was not to destroy the enemy but to exhaust the enemy's available options until he stopped his ostensible "aggression."

2. Both side's strategies were essentially *psychological*—designed to break the will of the other to continue the fight.

3. Both strategies were *reactive*. Each side believed, at each point in the process of escalation, that the initiative rested with the other side. In a sense, each side was trying to "educate" the other by a process of punishing unacceptable actions. But since neither side understood that the other had this view, each regarded the other's actions as gratuitous and aggressive moves, which in turn required "responses." And so on, up the ladder of escalation.

4. Each sought to *signal* the other using military means. Instead of using bombing runs and infiltration rates to send "signals" to each other—signals that neither side could decipher—could we not have found a way to *contact* each other, to talk about these matters?

5. Each side came to believe that the other's objective was total victory—requiring an *unconditional surrender* of its own minimum goals—regarding the Saigon government. If each side had known or believed that the

other would have been satisfied with a lesser result, a resolution might have been possible in those terms.

6. Neither side understood that it was the *interaction* of two strategies of attrition that produced the spiral of escalation and a kind of World War I–like stalemate for nearly an entire, incredibly destructive decade.

Taken together, these misunderstandings reveal fundamental ignorance on each side with regard to the motives and intentions of the other.

There were also specific opportunities missed by each side to arrest and reverse the process of escalation toward a major war:

- *January 1961:* Our view was that the war in South Vietnam was supplied and directed by Hanoi and that Hanoi was therefore waging a war of aggression. Hanoi, in contrast, believed that by January 1959—when Resolution 15 was passed, endorsing armed violence in the South—it was in danger of losing the South forever, so effective had Diem seemed to them to have been in eliminating their allies south of the 17th parallel. The founding of the NLF, which was announced in late January 1961, was the organizational response to this fear in Hanoi—that they were in danger of losing any chance of reunifying their country. To us in the new Kennedy administration, we saw Diem as being incapable of dealing with what we saw as aggression from the North without outside help.

- *November–December 1963:* The Kennedy administration erred profoundly in authorizing the coup against Diem and Nhu, having no plan for who or what would follow them. This was not John Kennedy's finest hour, nor do those events reflect favorably on those of us who advised him. A thoughtless, counterproductive mistake was made.

  However, as has been pointed out above, there were opportunities to reverse the escalation both *before* and *after* the removal of Diem and Nhu. *Both* sides now understand this. We in Washington should have fully explored the possibility of involving Diem in some sort of neutral solution rather than in authorizing his removal because of his bureaucratic incompetence and difficult personality. He may have been personally interested in such a prospect, as we now know. So was Hanoi. I was amazed to learn, during the course of our discussions with the Vietnamese participants, that an arrangement with Diem had been taken seriously in Hanoi. It was not out of the question. I wish we would have known.

  But perhaps an even greater tragedy was our failure—and I mean leaders in *Hanoi* as well as Washington—our failure to grasp the opportunity in the aftermath of Diem's removal to explore the possibility of a compromise neutral solution in Saigon. Instead, we developed a kind of "bunker mentality" on both sides. Washington increasingly supported anybody in Saigon who could control the army and the Buddhists. Moreover, as we have learned, the reaction in Hanoi to the removal of the Ngo brothers was—as we saw it in Washington—to *escalate* the war. I now understand that Le Duan and his colleagues did not see it this way. They believed they were preempting an American war that some in Hanoi already believed the Americans were determined to fight. But they were profoundly mistaken. It was *not* inevitable. Many of us did not even believe it was desirable.

So on either side of Diem's removal, there were major opportunities missed by both sides to reverse escalation toward war.

• *July–August 1964:* Of course, the revelations described above regarding the Tonkin Gulf affair represent a significant addition to the historical record. At the time, we in Washington were primarily concerned with whether the second attack, on August 4, had really occurred. Gen. Vo Nguyen Giap says it did not. I have no reason to believe he is in error. But the more interesting revelation, to me, is that the attack was ordered by a local torpedo-boat commander. My god! A local commander of three torpedo boats was making the kinds of decisions that contributed to a war in which millions of people died! But we didn't know. We assumed that Hanoi *must* be involved in any such decision. I don't believe this issue was ever raised, by anybody, at a senior level.

Yet the Tonkin Gulf episode is another illustration of two lessons we learned in the Cuban missile crisis project: First, covert operations almost always convey to those on the receiving end more hostile intent or capability than is meant or available. The 34-A operations against the North Vietnamese were just like Operation "MONGOOSE" against Cuba after the Bay of Pigs. We in Washington thought MONGOOSE was, as Mac Bundy once put it, merely "psychological salve for inaction."[122] The Cubans, however, believed it was a forerunner to an invasion by the United States. This was a factor leading them to seek assistance from the Soviets, which in turn led to the Cuban missile crisis.

Second, beware of the power in crisis situations of local commanders. The decision to shoot down a U-2 spy plane over Cuba on October 26, 1962, was made by a junior-level Russian antiaircraft officer, contrary to standing orders issued by Premier Khrushchev. That single act almost led to war between the Soviets and the United States. Likewise, the local commander's decision to attack *Maddox* was as important as any decision taken in

Hanoi or Washington—maybe more important—because we in Washington did not understand who had made the decision or why it had been made.

If Hanoi had only known: that *we* attributed virtually zero military significance to the 34-A program; and if we had known that *they* attacked *Maddox* based on the decision of a torpedo-boat commander who just thought he was doing his job, major escalatory actions would have been avoided. So these are major missed opportunities.

- *February 1965:* I regard the revelations regarding the attack on Pleiku on February 7, 1965, as having great significance. We in Washington would never have thought it possible that the attack that killed the Americans at Pleiku, during Mac Bundy's visit, could be the result of anything other than an order issued by the leadership in Hanoi. But according to Gen. Dang Vu Hiep, we were absolutely wrong to believe this. General Hiep and his colleagues were trying to split South Vietnam in two by destroying as many South Vietnamese facilities as possible, as quickly as possible. Why? This is the tragic and amazing truth: *to raise the odds that Hanoi might still be able to avoid a U.S.–North Vietnam war*. Le Duan felt an American war could still be avoided if the South Vietnamese Army were beaten quickly and completely. It is just unbelievable that General Hiep and his colleagues could have been carrying out their mission for that overall purpose, knowing what we know about American perceptions at the time.

  But Hanoi was equally wrong in its belief that the decision to bomb the north—to begin ROLLING THUNDER, or what was called in Hanoi "the war of destruction"—had *already been made* before the visit of Mac Bundy. It had not. But because Hanoi's leaders believed this so firmly they no doubt saw nothing to be lost by attacking bases all over South Vietnam, irrespective of whether Americans would be involved or not. Why would it matter, if Washington had already decided on an all-out war against North Vietnam? But they were wrong to believe this. As Chet Cooper showed at the February 1998 conference, a very different memorandum might have been written to President Johnson by Mac Bundy, when he returned, if the events at Pleiku had not intervened.

  So even then, as late as early February 1965, war between Washington and Hanoi was *not* inevitable. Neither side understood this because each had concluded that the other's objective would lead to war. Both were wrong.

Lyndon Johnson later recalled his reaction when he heard the news about the Pleiku. He said: "We have kept our guns over the mantel and our shells in the cupboard for a long time now. And what was the result?

They are killing our men while they sleep in the night."[123] Even though it made no sense to him, Johnson now believed "Old Ho"—as he referred to the leader in Hanoi—really wanted a war, a wider war with the U.S. "Suddenly," he later recalled, "I realized that doing nothing was more dangerous than doing something."[124] But he was wrong on both counts. Hanoi did not want that war. And after Pleiku, "doing nothing" would have been completely appropriate. But Johnson didn't know. Thus began another escalatory move in the Vietnam War.

So at each of these four crossroads, each side—Washington and Hanoi—adhered to its reactive strategy of minimal escalation, trying to signal to the other side its intention to punish the other if it did not cease to escalate the confrontation. Each side remained convinced—but could not convince the other—that it did not seek unconditional surrender of the minimum objectives of the other. Washington just could *not* bring itself to believe Hanoi was *not* a communist puppet bent on conquering all of Southeast Asia, beginning with South Vietnam. And Hanoi could *not* bring itself to believe that Washington was *not* a neoimperialist bent on destroying the Hanoi government and, with it, any possibility of a unified Vietnam. Erroneous mindsets drove the escalation. Misunderstandings facilitated it. Neither side showed sufficient courage and imagination, at any of the critical crossroads on the way to war, to examine the validity of either their own views or those of their adversary. And so a process ensued by which both sides were sucked into a spiral of continuing escalation.

September 1967. North Vietnam, after heated debate, turned down a proposal drafted by Robert McNamara that, with President Johnson's approval, had been passed to Prof. Kissinger for transmission to Ho Chi Minh by a French communist (Raymond Aubrac) whose daughter was Ho Chi Minh's god-daughter. The formula was put forward publicly by President Johnson in a speech in San Antonio, September 29, 1967, and was to become the basis for the start of negotiations between the U.S. and North Vietnam in Paris later that year.

6

Negotiating Initiatives, 1965–1967: Why Did They Fail?

We have tried over the past several years, in a variety of ways and through a number of channels, to convey to you and your colleagues our desire to achieve a peaceful settlement. For whatever reasons, these efforts have not achieved any results.

It may be that our thoughts and yours, our attitudes and yours, have been distorted or misinterpreted as they passed through these various channels. . . . I am [now] prepared to order a cessation of bombing against your country . . . as soon as I am assured that infiltration into South Vietnam by land and by sea has stopped. These acts of restraint on both sides would, I believe, make it possible for us to conduct serious private discussions leading toward an early peace.

Pres. Lyndon Johnson to Ho Chi Minh, February 8, 1967[1]

In your message you seem to deplore the suffering and the destruction in Vietnam. Allow me to ask you: Who is perpetrating these monstrous crimes? It is the American and satellite troops. The United States Government is entirely responsible for the extremely serious situation in Vietnam. . . .

The Government of the United States must stop the bombing, definitively and unconditionally, and all other acts of war against the Democratic Republic of Vietnam . . . and withdraw from South Vietnam all U.S. and satellite troops. . . .

The Vietnamese people will never submit to force; they will never agree to talks under the threat of bombs.

Pres. Ho Chi Minh to Lyndon Johnson, February 15, 1967[2]

Introduction

I often think of four lines from T. S. Eliot's poem "Little Gidding," which were brought to my attention by my wife, Margaret, just after the Kennedy administration assumed office. They are:

We shall not cease from exploration
And the end of all our exploring
Will be to arrive where we started
And know the place for the first time.[3]

I have not yet "ceased from exploration," particularly with respect to the Vietnam War. When I began this project, I did not see clearly why the war had started; why it had not ended sooner; and what its lessons were. When I proposed to the Vietnamese that we jointly reexamine the evolution of the war, I hoped for answers to these questions. In particular, were there missed opportunities for establishing negotiations that could have led to an earlier peace?

In this chapter, my coauthors and I present our findings.

. . .

In an appendix to his memoirs, President Johnson graphically portrayed the principal disappointment—in fact, the great tragedy—of his presidency: the failure to reach a negotiated end to the Vietnam War. In three lengthy lists, he summarized his efforts to terminate the war: sixteen partial or complete "Bombing Pauses Over North Vietnam" between May 1965 and November 1968; no fewer than seventy-two "Major Peace Initiatives" during the same period, almost all of which involved intermediaries from one or more countries other than the United States and North Vietnam; and seventeen bona fide "Peace Channels to North Vietnam," all but one occurring between May 1965 and November 1968.[4] We all know the results of these far-flung efforts: very close to nothing, or so it seemed at the time. The desired result never happened. The Washington, Hanoi, and Saigon governments, together with the NLF, did not agree to enter into formal peace talks until October 31, 1968, days before the election of Richard Nixon. Lyndon Johnson, profoundly exhausted by the war, then retired to his ranch in Texas. The war went on for nearly seven more years.

Therefore, in this chapter, we arrive at what was for me personally, and I believe for President Johnson and his other senior foreign policy advisers as well, the most frustrating aspect of the entire affair: the failure to deescalate the conflict, to move to direct talks and, ultimately, to a negotiated settlement during the Johnson presidency. Once we started down the path to a U.S.–North Vietnam War, we could not reverse the momentum until the conflict reached tragic proportions. Why couldn't we find a way out?

We learned in Hanoi from Tran Quang Co, who during the mid-1960s was chief of the "solutions" division of the Department of U.S. Affairs in Hanoi's Foreign Ministry, that all of the administration's efforts were believed to constitute a "U.S. intermediary campaign," a diplomatic adjunct to the military campaign. Not only did Hanoi regard U.S. efforts as lacking seriousness with regard to a peaceful settlement; Hanoi also saw a sinister U.S. plot behind the deluge of intermediaries—a plan to destroy or occupy Vietnam north of the 17th parallel and establish a colonial regime in Saigon on a permanent basis. As I told Tran Quang Co in Hanoi, I was amazed to hear this, since no senior member of the Johnson administration had anything remotely resembling such a view, let alone any plan to carry it out.

Where did *we* go wrong? I'll speak first to what I'll call *Washington's* failure. It was clear to some of us as early as 1965, when the first significant peace initiatives occurred, that the United States might well fail to achieve its political objectives in Vietnam through military means. There were fundamental questions we should have debated—but did not—with all the intensity and candor that marked our discussions in October 1962 during the Cuban missile crisis.

Nothing like this occurred during the Johnson years with regard to Vietnam. To this day, it is difficult to explain why I, and others, did not force the key issues to the surface, debate them fully, then proceed on the basis of our conclusions. Had we done so, our diplomatic effort would have been far more intense and far more effective. As it was, Hanoi believed it to be a trick.

Our failure to develop a reliable channel to Hanoi, and a realistic message for its leadership, did not occur in isolation. We were not alone. There were *Hanoi's* failures as well. Where did *they* go wrong in interpreting the offers alluded to in the appendix to President Johnson's memoirs? Why did they adhere so rigidly to conditions they demanded we accept *before* talks could even begin? Why did they not explore the possibilities of various bombing pauses and other gestures toward some sort of compromise that would allow us to begin talking with each other directly, not just via the intermediaries? In short, why did Hanoi not take even a small risk to move to peace negotiations, or at least to explore what was possible, rather than endure the terrible suffering (more than 3 million killed) and damage the war brought to their country? Neither President Johnson, nor I, nor any of the president's other senior advisers could answer these questions.

The circumstances under which this chapter was written have required an adjustment in the format we have used for Chapters 2–5. My coauthors and I concluded that each of the peace initiatives must be dealt with as a definable event, seen from both sides at more or less the same time, with each side constructing its individual explanations of failure, then moving on to the next such attempt. The Vietnam War is one of the most intensely studied—and most frequently written-about—episodes in the history of American foreign policy. Hundreds of books have been published on the war. But relatively little has been written on the failed peace initiatives.

What have we previously had to go on? Chester Cooper's scholarly memoir, *The Lost Crusade*, published in 1970, remains the best detailed account of the events by a participant in them, but it deals almost exclusively with U.S. decisionmaking.[5] *The Secret Diplomacy of the Vietnam War: The Negotiating Volumes of the Pentagon Papers*, edited by historian George Herring and published in 1983, is somewhat broader, for it includes, in addition to formerly classified U.S. documentation, a running account of broadcasts, published interviews, and speeches from Hanoi.[6]

What about the Hanoi side? What have we known about the motives, assessments, decisions, and all-important options that were considered in Hanoi, involving the many attempts to move to negotiations? Virtually nothing. We have known that the initiatives failed but not why. No one has had a clue as to how U.S. analyses matched, or did not match, the reality as seen by Hanoi. This is why, I speculate, there has been so little work—approaching nothing—conducted on the peace initiatives, relative to other aspects of the war, since the 1960s. Our meetings were a first step in this area, and what came out of them was surprising, frustrating, and at times heartbreaking.

In this chapter, we divide the material into three parts:

- *Four Points and Fourteen Points*. These are the annotated discussions between the U.S. and Vietnamese participants in our meetings in Hanoi regarding the absolutely fundamental issues raised by each side's formal statement of its negotiating position: Hanoi's "Four Points" of April 8, 1965; and Washington's "Fourteen Points" of December 29, 1965.

- *Key Misunderstandings*. These are the annotated discussions of what we regard as major misunderstandings that cut across all the failed initiatives: the use of intermediaries; each side's bottom lines in negotiations; the impact of casualties on Hanoi's willingness to negotiate; and the distinction, for purposes of moving to negotiations, between a conditional U.S. bombing pause and an unconditional bombing halt.

- *Six Peace Initiatives.* We do not, and cannot possibly, deal here with all of the failed initiatives. But we do cover what we believe—and what our Vietnamese colleagues also believe—were the most significant initiatives, in the sense that any one of them might possibly have succeeded but for misunderstandings by one side or the other (usually both) that prevented it.

Four Points and Fourteen Points

HANOI'S FOUR POINTS OF APRIL 8, 1965

In early February 1965, just days after sustained U.S. bombing of the North began, the Hanoi leadership met in emergency session to develop a statement of their fundamental position with regard to eventual negotiations with the United States. After nearly two months of intense discussion, debate, and drafting, they produced a document that became known as the Four Points. It was the result of daily consultations between the drafting committee and the three principal political leaders in Hanoi: Pres. and Chairman Ho Chi Minh, Party Secretary Le Duan, and Prime Minister Pham Van Dong. Consistent with the Vietnamese experience with foreign powers over many centuries, the Four Points are based on the premise that Hanoi cannot hope to "win" a military victory over the Americans; therefore, at a certain point, negotiations must begin. Toward this end, Hanoi must state its maximum position on basic issues and convey its determination to carry on the fight no matter how long and how hard that might be.

The Four Points were as follows:

1. Recognition of the basic rights of the Vietnamese people—peace, independence, sovereignty, unity, and territorial integrity. U.S. must remove its troops from South Vietnam; U.S. must stop its acts of war—i.e., the bombing—against North Vietnam.

2. Pending the peaceful reunification of Vietnam, the military provisions of the 1954 Geneva Agreements on Vietnam must be strictly respected. All foreign troops must leave the country. There must be no military alliances between either the Hanoi government or the Saigon government, and outside powers.

3. The internal affairs of South Vietnam must be settled by the South Vietnamese people themselves in accordance with the program of the NLF [National Liberation Front], without foreign interference.

4. The peaceful reunification of Vietnam is to be settled by the Vietnamese
people in both zones, without foreign interference.[7]

The Four Points were approved on April 7, 1965, and made public the
following day over Radio Hanoi, following an address of Pham Van Dong to
the Central Committee of the Party.[8]

Point three—that the affairs of South Vietnam would be settled "in accordance with the program of the NLF"—was destined to become the principal
stumbling block to U.S. acceptance of Hanoi's position. It appears to have
been a compromise between the views of the NLF and the Hanoi leadership.
On March 22, the NLF had issued a five-point statement expressing its
absolute refusal to enter into negotiations with the United States until all
American troops were withdrawn from the country.[9] The Four Point statement, in contrast, takes a more moderate stand on the issue. Point three does
not require that all U.S. troops leave the country before negotiations com-
mence—a condition the leaders in Hanoi must have recognized as impossible, since it would require Washington to, in effect, capitulate before talks
began, leaving them with no leverage in whatever talks might follow. One
can also understand the intensity of the NLF in putting forth their proposition. After all, it was they who, during the spring of 1965, were in actual
combat with the Americans.

Finally, a little-understood yet extremely important appointment had
been made just a few months before the release of the Four Points: At the
end of 1964, Nguyen Duy Trinh was appointed foreign minister. Nguyen
Duy Trinh, who was already a deputy premier, thus became the first Politburo member ever to be named foreign minister.[10] Moreover, as a longtime
member of the southern resistance, he could be expected to give full consideration to the needs and wishes of Hanoi's southern allies. It also meant—
though there is nothing in U.S. documents to suggest that this was picked up
by Washington—that Nguyen Duy Trinh would lead an intensive effort
within the newly empowered Foreign Ministry to develop strategy, tactics,
channels, and all other aspects of a comprehensive negotiating approach to
dealing with the Americans. Hanoi was preparing to negotiate well before
the United States decided to send combat troops to Vietnam.

From the moment they were announced, Washington was confused about
the meaning of the Four Points. Were they an opening bid in a negotiation?
Or were they a rigid set of unalterable "preconditions" to even entering into
negotiations? Particularly troubling to many in Washington was the wording
of Point Three: "The internal affairs of South Vietnam must be settled by the
South Vietnamese people themselves in accordance with the program of the

NLF, without foreign interference." Did this mean that all other groups—including members of the current Saigon government, for example—were to be excluded? That was how most in Washington read it. But there were exceptions. In fact, Richard Goodwin, then on the White House staff, wrote to President Johnson with this analysis:

> . . . (a) these were not set forth as conditions, (b) they were meant as a statement of ultimate objectives, just as we say any settlement has to provide for an independent South Vietnam, tied to no alliance, etc. . . . (c) they said this in order to reassure the Liberation Front that they would not sell them out at a conference, just as we say things to reassure Saigon.[11]

This analysis was basically an accurate view of Hanoi's intentions, as it happened.

Such sentiments, which were also shared in the White House by Chester Cooper, were overruled by the more skeptical views of higher-ranking officials. For example, McGeorge Bundy felt there would be no way to implement any negotiation with Hanoi under the terms of the Four Points.[12] And William Bundy believed they had been put forth only as propaganda and deserved no further analysis.[13] Dean Rusk had perhaps the strongest reaction of this sort, as he recalled in his memoirs. "The Four Point Program was quite deceptive; the third of those four points required the imposition of the program of the National Liberation Front upon all South Vietnam. To us this meant that Hanoi was never interested in talking seriously about peace."[14] Few seemed to know, or to care, that the much-discussed "program of the NLF" actually called for the establishment of a coalition government, dedicated to peace and neutrality, and that reunification was envisioned by the NLF members themselves as a long process, possibly taking decades.[15]

· · · ·

Chester Cooper opens the discussion by referring to President Johnson's April 7, 1965, speech in Baltimore, in which he pledged U.S. interest in "unconditional discussions" under any circumstances that might lead to a peaceful settlement.[16] Cooper wonders why Pham Van Dong didn't take Johnson up on the offer during his April 8 speech in Hanoi the following day. Luu Doan Huynh responds by pointing out that Pham Van Dong's speech had nothing to do with Johnson's Baltimore speech but was instead a statement of the Hanoi negotiating position.

Following further discussion, Luu Van Loi, who was one of those who drafted the Four Points, concludes by saying that he always felt the Four Points were a clear and unambiguous attempt to begin negotiations, not the ultimatum that Washington said they were. This led many in Hanoi, he said, to believe that Washington had no interest in negotiations because they still felt they could win the war. Chester Cooper then asks specifically about Point Three, in particular. Luu Doan Huynh responds again that Point Three was flexible and that all of the Four Points were designed to evolve from "the" basis for a settlement to "a" basis as the talks progressed. This is what happened in Paris, he points out, several years later.

❖

Dao Huy Ngoc: Mr. McNamara played an important role in these events, and therefore his personal opinions are important. We welcome them. However, Mr. McNamara claims that there were missed opportunities on *both* sides. But to be honest, up until this point we, on the Vietnamese side, have yet to find any opportunity that we missed.

Now I would like to invite others to comment.

Chester Cooper: . . . In April of '65 President Johnson *did* say he would go anywhere, anytime . . . to negotiate. He did *not* get an answer. Instead, he got your Four Points on April 8.

So in response to your remark, Mr. Chairman, about the Vietnamese side not having missed any opportunities—well, in addition to all the others that we have brought forward, here is one more—not responding to President Johnson's offer in April 1965, which, in hindsight, just might have been the last chance to avoid widening the war.

Luu Doan Huynh: I want to say something about this critical period—it seems to both sides that it *was* a critical period—of the first part of 1965. Our plan to win the special war was overturned by your bombing of North Vietnam and by your introduction of troops into Vietnam. We must be honest. You did this. Therefore, this presented us with a limited war—a new situation, a new problem. The problem was this: How do we deal with the most powerful country in the world that is full of confidence and full of the desire for success? And we have to ask ourselves: What do you mean by "success"? This might mean that you wanted us to give up the fight to liberate South Vietnam, that is, to surrender. And it seemed to us that you might even invade the North.

Now at that time—early in 1965—we did not have adequate plans for a limited war. So we had to think: What will be our objectives—our concrete objectives? And we decided: Our objectives would be to fight in order to defeat the U.S. air war, to exhaust the U.S. troops in the South, and to weaken the determination to fight of both American politicians and soldiers. These became our objectives. You must understand this. Ultimately, we would try to get the U.S. to withdraw its troops from Vietnam through negotiations. But we believed that the prerequisite conditions for withdrawal were as I have just stated: defeat the air war, exhaust the troops, and erode your aggressive will. If you had good intelligence—you Americans—you would have known this, because these objectives are lyrics to a popular song of Vietnam, but I am not going to sing it. [Laughter.]

North Vietnam's Four Points were set forth by Premier Pham Van Dong on April 8, 1965. . . . This is very important: The Four Points that we introduced were not a response to President Johnson's Baltimore statement of April 7. They were not. Instead, they were our fundamental diplomatic position toward the war as well as toward the resolution of the war. You see, all our calculations changed when the bombing started. We were concerned especially about U.S. self-confidence and your underestimation of Vietnam, which—this is how it looked to us—demanded that we surrender under your terms. The Four Points, therefore, have an important message for the *Vietnamese* people: They say you must not have any illusions—no illusions—but you must have instead a firm position; you must maintain your sovereignty; you must not negotiate under the U.S. terms; and you must not proceed down the path that the U.S. has invited us down. Furthermore, we must have a global strategy to win over international public opinion. This strategy must be based strictly on the situation on the battlefields. And we can proceed to negotiate only at a suitable time and under conditions which are suitable for us. . . .

Not only the Foreign Ministry, but the leadership also had to do homework. They had to have a Central Committee meeting in order to discuss how to conduct the diplomatic struggle. Now I'm about to say something that will disclose a secret, so I hope that those on the Vietnamese side will forgive me. In '66–67, I was given the responsibility of preparing the proper documents for negotiations with the U.S. Four other persons and I worked at it, and by August 1967, most of the files were ready, just in time. But then, because of exhaustion and illness, I had to ask for a transfer to the China division.

You see, with regard to the first of the Four Points, there are at least three conditions that are nonnegotiable. First, the rights of the Vietnamese—freedom, independence, self-determination—these eventually became the first point of the Paris Agreement. From these, there were two corollaries. One: The U.S. had to withdraw its troops from Vietnam. This also is nonnegotiable. Two: The U.S. had to stop bombing the North. This also is nonnegotiable. These were conditions that could not be changed or "negotiated" because they were the basis of our fight. We could not proceed without *assuming* these three points. If we did, that would be [Speaks in English.] "accepting your rationale for invading Vietnam. We could not accept it." [Resumes in Vietnamese.] The South is part of our country, of Vietnam, and all Vietnamese have the right and duty to fight in the South. Therefore, the bombing of the North is just as illegal as the U.S. waging a land war in the South. I guess you did not understand that. For us, there was no way we could withdraw from that point—that point and the corollaries.

[Speaks in English.] Your problem was that you could not stop bombing. That was your strength and your weakness. The bombing strengthened our resolve. It also strengthened world support for our cause. I don't know if you can understand this.

Nguyen Khac Huynh: It seems to me that underlying all your comments is the following question: Under what conditions would the U.S. initiatives have been acceptable and appealing to the Democratic Republic of Vietnam [DRV]—to Hanoi—and the NLF? The first two conditions are: cessation of bombing and no increase in ground troops. These were two conditions. I would add a third condition, a kind of "psychological condition"—maybe this is not the right term—but the *overall* condition of not requiring the other side—Hanoi—to abandon its minimum objectives. It seems to me that . . . it was always the same: You never, not even once, acknowledged the minimum objectives of our side. And what did this mean? It means—I am sorry, but it meant, to us—only one thing, and that is unconditional surrender.

Why do I say that your initiatives to negotiate really asked for unconditional surrender? Ask yourself: What were your demands? They were as follows: (1) unconditional negotiations; (2) cessation of armed conflict on the battlefront, or at least a radical decrease of armed conflict; and (3) the North must stop the infiltration of arms into the South. None of those demands considered the minimum objectives of Hanoi and the NLF. You were asking us to abandon our brothers in the South. *Abandon them!*

Therefore . . . the U.S. should have paid closer attention to the minimum objectives and requirements of the other side. Otherwise, no matter whether you *say* you are demanding the other side to surrender, this is the way you will be interpreted.

I would also like to make a more personal comment so that our American friends have a correct and precise understanding of our situation. The *bombing* was the key factor, and the cessation of the bombing was our key demand. You must understand that the U.S. bombing of the North was a serious challenge to our sovereignty. Our only choice was whether to submit or resist. Under these circumstances, every Vietnamese citizen would have felt ashamed if we had sat down and talked with you under the pressure of bombing. This is the reason why so long as you continued to bomb the North, there could be no negotiations. Just imagine what our people would think if the Hanoi government entered into formal talks while bombs were falling on our heads.[17]

Nguyen Co Thach: We were very, very weak, and we already knew that the United States was the strongest country in the world. We knew this. We knew you knew this—that the U.S. knew this. This had an impact on us—it affected our way of thinking. First, why in the world would the U.S. ever settle for less than they thought they could get militarily? Why? They would not, of course, because they thought they did not have to. Second, how can we ever prevail in a confrontation with the U.S. We cannot—we understood that we could not—in the strict sense. We would have to hold out, to resist, to find some way to carry on until you left us alone.

The Four Points were designed to provide a diplomatic framework for this resistance war. I think we should connect the Four Points of April 1965 with our theme of "missed opportunities." If you look back at the Paris Agreement on Vietnam in 1973, you will see that it is framed within the structure of the Four Points. If the U.S. had agreed to, or followed, the Four Points in April 1965, then could we not have prevented much bloodshed, as Mr. McNamara has emphasized? Think about it. We would not have had to wait eight years to sign the Paris Agreement on Vietnam. How many people died in those years? Many. Wasn't this a "missed opportunity"—missed by the United States?

. . .

Luu Van Loi: Perhaps we—the Americans and the [North] Vietnamese—were more similar than different, in our younger years, in at least one respect. You know the parable of the lover who cannot muster the courage to state his love for a woman, for fear of being rejected. But if he does not tell her of his love, then she will never know that he loves her. And vice-versa. . . .

As for the Four Points—I was among those who drafted them. The Four Points were not inflexible. They were not. You know, you on the U.S. side continue to express your perplexity at the "inflexibility" of the Four Points. . . . I must tell you that I have been perplexed for the past thirty years or more at why you Americans insist on interpreting the Four Points as somehow or other "inflexible"—even . . . that they constituted some kind of "ultimatum." This is just amazing to me.

So let me take just a minute to give you my view of the Four Points, as we who helped draft them understood our task. The first thing to be said is that the Four Points were really just a summary of the contents of the Geneva Accords of 1954. Nothing more, nothing less. Why start with the Geneva Accords? Because we consistently took the view from 1954 onward that the solution to the "Vietnam problem" lay in the implementation of the Geneva Accords. . . . We were not happy with all aspects of the accords. Not at all. But we believed that the Geneva Agreement was the best available basis for beginning to sit down and solve the problem.

Second, all of you are either historians or diplomats—or both, in the case of our friend Mr. Cooper—so you must understand that any good negotiator starts with his maximum demands. Everyone does this, as far as I know. The idea is of course that via talks each side reaches a better understanding of one another, of what is a possible compromise, and, finally, what the shape of an agreement might be. This is the process of any negotiation, no more, no less. Do we agree on this much? [Assent from the U.S. side.] Good.

At various times between 1965 and 1968, Mr. Pham Van Dong and Pres. Ho Chi Minh both explained—or attempted to explain—that the Four Points were *not* prerequisites for negotiations. They were *not!* Now, as to my perplexity. I remember at the time the Americans were terribly concerned about whether or not to "accept" the Four Points. We could not understand this, except to theorize that, perhaps, the U.S. government did not *want* to understand the Four Points and was simply "buying time," as the saying goes, in order to escalate the war. Why on earth, we asked ourselves, would the Americans believe that they have to "accept" the Four Points before the DRV would come to the negotiating table? I think that you could have trusted us on this because we had negotiated with the French to end the First Indochina War. But more to the point, we had also negotiated with *you* to reach a neutral solution for Laos. . . .

This is why, in short, we could make no sense out of the charge that our Four Points were "inflexible." The only "sense" we could make out of such a charge was that you were not serious about negotiations—not at that time, between 1965 and the end of 1967, the period we are talking about.

Chester Cooper: Listening to you [Gestures at Vietnamese participants.] this morning, I wonder what our grandchildren—yours and mine—will think of us when they discover that on matters of such importance, we were simply unable to communicate with one another.

Neither side was able to explore to any significant degree whether the other side was flexible or not, because we didn't communicate with one another. Let me give you an example in connection with the Four Points. When the Four Points were announced, a colleague of mine and I in the White House sat down and tried to analyze them, and we decided three of the points could be dealt with without much trouble, but the third point was going to be very difficult.

Point 3: "The internal affairs of South Vietnam must be settled by the South Vietnamese people themselves in accordance with the program of the NLF, without foreign interference."

Let me tell you why we found Point Three so difficult: It was because in our translation, the Four Points were said to be "the" basis for a political settlement, not "a" basis. Then, at the very end of your statement, Pham Van Dong said this: "Any approach other than the above-mentioned stand is inappropriate." Frankly, I cannot imagine any so-called negotiating position being more *inflexible* than this. Can you?

Luu Doan Huynh: . . . The Foreign Ministry started drafting the Four Point stand a few days after the U.S. bombing in early February 1965. It was under the direct supervision of Prime Minister Pham Van Dong (who consulted frequently on this with Pres. Ho Chi Minh and Mr. Le Duan). The Four Points is a direct result of their collaboration. The drafting was completed around the end of March. Thereafter, Prime Minister Pham Van Dong included the Four Points in his report to the National Assembly on April 8, 1965. It was not a reply to President Johnson's Baltimore speech of April 7. It had nothing to do with that speech but was instead our basic negotiating position with respect to the war and the solution of the war.

In his letter of May 1965 to NLF officials, Mr. Le Duan said that as compared with the Geneva Agreement the conditions put forth in the Four Points represented a retreat. The Geneva Agreement provided for the holding, two years after the signing, of elections throughout the country for the purpose of national reunification. Yet after ten years of untold suffering, North Vietnam asked only for a U.S. troop withdrawal from South Vietnam, the cessation of the bombing of the North, and allowing the Vietnamese to decide their own affairs. He said: "We are opening the way for the U.S. to withdraw." He meant we were providing a way for the U.S. to withdraw without losing face. . . .

Let me put it this way: The Four Points are absolutely central to a solution, because they comprise three sine qua nons for a settlement favorable to Vietnam's independence and unity. In fact, in addition to the important Point One of the Paris agreement ["respect for the sovereignty and territorial integrity of Vietnam"], there were only two others: unconditional cessation of bombing and the withdrawal of U.S. troops. That's it. We could talk about everything else. This means that we did not, by any means, require that all the Four Points have to be incorporated into any final agreement. Except for the three sine qua nons, everything else could be watered down to the satisfaction of both sides. That was the intent behind the Four Points.

Robert Brigham: Mr. Huynh, were they "the" basis for negotiations or "a" basis?

Luu Doan Huynh: At the beginning, they were "the" basis, but they became—they could become—"a" basis.

David Welch: Would the NLF have agreed that Point Three was negotiable?

Luu Doan Huynh: Sure, absolutely. The actual demand of Point Three was that the NLF must be a party to the negotiations and a party to the future government to be set up in South Vietnam. That was the real minimal demand. Never in the Paris talks did the NLF insist on Point Three being included in total. Point Three, which you Americans had the most trouble with, was actually the most flexible point of all—the *most* flexible. If we could only have found a way of making you understand this, things might have been different.

WASHINGTON'S FOURTEEN POINTS OF DECEMBER 29, 1965

By late 1965, the United States had nearly 200,000 combat troops in South Vietnam, and the bombing of the North continued unabated. During November 14–19, the fierce battle in the Ia Drang Valley between U.S. forces and North Vietnamese forces had shown that infiltration from north to south had been much greater than previously supposed. This revelation caused Gen. William Westmoreland to cable Washington on November 23 and double his estimate of the number of troops he would need.[18] Defense Secretary McNamara went to Saigon in late November 1965 to confer with General Westmoreland and others about Westmoreland's greatly increased requests for troops during upcoming 1966. When he returned, McNamara told the president that if he chose to honor Westmoreland's request, or anything like it, Washington ought to institute a pause—a temporary cessation—in the bombing of North Vietnam, in order to show seriousness in seeking a negotiated settlement—both to the Hanoi government and to the world at large. (For details on the origins of the bombing pause, see the section titled "PINTA/Christmas Bombing Pause," below.) Johnson agreed to the pause, which went into effect on December 22.

Johnson then sought to address the need for some sort of political program, something in writing that would contrast with Hanoi's Four Points and could be taken in hand by the dozens of intermediaries—official and unofficial—he was about to dispatch to 145 countries to advertise the fact that Washington desired peace, that the pause proved it, and that the United States had a plan that represented a reasonable basis for beginning negotiations.[19] In his inimitable way, Johnson was about to embark on a "peace offensive" that bore the unmistakable imprint of this master of the Senate, a politician who made deals by making offers people couldn't refuse. Johnson was, recalled Chester Cooper, acting in this episode "like a ringmaster of a three-ring circus."[20]

On December 19, Johnson requested a memorandum from Rusk regarding concrete plans for diplomatic action in concert with the pause. Rusk resisted at first, writing to Johnson in a same-day response that he wanted to make sure that "the European Communists fully understand our position and understand that Hanoi's insistence upon their four points (amounting to victory in South Vietnam) is the central obstacle to peace. The central point," Rusk wrote, "is that diplomacy cannot produce miracles if Hanoi remains determined to seize South Vietnam."[21]

Still, Rusk dragged his feet, so strongly was he opposed to any sort of démarche to Hanoi. Finally, Johnson instructed McGeorge Bundy to call Rusk and tell him to get moving because "there has been no noise over North Vietnam for four days" and the president wanted to get moving.[22] But Rusk remained, as Bundy told Johnson, "very resistant indeed" to the president's idea of a diplomatic offensive in connection with an extended bombing pause.[23]

At some point during this process, Rusk was called by a Hungarian diplomat, Janos Radvanyi (who would later defect to the West)—volunteering to be yet another intermediary in the search for a Washington-Hanoi formula for peace talks. Radvanyi told Rusk that all he needed was an authoritative statement of the U.S. negotiating position, to which Rusk responded that he would "give him some negotiating points, which we later released as our fourteen-point program for peace in Vietnam."[24] Rusk's deputy, George Ball, was highly skeptical of their worth, however, because it seemed to be devoted to forcing Hanoi's leaders into "crying 'Uncle' in a low voice and with minimal loss of face . . . when their interest was in forcing us to go home."[25] The Fourteen Points were enunciated publicly, in any event, at a press conference on December 29.[26]

The Fourteen Points are listed below, by Chester Cooper in his initial intervention on the topic. He cites Dean Rusk as having said, "We have put everything into the basket of peace except the surrender of South Vietnam."[27] This is a typical formulation by Rusk, indeed, by many State Department officials, in two respects: First, it states the central objective of preserving an independent South Vietnam that is unfriendly to Hanoi; and second, it assumes, implicitly, that Hanoi's central objective is to "conquer" South Vietnam by force. The latter was evidently in error, though this was not appreciated at the time.

Hanoi's point-by-point response to the Fourteen Points, broadcast in English over Radio Hanoi on February 1, 1966, was scathing. The piece was titled "Johnson Puts Everything into the Basket of Peace Except Peace," and it characterized the entire effort as a "smoke screen" and as a "bare-faced lie."[28] They reminded their listeners that it was "Dean Rusk himself who declared to the CBC [Canadian Broadcasting Company] on December 23 1965 that South Vietnam's neutrality might be realized after the Viet Cong have laid down their arms and accepted the amnesty."[29]

In a partial exception to nonstop agitprop, however, Hanoi's official radio "voice" addressed the controversial Point Three of the Hanoi Four Point stand. Noting that Washington had hinted from time to time that three of the Four Points would be acceptable, if only Hanoi would drop its insistence on Point Three—that the South must be run "in accordance with the program of the NLF"—the broadcast said the following:

> The National Front for the Liberation of South Vietnam, the only authentic representative of the South Vietnamese people, controls at present four-fifths of the territory, inhabited by 10 million people. Its program aims at realizing independence, democracy, peace and neutrality in South Vietnam and the eventual peaceful reunification in Vietnam. It envisages the setting up of a broad national union. If it is true that the U.S. government respects the Vietnamese people's right to self-determination, how can it justify its refusal to accept that third point?[30]

The answer, according to the broadcast, is obvious: The U.S. seeks to "turn South Vietnam into a U.S. military base and new-type colony."[31] In short, if the public response reflects accurately the private feelings in Hanoi toward Rusk's proposal, their leaders were offended, even insulted, by the proposal.

· · ·

The discussion that follows suggests not only that Hanoi's leaders were insulted by the Fourteen Points but also that the sources of their grievances against Washington remain somewhat obscure to Chester Cooper, whose job it was to proclaim the Fourteen Points to many of the dozens of intermediaries he briefed and debriefed during this period. Cooper opens the discussion with a recitation of the Fourteen Points and expresses considerable frustration with the Vietnamese participants in the conference. Why? Because, he says, it is apparent that officials in Hanoi had not seen—and were still unaccountably unable to see—in the Fourteen Points that a coalition government in Hanoi was "in the cards."

Nguyen Khac Huynh responds by addressing Point Thirteen, requiring Hanoi to "cease aggression." His voice ringing with emotion, Nguyen Khac Huynh tries to explain to Cooper why he and his colleagues in Hanoi were supremely insulted by Rusk's Fourteen Points. Cooper responds caustically that perhaps the two sides did not want to understand each other in those days. Nguyen Co Thach then asks why, if the United States could accept the Four Points as the basis for sitting down to negotiations in 1968, in Paris, why couldn't Washington bring itself to do so much earlier? Cooper responds by saying that, as they viewed the situation at the time, this would have required "unilateral surrender." Luu Van Loi concludes the discussion by hinting that Hanoi's reaction to the Fourteen Points may not have been entirely rational—that it was impossible, under the conditions of the moment, to seriously consider such a peace offer, when the bombs were about to fall, or were falling. This, he said, was regarded as extortion or blackmail, to which they were not about to submit.

❖

Chester Cooper: I want to get very specific—painfully specific—about this absolutely fundamental issue of whether we on the U.S. side were serious about negotiations. I sense that we have not so far been able to convince you Vietnamese participants that we were serious. We have had some discussion—interesting discussion—of your Four Points of April 1965. I want to summarize, if you will permit me, the U.S. negotiating position, represented by Dean Rusk's Fourteen Points, which he announced on December 29, 1965, and which were published about a week later by the State Department. This was our position. This was not put forward for propaganda. If you had accepted these—if you had responded productively to these—we would've simply have *had* to use these as the basis for negotiation, because our secretary of state had said so and said so publicly. We would've *had* to do it.

I'll read them as Rusk gave them. Now some of them, I don't necessarily agree with. And some, you wouldn't have agreed with. You know which are which. Here are the points:

1. The Geneva Agreements of 1954 and '62 are an adequate basis for peace;

2. We would welcome a conference on Southeast Asia or any part thereof;

3. We would welcome "negotiations without preconditions";

4. We would accept unconditional discussions;

5. A cessation of hostilities could be the first order of business at such a conference;

6. Hanoi's Four Points could be discussed along with any other points which others might wish to propose;

7. We want no U.S. bases in Southeast Asia;

8. We do not desire to retain U.S. troops in South Vietnam after peace is assured;

9. We support free elections in South Vietnam to give the South Vietnamese a government of their choice;

10. The question of reunification of Vietnam should be determined by the Vietnamese themselves;

11. The countries of Southeast Asia could be nonaligned or neutral if that be their option;

12. We would much prefer to use our resources for the economic reconstruction of Southeast Asia than war;

13. The Viet Cong would have no difficulty being represented and having their views represented if Hanoi decided she wanted to cease aggression;

14. We have said publicly and privately that we could stop the bombing of North Vietnam as a step toward peace, although there has not been the slightest hint of suggestion from the other side as to what they would do if the bombing stopped.

Now those are the Fourteen Points. Secretary Rusk worked these out himself. He felt strongly that this should have enticed you to the negotiating table. Later, he said: "We put everything into the basket except the surrender of South Vietnam." That's just the way he felt about it. That's the way I felt about it. That's the way we all felt about it. But there was no response. . . .

I promise you this: If negotiations had started and proceeded along those lines of the Fourteen Points, then there is absolutely no question in my mind that a coalition government, with the NLF, and with others, was in the cards. That was a "given," because we had already accepted the proposition that the NLF would be a party to the negotiations.[32]

Nguyen Khac Huynh: What was the position of the U.S.? Mr. Cooper has read us Rusk's Fourteen Points. We know about Rusk's Fourteen Points. I would like to respond in some way that gives our American colleagues insight into why the Fourteen Points were so totally—absolutely—unacceptable to us, no matter how reasonable they may appear to you. I don't have nearly enough time to go over all of the Fourteen Points, thus I will focus only on Point Thirteen—the thirteenth point. I apologize to you, Mr. Cooper, for focusing on Number Thirteen, for we know that the number thirteen is unlucky. [Laughter.] Point Thirteen says that the Viet Cong can be represented, and have their views represented, if Hanoi will "cease aggression" in the South. That is more or less the gist of it.

Mr. Cooper, I ask you, and your colleagues, to ask yourselves: What were you saying with this Point Thirteen? Now, to you, or to Rusk, perhaps you think this is more or less equivalent to the point about withdrawing DRV troops from the South. But the Viet Cong, Mr. Cooper, were part of the South! Put yourself in our shoes, reading this thirteenth point. What are we supposed to make of this? I will tell you what we made of it: We called it an insult. It *was* an insult. From this fact alone, we could conclude—we *did* conclude—that this was not a serious proposal of anything realistic.

This was our basic understanding: that the U.S. initiatives were "cover"— were smoke screens—for various efforts to escalate the war.

Chester Cooper: I am beginning to think that not only did we not understand each other, I'm beginning to think we did not *want* to understand each other. My reading of the Fourteen Points of January 1966 is that we would have begun negotiations without any preconditions. We would have unconditional discussions. The Four Points could be discussed together with anything else. Anything.

I mean, just look at the points. We supported free elections. We supported reunification of Vietnam on the terms of the Vietnamese themselves. And we supported a nonaligned—a neutral—South Vietnam. Okay, so your first reading of it was that it insulted you, for some reason. Perhaps we were insensitive. I already admitted that we didn't know anything about Vietnam. What I don't understand is why somebody didn't *ask*: "Well, what do you mean by this?" Or: "Could we discuss this point a bit further?" Or: "Perhaps you could clarify one of these points?" Nobody asked us. Nobody responded. Now one or two of you have said you were insulted because the tone of the Fourteen Points gave you to believe that we were treating you like children. Well, that was far from anything we intended. But as I have listened to this discussion, I am indeed reminded of a parallel to this situation. It was as if my five-year-old daughter, at the time, had written a letter to Santa Claus. There was no response whatsoever.

I get the impression, Mr. Nguyen Khac Huynh, that you are growing weary of explaining your Four Points to us. Well, I feel the same way in trying to get a satisfactory answer as to why the Fourteen Points—I don't understand why the spirit, or even the letter in the Fourteen Points, didn't arouse some reaction in Hanoi.

This was not some gentle probe through an intermediary that—as was often the case—neither of us really knew or perhaps even trusted. This was a direct message from the secretary of state to Hanoi. . . . I said that when we sent these proposals to Hanoi, I felt like my young daughter—then, thirty or thirty-five years ago—sending a letter to Santa Claus. But listening to Mr. Nguyen Khac Huynh's response, I felt like my *grand*daughter *now*, again writing a letter to Santa Claus. And the response she got, so to speak, wasn't any more informative than the one her mother got. It wasn't somehow relevant to my question. . . .

Nguyen Co Thach: I want to assure Mr. Cooper that he is not the only frustrated person at this conference. I personally sympathize with your perplexity at not getting the response you expected to the Fourteen Points in early 1966. With me—with us, on the Vietnamese side—the question goes back to April 8, 1965, six months earlier than your Fourteen Points.

So let me ask again: Why, in 1965—when the Four Points were first announced—did the U.S. do nothing about them—why did the U.S. not react to them. Why? From '68–73, the U.S. recognized the Four Points as valid and tried to work within their framework. Why did all those years pass before you could accept these Four Points?

Chester Cooper: Well, I am going to—forgive me, because this may not translate well—but I am about to sound like a broken record—I have to keep coming back to Secretary Rusk's Fourteen Points. [Laughter.] But in January of '66, in conjunction with the SUNFLOWER initiative, Secretary Rusk said that your Four Points could be a matter of discussion. Now, short of unilateral surrender—short of giving up everything we thought we were fighting for before even entering into negotiations—what else could he have said—what position could we conceivably have taken, to show our seriousness?

Luu Van Loi: You cannot separate our reaction to the Fourteen Points from our reaction to the continued bombing of the North. I mean: These can be separated analytically, of course. Bombing and diplomacy are different. But as for our reaction—the psychology of our reaction—all of these points, all of these proposals, all of these initiatives, all of these intermediaries—all of these efforts foundered, and could not be taken with total seriousness, because of the bombing.

Key Misunderstandings

"The U.S. Intermediary Campaign": Serious or Sham?

Serious discussions about moving to negotiations with the United States began in Hanoi's Foreign Ministry only in February 1965 and were concerned at first almost exclusively with the drafting of the Four Points. The preparation of a wider array of background papers, making contacts with friendly countries, and instituting other mainstays of diplomacy began only with the appointment of Foreign Minister Nguyen Duy Trinh—a southerner, a deputy premier, and a Politburo member—late in 1964.

From the beginning, the staff of the Foreign Ministry faced three problems that proved to be nearly insurmountable: First, they had no experience in the conduct of the sort of international diplomacy they believed was required for dealing with the United States. They had not a single diplomat of international standing who was personally familiar with his counterparts in the United States or in the West generally, with the partial exception of France. Second, they had few resources with which to inform themselves about the Americans. Even *The New York Times* proved too difficult to acquire on a regular basis. Initially, their information about U.S. decisions and actions in Washington came mostly via teletype (known as "tickers") and by monitoring broadcasts by the Voice of America and the British Broadcasting Corporation's "World Service." Junior staff members of the Foreign Ministry—the few who were reasonably fluent in English—monitored the broadcasts and prepared one-page summaries for the leadership. Third, they wished to deal with the United States alone, not via an international forum in which other big powers would participate. Leaders in Hanoi believed that the four big powers—including their two big friends—had imposed a solution (the partition of Vietnam) in Geneva in 1954, and they did not want to tempt fate again.

This is the background against which the Foreign Ministry in Hanoi began to receive messages from the first of a series of intermediaries seeking to broker a deal leading to peace talks between Washington and Hanoi. Messages arrived. Then applications for visas had to be processed. Investigations were required into the credibility of the various intermediaries— including many Americans who were not at the moment members of the U.S. government but who had been in the past. But they—the Vietnamese—had no resources, material or human, to apply to the situation. In principal, they could have turned to Moscow or Beijing for information and assistance, but this was immediately ruled out. The two communist giants were, by 1965, fast becoming their own number-one enemies, and each had already begun to try to leverage Hanoi into choosing sides—aligning with one and abandoning the other. But Hanoi needed the assistance of both for the conduct of the war—chiefly Chinese material and manpower, along with Soviet technology, such as jet fighters and especially surface-to-air missiles for antiaircraft batteries.

As the number and variety of those claiming to be intermediaries grew steadily, so did U.S. escalation of its involvement in the war. By the end of 1965, nearly 200,000 U.S. combat troops were in South Vietnam. Moreover, the bombing campaign was hitting targets increasingly farther north and closer to the major population centers of Hanoi and Haiphong. Just as their own military forces were helpless to prevent the U.S. escalation, the Foreign Ministry personnel were also virtually helpless as they tried to sort out the valid and potentially useful intermediaries from the thrill-seekers and those whom President Johnson derided as "Nobel Peace Prize seekers." Their instinct was to turn correlation into an inference of causation: In other words, the flood of intermediaries approaching Hanoi had, they concluded, been instigated by Washington for two reasons: to make the U.S. appear to be the sincere peaceseeker and the DRV the "aggressor"; and to confuse, possibly to entrap, Hanoi into a bargain that would not be in their interest. Thus, channels suggested in the U.S. "intermediary campaign" came to be distrusted as possible routes to a peaceful settlement. Hanoi would listen, but they remained skeptical throughout.

The conspiracy theory regarding intermediaries that developed in Hanoi's Ministry of Foreign Affairs bore no relation to the situation as viewed in Washington. On the one hand, President Johnson had never really abandoned the methods of political persuasion that propelled him from the Texas backcountry to the White House. David Kraslow and Stuart Loory, writing in 1968, called Johnson's use of intermediaries "fandangle diplomacy":

> Down on the Texas range, they have a form of entertainment that is as big as life. They call it a "fandangle" and it has just about everything in it—barroom brawls, shoot-outs, singing, dancing, herds of cattle, fireworks. A fandangle is a sight to behold, as rancher Lyndon Johnson well-knows. He has brought fandangles to the LBJ Ranch, in sparse hill country forty-eight miles west of Austin, to entertain important guests. Even the most sophisticated come away impressed.[33]

By late 1965, the authors note, "fandangle diplomacy was in full swing."[34] To Lyndon Johnson, America was like Texas and the world was like America.

In fact, the evidence suggests that Johnson was sincere in his expressed hope that one or more of the "acts" in his diplomatic fandangle really would lead to peace talks with Hanoi, and that he was deeply frustrated when the flood of intermediaries he unleashed came back with nothing useful. Already in April 1965 he complained: "I am a reasonably good cowboy, and I can't even rope anybody and bring them in who is willing to talk and settle this by negotiation. We send them messages through our allies—one country, two countries, three countries, four countries or five countries . . . and they say, we can't even talk to you."[35] Technically, Johnson put Averell Harriman and Chester Cooper in what he called his "peace shop" in 1966, in order to stay on top of all the peace initiatives. In fact, he did not give them the authority they needed to do a job he wanted to control himself.[36]

State Department professionals were also frustrated by this scattergun approach. Chester Cooper has recalled that during a brief period in the spring of 1966, he fielded offers from "Mrs. Ghandi, Tito, Nasser, Wilson, U Thant, Eden and a host of others."[37] And Washington had a conspiracy theory of its own, centered on UN Secretary General U Thant. On February 24, 1965, U Thant implied to the press that officials in Washington were lying about the war and that peace could be obtained if only Washington would be reasonable. Dean Rusk recalled many years later: "I thought he lied like a sailor. I never had much respect for U Thant's integrity." As Rusk pointed out on the basis of this affair, "sometimes intermediaries will say things to each side that go beyond the facts."[38]

The net result of all this activity was that Hanoi came to believe that

Washington had organized a campaign of intermediaries to help Washington win the war; and Washington came to believe, on the basis of dozens of failed attempts to make contact in Hanoi, that its leaders simply were not interested in a peaceful settlement on any terms other than a U.S. surrender.

. . .

The discussion is opened by Tran Quang Co, who was for a time in charge of oversight of the intermediaries in Hanoi's Foreign Ministry. In blunt language, Tran Quang Co states that the U.S. intermediary campaign was created for public relations purposes, showed the lack of seriousness in Washington, and was insulting to him and his colleagues in Hanoi. Chester Cooper, who had a job similar to Tran Quang Co's on the Washington side, disagrees strongly. Nearly all were sincere efforts to find a peaceful settlement, he says, and that is what made them so frustrating. In one of the most emotional statements of the June 1997 conference, he vehemently denies the charge that the initiatives were not serious. Tran Quang Co responds by saying, in equally fervent terms, that however well-meaning some Americans in Washington may have been, what was seen in Hanoi was the constant conjunction of intermediaries and the escalation of the war, with troops in the South and bombing in the North.

Robert McNamara supports Chester Cooper's claim about the basic motivation behind most of the initiatives: They were serious attempts, he says, and he is sure of it because he was the originator of many of them.

❖

Tran Quang Co: In the U.S. intermediary campaign, the U.S. clearly wanted to force North Vietnam to surrender—or the equivalent of surrender—all of its objectives in the conflict. . . .

The U.S. tried to use a very plentiful, very diverse group of intermediaries. There were dozens of them, from many countries. Some came from countries that were close to the U.S., such as Canada, England, and France. But there were also countries involved that belonged to the Third World, such as Egypt, such as Ghana, such as Algeria, and still others. These were not all. The U.S. even involved socialist countries in these efforts, such as the Soviet Union and the Eastern European countries.

So what was our analysis of this bewildering use of intermediaries by the U.S.? According to our analysis, this could only mean that the U.S., with its hunger for publicity, was seeking in every way available to tell the world that it was the U.S.—the U.S., not North Vietnam—that seeks a peaceful solution. Why did the U.S. feel it had to do this? In order to try to justify—in the eyes of the world—the bombing of the North. That is what these intermediaries were for—to help the U.S. justify its bombing. The basic argument that they tried to get across in this way was that North Vietnam was not concerned with peace—was belligerent—and so if North Vietnam wants war, then—according to this U.S. approach—then it will get it—it will get a war, until it realizes it had better start negotiating. . . .

With all this diplomatic activity, the U.S. tried to convince the international community to justify the fact that the U.S., a big and powerful country, was fighting a small, poor country, and was doing so with such violence. The U.S. hoped that the international community would conclude that the U.S. had no choice but to "punish" Vietnam with the bombing—especially with the bombing.

Chester Cooper: I want to argue with much of what was said by Mr. Tran Quang Co. I want to respond by explaining to you what the thinking was actually like in Washington during the time that these efforts to negotiate with you were going on. I'm not talking about what's in these documents. [Points to briefing notebook.] I'm talking about feelings, interpretations, "atmosphere," if you like—something Mr. Co emphasized. I want to tell you what it was like in Washington as we were frantically—and ineptly, as it turned out—looking for a way out of this terrible mess. . . .

You didn't like our use of intermediaries. Let me tell you why we used so many different intermediaries. It was because we couldn't—we really couldn't—get to you any other way. . . . We were desperate to find somebody who would deliver a message. Let me assure you—and if you didn't believe it then, I hope you will believe it now—that if anything promising had been proposed to us by you, we would have sent Averell Harriman or me, or both of us, directly to Hanoi to discuss it. That's how serious we were. But nothing serious was ever proposed. We couldn't even get a serious answer to our own proposals. That's the way we felt about it.

I want to respond to the charge that all this—all these efforts—were nothing but, or mostly nothing but, propaganda. That's wrong! . . . A concern for public relations was *not* what was driving this process. It was a sincere attempt to locate and make use of someone—anyone—who seemed to us to have the ability to get through to you. At a minimum, we hoped they would deliver messages faithfully and accurately and somehow convince you to respond in kind. That's what that effort was about. And given the way you organized your own affairs—I am not criticizing you, just stating what I think is a fact—the great secrecy in which you cloaked your own process—even today it seems this is the case—I can see why you might have thought that our public efforts, with people scurrying every which way, these speeches by the president talking about these efforts—I can see why you might have been suspicious. But I am here to tell you: You should have taken them seriously, because they were meant seriously. . . .

We were very serious. And the problem—the core problem—it seems to me in looking back on it is this: *We just could not find a way to have direct contact with each other!* Some of that was our fault. But some of it was certainly your fault as well. We never knew what you thought about the initiatives. These intermediaries should never have been sent. Many were not capable. I'm not even sure that some of them were trustworthy. At least some of them probably didn't understand what we were talking about. And some of these people got involved because they thought they might win the Nobel Peace Prize. [Laughter.] That was no way to run a negotiation.

Tran Quang Co: . . . I would like to . . . offer a few reactions to the discussion thus far, especially regarding a question raised so forcefully by Mr. McNamara, but also by others on the U.S. side. That question is: Were there "missed opportunities" during this period to end the war via one or more of these contacts which were initiated by the U.S.? I think the answer is "no," as I will now explain.

1. *"Peace Initiatives."* In 1965, the Vietnam War entered a new stage. One of the major features in this stage was the emergence of a series of "peace initiatives" by the U.S., some open and some secret, which had not previously been a feature of U.S. policy. Now, in this conference, the U.S. side has mentioned only six or seven major initiatives. However, according to detailed U.S. accounts, between February 1965 and April 1967, the U.S. side put forth forty-one peace probes. So, on average, the U.S. initiated two contacts per month during this period.

   What, then, was the substance of this increasingly hectic series of "peace initiatives," especially the secret ones? For what purpose were they put forward? And most important, were they really aimed at achieving peace, or were they part of the general U.S. strategy of escalating the war at that time?

2. *The Context.* Let us review the circumstances under which these "peace initiatives" took place. On the battlefield, the U.S. was vigorously shifting from the "special war" (or counterinsurgency) to "local war," beginning with the introduction of combat troops into South Vietnam. (The U.S. had a total of 23,000 men in South Vietnam by the end of 1964; by early 1967, nearly half a million U.S. and allied troops were present.) The U.S. was also expanding the air war and artillery attacks in the North, hoping to end the war within two years by achieving a military victory. . . .

3. *The U.S. Position.* What was the U.S. negotiating position? Through the open statements of U.S. officials, as well as the contents of the secret contacts between 1965–1967, one could summarize the U.S. position as follows: conditional cessation of bombing; unconditional negotiations modeled on the Geneva Accords of 1954 (which the U.S. had rejected ten years earlier, so that it could interfere directly in Vietnam). In this way, the U.S. made use of two trump cards: cessation of bombing of the North; and the contingent withdrawal of U.S. troops—which were used to exert pressure on North Vietnam, to make North Vietnam pay a price.

4. *U.S. Objective.* All these factors lead to the conclusion that the U.S. "peace initiatives" all aimed at two objectives: first, to serve the escalation of the war, by diverting world and U.S. domestic public opinion against the efforts to expand and escalate the war; and second, to press North Vietnam to choose either of two options—surrender or be destroyed. This conclusion seems to me inescapable. During the period under discussion, 1965–1967, the U.S. government was convinced that they would win the "local war" and therefore they did not think a negotiated solution was necessary. This is why I believe we cannot consider this period as having any significant "missed opportunities" for peace.

Robert McNamara: . . . I want to state without any qualifications whatsoever—and there's nobody in this room who can credibly dispute me on this—many, I'd say most, of the U.S. efforts toward negotiation [particularly in the period Mr. Co is referring to] were not—I repeat were *not*—directed primarily toward achieving a propaganda objective.[39] Now I say that without qualification, and I am absolutely sure of myself on the point, because I personally initiated several of those.

The "Bottom Lines": Why Weren't They Reconciled?

During most of the period under reexamination, Washington and Hanoi interpreted the terms of a peace settlement offered by one another as requiring the equivalent of an unconditional surrender. In the typical pattern, this interpretation led to angry rejoinders and rejections, which in turn seemed to confirm the assumptions of both: that the other was being so utterly unreasonable as to suggest that the adversary's stance ruled out compromise or even negotiation in any meaningful sense. This scenario was replayed a dozen or more times between mid-1965 and late 1967.

What did each side regard as the other's "bottom lines"—the minimum objectives acceptable at the end of a process of negotiation? Washington believed Hanoi would never settle for anything other than military conquest of South Vietnam and the unification of Vietnam under the rule of Hanoi's totalitarian dictatorship, followed by subsequent attempts by Hanoi to conquer the rest of Indochina in the same fashion. Since each of these supposed objectives was absolutely anathema to U.S. officials of all stripes, there was thought to be nothing to negotiate about. This is what Dean Rusk referred to when he said that with the announcement of his Fourteen Points, "We have put everything into the basket of peace except the surrender of South Vietnam."[40]

This interpretation of Hanoi's motives and mode of operation was embedded, moreover, in Western notions of how communists negotiated with liberal Western democracies. According to former CIA analyst Allan Goodman:

> For Communists, negotiating is a tactic of warfare. The American conception of negotiation is a process of bargaining and concession, and the outcome of negotiation is compromise, not victory. Americans expect to bargain, and we expect a military stalemate will cause our adversaries to do the same.
>
> Negotiating while fighting thus served Hanoi's purposes far better than it did Washington's. Hanoi used negotiation as a tactic of warfare, convinced that only a military victory, not concessions at a conference table, could end the war.[41]

This comparison is a caricature of the attitudes leaders in Washington and Hanoi had toward their own positions. Yet it accurately reflects the way Americans came to view the bottom line of their opponents in Hanoi. Henry Kissinger also came to this view. "Bismarck," he wrote, "had once said that German unity would never come about through talk but by 'blood and iron,' which was precisely Hanoi's views on Vietnamese unity."[42] In short, the Hanoi government was viewed as totally rigid, unyielding, and bent on conquest.

Hanoi's view of Washington's bottom line was, if anything, more extreme, even less likely to encourage an adversary's entry in negotiations. Moreover, Hanoi's estimate of Washington's bottom line was derived almost exclusively from the battlefield. This point has been made over and over again by Vietnamese participants in our joint project on the war: Deeds spoke louder than words, because their country was the theater of battle. That is the reality they had to deal with daily. Here is Prime Minister Pham Van Dong, speaking on August 31, 1965:

> We must consider not the statements by the U.S. ruling circles, but their deeds. What have they done? They have been intensifying the aggressive war

in South Vietnam and stepping up the escalation in the North. They have decided to dispatch all at once 50,000 more U.S. combat troops and still more in the future to South Vietnam and at the same time are making preparations . . . for expansion of the war in this area.

In a word, President Johnson talks about peace in an attempt to cover up his war schemes; the more he talks about peace the more he steps up the war.[43]

This was rhetoric, of course, but it was also more than that. Pham Van Dong was speaking to people who spent part of each day in bomb shelters, people who had doubtless already lost loved ones either to the war of destruction (the bombing of the North) or the war of aggression (U.S. troop activities in the South).

Moreover, given the paucity of reliable information on the United States available to the Hanoi leadership, it must have seemed natural to begin their assessment of U.S. bottom lines with their immediate reality. It is a pity, however, that they seem to have relied so heavily on it, to the exclusion of virtually every public statement made during the period by President Johnson or his senior advisers. To leaders in Hanoi, the U.S. bottom line was the utter annihilation of the Hanoi regime, a thought that no doubt made it difficult to pay attention to anything other than the brutal reality of bombs and bullets.

. . .

Robert McNamara initiates discussion on "bottom lines" with an unscheduled intervention. He begins by summarizing the argument given above by Allan Goodman: Communists don't approach negotiations expecting to compromise, whereas Westerners do. He then says that as he has been listening to the discussion at the June 1997 conference, he has sketched out what he takes to be the real, rather than the imagined, bottom lines of Washington and Hanoi. He divides each of them into three parts and notes that the bottom lines are not irreconcilable, as leaders on both sides believed between mid-1965 and late 1967.

Tran Quang Co responds that he believed during the 1960s—and he believes he was correct in this belief—that the real purpose served by ostensible U.S. interest in negotiations was to determine if Hanoi's will had yet been broken. Washington simply wished to know, he says, whether the Vietnamese people had been sufficiently punished.

Before anyone on the U.S. side can respond—many raised their hands wishing to speak—Nguyen Khac Huynh, amazed at the other part of McNamara's intervention—about the bottom lines—asks McNamara a question without going through the chairman. He says, first of all, that McNamara's delineation of Hanoi's bottom line is correct. He then asks whether McNamara discovered this years ago—when he was a member of the U.S. leadership—or more recently. McNamara responds by saying that he has come to this judgment only at this conference in Hanoi, a comment that is both humorous and tragic at the same time.

◈

Robert McNamara: I think I'm beginning to understand why the . . . peace initiatives failed. One of the reasons, I think, is that we each had a quite different approach to negotiations. I think that our approach involved compromise. We entered into the negotiating process expecting to have to compromise. In this sense, we conceived of negotiations as a situation in which each side would appraise the bottom line of the other side. Then, having established his own bottom line, each would examine the two bottom lines and see if they could be reconciled at acceptable cost. That was the way we conceived of the process. That was our basic assumption, going into any kind of possible negotiation.

Now what were your bottom lines? I see three of them:

1. Stop the U.S. bombing of the North.

2. Obtain withdrawal of U.S. troops.

3. Agree to bring the NLF into a coalition government—at a minimum—and establish a process that would lead to reunification of your nation.

Those were your objectives as we saw them.

What were our bottom lines? There were also three:

1. Obtain the return of U.S. prisoners.

2. Achieve participation of some of the members of the South Vietnamese government in a coalition government.

The third is the most important—and this goes back to our mindset and our basic objective. As I said yesterday, we were not opposed to a reunified Vietnam, we understood why you wanted it, we supported that. *But*:

3. Obtain assurances that a reunified Vietnam would not serve as a base for extension of Soviet and/or Chinese hegemony throughout Asia.

Now those were your bottom lines and our bottom lines. And as I sit here today, one of the most tragic thoughts in my mind is those were *not* irreconcilable! They *were* reconcilable! Just write them down and put them together and you can't help but notice that they are—they were reconcilable. But they weren't reconciled. The problem is that neither of us understood—or believed, neither of us believed—that these in fact *were* one another's bottom lines. But if we had known and accepted that they were, then they are not—and would not have been—irreconcilable. And it is not yet clear to me why they weren't reconciled.

Tran Quang Co: You say that in the Vietnamese view—in our view, therefore—the negotiation process was merely a tactic for war that sought to take advantage of time—of "buying time"—in order to increase the advantage of our military forces. If you take this point of view, then it must be the U.S. which is the one interested in peace and that North Vietnam did not care for peace—was not serious about peace.

To us, the situation looked like this. We realized your motives during the period of all these U.S. overtures for peace, between '65–68. We especially realized the U.S. intent during '65–67. Between '65 and '67 was the period of the greatest U.S. escalation. You were still optimistic about the effects of the bombing campaign in the North, at this point, because you thought we might sue for peace, or something like that. But from the end of 1967 and into early 1968, the U.S. began to have doubts as to whether the bombing of the North would accomplish this objective—of forcing North Vietnam to surrender or sue for peace on U.S. terms.[44] These doubts led the U.S. to consider peace. That is what we believed.

Why did we believe this? First: In what kind of atmosphere did the U.S. open up these initiatives—or try to open them up? It seems to us absolutely clear that the peace initiatives of '65–68, especially in '65 and '67, occurred simultaneously with the vigorous escalation of the U.S. war effort—step by step, gradually, according to the U.S. plan. So we had to ask ourselves: What is the meaning of the introduction of peace initiatives coinciding with an intensification of the U.S. military effort? We asked ourselves this question. The answer was not so hard to find: The U.S. was trying to pressure Vietnam militarily and was probing, every so often, to see if we thought we had been "punished" enough.

Nguyen Khac Huynh: . . . Mr. McNamara . . . you have presented very clearly the three minimum objectives of each side. From the Vietnamese side, I would say you have described our objectives—our minimum objectives—correctly. I would therefore like to ask you: At what point did you come to your understanding of these objectives—of these "bottom lines"? Just recently or during the war? And within the U.S. leadership, while you were still within the leadership, had anyone considered these minimum objectives? As scholars, we are concerned with the real situation at the time—what people actually had in their minds at the time. Did you or others think of this then, in the middle 1960s, as we have been discussing?

Robert McNamara: . . . I'll tell you the truth. I thought of them the night before last, on the basis of what I had heard in our discussions here at this conference. [Laughter.] That's a little late, I know. [Laughter continues.]

Now that's funny in one sense, but in another sense, it just emphasizes the tragedy of having missed all those opportunities—to try to merge or reconcile the bottom lines I described to you. We, like you, were under tremendous pressure in those days. I mean tremendous pressure. I have mentioned this in my book, but it comes home to me again here in Hanoi: We did not—we in the U.S. leadership did not—take nearly enough time to focus on these problems, at a point where maybe we could have reached some sort of compromise. In my book, I compare our performance during the Vietnam War with the way we handled the Cuban missile crisis. There was no comparison. In October 1962, we focused our minds totally on the problem, and we solved it. Just barely in time, as it turns out. But on Vietnam, we just never got our minds wrapped around the issues in the way that I presented them to you today, and that you say—and I thank you for telling me—is basically a correct view of what it would have taken to get our two sides together in—I'll say not later than 1965—and therefore prevent a lot of what happened later.

THE IMPACT OF CASUALTIES
ON HANOI'S READINESS TO NEGOTIATE

Under Robert McNamara, the U.S. Defense Department was the clearinghouse for hard information on how the war in Vietnam was going. McNamara and many of his staff had the disadvantage of having had little experience in international diplomacy and were often surprised and sometimes irritated by what they perceived as the unwonted niceties and "slow motion" of decisionmaking in the State Department. Yet the Defense analysts, led by McNamara himself, had the advantage of being relatively unblindered by ideology, by historical analogies (such as "Vietnam=Korea" or "Vietnam=Munich"), or by personal relations (of lack of them) with foreign leaders. They looked at the facts and drew their conclusions on the basis of what they saw.

This is the background for one of the most profound transformations of the war: the evolution of awareness at senior levels in the Department of Defense that the war could not be won at acceptable political cost. Few if any of those who came to hold this view began their involvement with the Vietnam War with this attitude. Many believed, like others in the government and in the United States as a whole, that (to use the shorthand of the day) "Ho Chi Minh could be bombed to the negotiating table." There were variations on this theme developed at U.S. military headquarters in Saigon. General Westmoreland spoke of a "crossover point" beyond which Hanoi and the NLF would be unable to replace their casualties at a rate that would adequately compensate for their losses. Westmoreland's deputy, Gen. William Depuy, spoke of a "threshold of pain" beyond which Hanoi and the NLF would give up the fight.[45] But of course these points, or thresholds, were never reached, though optimists in Saigon and Washington claimed regularly that the United States was—at last—within sight of bringing Hanoi and the NLF to its knees in this fashion.

McNamara and some members of his staff began early on to question some of the underlying military assumptions. It is evident in his communications with the Joint Chiefs of Staff (JCS). For example, on August 31, 1964, months before the sustained bombing campaign, and just after the Tonkin Gulf attack and retaliation, McNamara wrote the following to Air Force Gen. Curtis LeMay, the acting chairman of the JCS:

> I have examined with great interest and satisfaction your recent analysis of the 94 targets in North Vietnam. . . . If the destruction of the 94 targets were not to succeed in its objective of destroying the DRV will and capability, what courses of action would you recommend?[46]

Already we see the attention to detail and the hard questions being put to military people, like General Le May, unused to having to defend their choices to so rigorous a civilian chief. And already we see that the objective of the coming air war will be to break the will of Hanoi to carry on the fight.

But as sorties against targets in North Vietnam grew to hundreds and thousands and tens of thousands, it became clear to many in the Defense Department that, for whatever reason, the will of Hanoi would not, and could not, be broken in this fashion. By August 1967, McNamara went public with this conclusion in his controversial testimony to the Senate Armed Services Committee. This is summed up in *In Retrospect* as follows: "The case against expanding the air war was clear. All you had to do was look at the numbers."[47]

But in August 1967, this was precisely what many did not wish to do because, as he said in his testimony on August 25:

> There is nothing in the past reaction of the North Vietnamese leaders that would provide any confidence that they can be bombed to the negotiating table. . . .
>
> The capacity of the lines of communication and of the outside sources of supply so far exceeds the minimal flow necessary to support the present level of North Vietnamese military effort in South Vietnam that the enemy operations in the South cannot, on the basis of any reports I have seen, be stopped by air bombardment—short, that is, of the virtual annihilation of North Vietnam and its people.[48]

McNamara's statement was made public at a time when efforts to establish a cease-fire and move to negotiations were under way in the secret negotiations known by their U.S. code name, "PENNSYLVANIA."

At the end of the day he said:

> The tragic and drawn out character of the conflict in the South makes very tempting the prospect of replying to it with some kind of new air campaign against the North. But however tempting, such an alternative seems to me completely illusory. To pursue this objective would not only be futile, but would involve risks to our personnel and to our nation that I am unwilling to recommend.[49]

The conservative senators facing McNamara were incensed and called him a defeatist. Sen. Strom Thurmond responded by saying: "Mr. Secretary—your statement . . . is a statement of placating the communists. It is a statement of no-win."[50] But this was the reality, as McNamara saw it.

The salient point is that even though this was the conclusion of McNamara and some of his associates, based on their analyses of the willingness of Hanoi and its southern allies to carry on the fight after taking so much punishment, it astounded most military and civilian officials in the U.S. government. Few had believed at the outset that any people could take that much punishment and still not give up, or at least seek some sort of accommodation with an enemy possessing, in effect, infinitely more potential firepower than themselves. One of McNamara's associates at this time, Townsend Hoopes, described the U.S. dilemma in its starkest terms in 1969, shortly after he left government. Hoopes contrasts two "strategies"—the strategy of the strong, and the strategy of the weak. We who are militarily and economically strong, according to Hoopes, take this view:

We believe the enemy can be forced to be "reasonable," i.e., to compromise or even capitulate, because we assume he wants to avoid pain, death, and material destruction. We assume that if these are inflicted on him with increasing severity, then at some point in the process he will want to stop the suffering. . . .

In Vietnam, however, according to Hoopes, the United States encountered people whose only plausible option was what he calls the "strategy of the weak":

The strategy of the weak is therefore a natural choice of ideologues in Asia, for it converts Asia's capacity for endurance in suffering into an instrument for exploiting. . . . It does this, in effect, by inviting the West, which possesses unanswerable military power, to carry its strategic logic to its final conclusion, which is genocide.[51]

He concludes: "At that point we hesitate, for remembering Hitler and Hiroshima and Nagasaki, we realize anew that genocide is a terrible burden to bear."[52] This is exactly the point McNamara made in his August 1967 testimony. It is a point learned by a hard look at the data—and by no inconsiderable reflection on the hideous implications of "winning" in such a situation.

.   .   .

Robert McNamara leads off by asking a question that has been on his mind for more than thirty years: Why didn't Hanoi come forward, between mid-1965 and late 1967, and explore the possibilities of a negotiated settlement? With all the death and destruction that was occurring daily, he asks: Wouldn't it have been wise for Hanoi to have responded more favorably to the U.S. peace initiatives?

The stage is thus set for one of the pivotal moments of the June 1997 conference in Hanoi. Tran Quang Co understands McNamara not to be asking a question about the peace probes, which was his intent, but rather to be accusing the Hanoi leadership of crimes against their own people—insensitivity to the pain and suffering of their own people. Working up to a fever pitch of emotion, he suddenly switches into English and accuses McNamara of being "wrong, terribly wrong," if he believes that Hanoi's leaders did not appreciate the suffering of their people. These are the very words—"wrong, terribly wrong"—that had already become the most quoted words of McNamara's memoir, *In Retrospect*.[53] Tran Quang Co's intervention ends abruptly, followed by a long, total silence.

Dao Huy Ngoc, who is chairing the session, finally adds that he under-stands McNamara's perplexity, but that Vietnamese suffering must be understood against the background of 4,000 years of history, much of which has involved suffering at least as devastating, if not more so, than that which they endured in the American War. Nguyen Co Thach, the leader of the Viet-namese team, closes the discussion by saying that, of course, the leaders in Hanoi, and the Vietnamese people generally, wanted peace, "but not peace at any price."

❖

Robert McNamara: I really have two points to raise; one is a statement and the other is a question that follows from the statement. My statement derives from what I've heard here at this conference, from what I thought about at the time—now thirty years ago—and from what I've read since that time. It is this: that a negotiation between Hanoi and the U.S. at any time between the end of 1965 and March of '68 when President Johnson made his speech that led to—that started the negotiations—a serious negotiation anytime during that period would have led to a settlement roughly as favor-able to each side as that which eventually evolved and was signed in Paris in 1973. That's my belief—my statement. I just don't understand, from what I have heard yesterday and today, why it didn't occur.

I also have a question that follows from this belief. During that period—from the end of '65 to March of '68—Vietnam (and here I use Vietnam meaning North and South, military and civilian), but primarily the North, was suffering casualties at a tremendous rate. I don't have the exact casualty figures, but deriving them from the fatality figures which Hanoi has devel-oped, Vietnam was suffering casualties at the rate of roughly a million a year during that period. Now if you accept that as anywhere close to the correct figure—and I don't want to argue whether it's a million or six hundred thou-sand or a million two hundred thousand—it was a tremendous loss, a tremendous penalty to the Vietnamese people, particularly the North, but to the South as well. My belief is that there could have been negotiations between the end of '65 and '68 which would have led to a settlement that was roughly the same as the one that eventually occurred, but without that terrible loss of life.

Why didn't it occur? Were you not influenced by the loss of lives? Why didn't it move you toward negotiations? Weren't there, from your point of view, reasons to probe the degree to which you could have "manipulated" the negotiations in ways that would have been favorable to you? Why didn't you at least probe the degree to which we could have been persuaded to reduce the military pressure, to move toward a unified Vietnam, unaligned. Now in a sense that's what ultimately happened. But at a tremendous cost in human life. Why weren't the negotiations started earlier? I have not heard anything this morning that answers that question.

Tran Quang Co: I would like to answer Mr. McNamara's question. You imply that there was a difference in attitude toward the war between the people of North and the North Vietnamese leadership. You have this misconception that even though the Vietnamese people were suffering because of the war, still the Vietnamese leadership did not want peace, did not want to proceed to peace.

I must say that this question of Mr. McNamara's has allowed us to better understand the issue. During the coffee break, an American colleague asked me if I have learned anything about the U.S. during the discussions of the past few days. And I responded that I have learned quite a lot. However, thanks to this particular question, I believe we have learned still more about the U.S. We understand better now that the U.S. understands very little about Vietnam. Even now—in this conference—the U.S. understands very little about Vietnam.

When the U.S. bombed the North and brought its troops into the South, well, of course to us these were very negative moves. However, with regard to Vietnam, U.S. aggression did have some positive use. Never before did the people of Vietnam, from top to bottom, unite as they did during the years that the U.S. was bombing us. Never before had Chairman Ho Chi Minh's appeal—that there is nothing more precious than freedom and independence—go straight to the hearts and minds of the Vietnamese people as at the end of 1966.

But if Mr. McNamara thinks that the North Vietnamese leadership was not concerned about the suffering of the Vietnamese people, with deaths and privation, then he has a huge misconception of Vietnam. That would be [Speaks in English.] "wrong, terribly wrong." [Resumes in Vietnamese.] There was never any such thing. On the contrary, if at that time we had begun negotiations with the U.S., we would have had to explain to the people why we could negotiate with the U.S., to meet with the U.S., and host the U.S., while bombs fell on us. On the contrary, it must be said that at those moments, when the bombs were falling, there was a complete unity between the leaders and the people. There could be no negotiations under the pressure of the bombing. We have to keep in mind that the war occurred on Vietnamese soil, not in America. Because we suffered a thousand times more than you, we needed and sought peace all the more.

Dao Huy Ngoc: When you look at this question of the sacrifice made by Vietnam in the war, you must also consider the history of our country. When we gained our independence in 1945 we already had 4,000 years of history. For 1,000 years, we were under the feudalist control of the North [of China]. We had to fight in order to regain our independence. And 3,000 years later we had to fight to regain our independence again. Then after independence—after the August Revolution—we had to fight the French for nine years in order to protect our independence. Only then came the fight against the U.S.

So, yes, I would agree with what Mr. McNamara has said. The price that we had to pay is huge. But it is far larger, and has been going on for much longer, than Mr. McNamara referred to—during the three years of the Vietnam War—1965 to 1968. And so I am afraid that to understand the Vietnamese attitude or psychology about this issue of sacrifice, it is not enough to just look at the American War. If you focus only on the American War, you will not understand it. I agree with you and in fact I sympathize with your "perplexity," as you called it. But you must look at the entire process of our history, the way the Vietnamese people look at it—the way they looked at it during the war. You Americans "discovered" Vietnam in 1945 or 1954 or 1961—in any case, very recently. But we see these events we are discussing in a 4,000-year perspective. This makes a big difference. This is why Chairman Ho Chi Minh's declaration was a realization of the hopes of all Vietnamese people, not just the leadership.

Nguyen Co Thach: I ask you: Why on earth would Vietnam *not* be serious about peace? The war was on Vietnamese soil. Why would Vietnam not want peace? We wanted the war to end early—as soon as possible—the earlier the better, the less our people would have to suffer. I can assure you, we wanted peace very badly. But not at any price, not if we had to give up what we were fighting for. But still, we wanted—the Vietnamese people wanted—peace.

I wanted to emphasize this because, based on questions from some reporters outside this conference, and some things said by the participants here, some may have gotten the impression that Vietnam—that Vietnamese leaders—did not care about the lives of the Vietnamese people—that Vietnam would not think much about those Vietnamese who lost their lives—the many who lost their lives. Let me just say this: Those who believe this—if any of you believe this [Gestures at U.S. participants.]—this is wrong, this is very wrong—a complete misunderstanding of Vietnam.

Why a Bombing "Halt,"
Not an (Evolving) Bombing "Pause"?

On no issue was the U.S.-Vietnamese strategic disconnect more profound than that of the bombing of the North and its relation to the viability of any plan to move to negotiations. Officials in Washington regarded bombing as a device to raise the cost of Hanoi's support of their NLF allies in the South, that is, as something that could be used to coerce Hanoi into agreeing to move to a negotiated settlement. So Washington repeatedly stopped the bombing and offered not to resume, conditional on Hanoi's agreement to stop (or lessen or not increase— the formula varied from time to time) its resupply of their forces and NLF forces in the South. Virtually all top U.S. officials were positively mystified by Hanoi's stubborn recalcitrance on this single issue of the bombing.

The negotiating volume in the *Pentagon Papers* contains a telling formulation of the disconnect between Washington and Hanoi on this issue. On January 28, 1967, Hanoi Foreign Minister Nguyen Duy Trinh made the following announcement in an English broadcast over Radio Hanoi:

> It is only after the unconditional cessation of U.S. bombing and all other acts of war against the DRV that there could be talks between the DRV and the U.S.[54]

The author of the synopsis in the *Pentagon Papers* describes the dilemma this and similar announcements posed for U.S. officials. "Washington," the author laments, "is given very little notion of what it would get in exchange for a bombing cessation."[55]

The inability to understand Hanoi's position on this issue was perhaps the source of President Johnson's greatest perplexity with regard to the war. Hanoi's position violated everything he thought he knew about bargaining chips, the use of implied threats, and other techniques of which he was the U.S. Senate's acknowledged master before becoming president. Since Hanoi was deemed unresponsive to his attempts to "seduce Ho," as he liked to put it, with bombing pauses, Johnson became deeply disillusioned and confused. Already in December 1965, while discussing the merits of what would soon become the Christmas bombing pause, Johnson was pessimistic. A pause, he said,

> is more a sign of weakness than anything else. All we'll get is distrust from our allies, despair from our troops, and disgruntled generals. Hanoi and

Peking tell us we're weak—won't do anything if we pause. If we suffer a severe reverse as a result of this, we'd never explain it.[56]

This attitude was more like an albatross that he carried with him from mid-1965 until the end of his presidency.

How to account for Hanoi's behavior? Basically, their unyielding position seems to have been driven by two factors, one more "rational" than the other. First, there was a kind of unspoken vow taken by the leadership, but also understood and appreciated by the majority of citizens of North Vietnam as well, never to show weakness to the United States under any circumstances. Sensing their own total vulnerability to U.S. military power, their greatest fear seems to have been showing interest in the bombing pauses, because it was precisely in such situations that the Americans might just be checking to see if they were caving in. And if the Americans should believe this, Hanoi seems to have drawn the most dire conclusion: The Americans would "go in for the kill." Second, as is evident in the discussion that immediately follows, there was something humiliating and degrading about being bombed and having no ability to either prevent it or to respond in kind. Thus, for reasons of state and for somewhat more personal or psychological reasons, there seems not to have been much debate in Hanoi about their stand: The bombing must stop unconditionally, or no talks. Period.

These are not the sorts of beliefs that one typically finds committed to print in official documents. The following discussion, however, provides insight into the sources of what was, during the period in question, the single, most perplexing signal arriving in Washington from Hanoi.

❖

James Blight: I think from the point of view of the U.S. government, from April 1965, when the Four Points were announced, there was never any attempt, any response, from the Vietnamese side suggesting that the Hanoi government had any interest in a process by which a five day ... bombing pause might, by mutual agreement, become ten, or twenty or forty or whatever, and then finally evolve—that is the key element that they saw lacking—the possibility that an initiative might *evolve* into something permanent. The impression they had was this: that either the U.S. must comply with your ultimatum, or there would be no discussion between the two sides.

Nguyen Khac Huynh: First, let us return to the context of 1965–1967. The U.S. objective was twofold: to "break the back of the Vietcong," and to break the will of North Vietnam. We understood the Americans to be committed to a military victory. We anticipated the escalating commitment of troops, and the expansion of the war to the North. So we had to bear down. We believed that what happened on the battlefield would be the decisive determinant of what would happen at the negotiating table. So we decided resolutely to defeat Westmoreland's plan. We tried to shoot down as many U.S. planes as we could, and tried to reduce as much as possible the damage caused by U.S. bombing of the North. The United States used the diplomatic front in support of its military objectives, and we did the same. That is the first point: This was war and each side was trying to win, according to its own definition of "winning."

Second, it seems that you still do not fully understand our demand for a bombing halt before we could begin negotiations. . . . Let me try to explain our views one more time. The bombing of the North was an extremely serious violation of our national sovereignty. It demeaned our humanity. It wounded our national pride and our international reputation. So as long as the United States bombed the North, we could not seriously entertain the possibility of entering into negotiations, at the end of which would be a compromise. The demand that the United States cease bombing unconditionally was not—I repeat was *not*—a diplomatic ploy. It was a sincere and serious demand. As long as the United States bombed, there could be no official talks. We believed that when the American will to prosecute the war weakened, the United States might come to the table. But we could not talk while the bombs fell. We did not debate this among ourselves because there was no dissent. None. We all felt the same way.

Third, the longest pause was thirty-seven days in December–January 1965–1966. Our understanding of the bombing pauses was as follows: They were used by the U.S. to determine whether the will of the DRV had been broken. That was our understanding of their purpose. In other words, the U.S. more or less "checked the pulse" of the DRV by an occasional bombing pause.

Fourth, even in May 1968 we "sang the same song" to Averell Harriman and Cyrus Vance, as the will of the U.S. was in the process of breaking down. That song was: No negotiations without an unconditional bombing halt. Even then, in Paris, we had to sing that song for six months before we finally saw some movement, by October of 1968.

Fifth, I freely admit that you are, in a sense, right to say that we were "inflexible"—in regard to the requirement of an unconditional bombing halt. That is true. We did not budge for several years on that, no matter what you did and no matter who you sent to talk to us. But I ask you now, in the light of history, to consider the situation we found ourselves in. The war was in its initial stages and both sides still believed they could win.

Moreover, the negotiations did not mean the same thing to us as they meant to you. For you, for the U.S., negotiations would provide a way to stop a war that you discover you cannot win. But we cannot just walk away from the war, because of what the war is *about*—it is about our country, about whether our country will continue to exist or not. We felt our backs to the wall. Under these circumstances, how could we be "flexible"? We did not know how to be "flexible." So every time you "took our pulse," either in a bombing pause or by sending some intermediaries, we did everything in our power to show you that we were alive, that we could still defy you, that we could outlast you, and that you could not defeat us.

Chester Cooper: Let me say something about the bombing pauses. The problem was not that you didn't respond. The problem was that you *did* respond to the pauses. Every time we called a halt to the bombing, you increased the flow of troops and supplies to the South. Your response made life very difficult—virtually impossible—for those of us who were arguing for a bombing pause, or for an extension of a bombing pause.

The "phase A–phase B" formula [U.S. stops bombing; and following an interval, the DRV stops resupplying and infiltrating the South] was an attempt to address this problem—that you always took advantage of our bombing pauses. Mr. Luu Van Loi was one of the authors of the Four Points. I was one of the authors of the "phase A–phase B" formula. Our idea was as follows: that there would be no announced conditions for a bombing pause; it would be a secret arrangement between your government and our government. On a given day, agreed to by both sides, we would stop bombing. We would do so without any public indication that there were any conditions to our bombing halt. However, during the pause, we would observe very carefully the flow of reinforcements and supplies to the South. If we noticed a decrease in your resupply efforts, we would then be willing to begin serious negotiations. We understood that you would not be able to halt the resupply effort overnight. We understood this. But we would take this into account. The question phase A–phase B was supposed to answer was: Are you serious about entering into negotiations or not?

Luu Doan Huynh: North Vietnam never had any idea—any intention—of destroying its enemies. Never in our history—when fighting the French or the Chinese, for example. It was impossible because they were great powers. This was also the case—obviously the case—in the American War. We were facing the world's greatest power. So we had to craft the military and diplomatic struggle for this kind of context: We are small and weak, while you are big and powerful. In this context, if we had asked for a bombing pause, or cooperated with a bombing pause, you would surely have interpreted our response as weakness and bombed us more. If we had reduced our supplies to the South, you would have concluded that the bombing was effective, and you would have bombed us more. So we had to be very careful. We could not allow ourselves any illusions, any wishful thinking. We decided that we must prove to you that we could absorb the blows you inflicted on us. We knew we must show firmness, no matter what. We had to show you that our will would be stronger than yours.[57]

Nguyen Khac Huynh: I would like first to speak about this issue raised again by Mr. Chester Cooper—whether North Vietnam took advantage of bombing pauses. I would like to tell a personal story. During the bombing days, we were afraid to travel along Highway 1. So, during the pauses, we tried to travel as much as possible. Our logistics people were keen to take advantage of these pauses, as you can imagine, to ship supplies to our brothers in the South. This is natural.

However, an insoluble problem arose for us because the United States was still bombing on the southern side of the DMZ [demilitarized zone]—still killing our brothers in the South, for whom the supplies were meant. Imagine our position. If we stop supplying our brothers in the South, who are being bombed without letup, because for a few days or weeks *we* are spared the bombing, then what would our southern comrades think of us? They would be justified, I think you will agree, in considering us to be traitors. Therefore, it was impossible. Everyone knew it could not be done—we could not comply without betraying the cause for which we were fighting. . . .

Janet Lang asked me during the coffee break why we did not apply pressure to the U.S. to extend the bombing pauses. This was also the essence of Mr. McNamara's question, with which Mr. James Blight began the session this morning. Of course, we *wanted* longer bombing pauses. Absolutely. But as has been said here by all of us on the Vietnamese side, we felt that we must show you, we must demonstrate to you, that we would never give in, that we could absorb any punishment you could deliver to us. We believed—and I believe we were correct to believe this—that only in this way would we "win"—in our sense, which meant that the Americans would leave our country because they could not break our will in either the South or the North.

Six Peace Initiatives

MAYFLOWER: "A SMOKE SCREEN TO DIVERT ATTENTION"?

On April 20, 1965, Robert McNamara, Gen. Maxwell Taylor, Gen. William Westmoreland, and other civilian and uniformed U.S. leaders met in Honolulu in an atmosphere of deep crisis. A consensus had been reached within the military command that the war in Vietnam was being lost and lost badly, that the bombing of the North alone would be insufficient to reverse the momentum, and that the United States therefore faced this stark choice: Send in its own combat troops in large numbers, or risk imminent humiliation and defeat.[58] At a meeting the following day in Washington, the Honolulu findings were presented to President Johnson. In connection with them, McNamara proposed a bombing pause to explore the possibility of a negotiated settlement. Out of this was born the initiative code-named "MAYFLOWER."

MAYFLOWER consisted of two moves: First, an unpublicized pause in the bombing of the North; and second, an approach to Hanoi via the U.S. ambassador in Moscow, Foy Kohler, who was instructed to deliver a sealed message in person to Hanoi's ambassador. The message was drafted by Assistant Secretary of State William Bundy, signed by Dean Rusk, and sent to Moscow on the evening of May 11. In addition, Rusk met with Soviet Ambassador Anatoly Dobrynin the same evening, handing him a copy of the letter being sent to Moscow.[59] The letter read, in part, as follows:

> The highest authority in this Government has asked me to inform Hanoi that there will be no air attacks on North Viet-Nam for a period beginning at noon, Washington time, Wednesday May 12, and running into next week. . . .
>
> The United States Government remains convinced that the underlying cause of trouble in Southeast Asia is armed action against the people and Government of South Vietnam by forces whose actions can be decisively affected from North Vietnam. The United States will be very watchful to see whether during this period of pause there are significant reductions in such armed actions by such forces. . . .
>
> Moreover, the United States must point out that the decision to end air attacks for this limited trial period is one which it must be free to reverse if at any time in the coming days there should be actions by the other side in Vietnam which required immediate reply.[60]

The following day, May 12, President Johnson made a major speech urging Hanoi to consider a "political solution."[61]

Kohler called for an appointment to see the North Vietnamese ambassador but was told that, in light of there being no diplomatic relations between Hanoi and Washington, Kohler could not be received. An envelope was thus delivered to Hanoi's Moscow embassy, but it was returned apparently unopened shortly thereafter, in an envelope marked "US of A." After obtaining approval from Washington, Kohler then tried to get the Soviet Foreign Ministry to deliver it, but they also refused. Nevertheless, Kohler cabled Washington that he was sure the substance of the message had gotten through to Hanoi, by one means or another.[62] Three days later, on May 15 in Vienna, Soviet Foreign Minister Andrei Gromyko told Rusk that the bombing pause had been "insulting."[63]

These responses did nothing to increase President Johnson's enthusiasm for lengthening the pause. On May 18, the bombing resumed. That evening, Hanoi's Foreign Ministry denounced the pause as a "deceitful maneuver designed to pave the way for new U.S. acts of war." They also said that during the pause U.S. planes had still continued to violate North Vietnamese airspace "for spying, provocative and strafing activities."[64] Thus did the first concerted U.S. effort to combine a bombing pause and a diplomatic démarche come to naught. Several years later, William Bundy, the primary drafter of the ill-fated letter to Hanoi via Moscow, said in an understatement of historic proportions that the letter to Hanoi was "crisp, kind of a lawyer's document . . . not well handled."[65]

In fact, Washington had, in going about its business of peacemaking, committed several blunders that doomed it from the start. Many of these are taken up in the discussion that follows. Washington made no concrete proposal, in any case. But the attempt to go through Moscow, ultimately through the Soviet Foreign Ministry, though a natural enough maneuver to the Americans, was absolutely anathema to North Vietnam at this moment. Why? Because there would be no way to keep the secret from being leaked to the Chinese, upon whom Hanoi was fundamentally dependent in its conduct of the war and whose leaders were at that moment applying great pressure on Hanoi *not* to negotiate with the Americans. For example, according to Chinese documents, during the MAYFLOWER bombing pause Ho Chi Minh was in Beijing getting a lecture from Foreign Minister Zhou Enlai and Vice-Premier Deng Xiaoping, as follows:

❧

Zhou Enlai: The Soviet revisionists want North Vietnam to talk with the U.S., to put the NLF aside and sell out its brothers.

Deng Xiaoping: They [the Soviets] provide you some aid for their purposes. . . . In short, Soviet aid is aimed at serving their strategy. If North Vietnam finds it inconvenient to expose this fact, let us do it for you.[66]

❖

These remarks follow a conversation the day before between Ho Chi
Minh and Mao Zedong, at the conclusion of which Mao agreed to send Chinese engineering troops to North Vietnam to build six roads linking it with
its border areas, taking over the task from 30,000 North Vietnamese troops,
who could then be sent to the South, via the Ho Chi Minh Trail.[67]

This would not be the last time Washington would try to go through
Moscow, the other superpower, in an attempt to force Hanoi to negotiate, or
at least moderate its stance toward negotiations. But in May 1965, Moscow
and Beijing were splitting apart, and Hanoi was still trying to "play both
ends against the middle." At this time, no approach using the Soviets as
intermediaries would have worked, even if the letter from Dean Rusk had
not had the look and feel of an ultimatum.

❖

James Hershberg: During the MAYFLOWER bombing pause of 12–18
May 1965, why did the DRV refuse to accept a message from, or meet with,
the American ambassador in Moscow, Mr. Foy Kohler. Ambassador Kohler
tried repeatedly to deliver a message that could possibly have started a
direct dialogue—a dialogue between the U.S. and DRV that would not have
involved the problems with intermediaries that have been discussed here.

Luu Doan Huynh: We understood MAYFLOWER—the short bombing
pause—we understood all this in the context of Johnson's speech at Baltimore on April 7, 1965. We thought it was a smoke screen to divert attention
from the troop buildup that was under way. That, and the bombing of the
North, of course. The Baltimore speech said many things to us—many
things. Johnson set the tone, for us, when he referred to us as "Hanoi," not
as the DRV, which indicated to us that he still did not accept our right to
exist.

Now, we have all these documents connected to the Baltimore speech,
compliments of Brown University, and I have read them. And what do they
say? These documents say that Johnson did not want to negotiate—that he
did not think negotiating was even possible. The documents say that there is
no need to negotiate because the U.S. will not suffer great losses, get tired,
or retreat. So the documents are optimistic. The U.S. will be able to protect
Saigon. No problem. With that attitude, they would just follow their course
and "win the war," as Johnson said.

Let me tell you how we felt about this—what we thought of your attitude, the U.S. attitude in putting forward an offer like MAYFLOWER, connected to a bombing pause. It was if we were "naughty" little children and you told us that if we did not stop crying, there would be no candy, only "punishment." That is how we in Hanoi understood it. You will reward us—give us money to spend, if we are good "children." That is how we understood it. In the same way, U.S.-proposed "unconditional talks" would in our view have amounted to negotiations under the threat of continued bombing. In addition, Johnson firmly excluded the NLF from negotiations. So, negotiations under your terms were not considered possible by us. So you continued the bombing. So we got punished. Ah, but you see, we were stubborn. You didn't think about that.

Several people . . . have raised the question: If the U.S. had really wanted to get into negotiations, would North Vietnam take them seriously? I think there is something wrong with this question, because it is not really in line with our understanding of the situation at the time. We knew what you wanted. You wanted a negotiation on your terms, with bombing as an instrument of pressure. That was what you wanted. But if negotiations were to be held, then we would demand that you stop the bombing and that you would subsequently withdraw the U.S. troops. That was our thinking—that was our *definition*—of "serious," of what you *should* propose or believe, if you were serious. And since you never proposed such a thing—not at this time, not until much later—then we understood that you were not serious about seeking to begin negotiations with us.

Now I will speak specifically about MAYFLOWER. MAYFLOWER, in Hanoi's view, was an offer to stop the bombing. Okay. But in the light of Baltimore, stopping the bombing was a way to get the cessation of infiltration from the North. That, and favorable world opinion, which had been running against you. The world—most of it—had demanded the U.S. to stop the bombing, quit the war, and find peace. Thus, with MAYFLOWER, the U.S. could say: "You see, we have stopped bombing, but they refuse to negotiate, so we have to resume the bombing." It made no sense for us to participate in this kind of charade.

Second, MAYFLOWER was a way to force us to stop our assistance to the South. This would be the trade-off you required from us for stopping the bombing. Without any real negotiation, you just make this requirement. But in reality, gentlemen, what could stop you then from bombing? The message of Rusk was really addressed to North Vietnam. But that message to Vietnam—it didn't even have the name of our country, so to say, on the envelope, just "Hanoi." So we felt that, in this case also, you were threatening us and treating us like a child. The Soviet foreign minister [Andrei Gromyko] even had to tell Dean Rusk that the temporary bombing halt maneuver was "insulting."

Now how did I feel? (I should make clear that this might not be how others on our side might have felt.) I think our ambassador in Moscow was also a bit confused. In referring to Hanoi for instructions, the ambassador tossed the matter into the hands of the USSR's Foreign Ministry. On the one hand, the USSR rejected direct talks with the U.S., while on the other hand they held informal talks with them. Hanoi soon came to grips with the problem, and in the end the Soviet cochairman refused to act as a go-between for the DRV and U.S. Then, and thereafter, the DRV did not want to have contacts with the U.S. in Moscow, partly because China might come up with accusations of Soviet-U.S. collusion. We also had in mind, of course, that the USSR and U.S. were quite involved with each other on a lot of issues.

A statement of the DRV Foreign Ministry on May 18, 1965, described the bombing pause as a "trick," a deceitful maneuver, designed to pave the way for new U.S. acts of war. This statement, and a previous statement issued on May 15, affirmed North Vietnam's national rights and rejected the U.S. demand that NLF forces must stop attacking U.S. troops. Both statements emphasized that the Four Points were the unique basis for a solution but did not explicitly demand unconditional cessation of the bombing as a precondition for talks. This shows that we were then taking the first step in the process of applying the Four Points and improving our tactics relating to them.

Vietnamese MAYFLOWER Counterfactual: "A Diplomatic Move"?

One of the more remarkable developments in the course of our dialogues with the Vietnamese has been the sophistication with which some of our colleagues from Hanoi have embraced the notion of missed opportunities. The intervention below is a case in point. Luu Doan Huynh, who had delivered the condemnation of MAYFLOWER at the June 1997 conference in Hanoi, let his harsh comments stand, more or less as given, through the translation and editing process. But in addition, based on what he learned at the conference about U.S. decisionmaking, he subsequently submitted another statement involving a counterfactual—a hypothetical "What if?"—concerning the U.S. move of May 11, 1965.

Luu Doan Huynh's point of departure was learning, in U.S. documents and in conversation with U.S. historians and former officials, that a firm decision to send troops to Vietnam had *not* been made by May 1965. He had always thought that it *had* been made by then and that MAYFLOWER was therefore the mere "charade" he called it at the June 1997 conference. This leads him to speculate that at that moment, before the U.S. had committed itself to, in effect, assuming responsibility for the war in South Vietnam, it might just have been possible to establish a dialogue that could have avoided the tragic war that followed.

It is an intriguing and clever idea: Hanoi would receive the message from Washington; it would then split the central issues surrounding the Four Points into two parts—Point Three, dealing with the structure of the Saigon government, which most concerned the Americans at the time, and all the others. (He had not known in 1965 that the Americans had misinterpreted Point Three to indicate the total exclusion of all U.S. influence and allies in a coalition government led by NLF forces.)

Would it have worked? No one can say for sure, of course. But it is interesting to note that shortly after the failure of the MAYFLOWER bombing pause initiative, George Ball submitted a memorandum to President Johnson, at Johnson's request, urging that Washington make a radical move immediately, to cut its losses and make any sort of reasonable deal possible with Hanoi and the NLF.[68] Robert McNamara, also at the president's request, prepared a paper describing the level of U.S. involvement—much higher than had been previously discussed—that would be needed to prove to the NLF and Hanoi that they could not win the war in the South. William Bundy prepared a paper describing a "middle way" between these two options, as did McGeorge Bundy.

All four memoranda were submitted to the president with a cover note by McGeorge Bundy that said: "My hunch is that you will want to listen hard to George Ball and then reject his proposal. Discussion could then move to the narrower choice between my brother's course and McNamara's."[69] The question evoked by Luu Doan Huynh's MAYFLOWER counterfactual is this: *If* Hanoi had accepted the message of May 11; and *if* Hanoi had responded by offering to clarify its views on the single, most sensitive element of the Four Points—Point Three, on the Saigon government—what would have happened next? Almost surely McGeorge Bundy, George Ball, William Bundy, and McNamara all would have argued that Hanoi's reply should be explored and any plan to expand U.S. troops in Vietnam should be deferred.

❖

Luu Doan Huynh: Should we have rejected MAYFLOWER? In my view, North Vietnam had enough reasons to reject MAYFLOWER. After seeing some of the documents from this time, I feel that mid-1965 was like this: We were very angry. The bombing made us very angry. But there were still only about 46,000 U.S. troops in the South—I am talking about May. There was still not a consensus in Washington to begin a large escalation—a limited war. And it would take Johnson and his advisers more than two months of debate before coming to the decision of July 28, 1965, which increased the number of U.S. troops to 126,000, and then 183,000 by the end of the year. Thus, in May, it seems from the documents, the U.S. had not really decided to escalate. It seems like this. That is the way I read your documents.

Three arguments were being made at this time to Johnson. George Ball and Sen. Mike Mansfield recommended negotiations and an early withdrawal from the war. Maxwell Taylor advocated fighting an "enclave" war, with only 95,000 U.S. troops and preparing the Saigon troops to take over. The third view was that of Westmoreland, the JCS, CIA, and Walt Rostow, who advocated escalation of the war until Vietnam yielded. At that time— mid-1965—I believe you, Mr. McNamara, also subscribed to this belief.

Thus, the question that we should think about, in my opinion, is whether or not May 1965 was an appropriate time for Vietnam to prevent the U.S. from switching to a limited war—to the "Americanization" of the war—by making a diplomatic move, while continuing to fight on the battlefield. As I think about it, such a diplomatic move would have involved the following:

- Vietnam's ambassador in Moscow should receive and transfer to Hanoi Rusk's May 12 message.

- After some time, Vietnam's ambassador should schedule another meeting with his U.S. counterpart and respond as follows: Reject the May 12 proposal and insist on unconditional cessation of bombing; propose U.S.-DRV discussions on a neutral South Vietnam, involving a coalition government committed to peace and neutrality; cessation of hostilities in South Vietnam; U.S. troop withdrawal; status quo in Southeast Asia; and any other terms the parties may wish to discuss.

In my opinion, such a proposal at that time would have injected a new element into the U.S. in-house debate and would strengthen the position and views of advocates of the first and second schools of thought in U.S. political circles—that is, those advocating either withdrawal or an "enclave" strategy. Such a proposal might have produced either of two results:

- At best: avoidance of a big war and gradual achievement of a neutral South Vietnam.

- At least: a period of indecision among U.S. ruling circles, involving delay in sending substantial reinforcements to South Vietnam, which might have given us more time to make preparations for coping with new developments, including the Americanization of the war.

Perhaps because of our poor knowledge of the internal debates in U.S. circles, we missed an opportunity. Maybe we should have done this. Or maybe, by this time, it was already too late, because the Americans, for some reason, were determined to "break the back of the Viet Cong," with their troops, and to break the will of Hanoi, with the bombing. I don't know. This is what I believe we should think more about.

XYZ: "Something Unofficial, Something Preliminary"

What became code-named the "XYZ" initiative was in fact initiated by Hanoi, not Washington, as is sometimes claimed. At 9:00 A.M. Paris time, on May 19, 1965, approximately eight hours after the United States resumed bombing of North Vietnam, Mai Van Bo, head of Hanoi's commercial delegation in Paris and Hanoi's top-ranking diplomat in France, called on the French Foreign Ministry and spoke with Etienne Manac'h, director of Asian affairs and a longtime Indochina specialist. Mai Van Bo said he wished to clarify to the United States the meaning of the Four Points, which Washington evidently did not understand correctly.[70]

Mai Van Bo asked the French to convey the following messages to Washington: First, that the Four Points "were to be considered not prior conditions but rather as working principles for a negotiation which should, in the DRV view, represent the ultimate goal of settlement in Vietnam."[71] Second, he said that U.S. recognition of the "principles" in the Four Points would open the possibility of a conference modeled on that of Geneva in 1954.[72]

When these messages first arrived at the State Department in Washington, officials were flabbergasted as to why these messages came *after* the resumption of the bombing of the North, rather than during the bombing pause. In any event, Washington did not pursue or respond to the Mai Van Bo overture in any way. Then, on June 14, Mai Van Bo returned to inquire with Manac'h as to the status, as far as he knew it, of his inquiry with the Americans. Still there was no official response via the French to Mai Van Bo. But after the intercession of a businessman named Urah Arkas-Duntov, a discussion was begun on the issues raised by the Four Points. At this point, word of the discussions reached the upper levels of the State Department and White House. President Johnson gave to George Ball, who had been involved with the French government since World War II, responsibility for pursuing the initiative. Ball appointed Edmund Gullion, a former U.S. foreign service officer, who had served in Vietnam and who spoke fluent French (as did Mai Van Bo), to explore the possibilities in face-to-face discussions with Mai Van Bo. Gullion was still technically an intermediary, because he was not in the government at that point. But it was clear to both sides that Gullion was being sent by the U.S. government to engage in exploratory talks in Paris.

Mai Van Bo and Edmund Gullion met on four separate occasions: August 6, 15, and 18 and September 3, 1965. Bo announced at the outset that his task was to ensure that Washington understood the Four Points and their relation to the likelihood of moving to formal negotiations to end the war. He emphasized to Gullion that the Four Points were *not* "preconditions" to talks but were instead "principles," to which both sides must subscribe before negotiations could be productive.[73] The discussions seemed cordial and productive until the two men met on September 3. Mai Van Bo began by saying that "bombings must stop unilaterally, immediately, totally, and definitively. Then there would be a possibility of negotiations."[74] A fifth meeting, scheduled for September 7, was canceled by Mai Van Bo. The channel was thus closed abruptly and without adequate explanation, or so it seemed to Washington.

The author of the *Pentagon Papers* synopsis of the XYZ initiative writes: "The talks between X (Edmund Gullion) and R (Mai Van Bo) represent the most serious mutual effort to resolve matters of substance between the U.S. and the DRV before and since."[75] Historian George Herring expressed his agreement with this assessment in a recent reexamination. But still Hanoi chose to terminate the channel. Why? At the time, U.S. analysts speculated wildly. Was it the action of U.S. troops? No, they said, because the announcement of the troop deployments was made before Gullion and Mai Van Bo ever met. Was it the bombing of the North? No, they said, because "overall air activity in the north in August was not higher than the previous month, July."[76] Had the Chinese weighed in to prevent the channel from developing? That seemed doubtful, or in any case impossible to pursue. There this perplexing matter has rested from September 1965 until the present.

· · · ·

In the brief exchange that follows, Robert Brigham asks the Vietnamese participants why they broke off the XYZ channel. The first response is given by Tran Ngoc Kha, who was in 1965 a press correspondent and English-language interpreter for Mai Van Bo in Paris. After giving a short summary of events, he says that after four fruitless meetings, the mission was accomplished. He points out that this was the period of the greatest U.S. escalation of the war and that, no matter how cordial or how clear seemed to have been the understandings reached in Paris along the XYZ channel, the war went on in Vietnam. Thus, having explained the Four Points in detail to an American intermediary with connections to the top of the U.S. government, Hanoi could only assume that the United States now understood the Four Points, was ignoring them, and was now determined to conquer South Vietnam and destroy North Vietnam. That is more or less the argument of Tran Ngoc Kha.

Luu Van Loi, one of the drafters of the Four Points, was in the summer of 1965 monitoring the XYZ channel in Hanoi. He confirms that the sole purpose of opening the channel was to be sure that the Americans understood the Four Points. In other words, they understood that they are not preconditions and that there can be no negotiations of any kind without an unconditional halt of the bombing of the North. Luu Doan Huynh (who the following year would begin working on the Foreign Ministry preparing documents to be used in any eventual negotiations with the United States) adds that he believes Washington missed two of the signals Hanoi was trying to send: First, by approaching the United States *after* the resumption of the bombing on May 18, Hanoi intended that Washington understand that Hanoi would never negotiate under the threat of continued bombing; and second, that Hanoi wished to deal with the Americans directly, not via Moscow or some other intermediary. He correctly surmises that Washington missed both of these signals completely.

❖

Robert Brigham: In May '65, and throughout the summer of '65, Mai Van Bo meets in Paris with Edmund Gullion. George Herring has reconstructed these various efforts from the available U.S. records in the negotiating volume of the *Pentagon Papers*. In George's reconstructions, we can see that the Geneva Conference may very nearly have been reconvened. We also see that real progress seemed to be under way at these secret talks in Paris, all through the summer of 1965.

Suddenly, everything seemed to change. On September 3, 1965, these Paris talks stalled. It has seemed as if Mai Van Bo changed his position and we in the West have often wondered what happened—why his instructions were changed, or were they changed? . . .

I've wondered, for instance, if the September 3, 1965, meeting between Mai Van Bo and Edmund Gullion—in which Mai Van Bo all of a sudden seemed to have changed his position—whether this was a result of one of these groups within the Hanoi government that did *not* favor negotiations, having the floor that day—winning a consensus within the Political Bureau. Is this the case? Is this what happened? Was this followed by further internal bargaining within the Party about how to proceed on this dual track?

Tran Ngoc Kha: XYZ evolved in the following manner: In July 1965, President Johnson decided to increase the number of troops in South Vietnam to 175,000 and to prepare for the introduction of 100,000 more by early 1966. That was a decision to "go deeper into the war," as was stated at the time. Because of the increase of military forces, Johnson faced public criticism of his Vietnam policies. He therefore launched a diplomatic campaign aimed ostensibly at exploring the significance of Hanoi's (Pham Van Dong's) statement of the Four Points. Essentially, however, Johnson still maintained his scheme of negotiating from a position of strength, the goal being to preserve the South Vietnamese government, which was in a state of virtual collapse.

Deputy Secretary of State George Ball was designated to direct the contact in Paris between Edmund Gullion and Mai Van Bo. Gullion was the former U.S. consul in South Vietnam in the 1950s. He also spoke fluent French. He met Mai Van Bo in a private capacity four times: August 6, 15, and 18, and on September 3, 1965. Gullion was code-named "X" and Mai Van Bo was known as "R." (There was no "Y" or "Z.")

Gullion was instructed to be flexible, but at the same time to apply pressure. He expressed the desire to end the war "on the basis of the Four Points" and added that in a prolonged war the U.S. would be forced to expand the conflict, forcing China to intervene. In that event, Gullion said, China would control North Vietnam.

Gullion explored whether the Four Points were "preconditions" or a "base" for negotiating a solution, and whether South Vietnam would be allowed to participate in a Geneva conference. He also stressed that any solution should include the withdrawal of both U.S. and North Vietnamese troops from South Vietnam. Mai Van Bo responded simply by saying that the bombing of the North should stop immediately, completely, unconditionally, and for good and that the NLF was the only legitimate representative of the people of South Vietnam. After four fruitless meetings, Mai Van Bo refused to receive Gullion on September 7, 1965.

After that, in November 1965, Paul Sturm, former U.S. consul in Hanoi, met Vo Van Sung to convey the message that the U.S. would stop bombing if Hanoi ceased infiltration and pulled its troops back to the North. But this led nowhere.

In brief, XYZ was an effort by the U.S. to explore the possibility of negotiation, to attempt to understand the implications of the Four Points, and to discuss some technical aspects of a Geneva conference, such as the conditions and the duration of troop withdrawal, the timing of unification and of general elections. While the U.S. was intensifying the war, neither side was able to persuade the other. Therefore, it is obvious that the time was not appropriate for serious negotiations.

Luu Van Loi: Mr. Gullion came to visit Mr. Mai Van Bo to further understand the Four Points of North Vietnam. As Mr. Kha said, this was its purpose. It had the status—it was understood in Hanoi as having only the status—of something unofficial, something preliminary. It had the sole purpose, as far as I understand it, of informing the U.S., to the extent they were interested, of what we meant by the Four Points, which were evidently not well understood when Pham Van Dong gave them on April 8, 1965.

Luu Doan Huynh: After we rejected MAYFLOWER, there was a démarche by Mr. Mai Van Bo and the French Foreign Minister on May 18. Professor Hershberg has referred to this and asked what this was about. This, as I understand it, was just to tell the French and the U.S. that the DRV seriously intended to talk to the U.S. at some time in the future. This was quite different from "nibbling" at the U.S. message of May 12. I don't mean we held a grudge with you because of the message of May 12. No. Basically, we just wanted to tell you that the Four Points were the best basis for fruitful negotiations—to work within the framework of the Four Points would be most the most useful way to proceed. So according to this, the withdrawal of troops would depend on the conclusion of negotiations. I want this to be clearly understood. Do you understand what I am saying? [Gestures at U.S. participants.]

PINTA/Christmas Bombing Pause: "We Did Not Know Everything . . . "

It can now be seen quite clearly that late November to early December 1965 was one of the critical moments in the history of the war, at least from the U.S. perspective. During November 13–19 a fierce battle took place in the Ia Drang Valley, near the Cambodian border. When it was over, the United States had lost 300 men, North Vietnam more than 1,300. Based on these kinds of casualty figures, General Westmoreland had sent to Washington estimates of his troop needs for the following year. His estimate was revised upward by 200,000 men. The infiltration rate from the North had tripled. Things were going very badly. President Johnson sent Robert McNamara to Saigon at the end of November for an on-site assessment on the basis of which he was to suggest the best available options.[77]

On November 30, McNamara sent a memorandum to the president listing two alternatives: First, "a compromise solution . . . and hold further deployments to a minimum"; second, "stick with our stated objectives and with the war, and provide what it takes in men and material."[78] If the second course were to be pursued, McNamara recommended it be preceded by a bombing pause. This recommendation gave added weight to a suggestion made on November 24 by Soviet Ambassador Anatoly Dobrynin to McGeorge Bundy:

If the United States stopped the bombing for two to three weeks, the Soviets would see what could be done to get Hanoi to negotiate.[79] The first option—a compromise political solution—was not pursued. The ensuing two weeks were taken up with debating the merits of a bombing pause, in connection with plans to radically increase U.S. military involvement in the war in South Vietnam.

After considerable debate between the president and his senior advisers, Johnson agreed to a pause, which began at 5:30 A.M. on December 24, 1965, and was initially to hold only for the duration of a thirty-hour holiday truce.[80] Johnson then agreed to extend the pause for several more days. Then, following a visit by McNamara to Johnson in Texas, the president embraced an initiative of much wider scope, one that bore his personal imprint. Dean Rusk was called on to produce what became the Fourteen Points; diplomats were dispatched to no fewer than 145 countries to emphasize Washington's eagerness to move to negotiations; and a channel was opened in Rangoon, Burma, via U.S. Ambassador Henry Byroade to DRV Consul General Vu Huu Binh. (The latter segment bore the code name "PINTA.") Their first meeting was on December 29, 1965, when Byroade delivered an aide-mémoire to Vu Huu Binh, calling his attention to the bombing pause and expressing the hope that Hanoi would reciprocate by invoking a similar "pause" in its efforts to infiltrate men and equipment to the South.[81]

Byroade's efforts went unrewarded. He called on Vu Huu Binh repeatedly in January but received in return only a diatribe against the Fourteen Points—this time in writing—that Hanoi's representative had given him orally at their first meeting on December 29. On January 21, Vu Huu Binh told Byroade that he regarded the original message as an ultimatum and that he had heard nothing from Hanoi in response. The pause was terminated by President Johnson on January 31, having gotten no meaningful response from Hanoi via the PINTA-Rangoon channel or any other means. Then, on January 31, six hours after the resumption of the bombing of the North, Vu Huu Binh sent a message to Byroade asking him to call. Meeting some twelve hours after the resumption of the bombing, Vu Huu Binh delivered an aide-mémoire that made the familiar points about the centrality of the Four Points and concluded by saying since the United States rejects Point Three—that the Saigon government must be "in accordance with the program of the NLF"—this is equivalent to rejecting all Four Points. Conversations in this channel continued sporadically until February 19. At that point, Vu Huu Binh broke off the channel by telling Byroade that "since the U.S. has resumed the bombing, I hold that it is inappropriate to continue our talks at your request."[82]

In the end, nothing came of all the fandangle diplomacy—Johnson's whirlwind dispatch of U.S. diplomats to well more than 100 countries in search of some way to get his message through to Hanoi. Averell Harriman, his top diplomat in search of a formula for peace in Vietnam, had gone to Poland, because the Poles seemed particularly interested in trying to get through to Hanoi. But a Polish special envoy to Hanoi, Jerzy Michalowski, returned to Warsaw on January 16 and reported to the British ambassador: "God damn those Chinese," indicating that if not for their interference, talks might have begun.[83]

Did the Chinese make the critical difference? It is impossible to know for sure. But it is an interesting hypothesis in light of newly available Chinese documentation from the period. Here is part of a lecture given by Zhou Enlai to North Vietnamese Foreign Minister Nguyen Duy Trinh on December 19, 1965, at precisely the same time the Johnson administration was debating the bombing pause:

> We are not against the idea that . . . when the war comes to a certain point negotiations will be needed. But, the problem is that the time is not now ripe. . . . It means that we should not put forward unconditional cessation of bombing the North and cessation of violating North Vietnamese sovereignty and security as conditions. . . . It's very dangerous to have such a way of thinking. So what will the situation be if they accept? If they do, we will be in a passive position, and this will have a negative impact on our struggle and on our solidarity. If we put forward tough conditions, they will not accept. But because your conditions are not tough, they may accept them. We sincerely hope that North Vietnam's Party and government would think further on this issue. Otherwise, you may fall into the trap made by the U.S. imperialists, by the modern revisionists [i.e., the Soviets] and their followers.[84]

On the following day, Zhou Enlai lectured Tran Van Thanh, head of the resident NLF delegation in Beijing, on the evils of entering into negotiations with the Americans. Zhou argued that this would be a mistake. He urges the NLF instead to oppose negotiations and not to worry about the consequences if the United States expands the war even further. In that case, he says, "the Chinese people will face it, will accept it, and will fight the war until the end."[85]

Did the DRV Foreign Ministry, led by Nguyen Duy Trinh, wish to explore negotiations at that point, just before the bombing pause? Was Nguyen Duy Trinh possibly contemplating what later became known as the "Trinh formula" (if Washington ceases bombing, talks can begin) more than a year earlier than its January 27, 1967, announcement? Would Hanoi—might Hanoi—have given a different response in the PINTA-Rangoon channel but for fear of

Chinese reprisals? Jerzy Michalowski thought so. We're not sure. What can be said with assurance, however, is that Washington utterly misread Hanoi's relations with the Chinese, which were complex and, as these conversations indicate, difficult.

❖

James Hershberg: Why was the PINTA contact opened in December of 1965? And why was it closed—mysteriously, it seemed to the Americans involved in it—in February 1966? This would have provided another opportunity for dialogue without the use of intermediaries. Why close it down?

Luu Van Loi: PINTA—as an effort to find a peaceful settlement—was not believable. True, the bombing of the North was put on hold. But all other forms of escalation continued unabated. I mean, we are talking about the period of the biggest escalation in the presidency of Johnson. So, with the U.S. escalation so blatant and so massive, you—Professor Hershberg—ask: What was our attitude?

Let me be historically precise on this point. On December 27, 1965, the Central Committee of the Workers' Party of Vietnam held its Twelfth Plenum to assess the development of the war. Based on their discussions, the Party issued an appeal to the people, the soldiers, and all armed groups to resist the U.S. invasion with determination—to protect the North and the revolution in the South, at all costs. This was the answer. This was the answer to the U.S. bombing of the North. I would also like to remind you—to point out something significant—that this proclamation, this "answer," corresponded with the first important victories of the Viet Cong—the NLF—over the U.S. troops at Van Tuong [August 1965]; and at Plei Me [October–November 1965]. These were all "answers" to the so-called peace initiative. I am sure Hanoi would have had a different reaction—a less combative reaction—if they had believed the intention of PINTA had been serious—a serious attempt to find peace.

If I may say so, the basic issue at this time was *trust*—I should say *mistrust.* The U.S. was escalating. More U.S. troops continued to arrive in the South to fight the Viet Cong. The bombing of the North had continued since February 1965. Recently it had begun to hit the heart of Hanoi. These were the facts— the main facts, the important facts—to the people in Hanoi, leaders and people in Hanoi. We did not trust you when you said: "We will stop the bombing for a while and, if you—if we—stop doing this and that, then we will continue not to bomb you." But what kind of guarantees could you—would you—give us that you would cease the bombing? There were none. Which is why we had to demand—to require—an *unconditional* cessation of the bombing. And, of course, all the time the bombing is going on, your fighting troops continue to build in the South. So this is how the situation looked to us.

I have listened to Mr. McNamara and Mr. Cooper describe their own feelings, their own approach to these initiatives, including the PINTA initiative. But, you see, your efforts for peace could not outweigh—could not distract us from—these actions of escalation that kept coming and coming. Really: If President Johnson had decided to simply stop the bombing of the North; and had stated clearly on what day he wanted to negotiate and where he wanted to negotiate, well, I ask you, today—who would dare think that Hanoi would not take it seriously? Perhaps you gentlemen in Washington had thought of this—understood this—but were afraid that the North would take the opportunity to attack the South during the halt in bombing. So you see, you did not trust us either. And this is the point. On matters such as we are discussing—bombs are falling, troops are arriving, yours and ours, in the South—in these matters, in order to start negotiations, each side has to trust the other to respect a cease-fire, a cessation of taking advantage of the other. But there was not this trust, on either side. I think that there was none.

So Professor Hershberg asks why we—why *we*, the DRV—closed the door on negotiations in Rangoon, during PINTA. The answer is that we did *not* close the door. At Rangoon, your Ambassador Henry Byroade had already received a proposition from us. It said that talks would continue after President Johnson had ordered a cessation of bombing in the North. On December 29, 1965, Ambassador Byroade had already read over the Four Points and said that it would be possible to consider them as something that could be discussed in negotiations. Mr. Gullion had already brought this answer back to the Vietnamese, via Mai Van Bo. So, from the Vietnamese side, there did not appear to be a need for more answers to these probes. There was no need to answer anymore. Thus, actually, on February 19, 1966, the door was still open, even though our representative in Rangoon, Vu Huu Binh, said that further talks would be inappropriate, because the U.S. had resumed the bombing. In truth, our side was ready to begin that day, that hour, negotiating, on the basis of the Four Points.

I want to say just one more thing in conclusion. You see, we thought—it seemed obvious—that after the discussions between Gullion and Mai Van Bo, that the Four Points had been clarified to you. We thought this. If not then, then later, via PINTA/Rangoon. But I understand from what I have heard at this conference that, perhaps, even now, you Americans find something mysterious about the Four Points, something not clear, perhaps. This is what I wanted to say.

Robert McNamara: The bombing pause of December 1965 . . . , when it was extended, lasted something on the order of forty days. I started it, I went down to the LBJ Ranch and spoke with President Johnson during the Christmas holiday, and I managed to get it extended beyond its originally projected length. Now, why did I do this? It had nothing to do with a propaganda objective. In December 1965—and the record is very clear on this, it's in writing—in December I said to President Johnson: "The chances of achieving a military victory are one in three." And then I added, "At best one in two." And therefore we needed to move on a political track. There should be no misunderstanding, there might have been some propaganda benefits from some of these peace negotiations. And, of course, they would have been packaged in a way to maximize whatever propaganda benefits could be achieved. That's unavoidable. But they were not designed *primarily* for propaganda purposes! They were designed to end a tragic war that was decimating your people and your country, and for which we were also paying a very heavy price. That is a fact! So I don't think that's the issue—were they propaganda or were they meant to be real? They were meant to be *real!* They *failed!* And that's the tragedy.

Luu Doan Huynh: . . . In regard to PINTA, I have to say that we did not know everything that the U.S. intended. We knew nothing about Mr. McNamara's change in his assessment of the situation. Now we understand that in November 1965 Mr. McNamara already told Johnson the U.S. must alter its objectives in the war and must accept the participation of the Viet Cong in any coalition government that might be formed. If we had known this, who knows what we might have done? On the other hand, one should not forget that President Johnson and many other U.S. leaders were then advocating a very hawkish line.

The "Trinh Signal": "We Wanted to Explore"

On January 28, 1967, North Vietnamese Foreign Minister Nguyen Duy Trinh gave an interview to Australian journalist Wilfred Burchett, whom the Hanoi government often used when it wished to get special attention in the West for an announcement. During that interview, Nguyen Duy Trinh said the following: "It is only after the unconditional cessation of U.S. bombing and all other acts of war against the DRV that there could be talks between the DRV and the U.S."[86]

In effect, Nguyen Duy Trinh and his staff in Hanoi's Foreign Ministry had been preparing for this moment ever since he was named foreign minister in late 1964. For more than a year and a half, as the war raged on in the South and bombing continued in the North, the Foreign Ministry had been laying the foundation for eventual discussions with the United States. Their status had been recognized just before Nguyen Duy Trinh issued his statement, at the conclusion of the Thirteenth Party Plenum, when it approved the "Resolution on Stepping Up the Diplomatic Struggle."[87] From now on, according to the resolution, it would be "necessary to implement our diplomatic strategy flexibly and cleverly."[88]

The "Trinh signal," as we call it, was considered in Hanoi to have far-reaching significance. Taken literally, it meant that there need be no more quibbling about Point Three—concerning the NLF's role in any Saigon government, at least not to initiate peace talks. It had but one requirement for that, or so it seemed: Stop the bombing of the North. According to sources in Hanoi, the signal sent by Nguyen Duy Trinh was meant to be absolutely clear: It was time to talk, directly, face-to-face, and try to find a way to end the war.

Alas, this was not the signal received in Washington. In a tragicomic segment of his fine memoir of these events, Chester Cooper has described the "diplomatic melodrama" in which the Trinh signal played a major role. "For almost a year," according to Cooper, "the issue took on a Talmudic quality."[89] Much of the hair-splitting concerned whether Trinh's usage of "there could be talks" was the same as, or different from, "there will be talks," and whether the distinction made any functional difference. In other words, Washington was looking for a guarantee, but they got none. But in fact, as Cooper has pointed out, the analysts in Washington weren't ever sure "whether the North Vietnamese were actually aware of the significance of the word 'could.'"[90]

This time, Hanoi was taking no chances, however. During a visit to Paris to discuss the war with French Pres. Charles de Gaulle, Sen. Robert Kennedy was passed a message indicating that Nguyen Duy Trinh's comment was a major policy statement by Hanoi. On February 5, 1967, *Newsweek* magazine reported that Senator Kennedy had received a significant "peace feeler" from the DRV during his trip, the message having been passed to Kennedy from Mai Van Bo, via Etienne Manac'h—the same channel by which the XYZ initiative had been launched. President Johnson, who had been feuding with Robert Kennedy ever since Johnson assumed the presidency, reacted harshly to what he perceived as Kennedy's attempt to upstage him; he suspected Kennedy of having designs on the White House himself.[91]

This may have had the unfortunate side effect of stifling Johnson's interest in the Trinh signal. On March 2, Kennedy made a speech on the floor of the

Senate laying out his plan for moving to negotiations with Hanoi. It had three parts: First, the United States should declare an unconditional bombing halt; second, international assistance should be secured to prevent further escalation by either side; third, a phased withdrawal of combatants from both sides should begin, to be replaced with international forces. Cutting very close to the bone of Johnson's vulnerabilities, Kennedy went on to say this:

> If our enemy will not accept peace, it will not come. Yet we must also look to ourselves. We must have no doubt that it is not our acts or failures which bar the way. . . . We are not in Vietnam to play the part of an avenging angel pouring death and destruction on the roads and factories and homes of a guilty land.[92]

In the volatile discussion that followed the speech, Kennedy was asked by Sen. Frank Lausche, an Ohio Democrat, what could be gained by a bombing halt, after the failure of all the previous pauses. Kennedy responded: "I don't see what we lose."[93]

President Johnson asked several of his advisers to comment on Kennedy's proposal. Dean Rusk and Walt Rostow dismissed it out of hand.[94] But on March 9, Robert McNamara submitted a memorandum to the president that contained the following:

> We should soon make another effort to initiate negotiations. We have often said that a primary objective of the bombing was to assist in persuading the North to cease its aggression. Therefore, I would be prepared to terminate the bombing if negotiations, either public or private, were under way.[95]

But by now the Trinh signal was buried in interference coming to Johnson from several directions. Hanoi was unhelpful in clarifying the "could" versus "will" problem. Two of the three senior advisers (other than McNamara) who mattered most on this issue—Secretary of State Rusk and National Security Adviser Rostow—were adamantly opposed even to exploring it. And the public endorsement of the Trinh formula by Robert Kennedy made it even more difficult than it would otherwise have been for Johnson to take a clearheaded look at it.

In any case, by late February 1967, Hanoi seems already to have given up. Mai Van Bo, in a February 22 interview with *The New York Times*, said that his foreign minister had "made an important gesture of good will toward the United States" in his interview with Wilfred Burchett on January 28. Washington had not only failed to respond, added Mai Van Bo, but neither

President Johnson nor Secretary Rusk had bothered to cite Nguyen Duy Trinh's statement accurately. "This was proof," he said, "of bad faith since Hanoi's real position was fully known and understood in Washington."[96]

. . . .

Nguyen Khac Huynh leads off the following discussion by posing a question to the U.S. side: Why didn't Washington respond to the Trinh signal? He adds that he knows for certain that it was absolutely serious, and he alludes to the fact that planning for the Tet Offensive began during March 1967, strongly implying that there was a brief window from January 28 until sometime in March when a move to negotiations along the lines of the Trinh signal may have been possible for Hanoi. Luu Doan Huynh adds that the Trinh signal also was meant to indicate that Hanoi wanted bilateral talks with the United States, with no involvement of other big powers. They did not want to risk another betrayal, such as happened at Geneva in 1954.

Chester Cooper recounts some of the discussion in Washington in reaction to the Trinh signal—for example, the "Talmudic" exercises over "could" and "will"—but says also that Hanoi made it difficult for Washington to respond productively, because of the demand for an unconditional bombing halt. This was something that seemed terribly one-sided and therefore unacceptable to many, he says.

Nguyen Khac Huynh concludes with a kind of "confession." He says that from his position in the Foreign Ministry at the time, he did not know, first, that such American officials as Chester Cooper really wanted to move to negotiations; and second, that the increase in infiltration during bombing pauses actually *had* damaged chances in the long run for a mutually acceptable settlement. He didn't believe these things then, he says. But now he does.

❖

Nguyen Khac Huynh: . . . On January 27, 1967, our Foreign Minister Nguyen Duy Trinh stated for the first time that if the United States would cease bombing unconditionally, then talks can begin. I want to point out that our foreign minister did *not* say "if the U.S. ceases bombing unconditionally *and* agrees in full to all of the Four Points." He did not say this. So you see what was happening. We felt we were nearing a point of victory, and we wanted to explore whether the U.S. might be ready to sit down and negotiate with us on the basis of the Four Points. And in an attempt to signal to you that we were interested in talking, our foreign minister made a very simple, very straightforward statement.

But you did not respond productively, and so we knew that you were not ready to talk—that you had not reached the conclusion that you could not win. Mr. McNamara may have reached this conclusion—we know this from his book—but we had no knowledge of this in 1967. As I pointed out at the June conference, the planning for the Tet Offensive began in March, a little over a month after the foreign minister's statement. Tet, we believed, had the potential to make you come to the right conclusion: that you could not win and that it was time to discuss how to end the war on the basis of the Four Points.

Luu Doan Huynh: This is important: The January 1967 statement of Foreign Minister Nguyen Duy Trinh (if you stop bombing, we could talk) was partly designed to convey to you our desire to have bilateral talks. I don't think you understood this. These talks would not be like at Geneva—it would be nothing like the Geneva Conference. Then you expressed the desire—I mean as President Johnson did—on March 31, 1968, to have direct talks with Vietnam. What happened? We immediately seized the opportunity, thus relegating any Geneva-type conference to merely an international gathering which would support and guarantee the agreement concluded between Vietnam and the U.S. But the main thing was: It must just be between the U.S. and us.

Nguyen Khac Huynh: What did you think—what was the thinking in the U.S. government—about our demand for a cessation of U.S. bombing of the North as a condition for negotiations? In particular, what was the reaction to the announcement by our Foreign Minister Nguyen Duy Trinh on January 27, 1967, to that effect: You stop bombing, we start talking. All of us on the Vietnamese side wonder whether, if you were in our shoes at that time, you would have made the same demand?

Chester Cooper: Let me say first of all: We had no assurance from Hanoi that if the president had declared an unconditional stop to the bombing, that anything would happen—that there would be any negotiations. You never said we *will* negotiate until the very last minute. Your formulation was that you "could" negotiate—there "could be" negotiations—if we stopped the bombing. It was only in late 1967 that you changed the wording to say there "will be" negotiations. When you changed the wording from "could be"—a conditional formulation—to the words "will be," then we revised our whole approach to unconditional bombing.

The phase A–phase B formula was put forward in an effort to take account of your concern that we would stop the bombing only on the condition that you stop reinforcement *first*. We wanted to keep that formula quiet, so there would be no public condition placed on you if and when we stopped the bombing. This was the basic idea: It would take the form of a "gentlemen's agreement." We'd be quiet about it. The bombing would stop, at some point. Then three weeks, or maybe four weeks later, if you had reciprocated by stopping the reinforcement and resupply of the South, then we could start a negotiating process. When we first planned the phase A–phase B formula, it was so secret that only eight or ten people knew about it in Washington. We did not want to give the impression that conditions we being placed on you for a bombing pause.

That's what was behind our response to your announcement that if we stopped the bombing, talks could, or would begin. But we could never get you to reciprocate. . . .

This is what life was like for those of us on the other side of the argument—who said okay, let's try an experiment, like a bombing pause and see what the reaction is in Hanoi. But we knew so little about what was happening in Hanoi—almost nothing—that all we could do was take note of the fact that no matter whether we bombed or not, you didn't *seem* to notice, except for the fact that your rhetoric got even nastier than it had been before. In some ways, your policy of "no response" was a great help to those around Johnson who wanted to escalate the war even further. You must understand this. By doing what you did—or by not doing what we had hoped you might do—you were ensuring that the escalation of the war would continue. I am talking about the period between the middle of 1965 and the end of 1967.

Nguyen Khac Huynh: I very much appreciate Mr. Chester Cooper's remarks. I found them very illuminating. From his remarks, I draw two conclusions:

1. First, those Americans who wanted to explore with us prospects for moving to negotiations had many difficulties—difficulties we were not aware of at the time. I would say, in fact, that we knew absolutely nothing about the difficulties mentioned by Mr. Cooper.

2. Second, I also now understand that you in the U.S. government had deep concerns about the increase in reinforcements during the bombing pauses. For some people in Washington, including Mr. Cooper, the DRV response was not helpful to your cause. I understand this now. And I deeply appreciate your having told us about it.

Thank you, Mr. Cooper.

SUNFLOWER: "YOU WERE STILL BOMBING THE NORTH"

The release of the Trinh signal on January 28, 1967, was preceded by a flurry of diplomatic activity in Moscow, initiated by Washington. Throughout the month of January, the United States and DRV embassies traded aide-mémoire regarding the possibility of moving to peace talks in the near future. On January 27, the DRV sent an aide-mémoire responding to a U.S. probe of January 10. The key passage read as follows: "The unconditional cessation of U.S. attacks on the North being materialized, the DRV could then exchange views with the U.S. concerning the place or date for contact."[97] Here was a version of the Trinh signal, being sent along a confidential channel, just as Trinh was releasing it, via his January 28 interview in Hanoi with Wilfred Burchett: If the U.S. stops the bombing, then talks can begin. The U.S. replied on January 31, expressing its objection to Trinh's statement but offering to hold secret talks on terms of settlement before "finding a formula for stopping the bombing."[98]

Given Hanoi's intransigence regarding the mandatory bombing halt prior to any peace talks, and given Washington's rigidity on requiring a reciprocal cessation of infiltration by Hanoi, the matter would probably have ended at that point, or soon after, consistent with previous attempts. However, Soviet Prime Minister Alexei Kosygin arrived in London on a previously scheduled visit on February 6 for a week of talks with British Prime Minister Harold Wilson and other officials. Not unexpectedly, Kosygin and Wilson, the cochairmen of the Geneva Conference, turned immediately to Vietnam. Washington had sent Chester Cooper to London on February 3 to participate in the discussions. These two tracks—one in Moscow and the other in London—were code-named "SUNFLOWER" in the U.S. government.

The central issue was this: Would it be possible to find a formula close enough to the Trinh formula, but one that involved reciprocity by Hanoi, such that each side would agree to move to negotiations? Kosygin and Wilson threw themselves enthusiastically into the search for a solution. The best hope seemed to be an amended phase A–phase B formula, developed by Cooper and others in Washington: The U.S. would stop bombing first; Hanoi would reciprocate following some specified interval by ceasing infiltration; and—this was the element that gave cause for optimism—Hanoi's agreement to reciprocate would remain secret. There would be no announcement. Thus, it would appear as if the United States had met the stringent requirements of the Trinh formula but with proviso that might make the arrangement acceptable to Washington.

Chester Cooper has recalled the atmosphere in London, as the two prime ministers began to sense that it just might be possible to broker a deal:

> In his first session with Wilson on Monday afternoon Kosygin shared his worries about China and, as expected, stressed the importance the Russians attached to Trinh's "initiative." He suggested that Wilson join him in endorsing the North Vietnamese statement.
>
> Virtually the entire meeting the following day was devoted to Vietnam. Kosygin reminded the British again of Trinh's talk with Burchett. It was suggested that Wilson use the hotline to the White House to inform the president that he favored Trinh's proposal. Wilson pressed Kosygin as to just what he was supposed to say to Johnson; for example, was he to tell Johnson that Kosygin subscribed to Trinh's proposition that if the bombing stopped there was a possibility that talks could start? How seriously would Washington regard a British statement that simply suggested that he, Wilson, had faith in the fact that Kosygin had faith in the fact that Trinh's statement meant more than it seemed to mean? Would this be very meaningful to Washington? Or would Kosygin personally guarantee that talks would actually start if the bombing stopped? Kosygin apparently was unwilling to make such a commitment. Wilson then advanced his own suggestion—reconvening the Geneva Conference. He also put forward an abbreviated version of the phase A–phase B formula. Kosygin perked up his ears when he heard this and asked Wilson to let him see the formula in writing.[99]

But Washington was no more enthusiastic about the Trinh formula than before. According to Cooper: "I reported this to Washington that night and was instructed the next morning to try to urge Wilson to divert Kosygin from pressing the Trinh formula."[100] Moreover, U.S. intelligence—which was relayed to Cooper—indicated that within hours of the initiation of a U.S. bombing pause, which would last for the duration of Kosygin's visit to London, "the traffic proceeding south in North Vietnam . . . was like a Sunday on the New Jersey Turnpike."[101]

President Johnson had written to Wilson on February 6/7 suggesting the phase A–phase B formula, but he was vague as to which side was to act first. However, in response to the intelligence about Hanoi's stepped-up infiltration efforts, Johnson wrote to Ho Chi Minh demanding simultaneous deescalation. On February 10, this became known to Wilson and Kosygin, who were furious about what became known as "the battle of the tenses" or "the switching of the tenses." The difference was that the British version said: "The U.S. will stop bombing North Vietnam as soon as they are assured that infiltration from

North Vietnam to South Vietnam will stop." The revised version in Johnson's letter to Ho Chi Minh, however, changed the last two words to "has stopped."[102] Despite a good deal more hand-wringing and consultation, the battle of the tenses was not resolved to the satisfaction of Wilson and Kosygin. On February 15, Ho Chi Minh responded with considerable bitterness to Johnson by reasserting the necessity of the Trinh formula.[103] The initiative was formally terminated on April 6, when the DRV embassy returned a note from the U.S. embassy. The envelope was opened but marked "unacceptable."[104]

Might SUNFLOWER have worked if the tenses had not been changed? Wilson and Kosygin thought so.[105] And in light of new information, this is not quite the for-want-of-a-nail question it used to appear to be. There are several reasons for believing that, in effect, Kosygin might have been able to deliver Hanoi's approval of the arrangement on which he and Wilson were working. Kosygin was a cautious and careful diplomat who had developed very close ties with Hanoi.

In addition, by early 1967, Hanoi was moving away from the Chinese orbit and toward the Soviets, for several reasons. They desperately needed sophisticated Soviet surface-to-air missile systems to protect important cities like Hanoi and Haiphong as well as strategically important points such as bridges and dikes. In addition, the Chinese troops in the DRV had, in the view of the Hanoi leadership, begun to overstay their welcome. Already, by the spring of 1966, an incident had flared up between the Chinese and DRV over a ship that, according to Beijing, was held out of the port of Hon Gai for four days, presumably to use it as a kind shield to deter U.S. bombing. Le Duan was called to Beijing and made to listen to lectures by Zhou Enlai and Deng Xiaoping, the gist of which was that the DRV leadership were ungrateful and had been naively diverted from the proper revolutionary road by Soviet revisionists. Here is Zhou Enlai:

> There have been some changes since last year when North Vietnam started talks with the U.S. We should tell you straight away that those changes began when the new Soviet leadership took power, especially after the February 6–10, 1965 visit of Kosygin to Vietnam. After Kosygin returned from Hanoi the Soviets used their support to Vietnam to win your trust in a deceitful way. Their purpose is to cast a shadow over the relationship between Vietnam and China, to split Vietnam and China, with a view to further controlling Vietnam to improve [their] relations with the U.S. and obstructing the struggle and revolution of the Vietnamese people.[106]

In a subsequent conversation on April 13, 1966, Deng Xiaoping asks Le Duan and Nguyen Duy Trinh: "Are you suspicious of us because we have so much enthusiasm? Do the Chinese want to take over Vietnam? . . . If you have any problem, please tell us straightforwardly." Deng concludes by threatening to remove the 100,000 Chinese military personnel in the DRV.[107]

Le Duan does not suffer this abuse passively. He interrupts Deng Xiaoping:

> I would like to express some opinions. . . . We hold that the Soviet assistance to Vietnam is partly sincere, so neither do we ask whether the Soviets will sell Vietnam out nor do we say the Soviets slander China in the matter of transportation of Soviet aid across Chinese territory. . . . You are saying that the Soviets are selling out Vietnam but we don't say so. All other problems are rooted in this judgment.[108]

The Chinese have discovered that Kosygin has developed a special relationship with the Hanoi leadership, but they cannot persuade Le Duan even to give lip service to disowning this relationship. Kosygin is Hanoi's advocate in Moscow for much needed technical assistance and equipment. It was Kosygin who played the major role in an agreement reached in 1966 with Hanoi to deliver over 500 million U.S. dollars' worth of material to Hanoi, a figure that had actually exceeded 1 billion U.S. dollars by 1968.[109] In addition, several thousand specialists received training each year in Moscow, and many were sent directly to the South when they returned to Vietnam, though this was a fact the Soviets did not want Hanoi to publicize for fear it would disrupt their efforts to improve Soviet-American relations.[110]

So, might SUNFLOWER have worked? Might Kosygin have been able to deliver the DRV's agreement, however reluctant it might have been, to something like the original phase A–phase B formula, which included both U.S. initiation of the bombing pause and secrecy regarding Hanoi's reciprocal actions with regard to infiltration? Kosygin thought so. His deputy, interpreter, and close confidant, Viktor Sukhodrev, said shortly after the London episode that this was in fact the case.[111] The timing and the intermediary may have been just right but for the "switching of the tenses."

· · ·

Luu Van Loi leads off the following discussion by saying that he believed SUNFLOWER might well have succeeded. He points out that the initiative took place on the heels of the Thirteenth Plenum of the Central Committee in Hanoi, which was devoted to developing the "diplomatic struggle" on equal terms with the political struggle and military struggle. Luu Van Loi was present at the Foreign Ministry in Hanoi when the "changing of the tenses" message came through, via the letter from President Johnson to Chairman Ho Chi

Minh. In addition to all the other affronts, he points out that Hanoi was given only nine hours to respond—it was an ultimatum, in other words.

Robert McNamara then argues that despite all the tactical bungling on the U.S. side the offer made during SUNFLOWER was very close, as he sees it, to what Hanoi was demanding. Nguyen Co Thach disagrees. He says that the United States was still bombing the North, which was unacceptable. McNamara responds by saying that though it is true that the bombing continued, the basic package being offered clearly included everything Hanoi was asking for. Nguyen Co Thach restates his disagreement. He says nothing was going to happen until the bombing was halted unconditionally. Chester Cooper then laments that in listening to this conversation, thirty years after the fact, he has almost become convinced that his entire professional life during this period was wasted. The discussion concludes with an exchange between Cooper and Luu Doan Huynh regarding who, ultimately, is to blame for the failure of SUNFLOWER.

❖

Luu Van Loi: I want to say something about a contact that, it seems to me, could have succeeded, but did not. This was the SUNFLOWER initiative. [Speaks in English.] This is SUNFLOWER. . . .

So why did the DRV engage in this activity with the U.S. at this time? The direct reason is the Thirteenth Central Committee Plenum, January 23–26, 1967, which decided to open a diplomatic front to coordinate with the military and political fronts. Implementing that resolution on January 28, Foreign Minister Nguyen Duy Trinh announced that if the U.S. called an unconditional bombing halt, then the U.S. and the Democratic Republic of Vietnam would be able to talk directly to each other. In the West this was called the "Trinh formula."

Nguyen Duy Trinh's position had been stated earlier by Prime Minister Pham Van Dong, on January 2, 1967, in an interview with Harrison Salisbury, a correspondent for *The New York Times*. Pres. Ho Chi Minh confirmed this in an interview with Mr. Harry Ashmore on January 17, 1967. This was a very clear diplomatic message. Unfortunately, President Johnson did not wait for Chairman Ho Chi Minh's response and on February 14, 1967, resumed the bombing of the North after a seven-day temporary pause. So on February 15, 1967, the Foreign Ministry of the DRV published the letters. . . .

Now, about the Wilson-Kosygin talks in London. They occurred during the week of February 6–13, 1967. As the two cochairmen of the Geneva Conference of 1954, they naturally discussed the situation in Vietnam from time to time. At this time, the White House had sent Mr. Chester Cooper to introduce the phase A–phase B plan to Wilson to discuss with Kosygin. Mr. Cooper has told this story very well in his book, *The Lost Crusade,* and of course he is here to answer questions about it. I would just like to add that President Johnson had said that he welcomed the announcement made by Nguyen Duy Trinh on January 28. So Wilson and Kosygin collaborated on a plan for the cessation of bombing and negotiations between the DRV and the U.S. and sent a copy to Washington.

But two days later Washington sent Wilson a new text of Johnson's response that was completely different. According to the new text, the U.S. would stop bombing the North, and stop sending troops to the South, only *after* receiving a guarantee that the DRV will stop its infiltration into South Vietnam. In other words, the sequence of the two-phase plan was reversed: B first, A after. Washington said the new plan was operative and gave the DRV only until 10:00 A.M. London time to respond. It was already 1:00 A.M. when Wilson and Kosygin heard about this. Mr. Cooper and Ambassador David Bruce were astounded by the change of plans by the White House and did not sympathize with the request that Hanoi respond before 10:00 A.M.

On the afternoon of February 13, President Johnson ordered the resumption of the bombing. I would like to quote a passage from his communiqué: [Speaks in English.] "Regardless of our efforts, and those from third parties, there was no response from Hanoi. But the door is still open and we are ready at any time to go more than halfway in order to obtain an equal response from the other side." [Resumes in Vietnamese.] This is how SUNFLOWER failed in London.

Robert McNamara: Let me speak about SUNFLOWER. The U.S. put forward a proposal. It was our understanding that the Russians came to the U.S. and said that they would be willing to put a proposal to the Vietnamese, or perhaps the U.S. would put a proposal to the Vietnamese. The Russians said they believed such a proposal would lead to serious talks. So we put a proposal in Moscow to the Vietnamese representative there. The proposal was subsequently discussed in London between Prime Minister Alexei Kosygin and Prime Minister Harold Wilson. U.S. Ambassador David Bruce and Chet Cooper were there. This was a very serious, very extensive negotiation or discussion, stimulated by the Russians coming to us saying they believed Hanoi would be interested in receiving a proposal from us.

What was our proposal? These were the major points: A cease-fire, troop withdrawals, elections, political participation by the NLF, reunification of North and South Vietnam. That sounds to me very close to your Four Points. In my mind, at least, this proposal sounds like something that would have been of interest, at least for further discussion. But it got none—not even a show of interest. Nothing. Why?

Nguyen Co Thach: You were still bombing the North.

Robert McNamara: Yes, we *were* bombing the North, that's true. But we were proposing, in a sense (subject, perhaps, to some further discussion), to accept your Four Points. I didn't understand then, and I don't understand today, why you didn't just say: "OK, Mr. United States of America, we've got you by the tail. You've accepted our Four Points. We'll meet you tomorrow and we'll work out a text." I mean, just *look* at the elements in this proposal: cease-fires, troop withdrawals, elections, political participation by the NLF, and reunification of North and South. Now that was in January 1967. Was anything better than that obtained in 1973, six years later, after hundreds of thousands of additional people were killed? I think not.

Nguyen Co Thach: I must remind you again that we did not accept any proposal while you were bombing us.

Robert McNamara: But, just a minute, the first proposal *was* a cessation of bombing—a cease-fire. It was right there in black and white. And this was in 1967, not 1973.

Nguyen Co Thach: But a cease-fire could not just apply to the bombing. The fighting in the South was absolutely linked to the bombings of the North. You bombed the North because you were losing in the South.

Robert McNamara: But the cease-fire included what we took to be your central requirement—cessation of bombing in the North. I just don't understand why you weren't willing to discuss it, to pursue it, to see how far you could push us. What in the world did you have to lose?

Nguyen Co Thach: We were always willing to negotiate anything but our basic principles, contained in the Four Points.

Chester Cooper: My sense is—and I may be wrong—but the sense that I get from the discussion thus far is that, in the last analysis, there was nothing that we could propose until 1968 that would elicit a positive, constructive response in respect to negotiations. I'm beginning to feel that much of my life during that period was wasted.

Nguyen Co Thach: But you see, in 1968, President Johnson agreed to abide by the Four Points and therefore cease the bombings of the North. Then we could begin to negotiate, and we did. But that is different than the Fourteen Points of 1966 that you are talking about. Completely different.

Robert McNamara: The point I want to make is: *This is a missed opportunity!* In essence, the deal that was finally made six years later, after hundreds of thousands more people were killed—yours and ours—it was essentially the same deal. I am not arguing that this is your fault. Please don't misunderstand me. I am arguing that together, we missed an opportunity. That's the point I want to make.

Luu Doan Huynh: On the subject of Kosygin and Wilson—on SUN-FLOWER—I don't understand how you, Mr. McNamara, can say that it was only North Vietnam that did not want to accept the conditions you just described. Don't forget that Johnson brought new conditions. Chester Cooper, you write about this in your book—how the White House changed the conditions—[Speaks in English.] Johnson changed the tense . . . there was a changing of the tense. [Resumes in Vietnamese.] Now, with this new thing from Walt Rostow, phase A comes second and phase B comes first. So we must stop helping our friends in the South *before* you stop the bombing. So if we are talking about SUNFLOWER, then the Americans are to blame. The Americans!

Chester Cooper: . . . I can't argue with what you just said.

Luu Doan Huynh: [Speaks in English.] You . . . you . . . you are the man to speak. [Laughter.]

Robert McNamara: We got a new chairman, Chet, and he's ordering you to speak up. [Laughter.]

Chester Cooper: Okay, I just want to ask you: When you said to us "no negotiations unless there is an unconditional cessation of bombing"—isn't that an ultimatum?

Luu Doan Huynh: [Speaks in English.] No, I don't think so. . . .

PENNSYLVANIA: "CLOSE, BUT NOT YET CLOSE ENOUGH"

On June 28, 1967, Raymond Aubrac, a hero of the French Resistance then working at the UN's Food and Agriculture Organization office in Rome, received a call from a friend, who asked him to come immediately to Paris but offered no explanation for why he should do so.[112] Aubrac left the next day and, upon arrival, was taken to the home of Etienne Bauer, a friend from the days of the Resistance who was at that time director of France's Institute for Nuclear Science. Bauer had assembled a group of scientists belonging to Pugwash, a group organized by American industrialist Cyrus Eaton in 1957 out of a concern for nuclear danger, but which had since gotten involved in a wider array of peace initiatives, both formal and informal. Bauer told Aubrac that the group wanted to speak to him about taking a peace proposal from the American government directly to Ho Chi Minh, whom Aubrac knew personally and who was in fact godfather of Aubrac's daughter.

Two others present—both members of Pugwash—would also be intimately involved with Aubrac. One was Henry Kissinger, a Harvard professor of government and a consultant to both the White House and State Department, who was familiar with Washington's Vietnam dossier. Kissinger would be the intermediary with Washington. The other person was Herbert Marcovitch, a microbiologist, who would accompany Aubrac to Hanoi, via Phnom Penh, where Marcovitch would allegedly be touring the Pasteur Institute.[113] It was in Phnom Penh that they would receive their visas for the journey to Hanoi. This was the proposition put to Aubrac: Would he deliver to Ho Chi Minh an offer from President Johnson? Astonished, Aubrac nevertheless said he would.

The initiative, which Kissinger had brought to the attention of William Bundy and Dean Rusk in June, had been left to languish in the State Department until Robert McNamara examined a copy of a cable sent to Rusk from Kissinger, with a copy to himself. After discussion with his deputy, John McNaughton, McNamara decided to bring Kissinger's proposal up to Rusk and Johnson at lunch the following day. They expressed skepticism but told McNamara that if he thought it might work then they accepted his offer to take charge of it. Thus began the strange saga of this extraordinarily complex and sensitive peace initiative, overseen from Washington by the U.S. secretary of defense.[114]

Aubrac and Marcovitch set off for Hanoi via Phnom Penh. After some difficulty in Phnom Penh about the visas, Aubrac and Marcovitch eventually met once with Ho Chi Minh, who was then ill (on the afternoon of July 24,

1967), and twice with Prime Minister Pham Van Dong (on July 24 and 25). They returned to Paris on July 28 and were debriefed by Kissinger during the course of a meeting lasting fifteen hours, according to Aubrac. Kissinger promptly wrote up his notes and submitted them to the State Department, where they were received by Chester Cooper, who read them and covered them with a brief memorandum summarizing their contents for the "Negotiations Committee," led by Averell Harriman and Walt Rostow.

The discussion with Ho Chi Minh was not substantive. But the discussions with Pham Van Dong were highly substantive. Kissinger's notes of those conversations provide some insight into what was and was not possible at that time between Washington and Hanoi. The following exchange took place on the morning of July 24:

> Aubrac asked what Pham Van Dong meant by unconditional bombing halt. Pham Van Dong replied that North Vietnam could not negotiate while being bombed. Aubrac asked whether Pham Van Dong wanted an official declaration that the bombing had stopped, or would he be satisfied with a de facto end of bombing. Pham Van Dong replied that a de facto cessation would be acceptable. Aubrac asked whether there should be some delay between the end of bombing and the beginning of negotiations. Pham Van Dong replied: "This is not a problem." Aubrac asked what channels could be used. Pham Van Dong replied: "This is not a problem but it should be someone authorized by both parties." He then went on to say initial negotiations could be on those matters affecting the United States and North Vietnam as principals. When issues affecting South Vietnam were raised, the NLF would have to be present.
>
> Pham Van Dong then closed the meeting with a little speech: "You see dear friends, that the problem is very complicated. You may think your travels are useless. In fact you have given us much to think about."[115]

Kissinger then adds that Marcovitch's "cover," the minister of health, told Aubrac and Marcovitch at lunch that "the two-step bombing proposal should be discussed officially rather than informally."[116]

This looked very interesting to McNamara. He dictated a new message for Pham Van Dong, to be given by Kissinger to Aubrac and Marcovitch, which they would deliver to Pham Van Dong on a subsequent trip to Hanoi, as follows:

> The United States is willing to stop the aerial and naval bombardment of North Viet-Nam with the understanding that this will lead promptly to

productive discussions between representatives of the United States and the Democratic Republic of Viet-Nam, looking toward a resolution of the issue between them. While discussions proceed either with public knowledge or secretly, the United States would assume that the Democratic Republic of Viet-Nam would not take advantage of the bombing cessation.[117]

President Johnson approved the draft on August 11, and Kissinger and Chester Cooper flew to Paris for meetings with Aubrac and Marcovitch, beginning August 17.[118] Aubrac and Marcovitch asked for and received a guarantee that the United States would suspend bombing within a ten-mile radius of Hanoi from August 24 to September 4, when the French interme-diaries were expected to be in Hanoi.

However, on August 20, U.S. planes hit Hanoi hard in a series of sorties that had been scheduled long before but was delayed due to bad weather. Aubrac and Marcovitch were informed by Hanoi that as a result of the bombing they should not come to Hanoi due to safety considerations. Instead, on August 25, the U.S. proposal was delivered by the two French intermediaries to Mai Van Bo, with the request that it be sent to Hanoi. Mai Van Bo read it and said it was "clearly significant."[119] But no word came back from Hanoi. On September 9, Aubrac and Marcovitch again visited Mai Van Bo and asked for an answer. The reply was that they "must realize that the DRV situation is quite complex."[120] Mai Van Bo then said: "What I really want to know is whether the August 25 message is still valid." He was told that it was and that the bombings in Hanoi were not related to the August 25 message.[121] Finally, on September 11, a message came through from Hanoi: No deal. The bombing, and the threat of bombing, it said, "con-stitutes an ultimatum to the Vietnamese people. . . . It is only after the unconditional stopping by the United States of all acts of war against the Democratic Republic of Viet-Nam, that it would be possible to engage in conversations."[122]

Discussions of various sorts carried on well into October, but the channel was effectively closed following the September 11 message. President John-son publicized the approach on September 29 in a speech in San Antonio, Texas, following which the August 25 proposal became widely known as the "San Antonio formula."[123] It became the basic formula that, on April 3, 1968, led Hanoi to agree to enter into peace talks with Washington, in Paris, in exchange for a partial bombing halt.

·   ·   ·

The following discussion begins with a query from James Blight regard-ing the reception of the PENNSYLVANIA initiative in Hanoi. Luu Doan

Huynh responds by discussing the complications involved when Hanoi received Aubrac and Marcovitch in late July, when the planning for the Tet Offensive was well under way. In addition, Gen. Nguyen Chi Thanh, the principal originator of the idea for the Tet Offensive, died of a heart attack on July 8, throwing the entire leadership into a crisis over how the Tet Offensive should be organized and who should be in charge of it. In short, this was not a good time to come to Hanoi to talk about peace negotiations, when the entire leadership was geared for an intensive escalation of the war.

He concludes, however, by pointing out that even though Hanoi rejected PENNSYLVANIA, he and his colleagues in the Foreign Ministry did so quietly, without harsh rhetoric, as had usually been the case. They had hoped that this would be noticed by the Americans. But of course it wasn't.

Nguyen Khac Huynh, who dealt with all the initiatives from within the Foreign Ministry, alludes to something that has come up informally: At about this time, the summer of 1967, the Foreign Ministry task force on negotiations with the United States had finished its preliminary work and was, in fact, ready to move to negotiations, if an acceptable offer was forthcoming. In fact, he says that even in August 1967 he believes negotiations would have gotten under way, if the United States had agreed to an unconditional bombing halt. But because Washington would not agree to this, PENNSYLVANIA became, as he says, the main part of "post-Tet planning." What he does not say, of course, is that the post-Tet phase of the war—1968–1975—was more deadly than the years leading up to it. One gets the impression that the people within the Foreign Ministry in charge of negotiations, led by Foreign Minister Nguyen Duy Trinh, fought hard between August 25 and September 11 with those who favored delaying a response to PENNSYLVANIA until after Tet. Mai Van Bo's exchanges with the French intermediaries during this period suggest as much. But the advocates of moving to negotiations lost the battle.

❖

James Blight: PENNSYLVANIA, known in its public phase as the San Antonio formula . . . was in some sense a last ditch effort by people like Bob McNamara, Chet Cooper, and Nick Katzenbach to find a negotiated solution. We know quite a lot about the U.S. side of it—from the several U.S. participants in it. Chet Cooper told this story in *The Lost Crusade*. Bob McNamara described his role in *In Retrospect*. Henry Kissinger, who acted as a go-between, mentions his role briefly in his book *Diplomacy*. And Raymond Aubrac has recently published his memoirs, containing a chapter on the PENNSYLVANIA initiative, focused on his trip with Herbert Marcovitch to

Hanoi to discuss the U.S. proposal with Ho Chi Minh and Pham Van Dong.

However, we in the West know little about what sort of discussion—if any—the initiative stimulated here in Hanoi. Again, I stress the significance of PENNSYLVANIA because it really was regarded at the time as the last chance that those in the Johnson administration favoring negotiations would have to make their case to you, via these intermediaries. We would therefore like to hear your assessment of PENNSYLVANIA.

There is a second reason for wanting to get your thoughts about PENN-SYLVANIA. As Ambassador Nguyen Khac Huynh told us in June, the summer and fall was also a period of very intense planning for the Tet Offensive—something that the Americans of course knew nothing about at the time. So the question arises: How did North Vietnam balance the reception of a peace initiative with the planning for a major offensive of the war? Did the planning for Tet destroy any chance that PENNSYLVANIA might otherwise have had for success? Or were other factors involved in North Vietnam's disinterest—or what appeared in Washington to be DRV disinterest—in the secret contact?

Luu Doan Huynh: I think it might be helpful if we explained a little bit about how the Tet planning and PENNSYLVANIA came together—how they interacted.

The PENNSYLVANIA initiative took place against the background of our preparations for the Tet Offensive. That is a fact. We don't want to hide that from you. Planning for Tet started in March or April 1967. And you may know that because of the untimely death of Gen. Nguyen Chi Thanh, we had some difficulty. Anyway, by October the final instructions were given. So that is the background. That is what we were doing.

On your side, I wonder whether any of you can tell me whether the PENN-SYLVANIA initiative is a reaction to the statement of Foreign Minister Nguyen Duy Trinh in January 1967—about negotiating at the moment you stop the bombing. Because, you see, when . . . these two gentlemen, Raymond Aubrac and Herbert Marcovitch, proposed the phase A–phase B formula in Hanoi, it was rejected by Prime Minister Pham Van Dong. He argued that there must be unconditional cessation of bombing. But then, as you know, on August 25, you put forward a proposal—we have been discussing the contents—mentioning that discussions must be "productive" and that we must not "take advantage." So this is a bit closer, you see, but still these two words—"take advantage"—make us suspicious. In Vietnam we say that this is like when you say we are going to deliver your cow to you, but we don't give you the string to take the cow out of the shed. . . . [Laughter.]

In the course of the secret contact, we rejected the August 25, 1967, proposal by putting an end to discussions on October 20. However, no attack was made against the proposal either in our official statements or media commentaries. Neither did we attack President Johnson's statement in San Antonio on September 29, which also reflected the PENNSYLVANIA proposal—at least until December 1967. Indeed, articles by the commentator of *Nhan Dan* continued to attack many of President Johnson's other statements about the war, but not his San Antonio speech. It was not until October 20, 1967, that the Australian journalist Wilfred Burchett published an article that reflected our views: Our absolute refusal to offer anything except talks in exchange for cessation of the bombing. We said that the fruitfulness of the talks would depend on the U.S.

But then beginning at the end of December 1967—that is, two months later—we did attack the San Antonio speech directly. Yet even in December, we did not attack the substance of the San Antonio speech. The attack came in our foreign minister's speech of December 29, 1967, which mentioned the recent bellicose San Antonio speech and other recent blatant statements in which President Johnson pretended to "desire peace," but used the pretext of "defending U.S. security" in order to intensify the war and cling to South Vietnam. Notice: No attack on the substance of the San Antonio speech. Later, the statement of our foreign minister put forth the further improved proposal: talks, an unconditional cessation of bombing and all other acts of war. We are familiar with all of this.

Thus the proxy article of Burchett and the foreign minister's speech implied that North Vietnam understands the San Antonio "formula" but we prefer our own formula, and we would like you to examine and respond to our formula. On January 21, 1968, the *Nhan Dan* commentator attacked President Johnson's State of the Union message yet also made some comments about the San Antonio formula. It said that the U.S. was trying to compel Vietnam to accept the San Antonio formula, requiring Vietnam to pay a price for U.S. aggression—the usual U.S. trick of equating the aggressor and the victim of aggression, and thus trying to compel Vietnam to give up its struggle for national salvation. (You see: No attack on the substance of the San Antonio proposal.) And so my impression, in hindsight, is that there was no unequivocal North Vietnamese rejection of the PENNSYLVANIA or San Antonio proposals.

But you should have paid attention to our reaction to the San Antonio speech. Our reaction to it shows that we did not want to encourage your hawks by trying to be more flexible—if we tried to be more flexible we would encourage your hawks, because they will think they are winning. But we also tried not to appear too tough—too rigid and inflexible—in order to avoid discouraging your doves. So you see, we left things pending. We left things pending like that, because we were waiting for the results of the Tet Offensive. . . .

Please: I would like someone on the American side to answer . . . was the PENNSYLVANIA initiative stimulated or provoked in any way by the statement of Foreign Minister Nguyen Duy Trinh in January 1967? That is my question.

Chester Cooper: The statement McNamara gave Kissinger *was* very different. When Kissinger was about to talk to Aubrac and Marcovitch in Paris, we decided to give him something new—something different from the same old formula. Kissinger passed that statement on to Marcovitch and Aubrac in Paris. Kissinger, of course, had no official position at the time—in the United States government. Aubrac and Marcovitch realized that the message was significantly different from what had been discussed before, so they wanted to make sure it really was an official U.S. offer. So I made a secret trip to Paris to meet with Aubrac, Marcovitch, and Kissinger to assure them that, yes, this was now the official U.S. position.

Luu Doan Huynh: Thank you. Now, may I also give you my impression? The contents of the proposal of PENNSYLVANIA and the San Antonio speech came very close to meeting our position on cessation of bombing as the principal condition for beginning talks—much closer than any other proposal made by the U.S. In particular, it was far—very far—from the ultimatum given to us by President Johnson in connection with the Kosygin visit. But we rejected PENNSYLVANIA, however. You know this. We did not reject it so loudly as before, but in a rather vague manner. And then later on came this statement by my Foreign Minister Nguyen Duy Trinh at the end of December 1967.

It was only two months after the end of PENNSYLVANIA that there came Clifford's statement—do you remember this statement by Clark Clifford on January 25 . . . ? Clifford said that the words "take advantage," in his view, did not require a cease-fire, and during the pause the DRV could continue to maintain the same flow of supplies to the South. He said this would not constitute a violation of the agreement. Clifford said this in late January 1968.

But unless I committed an oversight in checking up, I believe we had no reaction to this statement. Either we missed it or we deliberately did not react. I do not personally know the reason. It was more or less—it more or less fulfilled 90 percent of what we wanted. I presume that we did not want to make any reaction that would discourage the doves. You see, this was a tricky and difficult business—to establish conditions that are best for the negotiations—*but after Tet!* We also did not want to encourage the hawks. So we left things pending until after the Tet Offensive. . . .

Nguyen Khac Huynh: Before the break, Mr. James Blight raised some questions about our negotiating strategy. Specifically, you asked whether PENNSYLVANIA and the San Antonio formula were close to our position—I mean what it would take to move to formal negotiations. Partly, I think, this is an issue of semantics: What do we mean by "close" or "closer"? I would say we thought the San Antonio formula was closer—much closer than before. But I would also say that while it was close, it was not yet close enough. The problem was that neither the PENNSYLVANIA initiative nor the San Antonio formula met our demand for an unconditional bombing halt.

I followed all the secret peace contacts from the very beginning, from within the Foreign Ministry. I can tell you that with each new contact, each new intermediary, each slightly altered U.S. position presented to us—all of this was very confusing and complicated. This was especially true of your different positions on the role of the NLF, but it was true to one degree or another of all the initiatives. It was very difficult for us, with very little information and few contacts with the U.S.—even indirect contacts—to determine what was true or false, what was a smoke screen, what was being put forward simply to satisfy U.S. domestic opinion. These factors made the evaluation of the proposals very complicated for us. In his book, Mr. McNamara says that one lesson he learned from the war was that for matters of war and peace like the Vietnam War, the government should have—I think he uses the phrase a "war cabinet," or something like this—a group that does nothing but try to understand all the facets of the war. We did this.[124] But even so, it was very, very difficult to understand what was going on.

Then there was a different problem: What was to be told to our friends and allies. As you know, and as we have said here, our relations with the Soviets and Chinese were not always so simple. Big problems arose over what we should tell each of them regarding, for example, the peace contacts. This was made even more complicated by the fact that the U.S. was also talking to them—especially to the Soviets—so we had to be careful. And then: What do we tell our enemies—not just the U.S., but the countries who supported the U.S. war effort against us? Please remember that we had few resources of our own but that we also made a firm decision to rely on our own judgment, in all cases, and that involved relying on our own sources of information, which were not many.

About San Antonio: We did not strongly criticize the U.S. position. In my opinion—this is my personal opinion; it is not found in documents—San Antonio made us believe that talks between the U.S. and Vietnam were now possible—were about to take place in the near future. We began, at this time, to prepare for negotiations with the U.S.—but only *after* the Tet Offensive. Our view was that, after Tet, the conditions would be favorable. I want to remind you of something I said earlier about our approach to negotiations. Our best source of relevant information—always—was the battlefield situation in the South. We had no way of knowing what to make of all these various "channels"—such as PENNSYLVANIA, for example, or all these intermediaries. Always, in planning our negotiating strategy, we analyzed the situation on the battlefield. This is where the planning for the Tet Offensive became important. We believed that Tet would decisively alter the situation in the South, demonstrate to everyone that the U.S. could not possibly prevail, and therefore you would seek to move to negotiations in a framework consistent with our Four Points. This is, in fact, what happened, in our opinion.

Our response to PENNSYLVANIA—which was very mild, as Mr. Luu Doan Huynh said—was our way of trying to encourage the doves in Washington, without encouraging the hawks to believe that you were on the verge of winning. In addition, in maintaining channels like the Aubrac channel in PENNSYLVANIA, we were able to explore the U.S. position and flexibility. To put it another way: PENNSYLVANIA, and our response to it, represented, for us, a critically important development in our *post-Tet* negotiating strategy.

In retrospect, we see that it took only from September 1967 to March 1968—just a few months—to get post-Tet negotiations started. Given the course of such a long war, a few months is not a very long time. In his book, Mr. McNamara says that PENNSYLVANIA came to an end in early October 1967. I can understand why he reached that conclusion, but it is a wrong conclusion, from our point of view. PENNSYLVANIA was very significant because it carried the message to us, we believed for the very first time, that the U.S. would soon be willing to sit down with us and negotiate. PENNSYLVANIA made negotiations seem possible.

James Blight: I gather, therefore, that you would not say that PENNSYLVANIA failed, would you?

Nguyen Khac Huynh: No, no. PENNSYLVANIA did *not* fail. PENNSYLVANIA proved to us in the Foreign Ministry of the DRV—and to the leadership—that talks were about to begin. As such, it gave tremendous support and encouragement to those of us who were at that moment working on a negotiating strategy. We were very encouraged. . . . PENNSYLVANIA succeeded several months after it was initiated, because it provided the basis for beginning the Paris peace process. There is your answer. Our ears were not "deaf." We "heard" you. And we gave our answer after Tet.

Conclusions

My general conclusion may strike some as obvious, but in light of the data in this chapter it cannot possibly be overemphasized: *There were a great many missed opportunities to move to a negotiated settlement of the Vietnam War between May 1965 and October 1967.* Now that we have the data to compare Washington's and Hanoi's views of each other's decisions and actions during the 1965–1967 period, the extent of missed opportunities is truly mind-boggling.

The main points are these: First, there are more missed opportunities for peace than I (or, I believe, anyone else) thought possible; and second, both sides missed opportunities every step of the way.

I will summarize the major missed opportunities as my coauthors and I have presented them in this chapter.

THE FOUR POINTS AND FOURTEEN POINTS

These are the absolutely *fundamental* missed opportunities. If the fundamental positions, inherent in Hanoi's Four Points and Washington's Fourteen Points, had been properly understood by each other, at any time in this process, I am convinced that we could have moved quickly to negotiations.

- *Washington's View of Hanoi's Four Points.* I am amazed at the repeated misunderstandings on the U.S. side with regard to Point Three: that the Saigon government would be arranged "in accordance with the program of the NLF." Looking back, it is obvious that the NLF's platform *had* to promote a government of neutrality because the NLF itself was composed of so many different groups, most of them noncommunist, at least in the beginning. Why did we miss it time and time again? Surely, our mindset, fearing the fall of dominoes, played a role. But so did the lack of sustained contact with North Vietnamese representatives, especially in the beginning, who might have been able and willing to explain it, had we been ready to listen.

- *Hanoi's Presentation of Their Four Points.* And what about the North Vietnamese? I understand that they only began preparing a staff and documents for negotiating in February 1965. But even so, Hanoi totally failed to make its meaning clear to us. It may be that some in the South felt it was not in their interest to be completely clear with us, fearing abandonment in another deal, such as that of Geneva 1954. If so, it still does not excuse the peremptory and often needless obfuscation engaged in by Hanoi's representatives.

- *Washington's Presentation of Its Fourteen Points.* The way the U.S. Fourteen Point proposal emerged was typical of our approach to the peace initiatives. In the middle of the Christmas bombing pause in 1965, the president suddenly wanted to know our negotiating position. Dean Rusk got a call from the Hungarian Janos Radvanyi, who wanted the same information. So Dean wrote them out one evening, and the result was the Fourteen Points. In contrast, Hanoi's Four Points were drafted by a team, supervised by Ho Chi Minh, Pham Van Dong, and Le Duan, during a two-month period, culminating in Pham Van Dong's Four Point speech on April 8, 1965. The Fourteen Point list borders on the incoherent. There is no clear program in it for moving to negotiations. Basically, Hanoi is asked to "pick" some things they like from the "basket of peace." We should have put a real proposal to them.

- *Hanoi's View of the Fourteen Points.* As I read the evidence, I can't understand why Hanoi did not even probe to see what might be developed from the "basket" of Fourteen Points. As Chet Cooper says in this chapter, once we acknowledged that the NLF could take part in a coalition government— and it is acknowledged in the Fourteen Points—then a coalition government, possibly much like the one envisioned in Point Three of Hanoi's Four Points, *had* to emerge. Why did Hanoi not see this? I don't understand it.

Washington was sloppy and disorganized, but Hanoi was defensive and rigid. Each misunderstood the other's intent to use the Points as a beginning, not an end of a process.

KEY MISUNDERSTANDINGS

There are four other key misunderstandings that contributed to a profound mistrust on each side. Progress on any one would have led to progress on the others, leading to talks.

- *Washington's Approach to Negotiations.* We were totally insensitive to the requirements of international diplomacy between combatants. Not all of this can be laid at President Johnson's doorstep, though it was his style to treat international affairs—indeed, domestic affairs as well—rather as if he were dealing with a group of American senators who were looking for something to trade. But the flood of intermediaries, initiatives, statements, and positions appears to have completely overwhelmed Hanoi's capacity to make sense—our sense—of what we meant to convey. In fact, we were desperate for a peace formula, whereas they saw our intermediary efforts as a plot to avoid negotiations, trap them, or even destroy them.

- *Hanoi's View of Negotiations.* There seems to have been an almost total disconnect between Washington and Hanoi. Preferring quiet, even secret talks, the North Vietnamese found themselves dealing with Lyndon Johnson, the embodiment of the American tendency to publicize and dramatize. But one finding in particular stands out: When in doubt of U.S. motives, as Hanoi usually was, they turned to their immediate reality— the bombing of the North and the arrival of U.S. troops in the South—as their primary evidence. That evidence said to them that Washington was escalating, therefore—they erroneously concluded—Washington was not interested in peace. If Washington was not interested in peace, then the intermediary campaign must be part of our war strategy, and therefore, Hanoi chose to fight our probes and offers, rather than—as I see it—treat them at face value—as initiatives motivated by the desire for peace.

- *Bottom Lines: Washington's Views.* Many in Washington came to believe at the time that Hanoi did not want, under any realistic scenario, a negotiated settlement to the war. In other words, Hanoi appeared to be asking for what amounted to an unconditional surrender, in the sense that we believed they wanted nothing less than the "conquest" of South Vietnam and instant reunification of the country on their own terms. Unaccountably, they seemed to actually *want* to fight on, rather than talk. In retrospect, it is possible to see that this was not the case at all, as the exchange in this chapter between myself and Nguyen Khac Huynh demonstrates. We didn't talk; we didn't know each other's bottom lines. And so the war continued.

- *Bottom Lines: Hanoi's View.* Hanoi too seems to have concluded early on that we in Washington would settle for nothing less than *their* surrender. This is evident in the way they defined the problem: "breaking the aggressive will" of the United States. But in fact, there was never any desire in Washington to "conquer" any of their territory or occupy it.

Neither side could decipher the other's bottom line and thus never under-stood—tragically—that it was not impossible to reconcile them in a way acceptable to both sides.

- *Impact of Casualties: Washington.* In a crude but not entirely inaccurate sense, U.S. strategy was aimed at inflicting sufficient "punishment" on Hanoi and its allies in the South to force them to this conclusion: Their objective—as we *mistakenly* understood it—was not worth the cost. I was hardly alone in my astonishment at the level of casualties Hanoi was will-ing to endure—that its people were willing to endure, in pursuit of their objective of reunification. We clearly lacked the understanding of Viet-namese history and culture that would have prevented us from believing that they would reverse course as a function of being "punished" by U.S. power.

- *Impact of Casualties: Hanoi.* In their own calculations, Hanoi was mis-taken to suspect that the U.S. motives were other than what we said they were. We were not colonialists, like the French. We were not their neigh-borhood Great Power, with long-term designs on them, like the Chinese. In fact, our motives were quite transitory and idealistic: We wanted to protect an ally we had helped create, called South Vietnam, until it could go it alone and was capable of avoiding being used as a pawn in the extension of Soviet and Chinese power. Hanoi made little or no attempt to appeal to these motives, by exploring the possibilities of dealing with us, or negotiating with us. Instead, they hunkered down for a war modeled, it seems, on their experience with the Chinese and French. Only this time they were dealing with a country whose capacity to inflict damage far sur-passed that of either of their traditional adversaries.

- *Bombing Halt or Pause: Washington's View.* We implicitly believed that the Hanoi government would pick up the signals we tried to send via our air war in the North. In particular, we felt we could signal our good faith and interest in negotiations by the *absence* of bombing, or by otherwise restricting it. As we indicated in this chapter, some in Washington felt the bombing was the blue chip for the United States in negotiations. It was anything but that. We did not understand that this approach, which we saw as an attempt to bargain with our adversary, would be regarded as an ultimatum and as unacceptable. To many in Washington, in turn, this response seemed to indicate a lack of seriousness regarding negotiations. It wasn't. We could never really appreciate the distinction Hanoi made between bombing pauses and an unconditional halt.

- *Bombing Halt or Pause: Hanoi's View.* Hanoi believed Washington was not serious about negotiations due in large part to two factors: First, Washington's use of pauses to (as Hanoi believed) coerce, threaten, and manipulate them; and second, because Washington appeared to refuse to meet their condition for an unconditional bombing halt. This was a complete misreading of U.S. intentions. It also showed very close to zero understanding of the needs of the advocates of the pauses in Washington, which was some minimal reciprocity from Hanoi on cutting back, or at least avoiding an increase in the rate of infiltration. They regarded this requirement as yet another way to ask them to surrender, because they apparently believed, as Nguyen Khac Huynh said, it would constitute the abandonment of their NLF allies in the South.

Six Peace Initiatives

The six key peace initiatives—four initiated by Washington, two by Hanoi—reexamined in this chapter by no means exhausts the number of initiatives that might be analyzed in this fashion. Nor does our analysis even reveal all the conceivable missed opportunities that one might find embedded in the six initiatives we do analyze. The point I want to emphasize is that *both* sides missed opportunities, in *every* initiative under analysis, and that in *each* case, had they not been missed by one or the other (or both), I believe serious peace talks could have begun soon thereafter.

- MAYFLOWER. *The brief bombing pause in May 1965, together with the démarche via Moscow to the DRV.*
Washington did not specify the length of the pause. We sent North Vietnam an insensitive, almost threatening aide-mémoire. We did not specify what sort of quid pro quo was being asked of Hanoi, in return for the pause. And we unwittingly chose a channel in the worst possible location at that moment—Moscow (due to Hanoi's fear of offending the Chinese, by seeming to be aligning themselves with the Soviets). Hanoi, in contrast, by refusing even to receive the note, seemed to signal its supreme disinterest in moving to negotiations, which in effect confirmed the views of officials in Washington who had opposed the bombing pause in the first place. Their action set back the cause of peace considerably.
Luu Doan Huynh is correct to assert that MAYFLOWER was the last chance for Hanoi to slow down U.S. decisionmaking with regard to the ground war. Hanoi should have tried it—should have responded, possibly as

he suggests, by addressing Point Three of the Four Points first. Both Washington and Hanoi radically misunderstood each other's responses. In fact, it seems that each side, at this early point, would have been amenable to the other's position, if it had only picked up the intended signals.

- XYZ. *The Paris channel, via Mai Van Bo, in August and September 1965.*

  Washington could not understand why Hanoi's approach was made immediately *after* the May bombing pause, rather than during the pause. We did not understand that Hanoi saw the purpose of the channel as strictly "pedagogical," in the sense that Mai Van Bo was simply supposed to "instruct" Edmund Gullion, the U.S. intermediary, about the Four Points. And we were blind to the inherent contradiction that Hanoi was bound to see in the escalation of the war in Vietnam and the discussions in Paris. Once again, we were insensitive to the importance of the fact that North Vietnam itself was the theater of operations, where peace "signals" would easily be drowned out by the noise and fog of war. Hanoi, in contrast, misunderstood U.S. motives—which were very serious (the initiative was, after all, directed by George Ball, an advocate of a negotiated settlement). And Hanoi was counterproductively obscure and self-defeating in the way it explained Point Three of the Four Points to Gullion.

  Although Washington mistook Hanoi's purposes in initiating the XYZ channel, Hanoi missed a golden opportunity by insisting that the only reason to talk to an American intermediary at that point was to instruct him about the Four Points. Washington in fact saw no contradiction between sending troops to Vietnam and engaging in peace probes, a fact that Hanoi did not pick up. But for this misunderstanding, the XYZ channel could easily have led to peace talks.

- PINTA. *The Christmas bombing pause and the Rangoon channel, December 1965–January 1966.*

  Washington and Hanoi *totally* misunderstood each other to an extent that is remarkable, even against the background of the ubiquitous misunderstandings revealed throughout this chapter. At the time, I had concluded that we were unlikely to achieve our objectives in Vietnam by military means and, therefore, we should put much greater emphasis on diplomatic actions. That was the thought behind the pause and opening the PINTA-Rangoon channel: to move to negotiations before we might find it necessary to pay that terrible price. Hanoi, in contrast, had just mistakenly concluded, at virtually the same time, that we had made a decision to escalate the war to the limit and to try not only to crush the NLF but also to destroy North Vietnam as well. This was an utter fantasy, fed by their repeated misreading of the motives of our "escalation" on the battlefield. We didn't even see it as "escalation" but as a set of minimal responses to *their* escalation. Of course, they saw it the other way around.

Neither side pushed hard enough to explore the possibilities of the bombing pause beyond the desultory and peripheral channel in Rangoon (between Henry Byroade and Vu Huu Binh). Both sides needed to talk at this point, rather than continue to signal with bombing pauses and troop movements. Hanoi was counterproductively rigid in its unwillingness even to discuss the possibility for a reciprocal arrangement: a bombing pause for a reduction in infiltration to the South. That is all we would have needed to make it work. But they missed the signal completely.

- The Trinh Signal. *The announcement on January 28, 1967, by Foreign Minister Nguyen Duy Trinh that if the bombing of the North stops, talks with the United States could begin.*

We in Washington did not understand at the time the increasing role of Hanoi Foreign Minister Nguyen Duy Trinh or the signal he tried to send in January 1967. We certainly did not know that Trinh had sponsored and directed a comprehensive effort, going back to his appointment as foreign minister in late 1964, to prepare for negotiations. In a sense, it is obvious that the January 28, 1967, announcement was his coming out party, so to speak. The search for a negotiated settlement had now become a high priority in Hanoi. We did not appreciate this. But I do not understand to this day why Nguyen Duy Trinh and his colleagues were so difficult, obscure, and noncommunicative about their demand for an unconditional bombing halt; why they had no understanding that in requesting this demand, without any sort of explanation for it, they were defeating those of us in Washington who wanted to move to negotiations. At the very least, they should have sensed that we needed and wanted to talk about it. But they refused even to discuss it or explain it.

However, we too dropped the ball on this one. As Chet Cooper said, the officials in the State Department got into a "Talmudic," hair-splitting exercise in an attempt to determine if "could" negotiate means "will" negotiate—or something else. This was irresponsible. But the North Vietnamese should have made much more of an effort to show us how the demand for an unconditional bombing halt squared with what appears, in retrospect, to have been a serious offer to move to talks. Since the planning for Tet began in March, this would have been one of the last opportunities to avoid a collision with the military planners in Hanoi.

- SUNFLOWER. *The dual démarche in Moscow, via the DRV ambassador, and in London, via Prime Ministers Harold Wilson and Alexei Kosygin, during January–February 1967.*

Based on the new information presented in this chapter, it appears as if SUNFLOWER was not only a missed opportunity but something like a *very* near miss as well. In fact, as I replay it in my mind, nine times out of ten SUNFLOWER leads to talks. All the conditions were right, at last, for intermediaries to succeed. Wilson was enthusiastic. Kosygin was well regarded in Hanoi at just the moment when the Soviets were replacing the Chinese as the principal backers of the Hanoi government in the communist world. Everything seems to have been in place. At the time, some thought Wilson and Kosygin exaggerated the significance of their initiative. But now, I think it was very, very close to a breakthrough, until the changing of the tenses—requiring Hanoi to cease infiltration *before* Washington instituted a bombing halt. Historian George Herring said at the June 1997 Hanoi conference that he had worked for six years, without success, trying to understand the origins of the changing of the tenses. It was tragic for President Johnson to reverse course at that point. But of course his reason points to the rigidity of Hanoi in refusing to reciprocate: He got a report that during our short bombing pause traffic heading south from the DRV looked like "the New Jersey Turnpike."

There is little question now that the decision leading to the shifting of the tenses, however it occurred in Washington, was decisive. It was terrible. It now appears that without it Wilson and Kosygin might have been able to pull off a new Genevalike arrangement. Yet if even a small amount of flexibility had been shown by Hanoi on the infiltration issue, talks might have begun.

- PENNSYLVANIA. *The channel via Paris, July–October 1967.*

PENNSYLVANIA, in light of the new information from the Vietnamese side, takes on the appearance of a Greek tragedy. Unknown to us in Washington, planning for the Tet Offensive was well under way by mid-June 1967, which is when I discovered Henry Kissinger's note on my desk—it was written to Dean Rusk, with a copy to me—regarding the offer from Henry and his friends from the Pugwash group. As I now read Pham Van Dong's discussion with Raymond Aubrac and Herbert Marcovitch on July 24, 1967, I see little or nothing in what he says that would have created a problem for us. The main requirement is the bombing halt, but he says that can be de facto. Of course, the previously scheduled bombing of Hanoi on August 20 was a costly blunder, particularly in light of what we have learned from the Vietnamese regarding their reliance on the *battlefield* as the index of Washington's intentions. Henry explained to them why it happened, but to no avail. As Luu Doan Huynh said at the February 1998 conference in Hanoi: "Blood speaks with a terrible voice."

But according to sources in Hanoi, a heated debate occurred during the two weeks following August 25, the day our position was communicated to Hanoi via Mai Van Bo. On the one hand, the military officials were well into finalizing the plan for the Tet Offensive and took a dim view of the wisdom of peace talks at that point. In fact, the Tet Offensive was, as they saw it, supposed to raise the odds of a negotiated settlement on their terms. Under these circumstances, Nguyen Duy Trinh and his deputies in the Foreign Ministry resorted to the only means of signaling that they felt was available to them—which was *not* responding harshly to PENNSYLVANIA and not responding at all to the San Antonio speech of President Johnson on September 29. But of course, no such signal was ever received.[125] Hanoi never received the signal we meant to send via bombing pauses—by *not* bombing. And we never received the signal they meant to send, via *not* responding to our offer with characteristically harsh rhetoric.

We in Washington should have appreciated, by mid-1967, the necessity for more careful coordination of military and diplomatic actions. Had we done so, we would have prevented the August 20 bombing of North Vietnam. In addition, we should have pushed harder in late August and early September to clarify our position, rather than simply waiting for Mai Van Bo to get in touch with Aubrac and Marcovitch, thence to Henry Kissinger. Yet those in Hanoi who favored moving to negotiations deluded themselves by thinking that we would pick up a "signal" as faint as "no response." And I strongly disagree with Nguyen Khac Huynh, who implies that the roughly six months between the time Hanoi rejected the PENNSYLVANIA proposal and the April 3, 1968, decision to open talks in Paris makes little difference. It made a huge difference, a tragic difference. In the summer of 1967, there was still time to move to talks and avoid Tet and its aftermath in Vietnam and in the United States—events that led to five more years of bloody war.

. . .

Finally, I want to pose a rhetorical question, then give my answer to it, as a wrap-up to my analysis of specific missed opportunities. *Is it possible, after reading the contents of this chapter, to reach any conclusion other than that if Washington and Hanoi had found a way to establish direct talks, then the war could have been terminated in 1965, if not earlier?*

I understand that in real time, bearing heavy responsibilities and operating under the pressures of time and circumstances, it is difficult to be perfectly candid with both allies and foes. I know what that pressure is like. So we cannot always expect in real time to have the kind of illuminating, productive discussions such as occurred in Hanoi in June 1997 and February 1998. I understand the point, and my experience confirms it.

But is it not likely—almost a certainty, in fact—that if the two sides had mustered the courage to establish a secret, high-level channel of communication in which each had confidence, with sustained face-to-face discussions taking place regularly, that any of the failed initiatives discussed in this chapter could have succeeded? If we didn't succeed during MAYFLOWER, then during PINTA. If not during PINTA, then during SUNFLOWER. If not during SUNFLOWER, then PENNSYLVANIA. I know there were large cultural, linguistic, and historical gaps between us in those days. But this is why we should have made an extra effort to take a small risk for peace.

Our experience during the Cuban missile crisis bears this out in two ways. First, by the time of the missile crisis, President Kennedy and Chairman Khrushchev had met and had developed an ongoing correspondence. These were *not* love letters. These were tough attempts to explain positions and to learn the true positions of each other. It is very fortunate that by October 1962 the two leaders had established such a channel. I believe that if such a channel could be established between the leaders of the two competing superpowers, at one of the most dangerous and difficult points of the Cold War, then President Johnson and Ho Chi Minh could, and should, have done likewise. Their exchange of acrimonious letters in February 1967 shows what happens when a channel is used without proper preparation.

Second, a back channel can be invaluable, providing it is believed to be secure and to provide accurate representations of the views of both sides. Anatoly Dobrynin, the Soviet ambassador in Washington, was the back channel during the most critical moments of the missile crisis. In what may have been one of the turning points—a meeting with Robert Kennedy on the evening of Saturday, October 27—Dobrynin conveyed a personal message from President Kennedy to Khrushchev that helped defuse the crisis. There was no "intermediary campaign," as Tran Quang Co called U.S. efforts to move to negotiations. We in the Johnson administration should have worked with Hanoi to establish just such a channel—perhaps via Mai Van Bo and Charles "Chip" Bohlen, our ambassador in Paris, who was very highly regarded by all of us. Here Hanoi could have been helpful, but it was not. As Henry Kissinger has recalled, Mai Van Bo had instructions during PENNSYLVANIA to avoid even speaking to Henry, who was at the time not even in the U.S. government. Possibly Hanoi feared leaks, which was not an irrational fear. But a channel should have been established that could have been used repeatedly throughout our attempts to move to negotiations.

As I read the evidence in this chapter—and I believe our Vietnamese colleagues will agree after they read this evidence—what was really lacking was the kind of nuanced understanding of the adversary that can occur only through repeated, direct contacts. Did this make a difference? It did. Hanoi's defense minister, Gen. Vo Nguyen Giap, said in a 1969 interview that military forces under Hanoi's command—North and South—had by 1968 suffered a half-million killed in battle in the American War.[126] They would by 1975 lose somewhere between 2 million to 3 million more. The United States had lost 19,562 killed in battle by December 31, 1967. Ultimately, 58,169 Americans would lose their lives in the war.[127] This means that the vast majority of war-related fatalities on both sides occurred *after* the failure of PENNSYLVANIA, which was the last serious attempt before the Tet Offensive to move to negotiations. In other words, even if Washington and Hanoi had failed in face-to-face talks time and again, yet had been able to move to negotiations by late 1967, most of those killed in the war would have been spared.

We didn't talk to each other directly; we were misinformed in basic ways about each other; we relied much too heavily on intermediaries and hit-or-miss contacts between lower-level officials to represent each leadership.

I am not the only senior participant in this research process to reach this conclusion. Another is Nguyen Co Thach, the former Vietnamese foreign minister and my counterpart as head of the Vietnamese team at the June 1997 Hanoi conference. The record of that conference, as it is contained in this book, is filled with blunt, no-holds-barred interventions by Nguyen Co Thach. Many of them, including one in this chapter's analysis of the SUNFLOWER initiative, involve exchanges with me. I was equally blunt, as the record shows.

The last regular session of the June 1997 conference was devoted to lessons of the war. As head of the visiting U.S. team, I was asked to go first. At the beginning of my remarks, I told the participants and observers that I would offer some reflections but that "before I draw additional lessons . . . I want to go home and reflect on what I have heard here." I then offered my reflections. Nguyen Co Thach was then asked to give the Vietnamese response. Given all the bitter history of our two countries, and on the heels of some very testy exchanges during the conference, none of us who were there will forget what happened next. The following was Nguyen Co Thach's response to my intervention on lessons:

> I had prepared a presentation, but after hearing everything that has been said here today, I no longer want to give my presentation. I do not want to read my presentation because I think that direct discussions between us would be better. I think that this morning's discussion has shown that we understand each other better than before, but also that there remain many

things that we do not understand—many things we do not understand about each other.

And perhaps the biggest lesson that should be drawn is the need for more meetings like this one, in order to talk, in order to explore in depth the thinking and understanding each of us has of one another. Therefore, I suggest that after this conference we should have more meetings in the future. This is the best lesson that I have drawn from this conference. [Speaks in English; gestures at McNamara.] I am glad we did not miss this opportunity. [Resumes in Vietnamese.] I will not give my presentation. I am done. Thank you. [Applause.]

I have thought a good deal since then about what Nguyen Co Thach may have meant by that gesture toward me at the end of his remarks. We had had lunch together each day during the conference, and in the course of our conversations we discovered that we had both dealt with various intermediaries—he in Hanoi, me in Washington—he having no idea at all that the U.S. defense secretary could possibly be involved in the search for peace, I with no knowledge of his own activities. He remarked at one point that it was too bad we couldn't have had lunch back then, as we were doing in Hanoi. I agreed.

I never saw Nguyen Co Thach again. After the conference he fell ill, and he died in April 1998. Thank god he lived long enough to—as we were later told—become the champion inside the Vietnamese government of my proposal for a collaborative project on the war and to muster the courage to exercise what freedom he felt he had been given by the Hanoi leadership to put that tough speech back into his briefcase on June 23, 1997, and thus draw our attention to the profound significance—the underrated significance—of dispensing with intermediaries and speaking face-to-face in matters of war and peace.

Some will say that such conclusions as those reached by Nguyen Co Thach and me are unrealistic—that it is too difficult to develop direct, credible channels for discussion under circumstances such as leaders in Washington and Hanoi found themselves during the Vietnam War. Skeptics will say, in fact, that our very failure to move to negotiations proves their point: that it couldn't have been done. I disagree totally with this point of view. Missed opportunities proliferated. Mistakes were made that were preventable.

The great American philosopher William James recorded in his journal on April 30, 1870: *My first act of free will will be to believe in free will.* He then gives himself some advice: "Care little for speculation," he says, and "much for the form of action."[128] This is also good advice for anyone wishing to lower the risk of such tragedies as the Vietnam War occurring in the twenty-first century.

7

U.S. Military Victory in Vietnam: A Dangerous Illusion?

The first, the supreme, the most far-reaching act of judgment that the statesmen and

commander have to make is to establish . . . the kind of war on which they are embarking;

neither mistaking it for, nor trying to turn it into, something that is alien to its nature.

This is the first of all strategic questions and the most comprehensive.

Carl von Clausewitz, *On War*[1]

If you know the enemy and know yourself; in a hundred battles, you will never be defeated.

When you are ignorant of the enemy but know yourself, your chances of winning and

losing are equal. If ignorant both of the enemy and of yourself, you are sure to be defeated

in every battle.

Sun Tzu, *The Art of War*[2]

Introduction*

Twenty-five years have passed since the U.S. military withdrew from Vietnam. During that quarter-century, scores of books on the war have been written by military authors. But no one of them has presented a definitive evaluation of U.S. military strategy, tactics, and operations, and none conclusively answers the central question: Could the United States have won militarily in Vietnam at reasonable cost in terms of human life and without an unacceptable risk of extending the war to China and/or Russia?

Although it was intended that the conference between U.S. and Vietnamese scholars and policymakers scheduled for June 1997 in Hanoi would

---

*With the exception of the introduction, written by Robert S. McNamara, the text of this chapter, including the conclusions, was written by Col. Herbert Y. Schandler.

July 1967. At a briefing to leaders in Washington, General William Westmoreland said: "The situation is not a stalemate. We are winning slowly but steadily, and the pace can accelerate if we reinforce our successes."

1984. In his scholarly memoir of the Vietnam war, *The Twenty-five Year War*, Gen. Bruce Palmer Jr. stated: "Not once during the war did the Joint Chiefs of Staff advise the commander-in-chief or the secretary of defense that the strategy being pursued most probably would fail and that the U.S. would be unable to achieve its objectives."

focus primarily on political issues, it was likely that some discussion of military matters would take place. I, therefore, invited Gen. William Y. Smith (U.S. Air Force, Ret.) and Lt. Gen. Dale Vesser (U.S. Army, Ret.) to join our group. General Smith had been an assistant to the chairman of the Joint Chiefs of Staff, Gen. Maxwell Taylor, during the early years of the war. General Vesser, after graduating from West Point, attended Oxford University as a Rhodes Scholar and later served 500 days in the jungles of Vietnam as a combat commander.

At the end of the June conference, the Vietnamese urged that further joint discussions be planned. Vesser, Smith, and I agreed that if such meetings were to occur a review of military operations should be placed on the agenda and a person capable of writing definitively on the subject should be added to the U.S. team. They recommended Col. Herbert Y. Schandler (U.S. Army, Ret.). Dr. Alfred Goldberg, chief historian of the Defense Department, concurred in their recommendation. Colonel Schandler graduated from West Point. After serving as a combat commander in Vietnam, he received his Ph.D. from Harvard during the mid-1970s. His doctoral studies focused on the war. Since that time, while serving as professor in the Department of Grand Strategy at the National Defense University, he has continued to write on Vietnam. At my request, he agreed to write an extended essay on U.S. military operations in Vietnam, focusing on the following question: Could the U.S. have won the war militarily at acceptable cost and risk?

I asked Colonel Schandler to address several subsidiary questions, including:

- Was President Kennedy correct in believing that, in the end, the South Vietnamese must carry the war themselves; that the United States could not do it for them?

- Was there anything that we did not do, which if we had done, would have equipped the South Vietnamese to win the war themselves? Or was corruption so rampant in the South Vietnamese Army, and political instability so characteristic of the South Vietnamese government, that the army was incapable of effectively combating the insurgency?

- Would an expanded program of support and assistance to South Vietnamese villages during the early years of the war—strengthening the strategic hamlet program, for example—have prevented the National Liberation Front (NLF) from developing bases and sanctuaries, which were essential foundations for further military action against the Saigon government?

- Would a change in U.S. military tactics in the South have resulted in more effective resistance to military pressure from the NLF and the North Vietnamese Army?

- Gen. William C. Westmoreland's military plan was based on a strategy of attrition. He assumed that the United States could inflict casualties upon North Vietnamese and NLF forces at such a rate that they would be unable or unwilling to continue the war in the South. Why did his strategy fail?

- It has been alleged that President Johnson and I severely constrained the bombing campaign north of the 17th parallel and that, as a result, it failed. For example, during hearings before the Senate Armed Services Committee in August 1967, Sen. Strom Thurmond stated, "Mr. Secretary, I am terribly disappointed with your statement [of the bombing program]. It is a statement of appeasing the communists. It is a statement of no-win." How effective was the bombing program? How serious were the constraints? Was there any way the bombing program could have been modified, in extent or time, which would have won the war?

- How unified were the Joint Chiefs in their recommendations regarding U.S. and South Vietnamese military strategy and tactics?

Over a period of years, I expressed doubt that the U.S. could achieve a military victory in Vietnam.In December 1965, the president and I had this exchange:

McNamara: A military solution to the problem is not certain— one-in-three or one-in-two. Ultimately we must find—a diplomatic solution.

President: Then, no matter what we do in the military field, there is no sure victory?

McNamara: That's right. We have been too optimistic. . . . [3]

❖

On June 23, 1966, I stated to Averell Harriman that an acceptable military solution was not possible and therefore we should "get in direct touch" with Hanoi and the NLF to work out the best settlement obtainable.[4]

On November 1, 1967, I delivered to the president a memo, which said: "Continuation of our present course of action in Southeast Asia would be dangerous, costly in lives, and unsatisfactory to the American people." Abe

Fortas, a Supreme Court justice (1965–1969) and a close friend of the president, after being shown the memo by the president, stated: "It must be appraised for what it is: A step in the process of withdrawal." Clark Clifford, later to be secretary of defense, also strongly disagreed with my recommendations. Clifford wrote: "I believe that the course of action suggested will retard the possibility of concluding the conflict."[5]

Did the Joint Chiefs share my views? If not, what was the basis for the different judgments?

There were other questions:

- Did the Joint Chiefs ever advise the president or the secretary of defense that the strategy being pursued would fail and that the United States would be unable to achieve its objectives?

- A majority (or at least a substantial number) of the books on the war by military authors concludes the United States could have won the war if the military had been unleashed. Is there merit to that position? For example, among the suggested traditional actions could have been undertaken are: land operations against the Ho Chi Minh Trail; extension of the war into Cambodia; and far more extensive bombing of North Vietnam. Would any one or more of these have led to a U.S. military victory?

- The Joint Chiefs, who at various times favored a U.S. invasion of North Vietnam, stated it might lead to war with Russia and China, in which case the United States might be forced to use nuclear weapons. How would the Chinese have responded to a U.S. invasion of North Vietnam?

- In September 1967, Richard Helms, director of the Central Intelligence Agency, sent President Johnson a report that concluded with the statement that "the risks [of U.S. withdrawal from Vietnam in defeat] are probably more limited and controllable than most previous arguments had indicated." Did the Joint Chiefs agree with that statement? Had they made any independent evaluation that supported or contradicted it?

Answers to these questions are vital if we are to determine whether a U.S. military victory in Vietnam at acceptable cost and risk was, as some continue to believe, a missed opportunity; or alternatively, whether it was (and remains) a dangerous illusion. In this chapter, Colonel Schandler addresses each of the constituent questions and answers them with reference to the available evidence—U.S., Vietnamese, and Chinese.

The Heart of the Illusion

The American failure in Vietnam has haunted and fascinated American political scientists, politicians, historians, journalists, and military officers at least since April 30, 1975, when Saigon fell to communist forces. To many, including former members of the Joint Chiefs of Staff (JCS, or Joint Chiefs), the outcome still seems scarcely believable. How could America have been defeated by one of the world's poorest countries, North Vietnam, even if one takes into account the support it got from its Soviet and Chinese allies? How and why could this have happened? Their assumption has most often been: The United States *should have* won militarily. Why it did not has therefore been a major issue in the retrospective assessment of the Vietnam War in military as well as civilian circles.

The claim most often made by military analysts and historians since 1975 is that the military was denied victory because of constraints placed on U.S. military power by political leaders in Washington. This view may be summarized as follows: The war in Vietnam was a war of aggression by communist-controlled North Vietnam against our noncommunist ally, South Vietnam. According to this view, more than sufficient U.S. military might and strategy were available to stop that aggression, to defeat North Vietnam, and thus preserve the independence of South Vietnam. That this did not occur is due to U.S. political leaders having "tied the hands" of the military. Military leaders and historians holding this view have bitterly denounced the policy of limited and gradual application of military force (in the air and on the ground, in both North and South Vietnam), as the principal cause of our failure to defeat the enemy and achieve a military "victory."

Had the U.S. military been allowed to attack at will and without limits, many believe, the U.S. victory would have come quickly and decisively. In this way, Hanoi's aggression would have been halted, and the territorial integrity of South Vietnam would have been maintained as a bulwark against the spread of communism in Southeast Asia.

Now, nearly twenty-five years after the end of the war, and nearly a half-century after the United States first became involved, the evidence points to the conclusion that to believe that the U.S. military was denied a victory it could have and should have won in Vietnam *is an illusion—a dangerous illusion if acted upon in future U.S. conflicts.*

For purposes of orienting the reader, the following are some of the unmistakable conclusions to be drawn from a comprehensive analysis of the data on military aspects of the war, conclusions that are incompatible with the illusion of a U.S. military victory in Vietnam. The heart of the illusion is the failure of U.S. military and civilian leaders alike to understand the nature of the war in which they became involved in Vietnam: It was a *people's war*—a civil war. Fundamentally, therefore, it was not simply a war of North Vietnamese aggression, as we viewed it at the time.

American leaders were inflexible in meeting the problems posed by people's war. Faced with a new challenge, the U.S. military responded in a conventional manner, attempting to follow doctrine and strategy that derived from its World War II experience. That is to say, they prepared to fight a conventional war based on doctrine designed for fighting on the plains of Western Europe in an all-out war.

In their desire to counter what they believed was a war of aggression from the North, U.S. military leaders gradually came to assume almost total responsibility for military operations in the South. Relative to U.S. military assistance, American attention to social programs and community organization in South Vietnam was trifling. This was a mistake that the communists fighting a people's war did not make. Indeed, their understanding of people's war suggested that it was first a *political* struggle; only secondarily, after proper political and social preparation, did it become an *armed* struggle.

Some historians and analysts of the Vietnam War reached these conclusions long ago. But they did so based almost exclusively on a reading of U.S. statements, declassified documents, memoirs, and other materials, which are voluminous and still growing. However, because of the dialogues that occurred in the context of the project of which this book is the first major publication, it is now possible to cite the views of former North Vietnamese officials—both military and civilian. As we shall see, this comparative analysis of military strategy and tactics now suggests that the North Vietnamese and their southern allies, the National Liberation Front, understood the nature of the war in Vietnam far better than we did. The documentation of this view occupies the remainder of this chapter.

Advisers: Defending the South Vietnamese "Domino," 1954–1960

After assisting the French effort against the Vietminh with money and supplies, the United States viewed the Geneva Accords of 1954 darkly, as bringing down the Iron Curtain on another country in Asia—North Vietnam—to the worldwide communist threat. The threat seemed omnipresent and exceedingly dangerous, as evidenced, for example, by the 1948 siege of

Berlin by Stalin, the communist takeover of China by communists under Mao Zedong in 1949, North Korean leader Kim Il Sung's decision to invade South Korea in 1950, and by the subsequent Chinese intervention in that war. These and similar events had convinced the Eisenhower administration that it faced a coordinated, worldwide communist conspiracy against the United States and its allies.

As discussed in Chapter 3, President Eisenhower and Secretary of State John Foster Dulles were convinced that the nationwide elections mandated by the 1954 Geneva Accords would, in fact, result in an all-Vietnam victory for the communists led by Ho Chi Minh. Thus from the outset, U.S. planning focused not on the elections but on providing necessary military and other assistance to the new entity called "South Vietnam"—everything it needed to defend itself against the communist threat from the North. This would be the fundamental objective of U.S. policy in the region from 1954 until the late 1960s: The South Vietnamese "domino" must not be allowed to "fall."

As we know, the elections of 1956 required by the Geneva Accords never occurred. Although the leader installed by the United States, Ngo Dinh Diem, was initially successful in this experiment in South Vietnamese nation-building, as it was called, his success (and popularity) was short-lived. As the Diem government intensified its efforts to consolidate its rule in South Vietnam, many of the individuals and groups being eliminated—some communist, some noncommunist—began to resist.

By 1957–1958, resistance to Diem and his brother, Ngo Dinh Nhu, South Vietnam's security chief, had intensified and was becoming increasingly violent. At the time, both Diem and his American advisers and supporters blamed the violence on communist infiltration of northerners. But we now know that the southern insurgency was by no means contrived in the North. The Diem regime alienated itself from one after another of the elements within South Vietnam that might have given it political support. Instead, Diem's remoteness, paranoia with regard to his personal security, and high-handedness made few friends and many enemies.[6] It is now clear that Hanoi neither instigated nor orchestrated anti-Diem violence in South Vietnam during 1957–1958.[7] On the contrary, as discussed in Chapter 5, leaders in Hanoi went to great lengths to discourage armed resistance by southerners during the 1950s, fearing a premature rebellion that Diem, aided by U.S. advisers, would be able to crush.

The North Vietnamese regime, denied the unification it had been promised, saw the Americans as the colonial successors to the French in Vietnam and the Saigon regime as illegitimate puppets of that colonial power. Conflict appeared to be inevitable. Ho Chi Minh would not long be denied the political victory he believed he had earned on the battlefield and had been promised during the peace negotiations, the goal that his nation had sought for so long—the unification and independence of Vietnam. Initially, however, beginning in 1954, the Hanoi government focused on its own internal recovery and consolidation.

U.S. military planning for the use of ground forces to defend Indochina began in 1956, when the Military Assistance and Advisory Group assumed the responsibility for training the South Vietnamese Army. The United States had inherited from France a poorly trained, ill-equipped South Vietnamese army of 250,000 with low morale and limited national spirit. With roughly $85 million per year, the United States provided the army with uniforms, small arms, tanks, and helicopters. It underwrote the entire cost of the training program, including officers' salaries. In its second year, the United States undertook a massive reorganization campaign, scaling the South Vietnamese Army back to 150,000 troops and creating a command school and an officer training program. U.S. officials in Saigon prepared the South Vietnamese for two diverse and, in retrospect, impossible missions: internal security and defending South Vietnam from a crossborder attack from the North.

The thinking among American leaders reflected the U.S. combat experience in Korea as well as Eisenhower's "New Look" military doctrine, with its emphasis on air, naval, and nuclear supremacy. The general outlook of U.S. Army doctrine was that revolution could not be instigated or be successful without the support of an external sponsoring power. Experience in Korea taught that guerrillas were the early warning of crossborder conventional attacks—a much greater danger. The focus of the army's doctrine of guerrilla warfare, therefore, was on the defeat and destruction of a crossborder invasion through mobility, firepower, and conventional combat.

Specifically, U.S. strategic planners in Saigon called for South Vietnamese troops to occupy invasion-blocking positions while American forces, generally those already based in the Pacific Command, would secure major air and sea facilities in South Vietnam, then deploy to occupy these blocking positions north and west of Saigon. After the invasion had been contained, a counteroffensive would be undertaken, featuring an ambitious joint airborne, amphibious, and ground attack into North Vietnam. To support these plans, provisions were made for selecting potential targets for nuclear strikes, for occupying key cities, and for interdicting the enemy's critical lines of communication. These plans anticipated, and were based upon, a mobilization of U.S. reserve units.[8]

It now seems clear that United States trained the South Vietnamese for the wrong mission. Instead of a crossborder conventional attack, the communists used the political struggle in the countryside from 1956 to 1959 to win the "hearts and minds" of the peasants. The insurgency during the early years of the war was homegrown, almost all cadres being southerners. Perhaps, as critics claim, the United States should have concentrated its efforts on the insurgency, but this was an alien type of war, and few in Washington or Saigon were prepared for its special qualities. Ultimately, U.S. strategy forced the South Vietnamese forces to the road, making them dependent on a motorized offensive force that was hard to resupply and totally inappropriate for the people's war in the countryside. Furthermore, the South Vietnamese were ill-prepared to fight the political war. Few of the top South Vietnamese military men had strategic training of any kind and were therefore incapable of directing a complex political and military struggle in the hostile countryside. Thus, the South Vietnamese Army continued to take heavy casualties in a futile attempt to spread government control throughout South Vietnam. Furthermore, Ngo Dinh Diem tended to promote officers based on their loyalty rather than merit, adding significantly to U.S. problems.

The American objective was clear and remained consistent throughout the long struggle: an independent, noncommunist South Vietnam. The Eisenhower administration sought to create a meaningful counterrevolutionary alternative south of the 17th parallel and thereby stop the spread of communism to neighboring countries. That understanding of the U.S. mission in Vietnam—preventing the fall of the South Vietnamese domino—would remain unchanged for the next fifteen years.

John Kennedy: Counterinsurgency—Winning Hearts and Minds

In response to the changing situation in Vietnam, Kennedy administration officials debated the merits of a new counterinsurgency proposal forwarded by Gen. Edward Lansdale three days before the end of the Eisenhower administration. The report, dated January 17, 1961, urged that Vietnam be treated "as a combat area of the cold war, as an area requiring emergency treatment." The report also suggested that the United States send its "best people" to Indochina, people who were "experienced in dealing with this type of emergency." One of the specific proposals was to increase South Vietnam's armed forces from 150,000 to 170,000 men, primarily for action against the National Liberation Front. The NLF, established in 1960, was designed to coordinate the southern insurgency and mobilize those in the South opposed to the Saigon regime. The additional 20,000 troops, Lansdale reported, should "meet the immediate and serious guerrilla threat."[9] The plan also required a substantial increase in the Civil Guard, increasing its total strength from 32,000 men to 68,000. The proposed changes would add $42 million to the $225 million per year already being spent by the United States to shore up the South Vietnamese government.[10]

At a January 28, 1961, meeting, Kennedy asked his top advisers if the new counterinsurgency plan under debate would "really permit a shift from the defense to the offense" or whether the deteriorating situation in Saigon was not "basically one of politics and morale."[11] Most concluded that there indeed was a problem with Diem; however, the administration seemed eager to show movement in Vietnam, so Kennedy approved Lansdale's counterinsurgency plan on January 30, 1961, in what was seen "as quite a routine action."[12] The Joint Chiefs, however, were not enthusiastic about creating special units for counterinsurgency efforts. They were especially concerned about the availability of American conventional forces for a conflict in Europe, and many thought that wars of national liberation in the developing world were a sideshow to distract the United States from the communists' main targets in the West. The Joint Chiefs rejected counterinsurgency as a special need and trained all infantry units in these tactics as an added duty. Army Chief of Staff George Decker is reported to have told Kennedy that "any good soldier can handle guerrillas." To which the president replied that counterinsurgency fighting was "a special art."[13]

Kennedy hoped to stop the insurgency through local and limited war. The goal was to find a means of containing Ho Chi Minh's communists while minimizing the risk of war with Ho's Soviet and Chinese allies. Kennedy proposed to limit the amount of force used to what was absolutely necessary to achieve political aims. The goal was not to crush North Vietnam but rather to persuade the communists to break off their support for the southern insurgency. Gen. Maxwell Taylor, former U.S. Army chief of staff, supported Kennedy's limited war concept. Taylor had retired in 1959 partly in protest over Eisenhower's New Look strategy. The general did not think that heavy reliance on nuclear arms was a viable strategy in the Cold War. "It was an all or nothing proposition," he once reported.[14] Taylor favored a more flexible response and one that would allow the United States to defend newly emerging nations from the communists.

Late in 1961, after a fact-finding trip to Vietnam, Taylor and White House aide Walt W. Rostow recommended a substantial expansion of American aid to stem the tide. They reported that additional American advisers could force a "much better, aggressive, more confident performance from the Vietnamese military and civilian establishment."[15] Finally, Taylor and Rostow recommended that the president consider sending an 8,000-man force to support South Vietnam.

In early November 1961, Secretary of Defense Robert S. McNamara and Secretary of State Dean Rusk sent the president a memorandum urging him not to send in troops, as Taylor and Rostow had requested. Both believed that, although additional U.S. forces might be necessary someday, the South Vietnamese Army would have to bear the burden of the fighting, particularly at this stage. "If there is a strong South Vietnamese effort," McNamara and Rusk suggested, "U.S. combat forces may not be needed. If there is not such an effort, U.S. forces could not accomplish their mission in the midst of an apathetic or hostile population."[16] Indeed, at the core of American strategy was the understanding that South Vietnam eventually had to defend itself and stand on its own. The president shared this view and stressed to others that the effort in Vietnam could only be as good as the Saigon regime. He warned, "to introduce U.S. forces, in large numbers there today, while it might have an initial favorable military impact would almost certainly lead to adverse political and, in the long run, adverse military consequences."[17]

After considerable debate, Kennedy ultimately rejected the Taylor-Rostow recommendations, favoring instead a more limited response. The president feared that sending in troops in 1961 was not prudent. "The troops will march in; the bands will play; the crowds will cheer," Kennedy told White House Special Assistant Arthur M. Schlesinger Jr., "and in four days everyone will have forgotten. Then we will be told we have to send in more troops. It's like taking a drink. The effect wears off, and you have to take another."[18]

Having decided against the use of American troops in late 1961, Kennedy then turned his attention to the insurgency in Vietnam. The CIA suggested a plan that would ostensibly help villagers defend themselves while also improving their living conditions. The strategic hamlet program, as this effort was called, was designed to develop support among the rural population for the Saigon government. The program was seen as a comprehensive, sequential plan, beginning with clearing the insurgents from an area and protecting the rural population, progressing through the establishment of a government infrastructure, and ultimately to the provision of services that would tie peasants to Saigon. The program borrowed many of its concepts from Sir Robert Thompson, the British counterinsurgency expert, who had years of experience in Malaya.

Similar guerrilla-led insurgencies in Malaya and the Philippines were put down, in part, by the successful implementation of the strategic hamlet concept. In Malaya, large-scale resettlement was used to isolate sympathetic ethnic Chinese from the guerrillas, thus depriving them of their essential source of food and protection. At the core of the government's success in Malaya was its ability to extend its administrative control over the entire population of the country. Government officials understood that "winning the hearts and minds" of the peasants was the key to success. Guerrillas needed the local population for food, shelter, and recruitment and thus they hoped to "turn passive acceptance into active support."[19] Officials in Saigon supported the strategic hamlet concept in Vietnam, and Diem's brother, Ngo Dinh Nhu, started construction in early 1961.

The Joint Chiefs condemned the concept, however, warning that "the insurgency in South Vietnam has developed far beyond the capacity of police controls."[20] This difference of opinion was common in the early years of the war as the Joint Chiefs in general objected to the Central Intelligence Agency arming and training the local defense forces. According to counterinsurgency specialist Douglas Blaufarb, the Joint Chiefs could not comprehend Kennedy's desire to "win over the population," instead supporting "the idea that priority must go to destroying the enemy's armed force, and doing it by familiar means of concentrating manpower and firepower at the right time and place."[21] These doctrinal differences meant that the United States was pursuing two—sometimes mutually exclusive—programs at once: strategic hamlets and a military effort to destroy the NLF. Furthermore, the divergent strategies represented sharp ideological differences that would continue to plague U.S. civilian and military leaders.

The Joint Chiefs were correct, however, in their assessment of the strength of the insurgency and the inability of the Saigon regime to deal with it effectively. At the height of the insurgency in Malaya, guerrillas managed to inflict a casualty rate of no more than seven per day. According to official U.S. sources, the NLF-led insurgency in Vietnam inflicted more than a hundred government and civilian casualties per day.[22] Furthermore, limited access to food supplies ultimately forced the Malayan guerrillas from the jungles to meet the full force of government troops. In Vietnam, in contrast, the NLF had easy access to the Mekong Delta's abundant food supply. The challenge in Vietnam also came from guerrillas who, unlike the ethnic Chinese in Malaya, were indistinguishable from peasants. Finally, throughout the program in Vietnam, corruption siphoned off needed resources and reimbursements to peasants who had been removed from their farmlands. Even Sir Robert Thompson was displeased with the effort of the South Vietnamese. "Basically, the Vietnamese seemed unable to understand that the establishment of strategic hamlets would accomplish nothing unless other necessary measures were taken to achieve their three objectives of protection, of uniting and involving the people, and of development." In the end, Thompson lamented, "The Vietnamese tended to confuse the means with the end. . . . In under two years in Vietnam 8,000 strategic hamlets were created, but no attention was paid to their purpose; their creation became the purpose in itself."[23]

Perhaps most damaging to the success of the strategic hamlet program, however, was the inability of the Saigon regime to convince rural Vietnamese that it was little more than a distant nuisance. The Saigon government did little to reform the land tenure system that left peasants paying high taxes and exorbitant rents on lands they had previously farmed without charge. Villagers viewed the hamlets as havens for corrupt government officials, and as a result they often conspired with NLF cadres. Since few leaders in the presidential palace in Saigon ventured much into the countryside, isolated security forces became the symbol of the government. The NLF often targeted Diem's appointees for assassination, adding to the belief that the Saigon regime could not secure the countryside. Nhu's personal interest in the program also led to its demise. According to Milton Osborne, an expert on the strategic hamlet program, Nhu's own civil servants feared his arbitrary use of power to such an extent that they failed to report the program's shortcomings accurately.[24]

The NLF's plan to defeat the strategic hamlets was simple: win the hearts and minds of the peasants in the 12,000 villages and hamlets throughout the South and foment urban unrest to topple Diem before the Americans could intervene directly. To accomplish this task, the NLF created mass associations at the village level organized around gender, age, occupation, and religion. These mass associations were the key to the political struggle during the early years of the war, as they helped organize the peasants at the "rice roots." The NLF's people's war was not a small-scale war but rather a political struggle with guns. Cadres highlighted the government's crimes and promised security in the countryside.

People's war, therefore, was the combination of various interests and actions, all designed to make the Saigon regime appear reactive and arbitrary. The Party exploited the government's oppressive policies by helping to organize the rural population in legitimate forms of protest. Simultaneously, NLF cadres sought to alleviate hardships by providing food, restoring land use rights, and tightening security in the countryside. People's war was an art form, requiring careful planning and timing. According to *Needs of the Revolution*, the most important communist document on the subject, every action and reaction was crucial:

> Timing is most important . . . choose the right moment to launch it . . . such as when the enemy is committing a mistake . . . or when the people's

rights have been endangered . . . by corruption, high taxation, forced money donations, land robbing, building strategic hamlets, forced membership in reactionary organizations, terror or killing, military draft. . . . Struggle movements can also be launched in favor of freedom of trade, freedom to move to a new part of the country. . . .[25]

As one former NLF official explained, "every military clash, every demonstration, every propaganda appeal was seen as part of an integrated whole; each had consequences far beyond its immediately apparent results."[26]

By the end of 1962, Kennedy understood that the strategic hamlet program was not enough to achieve American objectives in Vietnam. Accordingly, he dispatched White House aides Roger Hilsman and Michael Forrestal on a fact-finding mission. The Hilsman-Forrestal Report expressed serious doubts about the future of the strategic hamlet program, the effectiveness of the South Vietnamese Army, and the capabilities of the Diem regime. It concluded that the United States had experienced some success in the countryside but that the war "would probably last longer than we would like" and "cost more in terms of both lives and money than we had anticipated."[27] Indeed, as the Saigon regime suffered defeat after defeat in the hamlets, Kennedy approved requests for more firepower. American military aid to Vietnam more than doubled between 1961 and 1962, and it included more than 300 military aircraft. The number of American advisers in Vietnam totaled 9,000 by the end of 1962, an increase of nearly 6,000 from the previous year. In addition, Kennedy reorganized the American command system in Vietnam, replacing the old U.S. command post with the Military Assistance Command-Vietnam (MACV—"mack-VEE"). The president also endorsed initial plans to transfer all CIA paramilitary operations to MACV.[28]

MACV used the increased firepower and control to launch sweeps in the countryside with South Vietnamese Army units. Buoyed by early successes, Kennedy made plans to withdraw some American advisers by the end of 1963. Gen. Paul Harkins, MACV commander, even told the president that the war would probably be over by Christmas 1963.[29] The CIA's National Intelligence Estimates were much less optimistic, however, warning that the situation was far more precarious and unstable than reports from Saigon indicated. In one report, the CIA analyst warned, "the Viet Cong by and large retain de facto control of much of the countryside and have steadily increased the overall intensity of the effort."[30] By mid-1963, according to one official U.S. source, "the rate of Communist-initiated incidents and attacks increased by one third over the first half of 1963, and exceeded the average level of such activity sustained during 1962."[31] These reports proved prescient as the situation went from bad to worse in Saigon.

By November 1963, the U.S. troop level in South Vietnam was 16,500, but they seemed to do little to stem the tide of disintegration of the government in Saigon. The South Vietnamese Army, led by its generals and often taking heavy casualties, remained largely ineffective, and the political leadership of Ngo Dinh Diem was becoming more arbitrary, corrupt, remote from the populations, and unable to win the loyalty and support of the South Vietnamese people.

As discussed in Chapter 4, on November 1 Diem and Nhu were assassinated during the successful coup undertaken by some senior South Vietnamese military officers, followed three weeks later by Kennedy's assassination.

Diem's death marked a new phase in the Vietnam conflict. America's complicity in Diem's death haunted U.S. leaders during the years ahead, as they sought unsuccessfully to find a credible anticommunist leader of his stature in Saigon. In addition, whatever legitimacy the South Vietnamese government may have had before Diem's assassination quickly became undermined, both in South Vietnam and internationally. After November 1, 1963, therefore, the communists' claim that Saigon was ruled by "puppets" of the Americans seemed increasingly accurate to the South Vietnamese, especially to the rural population of South Vietnam, among whom the communists were extraordinarily active.

After Diem's assassination, the establishment of a stable, independent noncommunist South Vietnam, the principal goal of American policy, was a chimera—an illusion that became increasingly dangerous as the United States committed itself ever more deeply to the effort. The Saigon governments that followed Diem were weak, divided, ineffective, and seen by the population of South Vietnam as increasingly illegitimate. Writer Gertrude Stein's sarcastic description of Oakland, California, where she was educated after living abroad, also applies to the South Vietnamese governments after Diem: "There's no *there* there." After Diem, the survival of the South Vietnamese government would depend almost exclusively upon American arms and other direct military, political, and economic support.

Gen. William C. Westmoreland, the U.S. commander in Vietnam, noted this in *Report on the War* (1968):

> If any generalization can be made about the war in South Vietnam it is that the U.S. effort, both military and political, prospered to the extent that the government of Vietnam was strong, coherent, and active. The corollary, of

course, is that none of our efforts had any chance of success in the periods during which the government was weak, divided, and thus ineffective.[32]

This being the case, one wonders why the inevitable results of withholding or withdrawing U.S. military support to South Vietnam were not seen as clearly in 1964 as in 1974. But alas, they were not. So rather than begin to withdraw during 1964–1965, the U.S. political leadership, responding to General Westmoreland's requests for increasing numbers of U.S. combat troops, began to get more deeply involved.

Meanwhile, Diem's assassination also caused considerable concern in Hanoi. The NLF hoped eventually to overthrow Diem and liberate Vietnam south of the 17th parallel, yet certain minimum conditions had to be met before it could accomplish these goals. Throughout the struggle in the South, the Party carefully monitored events, not wanting to act prematurely and thereby destroy all that had been gained. At the time of Diem's death, the Party still considered him a useful foe.

As we learned in Hanoi, the North Vietnamese respected Diem's credentials as a nationalist and understood that he was unlikely to ask for or accept large numbers of American troops in the South. Therefore, the Party leadership in Hanoi did not want to wrest control of the South from Diem prematurely. He was a strong enough nationalist to resist the Americans right up to the point where the Party would remove him by force and liberate Vietnam. And the NLF, in the South, also wanted ultimately to remove Diem from power. But until they did, his policies filled cadre ranks and kept the Americans at bay. When Diem's own generals took his life, the NLF was not yet prepared to counter a more aggressive American ally.

Lyndon Johnson: "Everything necessary . . . only what is absolutely necessary . . ."

Shortly after assuming the presidency, Lyndon Johnson undertook a determined policy reassessment of the future American role in the war. On March 8, 1964, he dispatched Secretary McNamara and General Taylor, now chairman of the Joint Chiefs of Staff, to Vietnam on a fact-finding mission. They presented their report to the president on March 16, and it was approved the following day. The report, by U.S. civilian and uniformed military leaders, predictably focused on military issues. The program contained in this document, labeled National Security Action Memorandum (NSAM) 288, reasserted the American objective in Vietnam as an "independent non-Communist South

Vietnam." NSAM 288 publicly affirmed Washington's support for the government of Diem's successor, Gen. Nguyen Khanh, and warned that the Johnson administration was opposed to "any further coups."[33] It also called for a national mobilization plan in Vietnam, lifting overall troop levels and placing Saigon on a war footing. Johnson replaced the overly optimistic and ineffective U.S. field commander, Gen. Paul Harkins, with Westmoreland, a veteran of World War II and Korea. In response to the McNamara-Taylor suggestions, the president also assured Ambassador Henry Cabot Lodge in Saigon that he would have "whatever you need to help the Vietnamese do the job."[34] At a National Security Council meeting on March 17, the president's closest advisers expressed support and confidence that the increased military and economic aid would change the course of the war in Vietnam.[35]

The Joint Chiefs, with the notable exception of Taylor, expressed doubt throughout spring 1964 that actions called for in NSAM 288 would be enough to stop the insurgency. A JCS report recommended that the United States begin air attacks against North Vietnam and shift from training the South Vietnamese army to launching direct attacks by U.S. forces against the communists.[36] Additionally, they proposed the sustained bombing of the Ho Chi Minh Trail. They concluded that none of these actions would prompt the Chinese Communists to "introduce organized ground units in significant numbers into the DRV [the Democratic Republic of Vietnam—North Vietnam]" or inspire to the Soviets to think about nuclear war.[37] President Johnson and Secretary McNamara rejected the proposal because, at the time, Khanh and others in Saigon did not think the South Vietnamese government could withstand the counterattack that would follow the actions the JCS had recommended.

Saigon's poor performance, however, only led to more communist advances. In late 1963, North Vietnam's Communist Party approved a resolution at its Ninth Party Plenum to increase its military support for the southern insurgency. As a result, the People's Liberation Army Forces (PLAF—the NLF's army) increased its activity in preparation for a general offensive and uprising to lead to a complete victory. Party strategists had concluded that NLF forces should use their stronghold in the Central Highlands to launch additional attacks against the South Vietnamese in the Lowlands to "tighten the noose around the neck of the Saigon regime."[38] CIA intelligence detected the change in communist strength and concluded that "the situation in South Vietnam is very serious and prospects remain uncertain." Lyman D. Kirkpatrick, a high-ranking CIA official, and Peer de Silva, the new CIA bureau chief in Saigon, worried that the tide had turned quickly against an unstable Saigon regime. "Even with U.S. assistance," they concluded, "unless there is a marked improvement in the effectiveness of the South Vietnamese government and armed forces, South Vietnam has, at best, an even chance of withstanding the insurgency."[39]

Five months later, Khanh was still in power, but his government remained in a precarious position. Almost uninterrupted political upheaval in Saigon was reflected in military demoralization in the countryside. The civil administration continued in a state of disarray and ineffectiveness. Military forces were becoming more and more defensive and demoralized. Desertions increased, and combat operations ground to a halt.

The controversial Tonkin Gulf incident, August 2–4, 1964, precipitated the first U.S. reprisal against the DRV and provided the president with a broad congressional resolution of support. The swift military reprisal, and near-unanimous support in Congress, was a dramatic demonstration of the U.S. commitment to the South Vietnamese government, a commitment that was undertaken with little domestic criticism or questioning. These events established the precedent for direct U.S. military action against the North, and the raids themselves meant that Washington had crossed an important threshold in the war: They were a clear signal to Hanoi, marking American firmness and resolve and identifying what to expect if the current course of action continued. In fact, Johnson's popularity rating in the polls increased dramatically in the wake of the reprisal attacks, from 42 percent to 72 percent.[40]

Encouraged by the U.S. reprisal and dismayed by the continued political turmoil in the South, several officials and agencies within the administration argued that additional military action against the North was necessary. President Johnson held the line, however, noting that the situation in Saigon was deteriorating and Khanh was still opposed to such actions. On August 6, Khanh declared martial law and imposed severe restrictions on civil liberties. He enacted such measures to save his government from the growing urban unrest, but predictably they sparked even more protest. Under these circumstances, President Johnson concluded that it would be unwise to escalate the war, saying: "I am not going to enter the patient in a 10-round bout, when he is in no shape to hold out for one round."[41] Maxwell Taylor, the new U.S. ambassador in Saigon, agreed that it would be too risky "to overstrain the currently weakened Government of Vietnam [RVN] by drastic action in the immediate future."[42]

On August 13, McGeorge Bundy, writing on behalf of himself, the secretary of defense, and the secretary of state, sent the president a memorandum that was to drive discussion of Vietnam for the next several months. Although acknowledging that Khanh's staying power was questionable, it also contended that trying to negotiate a solution under these circumstances would be equivalent to surrender in the South.[43] Bundy also laid out possible plans of action:

> The larger question of action is whether there is any course of action that can improve the chances in this weakening situation. A number of contingency plans for limited escalation are in preparation. They involve three kinds of activities—naval harassment, air interdiction in the Laos panhandle, and possible U.S. fleet movements resuming a presence on the high seas in the Gulf of Tonkin. The object of any of these would be more to heighten morale and to show our strength of purpose than to accomplish anything very specific in a military sense—unless and until we move toward a naval quarantine.[44]

The Joint Chiefs agreed that the Johnson administration should prepare for U.S. air strikes against the North and the Ho Chi Minh Trail, with the objective of convincing Hanoi that it could not win the fight and should resist supplying the NLF. The Joint Chiefs thus formulated what became known as the 94 Targets List, an effort to identify which sites in North Vietnam must be knocked out in order to crush their industrial capacity. Several members of the JCS believed that U.S. airpower could knock out these essential targets in a matter of weeks, forcing Hanoi to quit the war. Johnson rejected this thinking, however, believing that such a massive air strike was impractical and dangerous. He reasoned that the Soviets and Chinese would not sit back idly while the United States launched such a massive campaign near Vietnam's northern border. He also doubted that Hanoi's war economy was as concentrated and industrialized as the Joint Chiefs seemed to suggest with their list.

In any event, Johnson called a meeting at the White House on September 9 to discuss the various proposals. In preparation for the meeting, William Bundy and Michael Forrestal drafted a working paper, "Courses of Action for South Vietnam," in which they summarized the emerging consensus of the president's top national security advisers. The paper called for the following military actions: (1) U.S. naval patrols in the Gulf of Tonkin; (2) covert operations by the South against the North; (3) limited South Vietnamese ground and air operations in the corridor areas of Laos; and (4) a tit-for-tat response against the North in the event of any attack on U.S. units or any special communist attack against the South—but no continuing attacks on the North.[45]

The president asked his advisers one by one to respond to the report. Ambassador Taylor commented that the situation in Saigon was as grave as ever; he therefore supported most of the proposals, agreeing there should be no major military operations against the North. Secretary McNamara agreed with Ambassador Taylor, adding that more could be done later if necessary. Secretary Rusk told the president that the decision to launch direct attacks against the North Vietnamese could be taken at any time but that now was not appropriate. The JCS split on the issue of direct action. Generals Wheeler (chairman) and Johnson (Army) were joined by Adm. David McDonald (Navy) in support of delaying any direct attacks, whereas Generals McConnell (Air Force) and Greene (Marines) believed that "time is against us and military action against the DRV should be taken now."[46]

As the president considered his options, events in Vietnam were forcing the administration's hand. On November 1, the NLF attacked the U.S. air base at Bien Hoa, killing four Americans and destroying several aircraft. Convinced now more than ever that the South was on the ropes and that the United States must respond to open aggression against Americans, the president ordered his advisers to formulate a plan for bombing the North. Johnson believed that "bombing was less risky than deploying ground forces" at this point in the war. Simultaneously, he asked Ambassador Taylor to do all he could to stabilize the Saigon government. The president correctly understood that American bombing raids against communist supply lines would prompt an immediate response from Hanoi, and he wanted to make sure that South Vietnam could withstand such an attack. "We don't want to send a widow woman to slap Jack Dempsey," the president told reporters.[47] On November 2, following the Bien Hoa bombing but before the election, the president appointed a working group to conduct a thorough review of Vietnam policy and to present him with viable options in Southeast Asia.

Finally, on December 1, the president was told that the working group had a two-phase proposal to suggest. Phase 1 would merely comprise a continuation of current actions, tit-for-tat reprisals against North Vietnam for attacks on U.S. forces in the South, and increased efforts to reform and strengthen the South Vietnamese government. When this had been accomplished or was well under way, Phase 2, a sustained and gradually increasing air campaign, would be undertaken against North Vietnam in an attempt to dissuade it from further support of the war in the South. These were not fundamentally new proposals, and no prospect was held out for speedy results. After almost a full month of deliberation, the president's advisers had failed to produce acceptable alternatives either in South Vietnam or in North Vietnam. The alternative of cutting American losses and abandoning a weak South Vietnamese government, which was demonstrably incapable of organizing its own defense, was briefly considered and quickly rejected.

Again the president emphasized the need to strengthen the Saigon government before beginning any military action against the North. He approved Phase 1 and gave assent, at least in principle, to Phase 2. The president did not at this time, however, make a commitment to expand the war, either in the air or on the ground. Looking back on November and December 1964, one sees that it constitutes a significant missed opportunity to *fundamentally* reassess the American commitment to the fatally flawed government in South Vietnam.

Toward what end was the expansion of the war to be directed? On April 7, 1965, President Johnson spoke at Johns Hopkins University in Baltimore and gave the answer that was to cause grave concern to some American decisionmakers in the future. Lyndon Johnson wanted a limited war with limited resources in a limited geographic area for limited diplomatic objectives. The objective, as stated, was itself unobjectionable: an independent, noncommunist South Vietnam. It was the president's caveat that was to frustrate some. "We will do everything necessary," the president said, "to achieve that objective, and we will do only what is absolutely necessary."[48] It was the "only" that would cause trouble, because it would come to seem to some U.S. leaders to indicate a less than all-out approach to winning the war militarily. But military victory over North Vietnam was not the American objective. As it turned out, the level of U.S. effort was, in fact, largely to be determined by North Vietnam. Its willingness to match American deployments to South Vietnam resulted in a gradual military escalation by both sides.

The Air War: The Futile Effort to Break Hanoi's Will

FEBRUARY 1965: PLEIKU TRIGGERS THE AIR WAR

As 1965 began, the Johnson administration remained beset by frustration and considerable anguish over the threat posed by the imminent collapse of the South Vietnamese government. As we have seen, however, debate in Washington focused on developing the means for generating more military pressure on North Vietnam. Discussion turned inevitably, therefore, to the possibility of moving to Phase 2 reprisal strikes against the North. The intelligence community continued to be skeptical, however, that such pressure would reduce Hanoi's support for its southern allies to any significant degree.

Those who favored turning up the military pressure against North Vietnam believed it would accomplish three major objectives: (1) it would boost the sagging morale in the South; (2) it would signal to North Vietnam the firmness of the U.S. commitment to its South Vietnamese ally; and (3) the increased human and material costs imposed upon North Vietnam would ultimately affect North Vietnam's will, as well as its ability to continue to support the NLF. This estimation of the potential impact of a U.S. air war against the North turned out to be wrong.

The long months of planning, hesitation, and agonizing debate reached a climax at 2:00 A.M. on February 7, 1965, when the NLF carried out raids against U.S. advisers' barracks and an American helicopter base near Pleiku. This was the most destructive attack to date against U.S. military installations in South Vietnam, and, as noted in Chapter 5, National Security Adviser McGeorge Bundy was in South Vietnam at this time. Telephoning from General Westmoreland's command post in Saigon, he recommended to the president that, in addition to immediate retaliatory strikes against the North, the United States should initiate Phase 2 of the previously planned military measures against North Vietnam.

This time the president showed the same decisiveness he had displayed six months earlier during the Gulf of Tonkin incident. The decision to retaliate against North Vietnam was reached in a seventy-five–minute meeting in the Cabinet Room of the White House on the evening of February 6 (local time), with Senate Majority Leader Mike Mansfield and House Speaker John McCormick present. Summarizing the views of those present, George Ball, the senior State Department representative present (Dean Rusk was traveling), told the president that everyone believed action must be taken. In fact, retaliatory air strikes were conducted by U.S. naval aircraft against North Vietnamese barracks and staging areas at Dong Hoi, just north of the demilitarized zone (DMZ—the 17th parallel), within fourteen hours of the presidential directive.[49]

This dramatic action, long on the U.S. planners' drawing boards, precipitated an escalating spiral of events that transformed the nature of the Vietnam War and the U.S. role in it. The sustained U.S. bombing of North Vietnam—which would become known by its code name, "ROLLING THUNDER"—would be the first U.S. move in the events of 1965 that, by December, would transform the war into a *U.S.* war against North Vietnam and its southern allies.

1965–1967: A Limited, Graduated Air War

Although the president's advisers had reached consensus by early 1965 that increased military pressure against North Vietnam was necessary, this consensus reflected neither a precisely defined strategy nor any commonly held expectation as to the results to be gained by such military pressure. Generally speaking, the military leaders advocated a dramatic and forceful application of military power against North Vietnam as the only feasible means for achieving satisfactory results. Most of the civilian officials favored a more gradual, restrained approach, progressively mounting in scope and intensity in which the prospect of greater pressure to come would be at least as important as the damage actually inflicted. The decision to use military power against the North, in the end, seems to have resulted as much from a lack of alternative proposals as from any compelling logic advanced in its favor.

The first and most obvious task of ROLLING THUNDER was that of interdicting the flow of men and supplies from the North into the South. This was to be done by striking lines of supply and communications. The objective would be to reduce the capability of North Vietnam to supply forces operating in the South—which U.S. leaders, both military and civilian, regarded as the most visible manifestation of Hanoi's aggression.

Predictions as to the effect of the interdiction campaign varied widely. Adm. U.S. Grant Sharp, commander in chief of U.S. forces in the Pacific (CINCPAC), bore ultimate military responsibility for air action over North Vietnam. Admiral Sharp, a zealous proponent of airpower, held the view that a properly executed bombing program "will bring the enemy to the conference table or cause the insurgency to wither from lack of support." A more cautious, but still optimistic, view was taken in a Special National Intelligence Estimate (SNIE) dated July 23, 1965. The SNIE estimated that a bombing program that included destruction of the petroleum facilities and military targets in the Hanoi-Haiphong area, combined with sustained interdiction of the lines of communication from China, could significantly reduce communist capabilities in the South. It reasoned that:

> If additional PAVN [People's Army of Vietnam—the North Vietnamese Army] forces were employed in South Vietnam on a scale sufficient to counter increased U.S. troop strength [which the SNIE said was "almost certain" to happen] this would substantially increase the amount of supplies needed in the South. The Viet Cong also depend on supplies from the North to maintain their present level of large-scale operations. The accumulated strains of a prolonged curtailment of supplies received from North Vietnam would obviously have an impact on the Communist effort in the South. They would certainly inhibit and might even prevent an increase in large-scale Viet Cong military activity, though they would probably not force any significant reduction in Viet Cong terrorist tactics of harassment and sabotage.[50]

Extended bombing programs, which might permit greater latitude in the field, were not approved, however. Bombing proposals from the Joint Chiefs were approved only in weekly target packages. Each target package, moreover, had to pass through a chain of approvals in the Department of Defense, the Department of State, and the White House that often included the respective department secretaries as well as the president himself.

From the outset of the air war, there was concern in the president's inner circle of advisers about a possible Chinese or Soviet response. The president himself often described this fear publicly as a "wider war." The ROLLING THUNDER campaign always had goals—such as avoiding a wider war, especially a nuclear war—that were explicitly political in nature. Thus, close control of the air war by the political leadership in the administration was entirely appropriate and necessary.[51]

Despite being under tight political control, however, the ROLLING THUNDER program was allowed to grow in intensity, in geographic coverage, and in the assortment of approved targets. By mid-1965, the number of target packages had increased from one or two per week to ten or twelve per week, and the number of sorties rose to about 900 per week, four or five times what they had been at the outset.

The Joint Chiefs were, from the very beginning, opposed to this gradual and limited bombing campaign. They argued repeatedly for a more forceful and continuous air campaign designed to force North Vietnam to its knees— to render it absolutely incapable of supporting the insurgency in the South. To accomplish this, the Navy and Air Force representatives on the Joint Chiefs sought from the president and secretary of defense complete freedom to pick targets in North Vietnam, the elimination of restrictive zones around Hanoi and Haiphong and the Chinese border, and expanded authority to strike in Laos and Cambodia. These requests for release from civilian control over targets were refused time and again.

The Air Force and Navy Chiefs were upset with an air campaign centered upon tactical interdiction rather than punishing the enemy. The latter approach would have been consistent with traditional uses of strategic airpower. Instead of attacking merely the infiltration system, the air chiefs preferred to inflict damage on the North Vietnamese economy as a whole. They objected, therefore, to the lack of approved targets in North Vietnam of the sort used by the United States in its strategic bombing campaigns over Europe and Japan during World War II—power plants, oil depots, factories, and transportation and harbor systems. Air planners believed, in effect, that U.S. airpower was not being used in the way that it best suited U.S. capability and strategy.

The Joint Chiefs continued to press throughout the autumn and winter of 1965–1966 for the right to expand the air war into a program of unlimited bombing aimed at all North Vietnamese industrial and economic resources *in addition to* all interdiction targets. The Joint Chiefs did so despite a steady stream of memoranda from the intelligence community expressing skepticism regarding the utility of any bombing campaign short of an attempt to destroy North Vietnam's population. Anything less, according to these memoranda, would not persuade Hanoi to negotiate a settlement on U.S. terms and not even effectively limit Hanoi's ability to infiltrate men and supplies into the South.

Writing to the secretary of defense on January 18, 1966, the Joint Chiefs repeated their November 1965 statement that numerous "self-imposed restraints" had limited the effectiveness of the bombing campaign. And again they proposed a substantial intensification of the bombing. They urged that future air operations be conducted in such a manner and be of sufficient magnitude, to "deny the DRV large-scale external assistance; destroy those resources already in NVN [North Vietnam] that contribute most to the support of aggression; destroy or deny use of military facilities; and harass, disrupt, and impede the movement of men and materials into SVN [South Vietnam]." It seems remarkable that these requests were made repeatedly, even though the U.S. intelligence community was stating at the time that most of the tasks were beyond the capability of airpower to accomplish.

On March 1, 1966, the JCS sent forward a memorandum stressing the special importance of an attack on North Vietnamese petroleum, oil, and lubricant (POL) storage areas. The Joint Chiefs had earlier singled out POL, writing the secretary in November 1965 that an attack on POL "would be more damaging to the DRV capability to move war-supporting resources within country and along infiltration routes to SVN than an attack against any other target system." Although causing relatively little damage to the civilian economy, it would, they stated, force a sharp reduction in truck and other traffic moving men and supplies southward. Secretary McNamara rejected this recommendation, not only because of a planned bombing pause (the Christmas bombing pause of December and January 1965–1966) but also because the CIA questioned the conclusions reached by the Joint Chiefs. The Board of National Estimates observed that, in regard to the POL system, "it is unlikely that this loss would cripple communist military operations in the South."

These requests by the JCS to expand the scope, intensity, and objectives of the bombing campaign, during April and May 1966, instigated a major policy debate within the administration. Increasing military pressure for POL strikes led finally to their approval, under certain circumstances, by the secretary of defense and the president. The POL strikes began on June 29,

1966, and continued into that autumn. They were initially hailed as highly successful. Strikes against POL storage sites were soon accepted as a routine part of the bombing program.[52]

These strikes made spectacular headlines everywhere. Hanoi charged that U.S. planes had indiscriminately bombed and strafed residential areas of Hanoi and Haiphong. The United Kingdom, France, and other European countries expressed official disapproval. However, by September, both the CIA and the Defense Intelligence Agency (DIA) were in general agreement that the POL strikes had failed, not only in their specific objective of inhibiting North Vietnamese support for the insurgency in the South but also in their unstated mission of affecting the will of the North Vietnamese leadership to support and supply the war in the South. Even as enthusiastic a proponent of airpower as Admiral Sharp reported that the campaign had reached the point of diminishing returns. Apart from some documented inconveniences, interruptions, and temporary shortages, there was no evidence that North Vietnam had at any time run short of POL. The failure of the POL strikes was reflected unmistakably in the undiminished flow of men and supplies from North to South, down the Ho Chi Minh Trail.[53]

Why did the POL strikes fail? First, according to an assessment made at the time, "NVN's dependence on the unloading facilities at Haiphong and large storage sites in the rest of the country had been greatly overestimated." Bulk imports continued, and tankers simply stood offshore and unloaded onto barges. More oil was also brought in already drummed. Thus, it was convenient for dispersed handling and storage. Second, "the difficulties of switching to a much less vulnerable but perfectly workable storage and distribution system, not an unbearable strain when the volume to be handled was not really very great, had also been overestimated." The key point was that "NVN's adaptability and resourcefulness had been greatly underestimated."[54]

After visiting South Vietnam in October 1966, Secretary McNamara sent the president a pessimistic report with respect to the air war. According to the secretary, the bombing had neither significantly reduced infiltration nor diminished Hanoi's will to continue the fight. He noted that the U.S. intelligence community had reached the identical conclusions. He now recommended that the president level off the bombing and seek other means of achieving U.S. objectives. Specifically, he recommended an electronic "barrier" across the DMZ and part of Laos (what became known as the McNamara Line). He further suggested that in order to improve the climate for negotiations the United States should make a dramatic gesture to indicate its good faith. As an example, he suggested a possible cessation or limitation of the bombing of North Vietnam. This was, in fact, a condition that North Vietnam had consistently insisted upon as a precondition to any negotiations.[55]

In November, the president adopted the McNamara recommendation for the stabilization of the air campaign, though he did not act on the secretary's suggestion of a dramatic gesture to stimulate a move to the negotiating table. For most of 1966, the president had resisted pressure from his military leaders for a major escalation of the war in the North. He had instead followed the restrained approach of his secretary of defense. Even so, a few inadvertent raids within the Hanoi area had mushroomed into media disasters and made it more difficult for U.S. allies to support the bombing campaign. Thus, the president was thrust into an unenviable position: He was able to please neither his hawkish critics within the military, nor his dovish critics in the United States and some foreign capitals. The carefully modulated middle course was becoming difficult to maintain.

In early 1967, a series of dispatches from Hanoi by Harrison Salisbury of *The New York Times* described civilian casualties caused by U.S. bombing. His reports touched off a storm of controversy as to the morality and effectiveness of the air campaign against North Vietnam.[56] In response, moderate student leaders, in a letter to the president, noted a disparity between American statements about Vietnam and American actions there, indicated confusion about basic U.S. purposes, and warned of a drift "from confusion toward disaffection." The public and the press were becoming increasingly wary of statistics and statements on the war coming out of Washington. In January 1967 a Louis Harris opinion poll showed that the public was just as likely to blame the United States for truce violations as the enemy. A credibility gap began to build, and the realization grew among the American public that the war was likely to be long and costly.[57]

Thus, as 1966 ended and 1967 began, the lines were again drawn for a debate within the administration over the effectiveness of the air campaign. Secretary McNamara's fears with respect to the air war were being realized: The results were totally unsatisfactory; the human costs were mounting for both North Vietnamese and U.S. pilots; there was the continued risk of a Chinese and/or Soviet response that might lead to a widening of the war; and finally, U.S. and world opinion was beginning to turn against the United States.

The U.S. military leadership, in contrast, by and large remained astonishingly indifferent to any of these considerations. In fact, they were becoming more insistent in their rationalization for why the bombing had failed: It was the fault of the civilian-imposed restraints on targets. Only this, they held, had prevented the successful interdiction of North Vietnamese infiltration to the South. And only civilian restraint—which they regarded as unnecessary—had prevented U.S. airpower from bringing the Hanoi regime to its knees. They insisted on these positions despite the fact that the U.S. intelligence community was virtually unanimous in predicting that this was an unattainable objective. Thus did the U.S. military leadership oppose both the specific proposals of Secretary McNamara regarding the air war and his rationale for them. Many still believed that if only (what they called) "political authority" would fully unleash U.S. airpower, a U.S. victory in Vietnam was still possible.

The argument within the administration concerning the conduct of the air war over North Vietnam continued unabated, and with few new arguments on either side, throughout 1967. There were some gradual enhancements of the military's operating authority, but the limited overall U.S. objectives were reiterated by civilian leadership in the Department of Defense. It appears that at no time during this period did U.S. military leaders accept the military, political, prudential, or moral rationales for limitations on bombing targets developed by their civilian superiors.[58] Instead, they simply continued to reiterate, over and over again, and in the complete absence of supporting data, that they could "win the war"—if only they were allowed to do so.

ANATOMY OF A FAILURE: ASSESSMENTS OF THE AIR WAR

The air war might theoretically have reduced Hanoi's support for its southern allies by four means: (1) the destruction of war-related industry and war-supporting facilities, such as weapons production and POL storage facilities; (2) general debilitation of the North Vietnamese economy, with the implied reduction of the willingness of its people to suffer further in support of that war effort; (3) attacking the lines of communications so that supplies would be slowed, stopped, or destroyed; and (4) destruction of the North Vietnamese military so that it could no longer support the war in the South. During the course of the war, all four approaches were tried, at one time or another, but none proved successful in reducing support for the war in the South.

During the war a number of comprehensive studies were made of the effectiveness of the bombing campaign in stopping North Vietnamese infiltration of men and supplies to the South. Two of the most important were carried out, at the direction of the secretary of defense, in 1966 and 1967 by a group of leading scientists under the auspices of the JASON Division of the Institute for Defense Analyses. Both studies reached strongly negative conclusions regarding the effectiveness of bombing. The 1967 study concluded that "as of October 1967, the U.S. bombing of North Vietnam has had no measurable effect on Hanoi's ability to mount and support military operations in the South."

The JASON studies concluded, in fact, that the bombing had not even achieved the limited goal of reducing the flow of supplies to the communists in South Vietnam. In an unqualified dismissal of claims of the airpower enthusiasts, it said:

> Since the beginning of the ROLLING THUNDER, air strikes on NVN, the flow of men and materiel from NVN to SVN has greatly increased, and present evidence provides no basis for concluding that the damage inflicted on North Vietnam by the bombing program has had any significant effect on this flow. In short, the flow of men and materiel from North Vietnam to the South appears to reflect Hanoi's intentions rather than capabilities even in the face of the bombing.[59]

The debate as to the effectiveness of bombing in interdicting the flow of supplies from the North was reflected in a document called the 1969 National Security Study Memorandum 1 (NSSM 1). MACV and the JCS held that the bombing had *succeeded*, whereas the U.S. State Department, CIA, and the Office of the Secretary of Defense all agreed that it had *failed*.

The debate over the attempt by MACV to block two key roads near the passes from North Vietnam into Laos during late 1968 illustrates the tension between the two views. MACV indicated that these roads had been blocked effectively 80 percent of the time and therefore permitted less traffic to get through. Defense, CIA, and State agreed that enemy traffic on the roads had been disrupted. However, they pointed out that the enemy used less than 15 percent of the available road capacity, that the enemy was constantly expanding that capacity through new roads and bypasses, and that U.S. air strikes did not actually block, but only delayed, traffic. Besides blocking the roads, of course, the bombing destroyed material in transit on them. MACV and the JCS interpreted this to mean that the material destroyed could not be replaced, leading to the conclusion that the air war had denied it to the North Vietnamese and NLF forces in South Vietnam. Defense and CIA, however, concluded that the enemy's needs in South Vietnam were so minimal and the supply of war material so ample that it could replace losses easily, increase traffic flows slightly, and thus ship just as many men, and as much materiel, through to the South regardless of the U.S. air war.[60]

On balance it is clear that even though the interdiction bombing in southern North Vietnam and Laos made the North Vietnamese logistical effort more difficult, costly, and time consuming, it did not and could not prevent Hanoi from meeting the supply needs of the communist forces in the South.

What about the northern half of North Vietnam? Theoretically, it would seem to offer more lucrative transportation targets, particularly railroads and harbors. In 1966, approximately two-thirds of North Vietnam's imports arrived by sea; the bulk of the remaining third came by rail from China. In the assessment of the air war in the far north, there was again a complete disconnect between MACV and the JCS, on the one hand, and CIA and the Office of the Secretary of Defense on the other. MACV and the JCS expressed the belief that if all imports by sea were denied, and land routes through Laos and Cambodia were attacked vigorously, the North Vietnamese would be unable to obtain enough war supplies to continue. Defense and CIA, however, concluded that the overland routes *alone* could provide North Vietnam enough material to carry on even in the face of an *unlimited* bombing campaign.[61]

Three factors stand out in these and other assessments as the most significant inhibitors of a successful air interdiction campaign. First, North Vietnam was an underdeveloped, mostly agricultural country. This greatly limited its susceptibility to the effects of strategic bombing. Second, the vast majority of material for its war effort originated not in North Vietnam but in Russia and China. North Vietnam served essentially as a conduit for supplies. In order to cut off the North Vietnamese war machine, therefore, it would have been necessary to "go to the source" in China and the USSR—an act that would risk war with those two countries. Third, the North Vietnamese demonstrated great resourcefulness and determination, far beyond anything the Americans envisioned at the outset of the air war in February 1965.

North Vietnam and U.S. Air Strategy: A Total Mismatch

It is worth noting just a few of the details concerning how, and why, North Vietnam was such a poor choice for the U.S. air campaign. Because it was an agricultural country, it had a very rudimentary transportation system and little industry of any kind. Nearly all of the people were rice farmers who worked the land with water buffaloes and hand tools and whose well-being at a subsistence level was almost entirely dependent on what they grew or made themselves. The so-called modern industrial sector of the economy was tiny even by Asian standards, producing only about 12 percent of a GNP of $1.6 billion in 1965. There were only a handful of industrial facilities.

When North Vietnam was first targeted, the JCS found only eight industrial installations worth listing on a par with airfields, military supply dumps, barracks complexes, port facilities, bridges, and oil tanks. Even by the end of 1965, after the JCS had lowered the standards and more than doubled the number of targets, the list included only twenty-four industrial installations, eighteen of which were power plants that were used mainly for such ordinary uses as lighting streets and pumping water.

In addition, North Vietnam's armed forces placed little direct reliance on the domestic economy for war material other than manpower. They produced only very limited quantities of simple military items, such as mortars, grenades, mines, small arms, and bullets. Moreover, such arms and munitions as were produced in North Vietnam were made in small workshops, which provided poor targets. Larger, more vulnerable arsenals that might have been lucrative targets from the air were nonexistent. The great bulk of its military equipment—all of the heavier and more sophisticated items— had to be imported. Meaningful targets were few, and those that existed were critical to neither the viability of the economy nor the prosecution of the war in the South. A less likely country to buckle under an air assault such as the United States undertook is difficult to imagine.

According to Lt. Col. Mark Clodfelter, a former professor of history at the U.S. Air Force Academy, the American bombing campaigns failed to produce the desired results in Vietnam because many U.S. military and political leaders "entered the war convinced that bombing's lethality assured political results."[62] Using the World War II bombing surveys and data gathered during the Vietnam War, Clodfelter concludes that no amount of bombing could have changed the political or military situation in South Vietnam. The communists' supply needs did not match the conventional war criteria that many U.S. political and military leaders placed on them. For example, the communists fought one day for every thirty and required only thirty-four tons of war material daily. Clodfelter concludes that "no amount of bombing could stop this meager amount from reaching the South."[63]

Why didn't U.S. airpower advocates understand this? Earl Tilford, a former U.S. Air Force officer and professor of military history at the U.S. Air Force Command and Staff College, has argued that Air Force leaders developed an uninhibited faith in the strategic bombing doctrine, blinding them "to the true nature of the war, which at its essence was a revolutionary conflict, and not a struggle between industrialized powers." The unconventional nature of the war confounded air war proponents, according to Tilford, and as a result Air Force leaders were unable to devise a plan that matched the war's needs. In the end, Tilford concludes, "technologically sophisticated weapons proved no substitute for strategy."[64]

U.S. airpower advocates were also influenced—perhaps one should say blinded—by their experience with strategic bombing in World War II. They seem to have viewed Vietnam as more or less equivalent to Germany or Japan, two highly integrated, urbanized societies. Thus, the U.S. Air Force and U.S. Navy had, in the 1950s, developed their forces and strategy believing that the next war would be much like World War II in the following sense: It would be directed against a highly developed industrial nation that produced large quantities of military goods and must sustain mass armies engaged in intensive warfare. The U.S. air war was therefore geared to wreck an enemy's economy, the intent being to produce a prostrate foe unable and unwilling to continue the fight. This never happened to the North Vietnamese. According to the best intelligence estimates, it never came close to happening. It remains remarkable that airpower advocates did not see this, if not at the outset of the air campaign, then soon after U.S. intelligence demonstrated that it was failing completely.

The mismatch between North Vietnam and U.S. air objectives aside, one must still marvel at North Vietnam's powers of recovery and overall resourcefulness. Its adjustments to the physical damage, disruption, and other difficulties brought on by the bombing were sufficient to maintain minimum living standards, meet transportation requirements, even improve its military capabilities. Given that one of the purposes of the sustained bombing of the North was to break the will of the Hanoi government to prosecute the war in the South, it must be said on this basis alone that the air war was a dismal failure.

The will of the Hanoi government was not broken, and as far as we know it never came close to breaking at any point during the air war. In fact, as we now know, the Hanoi government, in effect, turned the rationale for the air war—that it would break the will of Hanoi to fight—on its head. The Hanoi government was remarkably successful in using actual and threatened U.S. bombings to mobilize people behind the communist war effort. There is substantial evidence, for instance, that the people of North Vietnam found the hardships brought on by the war more tolerable when they faced daily dangers from the bombing. The bombing actually seems to have hardened the attitude of the people and rallied them behind the government's war effort.

Col. Quach Hai Luong, a former North Vietnamese air defense commander, now a historian at Hanoi's Institute for Strategic Studies, recently explained the situation as follows:

> One of the enduring images of that time was of a farmer working in his rice field with his rifle slung on his back. And the industrial workers toiled in the factories with guns on their backs. Many of the artillerymen were often both farmers and factory workers. Every time the U.S. air strikes came, the workers would leave their factories and operate the artillery, and the farmers

would also leave their rice fields and, in groups of three and five, they would man the antiaircraft batteries. Many people in the world still cannot understand how the U.S. planes were shot down by such farmers and factory workers—the people in every village who would fire at these planes.[65]

The persistence of the view that Hanoi's will could be broken by bombing is also inconsistent with what should have been known of the North Vietnamese leadership and history. Hanoi's top leadership was composed of longtime revolutionaries who were intimately involved with Vietnam's struggle for independence from the French. Their successful struggle, which lasted more than thirty years, should have indicated the presence of a tenacity and will not easily broken. Moreover, as both communists and nationalists, they believed that they had a mission to liberate what they considered to be the southern half of their country.

Civil Defense: Life Under the Bombs in North Vietnam

The air war troubled the North Vietnamese, but from the very beginning of the conflict, Hanoi had prepared its citizens for heavy pressure. Party officials warned of an American invasion and a war of destruction against the North, but when citizens saw that they could withstand the punishment, their morale actually improved. The Party had long anticipated heavy damage to the major cities in the North. In Hanoi, streets were lined with individual bomb shelters. The now famous one-person sanctuaries were constructed of concrete cylinders, just large enough for an adult. According to some estimates, North Vietnam constructed more than 21 million air raid shelters.[66] Every able-bodied person was involved in the civil defense war, building shelters under the slogan, "The Shelter Is Your Second Home."[67] According to historian William Duiker, the city of Hanoi contained an average of one shelter every six to thirty feet.[68] The ruling North Vietnamese Politburo often met in the bomb shelter next to Ho Chi Minh's private home. Air raid drills were an everyday occurrence.

The Party also supervised the dispersion of nonessential personnel. The city of Hanoi had a population of roughly 1 million people in 1965. After the bombing began, the population was reduced to approximately 200,000. One former member of Hanoi's Foreign Ministry remembers the evacuations:

During the Gulf of Tonkin incident, you bombed us. Sometimes you forget about that one. I am talking about August 4 and 5, 1964 and the bombing right after. So after August 5, the children in Hanoi were ordered to go to the countryside for dispersal. My young son was among these children who were quickly moved to the countryside, because we knew that the bombing—the real bombing in earnest—could begin at any time. Our Foreign Ministry, and many other ministries, organized boarding houses in the countryside for children and spouses.

So this means that in 1963 we realized—I would say for the first time—that the bombing is coming, at some point. In August 1964, we went on alert, so to speak, and evacuated spouses and children from Hanoi, in anticipation of the bombing. And the bombing began the following February.[69]

During Harrison Salisbury's late 1966–early 1967 visit to Hanoi, he found one school set up outside the city in which students moved from class to class in trenches. Each student had a foxhole under his or her desk and was provided with a helmet in case of attack.[70] According to some government reports, more than 4 million children continued their schooling uninterrupted.[71] Most fixed industries were completely destroyed by the bombings, but their essential ingredients had also been dispersed. Oil was stored in fifty-five–gallon tanks along minor roadways throughout the country. Small factories were entirely relocated to the countryside as well. Railroads and bridges were camouflaged, and there were permanent curfews and blackouts in the major cities.

The passive defense of the cities cut down on civilian casualties immensely. The active defense of Vietnam's skies gave the people an outlet for their rage. Beginning shortly after the Gulf of Tonkin incident, the North Vietnamese constructed a complex antiaircraft system. Using sophisticated weaponry from the Soviet Union and China, Hanoi created a practical combination of radar, defense missiles, antiaircraft guns, and surface-to-air missiles. The radar system consisted of long range search radar and shorter range tracking radar supported by a refined network of ground observers who reported to North Vietnamese Army control centers. When American aircraft approached within thirty kilometers, air raid sirens went off and civil defense instructions followed on the radio. During the three years of ROLLING THUNDER, the North Vietnamese shot down more than 900 American aircraft, increasing the cost of the war in human and material terms dramatically.[72]

Life under the bombs required enormous sacrifice, but at no time did the ordeal break Vietnam's will. Hardships were reduced by preparation and increased aid from socialist countries. The Hanoi government transferred many of the material costs imposed by the bombing back to its allies, which accepted them as their part in what was officially regarded as a fraternal struggle. From 1965 through the end of the war, it is estimated that socialist countries provided Vietnam in economic aid and military support more than four times what was lost in bombing damage. If economic criteria were the only consideration, therefore, North Vietnam would show a substantial net gain from the bombing, primarily in military equipment. Because of this aid, and the effectiveness of its countermeasures, North Vietnam's economy continued to function.[73] Immediate mobilization of the population to repair damage done by American bombing missions also reduced the hardship. By 1968, nearly 600,000 civilians were working in cleanup and rehabilitation efforts.[74] An estimated 500,000 laborers repaired roads and railroads.[75] And Chinese combat engineers aided in bridge repair.[76]

It appears, in short, that North Vietnam never faced a manpower shortage, even under the heaviest pressure of U.S. bombing. A study by the Systems Analysis Office of the Department of Defense reported, for example, that 90 percent of the North's manpower needs were met by normal population growth. The same study found, moreover, that bombing actually increased the supply of available labor.[77]

The Ground War: The U.S. Strategy of Attrition

WATERSHED AT DA NANG, MARCH 8, 1965

At approximately nine o'clock on the morning of March 8, 1965, a U.S. Marine Corps battalion landing team splashed ashore at Da Nang, in South Vietnam. A companion battalion landed by air later the same day. Although there were already more than 20,000 American servicemen in South Vietnam when the two Marine battalions arrived, this was the first time that an organized ground combat unit had been committed. The mission assigned to these two battalions was to secure the airfield and U.S. supporting installations and facilities. The orders were clear: "The U.S. Marine Force will not, repeat will not, engage in day-to-day actions against the Viet Cong."[78]

The mission assigned to these forces had been recommended by General Westmoreland on February 22, 1965. He was concerned about the ability of the South Vietnamese to protect the base from which American aircraft were conducting air strikes against the North and providing air support missions in the South. Although Ambassador Maxwell Taylor supported Westmoreland's request for the Marines at Da Nang, he also had deep reservations about it. He feared that once U.S. forces were assigned to a mission such as that at Da Nang then other missions for U.S. ground combat units would soon follow. With these reservations in mind, Taylor was informed on February 26 that the Marines were on the way.[79]

Whereas the decision to bomb North Vietnam was the product of a year of intense debate, this decision to introduce the Marines was made with relatively little discussion at the highest levels of the Johnson administration. The landing of U.S. ground combat units at Da Nang nevertheless represented a watershed event in the history of U.S. involvement in Vietnam. With the commitment of just those two battalions in March, the administration would begin to slide down a slippery slope of surprising steepness. By December nearly 200,000 U.S. combat troops would be deployed in South Vietnam, and more than 1,500 Americans would already have died there.

General Westmoreland and the Quick Shift to Offense

President Johnson held extensive discussions with his advisers on April 1 and 2, 1965. His decisions were recorded in NSAM 328 on April 6. Approval was given for the deployment of two additional Marine battalions, one to Phu Bai and one to Da Nang, and for an 18,000–20,000-man increase in U.S. logistical and support forces. Most significant, however, NSAM 328 sanctioned a change in mission for U.S. ground forces in Vietnam. The key passage in this regard was the following:

> The President approved a change of mission for all Marine battalions deployed to Vietnam to permit their more active use under conditions to be established and approved by the Secretary of Defense in consultation with the Secretary of State.[80]

This decision, although it did not yet clearly define the new mission, was a pivotal one. It marked the president's acceptance of the concept that U.S. troops could engage in offensive ground operations against an Asian foe. The language was cautious, indicating a desire to proceed slowly and carefully.

Missing from NSAM 328, however, was a coherent strategy for the actual use of U.S. ground forces in this new mode. Ambassador Taylor, among others, had raised the question as to whether Western troops could fight effectively in Vietnam. But NSAM 328 implied that a limited number of troops would be tested in offensive ground operations *before* a strategy was devised for using these forces.

At a conference in Honolulu on April 20, U.S. civilian and military leaders agreed that the key to success was to frustrate the enemy's strategy in the South. This marked the relative downgrading of air pressure against North Vietnam. Henceforth, first call on air assets would go to targets in the South. The objective was to "break the will of the DRV/VC by denying them victory in the South."[81] An increase of U.S. forces to a total of thirteen battalions and 82,000 men was agreed to. Thus, it should have been quite clear to participants in the Honolulu conference that "winning" militarily in Vietnam was not the stated objective.

The use of U.S. combat troops exclusively as defenders of U.S. assets in South Vietnam was seen as a defensive strategy, yielding the initiative to the enemy and merely designed to frustrate him, rather than defeat him. But the U.S. Army had been trained in offensive warfare. And therefore a defensive strategy, regardless of how well it suited American political objectives, was never enthusiastically accepted by American military commanders. This confusion as to the mission for American ground forces continued throughout the war. Frustrating the enemy was seen as a negative defensive mission unsuited to a combat force designed for offensive operations whose objective was to defeat the enemy.

Security, therefore, was never in fact the only mission of U.S. units. Yet it remained their primary one during the period immediately following the landing at Da Nang, as they consolidated and developed their coastal base areas. Patrol perimeters were pushed out, and an active defense was conducted. Failure to solve knotty problems concerning control and coordination between U.S. and Vietnamese forces, however, prevented for some months offensive operations in support of the South Vietnamese.

This period of relative quiet in the war in the South ended in May. Before the month was over, the South Vietnamese were decimated in a series of battles at Ba Gia, near Quang Ngai. In early June, two NLF regiments again defeated the South Vietnamese at Dong Xoai, inflicting heavy casualties. Although U.S. troops were nearby in both cases, in neither case were they committed to the battle in an attempt to prevent the South Vietnamese defeat.[82]

On June 7, 1965, shortly after the defeat at Ba Gia, General Westmoreland forwarded to Adm. U.S. Grant Sharp, the commander in chief of U.S. forces in the Pacific, "a broad review of force requirements . . . in light of the changing situation in Southeast Asia and within South Vietnam." Describing the South Vietnamese army as near collapse, reluctant to assume the offensive, with desertion rates running inordinately high, and with its steadfastness under fire coming into doubt, Westmoreland said he saw "no course of action open to the U.S. except to reinforce our efforts in SVN with additional U.S. or Third Country forces as rapidly as is practicable during the critical weeks ahead." In addition, he added, even greater forces should be prepared for deployment if required "to attain our objectives or counter enemy initiatives." He did not envision these forces merely as part of a defensive strategy, however. Rather, General Westmoreland said: "I am convinced that U.S. troops with their energy, mobility, and firepower can successfully take the fight to the NLF. The basic purpose of the additional deployments . . . is to give us a substantial and hard-hitting offensive capability on the ground."[83]

In his cable to CINCPAC, Westmoreland requested a buildup to a total of thirty-five maneuver battalions, with an additional nine battalions to be prepared for deployment if needed at a later date. In subsequent communications, the U.S. commander spelled out his plans for employing these forces. Dispensing with any pretense of a defensive strategy, Westmoreland saw these troops assuming the offensive and defeating the enemy. He saw the war developing in three distinct phases as follows:

- *Phase 1.* Commitment of U.S. (and other free world) forces necessary to halt the losing trend by the end of 1965.

- *Phase 2.* U.S. and allied forces mount major offensive actions to seize the initiative to destroy guerrilla and organized enemy forces. This phase would be concluded when the enemy had been worn down, thrown on the defensive, and driven back from the major populated areas.

- *Phase 3.* If the enemy persisted, a period of twelve to eighteen months following Phase 2 would be required for the final destruction of enemy forces remaining in remote base areas.[84]

General Westmoreland's recommendations stirred up a hornet's nest back in Washington. His request for reinforcements on this large a scale, together with the stated intention to put the troops on the offensive throughout South Vietnam, was devoid of the comforting restrictions that had always been part and parcel of the strategies previously considered. In fact, General Westmoreland was recommending a virtual American takeover of the war. There was little or no mention in General Westmoreland's request of South Vietnamese forces, or any program to utilize those forces, or to make them more effective. And so once again the specter of major U.S. military forces engaged in ground combat on the Asian mainland was about to become a reality. The implications for the United States in terms of lives and resources would be profound.

In American senior military colleges today, students are taught that an estimate of the situation such as that given by General Westmoreland—that "there is only one course of action open to us"—is never adequate and should always be viewed with suspicion. *Of course* there was more than one course of action open to the United States. But General Westmoreland's request was taken at face value by senior U.S. political leaders as well as military leaders. They seem to have believed, incorrectly, that they faced but two options: either to approve Westmoreland's recommendations or to reject them, leaving the United States without any strategy or prospects at all in Vietnam.

Before making a decision of this magnitude, however, President Johnson wanted to reexamine all his options. Secretary McNamara was asked to meet with General Westmoreland in Saigon to examine the alternatives and to determine the force requirements for the immediate future and through 1966.[85] But in a fait accompli, General Westmoreland was given authority on June 26 to commit U.S. ground forces anywhere in the country when, in his judgment, they were needed to strengthen South Vietnamese forces. Thus liberated from the restrictions imposed by the defensive mission, the first major operation by U.S. forces under this new authority was conducted on June 27 in War Zone D northwest of Saigon.[86]

In Saigon, General Westmoreland explained to Secretary McNamara that a buildup to forty-four battalions (now dubbed Phase 1 forces, totaling 175,000 men) would be needed in South Vietnam by the end of 1965. However, he also made it clear that this force and the new offensive strategy would prevent defeat only long enough to prepare the way for additional U.S. forces that, if approved, would allow him to seize the initiative from the Viet Cong sometime in 1966. He foresaw the necessity of some twenty-four additional combat battalions, plus associated combat support and support units, by the end of 1966 (the so-called Phase 2 forces, totaling 100,000 men). This force would enable him, he told the secretary, to take the offensive that year and, with "appropriate" (but unspecified) additional reinforcements (Phase 3), to defeat the enemy by the end of 1967.[87]

In his memoir of the war, *In Retrospect*, Secretary of Defense McNamara has characterized these discussions with General Westmoreland in Saigon as "superficial." Looking back, he says:

> I clearly erred by not forcing—then or later, in Saigon or in Washington—a knock-down, drag-out debate over the loose assumptions, unasked questions, and thin analyses underlying our military strategy in Vietnam. I had spent twenty years as a manager, forcing organizations to think deep and realistically about alternative courses of action and their consequences. I doubt if I will ever fully understand why I did not do so here.[88]

Secretary McNamara reported General Westmoreland's requests to the president on July 20. He recommended that General Westmoreland's Phase 1 request be met, with the understanding that additional troops would be needed in 1966. He also recommended asking Congress for authority to call up 235,000 reservists, not because they were needed militarily but to emphasize to the public the magnitude of the war effort.

ATTRITION: THE ILLUSION OF AN OFFENSIVE STRATEGY

On July 28, 1965, President Johnson approved the deployment to South Vietnam of the Phase 1 forces totaling 175,000 troops (later raised to 219,000). He refused to call up the reserves and made no decision about the deployment of Phase 2 forces (no decision was required at the time). In announcing these increases in U.S. forces to South Vietnam, the president stressed the continuity of the U.S. commitment to the defense of South Vietnam and indicated that he foresaw no quick solution to the problems there.[89] That was the public "face" the administration put on the president's decision of 28 July.

In their private discussions, all the participants likely realized that a major threshold had been crossed. A new course had been taken, the outcome of which was not in sight. No longer would U.S. strategy call for the concentration of troops in *enclaves*, from which they would be limited to defending essential U.S. and South Vietnamese assets from NLF attacks. In his memoir, General Westmoreland reported seeing it that way at the time:

> Explicit in my forty-four battalion proposal and President Johnson's approval of it was a proviso for free maneuver of American and allied units throughout South Vietnam. Thus the restrictive enclave strategy with which I had disagreed from the first was finally rejected.[90]

In his own memoir, President Johnson observed: "Now we were committed to major combat in Vietnam."[91]

Accompanying this change from enclave defense to offensive search-and-destroy operations, as they came to be called, was also a subtle, but extremely significant, change in emphasis. By rejecting the limited objective of simply denying the enemy victory and convincing him that he could not win, this new thrust in U.S. policy was to defeat the enemy on the ground in the South. However, the decision to use U.S. forces in an offensive strategy left the U.S. commitment to the defense of South Vietnam open-ended.

That is to say, the amount of U.S. force required to "defeat" the enemy depended entirely, in the end, on the enemy's response to the U.S. buildup and the enemy's willingness to increase its own commitment to the struggle. This is why the force approved by President Johnson in July 1965 was recognized as sufficient only to prevent the imminent collapse of the South Vietnamese government. In other words, the stage was being set for further U.S. troop deployments of such size as would be required *by the enemy's commitment to maintaining the struggle in the South*. And therein was the rub: Who knew—who could even have guessed—that the enemy's commitment was as deep and strong as it in fact turned out to be?

In the end, no matter what it came to be called, the U.S. ground war in Vietnam was a *war of attrition*. Success in this kind of war did not depend on the ability of American forces to inflict a decisive defeat on the enemy in South Vietnam. It depended instead on how long the North Vietnamese were willing to feed the war pipeline with men and material. If they were willing to pay the price, the enemy could keep large numbers of American forces tied up indefinitely and continue to inflict casualties on them.

.   .   .

Yet this failure to recognize the illusion of military victory in Vietnam may not have been the most significant shortcoming of the American strategy. There was also the failure to realize that General Westmoreland's request, and its approval by President Johnson, implied an irrevocable and complete loss of confidence in the South Vietnamese government to manage its own affairs. The supreme paradox of the Vietnam War, for those Americans who fought in the jungles of Vietnam, was that the American strategy for winning the war led to disdain for the South Vietnamese people themselves, on whose behalf the United States had ostensibly intervened in the first place. Thus did an insoluble contradiction exist between the overriding U.S. political objective of the war and the actual situation on the ground in South Vietnam.

The North Vietnamese were not blind to this contradiction. They understood the deployment of American troops to be fundamentally an admission of U.S. failure in what they called the "special war"—the war of Vietnamese against Vietnamese, with American advisers training and supporting the South Vietnamese. The deployment of U.S. troops signaled to North Vietnam that the United States had discovered what they already knew—that the Diem regime and its successors had been repudiated by the majority of the South Vietnamese people.[92]

Hereafter, the cost of adopting an offensive ground strategy in South Vietnam in pursuit of the illusion of military victory would mount quickly. How illusory was this pursuit? How misguided were the U.S. military commanders? The numbers tell the story graphically. By the end of 1967 the United States had 107 battalions, and a total of 525,000 men, in Vietnam, all the while mounting a virtually unprecedented bombing campaign against the North. But as we know, there was no U.S. victory in sight.

Just as the air war could not break the will of the Hanoi government and its people, the offensive strategy of ground war could not break the back of the NLF in the South. It appears that U.S. military leaders did not accept the political rationale for the constraints they believed had been placed on U.S. military power; but neither did they present political leaders with plausible alternative strategies.

LIMITATIONS OF THE STRATEGY OF ATTRITION

The potential costs of the policy the administration had adopted in July 1965 were made apparent by the North Vietnamese in November, at the battle of the Ia Drang Valley. Nearly 300 U.S. troops were killed. At least 1,300 North Vietnamese forces were killed. These results were sobering to an extent that went far beyond the strategic significance of the battle itself, for the North Vietnamese had shown their willingness to match or exceed the American buildup and also that they were apparently willing to take casualties at an appalling rate, without giving up the fight. U.S. officials now had to face squarely the implications of having adopted an open-ended, reactive strategy of attrition in Vietnam.

By April 10, 1966, President Johnson had approved a plan for the subsequent buildup of U.S. forces that did not require a reserve call-up. It projected U.S. strength in South Vietnam at the end of 1966 to be seventy battalions and 383,500 men. By the end of June 1967, the total U.S. strength in South Vietnam was scheduled to be 425,000. During the next three months, adjustments in these deployment capabilities raised the projected totals to seventy-nine maneuver battalions by the end of 1966, eighty-two battalions by June of 1967. Even this ambitious plan, called Program 3 (not to be confused with General Westmoreland's initial Phase 3 of June 1965), nevertheless involved fewer men than Westmoreland's original recommendations. But even before these figures had been published by the Department of Defense, the military commanders (on August 5, 1966) submitted new troop requirements for 1967. They called the additional troops "rounding out forces," whose purpose was to give a more balanced additional capability. If the request were to be approved, troop strength in Vietnam would be raised, according to the August 5 plan, to ninety maneuver battalions and 542,588 men by the end of 1967.[93]

Secretary McNamara did not seek to veto these new requirements. Instead, he gave the following guidance to the Joint Chiefs of Staff:

As you know, it is our policy to provide the troops, weapons, and supplies requested by General Westmoreland at the times he desires them, to the greatest possible degree. The latest revised CINCPAC requirements . . . are to be accorded the same consideration: valid requirements for SVN . . . will be deployed on a schedule as close as possible to CINCPAC/General Westmoreland's requests. Nevertheless, I desire and expect detailed line-by-line analysis of these requirements to determine that each is truly essential to the carrying out of our war plan.[94]

By "our war plan," Secretary McNamara meant the war plan developed by the Joint Chiefs of Staff and the military commanders in the Pacific. It was these military officials who were developing U.S. strategy in Vietnam and setting force requirements.

Thus, one can reasonably ask the following series of questions: Whose responsibility *was* it to articulate U.S. strategy for the ground war in Vietnam? And, accordingly, whose role should have been dominant in issues such as the regular requests for troop increases coming from General Westmoreland and MACV, which were routinely supported by the Joint Chiefs? Was it primarily a military or a civilian responsibility? The simple answer is that it was *both*. But the *simple* answer was not an *easy* answer to implement. It was extremely difficult to translate the political objective—preventing the enemy from destroying a viable, independent South Vietnam—into meaningful military strategy that did not carry risks of widening the war into a conflict with Russia and China.

The senior members of the civilian leadership did not believe they *should* supply detailed military guidance. From the civilians' point of view—and that includes the president—they were not qualified to pronounce on the technical problems of trying to conduct a war on the ground in Asia. Their view was this: Civilians set the overall political objectives, in line with their understanding of U.S. interests in Southeast Asia and the world at large; it falls to the military commanders to translate the stated objectives into concrete strategy and tactics.

The record suggests that the military commanders and the JCS saw the president's limited political objectives as essentially negative and ineffective. It was a no-win approach, in their view, that yielded the initiative to the enemy. If the United States was to go to war, then the Joint Chiefs believed a more ambitious objective should be pursued—that of decisively defeating the enemy in both North and South Vietnam. They therefore advocated the classic doctrine of pursuing such a victory via the rapid application of overwhelming military power through offensive action to defeat the enemy's main forces. The Joint Chiefs of Staff therefore opposed restrictions on the use of American force in North and South Vietnam and repeatedly sought their removal. They continued to request additional American troops for South Vietnam, increased bombing of North Vietnam, and the lifting of geographical restrictions on where American military power cold, and could not, be applied.

In addition, throughout this period, the JCS unsuccessfully advocated the call-up of U.S. reserve units, which they felt was necessary to protect U.S. interests elsewhere in the world. This question of whether to call up reserve forces hovered like a cloud in the background whenever additional troops requests were considered.

The Joint Chiefs, in their review of the 1967 force requirements, provided the secretary of defense with their analysis of the U.S. worldwide military posture in light of those force requirements. The JCS began with these assumptions: (1) there would be no call-up of reserve forces; (2) there would be no change in rotation policy (a one-year tour for U.S. personnel); and (3) resources for the proposed deployments would be taken from the active force structure. With these assumptions, the impact of meeting the 1967 requirements would, the Joint Chiefs concluded, be potentially devastating. Without a reserve call-up, they indicated, the services could not fully respond to the stated force requirements within the schedule prescribed. Moreover, they said that providing these forces on a delayed schedule was *not* a viable option either. Instead, they said, a delay would:

> Further impair the U.S. military posture and capability to maintain forward deployments to deter aggression worldwide. It would further reduce the capability to reinforce NATO rapidly, to provide forces for other contingencies, and to maintain a sufficient rotation and training base. . . . Of particular note in the case of the Army, equipment withdrawals from the Reserve components have substantially weakened the Army's reserve structure."[95]

With the JCS request in hand, Secretary McNamara again departed for Saigon to confer with General Westmoreland. Upon his return, on August 10, 1966, the secretary concluded that a reserve call-up was not needed to meet the field commander's request for troops in Vietnam or to strengthen U.S. forces in Europe. But he nonetheless recommended the call-up to underline the extreme magnitude of the war in Vietnam. The bottom line of his report to the president was this: He could "see no reasonable way to bring the war to an end soon."

Secretary McNamara's solution was to move to "getting ourselves into a military posture that we credibly would maintain indefinitely—a posture that makes trying to 'wait us out' less attractive" to the North Vietnamese and NLF. To achieve this, the secretary now recommended a five-step program vastly different from the war plan embraced by his military commanders. The five steps were:

1. Barring a dramatic change in the war, we should . . . level off at the total of 470,000 [U.S. ground forces];

2. An infiltration barrier should be constructed across the neck of South Vietnam near the 17th parallel and across the infiltration trails in Laos;

3. Stabilize the ROLLING THUNDER program against the North at present levels;

4. Pursue a vigorous pacification program;

5. Increase the prospects for a negotiated settlement of the war [he suggested several possible actions].

Even if these steps were taken, however, Secretary McNamara saw little likelihood of success in the near future. The solution, as he now saw it, was "to prepare openly for a longer war in order to give clear evidence that the continuing costs and risks to the American people are acceptably limited, that the formula for success has been found, and that the end of the war is merely a matter of time."[96]

It is important to note what had happened. By August 10, 1966, the U.S. secretary of defense had concluded the following:

- The U.S. strategy of attrition was a losing strategy that played to enemy strengths and must be replaced.

- The political objective of not widening the war, and the military's procedure of asking for endless increases in troops and equipment, were fundamentally in conflict with each other.

- A military "victory" in the normally accepted sense of the term was quite unlikely through offensive military action—in fact, was an illusion that could be maintained only if one turned a blind eye to the disconnects between predictions of the military commanders and actual results on the battlefield.

- The nature of the conflict in Vietnam—bluntly, that it was a *war*, and an especially brutal and destructive one at that, without an end in sight—must be made clear to the ultimate arbiters of U.S. security—the American people.

It is unlikely that this radically pessimistic view—maybe we should say rad-ically *realistic*—came to the secretary in a flash. He had long harbored doubts about the possibility of victory. He has indicated in his memoir, *In Ret-rospect*, that his doubts first crystallized in November 1965, after he received the results from the battle of the Ia Drang Valley, along with General West-moreland's simultaneous requests for greatly increased numbers of U.S. ground forces. "The message," he recalls, "came as a shattering blow."[97]

By August 10, 1966, Secretary McNamara had pulled his thoughts together and produced a strategy for the war that was new, that was realistic—but one that was absolute anathema to the Joint Chiefs and military commanders. His strategy did not merely say "no" to the Joint Chiefs; it also provided an alter-native strategy and criteria for success, as well as new assumptions about the meaning of *winning*.

To President Johnson, the prospect of reserve mobilization—if not required to support the forces in Vietnam—was not appealing. It would both encourage the hard-liners to demand action that carried the risk of widening the war and lead them to say, as well, that the war is getting bigger and more costly and therefore America must move to a war footing, as it had done in World War II. As he saw it, reserve mobilization would have been a crossover point, an outcome he wanted to avoid. For a president who, simultaneous with the war, was attempting to pass a Herculean set of social programs through the Congress, mobilization carried all the wrong messages.

After a series of conferences, the president approved on November 11 a new deployment program, Program 4, with an end strength of U.S. military personnel of 470,000, to be reached by June 1968 (as opposed to the origi-nal request for some 542,000 by the end of 1967). In explaining the reason-ing behind the Program 4 decisions, McNamara posed the U.S. strategic dilemma as precisely as he, or anyone, ever had:

> We now face a choice of two approaches to the threat of the regular VC/NVA [Vietcong/North Vietnamese Army] forces. The first approach would be to continue in 1967 to increase friendly forces as rapidly as possi-ble, and without limit, and employ them primarily in large scale "seek out and destroy" operations to destroy the main force VC/NVA units. . . .
>
> The second approach is to follow a similarly aggressive strategy of "seek out and destroy," but to build friendly forces only to that level required to neutralize the large enemy units and prevent them from interfering with the pacification program. It is essential to this approach that such a level be con-sistent with a stable economy in SVN, and consistent with a military posture that the U.S. credibly would maintain indefinitely, thus making a Communist attempt to "wait us out" less attractive.

I believe it is time to adopt the second approach for three reasons: (1) if MACV estimates of enemy strength are correct, we have not been able to "attrit" the enemy forces fast enough to break their morale and more U.S. forces are unlikely to do so in the foreseeable future; (2) we cannot deploy more than 470,000 personnel . . . without a high probability of generating a self-defeating runaway inflation in SVN, and (3) an endless escalation of U.S. deployments is not likely to be acceptable in the U.S., or to induce the enemy to believe that the U.S. is prepared to stay as long as it is required to produce a secure noncommunist SVN.[98]

The civilian decisionmakers in the Department of Defense, led by the secretary, had begun to see the objective of military victory in Vietnam for the illusion that it was.

By April 25, 1967, the issues would be squarely posed for the president. General Westmoreland returned to the United States on that date to address the Associated Press annual convention in New York. He and the chairman of the Joint Chiefs, Gen. Earle Wheeler, met with the president on April 27. General Westmoreland indicated to the president that if the troops he requested were not provided the war would not necessarily be lost, but progress would certainly be slowed. He admitted that it was likely that the enemy would also add more troops, although he felt the United States had reached the crossover point where "attritions will be greater than additions to the [enemy] force." General Westmoreland concluded by estimating that with 565,000 men the war could well go on for three years; but with a total of 665,000, as he had requested, it could start to wind down in two years. General Wheeler repeated to the president his concern about the possibility of military threats in other parts of the world.[99] In essence, the president was told the United States needed vastly more troops in Vietnam than Secretary McNamara had deemed necessary and that such a deployment was unthinkable without calling up reservists.

In his budget message to Congress on August 3, 1967, President Johnson at last disclosed plans to dispatch "at least 45,000" additional troops to South Vietnam in that fiscal year, bringing the total authorized troop strength in the war zone to 525,000 American forces. This was Program 5, officially published by the Defense Department on August 14. The press and the public, by now all too used to these sorts of announcements, seemed scarcely to notice.[100] Yet a threshold had quietly been crossed when the president chose not to grant the JCS's request. Although no change in concept or objectives was mentioned in the decision, the forces allocated, in numbers far below what the Joint Chiefs deemed necessary, would necessar-

ily compel the military to change the way the war was pursued on the battlefield. The illusion of military victory began, at that moment, to fade into the
distant future.

What amounts to the penultimate act in the exposé of "military victory"
as an illusion was played out in November and December 1967. The secretary of defense forwarded a personal memorandum to the president on
November 1, 1967, that explained in blunt language why he believed the
current course of action in Vietnam "would be dangerous, costly, and unsatisfactory to our people." In his memorandum, McNamara suggested alternative moves toward "stabilization of our military operations in the South . . .
and of our air operations in the North, along with a demonstration that our
air attacks on the North are not blocking negotiations leading to a peaceful
settlement."

Secretary McNamara concluded his memorandum with three recommendations, similar to the ones he had made in August 1966. First, he suggested
that the United States announce that it would not expand air operations in
the North, or the size of combat forces in the South, beyond those already
planned. Second, the secretary proposed a bombing halt before the end of
1967. Finally, he favored a new study of military operations in the South
aimed at reducing U.S. casualties and giving the South Vietnamese greater
responsibilities for their own security.[101]

In his memoir *In Retrospect*, Secretary McNamara explains that he
learned years later, while conducting research for the book, what happened
to his November 1 memorandum:

> I never received a reply from the president to my memorandum. Much
> later, I learned he had sent a copy of it to Dean Rusk for his reaction, with
> instructions to show it to no one. And he asked Walt Rostow to disclose [to
> various advisers] the memo's substance, but not its author. . . . Abe Fortas [a
> close personal adviser to the president] wrote . . . "in my opinion, it means
> not domestic appeasement, but domestic repudiation (which it would
> deserve); a powerful tonic to Chinese Communist effectiveness in the world;
> and a profound retreat to the Asia dominoes."[102]

Meanwhile, the president had asked the Joint Chiefs to recommend to
him what they thought could be done in Vietnam during the following four
months at current force levels and within existing policy limitations. On
November 27, 1967, they responded by, in effect, wringing their hands at
the shortage of manpower needed for the essential tasks and repeating again
their request, which Secretary McNamara had repeatedly refused, for an

additional 200,000 troops and for the removal of operational restrictions. "There are no new programs which can be undertaken under current policy guidelines," they said, "which would result in a rapid or significantly more visible increase in the rate of progress in the near term."[103] The illusion of an American "victory" on behalf of our South Vietnamese allies seems to have been abandoned by America's military leaders.

THE TET OFFENSIVE: THE ILLUSION IS FULLY EXPOSED

The U.S. government entered 1968 with a mood of cautious optimism concerning the course of the war in Vietnam. Although the press and Congress were becoming increasingly skeptical about the extent and the success of the American effort, the president and most of his principal advisers remained doggedly optimistic. Among the president's closest advisers, only Secretary McNamara expressed serious doubts about the course of the American War effort—which had led to his departure from the cabinet.

However, General Westmoreland's year-end assessment of the military situation, dated January 26, 1968, was not sanguine about the political situation in South Vietnam. He reported: "The GVN [government of Vietnam— the South Vietnamese government] is not yet a ready and effective partner with its own people. The Viet Cong [i.e., the NLF] infrastructure remains basically intact; and corruption is both corrosive and extensive."[104]

As noted above, the United States had boxed itself into a basically reactive position in Vietnam. Since March 1967, Hanoi and its NLF allies in the South had been planning the Tet Offensive—what the communists called the "general offensive, general uprising."

Hanoi sought a decisive victory in order to create the military, political, and psychological conditions that would destroy the political foundations of the Saigon regime in the South and political support for the war in the United States. Dramatic, large-scale attacks across South Vietnam, they believed, might precipitate a general uprising, destroying the Saigon government and, for the United States, making it psychologically and politically impossible to continue to pursue the war. Negotiations to end the war, they hoped, would follow.

A former North Vietnamese Foreign Ministry official, Luu Doan Huynh, recently explained the context of Tet planning as follows:

> The Tet Offensive must be viewed as part of a general move that involved both a diplomatic and a military offensive. From 23 to 27 January 1967, the

[Thirteenth Party Plenum] was held in Hanoi, and it was there that these issues were first discussed. A decision was taken at the Plenum that was designed to open a new stage of struggle; that is, to continue the armed struggle while preparing for the conditions favorable to peace negotiations. The resolution said that the success of the military and political struggle in South Vietnam must be the decisive factor for victory on the battlefield, and that this victory will serve as the foundation for success in the diplomatic field. That is: We can only win at the negotiating table what we have already won on the battlefield.[105]

Operationally, Hanoi's plan was to distract and overextend U.S. forces through massive attacks on the frontiers, far from the populated areas, thus leaving the urban areas vulnerable to attack. With Hanoi having thus diverted U.S. attention, the major attacks would be directed against government administrative structures in the towns and cities. With the collapse of the government and the expected general uprising of the population, the United States would, according to this scenario, be faced with a fait accompli—the government and army in South Vietnam would have been eliminated, leaving the Americans with nothing to support or defend.

Vietnamese historian and former North Vietnamese official Nguyen Khac Huynh recently revealed how those who planned the offensive envisioned the outcome. According to Nguyen Khac Huynh, the Hanoi government allowed for three possibilities:

1. *Very Big Victory.* This would compel the U.S. to enter negotiations, to seek an end to the war and to withdraw U.S. troops.

2. *Big Victory.* This would be a major setback for the U.S. military position. However, the U.S. would still be able to increase its troop strength and stabilize the situation. Fighting would continue.

3. *Limited Victory.* The U.S. would increase its troop strength, and even expand the war to the North, Cambodia, and Laos.[106]

By July, concrete plans were laid, and Hanoi began to make preparations. As early as October, the first stage of the communist plan was put into effect with a series of bloody battles in remote areas along the borders of South Vietnam.

As the NLF began extensive infiltration of South Vietnam's cities prior to attacking them, indications of the plan began to reach U.S. officials. An intelligence summary prepared in Saigon on December 8 accurately predicted a "general counteroffensive and general uprising" designed to lure allied units to the border areas, allow the communists to control the country's armed forces and local administration, and force the Americans "to withdraw from South Vietnam in a short period of time."

Indeed, the attack order for the communist offensive had been captured by American forces on November 19, 1967. The order stressed that strong military attacks would be used "in coordination with the uprisings of the local population to take over towns and cities." In releasing this document on January 5, 1968, however, U.S. officials cautioned that the document could not be taken as conclusive evidence that such an order had been given and might, in fact, represent merely an internal propaganda document "designed to inspire the fighting troops." Washington intelligence analysts were inclined to think the coming campaign would not really indicate anything new but only a continuation of past communist strategy.[107]

Although some sort of offensive action by the NLF and North Vietnamese forces was believed to be imminent, virtually no one in the American command, or anyone among South Vietnamese military officials, believed the action would come during the Tet holidays. Tet is the Vietnamese holiday celebrating the arrival of the Chinese lunar new year. And Saigon was, in fact, in its usual festive mood on the eve of Tet. For city dwellers, the war seemed remote. At least half the South Vietnamese Army had departed for home to celebrate Tet with families. Pres. Nguyen Van Thieu was celebrating in his wife's hometown, My Tho, in the Mekong Delta.[108]

But Tet is much more than a New Year's holiday. It has been described as "a combination All Souls' Day, a family celebration, a spring festival, a national holiday and an overall manifestation of a way of life."[109] Throughout Vietnam, it is the most important and most sacred holiday of the year, universally observed by every religious group and social class. The unique and peaceful nature of the Tet holiday had been stressed throughout the course of the Vietnam War. Beginning in 1963, the communists had proclaimed annual battlefield cease-fires for Christmas, New Year's Day, Buddha's birthday, and Tet. The Saigon government and the United States followed suit beginning with Christmas 1965. These recurrent holiday truces quickly became expected in Vietnam, although the U.S. command complained of massive communist violations and supply movements during the truce periods. There must have been very few Americans who were aware that the greatest feat of arms in Vietnam's history was considered to be the epic surprise attack by Nguyen Hue (Quang Trung) on the Chinese garrison in Hanoi during Tet of 1789.[110]

According to the lunar calendar, the Year of the Monkey was to begin on Tuesday, January 30. In an action that went unnoticed in the South, however, the North Vietnamese government announced that the celebration would begin one day earlier than usual. Thus, North Vietnamese families were able to celebrate the important first day of Tet together in peace.

During the early morning hours of January 31, 1968, the enemy launched a series of simultaneous and coordinated attacks against the major population centers in III and IV Corps Tactical Zones (CTZ). Attacks had been launched against the major cities of I and II CTZ the previous night. During the period January 30–31, thirty-nine of South Vietnam's forty-four provincial capitals, five of its six autonomous cities, and at least seventy-one of 245 district towns were attacked by fire and ground action. The offensive was aimed primarily at civilian centers of authority and military command installations.

In Saigon, the enemy attack began with a sapper assault on the U.S. embassy, rapidly followed by assaults on Tan San Nhut Air Base, the presidential palace, the Joint General Staff compound of the Republic of Vietnam Armed Forces, and other government installations. In addition, enemy forces that had infiltrated in large numbers into Hue managed to capture the Imperial Citadel and most of the city.

The American command had failed to anticipate the scope and intensity of the NLF attacks. General Westmoreland acknowledged this: "The extent of this offensive was not known to us, although we did feel it was going to be widespread. The timing was not known. I frankly did not think they would assume the psychological disadvantage of hitting at Tet itself, so I thought it would be before or after Tet. I did not anticipate that they would strike in the cities and make them their targets."[111]

A major purpose of the communist attack was clearly psychological. The attacks apparently were designed "to discourage the United States, to shake the faith of the people of South Vietnam in the ability of the United States and their own government to protect them, and to impress all concerned with the strength and popular support of the Viet Cong. This would leave Hanoi in a position of strength from which it could negotiate a cease-fire and the eventual withdrawal of American forces. The U.S. ambassador in Saigon, Ellsworth Bunker, took this view, saying that the "primary purpose of the operation . . . [was] psychological, rather than military."

In February 1968, General Westmoreland reported that the unfavorable psychological effects on the South Vietnamese people included the following: "Added fear and respect of Communist capabilities, more fence straddling by the uncommitted, and greater war weariness. . . . From a realistic point of view, we must accept the fact that the enemy has dealt the GVN a severe blow. He has brought the war to the cities and the towns and has inflicted damage and casualties on the population."[112] In the aftermath of the

Tet Offensive, President Johnson was of course anxious to send whatever additional forces were needed by his field commander in Vietnam to prevent a politically damaging defeat.

The Joint Chiefs of Staff, therefore, almost from the time that news of the Tet Offensive arrived in Washington, saw it not as a repudiation of past efforts in Vietnam but rather as an opportunity to obtain the number of troops they believed would allow them to achieve their basic objective: military victory. In this way, they thought they could convince the president to lift the hated restrictions on military operations that had hampered their military efforts to date.[113]

General Wheeler visited Saigon in February and returned with a recommendation that the president approve an additional 206,000 men by mobilizing the reserves. Some of these troops, according to Wheeler's plan, would be sent to Vietnam, whereas others would be used to reconstitute the strategic reserve in the United States. By stressing the dangers inherent in the Vietnamese battlefield, General Wheeler hoped to persuade the president and the new secretary of defense, Clark Clifford (known theretofore for his support of an aggressive American strategy in Vietnam), that the time had come for America to really try to "win" the war militarily.

The choices that General Wheeler presented to the president were not attractive. To accept General Wheeler's request for troops would mean a huge increase in the U.S. military commitment to South Vietnam, an even greater Americanization of the war, a large call-up of reserve forces, and a need to put the economy on a war footing—all during a presidential election year. The president understood, even if General Wheeler did not, that dissent, dissatisfaction, and disillusionment with the war was growing rapidly in the country. Yet to deny the request for troops would signal that an upper limit to the U.S. military commitment in South Vietnam finally had been reached—that the illusion of military victory had been discarded, even by the president himself, and that a satisfactory end to the war had become very unlikely.

On March 31, 1968, during a speech to the nation and the world, the president implied that he had, in fact, seen the pursuit of military victory in Vietnam for what it was—an illusion. During this televised speech, he announced four major decisions: (1) he would make only a token increase in the size of American forces in South Vietnam, repudiating the call from the Joint Chiefs and commanders for major reinforcements and the reconstitution of the strategic reserve; (2) he would make the expansion and improvement of the South Vietnamese forces the first priority of the U.S. effort in Vietnam; (3) he would order a halt to the bombing of North Vietnam north of the 20th parallel (thus sparing the major population centers), in the hope that Hanoi would move to peace talks immediately; and (4) he would not accept his party's nomination for another term as president.[114]

That speech is often remembered only for its dramatic and unexpected announcement that the president would not run for reelection. He said: "I shall not seek, and I will not accept, the nomination of my party for another term as your president."[115] In fact, however, Johnson's first three points constituted a great turning point, whereby the president decided to bring the U.S. commitment and strategy in Vietnam into line with political objectives and constraints, which had been present from the beginning but had been misunderstood and resented by his military advisers. The illusion of victory in Vietnam had now been fully exposed. Psychologically, U.S. withdrawal from Vietnam began at that moment, even though it took several more years to physically complete the task.

And back in Vietnam, notice was finally served to the government in Saigon that its theretofore open-ended claim on American resources and manpower was at an end. In the future, Saigon would have to shoulder an increasing share of responsibility for the war. The dangerous illusion of military victory *by the United States* was therefore dead. On April 4, Hanoi accepted President Johnson's offer to begin negotiations, which began in Paris on May 13, 1968. Paris, not South Vietnam, would henceforth become the venue in which the United States would pursue its objective, which the incoming Nixon administration would call "peace with honor" (not "peace through military victory").

Yet the Nixon administration fell victim to its own illusion, which it called "Vietnamization"—the idea that the United States could withdraw completely and that the South Vietnamese government would successfully defend itself against the NLF and North Vietnamese forces. Whereas during the Johnson years the military had blamed civilian leadership for American failure to defeat the enemy, Nixon administration officials blamed the U.S. Congress for refusing to grant it adequate funds to successfully pursue Vietnamization. As recently as September 1998, for example, former Secretary of State Henry Kissinger wrote:

> We did believe . . . that with adequate economic and military assistance, South Vietnam had a chance to preserve its independence. We did not consider it conceivable that the Congress would within two years at first drastically reduce and finally cut off aid to the country for whose freedom over 50,000 Americans had given their lives.[116]

But there is no evidence that the South Vietnamese would ever have been able to accomplish on their own what they failed to achieve with massive

American assistance. The level of congressional funding was irrelevant to the final outcome. The Nixon administration, like the Johnson administration before it, could not give the South Vietnamese the essential ingredient for success: genuine indigenous political legitimacy.

Conclusions: Implications of Rejecting the Illusion of Victory in Vietnam

The answer to the question posed in the title of this chapter—Was U.S. military victory in Vietnam a dangerous illusion?—is clear. *The achievement of a military victory by U.S. forces in Vietnam was indeed a dangerous illusion.* At no time, beginning with the increase of U.S. military advisers early in the Kennedy administration to the final withdrawal of American troops during the Nixon administration, would it have been possible at acceptable cost—in terms of American and Vietnamese lives lost and without the risk of war with China and/or Russia—to achieve a military victory in Vietnam. From 1964 forward, there did not exist an independent, noncommunist South Vietnam with the ability to provide services and security to the rural population of South Vietnam to thereby win over its loyalty. To put it bluntly, America's efforts to substitute for South Vietnam's government and army through force of arms were doomed to failure from the very beginning. Both Presidents Kennedy and Johnson at some point in the decisionmaking process stated that they would not send American boys to do what South Vietnamese boys should be doing. But for various reasons, and on the advice of their senior advisers, they did exactly that. And this nation found out, tragically, that 525,000 American soldiers—however courageous, however well-trained, -equipped, and -supplied—were not the answer to South Vietnam's political problems; the civil war—the Vietnamese "people's war"—could not be won by any external military force, no matter how powerful. From 1964 to 1973, the so-called Republic of Vietnam, that is, what we came to know as "South Vietnam," existed only because of the willingness of the United States to send soldiers to fight on its behalf. When U.S. support was removed, the inevitable results could have been predicted, whether in 1964, 1968, or 1973.

Americans saw the conflict in Vietnam as the aggression of one sovereign state (the North) against another (the South). But that aggression, from the viewpoints of Hanoi and the NLF, was nothing more than an attempt to complete the process of unifying Vietnam free from foreign rule and under a revolutionary government. In fact, unification was a process that had begun decades before, had already been won on the battlefield in the First Indochina War against the French, and had been promised in the armistice coming out of the 1954 Geneva Agreements.

American forces could win individual battles, but, as the French had discovered years before, military might could not overcome the ardor for unity and independence that burned in the hearts of the old nationalists of both North and South Vietnam. The American failure in Vietnam was not a failure caused by the limitations placed upon military action. Indeed, overwhelming American military power had been brought to bear, and the United States enjoyed complete control of the sea and air and had a striking superiority in material, weapons, and mobility on the ground. The American failure was caused by a lack of realization that military power could not solve what was fundamentally a political problem. Robert Komer, former special assistant to President Johnson and later director of the pacification program in South Vietnam, put it this way: "In the last analysis, the U.S. effort in Vietnam . . . failed largely because it could not sufficiently revamp or adequately substitute for a South Vietnamese leadership, administration, and armed forces inadequate to the task."[117]

Some retrospective analyses by American military leaders have recognized the mistake of seeking a military victory by making the war in Vietnam an *American* war; these analysts have made sober reappraisals of U.S. military strategy and leadership in Vietnam. Gen. Bruce Palmer Jr., for example, wrote this in 1984: "Not once during the war did the JCS advise the Commander-in-Chief or the Secretary of Defense that the strategy being pursued most probably would fail and that the U.S. would be unable to achieve its objectives."[118] And during a retrospective at the LBJ Library in Austin, Texas, in March 1991, General Westmoreland contrasted his view during the war with his understanding of the situation, given benefit of hindsight. "I felt at the time . . . that our hands were tied," he said. But, he added: "We have to give President Johnson credit for *not* allowing the war to expand geographically. One of his main objectives was to confine the war. He did not want it to spread."[119]

At any time after 1964, the United States could have attained peace by negotiating a settlement with Hanoi, or with the NLF, for a coalition government in the South that eventually would have sought unity with the North. Such a peace could have been achieved with far less harm to American international prestige and national security and domestic unity than was occasioned by a costly and eventually humiliating military debacle. CIA Director Richard Helms reported this very judgment to President Johnson in 1967, but Helms's memo was not circulated to the secretaries of state and defense or to the Joint Chiefs of Staff; neither was it acted upon by the president. One remarkable fact emerges clearly from a study of the American decisionmaking process during this nation's involvement in Vietnam: American strategic intelligence concerning North Vietnam was consistently and remarkably accurate, but senior military leaders seldom, if ever, believed or acted upon it.[120]

Sadly, the U.S. military and the American people may have learned the wrong lesson from the war. Many today believe that, in the future, American military forces should be used only where our advantage in firepower and mobility can be directed with overwhelming force against a massed enemy, thereby assuring victory; there will be no more gradualism, no more political limitations, no more sanctuaries, no more fighting without winning.

And thus today we can see the development of the so-called Vietnam syndrome, the idea that military force has limited utility and little public support in the conduct of American foreign policy in the modern world. "No more Vietnams!"—that has become the watchword for the military as well as for those generally opposed to U.S. military intervention anywhere.

On November 28, 1984, during the largest peacetime military buildup in American history, Secretary of Defense Caspar Weinberger enunciated six criteria to be applied for the use of American military force. These criteria in effect codified the Vietnam syndrome and seemed to be essential rules for avoiding another Vietnam in the future. These guidelines, of course, declared what not to do with military force rather than when to take bold and imaginative military action. The Weinberger criteria were thus designed to respond to criticisms of the conduct of the war by the American military. They ruled out the use of force except when there was a determination to achieve a military victory. They also demanded assurance of domestic support in advance of committing troops and called for clear political and military objectives.[121] These criteria constituted a hurdle to the use of force so high that Secretary of State George Shultz later remarked: "This was the Vietnam syndrome in spades, carried to an absurd level, and a complete abdication of the duties of leadership."[122]

The evolving global situation soon called into question the usefulness of Secretary Weinberger's criteria as a guide to action. After overseeing two major military operations in Panama and the Persian Gulf, Pres. George Bush reflected on the use of force during his December 1992 valedictory address at the United States Military Academy at West Point. The outgoing president argued against fixed rules and rigid criteria. Instead of relegating the use of force by the United States to a last resort in extreme circumstances, as Weinberger had seemed to do, Bush endorsed military action for important but less vital national purposes. The Bush criteria were put into action in the decisionmaking surrounding involvement in Bosnia and Somalia.

Through this evolution, new and more flexible criteria have been elaborated in current joint doctrine. For example, *Joint Publication 3.0: Doctrine for Joint Operations*, a 1995 document drafted by the Joint Chiefs of Staff, goes beyond earlier criteria by making significant distinctions among types of conflicts and alternative political goals. In war, the doctrine states, "the goal is to win as quickly and with as few casualties as possible, achieving national objectives and concluding hostilities on terms favorable to the United States." In "military operations other than war involving the use of force," however, the general goals are "to support national objectives, deter war, and return to a state of peace."

The document emphasizes that strategic direction for the employment of military forces comes from the National Command Authority through the chairman of the Joint Chiefs of Staff, and the necessity for military activities is "to be synchronized with other instruments of national power and focused on common national aims." The doctrine also places upon the National Command Authority, through the JCS chairman, the responsibility to ensure that "military objectives are defined, understood, and achievable."[123]

Thus, young leaders in the American military today, as they have moved into positions of leadership and responsibility in their respective services, have learned some of the lessons of Vietnam. They are transforming the American military, moving away from an inflexible focus on defeating the enemy at all costs toward open-mindedness, an outlook in which the services are more able and willing to undertake multiple, varied military and civil operations to achieve national objectives.

PREVENTING
DEADLY CONFLICT

Final Report
With Executive Summary

**CARNEGIE COMMISSION ON
PREVENTING DEADLY CONFLICT**

Can the lessons of the Vietnam War help reduce deadly conflict in the twenty-first century?

8

Learning from Tragedy: Lessons of Vietnam for the Twenty-First Century

Le Van Bang: *Each day, Ambassador Peterson and I must deal with the war. It is still the main fact of our U.S.-Vietnam relationship. We must try to get beyond it, but not to deny it, not to ignore the pain our people—yours and ours—still feel.*

Pete Peterson: *I agree. The pain is there. I still feel it. I am sure you do too, Mr. Ambassador. The point is: What do we* do *with that pain, that energy? I think we search for* lessons—*yours and ours—so that future wars of that magnitude can be prevented. It's what keeps us going, isn't it?*

Le Van Bang: *Yes—searching for something good and useful from the war. It is our responsibility.*

From the "Ambassadors' Dialogue" between the U.S. ambassador to Vietnam and the Vietnamese ambassador to the United States, November 17, 1997[1]

Introduction

This chapter represents the logical outcome of my approach to the history of the Vietnam War as I describe it in Chapter 1. In that introduction, I state that I believed the war was a tragedy for all concerned because it need not have turned out as it did—things might have been different, might have led to a better outcome, if Washington and Hanoi had not repeatedly missed opportunities to avoid the war or at least terminate it before the devastation reached tragic dimensions. The missed opportunities were *real*, I argued, and because they were real, because fallible human beings made mistakes along the way, and because events are *not* totally determined by outside pressures—no matter how intense they may be—lessons can be drawn and responsibly applied to efforts to avoid conflict now and in the twenty-first century. In other words, I believe that if things *might* have been different during the Vietnam War, then things *can* be different in the future, as long as we allow for conditions that may have changed due to the passage of time.

However, as I point out in Chapter 1, some historians deny that human actions can make such a difference.[2] This general view was stated forcefully at the July 1998 Bellagio conference by one of the participants who said, with regard to missed opportunities and lessons from Vietnam, "It is impossible to do good by doing history."[3]

That phrase—It is impossible to do good by doing history—has bothered me every since I heard it in Bellagio. It seems to imply that drawing lessons from a tragic war is some kind of pathetic exercise by do-gooders who, perhaps because they lack the professional credentials of academic historians, seek to draw lessons as a hobby taken up in retirement. I totally disagree with this point of view, and before getting into the missed opportunities and lessons themselves, I want to explain as clearly as I can why I believe that drawing lessons from this new history of the war is *necessary* and should be approached with a sense of urgency.

Toward the end of *In Retrospect* I tried to convey why I personally feel so strongly about drawing lessons from the war. "In the end," I said, "we must confront the fate of those Americans who served in Vietnam and never returned. . . . Let us learn from their sacrifice and, by so doing, validate and honor it."[4]

Let me give a more recent example to illustrate why I believe the search for lessons—for accurate, durable answers to the Vietnam War—is (or should be) at the core of any historical research on the war—the payoff, the ultimate justification for undertaking the research in the first place. On February 15, 1996, I gave a public lecture at Brown University, whose Watson Institute for International Studies had by then become the U.S. headquarters of the joint U.S.-Vietnamese project on the war. Toward the end of the question-and-answer period, a student asked me a question I have often been asked since the publication of *In Retrospect* in 1995: "Why," he asked, "did you not publish this book earlier?" I replied: "Because I did not know how to write chapter 11—'The Lessons of Vietnam.'" I said: "I simply could not answer the 'So what?' question—what did it all add up to? How could I justify opening the wounds of Vietnam all over again if I had nothing positive to contribute?"[5] I said that only when I had reached the point in my own thinking, where I was comfortable writing "The Lessons of Vietnam," did I feel I would be justified in moving ahead to tell the story, to write "the book I planned never to write," as I had called it.[6] The meeting was then adjourned and the exchanges with the audience ended.

At least I thought they had. As I was leaving the lectern, a large, middle-aged man in a jacket and cap that indicated he was a Vietnam veteran came charging toward the stage. Upon reaching the stage, he attempted to climb up and grab me but was prevented from doing so by security guards. But he shouted at me, letting loose with some portion of his pent-up rage, as he recounted it, at having been sent to Vietnam, having been made to suffer through the brutal fighting in Hue during the Tet Offensive of January–February 1968, having watched his close friends die miserable deaths, and he wanted to know: "For what?" It was heartbreaking. He wept. The 400 or so undergraduate students, most of whom were not yet born when the war ended in April 1975, looked on in horror and incomprehension at this outpouring of emotion.

I asked the security guards not to lead the man away, as they were attempting to do. I climbed down from the stage and asked him if he would like to discuss the war and what we ought to be doing about it now. He said he would. Gradually, our voices lowered and we had a serious conversation. The conversation lasted for about twenty minutes, or a little more. Finally, I said: "We both agree that the war was a tragedy. So hadn't we better do all we can to prevent something like the Vietnam War from ever occurring again? Shouldn't we," I asked him, "seek to give this gift—the gift of freedom from the horror of war that you have known all too well—to our children and grandchildren?" He said he agreed with this.

I dwell on the personal dimension here in an attempt to illustrate why I believe that, for the American people, drawing lessons from the Vietnam War is not just an option, not just a hobby of former officials such as myself. On the contrary, examples like this focus our minds on what I regard as the principal purpose of our historical work, all of it—the narrative history, the dialogues with the Vietnamese, the years of effort it has taken to create a new body of information that provides a uniquely balanced and comprehensive view of the war. At last, I believe, it is possible to begin to appeal to historical evidence, rather than intuition, regarding which views in our two nations, the United States and North Vietnam, were correct, and which incorrect, in their mutual assessments of each other. In other words, we now can say with much more confidence than ever before when mistakes were made. And it is just these mistakes and missed opportunities that point to *lessons*.

·   ·   ·

My coauthor of the body of this final chapter, Thomas Biersteker, made what was, in my opinion, a very constructive intervention at the June 1997 Hanoi conference. Asked to speak at the end of the discussions about the lessons of the war, professor Biersteker began by listing what he felt were the failures of *both* sides, evidence for which, he said, permits us for the first time to draw lessons from the war based on authoritative knowledge, rather than speculation and intuition, about North Vietnamese decisions. He stated why he believed the dialogues in Hanoi proved that both sides must bear some responsibility for the ubiquitous missed opportunities discussed during the three previous days.[7]

Professor Biersteker's statement was followed by a long period of total silence, which was finally broken by the chairman of the session, Ambassador Dao Huy Ngoc, who added: "Personally, I agree with many of the points that Professor Biersteker raised."[8] This drew smiles of approval from the participants on both sides. It was clear that in the future, any discussion of the failure to seize opportunities for peace, and of lessons to be drawn from such failures, would require a discussion of the responsibilities falling on the shoulders of the leaders and the people of both the United States and Vietnam.

Professor Biersteker and I have expanded on the remarks he made in Hanoi in the following section. I will conclude with some remarks on specific lessons I believe follow from the principal failures of both sides.

Fundamental Failures by the United States and North Vietnam

What the Dialogues Reveal

There are many ways to characterize the failures on all sides that resulted in what we in the United States call the "Vietnam War." During the war and since, many have found it impossible to avoid assigning blame for it, thereby attempting to explain the failure by *naming* those deemed to be the principal culprits. There is no need here to recite the list of those held responsible by various constituencies. Suffice it to say that one conclusion to be drawn from the U.S.-Vietnamese dialogues is that there is plenty of blame to go around, if blaming is to be done, not just in the United States and South Vietnam but in North Vietnam as well. This was recognized by the American and the Vietnamese participants in the dialogues.

In fact, the dialogues themselves reveal what seems to have been one of the central failures—perhaps *the* central failure—in both the United States and North Vietnam: a failure of *empathy*. Each side fundamentally misread the mindset of its enemy. The fact that they became and remained bitter enemies for a quarter-century is testament to the depth of the misreading, the utter inability of leaders in Washington and Hanoi to penetrate the thoughts, perspectives, and emotions of those on the other side. A classic statement of this phenomenon, empathy, is due to Michael Ignatieff:

> What is required, for the higher empathy, is something more than the comprehension of an alien argument. It means the intuitive grasp of the particular vision of the universe which lies at the heart of an enemy's thought.[9]

But this is just what was lacking in the U.S. and North Vietnamese comprehensions of each other: the "higher empathy," the ability to think and feel like the enemy.[10] And, of course, all attempts at persuading the other were done in vain—until the tragedy had reached monumental proportions.

FAILURE TO UNDERSTAND EACH OTHER

One of the most striking features of the dialogues is the profundity of mutual ignorance and its dangerous consequences. The level of ignorance that existed on both sides of the conflict, and in many ways still persists, was astounding. As Chester Cooper commented on the first day of the June 1997 conference, American ignorance of Asia was such that "we did not know what we did not know. And that was one of our problems when we got involved here in Vietnam."[11] Later in the same session, focusing on the mindsets of both sides during the early 1960s, Nicholas Katzenbach suggested that the ignorance was mutual and that "one of the reasons for the misconceptions in these various mindsets comes from the fact that . . . each country is focused on its own problems."[12] There is a natural tendency for a party to a conflict to focus disproportionately on its *own* problems and, therefore, to mistakenly attribute the actions and motivations of others to factors affecting one's own situation—but not the adversary's.

In every way, American ignorance of the history, language, and culture of Vietnam was immense. The chapters in this book are filled with illustrations of that ignorance. Even Pres. Ngo Dinh Diem of South Vietnam recognized that weakness. He told American journalist Marguerite Higgins that it was a delusion for the Americans to believe that blindly copying Western methods might work in Vietnam: "The Americans are breaking Vietnamese psychology and they don't even know they are doing it."[13] Americans in Vietnam and those concerned with Vietnam were mostly like Graham Greene's Quiet American: "Impregnably armoured by his good intentions and his ignorance."[14] Vietnamese ignorance of the United States and U.S. decisionmaking was at least as great. American participants in the U.S.-Vietnamese dialogues learned that most of Hanoi's direct information about the United States during the 1950s and 1960s came from international news agencies and weekly newsmagazines—not from sources like *The New York Times*, and certainly not from personal interactions with American leaders and officials. As a result, leaders in Hanoi had virtually no knowledge of the policy discussions on Vietnam in Washington during the mid-1960s. Since they didn't know which options the Americans were considering, they were helpless to affect any of them in ways they desired.

This profound mutual ignorance encouraged each side to project onto the other motivations and objectives that had little, if any, semblance to reality. Indeed, each projected onto the other motivations and intentions that ultimately proved to be tragically wrong. The U.S. leadership after World War II greatly feared the hegemonic impulses of the Soviet Union in Eastern Europe, even in Western Europe. Since it assumed that all communist countries operated according to the same logic (and perhaps even received orders from Moscow), the United States proceeded to project those presumed impulses onto Vietnam, assuming that Hanoi *must* be acting as a pawn of a global communist movement. Yet as Vietnamese scholar Luu Doan Huynh said pointedly to the Americans during one of the dialogues:

> If I may say so, you were not only wrong, but you had, so to speak, lost your minds. Vietnam a part of the Chinese expansionist game in Asia? For anyone who knows the history of Indochina, this is incomprehensible.[15]

Hanoi in and of itself was never a strategic threat to Indochina; neither did it intend to be a pawn used by China to knock over the dominoes in Indochina. U.S. leaders, however, tended to see their interests in Vietnam in a larger context dominated by the Cold War struggle between the United States and the Soviet Union. The stakes for the United States, therefore, appeared to be extremely high. In the worst-case analyses of the United States at the time, Vietnam was assumed to be a communist puppet doing the bidding of its friends in Moscow and Beijing throughout Southeast Asia. The American obsession with the global chessboard of the Cold War blinded leaders in Washington to the decisive importance of Vietnamese nationalism and the desire of the Vietnamese people for reunification.

Another unfortunate projection made by Washington was in its belief that a degree of centralized control—remarkably similar to that in Washington—existed in Hanoi's decisionmaking process. This was almost completely erroneous. As discussed in Chapter 5, it also had disastrous consequences. The United States, with its state-of-the-art technology and immense resources, made its decisions in a context entirely different from that of Hanoi's leaders or those of the National Liberation Front (NLF) deep in the jungles of Vietnam.

But projection in Vietnam was a two-way street. Hanoi, in effect, projected onto the United States a kind of colonial mode of operation not significantly different from that of the French, who had occupied the country for more than a century. However, unlike the French, Americans were ambivalent about their global role and were not colonialists in the way that the French could be characterized. Had Hanoi understood this—had it achieved a more empathetic understanding of U.S. fears and motivations—it could have appealed to a strong set of American motives emphasizing self-determination and anti-colonialism. But Hanoi did *not* understand this.

Luu Doan Huynh suggested during the course of our dialogues that the Americans should have read between the lines of Hanoi's pronouncements. Chester Cooper responded by saying that, alas, this is almost never done, especially when what is *in* the lines is so adversarial.

As this book has made clear, there are many—too many—examples of opportunities that were missed. On the issue of a neutral solution in Saigon, it is clear that the United States overestimated the extent to which Hanoi was either intent on, or capable of, subverting a neutral coalition government in Saigon. Misjudgments by Washington played critical roles in the American misassessment of the attacks in the Gulf of Tonkin in August 1964 and at Pleiku in February 1965. In both cases, the Americans concluded that deliberate attempts were made by Hanoi to escalate the war by specifically targeting Americans. Yet as was made clear by the Vietnamese during our dialogues, they conducted the war according to a decentralized command-and-control structure, and neither attack had been ordered by Hanoi. Both were actions of local commanders, taken for essentially local reasons. But of course all this becomes significant when one recalls that ROLLING THUNDER, the sustained bombing of North Vietnam, followed the Pleiku attack—was triggered by it, in fact.

The inability of Washington to understand the relationship between northern and southern communists contributed to profound American misjudgments. The NLF insurgency was never as consistent, predictable, or controlled as those of the regular North Vietnamese forces after they entered the war in significant numbers in 1965. The United States often failed to distinguish between them, usually attributing more control to Hanoi than actually existed.

Other American misjudgments include the widespread belief in Washington that bombing the North would weaken the will of the Hanoi government to prosecute the war, a misjudgment that flew in the face of events the Americans should have been aware of, such as the way Hitler's bombing of England stiffened the will of the British during World War II. The exchange between Col. Herbert Schandler and Col. Quach Hai Luong was instructive in this respect. Col. Schandler commented: "As you know, our strategy for the air war was based on the belief that we could destroy the will of the people in North Vietnam to continue to support the war in the South."[16] Col. Quach Hai Luong replied: "Every time you bombed the North, we said, we know we are succeeding in the South."[17] In this way, Hanoi's reverse psychology completely frustrated Washington's attempt to break its will, arguing successfully to its people that the U.S. bombing, whatever else it may have implied, meant that Hanoi and its allies were winning the war in the South.

Many retrospective analyses of the war focus on American misjudgments. But misjudging adversaries, exaggerating dangers, and misinterpreting behavior were not restricted to the American side during the war in Vietnam. The Vietnamese participants in the dialogues were initially reluctant to admit any misjudgments by Hanoi. But they came eventually to see that Hanoi's belief that the United States was a colonialist power, like the French, was wrong. This misjudgment significantly colored Vietnamese perceptions of American actions from a very early point, probably from 1950 onward.

Most Vietnamese participants in the dialogues also came to realize that the United States was probably *not* keen to carry out a military intervention in Vietnam in 1954. Our Vietnamese colleagues suggested, in fact, that they had been "misled" by their "friends" (i.e., the Chinese and Soviets) into believing the United States was intent on intervening. The Vietnamese communists, it appears, did not understand that the United States had refused to intervene to save the French at Dien Bien Phu in May 1954.[18]

Hanoi's failure in July 1962 to inform its foreign minister, Ung Van Khiem, of its own neutralist intentions in Saigon (see Chapter 4), is one of the most telling and unfortunate of its omissions. It was such a monumental error that, in hindsight, it is difficult to categorize—an oversight, perhaps, a flaw in the decisionmaking processes? In any case, it now appears to mark a kind of turning point, beyond which it would become progressively more difficult for the Americans to convince themselves that Hanoi was actually interested in a neutral solution and that such a solution might provide what in the Johnson administration was often referred to as a "decent interval" for the United States to withdraw.

Another significant failure by Hanoi was its inability to preempt a U.S. escalation of the conflict during the 1960s. As described in Chapter 5, one of the key strategic goals of Party Secretary Le Duan was to overthrow the

Saigon government *before* the Americans could take over the war effort in the South. Resolutions passed at the Ninth Party Plenum in December 1963 to this effect reflected a major misjudgment of U.S. capabilities and intentions. The United States could and eventually did take over the war effort, largely in the belief that Hanoi and the NLF had already decided to escalate the war. In less than a year, the American military intervention had begun.

These misjudgments prevented Washington and Hanoi from finding an effective strategy either for peace or for war. In Chapter 3, our Vietnamese colleagues recount just how ignorant they were during the immediate postwar period of the elements of diplomacy, as practiced by big powers like the United States. Neither was either side able to comprehend the signals being sent by the other, based as they were on fundamentally different kinds of strategic calculations. In this context of mutually incomprehensible signaling, it is not difficult to see why the secret contacts between 1965 and 1968 did not succeed in moving to the parties to the negotiating table. When Washington attempted to signal its good intentions via a bombing halt, Hanoi interpreted the gesture as an attempt to check its pulse, believing that the Americans would read any sign of weakness as a signal to go for the kill. In turn, Hanoi then reliably signaled its intention to keep fighting, to not surrender—usually by raising the level of support heading north to south down the Ho Chi Minh Trail—which the Americans read as an aggressive and defiant attempt to escalate the war to a still higher level. The Americans then responded by raising the intensity of the bombing—and so on in a spiral of escalation. The incomprehension seems to have been total and absolutely consistent. Washington and Hanoi, in other words, interpreted each other's behavior in this way very nearly 100 percent of the time and were thus wrong nearly 100 percent of the time, a remarkable statistic given the length of time we are considering, roughly early 1965 to late 1967.

Mutual ignorance in Vietnam, as we have seen, fueled inappropriate projections, creating systematic and repetitive misjudgments in a spiral of escalation leading to tragedy for all sides. The fundamental enemy—the root cause of the agony over the Vietnam War—was mutual ignorance, the inability of Washington and Hanoi to penetrate the outlook of the other side. Where facts are lacking, fears and fantasies often rush in. In Vietnam, the fears and fantasies of Washington and Hanoi combined to produce a self-fulfilling prophecy of destruction on a scale unimagined at the outset. Ultimately, victory tasted only slightly less ashen in Hanoi than defeat tasted in Washington.

The Vietnam tragedy demonstrates that empathy is not a luxury but a necessity in the conduct of foreign affairs if one is to avoid raising the risk of disaster fueled by misunderstanding, misjudgment, and misattribution.

Empathy implies a higher level of understanding and comprehension than is provided by books and briefing papers alone. Even linguistic competence in a language, as difficult as Vietnamese was (and remains) for most Americans, does not guarantee empathetic understanding of another culture or respect for another outlook on the world. It requires, above all, an effort to experience the world from the perspective of one whose outlook is radically different. This has proven particularly difficult for the United States, due to its rise in global dominance in the latter half of the twentieth century. And for this very reason U.S. leaders and citizens should seek to counter their triumphalist urges, their belief that everyone should establish a multiparty system and accept our mores. If Americans do not do this, it seems inevitable that Vietnams—tragedies rooted in mutual misunderstanding—will recur.

Failure to Communicate with Each Other

One of the most striking features of the U.S.-Vietnamese dialogues regarding the negotiating process—from Geneva in 1954 through the secret diplomatic initiatives between 1965 and 1967—is the mutual, retrospective astonishment at the lack of high-level contacts between the adversaries. Former officials on both sides cannot quite explain why one side or the other did not simply initiate direct discussions between leaders. The overuse of intermediaries by the United States, and the virtual absence of initiatives of any kind from Hanoi, can of course be explained to an extent: Washington did not know how best to contact such a secretive, communist country as North Vietnam; Hanoi, fearing it would appear weak to the infinitely more powerful United States, wanted the bigger power to initiate negotiations. Luu Van Loi compared the two countries to characters in a Victorian novel, each side being interested but, for various reasons, unable or unwilling to expose its real feelings and intentions to the other.

Intermediaries, however well-intentioned, were unreliable, often misrepresented the views of the protagonists, and ultimately proved to be ineffective channels of communication. In addition, intermediaries were not used creatively: Most were principally carriers of information; few, if any, were consulted for their insights about how to negotiate or to deal with existing adversaries. Raymond Aubrac, in whose house Ho Chi Minh had once lived, was unaccountably not asked by Washington (or Hanoi) to do anything other than carry the mail between Ho Chi Minh and Pham Van Dong, in Hanoi, and Henry Kissinger, the U.S. contact in Paris.[19]

Not all missed opportunities would have been avoided had there been direct, high-level contacts, of course. But direct contacts would certainly have reduced the probability of the sort of repeated major misunderstandings that characterized the feeble attempts of Washington and Hanoi to communicate. In hindsight, the participants in the dialogues were almost amazed at themselves and their former adversaries in equal measure for not having initiated the kind of meaningful dialogue during the war that we have established retrospectively during the past several years.

A second kind of failure by Washington and Hanoi to communicate lay in the reluctance of each to come forward with some kind of significant unilateral gesture that might have broken the stalemate of adversaries locked in an action-reaction dynamic. Each side was caught in a web of retaliatory moves in response to the last action of its adversary, and each was afraid to make the first move—Washington, because it felt that its pressure would eventually cause Hanoi to give way, Hanoi, because it worried about appearing weak to the Americans. The only way out of such a situation would have been a unilateral gesture of some substance, with enough time to be perceived as genuine.

A common thread linking all the failures to communicate is each side's failure to understand the recent history of the other—*as the other side understood it*—and the implications of that history for their attempts to communicate. Neither side, in other words, understood what *lessons* the other took away from significant events in which both participated. The Washington-Hanoi interpretations of each other after Geneva 1954 were merely knee-jerk responses, not to reality but to the worst fears regarding possible motives.

In Hanoi, for example, Geneva symbolized the dangers of accepting compromises that leave one vulnerable to the broken promises of ostensible friends. Accepting the 17th parallel as the *temporary* dividing line between North and South was an acceptable compromise at the time, because Hanoi was confident that reunification would follow in two years, in part because they believed the Chinese and Soviets would guarantee it. The leadership in Hanoi was especially careful, therefore, to avoid giving the appearance of violating the agreement.

Washington saw the resistance to Diem's actions in the South as evidence that Hanoi had simply found a different way to carry out the wishes of Beijing and Moscow—via guerrillas in this new entity called South Vietnam. Hanoi's leaders, knowing this was preposterous, refused to believe that the Americans actually believed it. But they *did* believe it, and Hanoi's failure to recognize this was a costly misjudgment. And leaders in Washington, knowing they had no interest in directly colonizing Vietnam, tossed aside as propaganda the endless stream of pronouncements from Hanoi and from the southern resistance movement condemning what Article 1 of the NLF Founding Platform called the "disguised (or camouflaged) colonialist regime" of Diem.[20] American officials refused to believe the Vietnamese communists believed it. But they did. In this way, collective monologues— rather than mature, successful communication via dialogue—led to disaster.

FAILURES OF GREAT AND SMALL POWERS

During the course of our U.S.-Vietnamese dialogues, there emerged a consensus as to one of the main reasons Washington and Hanoi were so ignorant of each other and failed on so many occasions to communicate. It was this: It is inherently difficult, though not impossible, for great powers and small countries to understand one another. Leaders in Washington saw every event in Vietnam, no matter how apparently inconsequential, as having possible global strategic significance. This is part of the so-called burden of hegemony that must be borne by a country like the United States, which is, as Joseph Nye has said, "bound to lead."[21] But in Hanoi, all events were interpreted according to whether they appeared to raise or lower the odds of achieving the principal objective of the government: reunification of Vietnam under the leadership of Hanoi. These are not so much incompatible as they are totally unrelated frameworks for understanding events in Southeast Asia. And much of the difference can be accounted for by the different perspectives of the two countries: great power and small country.

The Vietnam War was, in important respects, a failure of American unilateralism. The United States acted virtually alone after 1954, despite the creation of the Southeast Asia Treaty Organization (SEATO), John Foster Dulles's fig leaf of a multilateral organization. President Eisenhower had told President Kennedy the day before Kennedy's inauguration that he— Eisenhower—preferred unilateral U.S. intervention in Vietnam to any kind of neutral arrangement. This was typical of Washington's cavalier attitude toward involving others in its schemes in Southeast Asia.

The unilateral impulse intruded again in 1963, in response to French Pres. de Gaulle's offer to try to broker a neutralist arrangement in Vietnam, perhaps extending across all of Southeast Asia.[22] De Gaulle knew something about Vietnam. Moreover, the French, as a signatory to the SEATO treaty, carrying the same obligations as the United States, should have figured doubly important in Washington's consultative process. But they didn't. Thus, there was in essence *no* consultative process worthy of the phrase.

A second failure, rooted in the natural arrogance of the very powerful, was Washington's inability to appreciate the limitations of its high-tech warfare capability in confronting a "people's war" (the Vietnamese conception of armed resistance). Two aspects of this particular failure stand out: First, it seems to have been difficult for leaders in Washington and Saigon to even consider the possibility of suffering defeat at the hands of Vietnamese communists, whose war material was dwarfed by that of the United States; and second, U.S. civilian and military leaders did not anticipate—probably they could not even imagine—a people and an organization like the Vietnamese Communist Party, whose members and allies were willing to absorb horrific casualty rates yet carry the fight to the Americans.

A third failure of the American superpower in Vietnam reflects, perhaps, more arrogance than either of the first two: the erroneous belief that so-called nation-building is possible through the use of military force and economic support. The Vietnam experience proves that this is untrue. South Vietnam was a "failed state," virtually from its inception, as discussed at length in Chapters 3 and 7. Washington failed to understand that such a flawed state cannot be saved by external military forces, no matter how well-armed.

A fourth failure of the U.S. superpower is the failure to pursue in its foreign policy the democratic ideals it preaches and practices in its domestic political arrangements. One might have thought that the United States, given its history, would have been the last country in the world to sanction and sustain a royalist despot like Diem. Clearly this was what the Vietnamese participants in our dialogues believed followed from their reading of U.S. history and U.S. values, at least as proclaimed, from Jefferson onward. In effect, leaders in Washington, in supporting a despot, betrayed their own stated principles, in the name of fighting communism.

Fifth, and finally, American leaders failed to understand the tenuous relationship that often exists between the application of military force and the achievement of political or diplomatic objectives. Even during the Cold War, American citizens only occasionally felt themselves physically at risk, for example, during the Berlin crisis of 1961 or the Cuban missile crisis of 1962. Thus, it is perhaps not surprising that Americans, accustomed to the application of force elsewhere but unfamiliar with having it applied to themselves directly, should overestimate the political possibilities of using military force. Americans may be singularly unable to predict or understand the degree to which a people can and will resist having their political will bent through the application of military power.

One is reminded of this American failure in rereading the seemingly endless reports and requests made by Gen. William Westmoreland to Washington between 1964 and 1968. The point at which the application of force is predicted to bend, then break, the political will of the enemy constantly recedes, like a mirage in the desert, just beyond the horizon. In fact, it was a mirage, an illusion. At no time during Westmoreland's tenure in Saigon, it now appears, was there the slightest chance of reaching the famed crossover point beyond which the fortunes of the Vietnamese communists would begin to decline, leading them eventually to sue for peace.

Throughout the Vietnam War, Vietnamese communists, northern and southern, became famous the world over for their tenacity, their iron will, their willingness to suffer grievously in pursuit of a national ideal. They were a formidable opponent by any standard. Yet looking back on the events that brought such devastation to Vietnam, it is clear today that it was not necessary for the Vietnamese to have suffered to the extent they did. As the results of our analyses in the preceding chapters attest, the conviction and bravery of Hanoi and the NLF were not matched by their capacity to understand and manipulate the perceptions and, hence, the decisions of leaders in Washington. Their diplomacy seems, in retrospect, unimaginative given the stakes for the Vietnamese themselves. They gave little if any thought to the consequences of conveying to Washington, however inadvertently, the image of communist fanatics bent on conquering Southeast Asia on behalf of the world communist movement. They did almost nothing to dissuade Washington of the error of its perception. The results were tragic.

Hanoi proved unable to prevent the escalation of the war during the 1960s. In part this was because it did nothing to dissuade the United States from the view that the creation of the NLF in 1960 was an integral part of the Maoist strategy of creating and supporting united fronts for liberation movements led by communist parties throughout Southeast Asia. Similarly, if Hanoi really wanted Washington to believe that its attack in Laos at Nam Tha in early May 1962 was an attempt to increase the likelihood of a neutral settlement in South Vietnam, it should have communicated its intentions much more clearly and directly. And the North Vietnamese seemed all too ready to believe the worst about the United States—for example, that Washington was implacably bent on enslaving Vietnam—even when the source of these dark scenarios was located in Beijing. They did little or nothing to develop independent sources of information about Washington. Consequently, their strategies for dealing with the United States tended to become self-fulfilling prophecies.

All the American participants in the dialogues have, at one point or another, lamented the tight secrecy, the lack of openness, in which Hanoi and the NLF kept the details, even the general outlines, of their decisionmaking. The frustrating, fruitless exchanges connected with the many failed negotiating initiatives are filled with what appeared in Washington to be hair-splitting, obfuscating, deceptive, and ultimately uncommunicative messages from Hanoi. Nguyen Co Thach addressed this point at the June 1997 Hanoi conference this way:

> This implication of our peculiar history has not been sufficiently empha-sized here, I think—we are a small country that has always had large coun-tries trying to defeat us. With so many conflicts, secrecy has become a major part of our national security. You have your nuclear weapons. We have our secrecy. [Laughter.][23]

Nguyen Co Thach was, of course, correct to link secrecy with centuries of Vietnamese attempts to retain independence while surrounded by much larger powers. But some Vietnamese participants in the dialogues learned that openness need not be a source of weakness. Indeed, it can be a source of strength, a means to forge bonds among nations.

The Vietnamese people have contended with all of the major forces of the twentieth century—European imperialism, Japanese militarism, American global containment, Maoist internationalism, and Soviet hegemonism. They have survived all of them largely through sheer force of will, tenacity, and intense nationalism. Because of this history, the ostensible benefits of polit-ical openness are bound to be regarded with skepticism. Nguyen Co Thach's statement is perhaps a characteristic response of this sort.

Nevertheless, the next challenge confronting Vietnam is the challenge of globalization, for which there are few alternatives to openness and greater transparency. In this sense, the U.S.-Vietnamese dialogues during the past several years may have contributed to the political opening of Vietnam by providing a forum and agenda for an open reexamination—by both Ameri-cans and Vietnamese—of our shared, tragic recent history.

FAILURE OF U.S. DECISIONMAKING PROCESSES

The U.S.-Vietnamese dialogues have amply revealed the extent to which decisions in Washington and Hanoi were based on faulty understandings and information. The dialogues did not, however, focus explicitly on the decisionmaking *processes* of either side. Upon reflection, it is as important to understand the shortcomings of decisionmaking processes as it is to under-stand the failures they produce.

Although we have learned a great deal from the conversations with our Vietnamese colleagues, we are only beginning to understand the outlines of the decisionmaking processes within Vietnam during the war. Therefore, in this section we will concentrate on an assessment of the failures of U.S. decisionmaking processes, because we know them better and from firsthand experience. We hope our Vietnamese associates will be motivated to reflect similarly on the shortcomings of their own decisionmaking processes.

In the United States, decisionmaking was not organized to deal effectively with the extraordinarily complex range of political and military issues involved. Policymakers did not raise fundamental questions, did not address basic issues about policy choices, and did not recognize their failure to do so. In particular, they failed to address four basic issues: (1) the severity of the threat to U.S. security (i.e., the likelihood of a series of falling dominoes); (2) the requirements for and the likelihood of realizing a stable South Vietnamese political structure and an effective South Vietnamese military effort (essential as a foundation for U.S. intervention); (3) the potential effectiveness of U.S. military intervention in a conflict for which our experience left us ill-prepared; and (4) the appropriate channel and form of a U.S. diplomatic effort, once senior policymakers realized that the United States could not win militarily. These fundamental questions were not fully explored when the United States initially intervened, and they were not reviewed periodically as conditions changed during ensuing years.

This lack of reflection among U.S. policymakers stems from three sources. First, unless special arrangements are made, there is rarely enough time for considered reflection and debate in foreign policymaking. Second, there is a lack of institutional memory within the government and a recurring tendency for new officeholders to reject the insights of the past in favor of new ventures and initiatives. Third, the incremental nature of decisionmaking about intervention in Vietnam never allowed policymakers an opportunity to step back and evaluate the significance of what appeared at the time to be small, almost inconsequential decisions. Policymakers today need to learn from the past and find the time to identify and debate fundamental issues involved in regional conflicts, which are likely to be as plentiful as in the past and at least as dangerous. Conflicts like those between India and Pakistan, the actions of North Korea, or the ongoing conflicts in the Balkans, come to mind. As long as fundamental issues remain unresolved, it will be important to find a way to review and reassess policy options.

In the case of Vietnam, deep-seated disagreements among the U.S. president's most trusted advisers about how to proceed were neither surfaced nor resolved. One way to address this problem would be to create a small team of officials at the highest levels to meet regularly with the president for open-ended, uninterrupted discussions when the use of military force is being considered. Institutionalizing opposition within decisionmaking processes would be an alternative way to incorporate different views about the use of force. Some countries have routinely included members of the political opposition as part of official diplomatic delegations, not only to co-opt them but also to add their perspectives and different voices to official delegations.

The post–Cold War world is at least as complex as the world of the early 1960s, yet it is by no means clear that decisionmaking is organized any more effectively to address the extraordinarily complex range of today's political and military issues. The relative simplicity of the Cold War has given way to an emerging international system in which even the identity of the core actors has become fluid and unclear. The crisis in Bosnia illustrated the fluidity of actors and the difficulty of coordinating political and military policy. Yet core decisionmakers involved in the Dayton Accords, the U.S.-led talks in Ohio that led to a peace settlement in the former Yugoslavia, were rarely able to find the time while in office to reflect on historical foundations, ask fundamental questions, and address basic issues about policy choices. Moreover, the breakdown in foreign policy bipartisanship within the U.S. political system has made decisionmaking even more uncertain and complex.

Throughout the course of the Vietnam War, the United States government failed to engage the American public in a frank, full discussion before initiating its fateful actions. Moreover, once it became engaged, the U.S. government failed to explain fully its logic and rationale, and ultimately it lost the unity and support of the people. Before engaging in wars, limited or otherwise, the American people must understand the difficulties they will face; the American military must know and accept the constraints under which they will operate; and the American leadership (and their constituents) must be prepared to cut losses and withdraw if it appears that limited objectives cannot be achieved at acceptable risks and costs.

The principles that underlie the application of military force by the nations of the world should be subject to intense debate, over a period of years, within each nation, among great powers, and in the councils of international organizations, as discussed more fully below. Other than national defense, there is no internationally shared understanding of justifications for the use of military force. However, it is clear that some interventions, such as that in

Bosnia, are more legitimate and sustainable internationally because of their multilateral nature.

A particular failure of U.S. decisionmaking during the Vietnam War was the poor coordination of political and military decisions. After 1965, there was a significant disjuncture between U.S. political and military actions in Vietnam. The bombing of the North was initially introduced to achieve a military end; later, it was associated with attempts to move to negotiations, a political goal. However, as we have seen from the dialogues and other material in Chapter 6, the bombing missions in the North often were not coordinated with U.S. diplomatic overtures. At least as serious was the U.S. failure even to offer hints about what such negotiations might lead to.

FAILURE OF EMPATHY AND MISSED OPPORTUNITIES

Reflecting on the project and conferences described in this book, it should be overwhelmingly clear that one can no longer credibly write the history of the Vietnam War, or attempt to articulate its lessons, from the vantage point only of Washington or only that of Hanoi. The U.S.-Vietnamese dialogues show: It simply is not possible to understand the tragedy by analyzing the standpoint of only one or the other. Multiple perspectives need to be discussed openly by both parties in an effort to come to an uncoerced consensus about contested issues.

In fact, one way to judge the results of the dialogues is to compare the degree of empathetic understanding between U.S. and Vietnamese participants *now*, as we reexamine the war, and *then*, during the events we have been discussing. The events themselves were, as we have seen, filled with examples of monumental misunderstandings, projections, and other failures of assessment and judgment. But today, after seven sets of meetings in Vietnam and in Europe, the U.S. and Vietnamese participants in the dialogues have reached a remarkable degree of consensus regarding what went wrong and why.

During our dialogues we identified two categories of missed opportunities, which were different not in kind but rather in degree: *strategic* missed opportunities—possibilities seeming to require fundamental changes in the approach of one side or the other; and *tactical* missed opportunities—possibilities that were not realized due to bad timing, incorrect information, and so on. The failed attempts on both sides are filled with examples of both.

Revisiting the war in Vietnam after so many years has been sobering. It brings back bitter memories and strong emotions on both sides, as the participants recall what they believed at the time and discover how mistaken beliefs were connected to unfolding events. As the late Nguyen Co Thach observed quietly during a lunch between sessions at the June 1997 conference, "We both paid dearly for our misunderstandings." What he did not say, because he did not have to say it to all of us who already felt it, was this: Now—at this fortunate moment when both documentary materials and the memories of former officials can inform our dialogues on the Vietnam War—now is the time to face our past together so that those who follow us can learn from our experiences.

Conclusions

In the introduction to this chapter, I refer to a question put to me by a Brown University student in February 1996. He asked why I hadn't written *In Retrospect* earlier. I told him that I published the memoir only after I felt I could responsibly write the chapter titled "The Lessons of Vietnam." Yet I was handicapped in my effort to draw definitive lessons from Vietnam—and I knew it—due to my ignorance of the decisionmaking process in Hanoi and the way Hanoi's decisions may have been influenced by NLF supporters in the South and by their allies in Moscow and Beijing. I discovered I was far from alone in my lack of understanding of communist decisionmaking. And as I got further into the research for *In Retrospect*, particularly regarding the lessons that others in the West had drawn from the war, I began to appreciate the truth of a comment made by Joseph Lelyveld of *The New York Times*. "When we talk about Vietnam," he said (referring to Americans), "we are seldom talking about the country of that name or the situation of the people who live there. Usually we are talking about ourselves. Probably we always were."[24]

I said in my memoir that I believed we were wrong. But now—having thought about the lessons of our failures in Vietnam for a quarter-century or more; and having learned in more than three years of dialogues with the Vietnamese that the failures I had identified were, in fact, failures—I believe it is time to try to re-state the lessons of the Vietnam War as concisely as I know how.

Some will say that I oversimplify history in so doing, and they will be correct. But the lessons are not meant to stand alone; they must be understood in the context of everything in this book that precedes them. Others may say that I have stated the wrong lessons, and we can argue about that. But if we are to carry out the responsibilities discussed in my introduction to this chapter, I believe we must try to state what we have learned in capsule form, as well as at book length. If we were to boil down our findings, what is it that we most want to pass on to the citizens of the twenty-first century?

I will list six lessons. I am not certain that the list is exhaustive or that this is the only possible arrangement; it may not even be the best. In the Preface, I quote historian Pieter Geyl, who said, "History is an argument without end." So too, I believe, is the drawing of lessons from history. My hope is that the following list leads to reflection on the lessons of Vietnam for the twenty-first century.

1. Understand the Mindset of Your Adversary.

Our mutual ignorance was mind-boggling. That much, however, had been said before. What the dialogues demonstrate in great detail—over a host of issues, events, and decades—is the direct causal connection between the mutual ignorance and the escalation to confrontation, then to war, then to the frustrating and tragic inability of either side to arrest the momentum toward tragedy. The misjudgments, misreadings, mistaken estimations, and other misunderstandings are now exposed for all to see and acknowledged by scholars and former officials from both Vietnam and the United States.

What about the United States today and in the future? Do we understand the mindset of Islamic fundamentalists? Or are we more likely to disparage as simply "irrational" a mindset that leads to suicide bombings of innocent people, such as occurred during the summer of 1998 in Nairobi and Dar es Salaam? Or that leads to death threats to émigré authors like Salman Rushdie? Are we confident that we understand the workings of a mind like that of Saddam Hussein, who has demonstrated his willingness to take risks that seem far greater than any possible benefit he might attain? What about the mind of Kim Jong Il and his fellow North Korean leaders? Or do we, even now, during the post–Cold War era, believe we adequately understand Russian Slavophiles or the 1.25 billion Chinese people influenced by a history going back thousands of years? Or Hindu nationalists in India's Bharatiya Janata Party (BJP), who, on May 11, 1998, openly tested a nuclear weapon, followed by Pakistan shortly thereafter? Do we understand all these mindsets to the extent necessary to head off crises before they become catastrophic events? I think not. We remain ignorant at our peril.

2. Communicate with Your Adversary at a High Level.

Remarkably, I failed to address this among the failures listed in *In Retrospect*. The more I ponder the dialogues and supporting material in Chapter

6—on the failed attempts to move to negotiations—the more puzzled I
become by our failure—Washington's and Hanoi's—to communicate at the
highest levels. Not once during my seven years in the Kennedy and Johnson
administrations did we have even one hour of direct contact between high-
level representatives of the U.S. presidents and Pres. Ho Chi Minh. Why did
we settle for low-level contacts, even freelancing intermediaries? Why did
we not take the initiative and, for example, simply send Averell Harriman to
Hanoi to talk to Ho Chi Minh? Why did leaders in Hanoi fail to try to initiate similar high-level contact with us, even to respond in ways that a reasonable person in Washington might have interpreted as promising? Why, in
short, did leaders in both Washington and Hanoi stand off from each other
while the war came and escalated and became so terribly destructive? I
can't answer these questions to my satisfaction. Neither can the other participants in the U.S.-Vietnamese dialogues.

What about the United States today and in the future? We have come
close in recent years to war with Haiti and North Korea, saved at the last
moment by the personal and unofficial intervention of former U.S. Pres.
Jimmy Carter. More recently, we seem to have learned something important.
As I write this, in late 1998, U.S. special negotiator Richard Holbrooke has
just returned from having spent fifty hours with Slobodan Milosevic in Belgrade, thereby defusing, at least for the moment, a crisis in Kosovo that
might well have led to military intervention by one or more Western powers.
And in October 1998, Pres. Bill Clinton is said to have spent seventy-seven
hours in consultation at the Wye Conference Center in Maryland with Israeli
Prime Minister Benjamin Netanyahu, Palestinian leader Yasser Arafat, and
their staffs. The result was the signing of a land-for-peace deal that, if ratified and implemented, would be the continuation of a process begun several
years before with the signing of the Oslo Accords. These examples contrast,
however, with the lack of high-level, continuous communications with Cuba,
Iraq, and Iran. In different ways, the tragedy of Vietnam and some recent
U.S. diplomatic successes all point to the salience of this lesson: Communicate with your adversary at a high level.

3. In Foreign Policy, Practice the Democratic Principles We Preach.

The American system of government is based on the principle that individuals and institutions are fallible and that consultation and checks and bal-
ances are absolutely necessary to avoiding the mistakes associated with less
democratic states. But U.S. administrations often fail to act on this fundamental

principle; they fail to practice what they preach. Neither before nor after the Tonkin Gulf resolution of August 1964 did we *fully* involve the Congress, or the American people, in a discussion of the situation in Vietnam. We might have done so by calling up the military reserves, which surely would have sparked a spirited, overdue conversation on the price the American public was willing to pay in an attempt to save the state of South Vietnam.

4. Apply U.S. Power — Economic, Political, or Military — Only in a Context of Multilateral Decisionmaking.*

Since World War II, the United States has appeared to many, as Nguyen Co Thach said in his opening remarks to the June 1997 Hanoi conference, "as seeming to want to become the world's policeman."[25] Believing, since the 1940s, that we were the main barrier that prevented the communist movement from conquering the world, we have often acted unilaterally in applying sanctions or military power. Such unilateral actions tended to irritate our allies—whom we did not consult and whose views we did not seriously consider—and often worked to the detriment of the very groups and individuals we sought to assist. An example of such unilateralism occurred just weeks after the Kennedy administration took office: The Bay of Pigs invasion, which has been described as a "perfect failure." But to this day we continue to apply our power—particularly U.S. economic power—unilaterally. This often is seen in the form of economic sanctions that are always resented by friend and foe alike and usually are, in addition, ineffective and costly both to American manufacturers and to innocent people.

Throughout the 1950s and 1960s, the United States repeatedly ignored the advice and actions of its closest allies, Britain and France, as it escalated the conflict in Vietnam. I am still puzzled, even amazed, by our behavior toward France, which, after all, had occupied Indochina for more than a century and knew the territory in ways we never would. True, President de Gaulle was haughty and extremely difficult to deal with, as I discovered personally in our dealings over the North Atlantic Treaty Organization (NATO), from which de Gaulle withdrew France in 1966. But that should not have been the point. In fact, by failing to take seriously the views of more knowledgeable and experienced allies, by acting unilaterally, we condemned ourselves to repeating the mistakes of the French. We acted as though we thought we were omniscient. We weren't, we aren't, and we will not be in the

---

*The single exception to the rule of multilateralism should be the defense of the continental United States, Alaska, and Hawaii.

future. Although there may be exceptions, the rule should be the one we broke in Vietnam: Use power, particularly military power, only in a multilateral context.

But we should not go to the other extreme—we should not learn the *wrong* lessons—and be guided by the so-called Vietnam syndrome—the unwillingness ever to use military power in association with diplomacy. As discussed in Chapter 7, former Secretary of State George Shultz has correctly said that this would be "a complete abdication of the duties of leadership."[26]

5. Acknowledge That Some Problems in International Affairs Have No Solution, Particularly No Military Solution.

I wrote toward the end of *In Retrospect* that problems like those we encountered in Vietnam may have no solution, at least no solution that is worth the cost and risk. The statement struck many as naive, in the sense that everyone already knew this. Perhaps. But political leaders often feel they have been elected or appointed to solve difficult problems confronting their nation. Vietnam proved that this attitude, when carried to extremes, can be disastrous. We created the entity called South Vietnam in order to halt the advance of communism. We created a president, Ngo Dinh Diem, to lead this entity and to participate with us in nation-building. These were all attempts to solve what we took to be the problem of an advancing communist surge in Southeast Asia. As I look back, it is obvious, particularly in light of our dialogues with the Vietnamese, that our "solutions" became the problem.

This lesson will likely be crucial during the twenty-first century. We are likely to be eyewitnesses, thanks to mass media, to assorted atrocities, catastrophes, and other horrors around the world, live, in real time. Appalled, we will want our government to do something, to intervene, militarily if necessary, but anyway to get involved and stop the suffering, injustice, and cruelty. These are, of course, noble motives. No one should question that. But leaders do need to question whether each particular problem is *their* problem, that is, whether it has any solution that can be brought about by U.S. action, alone or in conjunction with other nations. May not such "solutions" lead to problems that may be more intractable than those that initially seemed to warrant an intervention?[27] These situations will provide supreme tests of judgment for leaders. The Vietnam experience teaches us the necessity to make hard choices as to which problems can and cannot be solved—particularly by military action—at reasonable cost and risk.

6. Organize to Apply and Administer Military Power with Intensity and Thoroughness.

During the Cuban missile crisis of October 1962, the Kennedy administration mobilized itself at the upper levels into a kind of war cabinet; through nearly two weeks of virtually continuous effort, it managed to defuse the crisis without a war. The intensity and thoroughness with which we analyzed and debated the relevant issues have been documented and much commented upon. However, many of the people in that informal war cabinet—Dean Rusk, McGeorge Bundy, George Ball, myself, and several others, including both President Kennedy and Vice President Johnson—were among those who were responsible for America's Vietnam policy after January 20, 1961. Unlike the way we focused on issues during the Cuban missile crisis, we tackled the Vietnam situation sporadically, inconsistently, without the kind of high-level specialists who had proved so essential to the defusing of the missile crisis. The difference in outcome speaks for itself. During the Cuban missile crisis, one American pilot lost his life as he was shot down in his U-2 spy plane over Cuba. In Vietnam, nearly 4 million people were killed. The question is: Why the difference?

As I look back with benefit of subsequent scholarship on the missile crisis, and as I reflect upon our dialogues with the Vietnamese, I conclude that two principal factors were involved. First, at no point during the Vietnam War did the U.S. government and the American people feel any danger to the U.S. homeland resulting from possible escalation of the war. This does not mean that the U.S. leadership did not think about it. On the contrary, it was often on our minds. Our policy was very cautious in this respect: We did not want to invite a Chinese intervention (as in Korea), which could lead to a war that would overspread the boundaries of Vietnam, even of Indochina, and might ultimately involve the Soviets. Because we kept the war limited by design, however, the riveting intensity and fear-driven singularity of purpose that characterized the missile crisis deliberations were lacking in our policy discussions concerning Vietnam.

A second factor, I believe, has to do with the insidious nature of what I will call *crises in slow motion*. Gen. Bruce Palmer Jr. has called the Vietnam War the "Twenty-Five Year War."[28] President Truman inherited it. So did Presidents Eisenhower, Kennedy, Johnson, Nixon, and Ford. It had no clear-cut starting point. Although it seems monumental in retrospect, the fact is that Vietnam was often left unattended at the highest levels for long periods of time, as we dealt with NATO, nuclear weapons policy, and crises in

Berlin, the Middle East, Turkey, Greece, and other parts of the world. There was never a point—not Pleiku in February 1965, not the Tet Offensive of January–February 1968, nothing—that focused officials on Vietnam as we had focused on the problem of Soviet missiles in Cuba.

And this is the point: Beware of crises in slow motion, watch out on the periphery, for events that have the potential for spiraling out of control. Learning and applying this lesson will be very difficult. However, the U.S. government must develop better procedures for conveying its institutional memory from one administration to the next, for it is in the nature of many problems—and Vietnam was one of these—that they are inherited. And it must learn as well how to organize to ensure high-level, consistent political and military responses, extending perhaps for a period of years, to such crises in slow-motion.

.   .   .

As I have thought about the lessons of Vietnam since beginning our dialogues with the Vietnamese, I have read and reread the many efforts others have made to state what they believe must not be forgotten—what must be learned and applied—regarding the tragedy.

One group includes many historians whose position is epitomized by professor Ernest May, whom I quote in Chapter 1. He is one of our nation's most eminent scholars in the fields of U.S. foreign policy and presidential decisionmaking, and a man whom I admire immensely. You will recall he said: "Given the assumptions generally shared by Americans in the 1960s, it seems probable that any collection of men or women would have decided as did members of the Kennedy and Johnson administrations."[29] He was right in the sense that the majority of Americans—academics, representatives of the media, members of Congress, and the public at large—all supported U.S. intervention in Vietnam until nearly the end of the decade. It would have been very difficult for any group of political leaders, during the early to mid-1960s, to act contrary to that body of opinion. But I have said before, and I want to repeat again: It is the responsibility of leaders to lead, not follow. It is their responsibility to resist the pressures of the majority if the majority is misinformed or fails to understand and properly evaluate the full range of options open to our country. Along with the majority of other Americans, we in the Kennedy and Johnson administrations did not possess that understanding. We were not that wise.

Few have understood and expressed as well what we have been seeking to accomplish in this project during the past four years as American journalist Frances FitzGerald. In a 1984 piece titled "How Does America Avoid Future Vietnams?" she wrote the following:

What the Vietnam veterans have taught the rest of us is this: We cannot simply write off our losses, declare failure, and get on with the matter, close the subject, because the young men we have sent to fight our wars for us will not forget. They will become our conscience. They will insist that there is responsibility. . . .

Most important . . . for us in general . . . the past is not simply for historians. Strength and endurance come from having a connection with one's own history. The past and future are balanced in the present, and you have one only to the extent you have the other.

You can have control over your future only to the extent that you are deeply and firmly attached to your own history.[30]

It is my hope that through this book, these U.S.-Vietnamese dialogues and these lessons from a costly war, we can become more firmly attached to, and have a much better understanding of, our own history, thereby entering the twenty-first century with more of the knowledge and caution it will take to make it less tragic than the twentieth.

Appendix A

Additions to History: Corrections to the Historical Record, 1945–1968

Much new information was put on the record for the first time by the Vietnamese participants during seven meetings between 1995 and 1998 involving former U.S. and North Vietnamese officials and scholars from both countries. The new information included revelations of two types: (1) information on the basic assumptions about the United States, on the basis of which leaders in Hanoi made their decisions; and (2) information about pivotal events contributing to the escalation of the war. Examples of both types are given below, framed by brief statements of the (heretofore) relevant received wisdom in the West, with a brief statement of the significance of the new information for our understanding of the war—and of missed opportunities to have avoided conflict. The titles of the subsections below mirror the titles for the "empirical" chapters in the book (Chapters 2–7).

The following corrections to the historical record represent a sampler in the sense that several such lists equal in length and historical significance to this appendix might have been assembled, with little or no overlap between the lists of events or issues. The inclusion of the current list thus does not mean that its entries are necessarily the most important, although we believe many are very important and require significant revisions in our understanding of the Vietnam War.

Neither does the inclusion of the items below indicate that the evidence supporting the claims is more (or less) convincing than the evidence for other revelations. In fact, we believe the evidence, deriving from having obtained unique access to Vietnamese documents and testimony, *is* convincing for every entry below. This does not mean, of course, that we believe the evidence is irrefutable and final. On the contrary, our objective here is to focus attention on what we believe have been fundamental errors of fact and interpretation made by Western officials, journalists, historians, and others with an abiding interest in this tragic conflict.

For all such individuals, we believe this much is clear: Nearly a half-century after the United States first became involved in Vietnam, and nearly a quarter-century after it withdrew, there is truly something new under the sun, something that we believe is both illuminating and important regarding this much-studied but insufficiently understood war. For the first time, we believe, it is possible to grasp its lessons with the accuracy and scope that comes with the comprehensive U.S.-Vietnamese understanding of its critical events. We hope the "argument without end" about the war continues, stimulated by, but by no means limited to, the sampler of claims that follows and the evidence presented throughout the book that supports them.

2

Enemies: Washington's and Hanoi's Mindsets at the Beginning of the Kennedy Administration

RECEIVED WISDOM IN THE WEST

By January 1961, Vietnamese communists constituted a unified movement, directed and controlled from Moscow and Beijing, whose objective was undermining U.S. security interests, that is, knocking over the dominoes in southeast Asia.

REVELATIONS

- Only in January 1959 did the indigenous southern resistance (the National Liberation Front, or NLF) secure Hanoi's backing for an armed rebellion against the regime of U.S.-backed Ngo Dinh Diem. Hanoi's support for an armed uprising was tempered by their fear of a U.S. intervention. *The United States believed Hanoi had supported and supplied the southern guerrillas since at least 1954.*

- The ultimate objective of the communist majority within the NLF was the reunification of Vietnam under Hanoi's leadership. However, leaders of the NLF, and in the Hanoi government, believed that a coalition government in Saigon—officially neutral, lasting ten to fifteen years, and including many noncommunist elements—could be a transitional step toward full reunification. *The United States believed that the NLF sought immediate reunification of Vietnam under Hanoi's communist rule and the total exclusion of elements from the South Vietnamese government.*

- President Kennedy's inaugural address was understood in Hanoi to indicate that a key U.S. objective was to become master of the world. *Instead, the Kennedy administration came to office believing the West faced a worldwide battle against communism.*

- Hanoi believed that the Kennedy administration sought to establish a neocolonialist regime in Saigon, as the French had done before 1954, and that they must therefore oust the Diem government quickly, before the United States could take over militarily. *The U.S. rationale for its presence in South Vietnam was to prevent "falling dominoes"—spread of communist influence—and had nothing to do with colonial ambitions.*

- Hanoi's principal objective after January 1961 was to carefully calibrate the activities of the NLF so that Diem would be removed and replaced before the Americans could successfully resist the transition. *This was a gross miscalculation by Hanoi regarding the extent to which the activities of the NLF could be controlled, or the response of the United States could be predicted, with precision.*

MISSED OPPORTUNITIES

A Washington-Hanoi confrontation need not have occurred if the Kennedy administration had understood Vietnamese nationalism and the Hanoi leadership had understood U.S. motives in Southeast Asia.

3

The Evolution of Washington's and Hanoi's Mindsets, 1945–1960

RECEIVED WISDOM IN THE WEST

Vietnamese communists, led by Ho Chi Minh, had from their earliest origins been pawns in the worldwide communist movement, and thus implacable enemies of the United States.

REVELATIONS

- Between 1945 and 1949, Vietnamese communists sent many signals to the United States indicating that they sought peaceful relations with Washington: via a half-dozen letters from Ho Chi Minh to President Truman; via an interview with American journalist Sol Sander in 1949; and via a 1947 diplomatic démarche to the U.S. ambassador to Bangkok. The Vietnamese communists interpreted the lack of U.S. response as proof of U.S. opposition to them. *At the time, top U.S. officials were over-*

whelmed with rebuilding Europe and countering Soviet expansionism in Europe and took little or no interest in Vietnam.

- During 1950–1954, Vietnamese communists regarded the United States as interventionists, due to U.S. financial support of the French effort to subdue them—but not yet as an implacable enemy. Many communist intellectuals were, in fact, strongly pro-American. *After the outbreak of the Korean War in 1950, Washington regarded the Vietnamese Communist Party, led by Ho Chi Minh, as communist puppets of Beijing and Moscow.*

- The Geneva Conference of 1954 was a watershed in the modern history of Vietnam, at which the Vietnamese communists were betrayed by the Chinese and Soviets, resulting in the division of Vietnam at the 17th parallel. The Vietnamese communists agreed to this only under tremendous pressure from the Chinese, including a secret meeting in China, July 3–5, 1954, between Zhou Enlai and Ho Chi Minh, at which Zhou argued that if the Vietminh did not agree to the partition of Vietnam the United States would intervene militarily in support of the French. *U.S. officials believed the result of Geneva was the "loss" of Vietnam above the 17th parallel to communism and had little or no awareness of the bitterness of Ho Chi Minh and his colleagues toward China and the USSR.*

- In January 1959, Hanoi agreed to authorize armed struggle by the southern resistance, only as a face-saving way to retain control over the southern resistance, whose members were bitter with Hanoi for selling them out in Geneva and whose goal was to establish their own neutralist, coalition government under southern control, not Hanoi's. *The U.S. government at the time, and later, had little or no understanding of the bitterness felt by southern communists toward their northern comrades for being "sold out" in Geneva in 1954.*

MISSED OPPORTUNITIES

The confrontation, leading to war, between Washington and Hanoi need not have occurred if each had correctly understood the other's perception of the evolution of the Cold War in Asia and the other's role in that evolution.

4

A Neutral Solution: Was It Possible?

RECEIVED WISDOM IN THE WEST

A neutralist government in Saigon, composed of a coalition of communists, anticommunists, and neutralists was never viable, because Hanoi's singular objective was to conquer South Vietnam and rule it from Hanoi.

REVELATIONS

*   Le Duan, a southern communist who in 1960 became Party secretary in Hanoi, established as twin objectives during 1961–1964: (1) the overthrow of the Diem government; and (2) the establishment of a neutral coalition government, made up exclusively of southerners. *Top U.S. officials were unaware of the significance of Hanoi's decision to put a southerner in charge of the war in South Vietnam—a decision that indicated support for armed struggle in the South yet recognized the desire of southerners themselves for considerable—even if transitional—independence from Hanoi. U.S. officials believed any government in Saigon formed by the NLF would instantly become a puppet of Hanoi.*

*   Between May and August 1962, Le Duan opened a "neutrality offensive" designed to convince the United States to apply the neutralist model adopted in Laos in July 1961 to South Vietnam. *Le Duan and his colleagues completely misunderstood the U.S. interpretation of the 1961 Laos Accords in Geneva—which was that the neutralist model had failed due to Hanoi's seemingly significant violations of it.*

*   Hanoi never took the initiative to explain its views to the Americans, despite several opportunities to do so at Geneva and elsewhere, because: (1) it feared appearing weak; and (2) it feared the wrath of the Chinese, who opposed any negotiated settlement between Hanoi and Washington. *Likewise, the United States never probed or even carefully examined Hanoi's interest in a neutral solution in Saigon, because it believed Hanoi was not interested in it.*

MISSED OPPORTUNITIES

A neutral solution in Saigon, with a coalition government in place, was possible at any point between 1961 and 1964, if only Washington and Hanoi had understood the concerns and objectives of each other.

5

Escalation: 1961–1965

RECEIVED WISDOM IN THE WEST

Escalation from confrontation to war between Washington and Hanoi was inevitable, given the conflicting interests of each side in South Vietnam and Hanoi's total disinterest in a compromise giving them anything less than total control over the South.

REVELATIONS

- Pressure to escalate the conflict in the South came almost exclusively from southerners who were being persecuted by the Diem regime. Leaders in Hanoi greatly feared, and tried to avoid, any escalation that would invite direct U.S. military intervention. For this reason, large numbers of Hanoi's regular combat units were withheld from the conflict in the South until 1965. *From the 1950s onward, U.S. officials believed U.S. presence in South Vietnam was required to combat an "invasion" from the North bent on conquering South Vietnam.*

- The coup and assassination of Ngo Dinh Diem in November 1963 caused consternation in Hanoi, because leaders feared the United States would decide to take over the war against the NLF from South Vietnamese forces. Decisions taken at the Party's Ninth Plenum in December 1963 resulted in further escalation by the NLF in an attempt to overthrow Diem's successors before the United States could mobilize. *At the time, U.S. officials viewed Hanoi's escalation of the conflict as a direct challenge to the U.S. right and authority to aid its ally in Saigon.*

- The August 2, 1964, attack by North Vietnamese patrol boats on U.S. ships in the Tonkin Gulf was ordered by a local commander who neither consulted nor informed leaders in Hanoi. The alleged "second attack" on August 4 never occurred. *U.S. officials assumed the events in the Tonkin Gulf constituted an intended escalation by Hanoi. The U.S. retaliated with the first U.S. air strikes on North Vietnam. Hanoi, knowing it had not ordered the attack, assumed the air strikes were an unprovoked attempt to intimidate them.*

- The NLF's attack on a South Vietnamese Army barracks at Pleiku on February 7, 1965, killing eight Americans and wounding more than a hundred, was ordered by a local commander of a thirty-man commando unit, without any consultation with leaders in Hanoi and without the knowledge that Americans were present at the base. *Believing the Pleiku attack to be a conscious attempt to target Americans and to embarrass National Security Adviser McGeorge Bundy, then visiting Saigon, President Johnson responded to the attack by launching what soon became the massive air campaign—code-named "ROLLING THUNDER"—against the North.*

MISSED OPPORTUNITIES

Escalation from confrontation to war between Hanoi and Washington was not inevitable, if only each had accurately understood the capabilities, intentions, and decisionmaking process of the other.

6

Negotiating Initiatives, 1965–1967: Why Did They Fail?

RECEIVED WISDOM IN THE WEST

U.S. efforts between May 1965 and October 1967 to initiate peace talks—including both diplomatic contacts and gestures such as bombing pauses—were doomed to failure because the Hanoi government was totally uninterested in any compromise resolution short of winning the war militarily.

REVELATIONS

- Hanoi's negotiating stance, in its Four Points of April 8, 1965, was drafted by Pres. Ho Chi Minh, Party Secretary Le Duan, and Prime Minister Pham Van Dong and was meant to be a relatively flexible restatement of the 1954 Geneva requirements for South Vietnamese autonomy. *U.S. leaders understood the Four Points to be a rigid restatement of Hanoi's intention to put the NLF in charge in Saigon, for a brief transitional period, before unifying Vietnam under the control of the communist government in Hanoi.*

- Point Three (of the Four Points), which required the government in Saigon to be "in accordance with the program of the NLF," appeared to the United States to be totally unacceptable. Over and over again, it was stated to be the main reason why the United States refused to move to negotiations based on the Four Points. The Vietnamese participants in the dialogues presented evidence to demonstrate that Point Three was the most flexible negotiating point of all, because it recognized implicitly the wish of the southern resistance for a neutral coalition government lasting at least ten years, possibly longer, which would have given the United States the cover it needed to withdraw honorably. *Hanoi never successfully communicated the meaning of Point Three to the United States, which misunderstood the point to imply that only southern communists completely loyal to Hanoi would be allowed to govern in the South.*

- The extensive use of intermediaries in the U.S. campaign to initiate peace talks, and its use of publicity to entice Hanoi to the negotiating table, was misunderstood in Hanoi to indicate that the entire effort was only a public relations ploy designed to turn Hanoi's friends—including its communist allies—against it. *U.S. use of intermediaries arose out of desperation due to Washington's inability to communicate directly with the Hanoi government, as well as Hanoi's seeming disinterest in any resolution other than the surrender of South Vietnamese forces and complete withdrawal of U.S. forces as prerequisites to peace talks.*

- U.S. pauses in the air war over North Vietnam, including the thirty-seven–day pause during December–January 1965–1966, were unacceptable to Hanoi for several reasons: They regarded it as a form of extortion (since Hanoi could not similarly threaten the U.S. directly); they were afraid of alienating the Chinese, whose assistance was vital to their prosecution of the war; and because they were convinced that the United States was only checking the pulse of Hanoi to determine if its will to fight had been eliminated. *The majority of the negotiating initiatives and/or bombing pauses were regarded as serious by many U.S. officials. These officials sought to use the initiatives to move to peace talks. Hanoi's inability to communicate its real position and constraints, however, led U.S. officials mistakenly to conclude that Hanoi was not interested in talks.*

- A U.S. bombing halt any time after January 27, 1967 (when it was announced by Hanoi Foreign Minister Nguyen Duy Trinh) would have resulted in immediate peace talks. *U.S. officials and specialists engaged in endless hair-splitting over the meaning of the January 27 statement and thus seemed to further confirm Hanoi in its belief that the United States was not serious about peace talks.*

- The last major U.S. initiative before the Tet Offensive of July–October 1968— code-named "PENNSYLVANIA"—was viewed in Hanoi as "nearly acceptable" during July–August 1967. But Hanoi's attempt to signal this response to the Americans—using less strident criticism than previously—was uninterpretable in Washington. *Leaders in Washington concluded that the initiative, like all the others, had fallen on deaf ears in Hanoi, a conclusion that played an important role in the decision of President Johnson, announced on March 31, 1968, not to seek reelection.*

MISSED OPPORTUNITIES

Washington and Hanoi could have moved successfully to peace talks at any time between May 1965 and October 1967 if each had understood the other's bottom lines—which were reconcilable—and their respective constraints on communicating their positions to each other.

7

U.S. Military Victory: A Dangerous Illusion?

RECEIVED WISDOM IN THE WEST

Many in the West believed during the war, and some continue to believe, that the United States could have "won" the war in Vietnam militarily, if only Washington had unleashed its vast military might.

REVELATIONS

- Hanoi began preparing for all-out war with the United States as early as 1963 by evacuating mothers and small children from Hanoi and sending them to the countryside; by beginning to build an elaborate and extensive system of bomb shelters; and by dispersing all essential war materials throughout the country. Hanoi had the intention and capability to prosecute its war effort at any level of U.S. bombing short of genocidal destruction. *U.S. bombing strategy was based on the mistaken belief that it could break the will of Hanoi to continue to support its NLF allies in the South; and also that it could so severely disrupt Hanoi's production and supply of essential war materials that Hanoi would be forced to capitulate.*

- According to an agreement reached by leaders in Hanoi and Beijing, any U.S. attempt to invade North Vietnam would have resulted in Chinese intervention, which occurred in Korea in 1950. Railroad track between the Chinese border and Hanoi was laid and made ready; and Chinese forces near the Vietnamese border were on alert throughout 1964–1968. *Some U.S. officials, civilian and military, argued that the United States should consider such an invasion of the North in order to "eliminate the problem at the source." They believed such action would not trigger a Chinese response. The result of such a move would have been catastrophic—for the U.S. forces, for North and South Vietnam, and for China.*

- With the important assistance of Chinese army engineers, Hanoi established six separate and independent means for infiltrating its forces and supplies from North to South, including two routes via water. *Many U.S. officials argued during the war, and some have continued to argue since the war, that cutting off the Ho Chi Minh Trail, at "choke points" in Laos, would have caused Hanoi to abort its war effort and sue for peace. However, Hanoi had made its resupply routes so numerous and redundant that any U.S. effort short of genocidal destruction would have been neutralized.*

- Hanoi calibrated its shipment and infiltration rates from North to South to correlate with the level of U.S. bombing of the North. In other words: Heavier bombing would lead to heavier infiltration of the South. This strategy was designed to send a signal to Washington that Hanoi understood the bombing to be a desperate measure taken by the United States because it was losing the war in the South and that no amount of bombing could cause them to reduce their support for the NLF. *Leaders in Washington believed that the bombing sent a signal to Hanoi's leadership: If they ceased, or at least significantly reduced, their efforts to supply the South, then peace negotiations would be possible. Instead, Hanoi used its response to the bombing to send the reverse signal to Washington: If the U.S. would cease bombing, peace negotiations would be possible.*

Missed Opportunities

None. For reasons relating to Hanoi's preparations and attitude, there were no missed opportunities for the United States to win the war militarily in Vietnam at a cost the United States was willing to bear and within moral bounds consistent with the precepts adhered to by the American people.

Three Alternative U.S. Strategies in Vietnam: A Reexamination Based on New Chinese and Vietnamese Sources

ROBERT K. BRIGHAM

Three alternative military strategies have been put forward since the end of the Vietnam War as missed opportunities for a U.S. military victory. They are: (1) invasion of North Vietnam; (2) incursion into Laos; and (3) concentration of U.S. forces on defense of "enclaves."

In Chapter 7, Col. Herbert Schandler concludes that each of these is seriously flawed as a strategy and would have carried negative consequences far beyond their intended results. When each is reexamined carefully, in light of recently released information from new Chinese and Vietnamese Sources, we find that none of them would likely have produced a better outcome for the United States.

Invasion of the North?

An invasion of North Vietnam was enthusiastically advanced by some in the U.S. Army.[1] They believed that the United States should have attacked the North directly, north of the demilitarized zone (DMZ) at the 17th parallel. Military leaders who supported this strategy, however, overlooked the threat of China and, on occasion, even appeared eager for a direct confrontation. Secretary of Defense Robert S. McNamara was convinced, in contrast, that an invasion of the North carried an unacceptable risk of bringing the Chinese into the war. He reasoned that Beijing would act in its own self-interest and would never surrender its buffer area to the West. Gen. Bruce Palmer Jr., Gen. William Westmoreland's deputy in Vietnam, agrees. He argues in his book *The Twenty-Five Year War* that "one cannot quarrel with the decision not to invade North Vietnam because it was too close to China."[2] In addition, as Palmer recognized, a war with China would have had little to do with American objectives in Vietnam and could even have led to millions of unnecessary deaths.

New documentary evidence from Hanoi and Beijing supports the worst U.S. predictions.[3] We now know that North Vietnam asked for and received security commitments from Beijing from 1960 onward. In 1962 a Vietnamese delegation headed by Ho Chi Minh and Gen. Nguyen Chi Thanh visited China, requesting aid for the southern struggle. The Chinese communists pledged an additional 230 battalions to the Vietnamese if needed.[4] The following year, Beijing's military chief of staff, Luo Ruiqing, visited Hanoi. He told Ho that if the Americans were to attack the North, China would come to its defense. In June 1964 the North Vietnamese Army's chief of staff, Van Tien Dung, received Beijing's pledge of "unconditional military support."[5] During the Tonkin Gulf crisis of August 1964, Chinese communists placed their naval units stationed in the area on combat readiness and ordered them to "pay close attention to the movement of American forces" and be prepared to "cope with any possible sudden attack."[6] The Chinese air command went on alert, and the Seventh Army's air force was moved to the Vietnamese border, where it remained for several years. Four other air divisions were also moved closer to the border, and Beijing built two new airstrips in anticipation of an American invasion. American intelligence reports also detected the Chinese movement of nearly forty MiG fighters to the North Vietnamese airfield at Phuc Yen.[7]

In 1965, when the sustained bombing of the North began under Operation "ROLLING THUNDER," the Chinese agreed to step up their commitment to Vietnam as a rear area and deterrent. Beijing pledged repeatedly that it would avoid a direct military conflict with the United States as long as possible, but it would not back away from a confrontation. On March 25, 1965, an editorial in the Party's official newspaper announced that China had offered Hanoi "any necessary material support, including the supply of weapons and all kinds of military materials." It stated further that, if necessary, China was prepared to "send its personnel to fight together with the Vietnamese people to annihilate the American aggressors."[8] Shortly after these statements, China sent the first wave of its combat engineers to Vietnam to aid in the construction of antiaircraft batteries, railroads, airports, bridges, and roads. By 1968, the number of Chinese serving within North Vietnam's borders reached 200,000.[9]

Gen. Doan Chuong, a Vietnamese specialist in military strategy and tactics, recently reported that Hanoi had several contingency plans for an American invasion:

We had to anticipate the worst possibility. . . . If the U.S. sent its troops to the North, it would have committed a serious mistake of strategic significance. . . . Countries having friendly relations with North Vietnam would give more support to the Vietnamese people. And militarily, the U.S. would put itself in an awkward situation, one in which they would be unable to solve the contradiction between concentrating and dispersing their troops. Moreover, the Northern troops would enjoy the advantage of fighting on their own territory. Because of all these factors, the U.S. would have been defeated by the "cobweb" of people's war. Also, we knew that the U.S. had to consider whether or not China or the USSR would intervene. On that point, we were utterly confident that the USSR and China would give more support to North Vietnam.[10]

Some analysts have suggested that China may have backed away from its military commitments to Vietnam during the Cultural Revolution.[11] New material from communist archives suggests, however, that China never would have allowed an American invasion of North Vietnam to go unanswered.[12] In fact, as Beijing looked inward during the mid-1960s, its line concerning the United States in Vietnam actually hardened. Until the end of 1964, China's official policy concerning U.S. planes flying into its airspace was to avoid a direct confrontation. By mid-1965, however, this policy had been reversed. Accordingly, there were nearly two hundred confrontations between China and the United States, resulting in the destruction of twelve American fighters.[13] Even after relations between Vietnam and China had soured, the evidence indicates that Beijing's own self-interest would have led it to defend its "buffer zone" in Indochina.

One former North Vietnamese Foreign Ministry official—and a leading scholar on the American War—has characterized China as a "credible deterrent." Luu Doan Huynh argues that Hanoi preferred to fight the war alone, but it had assurances from Beijing that China would intervene if the United States attacked across the 17th parallel. Huynh recalls:

I think that the Chinese factor must be understood as a real deterrent. And so we must have it in our hands, so to speak, for the purpose of deterrence. But deterrence does not mean that we are very eager to use it. We are not eager to use it. This kind of deterrence is also a historical legacy. You have to understand this: for many centuries, Vietnam was a colony and, after that, a tributary state of China. And as a legacy of that—China has always considered Vietnam, and in particular North Vietnam, as being within China's zone of security and influence. That is something that we cannot

deny. When France invaded and annexed southern Vietnam in the 19th century—in 1858—China kept quiet.

But as soon as the French troops invaded northern Vietnam—1875 and
1886—China, which was then very weak, still reacted militarily. So, I think
that China did anticipate the possible U.S. invasion of North Vietnam—particularly after the landing of U.S. Marines in Danang in 1965. Probably they
did not want to repeat the lack of adequate Chinese measures with respect to
North Korea in 1950, which they thought may have caused the U.S. to make
the decision to cross the 38th parallel.

In 1950, the Americans thought the Chinese were bluffing. This time, the
Chinese wanted you to know they weren't bluffing.[14]

China was motivated to aid Vietnam by its own foreign policy needs. Beijing hoped to use its support of the war in Vietnam to stimulate mass mobilization within China for the Cultural Revolution. Chinese leaders claimed
that Beijing was the center for continuous revolutions and that the United
States threatened that central role. China repeatedly claimed that it would
support Vietnam by any means necessary, "even at the expense of heavy
national sacrifice."[15] Accordingly, when a Vietnamese delegation visited
Beijing in April 1965, China pledged to aid Hanoi economically and militarily. Aid came in the form of armored vehicles, small arms and ammunition, uniforms, shoes, rice, and even recreation equipment for North
Vietnamese soldiers. Chinese communist sources claim that more than $200
million in material aid was sent to Hanoi annually beginning in 1965.

At the time, other considerations were also thought to preclude taking the
war to the North. During the early years of the war, the Sullivan Group, a
presidential advisory group, had concluded that attacking the North would
do little to reduce its support for the war in the South. For example, the
group predicted:

> It is not likely that North Vietnam would (if it could) call off the war in the
> South even though U.S. actions would in time have serious economic and
> political impact. Overt action against North Vietnam would be unlikely to
> produce reduction in Viet Cong activity sufficiently to make victory on the
> ground possible in South Vietnam unless accompanied by new U.S. bolster-
> ing actions in South Vietnam and considerable improvement in the govern-
> ment there.[16]

Indeed, the war had always been fundamentally about the political future
of Vietnam south of the 17th parallel, and a direct attack by U.S. ground

forces against North Vietnam would have had little or no positive effect on meeting this objective. The United States came to understand too late that the insurgency in the South was primarily indigenous. During the early days of the insurgency, we now know, it was the southern cadres who pressed Hanoi to allow them to move toward the armed struggle.[17] Attacking the North to stop the insurgency was strategically meaningless, given the U.S. objective of preserving the *South* Vietnamese government in Saigon. By 1968 it was understood in Washington that the NLF would have continued to carry the fight to the South Vietnamese Army, and it would have remained in control in the countryside no matter what happened in North Vietnam.[18]

Many southern cadres felt betrayed because of the 1954 partition of Vietnam, which left them vulnerable to the brutal efforts of the anticommunist Ngo Dinh Diem to exterminate them. Thereafter, the southerners tended to stress the need for a decisive battlefield victory prior to engaging in peace talks. Communist documents show overwhelmingly that southerners were more offensive-minded than many of their colleagues in Hanoi—in fact that they were prepared to carry on the struggle against the United States and its Saigon ally no matter what decisions were made by Hanoi.[19]

Writing after the war in a special issue of a military history journal, Le Duc Tho, a longtime member of the Party's political bureau, noted that southerners often engaged in offensive struggles "in spite of orders to the contrary by northern cadres."[20] This is especially true after Gen. Nguyen Chi Thanh became director of the Central Office South Vietnam—the mobile command post in the South—in 1965. Nguyen Chi Thanh was a southerner who had long advocated a more militant pursuit of the war effort. During the early 1960s, he argued that victory over the South Vietnamese and their American backers would come only on the battlefield. "If we feared the United States," Nguyen Chi Thanh declared, "we would have called on the people of southern Vietnam to wait and coexist peacefully with the U.S.-Diem clique. We are not afraid of the United States. . . ."[21]

As revealed in Chapter 5, the pivotal February 7, 1965, attack on the barracks at Pleiku was part of the regular "people's war" activities of district guerrillas. Nguyen Chi Thanh supported such actions. Throughout his career, he pressed for decisive action on the battlefield. He was a Maoist, believing that spirit and manpower always prevailed over firepower and technology. Whereas others grew cautious in the face of American escalation, especially in 1965, Nguyen Chi Thanh—an optimist to a fault—claimed instead that victory on the battlefield was at hand, if only the courage to confront the Americans could be mustered.[22] Until his death in July 1967, he never wavered from his view that "to attack unremittingly is the most active and effective method to maintain and extend our control of the battlefield."[23] With Nguyen Chi Thanh in charge of the southern forces, one can be absolutely certain than any attack on the North would have led to greatly increased offensive actions in the *South*, in addition to likely cata-strophic American casualties inflicted on any American expeditionary force north of the 17th parallel.

An attack against the North, therefore, was a losing strategy on several counts. It virtually guaranteed a war with China. If China intervened, one could only surmise what the Soviets would do, in an attempt to retain their leadership of the world communist movement. Neither did such a strategy take account of the irrelevance of an invasion of the North regarding saving the South Vietnamese government from collapse. And finally, neither did such a strategy acknowledge the probable consequences—north and south—for U.S. forces. The probable casualties would have dwarfed the actual U.S. casualties from the war, leading in all likelihood to severely hostile reactions in the U.S. Congress and American body politic.

Invasion of Laos?

Former U.S. Army Col. Harry Summers has long been one of the most outspoken advocates of the invasion of Laos.[24] Summers argues that a combined military action into Laos could have blocked the Laotian panhandle from being used as a base by North Vietnamese forces. After blocking the flow of men and supplies South, Summers contends, the South Vietnamese forces could have isolated the battlefield from communist incursions originating in Laos and destroyed the NLF.

The U.S. Army actually considered this proposal during the war but ultimately rejected it as unacceptable. When Army Chief of Staff Harold K. Johnson explored the option, he concluded that it would require support services beyond U.S. capabilities. For example, he found that such an operation demanded the astounding total of 18,000 engineer troops to make the operation feasible. Alas, the United States did not have available 18,000 engineer troops for assignment to Vietnam and Laos.[25] Furthermore, U.S. intelligence reports reliably reported that, until mid-1969, the majority of communist forces in the South were actually southerners, who had no need of a sanctuary in Laos in which they might prepare to "invade" South Vietnam. There were already there.

The Trong Son, or Ho Chi Minh Trail, ran through the Laotian panhandle. Advocates of the Laotian invasion strategy believe that by invading Laos the

United States could have effectively cut off the trail, stopped supplies heading from North Vietnam to South Vietnam, and thus won the war. But it is clear now, years later, that the southern insurgency could have survived without the Ho Chi Minh Trail. All the conditions that created the insurgency would still have been present. The NLF was never dependent on the North for its sustenance, in any case.

Finally, the force that Summers proposed would probably have met with the same fate as those U.S. forces who operated along the DMZ, nearest to North Vietnam's territory. These troops experienced unusually high casualty rates—mainly from mortars and heavy artillery. The same sort of phenomenon had already occurred in Laos, where U.S. combat losses were higher in a relative sense than those within the territory of Vietnam.[26] Thus, the "barrier across Laos" strategy ignores the reality of jungle war and the extraordinary disadvantages the U.S. would have had in such a war with the NLF and North Vietnamese.

Most strategic experts agree that extending the battlefield into Laos may have been the worst possible strategy. Sir Robert Thompson, the British counterinsurgency expert, noted that in a people's revolutionary war, such as the United States faced in Vietnam, "it is essential to keep the area of conflict confined and so limit the impact of the war."[27] Keeping resources limited is essential in a battle against people's war, according to Thompson, because it reduces human and material cost and permits control of the tempo of the war, that is, who has the initiative and who must respond. In people's war, guerrillas are always prepared to trade land for time. The objective of any counterinsurgency strategy worthy of the name must be, says Thompson, to reduce the control of the insurgency over the villages by denying it the time necessary to infiltrate. But a U.S. expansion of the Vietnam War into Laos would have done little or nothing in this regard. Thompson concludes that in the use of such strategies as the invasion of Laos, "successes will be almost irrelevant to the decision."[28] What are needed, according to Thompson and most other counterinsurgency specialists, are not the large units needed to carry the war into Laos but smaller, lighter, quicker forces for use in the southern villages.[29]

Leading military strategists in Hanoi agree that cutting off the Ho Chi Minh Trail via an invasion of Laos would have accomplished nothing for the United States. Gen. Doan Chuong, director of Hanoi's Institute for Strategic Studies, recently addressed the issue as follows:

If the supply route had been truly cut off during the war, this would have been a very serious development. That is why the strategic Truong Son Road

[Ho Chi Minh Trail] was constructed and involved such elaborate precautions, as you know. We not only had trails on land, we also had a "sea trail." In addition to the East Truong Son Road, there was a West Truong Son Road, with numerous criss-cross pathways, like a labyrinth. So it would have been hard to cut it off completely. As you know the U.S. applied various measures to block it: bombing, defoliating, sending in commandos, setting up a fence called "McNamara's Line," concentrating air strikes on the panhandle area, and so on. Still, the route remained open. . . . We could not, and in fact did not, allow the Trail to be cut off.[30]

During private discussions in Hanoi, Gen. Doan Chuong and several of his colleagues revealed that Hanoi was prepared for far more drastic measures in Laos, and with regard to the Ho Chi Minh Trails generally, than the United States actually took.

William C. Westmoreland, the U.S. field commander from 1964–1968, opposed the Laotian invasion strategy. In his memoirs, General Westmoreland recalls with amazement that many of his critics—within the military and without—"considered it practicable to seal land frontiers against North Vietnamese infiltration. . . . Yet small though South Vietnam is," he pointed out, "its land frontier extended for more than 900 miles." To have defended that entire frontier, according to General Westmoreland, would have required "many millions of troops."[31]

A cardinal error of advocates of the Laos incursion, it would appear, is their use of the U.S. experience in Korea as a model for what they believe should have been done in Vietnam. But the Korean Peninsula presented problems for the infiltration of men and supplies far different from what was faced in Vietnam. Surrounded by water on three sides, the actual Korean *frontier* was quite limited. Not only is the Vietnamese frontier, in this sense, almost 1,000 miles long, or roughly the distance from Boston to Chicago; in addition, the Truong Son Mountains of Indochina, along which supplies moved north to south, are home to the largest triple-canopy jungle in the world outside of the Amazon Basin. Detection and interdiction of the movement of supplies is nearly impossible in such conditions, which can create almost total darkness at noon on a sunny day.

The "Enclave" Strategy

A third alternative U.S. strategy in Vietnam—gathering U.S. forces into enclaves located in or near strategic assets—is in some ways more sophisticated than the invasion strategies directed at North Vietnam and Laos. Those advocating this strategy showed that they understood the nature of the war on the ground in South Vietnam: a fundamentally indigenous insurgency that could be successfully combated, if at all, by the application of counterinsurgency techniques in the South.

At the heart of this notion is the idea that U.S. troops would occupy a supporting role by controlling the densely populated coastal areas. The South Vietnamese forces would thereby be free to move inland from coastal bases, where they would confront the NLF. Proponents of the enclave strategy argued that U.S. troops could join the fight as long as the coastal bases remained protected and secure.

This strategy was based on some realistic assumptions about the war: (1) Basically, the war in the countryside had to be won by the South Vietnamese; and (2) the communists would never be strong enough to drive the U.S. Army into the sea. At worst, its adherents claimed (as some still claim), the enclave strategy would have bought time for South Vietnam to become stabilized, at minimum cost in American lives and material. An added feature, it is claimed, is that the insurgency itself would actually weaken once U.S. troops secured the heavily populated coast.

The enclave strategy, however, like the other alternatives, has not been without its strident critics. They assert that herding U.S. forces into enclaves would have disallowed the Americans from taking maximum advantage of their most potent weapon—superior firepower. Considerable doubt has also been expressed as to the ability of the South Vietnamese Army to carry the battle inland to the NLF. Time and again, the South Vietnamese proved they were no match for the NLF's committed guerrillas.

General Westmoreland was absolutely opposed to the enclave strategy. He believed bringing American combat troops into the major coastal cities of the South, including Saigon, would constitute a huge mistake. He saw the potential for them to get embroiled in the daily street demonstrations and other political conflicts that plagued the South. When Gen. Earle Wheeler, the chairman of the Joint Chiefs of Staff, recommended the enclave strategy to Westmoreland as one that would free the South Vietnamese for offensive operations in the countryside, the field commander pointed out that approximately 40 percent of the South Vietnamese forces were always available for, or committed to, combat operations in any case.[32] Gen. Maxwell Taylor recalled in his memoirs that "giving the U.S. the primary combat role and reserving the South Vietnamese Army for secondary combat missions was a mistake from the point of view of South Vietnamese psychology and U.S. domestic opinion."[33]

In fact, a variant of the enclave strategy had been tried before, by the

French, and it had failed miserably. Col. Quach Hai Luong, deputy director of Hanoi's Institute for Strategic Studies, recently argued that the Americans would have met a similar fate if they had withdrawn to enclaves: "That would conjure up a situation that was similar to what happened during the French war. The French had also concentrated their forces in the big cities. If you do that, then you would be able to control various outlets [i.e., ports] and economic and political headquarters. If you want to occupy a country for a long time, as the French did, then that's what you would do."[34] As Quach Hai Luong went on to point out, however, the Americans had no wish to occupy Vietnam in the traditional sense, as the French did. To him, this meant that the strategy of enclaves would make even less sense for the Americans than it did for the French. At least the French goal—long-term occupation of Vietnam—was consistent with the strategy, even though it failed. But for the Americans, he could see no benefits to it whatsoever.

Many who have compared the American and French military experiences in Vietnam agree. Bernard Fall, a French journalist and scholar with vast experience in Indochina, wrote in 1961 that the enclave strategy invited disaster because it concentrated conventional forces in an area where it could not dispense its weapons, for fear of alienating the local population. Revolutionaries, according to Fall, could isolate enemy forces for attack and simply use the village or rural area as a sanctuary. This was certainly the French experience along the central Vietnamese coast on Highway 1—*La Rue Sans Joie*, or "The Street Without Joy."[35]

. . .

After the war, Harry Summers recalled an encounter with a North Vietnamese general in which Summers said that the Americans won every battle in Vietnam. The general replied, "That may be so, but it is also irrelevant."[36] *Why* it was irrelevant is something that has been insufficiently grasped by advocates of one or more of the alternative strategies just reexamined. In short, the U.S. forces arrived in Vietnam prepared to turn back an invasion of South Vietnam by North Vietnam. If that had been the nature of the problem, the United States might have been successful. But what they encountered, and what some analysts still find it impossible to accept, is a war in the South that was fundamentally a war among southerners. Each side had a more powerful patron—the NLF was allied to Hanoi and the South Vietnamese government to the United States. And in this kind of war, the United States, along with its uninspired and hapless South Vietnamese allies, did not "know the territory."

Any strategy, including those just reexamined, would have required for its success a viable South Vietnamese government with credibility in the eyes of the South Vietnamese people. No government in Saigon after November 1963, when Diem was assassinated, was credible in this sense. From 1965, therefore, when U.S. combat troops first arrived, the situation in Saigon was politically untenable. In the end, no American strategy could have reversed the outcome in Vietnam, because the NLF and its North Vietnamese allies had committed to total war. Each was prepared to sustain casualties, far beyond American estimates, without giving up the fight. Any war would have been a war of attrition on the ground. And it is obvious, looking back, which side was willing, as John Kennedy said during his inaugural address, to "pay any price, bear any burden." The Vietnamese communists, North and South, were willing to pay that price. No alternative strategy, however clever, could have changed these fundamental facts of the matter.

Appendix C

Participants in "The Vietnam War Reexamined: Its History and Lessons"

A Conference in Bellagio, Italy, July 27–31, 1998

An international cast of scholars and former officials gathered in a conference sponsored by the Rockefeller Foundation, at the foundation's Villa Serbelloni Conference Center in Bellagio, Italy, July 27–31, 1998, to review an early version of the manuscript of this book. The authors wish to thank the Rockefeller Foundation for making the conference possible. We also thank the participants listed below for the lively interest and constructive criticism they provided at the conference.

Participants in the Bellagio Conference

Thomas J. Biersteker, Henry Luce Professor of Transnational Organizations, and Director, Watson Institute for International Studies, Brown University, Providence, RI, USA.

James G. Blight, Professor of International Relations (Research), Watson Institute for International Studies, Brown University, Providence, RI, USA.

Robert K. Brigham, Associate Professor of History, Vassar College, Poughkeepsie, NY, USA.

Chester L. Cooper, Deputy Director, Pacific Northwest National Laboratories, Washington, DC, USA; former analyst for Southeast Asia, CIA, State Department, and the National Security Council, 1945–1966; Special Assistant to Averell Harriman for Vietnam Negotiations, 1966–1968; and author of *The Lost Crusade: America in Vietnam*.

Frances FitzGerald, journalist and writer, author of *Fire in the Lake: The Vietnamese and the Americans in Vietnam*, New York, NY, USA.

Lawrence Freedman, Professor of War Studies, King's College, University of London, UK.

Gordon Goldstein, editor, Carnegie Corporation Project on McGeorge Bundy and the Vietnam War, New York, NY, USA.

Janet M. Lang, Associate Project Director, Watson Institute for International Studies, Brown University, Providence, RI, USA.

A. J. Langguth, Professor of Journalism, University of Southern California–Los Angeles, USA.

Le Hong Truong, Deputy Chief, Bureau for International Cooperation and Administration, Institute for International Relations, Hanoi, Vietnam.

Kathy Ngan Ha Le, Masters Candidate in Public Policy Program, John F. Kennedy School of Government, Harvard University, Cambridge, MA, USA.

Luu Doan Huynh, Senior Researcher and retired Foreign Service officer, Institute for International Relations, Hanoi, Vietnam.

Robert McNamara, Secretary of Defense to Presidents John F. Kennedy and Lyndon B. Johnson, Washington, DC, USA.

Nguyen Dinh Phuong, Ministry of Foreign Affairs, Hanoi, Vietnam, and retired Foreign Service officer, specializing in U.S. and European affairs.

Mari Olsen, Research Fellow, Peace Research Institute, Oslo, Norway.

Robert A. Pastor, Professor of Political Science, Emory University, Atlanta, GA, USA.

Svetlana Savranskaya, Lecturer in Political Science, Emory University, Atlanta, GA, USA.

Col. Herbert Y. Schandler (U.S. Army, Ret.), Professor in the Department of Grand Strategy, The National Defense University, Washington, DC, USA.

Waheguru Pal Singh Sidhu, Warren Weaver Fellow, The Rockefeller Foundation, New York, NY, USA.

Steve Smith, Director, Department of International Politics, University of Wales, Aberystwyth, Wales, UK.

Stein Tonnesson, Professor, Center for Development and the Environment, University of Oslo, Norway.

David Welch, Associate Professor of Political Science, University of Toronto, Ontario, Canada.

Odd Arne Westad, Research Director, Norwegian Nobel Institute, Oslo, Norway.

Representing the Bellagio Center: Gianna Celli, Acting Director of the Villa Serbelloni.

Representing Brown University: Leslie W. Baxter, Events Coordinator, Watson Institute for International Studies.

NOTES

CHAPTER 1. THE THEME AND STRUCTURE OF THE BOOK

1. This aphorism was often quoted by Robert F. Kennedy, for example, in his campaign stump speech during the Democratic presidential primary campaign in spring 1968.
2. Robert S. McNamara, with Brian VanDeMark, *In Retrospect: The Tragedy and Lessons of Vietnam*, rev. ed. (New York: Vintage, 1996; hardcover ed. publ. April 1995).
3. *Preventing Deadly Conflict: Final Report* (Washington, DC: Carnegie Commission on Preventing Deadly Conflict, 1997), p. xii.
4. Michael Sandel, quoted in *The New York Times*, December 31, 1989.
5. Carl Kaysen, "Is War Obsolete?" *International Security* (Spring 1990), vol. 14, no. 4, p. 63.
6. Joseph S. Nye Jr., "Ethics and Foreign Policy" (Washington, DC: Aspen Institute for Humanistic Studies, 1985), p. vii.
7. Gordon A. Craig, "Becoming Hitler," *The New York Review of Books* (May 29, 1997), vol. 44, no. 9, pp. 7–11, p. 7.
8. H. R. Trevor-Roper, "The Lost Moments of History," *The New York Review of Books* (October 27, 1988), vol. 35, no. 16, pp. 61–67, p. 67.
9. Ibid., p. 61.
10. See Philip E. Tetlock and Aaron Belkin, eds., *Counterfactual Experiments in World Politics: Logical, Methodological, and Psychological Perspectives* (Princeton: Princeton University Press, 1996). Although the contributions to this volume are mainly concerned with the ways in which policymakers use counterfactuals—or "What ifs?"—it also gives several examples of the way social scientists try to use alternative histories to deepen their own thinking about the causes of important events in recent U.S. foreign policy.
11. See Alexander L. George and Jane E. Holl, "The Warning-Response Problem and Missed Opportunities in Preventive Diplomacy," Carnegie Commission on Preventing Deadly Conflict, May 1997. The authors state two criteria they believe should be applied as one formulates hypothetical missed opportunities and attempts to evaluate them: "[First], was the alternative action that might have made a difference actually present at the time and known to be present, or was the alternative action associated with the belief in a missed opportunity something that one sees only in retrospect? If the latter, then the plausibility of the claim of a missed opportunity is weakened since it rests on the argument that alternative action could have and should have been seen at the time. . . . But [second], such claims should not be dismissed if one wants to draw useful lessons from such experiences. An after-the-fact identification of an action or strategy not known or considered at the time can still be useful in drawing lessons" (pp. 37–38, emphasis added). In this book, the phrase *missed opportunities* is often used in the second sense, because

the emphasis in not on speculating about historical probabilities but on drawing lessons from history.

12. Robert Legvold, quoted in the executive summary of the transcript of SALT II and the Growth of Mistrust (a conference of U.S. and Russian policymakers and scholars, held at Musgrove Plantation, St. Simons Island, GA, May 6–9, 1994), p. 10.

13. Ernest R. May, *"Lessons" of the Past: The Use and Misuse of History in American Foreign Policy* (New York: Oxford University Press, 1973), pp. 120–121.

14. Ernest R. May, "Comments by Professor Ernest R. May at the John F. Kennedy School of Government, Harvard University, April 25, 1995." Reprinted in the appendix to McNamara, *In Retrospect*, paperback edition, pp. 422–424, pp. 422–423.

15. See McNamara, *In Retrospect*, p. 323: "We thus failed to analyze and debate our actions in Southeast Asia—our objectives, the risks and costs of alternative ways of dealing with them, and the necessity of changing course when failure was clear—with the intensity and thoroughness that characterized the debates of the Executive Committee during the Cuban Missile Crisis."

16. This summary of the method of critical oral history is adapted from James G. Blight and David A. Welch, *On the Brink: Americans and Soviets Reexamine the Cuban Missile Crisis*, 2d ed. (New York: Hill and Wang, 1990), p. 6.

17. The complete transcripts of the audiotaped deliberations of the Executive Committee during the crisis are now available, thanks to the herculean efforts of Ernest R. May and Philip D. Zelikow, the editors of *The Kennedy Tapes: Inside the White House During the Cuban Missile Crisis* (Cambridge: Harvard University Press, 1997).

18. James G. Blight, Bruce J. Allyn, and David A. Welch, *Cuba on the Brink: Castro, the Missile Crisis, and the Soviet Collapse* (New York: Pantheon, 1993), pp. 56–63 and passim.

19. Gen. Anatoly Gribkov elaborated on these points in a meeting at the Woodrow Wilson Center, Washington, DC, on April 5, 1994.

20. The evidence from all sides is presented and evaluated in Aleksandr Fursenko and Timothy Naftali, *"One Hell of a Gamble": Khrushchev, Castro, and Kennedy, 1958–1964— The Secret History of the Cuban Missile Crisis* (New York: Norton, 1997). On why the three sides' intelligence services were so mistaken, see James G. Blight and David A. Welch, eds., *Intelligence and the Cuban Missile Crisis* (London: Cass, 1998).

21. See Anatoly Dokochaev, "Afterword to Sensational 100 Day Nuclear Cruise," *Krasnaya Zvezda*, November 6, 1992, p. 2; and V. Badurikin interview with Dimitri Volkogonov, "Operation Anadyr," *Trud*, October 27, 1993, p. 3.

22. In Blight et al., *Cuba on the Brink*, pp. 250–251.

23. In Blight et al., *Cuba on the Brink*, p. 251.

24. In Blight et al., *Cuba on the Brink*, p. 252.

25. Both the Canberra Commission (see Note 26, below) and the Carnegie Commission came to the same conclusion.

26. The disutility of nuclear weapons, except to deter others from using them, was endorsed in 1991 by the U.S. National Academy of Science and signed by eighteen security experts, including Gen. David C. Jones, former chairman of the U.S. Joint Chiefs of Staff; by the Henry L. Stimson Center's Panel on Nuclear Forces, chaired by Gen. Andrew Goodpaster, the former Supreme Allied Commander, Europe ("An Evolving Nuclear Posture," published in 1995); and by the Canberra Commission ("Report of the Canberra Commission on the Elimination of Nuclear Weapons," published in 1996). On the implications of the missile crisis data for contemporary nuclear nonproliferation policy, see McNamara, *In Retrospect*, pp. 337–346 ("The Nuclear Risks of the 1960s and Their Lessons for the Twenty-First Century"); and James G. Blight and David A. Welch,

"Risking 'the Destruction of Nations': Lessons of the Cuban Missile Crisis for New and Aspiring Nuclear States," *Security Studies*, vol. 4, no. 4 (summer 1995), pp. 811–850.

27. For accounts by three witnesses to the Havana conference, see Arthur Schlesinger Jr., "Four Days with Fidel: A Havana Diary," *New York Review of Books*, March 26, 1992, pp. 22–29; J. Anthony Lukas, "Fidel Castro's Theater of Now," *The New York Times*, January 20, 1992, p. 22A; and John Newhouse, "Socialism or Death," *New Yorker*, April 27, 1992, pp. 52–83.

28. See McNamara, *In Retrospect*, p. 231.

29. See for example, McNamara, *In Retrospect*, p. 252 (on the Christmas bombing pause of 1965–1966); or p. 320 (on the failure of another peace feeler sent through the British and Soviets in 1966).

30. McNamara, *In Retrospect*, p. 320.

31. The November 1995 visit was well covered in the press, thanks in no small part to the efforts of Ms. Karen Sughrue, who represented the Council on Foreign Relations in Hanoi during the visit. See, for example, Tim Larimer's pieces for *The New York Times*, many of which were carried in the *International Herald Tribune* (*IHT*): "McNamara Visit Sparks Pain in Vietnam" (*IHT*, November 7, 1995, p. 4); "McNamara in Hanoi for 'Dialogue,' Not to 'Tell' Ex-foe Anything" (*The New York Times*, November 9, 1995, p. A4); and "McNamara and Giap Revisit Gulf of Tonkin" (*IHT*, November 10, 1995, p. 1).

32. I learned in Vietnam that the Vietnamese edition of *In Retrospect* also contained all the endnotes, many of which contain references to formerly classified U.S. documents. Bob Brigham said he could not think of a single instance in which this had happened previously, indicating something of the interest with which the book was received. But it also indicated, as I would later learn, that some of the eventual Vietnamese participants in our joint project began, with their reading of the notes to my memoir, to comprehend for the first time the meaning of "document" and "documentation" as Americans use those terms.

33. There were six principal meetings, all of which played important roles in legitimizing the project in Hanoi. I met with the following: Gen. Vo Nguyen Giap, former defense minister; Vice-Pres. Madame Nguyen Thi Binh, a founder of the National Liberation Front; a seminar at the Institute for International Relations with approximately fifty of their top leaders from the war years, as well as their leading scholars of the war; Vice Prime Minister Phan Van Khai (now the prime minister); Nguyen Manh Cam, foreign minister; and finally with L. Desaix Anderson, the U.S. chief of mission in Hanoi. All endorsed the project.

34. For details on the Hanoi conference, see the following: David K. Shipler, "Robert McNamara and the Ghosts of Vietnam," *New York Times Magazine*, August 10, 1997, pp. 30–35, 42, 50, 56–57; and Norman Boucher, "Thinking Like the Enemy," *Brown Alumni Magazine*, November/December 1997, pp. 36–45. In addition, two documentary films based on the conference were produced: "Fighting Blind: The Vietnam War," which aired on CNN, December 23, 1997; and "Why Did We Fight the War?" produced by the NHK network (Japan) on August 2, 1998.

35. Ho Chi Minh quoted the U.S. Declaration of Independence during his Independence Day speech in Hanoi on September 2, 1945. Ho also sent several letters to President Truman, which were never answered.

36. The United States had supported French efforts to reclaim its pre–World War II colonies in Indochina; had financed the French war against the Vietminh resistance, led by Ho Chi Minh; and refused to become an official participant in the Geneva Conference during the summer of 1954. The conference resulted in the partition of Vietnam at the 17th

parallel, which marked the beginning of a more extensive U.S. role in South Vietnam, which led to the U.S. backing of the anticommunist government of Ngo Dinh Diem.

37. Eisenhower made this statement at a news conference in Washington on April 7, 1954.

Chapter 2. Enemies

1. John F. Kennedy, "Annual Message to Congress on the State of the Union," January 30, 1961. In *Public Papers of the Presidents* (Washington, DC: Government Printing Office, 1962), pp. 22, 23, 27.
2. "Founding Program of the National Liberation Front," announced in a Radio Hanoi broadcast, January 29, 1961. In Marvin E. Gettleman et al., eds., *Vietnam and America: A Documented History*, rev. and enlarged ed. (New York: Grove Press, 1995), pp. 188–192.
3. *International Herald Tribune*, November 10, 1995, pp. 1, 6.
4. Robert S. McNamara, with Brian VanDeMark, *In Retrospect: The Tragedy and Lessons of Vietnam*, rev. ed. (New York: Vintage, 1996; hardcover ed. publ. April 1995), p. 39.
5. Ibid., p. 128.
6. See ibid., pp. 129–136.
7. Excerpt from the transcript of the audiotaped exchange between Robert McNamara and Gen. Vo Nguyen Giap, Ministry of Defense, Hanoi, Vietnam, November 9, 1995. Translation by Pham Sanh Chau.
8. John F. Kennedy, "Inaugural Address," in *Public Papers of the Presidents, 1961*, pp. 1–3, p. 1.
9. Lloyd C. Gardner, *Pay Any Price: Lyndon Johnson and the Wars for Vietnam* (Chicago: Ivan R. Dee, 1995), pp. 40–64.
10. Thomas G. Paterson, ed., *Kennedy's Quest for Victory: American Foreign Policy, 1961–1963* (New York: Oxford University Press, 1989). See especially chapter 9 by Lawrence J. Bassett and Stephen E. Pelz, "The Failed Search for Victory: Vietnam and the Politics of War," pp. 223–252.
11. Henry Kissinger, *Diplomacy* (New York: Simon and Schuster, 1994), pp. 622–623.
12. Ibid., p. 641.
13. George C. Herring, *America's Longest War: The United States and Vietnam, 1950–1975*, 3d ed. (New York: McGraw Hill, 1996), p. 84.
14. W. W. Rostow, *The Diffusion of Power, 1957–1972: Men, Events, and Decisions That Shaped America's Role in the World—From Sputnik to Peking* (New York: Macmillan, 1972), p. 170.
15. Ibid., p. 298.
16. Nikita S. Khrushchev, "On Wars of National Liberation," January 6, 1961. Quoted in James A. Nathan and James K. Oliver, *United States Foreign Policy and World Order*, 2d ed. (Boston: Little, Brown, 1981), p. 254.
17. See James G. Blight and Pater Kornbluh, eds., *Politics of Illusion: The Bay of Pigs Invasion Reexamined* (Boulder: Lynne Rienner, 1998), pp. 63–64. At a 1996 conference on the Bay of Pigs, Schlesinger said that the Kennedy administration had what, in retrospect, seems to have been an "overreaction" to the Khrushchev speech. But at the time, he added, it gave the president and his advisers "the feeling that history was running against us" (p. 63).
18. William P. Bundy, unpublished manuscript, written in 1970–1972, chapter 3. Quoted in William Conrad Gibbons, *The U.S. Government and the Vietnam War: Executive and Legislative Roles and Relationships*, 4 volumes (Princeton: Princeton University Press, 1986), vol. 2, p. 41.

19. John F. Kennedy, "America's Stake in Vietnam," Speech to the American Friends of Vietnam, June 1956. Quoted in Gibbons, *U.S. Government and the Vietnam War*, vol. 2, p. 5.

20. Ibid., pp. 4–7.

21. See the memorandum of Clark Clifford, who attended the January 19 discussion between Eisenhower and Kennedy: "Memorandum of Conference on January 19, 1961, Between President Eisenhower and President-elect Kennedy on the Subject of Laos," in *The Pentagon Papers: The Defense Department History of United States Decisionmaking on Vietnam* (Gravel ed.), 4 volumes (Boston: Beacon Press, 1971), vol. 2, pp. 635–637. Also note Robert S. McNamara's memo on the same conference: McNamara, *In Retrospect*, p. 35.

22. Dwight D. Eisenhower, in a meeting of the National Security Council, December 31, 1960. Quoted in Gibbons, *U.S. Government and the Vietnam War*, vol. 2, p. 9.

23. Ibid.

24. Mao Zedong, cited in Odd Arne Westad et al., eds., "77 Conversations Between Chinese and Foreign Leaders on the Wars in Indochina, 1964–1977." In *Bulletin of the Cold War International History Project*, Working Paper No. 22, May 1998, p. 87.

25. Lyndon B. Johnson, quoted in Gibbons, *U.S. Government and the Vietnam War*, vol. 2, pp. 41–42.

26. National Security Action Memorandum (NSAM) 52, May 11, 1961, in *Pentagon Papers* (Gravel ed.), vol. 2, pp. 642–643; see also Gibbons, *U.S. Government and the Vietnam War*, vol. 2, pp. 39–41.

27. Kennedy, "Inaugural Address," in *Public Papers of the Presidents, 1961*, p. 1.

28. John F. Kennedy, "Address Before the American Society of Newspaper Editors," April 20, 1961. In *Public Papers of the Presidents, 1961*, pp. 304–306, p. 306.

29. Theodore C. Sorensen, *Kennedy* (New York: Harper and Row, 1965), p. 292.

30. John F. Kennedy, "Special Message to the Congress on Urgent National Needs," May 25, 1961. In *Public Papers of the Presidents, 1961*, pp. 396–406, p. 397.

31. Le Duan, Thu Vao Nam ["Letters to the South"] (Hanoi: Nha Xuat Ban Su That, 1986), p. 52. Quoted in William J. Duiker, *The Communist Road to Power in Vietnam*, 2d ed. (Boulder: Westview, 1996), p. 222.

32. Ibid., p. 214. Duiker is not precise about the date in January when the Politburo made its decision. But recent evidence suggests it occurred on January 31.

33. Vo Nguyen Giap, *Once Again, We Will Win* (Hanoi: Foreign Languages Publishing House, 1966), p. 29. Reprinted as "The Political and Military Line of Our Party," in Gettleman et al., eds., *Vietnam and America*, pp. 193–201, p. 194.

34. Truong Chinh, *The Resistance Will Win*, 3d ed. (Hanoi: Foreign Languages Publishing House, 1966, orig. publ. 1947), pp. 106–107. Quoted by Bernard B. Fall, *Street Without Joy* (Mechanicsburg, PA: Stackpole Books, 1961), pp. 372–373.

35. This is the central premise of chapter 15 ("The Future of Revolutionary War"), in Fall, *Street Without Joy*, pp. 369–382.

36. Bui Tin, *Following Ho Chi Minh: Memoirs of a North Vietnamese Colonel*, trans. by Judy Stowe and Do Van (London: Hurst, 1995), p. 42.

37. For an account of the Ben Tre uprising by a participant, see Mrs. Nguyen Thi Dinh, *No Other Road to Take: Memoir of Nguyen Thi Dinh*, trans. by Mai Elliott (Ithaca: Cornell University Data Paper 102, Southeast Asia Program, Department of Asian Studies, June 1976), pp. 17–19. Reprinted in Gettleman et al., eds., *Vietnam and America*, pp. 165–188. Mrs. Nguyen Thi Dinh later became deputy commander of the People's Liberation Army Forces. In addition, see To Minh Trung, "Ngon co dau cua phong trong dong khoi toan mien Nam Viet Nam" ["The first banner of the concerted uprising movement in all of South Vietnam"], *Nghien Cuu Lich Su 119* (February 1969), p. 49. See also Duiker, *Communist Road to Power in Vietnam*, pp. 204–206.

38. On Tay Ninh, see Eric M. Bergerud, "The Success of Communist Strategy at the Village Level." In Robert J. McMahon, ed., *Major Problems in the History of the Vietnam War: Documents and Essays*, 2d ed. (Lexington, MA: D.C. Heath, 1995), pp. 312–336, p. 321.

39. Lt. Gen. Samuel Williams, quoted in ibid., p. 321.

40. Ibid.

41. See Duiker, *Communist Road to Power in Vietnam*, pp. 205–206.

42. Truong Nhu Tang, "On the Origins of the National Liberation Front (1957–1959)." In McMahon, ed., *Major Problems in the History of the Vietnam War*, pp. 285–288 (quotation at pp. 287–288). The piece is excerpted from Truong Nhu Tang, David Chanoff, and Doan Van Toai, *A Vietcong Memoir* (New York: Harcourt, 1985).

43. Isaiah Berlin, *The Crooked Timber of Humanity: Chapters in the History of Ideas*, ed. by Henry Hardy (New York: Knopf, 1991), pp. 260–261.

44. Ho Chi Minh, "The Path Which Led Me to Leninism." In Gettleman et al., eds., *Vietnam and America*, pp. 20–22, p. 22. The piece originally appeared in 1960.

45. Le Duan, letter to Nguyen Van Linh, February 1961, in *Thu Vao Nam* [Letters to the South] (Hanoi: Nha Xuat Ban Su That, 1986), p. 35. Quoted in Duiker, *Communist Road to Power in Vietnam*, p. 206.

46. *Pentagon Papers* (Gravel ed.), vol. 1, p. 340.

47. Tran Van Giau and Le Van Chat, *The South Vietnam Liberation National Front* (Hanoi: Foreign Languages Publishing House, 1962), pp. 27–29. This "Founding Program of the National Liberation Front of Vietnam" is reprinted in Gettleman et al., eds., *Vietnam and America*, pp. 188–192.

48. Tran Van Gian and Le Van Chat, *National Front*, pp. 27–29. Reprinted in Gettleman et al., eds., *Vietnam and America*, p. 189.

49. On the Cuban missile crisis project, see James G. Blight and David A. Welch, *On the Brink: Americans and Soviets Reexamine the Cuban Missile Crisis*, 2d ed. (New York: Hill and Wang, 1990); and James G. Blight, Bruce J. Allyn, and David A. Welch, *Cuba on the Brink: Castro, the Missile Crisis, and the Soviet Collapse* (New York: Pantheon, 1993).

50. See Chapter 3, on the Geneva Conference and Geneva Accords of 1954.

51. George F. Kennan, "The Sources of Soviet Conduct," *Foreign Affairs*, vol. 25, no. 4 (July 1947), pp. 566–582.

52. Nikita Khrushchev, "On Wars of National Liberation," January 6, 1961. See Nathan and Oliver, *United States Foreign Policy and World Order*, p. 254, for the key passage.

53. Dean Acheson, quoted in *Pentagon Papers* (Gravel ed.), vol. 1, p. 51.

54. Dwight D. Eisenhower, "President's News Conference, April 7, 1954." In *Public Papers of the Presidents, 1954* (Washington, DC: Government Printing Office, 1955), p. 382.

55. Clark Clifford, "Memorandum," January 19, 1961. In *Pentagon Papers* (Gravel ed.), p. 636.

56. Kennedy, "America's Stake in Vietnam" (1956). In Gibbons, *U.S. Government and the Vietnam War*, p. 5.

57. Kennedy, "Inaugural Address," in *Public Papers of the Presidents, 1961*, p. 1.

58. "Would the Loss of South Vietnam and Laos Precipitate a 'Domino Effect' in the Far East?" A memorandum for CIA Director John McCone from Sherman Kent, Chairman of the Board of National Estimates, June 9, 1964.

59. Aleksandr Fursenko and Timothy Naftali, *"One Hell of a Gamble"*: *Khrushchev, Castro, and Kennedy, 1958–1964—The Secret History of the Cuban Missile Crisis* (New York: Norton, 1997).

60. On Resolution 15, see Chapter 3.

61. See "Ho Chi Minh: An Asian Tito?—A Summary." In *Pentagon Papers* (Gravel ed.), vol. 1, pp. 47–52.
62. Richard Harwood, "As Wrong as McNamara," *Washington Post*, April 19, 1995. Reprinted in McNamara, *In Retrospect*, pp. 387–390. The passage from Halberstam is on p. 389.
63. Susan Welch, quoted in ibid., p. 389.
64. W. W. Rostow, "The Case for the War," *Times Literary Supplement* (London), June 9, 1995. Reprinted in McNamara, *In Retrospect*, paperback edition, pp. 425–442 (quotation at pp. 427–428).
65. Graham Greene, *The Quiet American* (London: Penguin, 1962), p. 163.

CHAPTER 3. THE EVOLUTION OF WASHINGTON'S AND HANOI'S MINDSETS, 1945–1960

1. On page 32 of *In Retrospect*, I emphasized the considerable impact the top U.S. specialists on the Soviet Union had on President Kennedy and his senior advisers, and I stated we lacked their counterparts with respect to Vietnam. See *In Retrospect: The Tragedy and Lessons of Vietnam*, rev. ed. (New York: Vintage, 1996; hardcover ed. publ. April 1995).

When *In Retrospect* was published in 1995, two former U.S. intelligence officers from the State Department took issue with my statement. They stated that Presidents Kennedy and Johnson, and their senior advisers, did have access to accurate appraisals of events in Vietnam, that they—and in particular I—failed to take account of that information. I fear the point I wished to make has been lost. It is this: "Our top Soviet experts had associated both socially and professionally with the top Russian leaders, including Khrushchev" (*The New York Times*, September 14, 1995, reprinted in *In Retrospect*, pp. 397–399, p. 397). They knew Khrushchev and his people. They had known them for many years. In addition, they were esteemed and trusted by the presidents they served. They sat at the same table with the president and his senior associates; they were consulted; their views mattered.

And they were often right when the chips were down, for example, in October 1962, when Llewellyn "Tommy" Thompson disagreed point-blank with a puzzled John Kennedy's claim that Khrushchev would never remove missiles from Cuba without a public "trade" of U.S. missiles in Turkey. Tommy told the president he was wrong. On this basis, Kennedy transmitted a letter to Khrushchev suggesting removal of missiles in exchange for a noninvasion pledge as regarded Cuba. Khrushchev accepted, ending the most dangerous phase of the crisis. See James G. Blight, ed., and McGeorge Bundy, transcriber, "October 27, 1962: Transcripts of the EXCOMM Tapes," *International Security*, vol. 12, no. 3 (1987–1988), pp. 30–92, esp. pp. 57–60. Thompson is the unsung hero of the missile crisis, in my opinion.

Contrast this with Vietnam. Who knew Ho Chi Minh? Who knew many—or any—of his colleagues? Where was there a single individual who both had a nuanced understanding of the North Vietnamese—and their Chinese allies—and the friendship and respect of Presidents Kennedy and Johnson? The answer is obvious: There was no one. In their absence, we relied primarily on the CIA (which drew on experts from State, Defense, the NSC, etc.) for evaluation of North Vietnam's intentions and capabilities. It was not until September 12, 1967, that the CIA, in a report delivered to the president by CIA Director Richard Helms, predicted an unfavorable outcome to the war in Vietnam and stated that "if the U.S. accepts failure in Vietnam it will pay some price in the form of new risks which success there would preclude. . . . [But] the risks are probably more limited and controllable than most previous argument has indicated." Quoted in *In Ret-rospect*, p. 293. The president did not distribute the report, and I was not aware of its existence until my research assistant brought it to my attention in 1994, while I was drafting *In Retrospect* (see pp. 291–294). No doubt there were individuals in the U.S. government who held such views before September 1967, but they were not given the high-level attention accorded to the CIA reports.

2. Nguyen Co Thach died in early April 1998, following a long illness. He championed our collaborative project within the Vietnamese leadership. See *The New York Times*, April 12, 1998, for details of Nguyen Co Thach's career.

3. McNamara, *In Retrospect*, p. 29.

4. Dean Acheson, in *The New York Times Book Review*, October 12, 1969, p. 30; cited in Chester L. Cooper, *The Lost Crusade: America in Vietnam* (New York: Dodd, Mead, 1970), pp. 55–56.

5. Dean Acheson, quoted in *The Pentagon Papers: The Defense Department History of United States Decisionmaking on Vietnam* (Gravel ed.), 4 volumes (Boston: Beacon Press, 1971), vol. 1, p. 51.

6. Ibid.

7. National Security Council Report #68 (NSC–68). *Foreign Relations of the United States, 1950*, vol. 1, pp. 234 ff (Washington, DC: Government Printing Office, various years). Cited in Marilyn B. Young, *The Vietnam Wars: 1945–1990* (New York: HarperCollins, 1991), p. 25.

8. See George C. Herring, *America's Longest War: The United States and Vietnam, 1950–1975*, 2d ed. (New York: Knopf, 1986), pp. 3–42.

9. John Foster Dulles, Speech to the Overseas Press Club, New York City, March 29, 1954, in *Department of State Bulletin vol. 30* (April 12, 1954), pp. 539–540. Cited in Marvin E. Gettleman et al., eds., *Vietnam and America: A Documented History*, rev. and enlarged ed. (New York: Grove Press, 1995), p. 51.

10. Ibid.

11. Cooper, *Lost Crusade*, p. 76.

12. Townsend Hoopes, *The Devil and John Foster Dulles* (Boston, 1973), p. 222. Cited in Herring, *America's Longest War*, p. 40.

13. Ibid., pp. 37–38.

14. Cooper, *Lost Crusade*, p. 75.

15. John Foster Dulles, July 23, 1954. Cited in *Pentagon Papers* (Gravel ed.), vol. 1, p. 176.

16. Walter Bedell Smith, July 23, 1954. Cited in ibid., p. 176.

17. Ho Chi Minh, "Vietnam Declaration of Independence," September 2, 1945, in Ho Chi Minh, *Selected Works*, 4 volumes (Hanoi: Foreign Languages Publishing House, 1960–1962), vol. 3, pp. 17–21. Cited in Gettleman et al., eds., *Vietnam and America*, pp. 26–27.

18. For the history of Ho Chi Minh's efforts to contact President Truman, see *Pentagon Papers* (Gravel ed.), vol. 1, pp. 50–51. For the text of Ho's second letter to Truman, dated October 17, 1945, see Gettleman et al., eds., *Vietnam and America*, pp. 47–47.

19. Ho Chi Minh, cited in *Pentagon Papers* (Gravel ed.), vol. 1, pp. 49–50. There are various renderings of Ho's declaration, some more or less earthy than others.

20. Ho Chi Minh, interview given in May 1950. Cited in Robert J. McMahon, ed., *Major Problems in the History of the Vietnam War: Documents and Essays*, 2d ed. (Lexington, MA: D.C. Heath, 1995), pp. 84–85.

21. For a detailed analysis of Pham Van Dong's proposal to the Geneva Conference, see *Pentagon Papers* (Gravel ed.), vol. 1, pp. 118–120.

22. Ibid., p. 173.

23. Jean Chauvel, cited in *Pentagon Papers* (Gravel ed.), vol. 1, pp. 173. See also Cooper, *Lost Crusade*, pp. 99–100, especially his reference to U.S. Assistant Secretary of State William P. Bundy, who in 1967 recalled that at Geneva "we played a critical backstage role . . . keeping alive the possibility of U.S. military intervention." Cooper is unconvinced and believes that whatever role the United States may have played, it was due to the "state of confusion" in which the Eisenhower administration found itself (p. 100).

24. Averell Harriman, the head of the U.S. delegation to the Paris Peace Conference beginning in May 1968, did, however, work closely with the Soviets to launch the talks. He had particularly good relations with Anatoly Dobrynin and Valerian Zorin, who proved useful in getting Hanoi to show some signs of "restraint" as the talks were initiated. See Ilya V. Gaiduk, *The Soviet Union and the Vietnam War* (Chicago: Ivan R. Dee, 1996), pp. 156–193.

25. Ho Chi Minh, July 15, 1954, cited in *Pentagon Papers* (Gravel ed.), vol. 1, p. 172. See also Michael H. Hunt, *Lyndon Johnson's War: America's Cold War Crusade in Vietnam, 1945–1968* (New York: Hill and Wang, 1996), pp. 33–35.

26. Ho Chi Minh, cited in Hunt, *Lyndon Johnson's War*, p. 33.

27. Le Duan, "The Path of Revolution in the South" [Duong Loi Cach Mien Nam], 1956, trans. by Robert K. Brigham. For an analysis of the context in which the pamphlet appeared, see William J. Duiker, *The Communist Road to Power in Vietnam*, 2d ed. (Boulder: Westview, 1996), pp. 189–191.

28. Resolution 15, cited in *The Great Anti-U.S. Resistance War for National Salvation of the Fatherland, 1954–1975—Military Events* [Cuoc Khang Chien Chong My, Cuu Nuoc, 1954–1975] (Hanoi: Nha Xuat Ban Quan Doi Nhan Dan, 1988), p. 30. Not all sources are as unequivocal as the text of Resolution 15 regarding the role of revolutionary violence by January 1959. Differences of opinion—perhaps differences between North and South, between those who direct and supply and those who fight and die—are reflected between Resolution 15 and, for example, *Nhung Su kien su Dang* [Events in the history of the Party], 3 volumes (Hanoi: Thong tin Ly luan, 1984). According to this official history, military struggle was not elevated to the same level as political struggle until early 1961, with the announcement of the founding of the NLF.

    In any case, Resolution 15 was a watershed, after which armed struggle—violent revolution, ultimately supplied and even fought by northerners, as well as southerners—would become the rule rather than the exception.

29. Ibid., pp. 30–32.

30. For the full English text of the broadcast, see *Pentagon Papers* (Gravel ed.), vol. 1, pp. 339–341.

31. *Great Resistance War*, pp. 44–45.

32. "Founding Program of the National Liberation Front of South Vietnam," broadcast on Radio Hanoi, January 29, 1961. Foreign Broadcast Information Service (FBIS), February 13–14, 1961. The text is carried in full in Gettleman et al., eds., *Vietnam and America*, pp. 188–192 (Article 1 at p. 189).

33. Nguyen Chi Thanh, *Who Will Win in South Vietnam?* (Peking: Foreign Language Press, 1963), pp. 1, 4, 8. Reprinted as "On Communist Strategy," and excerpted in McMahon, ed., *Major Problems in the History of the Vietnam War*, pp. 299–301. Little is known about this shadowy figure. Bui Tin says that the Tet Offensive was largely his idea. See his *Following Ho Chi Minh: Memoirs of a North Vietnamese Colonel*, trans. by Judy Stowe and Do Van (London: Hurst, 1995), p. 61. Bui Tin also says that Nguyen Chi Thanh died of a heart attack. But see also Duiker, *Communist Road to Power in Viet-*

nam, pp. 282–288. Duiker speculates that Nguyen Chi Thanh may have died in a U.S. bombing raid while in Hanoi, discussing final plans for the Tet Offensive.

34. Nguyen Khac Huynh, in James G. Blight, ed., and Kathy N. Le and Quang M. Do, trans., *Missed Opportunities I: Revisiting the Decisions of the Vietnam War, 1961–1968* (the June 1997 Hanoi conference).

35. All subsequent excerpts in this section are from James G. Blight, ed., *Missed Opportunities II: Revisiting the Decisions of the Vietnam War, 1945–1968* (the February 1998 Hanoi conference).

36. The question of whether Ho Chi Minh could have been an "Asian Tito" is taken up in some detail in *Pentagon Papers* (Gravel ed.), vol. 1, pp. 47–52.

37. At the July 1998 study conference in Bellagio, Italy, Luu Doan Huynh expanded on this point. According to Vietnamese documents, he said, the Vietnamese communist representative in Bangkok, Nguyen Duc Quy, sought successfully to maintain good relations with personnel at the U.S. embassy. It was Nguyen Duc Quy who, in 1949, granted an interview to American journalists Sol Sander and Andrew Roth indicating that Ho Chi Minh and his fellow resistance fighters wished to remain neutral with regard to the East-West Cold War. Between 1950 and 1954, however, all contacts with the United States were cut off. It was clear by then, according to Luu Doan Huynh, that the U.S. support for the French made a rapprochement with the Americans impossible. In addition, the Thai authorities, probably encouraged by the United States, ordered Nguyen Duc Quy out of the country.

38. On July 13, 1954, as the Geneva negotiations were nearing their July 20 deadline set by the French, Pham Van Dong, according to Chester Cooper, told Pierre Mendes-France that "he would accept a line at the 16th parallel." But the French held out for the 18th parallel. Only on July 20 did all parties agree to the 17th parallel. Whether the United States, in its role as unofficial participant in the conference, would have immediately agreed to the 16th parallel is difficult to say. See Cooper, *Lost Crusade*, pp. 96–97.

39. Although the Eisenhower administration had decided against a U.S. intervention in Indochina, many in the administration, including Secretary of State Dulles, found it useful to leave open the possibility of U.S. intervention in their dealings with the Soviets and Chinese.

40. John Foster Dulles, cited in Young, *The Vietnam Wars*, p. 46.

41. Le Ly Hayslip and Charles Jay Wurts, *When Heaven and Earth Changed Places* (New York: Bantam, 1989), cited in McMahon, ed., *Major Problems in the History of the Vietnam War*, pp. 293–297, p. 297.

42. The U.S. Military Assistance Advisory Group (MAAG) was set up in 1954, just as similar offices were set up elsewhere in the world at the time, to provide military equipment to the forces of the host country and training by U.S. specialists on the use and maintenance of equipment. In this sense, the United States did have a military "presence" in the South by 1954.

43. See *Pentagon Papers* (Gravel ed.), vol. 2, pp. 23–25, "The Counterinsurgency Plan."

44. Gen. Maxwell D. Taylor, "Letter from the President's Military Representative to the President," November 3, 1961. In FRUS, 1961–1963, vol. 1, pp. 477–479.

45. NLF Founding Program, in Gettleman et al., eds., *Vietnam and America*, p. 189.

46. Luu Doan Huynh, in the June 1997 Hanoi conference.

Chapter 4. A Neutral Solution

1. T. S. Eliot, "Burnt Norton" (1935). In *Collected Poems, 1909–1962* (New York: Harcourt Brace, 1963), pp. 175–181, p. 175.

2. John F. Kennedy, quoted in Arthur M. Schlesinger Jr., *Robert Kennedy and His Times* (New York: Ballantine, 1978), p. 767.

3. Ibid., p. 774.

4. Robert S. McNamara, with Brian VanDeMark, McNamara, *In Retrospect: The Tragedy and Lessons of Vietnam*, rev. ed. (New York: Vintage, 1996; hardcover ed. publ. April 1995), p. 271.

5. See note 31, p. 483, of the paperback edition of *In Retrospect*.

6. See Marilyn B. Young, *The Vietnam Wars, 1945–1990* (New York: HarperCollins, 1991), pp. 46–47.

7. John Foster Dulles, cited in ibid., p. 47.

8. "Final Declaration of the Geneva Conference," in Marvin E. Gettleman et al., eds., *Vietnam and America*, rev. and enlarged ed. (New York: Grove Press, 1995), pp. 74–76, p. 75.

9. George W. Ball, *The Past Has Another Pattern: Memoirs* (New York: Norton, 1982), p. 362.

10. Ibid., pp. 361–362.

11. See Bernard B. Fall, *Street Without Joy* (Mechanicsburg, PA: Stackpole Books, 1964), chapter 13, "The Loss of Laos," especially pp. 334–336.

12. "Notes of Conversation Between President-elect Kennedy and President Eisenhower," January 19, 1961. In *Foreign Relations of the United States*, 1961–1963, vol. 24, pp. 19–20 (Washington, DC: Government Printing Office, various years). The quotation is from Evelyn Lincoln's transcription of notes dictated following the meeting by Kennedy.

13. "Memorandum for the Record," January 19, 1961. In ibid., pp. 20–22. The notes were taken by Eisenhower's assistant, Gen. Wilton Persons.

14. Theodore C. Sorensen, *Kennedy* (New York: Harper and Row, 1965), p. 640.

15. The options are paraphrased from detailed summaries given in ibid., pp. 639–642.

16. John F. Kennedy, "The President's News Conference," March 23, 1961. In *Public Papers of the Presidents, 1961* (Washington, DC: Government Printing Office, 1962), pp. 213–220, especially pp. 213–215.

17. Robert Lowell, "Fall 1961." In *Selected Poems* (New York: Farrar, Straus, and Giroux, 1977), p. 105.

18. See *The Pentagon Papers: The Defense Department History of United States Decision-making on Vietnam* (Gravel ed.), 4 volumes (Boston: Beacon Press, 1971), vol. 2, pp. 84–127, for the context, the text of the Taylor Report, covering letters, and response by Dean Rusk and Robert McNamara.

19. National Security Action Memorandum (NSAM) 111, in *Pentagon Papers* (Gravel ed.), vol. 2, pp. 117–120, and William Conrad Gibbons, *The U.S. Government and the Vietnam War: Executive and Legislative Roles and Relationships*, 4 volumes (Princeton: Princeton University Press, 1986), vol. 2, pp. 92–99.

20. Arthur M. Schlesinger Jr., *A Thousand Days: John F. Kennedy in the White House* (New York: Fawcett, 1965), p. 504. See also George McT. Kahin, *Intervention: How America Became Involved in Vietnam* (New York: Anchor, 1986), pp. 136–138.

21. Schlesinger, *Thousand Days*, p. 504.

22. Ibid., p. 503.

23. Averell Harriman, cited in Kahin, *Intervention*, pp. 136–137.

24. Averell Harriman, cited in ibid., p. 477.

25. John F. Kennedy to McGeorge Bundy, November 14, 1961. In Gibbons, *U.S. Government and the Vietnam War*, vol. 2, p. 93.

26. John F. Kennedy to Dean Rusk and Robert S. McNamara, November 14, 1961. In Kahin, *Intervention*, p. 137. Rostow's critique is in his Memorandum for the President, "Negotiations About Vietnam," November 14, 1961.

27. Schlesinger, *Thousand Days*, p. 503.

28. Kahin, *Intervention*, p. 137.

29. For the Kennedy administration's view, see Sorensen, *Kennedy*, p. 647; and Roger Hilsman, *To Move a Nation: The Politics of Foreign Policy in the Administration of John F. Kennedy* (Garden City, NY: Doubleday, 1967), pp. 140–141.

30. "Implications of the Fall of Nam Tha," Special National Intelligence Report (58–3–62), May 9, 1962, pp. 4–5.

31. Hilsman, *To Move a Nation*, p. 141.

32. Sorensen, *Kennedy*, p. 547. But see Fall, *Street Without Joy*, pp. 338–339, for a detailed account of the episode.

33. See Gibbons, *U.S. Government and the Vietnam War*, vol. 2, p. 120, for J. K. Galbraith's neutralist proposal of April 1962 and excerpts from the more than slightly horrified responses of the Joint Chiefs of Staff and also by Walt Rostow.

34. Chester L. Cooper, *The Lost Crusade: America in Vietnam* (New York: Dodd, Mead, 1970), p. 190.

35. Ibid.

36. William Sullivan, quoted in Gibbons, *U.S. Government and the Vietnam War*, vol. 2, p. 121. See pp. 120–122 for the context. Gibbons reports that Sullivan was unsure of the exact date of the meeting between Harriman and Ung Van Khiem. But sources in Hanoi have confirmed July 23, 1962, the day the Geneva Agreement was signed, as the day of the meeting.

37. William Sullivan, in ibid., p. 121.

38. For example, Chester Bowles made two more attempts to interest Kennedy in a neutral solution for Saigon; the last one, in the spring of 1963, failed even to get a response. See ibid., p. 121, note 122.

39. Chester Cooper, in James G. Blight, ed., and Kathy N. Le and Quang M. Do, trans., *Missed Opportunities I: Revisiting the Decisions of the Vietnam War, 1961–1968* (the June 1997 Hanoi conference), June 20, session 2: "Missed Opportunities Between 1945 and 1960."

40. Cooper, *Lost Crusade*, p. 191.

41. Dean Rusk, as told to Richard Rusk, *As I Saw It*, ed. by Daniel S. Papp (New York: Norton, 1990), p. 434.

42. See Stanley Karnow, *Vietnam: A History* (New York: Penguin, 1991), pp. 294–297. The statement by Madame Nhu is on p. 297.

43. See Hilsman, *To Move a Nation*, p. 498.

44. Roger Hilsman, "Memorandum of Conversation," September 3, 1963. In Gibbons, *U.S. Government and the Vietnam War*, vol. 2, pp. 164–165.

45. Mieczyslaw Maneli, *War of the Vanquished*, trans. by Maria de Gorgey (New York: Harper and Row), 1971.

46. Ellen J. Hammer, *A Death in November: America in Vietnam, 1963* (New York: E. P. Dutton, 1987).

47. Ibid., pp. 222–223.

48. Ibid., pp. 225–232.

49. Francis X. Winters, *The Year of the Hare: America in Vietnam, January 25, 1963–February 15, 1964* (Athens: University of Georgia Press, 1997), p. 44.

50. Mieczyslaw Maneli, in *The New York Times*, January 27, 1975. Cited in Hammer, *A Death in November*, p. 348.

51. Schlesinger, *Robert Kennedy and His Times*, pp. 777–778.

52. National Liberation Front proclamation of November 8, 1963. Cited in Kahin, *Intervention*, p. 186.

53. Lyndon B. Johnson, "New Year's Message to the Chairman of the Military Revolutionary

Council in South Viet-Nam," January 1, 1964. In *Public Papers of the Presidents, 1963–1964* (Washington, DC: Government Printing Office, 1965), p. 106.

54. See the responses of McGeorge Bundy and Walt Rostow in Kahin, *Intervention*, p. 191.

55. For example, see George Ball to the Saigon Embassy, December 16, 1963: "Nothing is further from USG [U.S. Government] mind than 'neutral solution for Viet-Nam.' We intend to win." See also the cable from the CIA Station in Saigon to Michael Forrestal, National Security Council officer for Southeast Asia, December 16, 1963: "On the subject of neutralism . . . and Sihanouk's gratuitous and unwelcome offer to 'federate' with South Vietnam, if only the latter would stop fighting and espouse a neutral foreign policy." Both available at the LBJ Library, Austin, Texas.

56. Duong Van Minh, interview in 1970 with George McT. Kahin. Cited in Kahin, *Intervention*, p. 185.

57. Nguyen Ngoc Tho, interview in 1970 with George McT. Kahin. In ibid., p. 185.

58. Ball, *The Past Has Another Pattern*, p. 378.

59. See Luu Doan Huynh, "Vietnam-U.S. Relations from September 1945 to July 1954," unpublished background paper prepared for the June 1997 conference in Hanoi (in English, 22 pp.). See also his recent review essay in *The Journal of American History*, March 1998, pp. 1464–1468.

60. See Huynh, "Vietnam-U.S. Relations."

61. Odd Arne Westad et al., eds., "77 Conversations Between Chinese and Foreign Leaders on the Wars in Indochina, 1964–1977." In *Bulletin of the Cold War International History Project*, Working Paper No. 22, May 1998.

62. The Non-Aligned Movement is often said to have been founded at the Bandung, Indonesia, conference in April 1955. But in discussions in Hanoi, it has become clear that the Hanoi leadership did not see it this way. To Hanoi, the Bandung meeting was really only a rallying point in support of the national independence of countries in Africa and Asia. Some participants at Bandung were neutral, whereas others, like China and Pakistan, were not. The Hanoi government regarded the Belgrade conference of November 1961 as the actual founding of a neutralist movement. All participants in Belgrade proclaimed a neutralist policy. Obviously, however, the neutralist plank in the founding platform of the NLF antedates the Belgrade meeting by almost two years. According to Vietnamese testimony, the real inspiration for Vietnamese neutralism at the time derived from the experiment in Laos, with which the Vietnamese were intimately familiar, and less so from Indonesia, Burma, and Cambodia.

63. See Huynh, "Vietnam-U.S. Relations."

64. This is obviously a very sensitive subject, one on which Vietnamese officials, past and present, are not inclined to comment for the public record. The substance of the preceding paragraph has, however, been confirmed by sources in both Hanoi and Ho Chi Minh City in interviews conducted between 1992 and 1998.

65. Excerpt from Resolution 15, January 1959 [Nhung su kien lich su Dang]. See also James G. Blight, ed., *Missed Opportunities II: Revisiting the Decisions of the Vietnam War, 1945–1968* (the February 1998 Hanoi conference), session 4, "A Neutralist Solution?" See also Bui Tin, *Following Ho Chi Minh: Memoirs of a North Vietnamese Colonel*, trans. by Judy Stowe and Do Van (London: Hurst, 1995), p. 41, for the role of Le Duan in the drafting of Resolution 15.

66. "Founding Program of the National Liberation Front of South Vietnam," in Gettleman et al., eds., *Vietnam and America*, pp. 189, 192.

67. Radio Hanoi broadcast in English to Europe and East Asia, February 2, 1962, 1530 GMT.

68. Tran Van Giau and Le Van Chat, *The South Viet Nam Liberation National Front* (Hanoi: Foreign Languages Publishing House, 1962), p. 31.

69. "A Threat to Peace: North Viet-Nam's Effort to Conquer South Viet-nam," U.S. Department of State White Paper, December 1961.

70. "Mot So Van Kien Cua Dang Ve Chong My, Cuu Nuoc, Tap I, 1954–1965" [Selected party documents related to the Anti-U.S. Resistance War for National Salvation of the Fatherland, vol. 1, 1954–1965] (Hanoi: Nha Xuat Ban Su That, 1985), pp. 136–156.

71. Nguyen Van Hieu, Liberation Radio clandestine broadcast in Vietnamese, June 12, 1962, 1400 GMT.

72. See William J. Duiker, *The Communist Road to Power in Vietnam*, 2d ed. (Boulder: Westview, 1996), pp. 222–223, for a synopsis of the key passages.

73. This account follows that of Luu Doan Huynh in his intervention on the topic at the June 1997 Hanoi conference, June 20, session 2, "Missed Opportunities Between 1945 and 1960."

74. Quoted in an intervention of Luu Doan Huynh at the February 1998 Hanoi conference, February 24, session 4, "A Neutralist Solution?"

75. Le Duan, letter to Nguyen Van Linh, *Thu Vao Nam* [Letters to the South] (Hanoi: Nha Xuat Ban Su That, 1986), letter of July 1962.

76. Editorial in *Nhan Dan* (Hanoi), July 24, 1962. Cited by Luu Doan Huynh in an intervention during the February 1998 Hanoi conference, February 24, session 4, "A Neutralist Solution?"

77. Referred to by Luu Doan Huynh, in ibid.

78. Bui Tin, *Following Ho Chi Minh*, p. 33.

79. Ball, *The Past Has Another Pattern*, pp. 361–362.

80. This does not mean, as several interlocutors in Hanoi have argued to us, that Le Duan was ignorant of important differences between the conditions affecting the success or failure of a neutral solution in Laos and South Vietnam. He could have had no doubt that South Vietnam would be the tougher case, due to all sorts of reasons, not least of which was the presence of Diem, who vigorously opposed the concept (at least in exchanges with his U.S. patrons). Le Duan's error lay elsewhere—in his assumption that Washington viewed the Laos agreement as: (1) important; and (2) a "model" to be applied in South Vietnam. This was manifestly *not* the Kennedy administration's view of the matter. Laos did not matter, relative to South Vietnam; more importantly, the Laotian arrangement was *not* to be repeated.

81. Duiker, *Communist Road to Power in Vietnam*, pp. 223–224.

82. The list is a distillation of interviews conducted in Hanoi with former officials who drew on their experience in this and similar episodes. See also Robert K. Brigham, *Guerrilla Diplomacy: The NLF's Foreign Relations and the Vietnam War* (Ithaca: Cornell University Press, 1998), especially chapter 2, "Our Friends Around the World."

83. Hammer, *A Death in November*, p. 222.

84. See Kahin, *Intervention*, p. 186.

85. Quoted in ibid., p. 186.

86. Memorandum from CIA Director John McCone, "Highlights of Discussions in Saigon, 18–20 December 1963," dated December 21, 1963. See Kahin, *Intervention*, p. 186.

87. Duiker, *Communist Road to Power in Vietnam*, p. 244.

88. John F. Kennedy, quoted in Schlesinger, *A Thousand Days*, p. 757. Schlesinger, writing in 1965, quotes Kennedy as saying "there's always some so-and-so who doesn't get the word." The quotation in the text is accurate, as Schlesinger and others have confirmed.

89. W. B. Yeats, in *The Collected Poems of W. B. Yeats*, definitive edition with author's final revisions (New York: Macmillan, 1950), p. 98.

CHAPTER 5. ESCALATION

1. Lyndon B. Johnson, "Address to the American Alumni Council," July 12, 1966. In *Public Papers of the Presidents, 1966*, vol. 2 (Washington, DC: Government Printing Office), pp. 718–722, p. 720.
2. Ho Chi Minh, "Letter to Martin Niemoeller," December 1966. Cited in Marilyn B. Young, *The Vietnam Wars: 1945–1990* (New York: Harper, 1991), p. 172.
3. Robert S. McNamara, with Brian VanDeMark, *In Retrospect: The Tragedy and Lessons of Vietnam*, rev. ed. (New York: Vintage, 1996; hardcover ed. publ. April 1995), p. 96.
4. Barbara W. Tuchman, *The Guns of August* (New York: Vintage, 1962).
5. McNamara, *In Retrospect*, p. 96.
6. John F. Kennedy, quoted in Robert F. Kennedy, *Thirteen Days: A Memoir of the Cuban Missile Crisis* (New York: Norton, 1969), p. 105.
7. See, for example, James G. Blight, Bruce J. Allyn, and David A. Welch, *Cuba on the Brink: Castro, the Missile Crisis, and the Soviet Collapse* (New York: Pantheon, 1993); Aleksandr Fursenko and Timothy Naftali, *"One Hell of a Gamble": Khrushchev, Castro, and Kennedy, 1958–1964—The Secret History of the Cuban Missile Crisis* (New York: Norton, 1997); and Ernest R. May and Philip D. Zelikow, eds., *The Kennedy Tapes: Inside the White House During the Cuban Missile Crisis* (Cambridge: Harvard University Press, 1997).
8. From among a vast literature, one might begin by consulting the following: Lloyd C. Gardner, *Pay Any Price: Lyndon Johnson and the Wars for Vietnam* (Chicago: Ivan R. Dee, 1995), holds that Johnson was determined to assert his manhood in Vietnam; H. R. McMaster, *Dereliction of Duty: Lyndon Johnson, Robert McNamara, the Joint Chiefs of Staff, and the Lies That Led to Vietnam* (New York: HarperCollins, 1997), holds that a vast conspiracy, with Johnson in the middle, was behind American involvement in Vietnam; and Jeff Shesol, *Mutual Contempt: Lyndon Johnson, Robert Kennedy, and the Feud That Defined a Decade* (New York: Norton, 1997), holds that Johnson's paranoia regarding the Kennedys, especially Robert Kennedy, drove him to try to "win" the Vietnam War.
9. Sen. Richard Russell, from a transcript in Michael R. Beschloss, ed., *Taking Charge: The Johnson White House Tapes, 1963–1964* (New York: Simon and Schuster, 1997), p. 364.
10. McGeorge Bundy, from a transcript in ibid., p. 370.
11. Ibid., p. 371.
12. Ibid.
13. Robert S. McNamara, "The Military Role of Nuclear Weapons: Perceptions and Misperceptions," *Foreign Affairs*, vol. 62, no. 1 (Fall 1983), pp. 59–80, p. 79.
14. Maxwell D. Taylor, *The Uncertain Trumpet* (New York: Norton, 1959).
15. The speech was delivered, in classified form, on May 5, 1962, at a meeting in Athens of NATO defense ministers and given in unclassified form later in the month in a commencement address to the University of Michigan in Ann Arbor, a city in which McNamara had resided for nearly fifteen years while working at the Ford Motor Company in Detroit. See Fred Kaplan, *The Wizards of Armageddon* (New York: Simon and Schuster, 1983), pp. 263–285.
16. Thomas C. Schelling, *The Strategy of Conflict* (Cambridge: Harvard University Press, 1960).
17. Ibid., p. 15.
18. See Lawrence Freedman, "Vietnam and the Disillusioned Strategist," *International Affairs* vol. 72, no. 1 (1996), pp. 133–151; and Kaplan, *Wizards of Armageddon*, chapter 18.

19. William C. Westmoreland, *A Soldier Reports* (Garden City, NY: Doubleday, 1976), p. 410.

20. Ted Gittinger, *The Johnson Years* (Austin: University of Texas Press, 1993), p. 76 (emphasis in original).

21. Mike Mansfield, quoted in McNamara, *In Retrospect*, p. 42. See also Ernest K. Lindley, "An Ally Worth Having," *Newsweek*, June 29, 1959, p. 31.

22. Cited in William Conrad Gibbons, *The U.S. Government and the Vietnam War: Executive and Legislative Roles and Relationships*, 4 volumes (Princeton: Princeton University Press, 1986), vol. 1 (1945–1960), p. 233.

23. Cited in ibid., p. 334.

24. Bernard B. Fall, cited in *The Pentagon Papers: The Defense Department History of United States Decisionmaking on Vietnam* (Gravel ed.), 4 volumes (Boston: Beacon Press, 1971), vol. 1, p. 334.

25. Fall, cited in ibid., p. 336.

26. Ibid., p. 337.

27. Douglas Pike, cited in ibid., p. 337.

28. Ibid.

29. Pike, cited in ibid., p. 346.

30. This history is summarized in ibid., vol. 2, pp. 23–30.

31. Ibid., vol. 2, p. 25.

32. See, for example, Ellen J. Hammer, *A Death in November: America in Vietnam, 1963* (New York: E. P. Dutton, 1987); and Francis X. Winters, *The Year of the Hare: America in Vietnam, January 25, 1963–February 15, 1964* (Athens: University of Georgia Press, 1997).

33. Ngo Dinh Diem, cited in Winters, *Year of the Hare*, pp. 49–50. See also, on Ngo Dinh Nhu's views at that moment, Hammer, *A Death in November*, pp. 244–245.

34. Bui Tin, *Following Ho Chi Minh: Memoirs of a North Vietnamese Colonel*, trans. by Judy Stowe and Do Van (London: Hurst, 1995), pp. 59–60.

35. Ibid., p. 58 (emphasis added).

36. National Security Action Memorandum (NSAM) 273, cited in McNamara, *In Retrospect*, pp. 102–103.

37. Robert S. McNamara, "Memorandum for the President," December 21, 1963. In *Pentagon Papers* (Gravel ed.), vol. 3, pp. 494–496, p. 496.

38. "Working Paper on the North Vietnamese Role in South Viet-Nam: Captured Documents and Interrogation Reports," Department of State, May 1968. Cited in William S. Turley, *The Second Indochina War* (New York: Mentor, 1986), p. 44.

39. Maxwell D. Taylor to Dean Rusk, August 3, 1964. Cited in Beschloss, *Taking Charge*, p. 493.

40. See McNamara, *In Retrospect*, p. 128; and Tim Larimer, "McNamara and Giap Revisit Gulf of Tonkin," *International Herald Tribune*, November 10, 1995, p. 1.

41. The phrase is McNamara's. See *In Retrospect*, p. 128.

42. "Minutes of National Security Council Meeting," August 4, 1964. In George McT. Kahin, *Intervention: How America Became Involved in Vietnam* (New York: Anchor, 1986), pp. 224–225. (Notetaker, Bromley Smith.)

43. *Pentagon Papers* (Gravel ed.), vol. 3, p. 291.

44. Ibid., pp. 288–289.

45. Ibid., p. 671.

46. Ibid., p. 672.

47. Cited in Ibid., p. 289.

48. Ibid.

49. Ibid., pp. 289–290.

50. "The situation" is discussed by Philip B. Davidson, *Vietnam at War: The History, 1946–1975* (New York: Oxford University Press, 1991), p. 333.
51. Lyndon B. Johnson to Maxwell D. Taylor, December 30, 1964. In Kahin, *Intervention*, p. 259.
52. See Ibid., p. 272, on this reversal of incentives.
53. McGeorge Bundy to Lyndon B. Johnson, January 27, 1965. In Gibbons, *U.S. Government and the Vietnam War*, vol. 3, p. 48.
54. Ibid.
55. Ibid., p. 49.
56. See Davidson, *Vietnam at War*, pp. 335–336, for details of the bombing programs.
57. Chester L. Cooper, *The Lost Crusade: America in Vietnam* (New York: Dodd, Mead, 1970), p. 259.
58. Ibid., pp. 259–260.
59. Ibid., p. 260.
60. Cited in *Pentagon Papers* (Gravel ed.), vol. 3, p. 303.
61. Ibid., p. 203.
62. Ibid., p. 286.
63. McGeorge Bundy, quoted in Townsend Hoopes, *The Limits of Intervention*, updated ed. (New York: Longman, 1973), p. 30.
64. *Pentagon Papers* (Gravel ed.), vol. 3, p. 306.
65. See David W.P. Elliott, "Hanoi's Strategy in the Second Indochina War." In Jayne S. Werner and Luu Doan Huynh, eds., *The Vietnam War: Vietnamese and American Perspectives* (Armonk, NY: M. E. Sharpe, 1993), pp. 66–94, p. 68.
66. Le Duan, quoted in ibid., p. 73. Elliott is citing Le Duan, *Duong loi cach mang Mien Nam* [The path of revolution in the South], Party Document, ca. 1956.
67. Tran Van Tra, *Vietnam: History of the Bulwark B2 Theatre* (Ket Thuc Chien Tranh 30 Nam). (Ho Chi Minh City: Joint Print Plant, 1982), p. 78.
68. See Elliott, "Hanoi's Strategy," p. 70.
69. Tran Van Tra, *Vietnam*, p. 78.
70. Elliott, "Hanoi's Strategy," p. 70.
71. Ibid.
72. William J. Duiker, quoted in Elliott, "Hanoi's Strategy," p. 74.
73. Bui Tin, *Following Ho Chi Minh*, p. 45.
74. *Pentagon Papers* (Gravel ed.), vol. 1, p. 311.
75. Ibid.
76. Le Duan, *Duong loi cach mang Mien Nam* [The path of revolution in the South], quoted in Kahin, *Intervention*, p. 106.
77. See Kahin, *Intervention*, p. 107.
78. See Kahin, *Intervention*, p. 111.
79. "The Legal Underpinnings of Government Terror in South Vietnam: Law 10/59." In Marvin E. Gettleman et al., eds., *Vietnam and America: A Documented History*, rev. and enlarged ed. (New York: Grove Press, 1995), pp. 156–159.
80. Tran Van Giau, quoted in William J. Duiker, *The Communist Road to Power in Vietnam*, 2d ed. (Boulder: Westview, 1996), p. 196.
81. Tran Van Tra was placed under house arrest for publicizing his bitterness toward the Hanoi government and was forbidden to continue his five-volume history of the war. Tran Van Tra died in April 1996.
82. Tran Van Tra, "The War That Should Not Have Been." In Werner and Huynh, eds., *Vietnam War*, pp. 233–242, p. 235.

83. Tran Van Tra, *Vietnam: History of the Bulwark B2 Theatre*, p. 34.
84. Tran Van Tra, "The War That Should Not Have Been," p. 34.
85. Ibid., p. 236.
86. Tran Van Tra, *Vietnam: History of the B2 Theatre*, p. 53.
87. After early 1961, the Hanoi government would quickly begin to articulate and implement a policy of matching violence with violence. Perhaps the most far-reaching of these actions was the establishment of the Central Office South Vietnam (COSVN), in a decision of January 23, 1961. It would be from this mobile command center that the struggle in the South would be coordinated. Gen. Tran Van Quang was named a member of COSVN and also named commander of the People's Liberation Army Forces, which was established in a decision of February 15, 1961. Gen. Tran Van Quang traveled south from Hanoi in May 1961 to assume his command.
88. Lyndon Johnson was bombarded with memoranda by McGeorge Bundy, Walt Rostow, and others arguing that any move toward neutralization would be a betrayal of the South Vietnamese anticommunists. In addition, the U.S. embassy in Saigon was reporting that one member of the junta, Gen. Ton That Dinh, "is considering how to accommodate himself to a neutral solution for Vietnam" (Kahin, *Intervention*, p. 192). See also Duiker, *Communist Road to Power in Vietnam*, pp. 237–238; and Turley, *Second Indochina War*, pp. 56–67.
89. See Davidson, *Vietnam at War*, pp. 287–291.
90. See Bui Tin, *Following Ho Chi Minh*, pp. 44–46; Davidson, *Vietnam at War*, pp. 304–306; and Duiker, *Communist Road to Power in Vietnam*, pp. 239–241.
91. Bui Tin, *Following Ho Chi Minh*, p. 44.
92. U.S. Embassy (Saigon) Vietnam Documents, 1972. Cited in Davidson, *Vietnam at War*, p. 306.
93. U.S. Embassy (Saigon) Vietnam Documents, 1972. Document 96, p. 2.
94. Ibid., p. 1.
95. Ibid.
96. Bui Tin, *Following Ho Chi Minh*, p. 52.
97. *Vietnam: The Anti-U.S. Resistance War*, p. 60. See also Turley, *Second Indochina War*, pp. 60–61.
98. *The Great Anti-U.S. Resistance War for National Salvation of the Fatherland, 1954–1975—Military Events* [Cuoc Khang Chien Chong My, Cuu Nuoc, 1954–1975] (Hanoi: Nha Xuat Ban Quan Doi Nhan Dan, 1988), p. 61.
99. See Thomas D. Boettcher, *Vietnam: The Valor and the Sorrow* (Boston: Little, Brown, 1985), p. 245.
100. Duiker, *Communist Road to Power in Vietnam*, pp. 249–250.
101. See Turley, *Second Indochina War*, p. 60.
102. See Duiker, *Communist Road to Power in Vietnam*, p. 250.
103. Ibid.
104. For details, see *Vietnam: The Anti-U.S. Resistance War*, pp. 64–66; for an account of these events as a critical "turning point," see Turley, *Second Indochina War*, pp. 64–66.
105. Duiker, *Communist Road to Power in Vietnam*, p. 261.
106. Le Duan to Nguyen Chi Thanh, February 1965. In Thu Vao Nam [Letters to the South] (Hanoi: Nha Xuat Ban Su That, 1986), pp. 93–95. Cited in Duiker, *Communist Road to Power in Vietnam*, pp. 261–262.
107. Nguyen Khac Huynh of Hanoi's Institute for International Relations has reported that the ten-to-fifteen–year figure appears often in North Vietnamese government documents from the period.

108. Duiker, *Communist Road to Power in Vietnam*, p. 262.

109. Kahin, *Intervention*, p. 277.

110. Thomas D. Boettcher, *Vietnam: The Valor and the Sorrow*, pp. 226–227.

111. Kahin, *Intervention*, p. 277.

112. Boettcher, *Vietnam: The Valor and the Sorrow*, p. 227.

113. Bui Tin, *Following Ho Chi Minh*, pp. 48–49.

114. Duiker, *Communist Road to Power in Vietnam*, p. 262.

115. A good deal of pressure was put on the junta regarding the use of U.S. advisers (the junta wished to limit their influence) and the prospect of bombing North Vietnam (the junta opposed it as militarily ineffective and harmful to the Vietnamese nation as a whole). A senior South Vietnamese general, Nguyen Van Chuan, put the junta's case this way: "The Americans said it was necessary to bomb North Vietnam. The [South Vietnamese] Armed Forces Council represented . . . by General Duong Van Minh, disagreed with the American policy. . . . General Minh gave two reasons: (1) bombing North Vietnam would not produce good military results; on the contrary, it would do more harm to innocent Vietnamese; (2) by such bombing we would lose the just cause because we had [thus far] held that we were fighting a defensive war and had ascribed the role of the aggressor to the communists." Kahin, *Intervention*, p. 188. General Huan's interview was in *Hoa Binh*, a moderate Catholic newspaper in Saigon, July 20, 1971. His account was corroborated in George Kahin's subsequent interview of Gen. Tran Van Don, who attended the meeting in question. Moreover, the junta could have had no doubt that the U.S. government and, in particular, the Saigon embassy were strongly opposed to any move toward a neutral coalition. But there is no documentary evidence of direct pressure on the junta to avoid leaning toward a neutral solution. Probably, there was no need for direct pressure, since U.S. views were so well known and so vehement on the issue. See Kahin, *Intervention*, pp. 188–193, on the issue of the Duong Van Minh junta and the contentious issues of U.S. advisers, the bombing of the North, and neutrality.

116. McNamara, *In Retrospect*, p. 128.

117. Ibid.

118. McGeorge Bundy to President Lyndon B. Johnson, February 7, 1965. In *Pentagon Papers* (Gravel ed.), vol. 3, p. 309.

119. Lyndon B. Johnson, *The Vantage Point: Perspectives of the Presidency, 1963–1969* (New York: Holt, Rinehart, and Winston, 1971), pp. 126–127.

120. Herbert Butterfield, quoted in Robert Jervis, *Perception and Misperception in International Politics* (Princeton: Princeton University Press, 1976), p. 69.

121. Ibid., p. 66 (emphasis added).

122. McGeorge Bundy, remarks at a forum at the Kennedy School of Government, October 12, 1987.

123. Lyndon Johnson, quoted in Doris Kearns, *Lyndon Johnson and the American Dream* (New York: Signet, 1976), p. 273.

124. Ibid., p. 275.

Chapter 6. Negotiating Initiatives, 1965–1967

1. Lyndon Johnson to Ho Chi Minh, February 8, 1967. In Lyndon B. Johnson, *The Vantage Point: Perspectives of the Presidency, 1963–1969* (New York: Holt, Rinehart, and Winston, 1971), p. 592.

2. Ho Chi Minh to Lyndon Johnson, February 15, 1967. The basic text is in ibid., pp.

594–595. The passage from Ho Chi Minh used in the epigraph, however, has been amended slightly by our Vietnamese colleague, Mr. Luu Doan Huynh, so that it more accurately reflects the meaning of the Vietnamese original.

3. T. S. Eliot, "Little Gidding." In *Collected Poems, 1909–1962* (New York: Harcourt, 1963), pp. 200–209, p. 208.

4. Johnson, *Vantage Point*, pp. 578–591.

5. Chester L. Cooper, *The Lost Crusade: America in Vietnam* (New York: Dodd, Mead, 1970).

6. George C. Herring, ed., *The Secret Diplomacy of the Vietnam War: The Negotiating Volumes of the Pentagon Papers* (Austin: University of Texas Press, 1983).

7. See Marvin E. Gettleman et al., *Vietnam and America: A Documented History*, rev. and enlarged ed. (New York: Grove Press, 1995), pp. 276–278.

8. On the evolution of the Four Points, see George McT. Kahin, *Intervention: How America Became Involved in Vietnam* (New York: Anchor, 1986), pp. 325–326.

9. On the NLF's Five Point Stand of March 22, 1965, consult Kahin, *Intervention*, p. 325; and William J. Duiker, *The Communist Road to Power in Vietnam*, 2d ed. (Boulder: Westview, 1996), p. 263.

10. See Kahin, *Intervention*, pp. 326–327. Kahin is correct about the significance of Nguyen Duy Trinh's appointment as foreign minister but wrong about the date of his appointment. Nguyen Duy Trinh was not appointed on April 7, 1965, in conjunction with Pham Van Dong's speech giving the Four Points, but earlier, at the end of 1964. At the Bellagio study conference in July 1998, both Ambassador Nguyen Dinh Phuong and Luu Doan Huynh reported to us that, in fact, they had both flown with their new Foreign Minister Nguyen Duy Trinh to the second (and abortive) Afro-Asian conference in Algiers in February 1965.

11. Richard Goodwin, "Memorandum for the President," April 27, 1965. In Kahin, *Intervention*, p. 328.

12. McGeorge Bundy, cited in William Conrad Gibbons, *The U.S. Government and the Vietnam War: Executive Roles and Relationships*, 4 volumes (Princeton: Princeton University Press, 1986), vol. 2, p. 362.

13. Gibbons, *U.S. Government and the Vietnam War*, vol. 3, p. 237.

14. Dean Rusk, as told to Richard Rusk, *As I Saw It*, ed. by Daniel S. Papp (New York: Norton, 1990), p. 460.

15. See the alternative translation by George McT. Kahin, in David Kraslow and Stuart H. Loory, *The Secret Search for Peace in Vietnam* (New York: Random House, 1968), p. 37, which is even closer to the U.S. position at the time.

16. See Johnson, *Vantage Point*, p. 133.

17. Nguyen Khac Huynh does not at this point address the question as to why the Hanoi government rejected the U.S. invitation to move to negotiations during the thirty-seven–day bombing pause of December 1965–January 1966. It is addressed directly in the second section, "Key Misunderstandings," in the passages discussing Washington-Hanoi differences in perceptions of conditional U.S. bombing pauses versus an unconditional bombing halt.

18. See Robert S. McNamara, with Brian VanDeMark, *In Retrospect: The Tragedy and Lessons of Vietnam*, rev. ed. (New York: Vintage, 1996; hardcover ed. publ. April 1995), p. 221.

19. See Rusk, *As I Saw It*, p. 445, on some of the challenges of reaching 145 countries over the Christmas holidays.

20. Cooper, *Lost Crusade*, p. 296.

21. Dean Rusk, "Memorandum for the President," in Gibbons, *U.S. Government and the Vietnam War*, vol. 4, p. 124.

22. McGeorge Bundy, "Memorandum for the President," December 27, 1965. In Gibbons, *U.S. Government and the Vietnam War*, vol. 4, p. 126.

23. Ibid.

24. Rusk, *As I Saw It*, p. 464.

25. George W. Ball, *The Past Has Another Pattern: Memoirs* (New York: Norton, 1982), p. 404.

26. The Fourteen Points proposal was published in the *Department of State Bulletin*, February 14, 1966, p. 225.

27. Rusk, *As I Saw It*, p. 465.

28. Herring, ed., *Secret Diplomacy of the Vietnam War*, pp. 143–149.

29. See ibid., p. 147.

30. Ibid., p. 148.

31. Ibid.

32. This is an excellent example of the way lack of communication between the two sides, with their fundamentally different approaches to beginning negotiations, proved to be insurmountable. Chester Cooper knows, as an American negotiator, that the United States was willing to deal on all of the Fourteen Points, so long as Hanoi showed some flexibility as well. But the Hanoi leadership did not know this and felt they could not take it for granted. So they demanded transparent clarity on *all* points before agreeing to sit down with the Americans, a position the U.S. side felt was rigid to the point of caricature. And so instead of facilitating negotiations, the publication of the Fourteen Points only served to deepen the suspicions that each side already held toward the other.

33. Kraslow and Loory, *Secret Search for Peace in Vietnam*, p. 137.

34. Ibid., p. 145.

35. Lyndon Johnson, quoted in *The Pentagon Papers: The Defense Department History of United States Decisionmaking on Vietnam* (Gravel ed.), 4 volumes (Boston: Beacon Press, 1971), vol. 3, p. 363. In addition, the problem was exacerbated by the regular visits to Hanoi of "freelancers" who represented themselves as U.S. envoys but whose connection to the Johnson administration was tangential or nonexistent.

36. The point is emphasized by George C. Herring, in *LBJ and Vietnam: A Different Kind of War* (Austin: University of Texas Press, 1994), p. 103.

37. Cooper, *Lost Crusade*, p. 308.

38. Rusk, *As I Saw It*, p. 463.

39. Bracketed phrase added to the original transcript for the sake of clarity.

40. Rusk, *As I Saw It*, p. 465.

41. Allan E. Goodman, *The Lost Peace: America's Search for a Negotiated Settlement of the Vietnam War* (Stanford: Hoover Institution Press, 1978), p. 5. Our colleagues in Hanoi have emphasized to us, however, that the "fight and talk" strategy of the Vietnamese communists antedated communism by centuries and is, in fact, the characteristic Vietnamese method of dealing with a larger invading enemy. A favorite example is the Vietnamese resistance to the Ming invaders of the fifteenth century, which involved guerrilla tactics that limited reinforcements from China, combined with a pledge ceremony in which both sides agreed to make peace—the Chinese would withdraw and promise not to return; the Vietnamese would allow them safe passage back to China. Episodes like these, according to colleagues in Hanoi, constitute the history behind expressions often used in the American War, such as "rolling out the red carpet" for the United States to withdraw its troops, a particular favorite of Le Duan.

42. Henry Kissinger, *Diplomacy* (New York: Simon and Schuster, 1994) p. 662.

43. Pham Van Dong, quoted in Herring, ed., *Secret Diplomacy of the Vietnam War*, p. 105.

44. Many in the U.S. government had such doubts much earlier. See McNamara, *In Retrospect*, paperback edition, pp. 220–225, dealing with the origins of the author's doubts in November and December 1965.

45. For a critique of these views, see Philip B. Davidson, *Vietnam at War: The History, 1946–1975* (New York: Oxford University Press, 1991), pp. 795–812.

46. Robert S. McNamara to General Curtis LeMay, August 31, 1964. In *Pentagon Papers* (Gravel ed.), vol. 3, pp. 555–556.

47. McNamara, *In Retrospect*, p. 289.

48. Robert S. McNamara, Testimony Before the Senate Armed Services Committee, August 25, 1967. In *Pentagon Papers* (Gravel ed.), vol. 4, p. 202.

49. McNamara, *In Retrospect*, p. 290.

50. Ibid.

51. Townsend Hoopes, *The Limits of Intervention* (New York: Longman, 1969), pp. 128–129.

52. Ibid.

53. McNamara, *In Retrospect*, p. xx.

54. Nguyen Duy Trinh, Broadcast statement (in English), Radio Hanoi, January 28, 1967. In Herring, ed., *Secret Diplomacy of the Vietnam War*, p. 384.

55. Ibid.

56. Lyndon Johnson, in a meeting on December 21, 1965 (verbatim notes by Jack Valenti). In Gibbons, *U.S. Government and the Vietnam War*, vol. 4, pp. 124–125.

57. At the Bellagio, Italy, study conference in July 1998, Luu Doan Huynh added that the Americans failed sufficiently to understand how the experience of the French war had conditioned the Vietnamese. He said that the Vietnamese attitude toward U.S. bombing, and toward its offers of bombing pauses, reminded many at the time of French tortures in which the Vietnamese would be forced to reveal certain secrets, following which *more* torture would be applied, in the hope of extorting more information. In such a case, he said, it was clear to the Vietnamese that to remain silent was the best of the available options. This, according to Luu Doan Huynh, was basically the way the Hanoi government, and the people of North Vietnam, viewed the bombing and the offers of bombing pauses.

58. See McNamara, *In Retrospect*, pp. 182–183; and *Pentagon Papers* (Gravel ed.), vol. 4, pp. 21–22.

59. See *Pentagon Papers* (Gravel ed.), vol. 3, pp. 369–370.

60. Ibid., p. 369.

61. Ibid., p. 370.

62. Ibid., p. 374.

63. Ibid., p. 377.

64. Herring, ed., *Secret Diplomacy of the Vietnam War*, p. 71.

65. William P. Bundy, quoted in Kahin, *Intervention*, p. 330.

66. Zhou Enlai and Deng Xiaoping (in conversation with Ho Chi Minh), Beijing, May 17, 1965. In Odd Arne Westad et al., eds., "77 Conversations Between Chinese and Foreign Leaders on the Wars in Indochina, 1964–1977." In *Bulletin of the Cold War International History Project*, Working Paper No. 22, May 1998, p. 87.

67. Conversation Between Mao Zedong and Ho Chi Minh, May 16, 1965. In ibid., pp. 86–87. See also the interesting account of this conversation in John Prados, *The Blood Road: The Ho Chi Minh Trail and the Vietnam War* (New York: Wiley, 1999), pp. 124–125.

68. See McNamara, *In Retrospect*, p. 193.

69. Ibid., p. 195.

70. See Herring, ed., *Secret Diplomacy of the Vietnam War*, p. 77.

71. Ibid., p. 78.
72. Ibid., p. 87.
73. Ibid., p. 79.
74. Ibid., p. 81.
75. Ibid., p. 78.
76. Herring, ed., *Secret Diplomacy of the Vietnam War*, p. 86.
77. See McNamara, *In Retrospect*, pp. 220–231, for an account of the main events of the PINTA/Christmas bombing pause.
78. Robert S. McNamara, "Memorandum for the President," November 30, 1965. In Gibbons, *U.S. Government and the Vietnam War*, vol. 4, p. 107.
79. See McNamara, *In Retrospect*, p. 223.
80. For a narrative of the events of the Christmas bombing pause, with primary documentation, see Gibbons, *U.S. Government and the Vietnam War*, vol. 4, pp. 113–117, and McNamara, *In Retrospect*, pp. 218–229.
81. See Herring, ed., *Secret Diplomacy of the Vietnam War*, pp. 123–125, for a brief chronology of the PINTA-Rangoon channel.
82. Ibid., p. 125.
83. Kraslow and Loory, *Secret Search for Peace in Vietnam*, p. 149.
84. Zhou Enlai (in conversation with Nguyen Duy Trinh), Beijing, 10:30 A.M., December 19, 1965. In Westad et al., eds., "77 Conversations," p. 92.
85. Zhou Enlai (in conversation with Tran Van Thanh), in Westad et al., eds., "77 Conversations," pp. 92–93.
86. Nguyen Duy Trinh, quoted in Herring, ed., *Secret Diplomacy of the Vietnam War*, p. 384.
87. "Resolution on Stepping Up the Diplomatic Struggle," January 23–26, 1967. In *Vietnam: The Anti-U.S. Resistance War for National Salvation, 1954–1975: Military Events* [Cuoc Khang Chien Chong My, Cuu Nuoc 1954–1975: Nhung Su Kien Quan Su] (Hanoi: People's Army Publishing House, 1980), pp. 92–94.
88. Ibid., p. 93.
89. Cooper, *Lost Crusade*, pp. 350, 353.
90. Ibid., p. 352.
91. See Gibbons, *U.S. Government and the Vietnam War*, vol. 4, pp. 551–553; and Arthur M. Schlesinger Jr., *Robert Kennedy and His Times* (New York: Ballantine, 1978), pp. 768–769.
92. Robert F. Kennedy, speech on the floor of the U.S. Senate, March 2, 1967, quoted in Jeff Shesol, *Mutual Contempt: Lyndon Johnson, Robert Kennedy, and the Feud That Defined a Decade* (New York: Norton, 1997), p. 372.
93. Ibid., p. 373.
94. Ibid., pp. 376–377.
95. Robert S. McNamara, "Memorandum for the President," quoted in ibid., p. 377.
96. Mai Van Bo, February 22, 1967, interview with *The New York Times*. In Herring, ed., *Secret Diplomacy of the Vietnam War*, pp. 490–491.
97. DRV aide-mémoire, January 27, 1967. In ibid., p. 380.
98. Ibid.
99. Cooper, *Lost Crusade*, pp. 356–357.
100. Ibid., p. 357.
101. Ibid; see also Johnson, *Vantage Point*, pp. 252–253.
102. Herring, ed., *Secret Diplomacy of the Vietnam War*, pp. 397–398.
103. The letters are in Johnson, *Vantage Point*, pp. 592–595.

104. Herring, ed., *Secret Diplomacy of the Vietnam War*, p. 381.
105. See McNamara, *In Retrospect*, pp. 250–252.
106. Zhou Enlai (in conversation with Deng Xiaoping and Le Duan), Beijing, March 23, 1966. In Westad et al., eds., "77 Conversations," p. 93.
107. Deng Xiaoping to Le Duan and Nguyen Duy Trinh, April 13, 1966, in ibid., pp. 94–95.
108. Le Duan to Deng Xiaoping and Zhou Enlai, in ibid., pp. 96–97.
109. Ilya Gaiduk, *The Soviet Union and the Vietnam War* (Chicago: Ivan R. Dee, 1996), p. 59.
110. Ibid., p. 60.
111. See Herring, ed., *Secret Diplomacy of the Vietnam War*, p. 399.
112. This follows the account of Raymond Aubrac, *Ou La Memoire S'Atarde* [Where memory lingers] (Paris: Gallimard, 1996); see also Kissinger, *Diplomacy*, pp. 663–665.
113. Herbert Marcovitch's surname has in scholarly accounts been spelled without the *t* ever since the publication of the negotiating volumes of the *Pentagon Papers* in 1983 (Herring, ed., *Secret Diplomacy of the Vietnam War*), presumably because this is the way Henry Kissinger spelled it in his transcription of conversations with Aubrac and Marcovitch in Paris. But in his recent memoir, Aubrac spells his friend's name with the *t*. See Aubrac, *La Memoire S'Atarde*; see also the interview of Aubrac and review of his memoir by Barry James, "'Simply the Postman': Ho's French Friend," *International Herald Tribune*, December 7–8, 1996, p. 22.
114. See McNamara, *In Retrospect*, pp. 297–302. One can perhaps see Dean Rusk's level of interest in the fact that he never mentions either PENNSYLVANIA or the San Antonio formula in his memoir, *As I Saw It*.
115. Herring, ed., *Secret Diplomacy of the Vietnam War*, pp. 720–721.
116. Ibid., p. 721.
117. Robert S. McNamara, quoted in ibid., p. 731.
118. McNamara, *In Retrospect*, pp. 298–299.
119. Herring, ed., *Secret Diplomacy of the Vietnam War*, p. 730.
120. Ibid., p. 736.
121. Ibid.
122. Ibid., p. 738.
123. See Johnson, *Vantage Point*, p. 267.
124. The high-level focus on the war effort described by Nguyen Khac Huynh contrasts markedly from the way the U.S. government dealt with the war. The war was always the first order of business for the leadership in Hanoi throughout the period covered in this chapter. The U.S. government was organized in a similar fashion during the Cuban missile crisis of October 1962. (The Executive Committee of the National Security Council, or EXCOMM, lead by President Kennedy, met every day, sometimes all day, during the crisis until it was resolved peacefully on October 28.) The EXCOMM had no analogue in Washington's handling of the Vietnam War, where many groups, at various times, met to deal with various aspects of the war. There was no "war cabinet" in any meaningful sense.
125. Colleagues from the Ministry of Foreign Affairs in Hanoi, having read this passage, have pointed out that in conventional diplomacy one way of communicating goes by the name "conspicuous absence," that is (they say), there was a conspicuous absence of the harsh rhetoric with which Hanoi typically responded to U.S. offers. They count three such conspicuous absences: (1) in reaction to PENNSYLVANIA on October 20, 1967; (2) in reaction to San Antonio on December 29, 1967; and (3) in reaction to President Johnson's State of the Union Address on January 21, 1968. Unfortunately, these absences of harsh rhetoric were *not* conspicuous, at least not in Washington. And I doubt whether even our specialists noticed anything as subtle as what our Vietnamese colleagues are sug-

gesting was a real attempt to communicate to us that the PENNSYLVANIA–San Antonio approach could have led to peace talks in late 1967 or early 1968, at the latest. This knowledge only adds to the tragedy of the war and the importance of drawing lessons from it regarding how adversaries ought to try to communicate.

126. Gen. Vo Nguyen Giap. In Oriana Fallaci, *Interview with History*, trans. by John Shepley (Boston: Houghton-Mifflin, 1976), p. 82.
127. Figures cited in Maurice Isserman, *Witness to War in Vietnam* (New York: Berkley, 1995), pp. 114, 211.
128. William James, journal entry, April 30, 1870. In John J. McDermott, ed., *The Writings of William James: A Comprehensive Edition* (Chicago: University of Chicago Press, 1977), pp. 7–8.

Chapter 7. U.S. Military Victory in Vietnam

1. Carl von Clausewitz, *On War*, trans. by M. Howard and P. Paret (Princeton: Princeton University Press, 1976).
2. Sun Tzu, *The Art of War*, trans. by Samuel B. Griffith (London: Oxford University Press, 1963).
3. Robert S. McNamara, with Brian VanDeMark, *In Retrospect: The Tragedy and Lessons of Vietnam*, rev. ed. (New York: Vintage, 1996; hardcover ed. publ. April 1995), pp. 224–225.
4. Ibid., p. 262.
5. Clark Clifford, quoted in McNamara, *In Retrospect*, p. 310.
6. *U.S.-Vietnam Relations, 1945–1967*. Prepared by the Department of Defense and printed by the House Committee on Armed Services, Washington, DC, 1971, 12 volumes. Also known as the "DOD Pentagon Papers," this will be cited hereafter in this chapter as *U.S.-Vietnam Relations*. Citation is to vol. 2, sec. IV. A. 5., p. 2.
7. Ibid., pp. 28–30.
8. BDM Corporation, *A Study of Strategic Lessons Learned in Vietnam, Volume 5: Planning the War* (McLean, VA: BDM Corporation, 1980), 3:1–3:2.
9. "Lansdale's Report," *U.S.-Vietnam Relations*, vol. 2, pp. 66–77.
10. William C. Gibbons, *The United States and the Vietnam War: Executive and Legislative Roles and Relationships*, 4 volumes (Princeton: Princeton University Press, 1986), vol. 2, p. 14.
11. "Memorandum from Walt Rostow to McGeorge Bundy, January 30, 1961," National Security File, Country File-Vietnam, Box 192, John F. Kennedy Presidential Library.
12. *The Pentagon Papers: The Defense Department History of United States Decisionmaking on Vietnam* (Gravel ed.), 4 volumes (Boston: Beacon Press, 1971), vol. 2, p. 27.
13. Lloyd Norman and John Spore, "Big Push in Guerrilla Warfare," *Army* (March 1962): 34.
14. *The New York Times*, January 4, 1960.
15. Walt Rostow, *The Diffusion of Power: An Essay in Recent History* (New York: Macmillan, 1972), p. 275.
16. McNamara, *In Retrospect*, p. 39.
17. *U.S.-Vietnam Relations*, vol. 3, pp. 1–2.
18. As quoted in George C. Herring, *America's Longest War: The United States and Vietnam, 1950–1975*, 3d ed. (New York: McGraw Hill, 1996), p. 92.
19. Milton E. Osborne, *Strategic Hamlets in South Viet-Nam: A Survey and Comparison*

(Ithaca: Cornell University, Southeast Asia Program, Department of Asian Studies, Data Paper Number 55, April 1965), p. 2.

20. *U.S.-Vietnam Relations*, vol. 11, p. 325.
21. Douglas Blaufarb, *The Counterinsurgency Era* (New York: Free Press, 1977), p. 119.
22. Osborne, *Strategic Hamlets in South Viet-Nam*, p. 53.
23. Robert Thompson, *Defeating Communist Insurgency* (New York: Praeger, 1966), pp. 141–142.
24. Osborne, *Strategic Hamlets in South Viet-Nam*, p. 56.
25. *Needs of the Revolution*, Party Document, Luu Tru I-Hanoi [National Archives I-Hanoi]. For access to this and other Vietnamese-language documents, I am grateful to my coauthor, Robert Brigham.
26. Truong Nhu Tang, *A Viet Cong Memoir: An Inside Account of the Vietnam War and Its Aftermath* (New York: Vintage Books, 1985), p. 87.
27. "Hilsman-Forrestal Report, January 25, 1963," *The Foreign Relations of the United States, Vietnam, 1961–1963, Volume 3: Vietnam, January–August 1963* (Washington, DC: Government Printing Office, 1991), pp. 50–52.
28. The transfer of responsibility was known as Operation "SWITCHBACK" and was completed on November 1, 1963.
29. Herring, *America's Longest War*, p. 103.
30. *Foreign Relations of the United States, Vietnam, 1961–1963, Volume 4: Vietnam, August–December 1963* (Washington, DC: Government Printing Office, 1991), p. 707.
31. "Trends of the Communist Insurgency in South Vietnam," National Security Files, Special Subjects, Vietnam, Reel 18, Lyndon Baines Johnson Presidential Library, Austin, Texas.
32. Gen. William C. Westmoreland, *Report on the War in Vietnam, Section 2: Report on Operations in South Vietnam, January 1964–June 1968* (Washington, DC: Government Printing Office, 1968), p. 71.
33. *Foreign Relations of the United States, Vietnam, 1964–1968, Volume 1: Vietnam, 1964* (Washington, DC: Government Printing Office, 1992), p. 154.
34. "Johnson to Lodge, April 4, 1964," Johnson Papers, National Security File, Country File-Vietnam, Box 3, Lyndon Baines Johnson Presidential Library, Austin, Texas.
35. *Foreign Relations of the United States, Vietnam, 1964–1968, Volume 1: Vietnam 1964*, p. 165. A significant exception was Secretary of Defense McNamara. He reports in his memoir that after his tour of South Vietnam with General Nguyen Khanh in March 1964 he became convinced that Khanh's support was weak and that U.S. aid alone would be unlikely to reverse the downward spiral of events triggered by the assassination of Ngo Dinh Diem and Ngo Dinh Nhu. See *In Retrospect*, pp. 113–117.
36. McNamara, *In Retrospect*, p. 109.
37. *Foreign Relations of the United States, Vietnam, 1964–1968, Volume 1: Vietnam, 1964*, pp. 112–118.
38. William J. Duiker, *The Communist Road to Power in Vietnam*, 2d ed. (Boulder: Westview, 1996), p. 245.
39. *Pentagon Papers* (Gravel ed.), vol. 3, pp. 41–42.
40. Herring, *America's Longest War*, p. 137.
41. "McGeorge Bundy Memorandum for the Record, September 14, 1964," Johnson Papers, National Security File, Country File-Vietnam, Box 6, Lyndon Baines Johnson Presidential Library, Austin, Texas.
42. As quoted in Herring, *America's Longest War*, p. 138.
43. See McNamara, *In Retrospect*, pp. 151–152.
44. As quoted in Gibbons, *U.S. Government and the Vietnam War*, vol. 2, pp. 349–350.

45. *Pentagon Papers* (Gravel ed.), vol. 3, pp. 561–562.

46. As quoted in Gibbons, *U.S. Government and the Vietnam War*, vol. 2, p. 352.

47. As quoted in Herring, *America's Longest War*, p. 141.

48. *Public Papers of the Presidents: Lyndon B. Johnson, 1965*, vol. 1 (Washington, DC: Government Printing Office, 1966), p. 395.

49. *U.S.-Vietnam Relations*, vol. 4, p. 23; Lyndon B. Johnson, *The Vantage Point: Perspectives of the Presidency, 1963–1969* (New York: Holt, Rinehart, and Winston, 1971), pp. 123–124; William C. Westmoreland, *A Soldier Reports* (Garden City, NY: Doubleday, 1976), pp. 115–116; Robert Shaplen, *Bitter Victory* (New York: Harper and Row, 1986), p. 305.

50. *U.S.-Vietnam Relations*, vol. 6, pp. 23–24.

51. Col. Dennis M. Drew, *Rolling Thunder 1965: Anatomy of a Failure* (Air University Press, Maxwell AFB, AL, 1986), p. 31; John Prados, *The Hidden History of the Vietnam War* (Chicago: Ivan R. Dee, 1995), p. 189.

52. Mark Clodfelter, *The Limits of Airpower: The American Bombing of North Vietnam* (New York: Free Press, 1989), pp. 92–99.

53. Ibid., pp. 138–139.

54. United States Congress, Senate, Committee on Foreign Relations, *Bombing as a Policy Tool in Vietnam: Effectiveness*, 92d Congress, 2d sess., October 12, 1972, pp. 6–7; *U.S.-Vietnam Relations*, vol. 6, pp. 142–145.

55. *U.S.-Vietnam Relations*, vol. 6, pp. 163–166.

56. Harrison Salisbury, *Behind the Lines—Hanoi, December 23–January 7* (New York: Harper and Row, 1967).

57. Herbert Y. Schandler, *The Unmaking of a President: Lyndon Johnson and Vietnam* (Princeton: Princeton University Press, 1977), pp. 47–49. See also Salisbury, *Behind the Lines*.

58. *U.S.-Vietnam Relations*, vol. 6, pp. 1–2.

59. Ibid., pp. 124–125.

60. National Security Council, NSSM 1, "Summary of Responses to NSSM 1—The Situation in Vietnam," *Congressional Record*, vol. 118, no. 76 (May 10, 1972), p. E4981; quoted in U.S. Senate Committee on Foreign Relations, *Bombing as a Policy Tool in Vietnam*, p. 12.

61. Ibid., p. 12.

62. Clodfelter, *The Limits of Air Power*, p. 203.

63. Ibid., p. 205.

64. Earl H. Tilford, *Setup: What the Air Force Did in Vietnam and Why* (Maxwell Air Force Base, AL: Air University Press, 1991), pp. 330–333.

65. Transcript of the Proceedings of a Conversation Between Col. Herbert Y. Schandler and Col. Quach Hai Luong, trans. by Kathy N. Le, Institute for International Relations, Hanoi, Vietnam, February 23–26, 1998, p. 26.

66. Vu Can, *North Vietnam: A Daily Resistance* (Hanoi: Foreign Languages Publishing House, 1975), pp. 24–35.

67. *Phong khong va khong quang: Ky su* [Air and air defense forces: Chronicle], vol. 3 (Hanoi: Bo Tu Lenh Quan Chung Phong Khong, 1978), p. 23.

68. William Duiker, *Sacred War: Nationalism and Revolution in a Divided Vietnam* (New York: McGraw Hill, 1995), p. 200.

69. Luu Doan Huynh, in James G. Blight, ed., *Missed Opportunities II: Revisiting the Decisions of the Vietnam War, 1945–1968* (the February 1998 Hanoi conference).

70. Salisbury, *Behind the Lines*, p. 114.

71. Vietnam News Agency, June 5, 1971.

72. John T. Smith, *Rolling Thunder: The American Strategic Bombing Campaign Against North Vietnam, 1964–1968* (Surrey, England: Air Research Publications, 1994), p. 178.

73. *U.S.-Vietnam Relations*, vol. 4, p. 125.
74. Vietnam News Agency, December 12, 1967.
75. *Ban roi tai cho may bay B-52* [Shooting down B-52 aircraft] (Hanoi: Nha Xuat Ban Quan Doi Nhan Dan, 1978), p. 29.
76. Chen Jian, "China's Involvement in the Vietnam War," *China Quarterly*, vol. 142 (June 1995): 356–387.
77. U.S. Senate Committee on Foreign Relations, *Bombing as a Policy Tool in Vietnam*, pp. 8–10; *U.S.-Vietnam Relations*, vol. 6, pp. 130–131.
78. *U.S.-Vietnam Relations*, vol. 4, p. 1.
79. Ibid., pp. 2–6; Westmoreland, *A Soldier Reports*, pp. 123–124.
80. *U.S.-Vietnam Relations*, vol. 4, pp. 68–69, 124–126; see also Johnson, *Vantage Point*, pp. 140–141.
81. *U.S.-Vietnam Relations*, vol. 4, pp. 99–101, 71–79; see also Maxwell D. Taylor, *Swords Into Plowshares* (New York: Norton, 1972), pp. 342–343.
82. Westmoreland, *Report on the War in Vietnam*, p. 109.
83. *U.S.-Vietnam Relations*, vol. 4, p. 7.
84. *U.S.-Vietnam Relations*, vol. 5, pp. 8–9; Westmoreland, *A Soldier Reports*, p. 142.
85. Just before Secretary McNamara left for Saigon, he received a report he had commissioned by a group led by a member of the Joint Staff (and President Eisenhower's former national security assistant), Gen. Andrew Goodpaster. The study addressed the question of whether the United States could expect to win the war if "we do everything we can." It concluded that there was no reason to suppose the United States could not win such a war, but it also contained an important caveat: Much would depend on whether the U.S. forces could perform adequately in offensive operations in South Vietnam. "Intensification of the Military Operations in Vietnam, Concept and Appraisal," LBJ Library, pp. ii, J-1. See also McNamara, *In Retrospect*, pp. 202–203.
86. *U.S.-Vietnam Relations*, vol. 4, p. 7; Westmoreland, *A Soldier Reports*, p. 141.
87. *U.S.-Vietnam Relations*, vol. 5, pp. 8–12, and vol. 4, pp. 117–119; Taylor, *Swords and Plowshares*, pp. 348–349; McNamara, *In Retrospect*, p. 203.
88. McNamara, *In Retrospect*, p. 203.
89. *Public Papers of the Presidents, 1965*, vol. 2 (Washington, DC: Government Printing Office, 1966), pp. 794–799.
90. Westmoreland, *A Soldier Reports*, pp. 144, 146–152.
91. Johnson, *Vantage Point*, p. 153.
92. Col. Quach Hai Luong, in transcripts of the February 1998 Hanoi conference.
93. *U.S.-Vietnam Relations*, vol. 5, pp. 34–41.
94. Ibid., pp. 53–54.
95. Ibid., pp. 80–81.
96. Ibid., pp. 83–93.
97. McNamara, *In Retrospect*, p. 221.
98. Ibid., pp. 108–110.
99. Ibid., pp. 82–85.
100. *U.S.-Vietnam Relations*, vol. 5, pp. 214–215, 93–100.
101. Henry Trewhitt, *McNamara: His Ordeal in the Pentagon* (New York: Harper and Row, 1971), pp. 227–245; Johnson, *Vantage Point*, p. 372.
102. McNamara, *In Retrospect*, pp. 309–310.
103. Ibid., p. 226.
104. *U.S.-Vietnam Relations*, vol. 5, p. 2.
105. Luu Doan Huynh, in James G. Blight, ed., and Kathy N. Le and Quang M. Do, trans.,

Missed Opportunities I: Revisiting the Decisions of the Vietnam War, 1961–1968 (the June 1997 Hanoi conference).

106. Ibid., pp. 68–69.

107. Harold P. Ford, *CIA and the Vietnam Policymakers: Three Episodes, 1962–1968* (Washington, DC: Central Intelligence Agency, 1998), pp. 104–123.

108. Pham Van Son, *The Vietcong Tet Offensive, 1968* (Saigon: Printing and Publications Center, RVNAF, 1968), pp. 25–26.

109. Dennis J. Duncanson, *Government and Revolution in Vietnam* (London: Oxford University Press, 1968), p. 53.

110. Ibid.

111. Westmoreland, *Report on the War in Vietnam*, p. 157.

112. MACV 01614, 040959Z, February 1968, General Westmoreland to General Wheeler.

113. *U.S.-Vietnam Relations*, vol. 5, pp. 12–16.

114. Schandler, *The Unmaking of a President*, p. 290; *U.S.-Vietnam Relations*, vol. 5, pp. 80–88.

115. Johnson, *Vantage Point*, p. 435.

116. Henry Kissinger, "The Tangled Web: An Exchange." *New York Review of Books*, vol. 45, no. 14 (September 24, 1998), pp. 78–80, p. 78.

117. Robert Komer, *Bureaucracy Does Its Things: Institutional Constraints on U.S.-GVN Performance in Vietnam* (Santa Monica, CA: Rand Corporation, 1972), p. 18.

118. Bruce Palmer Jr., *The Twenty-Five Year War: America's Military Role in Vietnam* (Lexington: University of Kentucky Press, 1984), p. 46.

119. William Westmoreland, in Ted Gittinger, ed., *The Johnson Years: A Vietnam Roundtable* (Austin, TX: LBJ School of Public Affairs, 1993), p. 76.

120. "Memorandum for the President from Richard Helms, September 12, 1967," National Security Files, Country File-Vietnam, Box 259, Lyndon Baines Johnson Presidential Library, Austin, Texas. The memorandum did not come to light until Secretary McNamara's research assistant came across it at the LBJ Library while working on *In Retrospect*.

121. Office of the Assistant Secretary of Defense, Public Affairs, News Release No. 609–84. "The Uses of Military Power," Remarks Delivered by Secretary of Defense Caspar Weinberger at the National Press Club, November 20, 1984.

122. George P. Shultz, *Triumph and Turmoil: Diplomacy, Power, and the Victory of the American Ideal* (New York: Simon and Schuster, 1993), p. 650.

123. *Joint Pub 3–0' Doctrine for Joint Operations*, The Joint Chiefs of Staff, Washington, February 1, 1995, pp. viii, I-2–I-4.

Chapter 8. Lessons of Vietnam for the Twenty-First Century

1. The "Ambassadors' Dialogue" took place in Brown University's Salomon Auditorium on November 17, 1997, as part of Brown's Stephen A. Ogden Memorial Lecture Series, moderated by Ralph Begleiter, world affairs correspondent for Cable News Network (CNN). The dialogue marked the first joint public appearance of Ambassador Peterson and Ambassador Le Van Bang since President Clinton's decision of July 1995 to normalize U.S.-Vietnam relations.

2. See Chapter 1, Note 13, for the citation from Ernest R. May, *"Lessons" of the Past: The Use and Misuse of History in American Foreign Policy* (New York: Oxford University Press, 1973), pp. 120–121.

3. The conference was held July 27–31, 1998. See Appendix C for the list of participants.

4. Robert S. McNamara, with Brian VanDeMark, *In Retrospect: The Tragedy and Lessons of Vietnam*, rev. ed. (New York: Vintage, 1996; hardcover ed. publ. April 1995), p. 333.

5. The lecture took place in Salomon Auditorium on the campus of Brown University, February 15, 1996.

6. McNamara, *In Retrospect*, p. xix.

7. The entire presentation may be found in James G. Blight, ed., and Kathy N. Le and Quang M. Do, trans., *Missed Opportunities? I: Revisiting the Decisions of the Vietnam War, 1961–1968* (the June 1997 Hanoi conference), pp. 201–206.

8. Ibid., p. 206.

9. Michael Ignatieff, "The Ends of Empathy," *New Republic*, April 29, 1991, pp. 31–37, pp. 33–34. Ignatieff, though not a student of Isaiah Berlin, was much influenced by Berlin's work on *einfuhlung* (empathy) in the work of Johann Gottfried Herder.

10. This was the theme of Norman Boucher's piece on the June 1997 conference in Hanoi. See "Thinking Like the Enemy," *Brown Alumni Magazine*, November/December 1997, pp. 36–45.

11. Chester Cooper, quoted in June 1997 Hanoi conference, p. 24.

12. Nicholas deB. Katzenbach, in ibid., p. 32.

13. See Chapter 5, p. 163.

14. Graham Greene, *The Quiet American* (London: Penguin, 1955), p. 163.

15. Quoted in Chapter 3, p. 79.

16. Chapter 5, p. 192.

17. Chapter 5, p. 193.

18. See Chapter 3, pp. 77–78, for Luu Van Loi's account.

19. Raymond Aubrac, *Ou La Memoire S'Atarde* [Where memory lingers] (Paris: Gallimard, 1996).

20. The NLF Program is discussed in Chapters 2 and 3. See "Founding Program of the National Liberation Front of South Vietnam." In Marvin E. Gettleman et al., eds., *America and Vietnam: A Documented History*, rev. and enlarged ed. (New York: Grove Press, 1995), pp. 188–192, p. 189.

21. Joseph S. Nye Jr., *Bound to Lead: The Changing Nature of American Power* (New York: Basic Books, 1990).

22. There was confusion in the Kennedy administration when, on August 29, 1963, President de Gaulle issued a statement in which he appeared to offer the services of France to the two Vietnams in order to reunify the country. Secretary of State Rusk quickly summoned French Ambassador to the United States Herve Alphand, who explained to Rusk that the goals mentioned by de Gaulle—peace and reunification—should be regarded as long-term in character. See Gareth Porter, *A Peace Denied: The United States, Vietnam, and the Paris Agreement* (Bloomington: University of Indiana Press, 1975), p. 45. See also George McT. Kahin, *Intervention: How America Became Involved in Vietnam* (New York: Anchor, 1986), pp. 190–191. There is general agreement among scholars that de Gaulle's statement was the tip of an iceberg of French activity devoted to playing a major role in the neutralization of Vietnam, probably as part of a scheme for the neutralization of all of Indochina, a scheme that was also supported by Prince Sihanouk of Cambodia.

23. Nguyen Co Thach, in the June 1997 Hanoi conference, p. 232.

24. Joseph Lelyveld, quoted in Arnold R. Isaacs, *Vietnam Shadows: The War, Its ghosts, and Its Legacy* (Baltimore: Johns Hopkins University Press, 1997), p. 137.

25. Nguyen Co Thach, quoted in the June 1997 Hanoi conference, p. 18.

26. George P. Shultz, *Triumph and Turmoil: Diplomacy, Power, and the Victory of the American Ideal* (New York: Simon and Schuster, 1993), p. 650.

27. See Michael Ignatieff, "Is Nothing Sacred? The Ethics of Television." In *The Warrior's*

Honor: Ethnic War and the Modern Conscience (New York: Metropolitan Books, 1997), pp. 9–33.

28. Bruce Palmer Jr., *The Twenty-Five Year War: America's Military Role in Vietnam* (Lexington: University of Kentucky Press, 1984).

29. See Chapter 1 for a discussion of the passage from Ernest May; see Note 13 for the full reference.

30. Frances FitzGerald, "How Does America Avoid Future Vietnams?" In Harrison E. Salisbury, ed., *Vietnam Reconsidered: Lessons from a War* (New York: Harper, 1984), pp. 300–305, pp. 304–305.

NOTES TO APPENDIX B

1. Andrew F. Krepinevich, *The Army and Vietnam* (Baltimore: Johns Hopkins University Press, 1986), p. 261.

2. Bruce Palmer Jr., *The Twenty-Five Year War: America's Military Role in Vietnam* (Lexington: University Press of Kentucky Press, 1984), p. 177.

3. See Odd Arne Westad et al., eds., "77 Conversations Between Chinese and Vietnamese Leaders on the Wars in Indochina, 1964–1977," Working Paper No. 22 of the Cold War International History Project (May 1998), Woodrow Wilson Center, Washington, DC.

4. Guo Ming et. al, *Zhongyue guanxi yanbian sishinian* [Forty-year evolution of Sino-Vietnamese relations] (Nanking: Guangiz People's Press, 1992), p. 69. See also Chen Jian, "China's Involvement in the Vietnam War, 1964–1969," *China Quarterly*, vol. 142 (June 1995): 359.

5. *Junshi shilin* [The circle of military history], vol. 6 (1989), p. 40.

6. As quoted in Chen Jian, "China's Involvement in the Vietnam War," p. 364.

7. Alan Whiting, *The Chinese Calculus of Deterrence* (Ann Arbor: University of Michigan Press, 1975), p. 176.

8. *People's Daily* (Beijing), March 25, 1965.

9. Chen Jian, "China's Involvement in the Vietnam War," pp. 372–377.

10. Gen. Doan Chuong, in transcript of *Missed Opportunities? I: Revisiting the Decisions of the Vietnam War, 1961–1968* (hereinafter: "the June 1997 Hanoi conference").

11. Edgar Snow, *The Long Revolution* (New York: Random House, 1971), pp. 215–219. See also Harry G. Summers, *On Strategy: A Critical Analysis of the Vietnam War* (Novato, CA: Presidio Press, 1982), pp. 93–94, 96.

12. Li Ke and Hao Shengzhang, *Wenhua Dageming Zhong de Renmin Jiefangjun* [The People's Liberation Army during the Cultural Revolution] (Beijing: Chinese Communist Party's Historical Materials Press, 1989).

13. *Mao Zedong junshi wenji* [A collection of Mao Zedong's military papers], vol. 6 (Beijing: Military Science Press, 1993), p. 403.

14. Luu Doan Huynh, quoted in the transcript of the June 1997 Hanoi conference.

15. Chen Jian, "China's Involvement in the Vietnam War," p. 386.

16. *The Pentagon Papers: The Defense Department History of United States Decisionmaking on Vietnam* (Gravel ed.), 4 volumes (Boston: Beacon Press, 1971), vol. 3, p. 156.

17. This is taken up at length in Chapter 5.

18. Tran Bach Dang, "Mau Than: Cuoc tong dien tap chien luoc," [Tet Offensive: A strategic rehearsal] *Tap Chi Lich Su Quan Su* (February 1988), pp. 57–64. See also *Lich su Dang Bo Dang Cong san Viet Nam tinh Ben Tre, 1930–1985* [History of the Communist Party Provincial Committee of Ben Tre, 1930–1985] (Ben Tre: Ben Nghien Cuu Lich Su Dang Ben Tre, 1985).

19. See "Tinh hinh phong trao dau tranh chinh tri o Nam Bo tu hoa binh lap lai den bien nay" [The situation of the political struggle movement in Nam Bo from the restoration of peace to the present], ca. 1960, Trung Tam Luu Tru Quoc Gia–1 [National Archives Center 1], Hanoi; "Tinh hinh va nhiem vu 59," [The situation and tasks for 1959], ca. 1959, Trung Tam Luu Tru Quoc Gia–1 [National Archives Center 1], Hanoi; *Mot so van kien cua Dang ve chong My, cuu nuoc* [Selected Party documents related to the anti-U.S. resistance war for national salvation of the fatherland], 2 volumes (Hanoi: Nha Xuat Ban Su That, 1985); *South Vietnam National Front for Liberation: Documents* (Saigon: Giai Phong, 1968); Hoang Van Thai, *How South Vietnam Was Liberated* (Hanoi: Foreign Languages Publishing House, Gioi, 1992); and Nguyen Thi Dinh, *Khong con duong nao khac* (Hanoi: Nha Xuat Ban Van Hoc, 1963).

20. "Dong Chi Le Duc Tho noi ve mot so van de tong ket chien tranh va bien soan lich su quan su," [Comrade Le Duc Tho discusses a number of questions on the general assessment of the war and the writing of military history], *Tap Chi Lich Su Quan Su* (March 1988), pp. 1–10.

21. Nguyen Chi Thanh, *Who Will Win in South Vietnam?* (Peking: Foreign Languages Press, 1963), pp. 8–9.

22. Nguyen Chi Thanh, "Cang thuoc tu tuong cong viec giua luc luong vu trang va nhan dan of mien Nam va 1965–66 kho mua thang loi," [The ideological task among the armed forces and people of our South and the 1965–1966 dry season victories] *Hoc Tap* 12 (July 1966), pp. 1–10.

23. As quoted in William Duiker, *Sacred War: Nationalism and Revolution in a Divided Vietnam* (New York: McGraw Hill, 1995), p. 188.

24. See especially Summers, *On Strategy.*

25. Krepinevich, *The Army and Vietnam*, p. 263.

26. John Prados, *The Hidden History of the Vietnam War* (Chicago: Ivan R. Dee, 1995), p. 234.

27. Robert Thompson, *No Exit from Vietnam* (New York: David McKay, 1969), p. 69.

28. Ibid.

29. Albert L. Fisher, "How to Beat the Guerrillas at Their Own Game," *Military Review*, vol. 43 (December 1963), pp. 81–86.

30. Gen. Doan Chuong, quoted in transcript of the June 1997 Hanoi conference.

31. William C. Westmoreland, *A Soldier Reports* (Garden City, NY: Doubleday, 1976), p. 147.

32. Westmoreland Papers, "Westmoreland MAC 3275 to Wheeler," COMUSMACV Message File, HRB, Center for Military History.

33. Gen. Maxwell Taylor, *Swords and Plowshares* (New York: Norton, 1972), p. 364.

34. Interview with Col. Herbert Schandler, Hanoi, February 1998.

35. Bernard Fall, *Street Without Joy* (Mechanicsburg, PA: Stackpole Books, 1961).

36. Summers, *On Strategy*, p. 1.

Photograph Notes and Credits

Chapter 1.

Photo of Woodrow Wilson courtesy of CORBIS.

Chapter 2.

Eisenhower and dominoes. In *Public Papers of the Presidents*, 1954 (Washington, DC: United States Government Printing Office, 1955), p. 382. Photo courtesy of UPI/CORBIS-Bettmann.

Khrushchev: "We will bury you." Cited in John Mueller, *Retreat From Doomsday: The Obsolescence of Major War* (New York: Basic Books, 1989), pp. 145–146. Photo courtesy of CORBIS/Bettmann.

Kennedy's Inaugural. In *Public Papers of the President*, 1961 (Washington, DC: Government Printing Office, 1962), p. 1. Photo courtesy of CORBIS/Bettmann.

Chapter 3.

Ho Chi Minh's Inaugural. "Vietnam Declaration of Independence" (September 2, 1945). In Marvin E. Gettleman, *Vietnam and America*, rev. ed. (New York: Grove Press, 1995), pp. 26–28, p. 28. Photo courtesy of CORBIS/Bettmann.

Dulles in Geneva. Cited in George C. Herring, *America's Longest War: The United States, Vietnam and the Paris Agreement* (Bloomington, Indiana: University of Indiana Press, 1975), p. 45. Photo courtesy of UPI/CORBIS-Bettmann.

Chapter 4.

Charles de Gaulle's statement is quoted in Gareth Porter, *A Peace Denied: The United States, Vietnam and the Paris Agreement* (Bloomington, Indiana: University of Indiana Press, 1975), p. 45. Photo courtesy of CORBIS/Bettmann.

Chapter 5.

Pres. Lyndon Johnson quotes: In Robert Dallek, *Flawed Giant: Lyndon Johnson and His Times* (New York: Oxford, 1998), p. 246; and Doris Kearns, *Lyndon Johnson and the American Dream* (New York: Signet, 1976), p. 263. Photo courtesy of CORBIS/Bettmann.

Ho Chi Minh and Mao Zedong. Transcript of discussions between Mao Zedong and Ho Chi Minh, May 16, 1965. In Odd Arne Westad, et al., *77 Conversations* (Working Paper No. 22 of the Cold War International History Project, The Woodrow Wilson Center, Washington, DC), pp. 86–87. Photo of Mao Zedong courtesy of CORBIS/Hulton-Deutsch Collection. Photo of Ho Chi Minh courtesy of CORBIS/Bettmann.

Photo of Robert McNamara and General Giap courtesy of Monica d. Church.

Chapter 6.

The Kissinger-Aubrac channel via Paris is described in George C. Herring, ed., *The Secret Diplomacy of the Vietnam War: The Negotiating Volumes of the Pentagon Papers* (Austin: University of Texas Press, 1983), pp. 717–771. Photo courtesy of CORBIS.

Chapter 7.

General William C. Westmoreland, quoted in "Vietnam Sec Def Briefings, 7–8 July 1967—COMUSMACV Assessment," Department of State, Lot File 70 D 48. Photo courtesy of CORBIS.

General Bruce Palmer, Jr. is cited from his book, *The 25 Year War: America's Military role in Vietnam* (Lexington: University of Kentucky Press, 1984), p. 46. Photo from the collection of the author.

Chapter 8.

Reference is to: Cyrus R. Vance and Dr. David A. Hamburg, co-chairs, *Preventing Deadly Conflict* (the Final Report of the Carnegie Commission on Preventing Deadly Conflict, 1997). Book cover courtesy of the Carnegie Endowment for International Peace.

Acronyms

CIA	Central Intelligence Agency
CINCPAC	commander in chief of U.S. forces in the Pacific
COSVN	Central Office South Vietnam
CPV	Communist Party of Vietnam
CTZ	Corps Tactical Zones
DIA	Defense Intelligence Agency
DMZ	demilitarized zone (the 17th parallel)
DRV	Democratic Republic of Vietnam
IIR	Institute for International Relations
INR	Intelligence and Research
ISS	Institute of Strategic Studies
JCS	Joint Chiefs of Staff
MAAG	Military Assistance Advisory Group
MACV	Military Assistance Command-Vietnam
NAM	Non-Aligned Movement
NATO	North Atlantic Treaty Organization
NIE	National Intelligence Estimate
NLF	National Liberation Front
NSAM	National Security Action Memorandum
NSSM	National Security Study Memorandum
NVN	North Vietnam
OPLAN	Operational Plan
PAVN	People's Army of Vietnam—the North Vietnamese Army
PLAF	People's Liberation Army Forces
POL	petroleum, oil, and lubricant
PRG	Provisional Revolutionary Government
SEATO	Southeast Asia Treaty Organization
SIOP	Single Integrated Operational Plan
SNIE	Special National Intelligence Estimate
SVN	South Vietnam

ACKNOWLEDGMENTS

Although the project upon which this book is based was originally my idea, neither the project nor the book would have been possible without the diverse contributions of dozens of people in several countries. The intellectual, institutional, logistical, linguistic, cultural, financial, and even psychological challenges involved have been considerable. The U.S.-Vietnamese dialogues in this book derive from three conferences: in June 1997 in Hanoi; February 1998 in Hanoi; and July 1998 in Bellagio, Italy. But the dialogues occurred and were productive only because the right people were in the right seats in the right place at the right time. I want here to note what I regard as the most significant of the contributions by this large and varied group.

Leslie Gelb, Karen Sughrue, and Lisa Greenberg at the Council on Foreign Relations in New York were receptive and supportive when I asked Les in early 1995 to probe the willingness of Vietnamese scholars and policymakers to join with their American counterparts to review the decisionmaking on both sides during the Vietnam War. My first trip to Hanoi in November 1995 was taken under the auspices of the Council.

When the Council withdrew from the project after I returned from Vietnam, Brown University's Thomas J. Watson Jr. Institute for International Studies stepped in to fill the void. The Watson Institute's director, professor Thomas Biersteker, supported the project in many ways, not least of which was his willingness to allocate substantial resources to the project after it became clear that it, like the war we proposed to study, was very controversial—too controversial for many U.S. foundations. Professor Biersteker eventually received support from many others at the university, including Brown's (then) President Vartan Gregorian, his successor, E. Gordon Gee, Vice President for University Relations Robert Reichley, and his successor, Laura Freid.

Janet M. Lang, the project's associate director, was the person at Brown who oversaw the day-to-day operations. She received able assistance at the Watson Institute from Leslie W. Baxter, Sheila Fournier, Kathy N. Le, Phuc Le, Jean Lawlor, Nancy H. Soukup, and Patricia Monahan. In addition, the project was aided by the efforts of Brown News Bureau Director Mark Nickel and his staff, and by Director of Special Events William Slack, Associate Director M. L. Farrell, and Norman Boucher, editor of *Brown Alumni Magazine.*

The Watson Institute's sister institution in Vietnam has been the Institute for International Relations in Hanoi, directed by Ambassador Dao Huy Ngoc. He was assisted by a hardworking staff, especially Bui Thanh Son, Le Linh Lan, and Le Hong Truong. Ambassador Ngoc had the support of two other Vietnamese institutions: the Institute of Military History, directed by Gen. Nguyen Dinh Uoc; and the Institute for Strategic Studies, directed by Gen. Doan Chong.

The efforts to arrange the two conferences in Hanoi were facilitated at crucial moments by both the U.S. and Vietnamese governments. At the U.S. State Department, Donald Coleman and Robert Carlson were especially helpful. Ambassador Pete Peterson made his entire staff available to us whenever we were in Hanoi. Particularly helpful were James Hall, deputy chief of mission; Col. Edward O'Dowd, military attaché; William Bach, U.S. Information Agency officer; and Jean Smith, Ambassador Peterson's executive assistant. Their efforts were matched in Washington by Ambassador Le Van Bang and his staff, led by Ha Huy Thong, deputy chief of mission, and Tran Trong Khanh, chief of political affairs.

Dr. Thomas Graham, director of international security at the Rockefeller Foundation, spearheaded an extraordinarily difficult effort to find a way for Rockefeller, which does not usually fund projects such as this one, to provide support for it. Dr. Graham was supported by the (then) president of Rockefeller, Peter Goldmark, and also by Joan Shigekawa, Chong Ae-Yu, Rebecca Rittgers, and George Soule. I am profoundly grateful to all of them.

Rockefeller's contribution extended to its decision to award the Watson Institute the funding for a manuscript review conference at their conference facility in Bellagio, Italy, in July 1998. We thank Susan Garfield, head of Rockefeller's New York office, for Bellagio events, and Gianna Celli, acting director of the Villa Serbelloni Center in Bellagio.

The contributions of the participants in the two Hanoi conferences— nearly fifty in all—are noted in the front of this book. The participants in the Bellagio conference in July 1998 are listed in Appendix C.

But before getting to the conferences, we had to identify, translate, and transport declassified U.S. documents and Vietnamese materials in our possession to our colleagues in Vietnam. My coauthor Robert Brigham was the key player in this regard, but he was ably assisted by Malcolm Byrne and Thomas

Blanton of the National Security Archive, located at George Washington University; and by James Hershberg, David Wolff, and Christian Ostermann at the Cold War International History Project, located at the Woodrow Wilson Center in Washington, D.C. Brian VanDeMark assisted by providing a critique of some of the more technical matters on the U.S. side, as did Alfred Goldberg, director of the Office of the Historian of the Department of Defense.

After my coauthors and I reached a decision to move ahead with the book, I called Peter Osnos, who along with his editorial chief, Geoffrey Shandler, had done a superb job as publishers of my memoir, *In Retrospect*. I asked if he would be interested in publishing the book. He was. My coauthors and I decided not to "shop" the book around, because, in my opinion, the ablest publisher I know of already wanted to handle the project. We signed the contact and that was that.

Also, I want to acknowledge the contributions of my coauthors.

Although the conception of the project and the theme and structure of the book were mine initially, the drafting of this book is the result of a team effort in every sense. Professor Biersteker brought to our analysis of the lessons of the war a keen analytical mind and balanced sensitivity to both U.S. and Vietnamese lessons. Colonel Schandler has produced what I believe is a significant addition to the literature on military aspects of the war by combining U.S. data and scholarship with the new revelations contained in our dialogues with the Vietnamese. Professor Brigham is the only one among us who speaks and reads Vietnamese; he is thus conversant with the Vietnamese-language materials, against which it has often been possible to check the accuracy of statements made by our Vietnamese colleagues. At each stage of our work, Professor Brigham was given full veto power by all the other authors, including myself, if anything we had written did not, in his view, stand up to historical fact. Professor Brigham had valuable support at his institution, Vassar College, from Vassar President Frances Fergusson, and able assistance from Monica D. Church. I believe Professor Brigham has more than lived up to his reputation as America's outstanding young historian of the Vietnam War.

Finally, I must acknowledge the contributions made by Professor Blight.

It is difficult to know where to begin or how convey in a few words the ways his monumental efforts contributed to the success of the project. He got it funded, kept it going, and served as the honest broker a project like this needs if former enemies are to come together with the expectation that if they speak the truth those on the other side will reciprocate. Everyone on both sides knew that Professor Blight was such a person.

But Professor Blight's contributions were by no means limited to organizing and facilitating. He is also a graceful writer, and it is with him that I personally worked most closely on the manuscript, as all five of us drafted our various contributions. Indeed, so often have he and I exchanged drafts of material of which I am author; and so often have we, in addition, exchanged the monologues and dialogues sections, of which he is primary author; that neither of us is sure anymore who was initially responsible for what. It doesn't matter. This book would not exist—in fact, I doubt I would have even considered getting involved in it—were it not for Professor Blight's participation.

ROBERT S. McNAMARA

Washington, DC

INDEX

PUBLICAFFAIRS is a new nonfiction publishing house and a
tribute to the standards, values, and flair of three persons who
have served as mentors to countless reporters, writers, editors,
and book people of all kinds, including me.

I. F. STONE, proprietor of *I. F. Stone's Weekly*, combined a
commitment to the First Amendment with entrepreneurial
zeal and reporting skill and became one of the great independent journalists in American history. At the age of
eighty, Izzy published *The Trial of Socrates*, which was a
national bestseller. He wrote the book after he taught himself ancient Greek.

BENJAMIN C. BRADLEE was for nearly thirty years the
charismatic editorial leader of *The Washington Post*. It was
Ben who gave the *Post* the range and courage to pursue such
historic issues as Watergate. He supported his reporters with
a tenacity that made them fearless, and it is no accident that
so many became authors of influential, best-selling books.

ROBERT L. BERNSTEIN, the chief executive of Random
House for more than a quarter century, guided one of the
nation's premier publishing houses. Bob was personally
responsible for many books of political dissent and argument that challenged tyranny around the globe. He is also
the founder and was the longtime chair of Human Rights
Watch, one of the most respected human rights organizations in the world.

　　　　·　　·　　·

For fifty years, the banner of Public Affairs Press was carried
by its owner Morris B. Schnapper, who published Gandhi,
Nasser, Toynbee, Truman, and about 1,500 other authors. In
1983 Schnapper was described by *The Washington Post* as
"a redoubtable gadfly." His legacy will endure in the books
to come.

Peter Osnos, *Publisher*